Human-AI Collaboration and the Evolving Role of Educators

Belqes Al-Sowaidi
https://orcid.org/0000-0002-3752-2684
Two Oceans Graduate Institute, South Africa

Tawffeek Mohammed
https://orcid.org/0000-0002-7314-9688
University of the Western Cape, South Africa

IGI Global
Scientific Publishing
Publishing Tomorrow's Research Today

Vice President of Editorial Melissa Wagner
Director of Acquisitions Mikaela Felty
Director of Book Development Jocelynn Hessler
Production Manager Mike Brehm
Cover Design Jose Rosado

Published in the United States of America by
IGI Global Scientific Publishing
701 East Chocolate Avenue
Hershey, PA, 17033, USA
Tel: 717-533-8845 | Fax: 717-533-7115
Website: https://www.igi-global.com E-mail: cust@igi-global.com

Library of Congress Cataloging-in-Publication Data

LCCN: 2025027637 (CIP Data Pending)
ISBN13: 9798337345215
Isbn13Softcover: 9798337345222
EISBN13: 9798337345239
British Cataloguing in Publication Data
A Cataloguing in Publication record for this book is available from the British Library.

Table of Contents

Detailed Table of Contents

This chapter contributes to contemporary debates on the implications of AI tools for academic writing and the preservation of academic integrity within HEIs. Traditionally, academic librarians have led efforts to promote academic integrity through various means. However, the rapid adoption of AI has disrupted the established roles of academic librarians and called for new approaches to ensure ethical and responsible academic engagement. In particular, questions arise about how academic librarians have adapted their technological support services. Using a PRISMA SLR and adapting the Digital Education Council (DEC) AI Literacy Framework (2025), the study identifies the range of AI-related literacies currently embedded within library services, as well as notable gaps in provision. Findings indicate that AI training and implications for academic integrity are multifaceted and evolving, suggesting that AI training and academic integrity should not be isolated, but integrated into existing structures - placing academic librarians at the forefront of such transformative practices.

The rapid adoption of artificial intelligence tools in education has outpaced systematic risk assessment development. Teachers lack practical frameworks to evaluate potential harms in classroom applications. While UNESCO, OECD, the EU AI Act, and NIST provide institutional guidelines, these remain inadequately operationalized for individual teaching practice. Through comparative analysis of international standards, a teacher-centered risk assessment framework is developed. Regulatory requirements are translated into a four-step methodology comprising inventory creation, risk prioritization, mitigation strategies, and monitoring. Implementation barriers are identified, including time constraints, digital literacy gaps, legal uncertainties, and institutional resistance. The framework demonstrates

As a result of rapid technological advances and shifting expectations in education, integrating Artificial Intelligence (AI) has gained importance, particularly in English Language Teaching (ELT). This mixed-methods study explores the relationship between EFL instructors' digital competencies and their perceptions of using AI in instructional settings. Data were collected from 51 EFL instructors at preparatory schools of four state universities using the AI and English Language Teaching Scale (Edmett et al., 2023) and the Teachers' Digital Competencies Scale (Ergül & Taşar, 2023), along with semi-structured interviews. Quantitative findings revealed that instructors with higher digital competence held more positive views on AI use in teaching, while those with lower competence expressed reservations. Thematic analysis showed that AI integration presents both opportunities and challenges. The study concludes that enhancing instructors' digital competencies may foster more positive attitudes and effective AI integration, emphasizing the need for targeted professional development.

The study investigated the impact of human-machine collaboration (HMC) in English-Arabic translation, examining both its benefits and challenges. A mixed-methods research design was employed, incorporating both quantitative and qualitative techniques. Sixty-four participants were involved, with four excluded due to a lack of experience with machine translation systems. Data was collected using a semi-structured questionnaire via the Google Forms platform. The findings indicated that HMC offers three major benefits: enhancing expertise in HMC, providing system feedback and optimizing job satisfaction. Despite these benefits, the key accuracy challenges were primarily linked to fundamental linguistic differences, including grammatical, lexical, and contextual variations. Culture and technical differences also posed significant difficulties for collaboration in translation and post-editing processes.

The widespread adoption of generative artificial intelligence is fundamentally transforming academic knowledge practices and presents significant challenges for higher education institutions globally. This chapter investigates the impact of generative AI on the epistemic foundations of university teaching, advancing beyond perspectives that regard AI solely as a technical instrument or regulatory concern. Generative AI is conceptualized as a catalyst for an epistemic paradigm shift, with implications for didactics, assessment, and institutional governance. The chapter employs a conceptual and theory-driven methodology, drawing on Kuhn's paradigm theory, epistemic culture research, distributed cognition, and actor-network theory. The findings indicate that generative AI disrupts reproduction-oriented models of academic performance and shifts epistemic authority toward critical judgment within hybrid human machine contexts. Prompt literacy is identified as a crucial epistemic competence, while control-oriented assessment frameworks are increasingly invalid.

Gamification, the strategic integration of game design elements into non-game contexts, has emerged as a powerful pedagogical approach aimed at enhancing motivation, engagement, and learning outcomes in educational environments. This chapter is designed to introduce educators to the fundamental concepts, theoretical foundations, and practical applications of gamification. It begins by defining key components such as points, badges, leaderboards, challenges, narratives, and feedback systems, illustrating how these elements can be tailored to support diverse learning objectives and student profiles.

This chapter is based on an argument that while AI offers opportunities for adaptive and on-demand learning, it tends to reduce the scope of the curriculum. A dataset collected through semi-structured interviews with twenty university-level TESOL educators from fifteen countries was analyzed qualitatively. Three interconnected themes surfaced from this analysis: bias in content selection, reduced critical engagement, and teacher mediation. As AI tools work on measurable skills rather than critical thinking and cultural depth, they risk narrowing language curricula to quantifiable features, underscoring the importance of pedagogical strategies for holistic development. Positioning educators as active agents helps in shaping inclusive and reflective language learning, preserving cultural depth, critical engagement, and holistic learning outcomes in AI-enhanced environments.

The integration of Digital Humanities (DH) into postgraduate education offers transformative possibilities for advancing research methodologies in Arabic and Islamic Studies. This chapter investigates how digital tools, computational approaches, and interactive platforms can enrich traditional modes of scholarly inquiry. By examining applications such as text mining, digital manuscript preservation, corpus-based linguistic analysis, and data visualization, the study highlights how DH fosters interdisciplinary exploration and critical engagement with classical and contemporary sources. In addition, the chapter proposes a technology-enhanced learning (TEL) prototype designed specifically to support research methodology training in Arabic and Islamic Studies. The prototype integrates digital research environments, collaborative annotation tools, and multilingual data resources to cultivate students' digital literacy and methodological innovation.

The integration of Artificial Intelligence (AI) into digital education marks a major shift in pedagogy, learner engagement, and institutional functions. AI-driven systems such as intelligent tutoring, adaptive learning, and learning analytics are transforming how knowledge is delivered and assessed. This chapter explores AI's role in creating adaptive learning environments, supporting both cognitive and emotional assessment, and improving institutional efficiency through automation. Global platforms including Squirrel AI, Carnegie Learning, Duolingo, and DIKSHA are examined. The chapter also addresses ethical, technical, and infrastructural

Understanding teachers' hopes and fears about AI is necessary as they are at the frontline of education. This will help how to successfully navigate AI integration into classrooms. This chapter involves interviewing eleven teacher-educators about their thoughts on AI impact in schools. The result shows that participants recognized AI's strong potential to improve teaching, provide personalized instruction for students, and improve access to learning resources. AI can lessen workload through content generation leading to enhanced lessons and assessment. Teachers also recognize the AI potential to help students by providing access to learning materials. On the other hand, they expressed concerns about the AI potential misuse such as the risk of plagiarism, the erosion of students' critical-thinking skills, and diminishing human interaction. They also recognized the lack of teachers' preparation and absence of clear policies pose challenge for the full adoption of AI. In closing, the chapter outlines actionable recommendations for seamless integration of AI in schools.

Preface

INTRODUCTION

The transformative rise of artificial intelligence (AI) is reshaping the educational landscape at a pace and scale unprecedented in modern history. AI systems are now central to teaching, learning, assessment, and curriculum design, no longer just on the edges. Educators are now being asked to reconsider their roles in evolving, hybrid human-AI learning settings, which include automated feedback tools, adaptive learning platforms, AI-driven research assistants, and frameworks for ethical governance.

This edited volume, Human-AI Collaboration and the Evolving Role of Educators, arises from a shared recognition that the AI revolution in education must not be reduced to technical integration alone. Instead, it demands sustained critical engagement with pedagogy, ethics, access, and equity. As editors, we were driven by the urgency to amplify global perspectives, particularly those from the Global South, and to offer a space for scholars, practitioners, and policymakers to reflect on both the risks and possibilities of AI-enhanced education.

Far from presenting AI as a threat or replacement, this book explores how AI can serve as a collaborator-augmenting human judgment, extending teacher capacities, and enabling new forms of inclusive, data-informed learning. Across the chapters, contributors reimagine the educator's role not as diminished by AI but as evolving into that of a cognitive architect, ethical mediator, and agent of equity in digital ecosystems.

CHAPTER OVERVIEW

Chapter 1 examines AI literacy and academic integrity through the lens of academic libraries, presenting a systematic review of how librarians are adapting support services in higher education. By aligning findings with the Digital Education Council AI Literacy Framework, the chapter positions librarians as key institutional actors in promoting ethical and responsible AI use.

Chapter 2 addresses the need for classroom-level AI risk assessment by introducing a teacher-centered framework. Drawing on international regulatory standards, it translates governance principles into practical steps that enable teachers to evaluate AI tools while maintaining professional autonomy.

Chapter 3 explores digital learning environments from a developing country perspective, analysing how AI tools affect student performance, self-efficacy, creativity, and originality. Grounded in self-efficacy, constructivist, and digital divide theories, it highlights structural inequities and proposes strategies to bridge the AI divide.

Chapter 4 reconceptualises educators as cognitive architects in AI-augmented learning environments. Using distributed cognition and TPACK, it advances a framework for pedagogical co-performance between humans and intelligent systems, emphasizing agency, ethics, and institutional support.

Chapter 5 investigates EFL instructors' digital competencies and their perceptions of AI integration in language teaching. Using a mixed-methods approach, the chapter demonstrates how professional development influences attitudes toward and effective use of AI tools.

Chapter 6 examines human–machine collaboration in English–Arabic translation, highlighting both efficiency gains and persistent linguistic, cultural, and technical challenges. The findings underscore the complementary relationship between human expertise and machine systems.

Chapter 7 argues that generative AI represents an epistemic paradigm shift in higher education. Drawing on paradigm theory and socio-technical perspectives, it reframes prompt literacy as a core academic competence and challenges traditional assessment models.

Chapter 8 analyses gamification, the strategic integration of game design elements into non-game contexts, which has emerged as a powerful pedagogical approach aimed at enhancing motivation, engagement, and learning outcomes in educational environments. This chapter is designed to introduce educators to the fundamental concepts, theoretical foundations, and practical applications of gamification. It begins by defining key components such as points, badges, leaderboards, challenges, narratives, and feedback systems, illustrating how these elements can be tailored to support diverse learning objectives and student profiles.

Chapter 9 presents TESOL professionals' perspectives on generative AI and the narrowing of language curricula. Based on international interviews, it emphasizes teacher mediation to preserve critical engagement, cultural depth, and holistic language learning.

Chapter 10 explores the integration of Digital Humanities into postgraduate research methodologies in Arabic and Islamic Studies. It demonstrates how digital tools enrich traditional scholarship and proposes a technology-enhanced learning prototype to foster methodological innovation.

Chapter 11 provides a synthesis of AI-driven transformations in digital education, examining adaptive learning, learning analytics, emotional assessment, and institutional efficiency. Ethical and learner-centred considerations frame future directions.

Chapter 12 introduces a policy-by-design framework for regulating human–AI collaboration in higher education. It advocates anticipatory governance models that embed ethical and pedagogical foresight into institutional policy.

Chapter 13 presents a systemic mixed-methods analysis of student use of AI-enhanced research tools across Global South universities. It identifies institutional disparities and proposes equity-focused pedagogical interventions.

Chapter 14 evaluates the impact of AI and EdTech tools on learning outcomes across diverse contexts. Integrating theory and empirical evidence, it offers recommendations for inclusive and pedagogically sound adoption.

Chapter 15 examines smart learning through educational robotics, emphasizing constructivist and constructionist approaches. It highlights robotics' potential for STEM education, inclusion, and real-world problem solving, while stressing teacher readiness.

Chapter 16 applies the Capability Approach to analyse teachers' roles in a tech-driven world, identifying essential capability sets needed to achieve quality education amid rapid technological change.

Chapter 17 explores the future of teachers' roles through the Technology Acceptance Model, reflecting on lessons from the COVID-19 pandemic and evolving demands for digital professional development.

Chapter 18 concludes the volume by examining teachers' hopes and fears regarding AI in classrooms. Through interviews, it captures tensions between opportunity and risk, offering actionable recommendations for ethical and effective AI integration.

CONCLUSION

This volume demonstrates that human-AI collaboration in education is neither uniform nor automatic-it is shaped by policy environments, institutional readiness, cultural values, and the agency of educators. The chapters collectively underscore that the role of the educator is not being replaced, but reframed. Educators are emerging as curators of ethical practice, designers of digitally mediated learning experiences, and critical agents in shaping equitable AI adoption.

What threads these contributions together is the conviction that *how* we integrate AI matters as much as *what* we integrate. Ethical governance, inclusive policies, critical digital pedagogy, and teacher agency are central to shaping AI futures that enhance rather than erode educational purpose. The risks of technological determinism-where systems dictate pedagogy-must be actively countered with frameworks that embed human values, justice, and critical inquiry.

As editors, we hope this book serves not only as a reference but also as a provocation, challenging institutions to center educators, not algorithms, in their AI strategies. By focusing on collaboration, contextual responsiveness, and critical reflection, this volume contributes to the collective task of forging human-AI partnerships that advance both excellence and equity in education.

Chapter 1

AI Literacy and Academic Integrity: A Systematic Review of Academic Libraries' Support Services in Higher Education

Tendai Mataranyika
https://orcid.org/0000-0002-9886-8996
Two Oceans Graduate Institute, South Africa

Lesego Makhafola
https://orcid.org/0000-0001-5934-384X
University of Pretoria, South Africa

Amber Clarke
https://orcid.org/0009-0008-3545-4463
Two Oceans Graduate Institute, South Africa

ABSTRACT

This chapter contributes to contemporary debates on the implications of AI tools for academic writing and the preservation of academic integrity within HEIs. Traditionally, academic librarians have led efforts to promote academic integrity through various means. However, the rapid adoption of AI has disrupted the established roles of academic librarians and called for new approaches to ensure ethical and responsible academic engagement. In particular, questions arise about how academic librarians have adapted their technological support services. Using a PRISMA SLR and adapting the Digital Education Council (DEC) AI Literacy Framework (2025), the study identifies the range of AI-related literacies currently embedded within library services, as well as notable gaps in provision. Findings

DOI: 10.4018/979-8-3373-4521-5.ch001

indicate that AI training and implications for academic integrity are multifaceted and evolving, suggesting that AI training and academic integrity should not be isolated, but integrated into existing structures - placing academic librarians at the forefront of such transformative practices.

1. INTRODUCTION

Academic integrity is essential to the core activities of teaching, learning, and research in higher education institutions (HEIs). However, there is no universally accepted definition of academic integrity, although common themes are present in descriptions of it. In 2021, the Australian Tertiary Education Quality and Standards Agency defined academic integrity as "the expectation that teachers, students, researchers, and all members of the academic community act with honesty, trust, fairness, respect, and responsibility" (Gunton, 2022, p. 157). Balalle and Pannilage (2025) emphasise that academic integrity signifies the value of the qualifications offered by institutions and reflects the honesty, trust, and ethical conduct of students, as well as the processes employed by institutions. The European Network for Academic Integrity (ENAI) presents a glossary that highlights various dimensions through which academic integrity can be defined and interpreted (Tauginienė et al., 2018). This interpretation aligns with ethical and professional principles, standards, and practices that support the core values of research and scholarship. Balalle and Pannilage (2025) reiterate that academic integrity is a commitment to honesty and moral conduct, both by students and academic staff. This collective effort cannot be achieved individually. Elaiess (2024) elaborates that academic integrity reflects honesty, trust, fairness, respect, and responsibility in the academic community. Academic integrity constitutes the moral fibre and essence of the higher education enterprise, underpinning teaching, learning, and research. The ethos of academic integrity serves as the foundation that upholds the rigour and credibility of the output of HEIs, such as publications, graduates, and qualifications.

Authorities have noted that university students often struggle with academic integrity, particularly as they begin their higher education studies. This places demands on those responsible for providing support in this area. According to Hossain et al. (2025), research on academic integrity shows that at the start of students' university careers, they often lack the skills required to cite, reference, paraphrase, and avoid plagiarism. Lowe (2024) shares similar views, stating that evidence shows that students have a limited understanding of what constitutes academic dishonesty and the meaning of academic integrity. From an academic integrity perspective, the widespread use of AI tools raises questions about AI detection, the development and enforcement of policies, authorship, cheating, and plagiarism (Moya et al., 2024).

Lowe (2024) emphasises that assuming students understand what counts as cheating and plagiarism is incorrect. Therefore, in the context of AI tools and the longstanding focus of academic librarians on information and digital literacies, many of these concerns should be addressed. The importance of academic integrity to academic excellence, research quality, teaching, and learning makes it a key concern for all involved parties, both within and beyond academia.

Academic librarians have long promoted academic integrity. For instance, Gunton (2022) emphasises that a holistic approach provides librarians with the opportunity to foster institution-wide collaborations. Furthermore, academic libraries are vital in equipping students and faculty with the skills and ethical understanding necessary to uphold academic integrity (Lo & Lo, 2025; Lowe, 2024; Miron et al., 2024). Gunton (2022) observes that librarians involved in teaching and learning activities are among the primary contributors in helping students to avoid academic misconduct. Filson and Atuase (2024) state that academic librarians promote integrity in HEIs by equipping students with information literacy skills, providing training, and offering guidance on the responsible and legal use of information through the use of citations and referencing, and by avoiding plagiarism. Michalak (2023) further emphasises that academic librarians are experts with extensive experience in areas such as information ethics, privacy, and intellectual freedom, making them authoritative voices on academic integrity. Miron et al. (2024) highlight that addressing the challenges that AI poses to academic integrity necessitates collaboration among faculty, administrators, instructional designers, librarians, and other stakeholders. Filson and Atuase (2024) recommend that, as technologies increasingly shape the higher education landscape, academic librarians should expand their roles and develop innovative strategies for managing academic integrity and enhancing learning experiences for their users. The shared focus on the intersection between the values of academic integrity and the skills embedded in information literacy training underscores the importance of academic librarians as key stakeholders in championing AI-related competencies in HEIs.

Academic librarians, who are already experienced in delivering information and digital and media literacy to students and academics at HEIs, are well-positioned to champion the design, development, and delivery of AI literacy. Their information literacy skills have long been hailed as critical for academic integrity and lifelong learning. Librarians, and academic librarians in particular, therefore play a key role in facilitating AI technical knowledge, ethical awareness, critical thinking, practical skills, and the evaluation and appreciation of societal impact (Leo, 2025). In addition, they have a history of forging campus-wide networks and partnerships, which are much needed in the integration of AI into higher education curricula. Partnerships with faculty and university technology units have been suggested as ways for academic librarians to integrate AI literacy into courses and facilitate learning communities.

The ubiquity and widespread use of AI tools in learning, teaching, and research require campus-wide support structures for both staff and students. There is a growing demand for AI-related support at HEIs. For example, in Australia, three-quarters of the staff at top universities indicate they need support, feeling that there is a gap in what universities currently provide (Lee et al., 2024). This underscores the vital role of academic librarians' expertise and support in addressing current and emerging challenges related to the ethical use of AI tools and in maintaining academic integrity at HEIs. While there is anecdotal evidence showing that librarians are key stakeholders in the design and delivery of AI literacy, there are limited studies that have specifically addressed how academic librarians across various geographic regions have responded to the integration of AI through the design and implementation of AI-related services, the strategies adopted, the challenges faced, and the resultant recommendations.

1.1 Problem Statement

The role of academic libraries in supporting the use of artificial intelligence by students and staff in higher education remains contested and insufficiently defined. Grote et al. (2024) point out that AI use in HEIs presents complexities that have led to questions about the legitimacy of the research support services offered by libraries and their role in this regard. Furthermore, there is a lack of literature on how academic library support services have responded to and reconfigured their offerings to support and promote the use of AI by students and staff at universities. To address this gap, this study explored the roles of academic librarians and the current strategies employed by them in delivering AI literacy support services at different universities. In this chapter, a structured and systematic literature review is conducted to examine how the roles of academic librarians are articulated in the literature and to establish the documented strategies that academic libraries have applied to date, as well as the challenges they face in fulfilling this mandate.

1.2 Objectives

The primary objective of this chapter is to systematically establish how the role of academic librarians in supporting AI usage by students and staff is portrayed in the literature and how this role has evolved over the years. Furthermore, the study aims to identify the challenges faced by academic librarians as they provide AI-related support services and recommend best practices that may enhance the effectiveness of their roles. The research endeavours to answer the following research questions (RQs):

1. How are academic librarians represented in the scholarly and professional literature as responding to AI and academic integrity challenges?
2. What strategies and initiatives are publicly communicated by university libraries to support AI literacy and its ethical use?
3. What challenges are academic libraries experiencing in imparting AI-related skills and competencies?
4. What best practices and frameworks can be distilled from the literature worldwide?

2. METHODOLOGY

This chapter presents a systematic literature review. It was conducted using comprehensive and reproducible search methods and a structured screening, appraisal, and synthesis workflow. Reporting of the results follows PRISMA-style conventions where applicable (for example, identification, screening, eligibility, and inclusion), recognising that the results span peer-reviewed literature relevant to academic libraries and higher education. To enhance reliability, screening and extraction decisions are documented with the justification for their inclusion or exclusion at full-text screening.

2.1 Information Sources and Search Strategy

Five sources were selected for balanced coverage and to reduce database bias, including Scopus, Web of Science (Core Collection), EBSCOhost, and ProQuest. A single, concept-clustered Boolean string structured around the population or context (in this case, higher education), the phenomenon (academic integrity or information ethics), the intervention technology (including AI, GenAI, and large language models [LLMs]), and the professional lens (libraries, librarianship, and AI literacy) was developed and piloted in Scopus and Web of Science, then adapted to other platforms, using field tags, wildcards, and phrase-handling adjustment as required.

2.1.1 Search String

The following search string was used across the selected databases:

[(“artificial intelligence” OR AI OR “generative AI” OR GenAI OR “large language model*” OR ChatGPT)] AND [(“academic integrity” OR plagiarism OR “information ethics” OR “academic misconduct” OR “ethical use”)] AND [(librarian* OR “academic library” OR “library services” OR “digital literacy” OR “AI literacy”)] AND [(“higher education” OR universit* OR college OR “tertiary education”)]

The search language was limited to English. Searches queried metadata fields (titles, abstracts, keywords or descriptors), including English-language dissertations and reports, and were last executed on 17 September 2025. No date limits were imposed to capture the rapid pre- and post-GenAI evolution.

Reference lists of the included studies and key policy documents were hand-searched.

2.1.2 Record Management and De-Duplication

All the results were exported in RIS (research information systems) file format, combined, and then de-duplicated using database-level tools, Covidence's automatic duplicate removal function. Manual duplicate removal was also performed. The 368 unique records progressed to title/abstract screening. Five duplicates were manually identified and removed, resulting in a total of 368.

The results from each of the databases searched are summarised in Table 1.

Table 1. Summary of the Results From Each of the Databases Searched

Database	Initial search results	Duplicates removed	Results for screening
EBSCOhost	154	37	117
ProQuest	180	54	126
Scopus	118	0	118
Web of Science	73	61	12
Total	525	157	368

2.1.3 Eligibility Criteria

The eligibility criteria were determined before screening commenced and refined after the initial search to ensure relevant results were retrieved. The inclusion and exclusion criteria were:

2.1.3.1 Inclusion Criteria

- Focus on artificial intelligence (including generative AI and large language models such as ChatGPT) in relation to academic integrity, information ethics, ethical use, or academic misconduct.
- Substantial engagement with librarians, academic libraries, library services, digital literacy, or AI literacy.
- Context was higher education (universities, colleges, and tertiary institutions).

- Source types: peer-reviewed journal articles, conference papers, dissertations and theses, policy papers, institutional reports, and professional guidelines.

2.1.3.2 Exclusion Criteria

- K-12 (primary and high school) and non-tertiary contexts; corporate and industry settings with no linkage to higher education.
- AI use unrelated to integrity or ethics (for example, solely automation of back-office library workflows without ethical framing).
- Purely technical papers without educational or library implications.
- Non-English documents (unless an English version or translation was available).

When uncertainty remained, the full text was retrieved and assessed against the same criteria.

2.1.4 Screening and Selection of Sources

The four databases were searched using the constructed search string. The results were exported in RIS file format and imported into Covidence to initiate the screening process. Duplicates across the database were identified upon importing the records into Covidence, and the duplicates were manually identified and removed.

The screening proceeded in two stages:

1. Title/abstract screening of the 368 unique records was done using the inclusion or exclusion criteria to exclude irrelevant records.
2. Full-text eligibility of the records retained from Stage 1 was assessed, and the full texts were retrieved and evaluated, documenting reasons for exclusion (for example, no full text, incorrect population, insufficient library linkage, and poor language).

Finally, the included literature was extracted for in-depth analysis.

A PRISMA-style flow diagram (Figure 1) summarises counts at each stage, along with reasons for full-text exclusions.

Figure 1. PRISMA-Style Flow Diagram For Literature Review

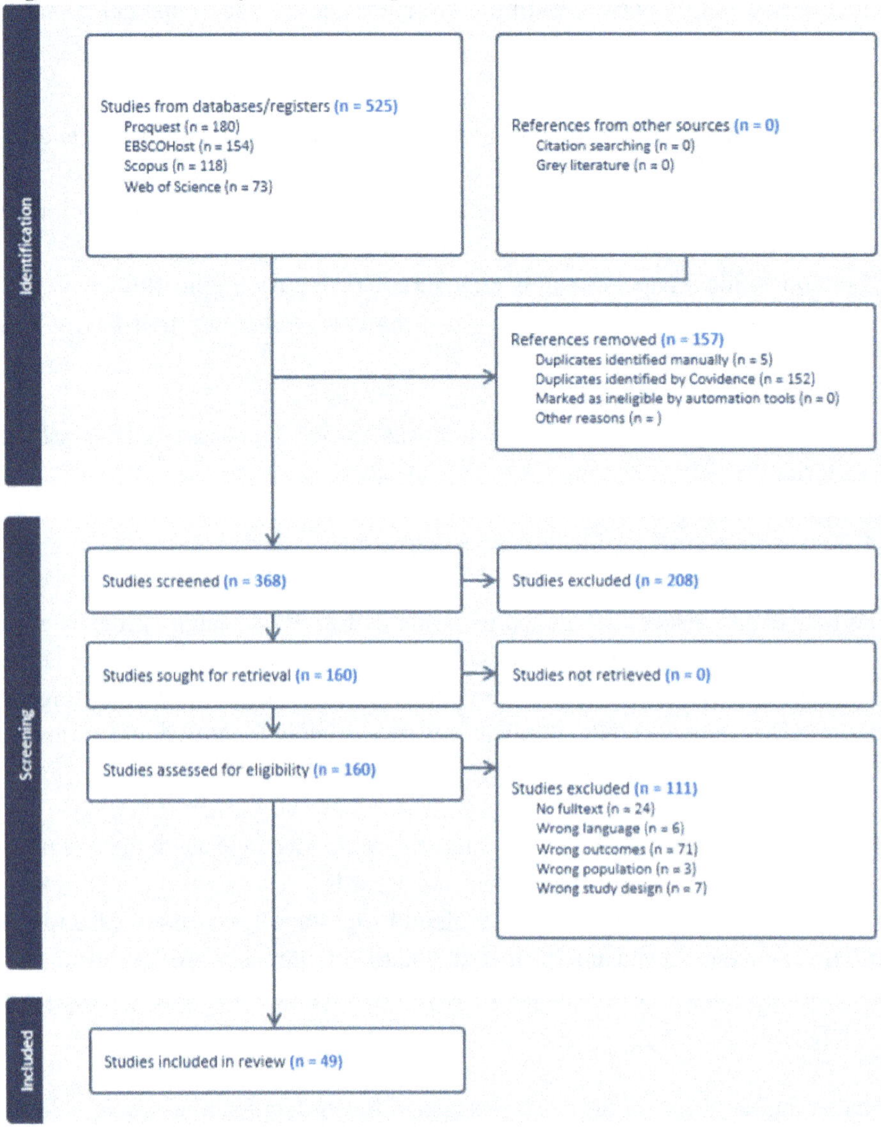

2.2 Data Extraction and Coding

A structured extraction template captured bibliographic and methodological details, as well as the substantive constructs necessary for synthesis, including citation details, study type, study design, AI focus, research integrity/ethics, library role, outcomes, challenges, opportunities, and recommendations. The data were coded thematically, focusing on the following:

- Role of librarians in AI and academic integrity
- Types of AI literacy initiatives
- Opportunities and challenges
- Best practices and gaps

2.3 Data Analysis

Given the variation in designs and outcomes, a narrative thematic analysis was undertaken. This approach emphasises patterns of meaning across texts while preserving contextual nuances (such as institutional type, discipline, policy maturity) relevant to academic libraries and higher education.

2.4 Validity and Reliability

Validity in qualitative research refers to the use of procedures that verify the accuracy and credibility of research findings (Creswell, 2014; Flick, 2015; Silverman, 2013). Validity helps to show that a study was conducted thoroughly and ethically. Reliability is used to assess the rigour of qualitative research, examining its theoretical foundations and methods, essentially checking the dependability of the data and data collection and analysis procedures (Flick, 2015). The results of this research are not generalisable, as the study focuses on particular cases in which views and opinions are likely to change over time.

2.5 Limitations

The limitations include English-language restriction. The authors used English because it is the language they are familiar with. Since primary data were not collected, the findings may differ from what is reported in this chapter. This leaves room for further investigation.

3. INTRODUCING AI LITERACY

There is no universally accepted definition of AI literacy, but there are common skills and competencies that constitute it. It is important to note that AI literacy has not developed in isolation; instead, it is closely related to previously defined literacies such as information and media literacies (Chiu et al. 2024; Long & Magerko

2020; MacCallum et al. 2023). Almatrafi et al. (2024) explain that the definition of AI literacy is elusive and constantly evolving due to AI's broad application across various sectors and the numerous interventions being introduced. Almatrafi et al. (2024), MacCallum et al. (2024), Ndungu (2024), and Zhao et al. (2024) agree that, although there is no globally accepted definition of AI literacy, the definition proposed by Long and Magerko in 2020 has gained widespread recognition. Long and Magerko (2020, p. 2) define AI literacy as "a set of competencies that enables individuals to critically evaluate AI technologies, communicate and collaborate effectively with AI, and utilise AI as a tool online, at home and in the workplace". Annapureddy et al. (2024) note that AI literacy has become a fundamental set of competencies necessary for individuals to function effectively in the era of AI.

Tadamilla and Maher (2024) introduce other dimensions of AI literacy, namely: technical (the understanding and development of AI systems), GenAI (understanding and interacting with AI systems such as ChatGPT, Bing, and SORA), general (skills for everyday use and interaction with AI systems), ethical and social (the ethical impact of AI such as privacy, security, fairness, and transparency); and cognitive and metacognitive (the cognitive skills needed to interact and adapt AI systems). From these converging definitions and perspectives, AI literacy skills and competencies transfer are characterised by a multiplicity of stakeholders and audiences, a factor giving rise to holistic approaches.

The role of AI literacy in the effective and efficient adoption and adaptation of AI in different socio-economic sections of society can never be underestimated. Tadimalla and Maher (2024) point out that AI literacy must not be confined to academics only, but should be regarded as a key component of informed citizenship and professional competence in the 21st century. In 2022, the World Economic Forum famously declared, "Without universal AI literacy, AI will fail us" (World Economic Forum [WEF], 2022). AI literacy is recognised as a vital component for deploying and realising AI across various sectors (Almatrafi et al., 2024; MacCallum et al., 2023 Miltenoff, 2024; Ndungu, 2024). Mansoor et al. (2024) explain that AI literacy, besides being a human rights issue, is a prerequisite for society's development and stability. The UNESCO International Forum on AI associates the concept of AI literacy with the general population, stating that global citizens must be educated about AI's impact, capabilities, and benefits, and how it can be utilised for the common good (Miao & Holmes, 2021). Miltenoff (2024) details how governments, international bodies, and institutions have integrated AI literacy into their AI governance policies and frameworks – examples include United Kingdom universities' guiding principles on AI, the United States federal, state, and local governments (National AI Institute Act of 2020), the European Union Council and Parliament, the Australian Framework for GenAI in Schools 2024, the Canadian AI and Data Act of 2023, and Israel's AI Regulation and Ethics Policy

2023. Wang (2025) highlights that different regions show variations in their AI literacy frameworks. It is crucial to recognise that AI literacy has gained prominence as a requisite skill and knowledge not only for academic endeavours, but also for professional and everyday life.

4. THEORETICAL FRAMEWORKS

Two theoretical frameworks informed this study: The Joint Information Systems Committee (Jisc) digital capabilities framework, first developed in 2015 and revised in 2019, and the Digital Education Council's (DEC) AI literacy framework, published in March 2025, which serves as the supporting framework. The two frameworks address different dimensions of the research problem; therefore, their combination provides a comprehensive conceptualisation of the research challenge. The Jisc digital capabilities framework demonstrates that digital capabilities give a baseline for technological literacy and use, while the DEC AI literacy framework, which applies specifically to this study, although with lesser known adoption, specifies the development of AI skills and competencies.

The Joint Information Systems Committee (Jisc) digital capabilities framework, first developed in 2015 and revised in 2019, is regarded as a comprehensive conceptualisation of the functional needs of university staff and students within digital educational systems. Beetham and Sharpe (2013) explain that digital literacy extends far beyond the mere functional IT skills students require to succeed in the digital era. In this framework, ICT, representing digital proficiency, is defined as the use and adoption of ICT devices, applications, software, and services, along with an understanding of basic computing, coding, and information processing. In contrast, digital productivity refers to the ability to select suitable devices, applications, software, and systems for different tasks based on their advantages and limitations (Jisc, 2019). The Jisc digital capabilities framework (2015 version) consists of six elements: digital (ICT) proficiency and productivity (functional skills), information, data and media literacies (critical use), digital creation, problem-solving and innovation (creative production), digital communication, collaboration and participation (participation), digital learning and development (learning), and digital identity and well-being (self-actualisation) (Jisc 2019).

Figure 2. Jisc Digital Capabilities Framework

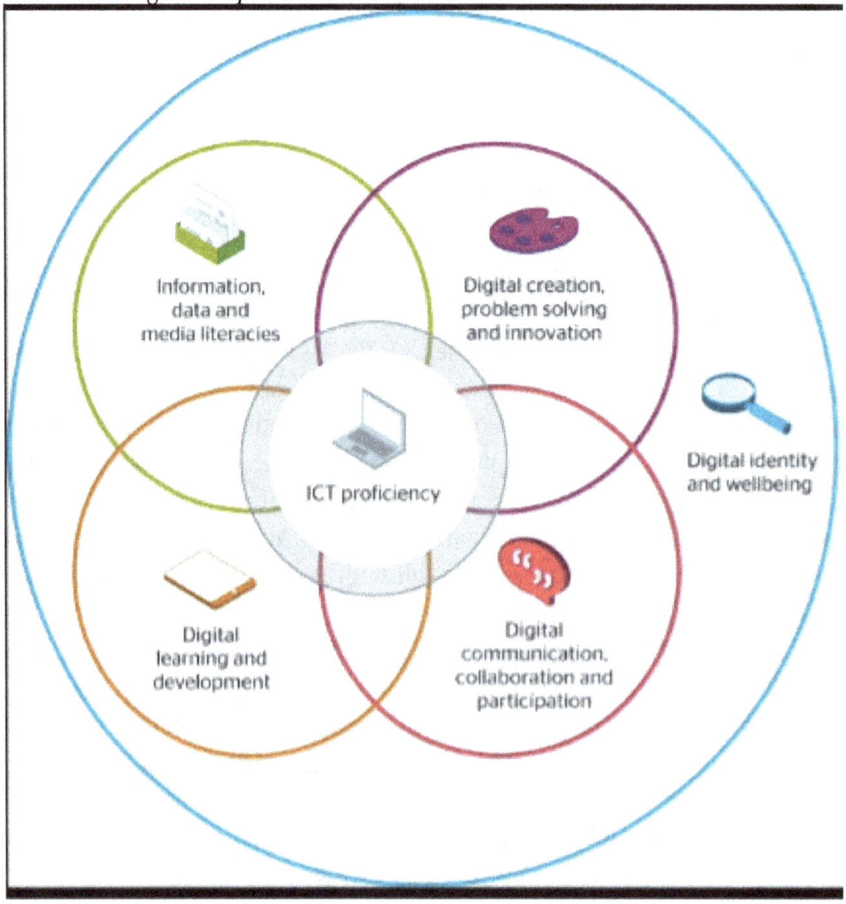

Note. Sourced from Jisc (2019)

Regarding AI support interventions and literacy skills, the six elements of the Jisc digital capabilities framework can be understood as follows: digital (ICT) proficiency and productivity (navigating AI-powered tools), information, data, and media literacies (assessing AI-generated outputs and sources), digital creation, problem-solving, and innovation (using AI in academic work and research), digital communication, collaboration, and participation (AI-based scholarly collaboration), digital learning and development (applying AI to lifelong learning and professional development), and digital identity and well-being (understanding AI ethics). As such, this primary theoretical framework provides a foundational perspective through which the digital capabilities required for engaging with AI tools can be assessed, offering a structure for evaluating AI support services in academic libraries for staff and students, as well as for integrating AI competencies into curriculum design and related objectives.

The DECA AI literacy framework outlines the essential knowledge and skills needed to understand, engage with, and critically evaluate AI technologies. AI literacy includes the ability to use AI tools effectively and ethically, assess their output, ensure humans remain central to AI, and adapt to the changing AI landscape in both personal and professional contexts (Digital Education Council [DEC], 2025). The framework presents five dimensions of AI literacy: understanding AI and data, critical thinking and judgement, ethical and responsible AI use, human-centricity, emotional intelligence, and creativity and domain expertise (DEC, 2025). This framework outlines the levels of competency of each of the five domains as shown in Figure 3.

Figure 3. DEC AI Literacy Dimensions and Competency Levels

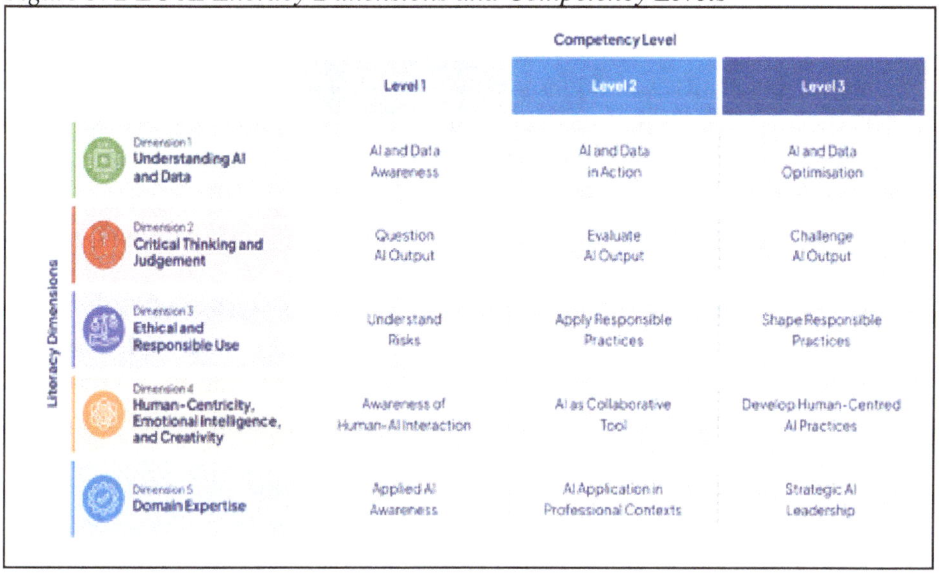

***Note**. Sourced from the DEC (2025, p. 10)*

The five AI literacy dimensions – understanding AI and data; critical thinking and judgement; ethical and responsible use; human-centricity, emotional intelligence and creativity; and domain experience – along with their associated progression levels, provide a foundation for enhancing the content and competency focus of AI literacy. As such, the theoretical combination of the Jisc digital capabilities framework and the DEC AI literacy framework provides a more comprehensive conceptualisation of technical capabilities and ethics-oriented skills, which aids in understanding and evaluating the AI support services and initiatives of academic libraries.

The Jisc framework already defines digital capabilities and role profiles for library and learning support staff. Therefore, institutions can use it to set minimum AI-related expectations for students and staff, formally recognise academic librarians as key AI literacy trainers, and integrate AI use and academic integrity into existing digital skills and information literacy policies rather than creating separate AI initiatives. The DEC framework, on the other hand, adds AI-specific dimensions, such as understanding AI and ethical and responsible use, which can be directly referenced in policies addressing the acceptable use of AI, transparency in assessments, and the ethical evaluation of AI outputs. In low-resource contexts, its tiered levels support minimum policy targets such as basic awareness and ethical use, which libraries deliver through how librarians are represented, the challenges they face, and the best practices and models which can be expanded to academic libraries globally.

Taken together, the Jisc and DEC frameworks provide the study with a strict reference point for (a) analysing how libraries frame their AI and integrity responses in the public sphere, (b) bringing to light structural challenges around resources, staff capabilities, and equity, and (c) proposing policy-linked, scalable models through which academic librarians act as brokers in HEIs between high-level AI strategies and everyday AI use by students and staff. In short, AI literacy frameworks such as the Jisc and DEC frameworks act as "translational tools" between theoretical AI skills and concrete institutional policies, which would be useful in resource-limited settings.

It is worth noting that different academic libraries have adopted different approaches and use of AI literacy frameworks in guiding the design and implementation of their instructional services, and their main emphasis is on evaluation, ethics, and usage of AI tools. Examples of institutions already applying different frameworks are shown in Table 2.

Table 2. Institutions That Apply Different Frameworks

Framework	Key Features	Example of Implementing Universities
UGM AI Literacy (prepare-understand-apply-responsible)	Four-step progression building on academic/ICT/digital skills for GAI	University of Bolton, UK (online, co-designed with students)
AI Literacy Framework	Recognise/understand, use/apply, evaluate/critique, reflect/respect	University of Adelaide Library (guides and webinars)
User-Perspective AI Digital Literacy	Instructional strategies, interactive experiences, and resources	McGill University Library, Canada (AI training programs) and Bindura University of Science and Technology, Zimbabwe

continued on following page

Table 2. Continued

Framework	Key Features	Example of Implementing Universities
Library 3.0-Inspired Information Literacy, Digital Literacy, and AI Literacy	Participation, interactivity, adaptability; workshops and makerspaces	Linköping University Library (DigiMaker makerspace, AI workshops)
AI Literacy Training Strategies	AI tools piloting, LibGuides, citation guidance, expert collaborations	University of Cape Town Libraries, South Africa

5. LITERATURE REVIEW FINDINGS

The findings from the literature review are presented in the ensuing section.

5.1 Synthesis of the Results

The study aimed to examine how the roles of academic librarians in supporting AI use by university students and staff are portrayed in the literature and to identify initiatives and strategies they have implemented in this area. Additionally, the study explored articulated challenges faced by academic librarians in providing AI-centred support services, along with best practices and frameworks emerging from the literature under review.

The 49 articles selected for this study were distributed as shown in Table 3.

Table 3. Distribution of Selected Articles by Year

Year	Number of Articles
2023	7
2024	16
2025	26
Total	49

The greatest number of articles was published in 2025 (n=26), followed by 2024 (n=16), and then 2023 (n=7). Between 2023 and 2024, the figure increased exponentially, with more than double the number of articles having been published in 2023. This shows an increasing trend in the number of articles about AI available in academic libraries.

In this study, four general themes were identified to address the research issues: the academic librarian's role in AI literacy and academic integrity as outlined in the literature; academic libraries' AI initiatives and strategies designed to support students and staff in using AI; challenges faced by academic librarians as they endeavour to provide AI-centred support services to faculty; and proposed best practices and frameworks that emphasise emerging recommendations from the literature for the design and delivery of AI-centred support services. Each paper was analysed to extract information related to any of these four themes. The distribution of documents covering these themes is shown in Table 4.

Table 4. Percentage of Papers Per Theme

Theme	**Percentage of papers covering each theme (%)**
Academic librarians' role in AI literacy and academic integrity	27
Challenges experienced by academic libraries	24
Academic libraries' AI strategies and initiatives	16
Proposed best practices and frameworks	38

Table 4 shows that the most common theme was *proposed best practices and frameworks*, appearing in 38% of the included papers. This was followed by academic librarians' role in AI literacy and academic integrity, which covered 27% of the papers. Following closely were the challenges experienced by academic libraries at 24%, and the least discussed theme was academic libraries' AI strategies and initiatives, which accounted for 16% of the papers.

5.2 Role of Academic Librarians in AI Literacy and Academic Integrity

It was found that 27% of the papers analysed contain information suggesting that academic librarians play a significant role in the upskilling of students and staff at universities. The documents that contained prominent assertions of this sentiment are stated in Table 5.

Table 5. The Role of Academic Libraries in AI Literacy and Academic Integrity

Assertion and Context	Authors
Librarians have a role to play in sustaining research integrity (Ghana)	Filson and Atuase (2024)
Librarians have a role in promoting ethical, practical, and literate use of GenAI through training and support (Hong Kong)	Yeung et al. (2025)
Academic librarians play a key role in AI training for academic integrity (Ghana)	Akakpo et al. (2025)
Academic librarians are engaged in disseminating AI literacy, where it is a component of information literacy (South Africa)	Bangani (2025)
Librarians should provide guidance on AI use in research, such as guidelines (not specified)	Huihui et al. (2023)
Libraries are uniquely positioned to help users mitigate the ethical complexities and verification challenges of GenAI.	Giray et al. (2025)
Emphasis is on the leading role of librarians and information specialists in the process (Europe)	Miltenoff (2024)
Librarians must address the equity concerns of the digital and AI divides and fight against misinformation (United States of America)	Sheppard (2025)
Librarians to deliver digital safety competence training (not specified)	Ma et al. (2025)

Table 5 indicates a strong consensus that academic libraries and librarians are central to AI literacy and academic integrity. Across the studies analysed, librarians were repeatedly positioned as key role-players in sustaining research integrity (for example, Ghana) and promoting ethical and literate use of GenAI through training and support (for example, Hong Kong). The focus was also on delivering AI-focused instruction tied to academic integrity (for example, Ghana and South Africa, where AI literacy is framed as part of information literacy).

The responsibility of librarians to provide practical guidance and formal guidelines on AI usage was stressed by several authors, along with helping students and staff to navigate ethical and verification challenges, and taking leadership roles in institutional responses. Beyond training, Table 5 highlights that librarians' broader societal role in addressing equity issues was linked to digital/AI divides, strengthening digital safety competence, and countering misinformation (which was particularly noted in the USA). Overall, the research positions academic librarians as educators, ethical stewards, and advocates who ensure that AI is used responsibly and fairly in academic contexts. As such, the literature considered in this study shows a significant assertion that academic librarians have a role to play in the design and delivery of AI-centred support services for staff and students at HEIs.

5.3 Challenges Faced by Academic Librarians in Teaching AI-Related Skills and Competencies

Academic librarians face numerous challenges in their efforts to develop and deliver AI-focused skills to university communities. Of the articles reviewed, 24% (in the USA, Norway, Nigeria, South Africa, and Zimbabwe) highlighted these challenges.

The legitimacy of academic librarians in terms of providing AI-centred research support services to students and staff, in one aspect, is shrouded in controversy. Michalak and Ellixson (2025) note that even at prominent universities in the USA, academic libraries do not offer mainstream AI training programmes but rather support and collaborate with other departments, such as the Office of Teaching Effectiveness and Innovation and the Centre for Career and Professional Development. In such partnerships, the role of the academic library is to curate AI research guides and instructional resources, ensuring that students and faculty have access to credible information (Michalak & Ellixson, 2025). Dabirian et al. (2025) echo these sentiments, pointing out that librarians at California State University in the USA are excluded from campus-wide initiatives, suggesting that academic librarians face exclusion in the implementation of strategic AI initiatives such as policy formulation (Michalak, 2023).

Academic librarians' lack of adequate AI skills and competencies is another challenge identified in the literature. In their discussion of this topic, Grote et al. (2024) note that in Norway, questions arise about the authority, credibility, and reliability of academic librarians' capacity to design and deliver holistic AI training and related support services. As such, academic librarians are said to be in dire need of credible training and upskilling in AI for them to be effective in offering research support to students and staff at universities (Alzubaidi, 2025; Bangani, 2025; Filson & Atuase, 2024; Moorhouse et al., 2023; Olusipe & Adetayo et al.,2024; Tsekea & Mandoga, 2025). Without such professional upskilling, the lack of skills and competencies may raise questions regarding the credibility of academic librarians in providing research support related to AI. An alternative approach can be seen in resource-advantaged countries such as Europe, where some university libraries are reportedly opting to employ AI specialists to serve in academic libraries (Buitrago-Ciro et al., 2025). This introduces an additional challenge – preventing academic librarians from embarking on AI-related professional development, both in terms of resource availability and funding. For example, in Nigeria and Zimbabwe, academic librarians reportedly lack budgetary provision for capacity-building and professional development related to AI (Olusipe et al., 2024; Safana & Fari, 2025; Tsekea & Mandoga, 2025).

In summary, the challenges faced by academic librarians in developing capacity begin at the operational level, but extend to structural limitations through their exclusion from institutional AI policy development. Such exclusion undermines academic librarians' legitimacy as AI educators and leaders, positioning them as circumstantial support structures. In addition, uneven access to professional upskilling opportunities and resource constraints, particularly in low- and middle-income contexts, exacerbate disparities in the provision of AI support by academic librarians. Taken together, these challenges are critical in relating directly to the provision of consistent, appropriate, and sustainable AI literacy support for students and staff. These challenges determine whether academic libraries can meaningfully contribute to safeguarding academic integrity in an increasingly AI-driven higher education landscape.

5.4 Public Strategies and Initiatives University Libraries Use To Support AI Literacy and Ethical Use

While significant challenges have been acknowledged, 16% of the articles reviewed mention strategies and initiatives that academic libraries have adopted to provide AI-focused services. One study investigated AI integration and outreach activities by academic libraries of the top 10 highest-ranked universities across Europe, North America, sub-Saharan Africa, Latin America, and the Caribbean. It found that 50% of these libraries offer educational materials, 42.5% organise educational activities, and 12.5% have policies related to AI (Buitrago-Ciro et al., 2025). Yet academic libraries in Latin America and Sub-Saharan Africa are reportedly falling behind in integrating AI into their courses compared to those in Europe and North America, and these gaps might be linked to socio-economic factors, social inequalities, and technological disparities (Buitrago-Ciro et al., 2025). The papers analysed in this section of the study provide further evidence of initiatives and strategies that academic librarians are implementing.

Academic librarians in the USA are advanced in their initiatives and strategies for providing AI-centric support services to the university community. According to Michalak & Ellixson (2023), in large universities across the USA, academic librarians offer training in partnership with departments such as Faculty Development Centres. For example, at Clemson University, AI training is delivered through collaboration between the Office of Teaching Effectiveness and Innovation, the Centre for Career and Professional Development, and the Clemson University Libraries, which is responsible for curating AI research guides and instructional resources. At mid-sized universities, academic libraries organise workshops and participate in cross-campus collaborations. At the same time, smaller colleges often adopt a library-led, practical approach, integrating AI training into specific courses and faculty partnerships

(Michalak & Ellixson, 2025). For instance, Golden-Beacom College manages AI tool adoption and training independently (Michalak & Ellixson, 2025), whereas at California State University, academic librarians are responsible for raising awareness of AI, developing AI literature, and integrating AI (Chaudhuri & Terrones, 2025; Dabirian et al., 2025). Michalak & Ellixson (2025) further elaborate that Hirons Library at Golden-Beacom College provides access to AI technologies by removing financial barriers to licensed tools, such as Grammarly, Scholarcy, and Litmaps. Harvard University and the University of Toronto Libraries are reportedly leading literacy programmes and integrating AI tools into their services (Buitrago-Ciro et al., 2025). However, while access to such technologies is imperative, it remains a double-edged sword, with academic librarians in the United Kingdom and Turkey reportedly struggling with students' limited technical abilities and understanding of AI mechanisms (Freeman, 2025; Hossain et al., 2025).

Elsewhere, academic librarians are undertaking notable initiatives and strategies. In Norway, academic librarians are reportedly focusing on AI literacy, including bias, plagiarism, cheating, and copyright violations (Grote et al., 2024). In Ghana, academic librarians are said to be engaged in AI advocacy and the ethical use of AI for students and faculty (Filson & Atuase, 2024). However, the efforts of academic librarians in Ghana are considered insufficient, and there is a need for extensive AI literacy training programmes (Akakpo et al., 2025). Alzubaidi (2025) reiterates that most academic libraries are using AI guides to promote responsible use among students and staff. This view is supported and corroborated by Bangani (2025), who details initiatives by academic librarians in South Africa and notes that 12 university libraries have publicly accessible student AI guides that explain AI and the related ethical considerations, but only six university libraries have dedicated AI Libguides. These institutions include the Central University of Technology, Nelson Mandela University, the University of Cape Town, the University of the Free State, the University of Johannesburg, and the University of the Western Cape (Bangani, 2025). Furthermore, this study found that six university libraries have dedicated AI pages and links. These are the Cape Peninsula University of Technology, Sol Plaatje University, University of Fort Hare, University of KwaZulu-Natal, and the University of South Africa.

The lack of AI initiatives and strategies in some HEIs is a prominent issue in the literature. In South Asia (Bangladesh, India, and Pakistan), there is a clear need for robust AI literacy education at universities. In El Salvador, digital literacy to support students is reportedly lacking. In the Philippines, rural college students are required to take part in AI literacy programmes in higher education. The same situation is noted in Peruvian universities, where 56.8% of faculty and 49.7% of students have not received training in the use and ethical implications of AI (Hossain et al., 2025; Marín and Angulo Mendoza, 2025; Sustaningrum & Haldaka, 2025; Valdivieso

& González, 2025). In Zimbabwe, academic libraries are reportedly preoccupied with the adoption of AI and the development of related policies, but show little to no significant involvement in training programmes (Tsekea & Mandoga, 2025).

The literature discussed in this section reveals that while a range of AI-focused strategies and initiatives are emerging within academic libraries, their implementation remains highly uneven across both institutional and regional contexts. Well-resourced universities, particularly in Europe and North America, demonstrate more structured, supported, and collaborative approaches than other institutions, such as those in Latin America, Asia, and sub-Saharan Africa, which are characterised by fragmented, awareness-based interventions. This uneven landscape suggests that the presence of AI guides, workshops, or tool access alone is insufficient to ensure meaningful AI literacy development amongst staff and students. Rather, sustainable and equitable AI support requires targeted integration into existing library and teaching infrastructures, attention to local socio-economic conditions, and investment in staff capacity. These findings underscore the need for context-sensitive and scalable models of AI literacy support that move beyond isolated, in-house initiatives and enable academic libraries to contribute more effectively to ethical AI use and academic integrity.

5.5 Emerging Best Practices and Frameworks Guiding Scalable Models for Global Academic Libraries

The findings from this study show that 38% of the articles proposed different pathways as future considerations for developing and delivering AI-focused training activities and strategies. These suggestions were not necessarily presented as models or frameworks but rather as best practice considerations aimed at addressing current gaps in AI support services at universities. Four categories of considerations can be derived from the literature: approaches to AI training, the structure and components of AI training, best practices in upskilling and empowering academic librarians regarding their AI skills and competencies, and approaches to AI policy formulation.

Authorities suggest that the development and delivery of AI training and support services should adopt tailored approaches to meet the individual needs of users. In their study, Tadimalla and Maher (2025) introduced a socio-technical AI literacy framework designed to ensure that the students understood the ethical, societal, and future implications of AI, based on a four-pillar technical model of AI education. This model covered how the students interacted with GenAI, alongside principles of critical, ethical, and responsible AI use, as well as the analysis of AI's societal impacts (Tadimalla & Maher, 2024). This four-pillar model covered technical aspects, such as how students interacted with GenAI, alongside principles of critical, ethical, and responsible AI use, and the analysis of AI's societal impacts (Tadimalla

& Maher, 2024). Michalak and Ellixson (2025) support this approach, arguing that academic libraries should balance "technical proficiency, critical engagement and ethical considerations" in their AI training efforts. Espinoza-Vidaurre et al. (2024) suggest that in the context of AI use, a contextualised approach is required to address academic integrity, taking into account socio-economic and educational disparities and tailoring training to the specific realities and needs of each country. This idea is further reinforced by Michalak and Ellixson (2025), who state that AI literacy must be scalable and relevant to institutional needs. He proposes that AI training should be basic for beginners, advanced for faculty who may attend workshops, and practical for students. According to Daly et al. (2024), AI training in which learners develop a foundational understanding of models and tools should focus on specific tools, along with critical thinking skills. Chaudhuri and Terrones (2025) also affirm that AI literacy must encompass topics such as bias, misinformation, and ethical use, while ensuring that such training is accessible for those it is intended for.

Several recommendations have been made to enhance academic librarians' AI skills and competencies. Central to acquiring these skills is Halvorson's (2024) suggestion that librarian training schools should include data privacy, algorithmic bias, and ethical use in their curricula. Moreover, Bangani (2025) advocates seminars and conferences as essential for sharing best practices among academic librarians, thereby boosting AI capacity-building. Universities are called upon to finance the capacity-building and hence the academic integrity and professional development of academic librarians, through AI workshops and formal training (Bangani, 2025; Filson & Atuase, 2024). Finally, the structure and location of AI training for students are additional aspects discussed in the reviewed literature, with the consensus being that AI literacy should not be a standalone module, but rather an extension of information literacy (Bangani, 2025; Michalak & Ellixson, 2025). Michalak and Ellixson (2025) made a clear call to incorporate AI literacy into existing support structures, emphasising integration rather than isolation as part of AI literacy development.

When viewed collectively, these emerging practices highlight a growing consensus amongst researchers that adequate AI literacy support in higher education requires more than isolated training sessions or interventions. The findings suggest that integrated, scalable, and context-sensitive approaches with tailored AI training should be explored. Importantly, such recommendations foreground the role of academic librarians in shaping responsible AI engagement and training, in which established structures should be transformed and strengthened to include AI literacy development.

6. DISCUSSION

The systematic literature review in the previous section, comprising 49 journal articles published between 2020 and 2025, focused on the defined roles of academic librarians in developing and delivering AI-focused training to enhance academic integrity. The study aimed to identify various initiatives and strategies used by librarians, as well as to profile the challenges they faced. Furthermore, it identified emerging best practices and frameworks for the development and delivery of AI-centred support services to university students and staff.

The evidence across the articles suggests that effective library responses to GenAI-related academic integrity pressures are inherently multipronged. They require (a) integration of AI literacy into established information/digital literacy practices (rather than isolated, optional sessions), (b) cross-campus collaborations that align library guidance with teaching and learning centres, academic development units, and governance structures (for example, incorporating core components of AI training into curricula to prepare academic librarians), and (c) practical, accessible interventions or resources (guides, consultations, workshops, conferences, and communities of practice) that translate institutional principles into daily practices of students and staff. Of the papers reviewed, 27% confirmed that academic librarians serve as key figures and legitimate educators who play a vital role in developing and delivering AI research support services for students and staff at HEIs. For example, in Europe and North America, academic librarians are engaged in AI literacy both independently and in collaboration with academic centres or other departments, depending on the size of the university. In developing countries, such as those in sub-Saharan Africa, Latin America, and Asia, the involvement and representation of academic librarians in AI training and academic integrity are limited, with notable exceptions being South African public universities.

Analysis of the empirical papers highlighted the challenges faced by academic librarians in providing AI-focused research support to students and staff. Since AI is a complex, multifaceted, and rapidly evolving field, the skills and competencies needed to stay current with these technologies can undermine the role and authority of academic librarians. In one respect, the legitimacy of academic librarians in delivering AI-centred research support services remains debatable. Several less common observations in the analysed articles point to under-explored dimensions that warrant targeted research. First, there was a reported move by European libraries to employ dedicated AI specialists, rather than relying solely on general upskilling. This raises questions about professional identity, sustainability, and the long-term division of labour in academic libraries. Second, the recurring outlier finding that librarians are sometimes excluded from campus-wide AI initiatives and policy formulation suggests that the core challenge may have less to do with librarians' willingness to lead and more to do with institutional governance and legitimacy. Third, articles that highlight misinformation, digital safety, and the AI divide go beyond just plagiarism and citation practices, demonstrating a need for further research on AI literacy as part of student well-being, information resilience, and programmes around equity and equitable access. These outliers are essential because they show that "what works" may not be solely a question of training content, but also of organisational positioning, procurement choices, how libraries position themselves, and the role they play in institutional AI governance.

The results of the analysis of the reviewed articles are laid out thematically and sequentially; however, further interconnections on themes also exist across geographical divides. The literature suggests similarity in the role of academic librarians in terms of their contribution to AI literacy and academic integrity. Articles presenting cases from Ghana, South Africa, Hong Kong, Europe, and the USA clearly illuminated this role. Furthermore, while the development and adoption of AI technologies in the Global North and the Global South are at variance due to differences in socio-economic and technological factors, in general, academic librarians are regarded as key players. A lack of skills and the inability of institutions to fund the training of academic librarians in AI seem to be prevalent in the Global South. Countries such as Ghana, South Africa, and Zimbabwe cite a lack of financial resources and budgetary constraints as barriers to the implementation of AI-driven academic library services. However, in resource-rich countries such as the USA and Norway, the question of skills takes on a different dimension. In the USA, the issue of skills does not even arise; instead, some academic libraries have closed the skills gap by employing AI experts. What concerns the USA and Norway is the exclusion of academic libraries from the implementation of AI initiatives in mainstream universities. Furthermore, in Norway, the authority and credibility of academic librarians to participate in such initiatives are questioned.

Thus, training initiatives and strategies for rebooting academic libraries in response to AI are varied, with clear-cut differences between developed and developing countries. In Europe and North America, academic librarians are engaged in AI literacy both independently and in collaboration with academic centres or other departments, depending on the size of the institution. By contrast, in developing countries, such as those in sub-Saharan Africa, Latin America, and Asia, the involvement and representation of academic librarians in AI training and academic integrity are limited, although notable exceptions have been observed at South African public universities. The thematic interconnections emerging from the literature show that while there is AI integration in the design and delivery of academic library services, there are marked differences between the Global North and Global South in what academic librarians are dealing with. However, issues such as exclusion, credibility, and perceptions of authority are common to all.

7. SUMMARY AND KEY INSIGHTS

This chapter contributes to and extends the current discourse on the implications of AI and GenAI tools for academic writing and the preservation of academic integrity in higher education. By highlighting the profound and evolving role of academic librarians as key stakeholders in the development of AI literacy, the need for institutional recognition and investment in these roles is emphasised. Drawing on a PRISMA-informed systematic literature review of 49 publications between 2020 and 2025 and guided by the Jisc digital capabilities framework and the DEC AI literacy framework, this chapter demonstrates that academic librarians are well-positioned to be critical change agents in equipping students and staff with the competencies required to engage ethically and effectively with AI tools.

The analysis revealed four broad themes: (1) the role of academic librarians in AI literacy and academic integrity, with librarians being framed as educators, advocates, and leaders of ethical AI use; (2) a diverse range of AI-focused strategies and initiatives, from LibGuides, workshops, and cross-campus collaborations at well-resourced institutions in Europe and North America, to emergent and uneven implementation in Latin America, Asia, sub-Saharan Africa, and other resource-constrained contexts; (3) significant challenges, including questions about the legitimacy and authority of academic librarians in AI training, their exclusion from institutional AI policy processes, gaps in their AI-related skills and competencies, and persistent resource and capacity constraints, and (4) emerging best practices that emphasise the integration of AI literacy into the existing provision of information and digital literacy, tailoring training to target institutional and regional contexts and investment in professional development. Taking these themes together, this systematic review argues that, when supported by robust AI literacy frameworks, academic librarians are well-positioned to act as institutional bridges between the implementation of AI policy and everyday academic practice, thereby strengthening institutional responses to challenges regarding academic integrity in an evolving higher educational landscape.

8. CONCLUSION

The primary objective of this review was to systematically identify the role of academic librarians in supporting the use of AI by students and staff, and to examine how this role is portrayed in the literature. Additionally, the study aimed to identify the challenges faced by academic librarians when providing AI-related support services and to propose best practices that could enhance the effectiveness of their roles. The findings from the reviewed literature position academic librarians as both educators and ethical stewards in a rapidly evolving scholarly ecosystem, but also show that academic integrity in AI literacy cannot be a single, one-size-fits-all intervention. The diversity of the initiatives and strategies of academic libraries for AI training and academic integrity calls for intentionally designed, multipronged approaches rather than isolated, erratic efforts lacking form and structure. These approaches can take the form of embedding AI literacy into information literacy instruction, institution-wide partnerships, interventions to upskill librarians, accessible guides, and equity-focused measures informed by the conditions shaping AI usage. University libraries must address gaps in their AI skills capacity to establish authority, credibility, and legitimacy as AI instructors. This study may assist university libraries in various contexts with the redesign and recruitment of their AI research support services, as well as in identifying the necessary staff upskilling requirements.

Furthermore, the review showed that academic librarians are involved in AI training and support services at various levels depending on the geographical context. In developed countries, such as those in Europe and North America, there is substantial documentation of the role of academic librarians in developing and delivering AI training and support services. In less developed countries, such as those in Latin America, Asia, and sub-Saharan Africa, there is limited or basic engagement by academic librarians in terms of AI training. This imbalance matters because best practices may rely on policy maturity, available resources, and/or infrastructure, without considering case-based evidence from resource-constrained countries or regions, which risks the guidance being aspirational rather than actionable.

Future research should move beyond describing AI guides and workshops to testing and comparing entire institutional configurations, for example, examining whether the inclusion of academic librarians in AI policy processes changes the uptake, or if licensing strategies reduce inequalities in access and outcomes, or how different staffing models (general upskilling versus hiring AI specialists) affect the credibility and sustainability of institutions. Finally, the emphasis on misinformation, digital safety, and well-being suggests that understanding support for AI literacy is an important research topic, not only as an academic intervention, but as part of an academic librarian's broader role in cultivating trustworthy knowledge practices in the age of AI-driven practices in higher education.

REFERENCES

Akakpo, M. G., Ahardy, D. O., & Kumankumah, S. S. (2025). Towards digital information literacy guidelines for African libraries: A survey of the relationship between digital and information literacy of university students in Ghana. *Journal of Academic Librarianship*, *15*(4), 103067. Advance online publication. DOI: 10.1016/j.acalib.2025.103067

Almatrafi, O., Johri, A., & Lee, H. (2024). A systematic review of AI literacy conceptualization, constructs, and implementation and assessment efforts (2019–2023). *Computers and Education Open*, *6*(June), 100173. DOI: 10.1016/j.caeo.2024.100173

Alzubaidi, K. (2025). The role of generative AI in higher education: Institutional guidelines, generational gaps, and the Grok 4 challenge. *Arab World English Journal (AWEJ). Special Issue on CALL*, *11*(11), 1–4. DOI: 10.24093/awej/call11.1A

Annapureddy, R., Fornaroli, A., & Gatica-Perez, D. (2024). Generative AI literacy: Twelve defining competencies. *Digital Government: Research and Practice*, *6*(1), 1–21. DOI: 10.1145/3685680

Balalle, H., & Pannilage, S. (2025). Reassessing academic integrity in the age of AI: A systematic literature review on AI and academic integrity. *Social Sciences & Humanities Open*, *11*, 101299. DOI: 10.1016/j.ssaho.2025.101299

Bangani, S. (2025). Artificial intelligence integration in academic libraries in South Africa: A web analysis. *Digital Library Perspectives*, *41*(4), 694–707. DOI: 10.1108/DLP-03-2025-0042

Beetham, H., & Sharpe, R. (2013). *Rethinking pedagogy for a digital age: Designing for 21st century learning* (2nd ed.). Routledge. DOI: 10.4324/9780203078952

Buitrago-Ciro, J., Samokishyn, M., Moylan, R., Hernández Pérez, J., Bakare-Fatungase, O., & Firdawsi, C. (2025). Bridging the AI gap: Comparative analysis of AI integration, education, and outreach in academic libraries. *IFLA Journal, 51*(3), 682-702. https://doi.org/ (Original work published 2025)DOI: 10.1177/03400352251325274

Chaudhuri, J., & Terrones, L. (2025). Reshaping academic library information literacy programs in the advent of ChatGPT and other generative AI Technologies. *Internet Reference Services Quarterly*, *29*(1), 1–25. DOI: 10.1080/10875301.2024.2400132

Chiu, T. K. F., Ahmad, Z., Ismailov, M., & Sanusi, I. T. (2024). What are artificial intelligence literacy and competency? A comprehensive framework to support them. *Computers and Education Open*, *6*, 100171. DOI: 10.1016/j.caeo.2024.100171

Creswell, J. W. (2014). *A concise introduction to mixed methods research*. SAGE Publications.

Dabirian, H., Swarat, C., & Swarat, S. (2025). Necessary but not perfect: Changes in AI perception at a large university. *IT Professional*, *27*(4), 13–18. DOI: 10.1109/MITP.2025.3585226

Daly, O.; Fogarty L.; Furlong E.; Vasquez del Aguila E.; Farrell R.; Morton S.; Woods A.; Digital Education Council. *Digital Education Council AI literacy framework*. Digital Education Council. https://www.digitaleducationcouncil.com/post/digital-education-council-ai-literacy-framework.

Elaiess, R. (2024). Academic integrity in the age of artificial intelligence: Exploring ethical challenges in a digital era. *International Journal of Academic Multidisciplinary Research*, *8*(11), 12–15. http://ijeais.org/wp-content/uploads/2024/11/IJAMR241103.pdf

Espinoza Vidaurre, S. M., Velásquez Rodríguez, N. C., Gambetta Quelopana, R. L., Martinez Valdivia, A. N., Leo Rossi, E. A., & Nolasco-Mamani, M. A. (2024). Perceptions of artificial intelligence and its impact on academic integrity among university students in Peru and Chile: An approach to sustainable education. *Sustainability (Basel)*, *16*(20), 9005. Advance online publication. DOI: 10.3390/su16209005

Filson, C. K., & Atuase, D. (2024). Artificial intelligence and academic integrity: The role of academic librarians. *Information Development*, *41*(3), 781–793. DOI: 10.1177/02666669241284230

Flick, U. (2015). *Introducing research methodology: A beginner's guide to doing a research project* (2nd ed.). SAGE Publications.

Freeman, J. (2025). *Student Generative AI Survey 2025* (Policy Note No. 61). Higher Education Policy Institute. https://www.hepi.ac.uk/wp-content/uploads/2025/02/HEPI-Kortext-Student-Generative-AI-Survey-2025.pdf

Giray, L., Fabros, B., Villarama, J., Gumalin, D. L., & Saavedra, J. B. (2025). Acceptance of and satisfaction with ChatGPT as a learning tool in higher education through the technology acceptance model (TAM): A Case from the Philippines. *Internet Reference Services Quarterly*, *29*(4), 527–546. DOI: 10.1080/10875301.2025.2542212

Grote, M., Faber, C. H., & Gasparini, A. (2024). Artificial intelligence in PhD education: New perspectives for research libraries. *LIBER Quarterly*, *34*(1), 1–29. DOI: 10.53377/lq.18137

Gunton, L. (2022). Librarians as drivers of academic integrity for student success at university. *Journal of the Australian Library and Information Association, 71*(2), 156–170. DOI: 10.1080/24750158.2022.2063101

Halvorson, O. H. (2024). AI in academia: Policy development, ethics, and curriculum design. *School of Information Student Research Journal, 14*(1). Advance online publication. DOI: 10.55917/2575-2499.1533

Hossain, Z., Biswas, M., & Khan, G. (2025). AI literacy of library and information science students: A study of Bangladesh, India and Pakistan. *Journal of Librarianship and Information Science, 0*(0), 09610006241309323. Advance online publication. DOI: 10.1177/09610006241309323

Jisc. (2019). *Guide to using the Jisc digital discovery tool for individual users.* https://digitalcapability.jiscinvolve.org/wp/files/2017/11/Guidance-for-end-users-REVISED.pdf

Lee, D., Arnold, M., Srivastava, A., Plastow, K., Strelan, P., Ploeckl, F., Lekkas, D., & Palmer, E. (2024). The impact of generative AI on higher education learning and teaching: A study of educators' perspectives. *Computers and Education: Artificial Intelligence, 6*(June), 100221. DOI: 10.1016/j.caeai.2024.100221

Lo, L. S. (2025). AI literacy: A guide for academic libraries. *College & Research Libraries News, 86*(3), 120. DOI: 10.5860/crln.86.3.120

Long, D., & Magerko, B. (2020). What is AI literacy? Competencies and design considerations. In *Proceedings of the 2020 CHI Conference on Human Factors in Computing Systems* (pp. 1–16). DOI: 10.1145/3313831.3376727

Lowe, M. (2024). The more things change: The ethical impacts of artificial intelligence in higher education. *Research Issues in Contemporary Education, 9*(2), 19–56. https://files.eric.ed.gov/fulltext/EJ1435770.pdf

Ma, C. M. S., Shek, D. T. L., Fan, I. Y. H., Zhu, X., & Hu, X. (2025). The impact of digital safety competence on cognitive competence, AI self-efficacy, and character. *Applied Sciences (Basel, Switzerland), 15*(10), 5440. DOI: 10.3390/app15105440

MacCallum, K., Parsons, D., & Mohaghegh, M. (2023). Identifying the components of foundational artificial intelligence (AI) literacy: Early results from a Delphi study. In T. Cochrane et al. (Eds.), *People, partnerships and pedagogies: Proceedings of ASCILITE 2023*. DOI: 10.14742/apubs.2023.672

Mansoor, H. M. H., Bawazir, A., Alsabri, M. A., Alharbi, A., & Okela, A. H. (2024). Artificial intelligence literacy among university students: A comparative transnational survey. *Frontiers in Communication, 9*, 1478476. DOI: 10.3389/fcomm.2024.1478476

Marin, V. I., & Angulo Mendoza, G. A. (2025). Digital competence in Quebec's teacher education programs: Toward a critical perspective. *Journal of Teaching and Learning, 19*(5), 45–74. DOI: 10.22329/jtl.v19i5.8957

Miao, F., & Holmes, W. (2021, December 7–8). *International forum on AI and the futures of education: Developing competencies for the AI era: Synthesis report.* UNESCO. https://unesdoc.unesco.org/ark:/48223/pf0000377251

Michalak, R. (2023). From ethics to execution: The role of academic librarians in artificial intelligence (AI) policy-making at colleges and universities. *Journal of Library Administration, 63*(7), 928–938. DOI: 10.1080/01930826.2023.2262367

Michalak, R., & Ellixson, D. (2025). Fostering ethical AI integration in first-year writing: A case study on human-tool collaboration in artificial intelligence literacy. *Journal of Library Administration, 65*(3), 361–377. DOI: 10.1080/01930826.2025.2468136

Miltenoff, P. (2024). Academic librarians in times of AI and AI literacy: Tasks, responsibilities, and leadership. *The International Information & Library Review, 56*(3), 296–305. DOI: 10.1080/10572317.2024.2381182

Miron, J., O'Neill Maher, M., Seeland, J., Oyarzun, J., & Virgo, I. (2024, December 14). *The collaborative librarian: Guardian of integrity.* International Center for Academic Integrity. https://www.academicintegrity.org/aws/ICAI/page_template/show_detail/583734?model_name=news_article&utm=

Moorhouse, B. L., Yeo, M. A., & Wan, Y. (2023). Generative AI tools and assessment: Guidelines of the world's top-ranking universities. *Computers and Education Open, 5*, 100151. DOI: 10.1016/j.caeo.2023.100151

Moya, B. A., Eaton, E. S., Pethrick, H., Hayden, A. K., Brennan, R., Wiens, J., & McDermott, B. (2024). Academic integrity and artificial intelligence in higher education (HE) contexts: A rapid scoping review. *Canadian Perspectives on Academic Integrity, 7*(3). Advance online publication. DOI: 10.55016/ojs/cpai.v7i3.78123

Ndungu, M. W. (2024). Integrating basic artificial intelligence literacy into media and information literacy programs in higher education. *Journal of Information Literacy, 18*(2), 122–139. Advance online publication. DOI: 10.11645/18.2.641

Olusipe, A. A., Adetayo, A. J., Enamudu, A. I., & Babalola, O. O. (2024). Safeguarding the digital economy: Librarians' perspectives on data privacy and ethical use of public AI chatbots. *Journal of Electronic Resources Librarianship, 36*(4), 257–270. DOI: 10.1080/1941126X.2024.2414706

Safana, A. S., & Fari, S. A. (2025). Application of artificial intelligence (AI) for information services delivery: Exploring the readiness and challenges in some university libraries in Katsina State. *Samaru Journal of Information Studies, 24*(2), 334–360. https://www.ajol.info/index.php/sjis/article/view/291763

Sheppard, A. (2025). Equity and ethical concerns regarding artificial intelligence in libraries. *Journal of Information Ethics*, *34*(1), 40–49.

Silverman, D. (2013). *Doing qualitative research: A practical handbook.* SAGE Publications.

Sustaningrum, R., & Haldaka, M. (2025). Student utilization and perceptions of AI technology for academic purposes: A mixed-method analysis. *Cogent Education, 12*(1), 2553835. Advance online publication. DOI: 10.1080/2331186X.2025.2553835

Tadimalla, S. Y., & Maher, M. L. (2024). AI literacy for all: Adjustable interdisciplinary socio-technical curriculum. *IEEE Frontiers in Education Conference (FIE)*, Washington, DC, USA, 2024, pp. 1–9. DOI: 10.1109/FIE61694.2024.10893159

Tauginienė, L., Gaižauskaitė, I., Glendinning, I., Kravjar, J., Ojsteršek, M., Ribeiro, L., Odiņeca, T., Marino, F., Cosentino, M., Sivasubramaniam, S., & Foltýnek, T. (2018). *Glossary for academic integrity* (ENAI Report 3G, revised version). *European Network for Academic Integrity*. https://www.academicintegrity.eu/wp/wp-content/uploads/2023/02/EN-Glossary_revised_final_24.02.23.pdf

The University of Adelaide. (2024). *Artificial intelligence literacy framework*. https://www.adelaide.edu.au/library/system/files/media/documents/2024-10/ua31352_ai-literacy-framework-doc-v2.pdf

Tsekea, S., & Mandoga, E. (2025). The ethics of artificial intelligence use in university libraries in Zimbabwe. *Frontiers in Research Metrics and Analytics*, *9*, 1–7. DOI: 10.3389/frma.2024.1522423 PMID: 39897937

University of Cape Town News. (2025, December 8). *UCT Libraries*. University of Cape Town. https://www.news.uct.ac.za/article/-2025-12-08-uct-libraries

Valdivieso, T., & González, O. (2025). Generative AI tools in Salvadoran higher education: Balancing equity, ethics, and knowledge management in the Global South. *Education Sciences*, *15*(2), 214. DOI: 10.3390/educsci15020214

Wang, L. (2025). A review of artificial intelligence literacy education and AI Skills development in Chinese universities. *Lecture Notes in Education. Psychology and Public Media*, *89*, 75–81. DOI: 10.54254/2753-7048/89/2025.22815

World Economic Forum. (2022, March 17). *Without universal AI literacy, AI will fail us.* https://www.weforum.org/stories/2022/03/without-universal-ai-literacy-ai-will-fail-us/

Yeung, R. S. K., Tian, R., Chiu, D. K. W., & Choi, S. P.-M. (2025). University students' perceptions on how generative artificial intelligence shape learning and research practices: A case study in Hong Kong. *Journal of Academic Librarianship*, *51*(5), 103082. Advance online publication. DOI: 10.1016/j.acalib.2025.103082

Zhao, X., Cox, A., & Cai, L. (2024). ChatGPT and the digitisation of writing. *Humanities & Social Sciences Communications*, *11*(482), 1–9. DOI: 10.1057/s41599-02402904-x

Chapter 2
AI Risk Assessment Framework for Teachers

Abdullah Yasin Gunduz
https://orcid.org/0000-0003-2370-6199
Usak University, Turkey

ABSTRACT

The rapid adoption of artificial intelligence tools in education has outpaced systematic risk assessment development. Teachers lack practical frameworks to evaluate potential harms in classroom applications. While UNESCO, OECD, the EU AI Act, and NIST provide institutional guidelines, these remain inadequately operationalized for individual teaching practice. Through comparative analysis of international standards, a teacher-centered risk assessment framework is developed. Regulatory requirements are translated into a four-step methodology comprising inventory creation, risk prioritization, mitigation strategies, and monitoring. Implementation barriers are identified, including time constraints, digital literacy gaps, legal uncertainties, and institutional resistance. The framework demonstrates how teachers can systematically evaluate AI tools while maintaining professional autonomy within institutional policy contexts. This study establishes a bridge between high-level governance frameworks and classroom-level decision-making, offering actionable guidance for teachers.

1. INTRODUCTION

The widespread adoption of artificial intelligence in educational institutions has brought the need for systematic management of unforeseen risks to the agenda. Following the public release of large language models, educational institutions have been compelled to adopt technologies whose pedagogical and ethical implications

DOI: 10.4018/979-8-3373-4521-5.ch002

have not been fully evaluated (Chan & Hu, 2023). This rapid adoption process has occurred in an environment where most teachers lack adequate preparation in AI literacy. This mismatch between the pace of technology and institutional readiness creates significant risk gaps in educational processes.

The increased familiarity with digital tools following the COVID-19 pandemic has facilitated faster acceptance of AI technologies (Trust & Whalen, 2021). However, this digitalization process has occurred before the development of risk assessment mechanisms. Educational institutions have adopted applications without yet having frameworks to identify the unique risks of AI. Traditional information technology risk frameworks fall short due to the stochastic nature of AI and the opaque structure of its decision-making processes (Brundage et al., 2020; Mökander & Floridi, 2021).

On the other hand, student usage rates of AI tools significantly exceed teacher usage rates. While the vast majority of high school and university students are aware of generative AI tools (Sullivan et al., 2023), this rate remains at 9% among instructors (Tyton Partners, 2023). This asymmetry shows that students are actively using tools in an environment where teachers have limited capacity to assess and manage technology-related risks. Teachers find themselves in a position to provide guidance without fully understanding the risks students face.

The risk profile of AI use in education displays a complex structure due to the diversity of applications. Learning analytics platforms create data privacy issues, while automated assessment systems carry algorithmic bias risks. Personalized learning tools affect student autonomy, and chatbots challenge academic integrity standards. Each application category contains different types of risks, and the magnitude of these risks varies according to context. Therefore, this multi-layered risk structure necessitates the development of systematic assessment tools.

1.1 The Emergence of Risk Assessment Need

The risks created by AI in education manifest across a broad spectrum, from academic integrity to student autonomy, from data security to pedagogical effectiveness. These risks form interconnected layers. While issues of academic integrity and assessment reliability appear in the most visible layer, deeper layers contain threats to the authenticity of learning processes and student autonomy. Technical risks such as data privacy and algorithmic bias are intertwined with pedagogical and ethical concerns. Uncertainty in teachers' professional roles and the rapid evolution of AI technologies further complicate this risk structure. However, the most critical problem is the lack of practical tools that teachers can use to systematically assess these risks.

Risk management frameworks developed at the international level provide valuable guidance for institutional policy development, but contain significant gaps in adaptation to individual teacher practice. Most frameworks address institutional decision-makers and fail to respond to concrete dilemmas encountered at the daily classroom level (Holmes et al., 2024). There is a need for operational tools to assess the risk profiles of specific tools used by teachers, consider student context, and make decisions aligned with pedagogical goals.

1.2 Purpose, Scope and Research Questions

This study is designed as a conceptual-theoretical model and does not involve empirical data collection. Based on literature review and comparative analysis of international standards methodology, the study develops a context-specific assessment model that adapts the principles of international risk management frameworks to teacher practice. The main contribution of the study is its transformation of frameworks designed at the institutional level into individual teacher context. The model categorizes AI tools frequently used by teachers in educational processes, identifies possible risk scenarios for each category, and presents concrete questions for teachers to assess these risks. The proposed tools are designed to account for teachers' limited time and varying levels of technical knowledge.

The section addresses four fundamental questions. The first question concerns identifying risk categories of AI tools used in education and systematic classification of ethical, pedagogical, technical and institutional risk types. The second question addresses how the principles of international frameworks can be operationalized for teachers making daily decisions at the classroom level. The third question involves designing practical tools that teachers can use in the processes of identifying, analyzing, prioritizing and mitigating risks. The fourth question concerns identifying structural, cognitive and institutional barriers in risk assessment practice and developing strategies to overcome these barriers.

The scope of the study is limited to risk assessment of AI tools used or considered for use by individual teachers. Institutional-level policy development, large-scale system implementation or AI algorithm design are outside the scope. The proposed framework aims to support teachers in making informed decisions while preserving their professional autonomy within the context of their existing duties and responsibilities, and to complement institutional policy development processes.

2. THEORETICAL FRAMEWORK AND RISK TAXONOMY

The theoretical foundations of risk assessment methodologies derive from traditional risk management discipline and have been developed in the field of information technology security. However, the unique characteristics of AI systems require the adaptation and expansion of existing risk frameworks (Floridi & Cowls, 2019; Mittelstadt et al., 2016). This section examines the taxonomies that form the conceptual foundations of AI risk assessment, specific risk types that emerge in educational context, and factors affecting teachers' technology acceptance processes.

2.1 AI Risk Definition and Dimensions

AI risk refers to the potential to create negative effects on individuals, institutions or society during the design, development or use of the system. The NIST AI Risk Management Framework emphasizes that risks should be addressed through governance, mapping, measurement and management phases (NIST, 2023). The NIST framework is adapted from industry-standard risk management methodologies and customized according to AI's specific features (Hubbard & Seiersen, 2016).

The governance function involves establishing organizational-level risk culture and accountability structures. The mapping function requires creating a map of the AI system's technical features, usage context, and potential risks. The measurement function encompasses quantitative or qualitative assessment of probability and impact parameters of identified risks. The management function refers to implementation of strategies for accepting, reducing, transferring or eliminating risks.

This framework proposes assessment of AI systems in terms of fundamental features such as reliability, accuracy, explainability, privacy, security and resilience. In the education sector, each of these features corresponds to different risk scenarios in teachers' daily practices.

In educational context, AI risk refers to technical or practice-based problems that prevent achievement of pedagogical goals, threaten student safety or privacy, or undermine educational equity (Holmes et al., 2022). This definition includes different fundamental dimensions of harm at individual student level (such as incorrect assessment, data breach), disruptions at pedagogical process level (such as decline in learning quality), and inequalities at systemic level (such as systematic disadvantage of certain groups).

2.1.2 AI Risk Assessment Approaches

The rapid spread of AI technologies has necessitated development of regulatory frameworks at national and international levels. In the last five years, multilateral organizations, regulatory authorities and standards development organizations have established normative frameworks for responsible use of AI. This section examines frameworks that have direct or indirect applications for the education sector. The conceptual foundations of each framework, education-specific provisions and applicability at teacher level are evaluated.

2.1.3 UNESCO's Ethics-Based Approach and OECD's Principles-Based Model

UNESCO's Recommendation on the Ethics of Artificial Intelligence, adopted by 193 member countries in 2021, provides a comprehensive framework for ethical governance of AI (UNESCO, 2021). The recommendation is structured around four core values of human well-being and environmental protection, human oversight and control, transparency and explainability, and responsibility and accountability. These values manifest in educational context as protection of student welfare, preservation of teacher professional judgment, and operation of accountability mechanisms in cases of student harm. OECD's (2022) Framework for the Classification of AI Systems proposes analysis of systems across five dimensions including human and environmental impacts, economic usage context, data sources, model architecture and tasks performed.

2.2.4 European Union's Risk-Based Regulation

The European Union Artificial Intelligence Act came into force in August 2024, becoming the first comprehensive regulation to bring legally binding rules for AI (EU, 2024). Unlike UNESCO and OECD's non-binding soft law instruments, the AI Act establishes legal obligations and includes sanctions for non-compliance. Although the law is not directly binding for educational institutions outside the EU, the standards it sets for AI providers operating in the EU market influence global practices.

The law adopts a risk-based approach, classifying AI systems into four categories. Unacceptable risk (prohibited), high risk (regulated), limited risk (transparency obligations) and minimal risk (unregulated). For the education sector, the most critical category is the high-risk systems category.

According to the AI Act, four categories of AI systems in education and vocational training are classified as high risk (EU, 2024). The first category covers systems used in student admission or placement processes to educational institutions. The second category includes systems that assess student performance in formal examination environments where assessment results directly affect the student's educational path. This encompasses high-stakes assessments such as diploma acquisition, university admission or professional certification. Daily homework assessments or classroom formative assessment tools fall outside this category. The third category comprises systems that determine individuals' educational level or competence. The fourth category consists of proctoring systems that monitor student behavior in examination environments. Underlying this classification is the idea that AI decisions can determine students' access to educational opportunities and consequently their future life paths. Systems falling into the high-risk category are subject to strict regulatory requirements because they have the potential to directly affect students' fundamental rights (EU, 2024).

Providers of high-risk systems are under extensive obligations under the AI Act. These obligations cover the entire lifecycle from system design to decommissioning and include areas of risk management, data quality, technical documentation, record keeping, user training, human oversight and cybersecurity (EU, 2024). The critical point for educational institutions and teachers is to understand the risk category of AI systems they use and to verify that providers fulfill these obligations when high-risk systems are involved. However, currently, many educational technology providers' AI Act compliance processes are ongoing, and teachers have the right to request compliance documents from providers.

The AI Act prohibits the use of emotion recognition systems in workplaces and educational institutions. Although limited exceptions are provided for medical or security purposes, in general educational context, AI systems cannot be used to monitor students' emotional states. This ban stems from concerns about the scientific reliability of emotion recognition technologies, risk of manipulation and the need to protect student privacy. Educational institutions are obliged to inspect whether learning analytics platforms or student monitoring systems contain emotion recognition features and to disable these features if they do.

2.2.5 NIST Artificial Intelligence Risk Management Framework

The NIST Artificial Intelligence Risk Management Framework presents a four-function cyclical methodology for operational risk management (NIST, 2023). The framework is an adapted version of the widely used NIST Cybersecurity Framework in the cybersecurity field applied to AI. Although each of the governance, mapping, measurement and management functions is designed at organizational level, it can be adapted to individual teacher practice.

Operationalizing the NIST framework at teacher level requires translation of each function into educational context. Table 1 shows how the four core functions of the NIST AI Risk Management Framework (2024) are adapted to teacher practice.

Table 1. Adaptation of NIST Functions to Teacher Level

NIST Function	Institutional Level	Equivalent at Teacher Level
Governance	Creating risk culture, policy setting, organizational structures	Compliance with professional codes of ethics, adherence to institutional policies, determining personal risk tolerance
Mapping	System documentation, technical specifications, data flows	Pedagogical purpose of tools used, data flows, risk scenario inventory
Measurement	Quantitative calculation of risk metrics, statistical analysis	Probability and impact assessment (qualitative), determining student harm potential
Management	Institutional-level risk mitigation strategies, legal compliance mechanisms	Preventive controls (transparent policy, training) and compensatory controls (human oversight, multiple tools)

At individual teacher level, the governance function manifests as compliance with professional codes of ethics, adherence to institutional policies, and determination of personal risk tolerance. The mapping function involves documenting the pedagogical purpose, data flows, technical features and potential risk scenarios of each AI tool the teacher uses. The measurement function requires assessing the probability of occurrence of each identified risk and its potential impact in terms of student harm. The management function encompasses developing and implementing mitigation strategies for high-priority risks.

For example, mapping the risk profile of an automated assessment system used by a teacher involves understanding what student data the system collects, how the algorithm works, and potential bias sources. In the measurement phase, the teacher can assess the system's accuracy rate, frequency of false positive and false negative results, and performance differences across different student groups.

The comparative analysis of AI risk assessment approaches (UNESCO, OECD, EU and NIST) detailed so far is presented in Table 2.

Table 2. Comparative Analysis of International AI Frameworks

Framework	Type	Core Focus	Education-Specific Provisions	Teacher-Level Application Tips
UNESCO AI Ethics Recommendation (2021)	Ethical Recommendation	Human rights and human dignity	• AI literacy programs, • Teacher training and preparation, • Ethical impact assessment tools	Integration of ethical principles (autonomy, non-maleficence, justice, openness) into teaching processes and basing decision-making on them
OECD AI Classification Framework (2022)	Classification Framework	Economic innovation and responsible development	• Multi-dimensional system analysis, • Data sources and quality, • Model architecture transparency, • Task and human-environment impact assessment	Systematically documenting technical features, data sources and pedagogical tasks of AI tools used
EU AI Act (2024)	Legal Regulation	Risk-based regulation and legal compliance	• High-risk systems for admission and placement, performance assessment, competence determination, surveillance systems; • Prohibited applications including emotion recognition systems in educational institutions; • Provider obligations for risk management, data quality, technical documentation	Determining risk category of tools used, requesting compliance certificates from providers for high-risk systems, avoiding prohibited applications
NIST AI RMF (2023)	Operational Risk Management Framework	Risk management cycle and reliability	• Four functions of governance, mapping, measurement, management; • Reliability features of accuracy, explainability, privacy, security, resilience; • Generative AI profile (2024) for hallucination, harmful content, copyright risks	Integrating governance (ethical code compliance), mapping (tool inventory), measurement (risk prioritization) and management (mitigation strategies) steps into daily professional routines

This comparison helps teachers understand the complementary nature of different frameworks. All four frameworks converge on protection of human rights, transparency in decision processes, algorithmic justice and the necessity of accountability mechanisms. However, emphasis points differ. UNESCO prioritizes ethical values, OECD economic innovation, the EU legal compliance, and NIST operational risk management. The practical consequence for teachers is that these frameworks can be used complementarily. UNESCO's ethical principles provide the normative basis of assessment, OECD's classification provides the analytical framework, the EU AI Act provides legal boundaries, and NIST methodology provides operational steps. This multi-perspective approach enables comprehensive assessment of AI risks.

3. AI APPLICATIONS IN EDUCATION AND RISK AREAS

AI use in education encompasses a wide range of applications. Below, five different application categories most frequently encountered by teachers in daily practice are examined. For each category, the technology's functioning, pedagogical purpose of use and specific risk profile are analyzed. Risk scenarios are derived from problems observed in actual educational settings.

3.1 Learning Analytics and Student Data Use

A high school teacher sees in the learning management system's weekly report that a student has not logged into the platform for the last seven days, has not submitted assignments, and has not participated in the forum. This information appears valuable for pedagogical intervention, but the teacher faces a dilemma about how to use this data. Would sharing the data with parents violate student privacy? Is the student's passivity on the platform a sign of a problem in their private life, or do they simply prefer a different learning method?

This scenario exemplifies the fundamental risk of learning analytics platforms. Learning management systems like Google Classroom and Moodle systematically monitor student behaviors, performance and interaction patterns. These systems collect detailed data such as last login time, pages clicked, assignment submission time and duration of interaction with online materials. As Hoel et al. (2018) emphasized, learning analytics is not merely an administrative task but a pedagogical activity that directly affects students.

3.2 Automated Assessment and Feedback Systems

Automated assessment systems offer teachers two advantages of time savings and consistent grading. In reality, these promises are intertwined with complex problems.

The promise of time savings materializes in simple multiple-choice questions but reverses in open-ended questions. The system quickly evaluates answers following the standard solution path. However, answers exhibiting original approaches are scored incorrectly because they fall outside the system's training data. The teacher is forced to manually check every answer to correct these errors. The result is additional workload instead of expected time savings.

The promise of consistent grading claims to eliminate subjective teacher judgment. In reality, the system creates a different type of inconsistency. In a mathematics problem, two students reach the solution equally correctly but with different methods. The system gives full marks to the method matching its algorithm, zero to the other. Potential subjectivity in human assessment has been replaced with algorithmic rigidity.

A more critical risk is the discouragement of creative thinking. As students learn the standard approaches the system expects, they stop trying alternative solution paths. Assessment shapes learning but toward the undesired direction of conformism.

3.3 Plagiarism Detection and Academic Integrity Tools

The claim that plagiarism detection systems can identify AI-generated content has gained widespread acceptance by educational institutions. This belief rests on three assumptions. That AI texts have distinctive linguistic features, that these features can be detected algorithmically, and that detection results are reliable.

However, empirical evidence does not support these assumptions. Weber-Wulff et al.'s (2023) comprehensive evaluation of AI detection tools revealed high false positive rates. Original student work, especially texts conforming to academic writing conventions, is frequently marked as AI-generated. Conversely, students' slight editing of AI outputs can circumvent detection systems.

The more fundamental problem is the inadequacy of the detection paradigm. AI use is not binary. The student may have used AI for drafts but written the final text themselves; AI may have been used for research but writing done by the student; or the student may have critically evaluated and integrated AI suggestions. Detection systems cannot capture these nuances.

Academic integrity literature acknowledges the unreliability of detection technologies and recommends rethinking assessment approaches. Rather than relying on AI detection tools, assessment designs that make AI use transparent should be developed.

3.4 Personalized Learning Platforms

The functioning of adaptive learning platforms is based on a three-stage cycle. In the first stage, the student's initial skill level is assessed. In the second stage, the algorithm selects content appropriate to the student's level. In the third stage, the student's performance is monitored and the algorithm adjusts the next content. This cycle repeats continuously.

Risk begins in the first stage. Initial assessment measures the student's current performance but does not evaluate potential. A student performing poorly on a bad day is placed in a low skill group. The algorithm offers easy content to the student based on this early classification. The student succeeds at these easy questions and the algorithm thinks the classification is correct.

In the second stage, risk deepens. The student is never exposed to challenging content because the algorithm optimizes for keeping the student at their current level. Vygotsky's concept of zone of proximal development is violated. The student should experience challenges slightly beyond their current competence, but the algorithm does not present this challenge.

In the third stage, the outcome crystallizes. The student never realizes their potential because the system keeps them at the initial classification. The more insidious dimension is the embedding of socioeconomic bias. Students from families with disadvantaged educational backgrounds are more likely to perform poorly on initial tests. The algorithm codes this structural disadvantage as individual low ability and constrains the student.

3.5 Chatbots, Virtual Assistants and Academic Ethics

The widespread use of generative AI tools by students brings to the agenda the fundamental question of education regarding what constitutes a student's "own work."

The traditional view assumes that original work is what the student produces individually, without external help. This view is inherited from the Romantic concept of genius. Originality springs from the isolated creator's mind. However, this view ignores the social nature of learning. Students continuously draw inspiration from teachers, books, peers, and ideas are constructed through social interaction.

The alternative view centers student engagement in the understanding process. From this perspective, AI use is legitimate if the student critically evaluates AI suggestions, compares alternative approaches, and makes informed choices. The problem is passive consumption of AI. When the student accepts AI output without questioning, learning does not occur.

The pragmatic view focuses on the purpose of assessment. If homework aims to measure the student's independent problem-solving capacity, AI use defeats this goal. If homework aims to develop research and synthesis skills, using AI as a tool may be appropriate. The critical point is alignment of assessment design with pedagogical goals.

This philosophical uncertainty leads to practical difficulties. When a teacher observes suddenly improved language in a student's homework, they suspect, but evidence is unclear. Two possible explanations exist; the student genuinely improved or used AI. Since detection tools are unreliable, the teacher is forced to question the student's intent. This process creates trust erosion and damages the teacher-student relationship.

Student views on AI use lie at the very center of this ethical debate. In interviews conducted by Sullivan and colleagues (2023) with higher education students, most students stated they viewed AI support as a "thought partner" but expressed discomfort with the unclear boundaries of academic integrity. Students indicated they struggled to understand which uses were acceptable when teachers did not provide clear guidance, and this uncertainty created anxiety. This situation emphasizes the necessity of actively including student perspective in the risk assessment process.

In light of these different applications frequently encountered by teachers in practice, risks arising from AI use in education can be presented at multiple levels and interacting categories. The classification given below is constructed from synthesis of Zeng et al.'s (2024) AIR 2024 taxonomy with Holmes et al.'s (2022) education-specific risk framework. Each risk category is examined with its theoretical definition, manifestation in educational context and concrete examples.

Table 3. Taxonomy of AI Risks in Education

Risk Category	Theoretical Definition	Manifestation in Educational Context	Example Scenarios
Ethical Risks	Potential to produce outcomes contrary to moral principles	• Data ethics involving data collection without consent and use beyond purpose; • Algorithmic ethics involving lack of transparency in decision processes; • Application ethics involving violation of student autonomy	Student data being processed in learning analytics platforms without parental consent and shared with third parties
Pedagogical Risks	Harms arising from incompatibility of AI applications with learning theories and educational goals	• Excessive interference with deep learning processes; • Hindering development of metacognitive skills; • Violation of zone of proximal development principle	Weakening of students' critical thinking and problem-solving capacities as a result of overdependence on AI-assisted homework tools
Technical Risks	Failures arising from AI systems' architecture, training data or implementation environment	• Model errors including hallucination, false positive and negative results; • Data quality issues involving incomplete, biased or contaminated training data; • Security vulnerabilities involving adversarial attacks and data poisoning; • Performance inconsistencies involving varying accuracy rates across different groups	Plagiarism detection system incorrectly marking original student texts as plagiarism or failing to detect AI-generated texts
Institutional Risks	Potential of AI applications to threaten educational institutions' legal, financial and reputational capital	• Legal compliance risks involving violation of regulations like GDPR, KVKK; • Financial risks involving high implementation costs and vendor dependency; • Reputational risks involving loss of trust following student harm; • Operational risks involving system failures and data losses; • Strategic risks involving wrong technology investments	Institution facing legal sanctions and losing public reputation as a result of personal data breach arising from AI tool use

This taxonomy facilitates teachers' systematic categorization of risks they encounter and development of appropriate intervention strategies for each category.

4. AI RISK ASSESSMENT FRAMEWORK PROPOSAL FOR TEACHERS

The risk assessment framework presented in this section derives from adaptation of the four functions of NIST AI RMF summarized in Table 2 to individual teacher practice. The framework adopts the cyclical approach (plan-do-check-act) common in institutional risk management literature but presents a simplified methodology considering teachers' time constraints, levels of technical expertise and pedagogical priorities. Although the four steps are presented sequentially, in practice they are iterative and cyclical. Findings from each step may require revision of previous steps. The framework's basic assumption is that teachers have the capacity to assess AI risks with their professional judgment but need a systematic structure and checklists.

4.1 Step 1: Risk Identification and Inventory Creation

The first step of risk assessment is inventory creation because unidentified risks cannot be managed. The teacher should identify tools directly used (assessment systems, lesson preparation assistants) and systems indirectly exposed to (learning management platforms, institutional data analytics).

The inventory should go beyond visible tools. Embedded AI features that teachers use unknowingly (such as email platforms' automatic response suggestions, notebooks' smart correction systems) should also be included because these "invisible" systems also carry risk.

A typical teacher's inventory may include tools in the following categories; learning management systems (Google Classroom, Moodle), automated assessment tools (Turnitin, Ithenticate), communication platforms (Microsoft Teams, Zoom), personalized learning applications (Khan Academy, Duolingo) and generative AI tools (ChatGPT, Claude). For each tool, it should be determined what pedagogical need it meets, whether alternative methods exist, and whether use is mandatory or optional.

When determining risk areas for each tool, dimensions of data flow, algorithm transparency, performance equity, user control and regulatory compliance should be examined. In the data flow dimension, the teacher should ask what data is collected, with whom it is shared, how long it is stored. In the algorithm transparency dimension, can the system's decisions be explained, how frequently do incorrect results occur. In the performance equity dimension, does the system show different accuracy rates across different student groups, are certain demographic groups systematically disadvantaged. In the user control dimension, can students view, correct and delete their data. In the regulatory compliance dimension, is the system compliant with local regulations like KVKK and if applicable international standards like the EU AI Act.

Answers to these questions can be obtained from provider documentation, privacy policies or direct queries to the provider. However, providers are generally reluctant to share algorithm details; in this case, the teacher can conduct behavioral risk analysis by observing the system's outputs.

4.2 Step 2: Risk Analysis and Prioritization

Risk analysis requires assessing each risk's probability of occurrence and potential impact. Quantitative methods common in institutional risk management are not applicable at teacher level. Therefore, the method proposed here is based on qualitative assessment. For each risk, probability (rare, possible, likely) and impact (low, moderate, severe) categories are determined.

Risk score is positioned in a priority matrix derived from multiplication of probability and impact categories. Figure 1 shows the risk prioritization matrix teachers can use. Each cell represents the risk level of the relevant probability-impact combination.

Figure 1. Risk Prioritization Matrix

IMPACT ↓ PROBABILITY →	**Low Impact**	**Moderate Impact**	**Severe Impact**
Likely (Weekly)	Moderate Risk (4)	High Risk (7)	Critical Risk (9)
Possible (Semesterly)	Low Risk (2)	Moderate Risk (5)	High Risk (8)
Rare (Yearly)	Minimal Risk (1)	Low Risk (3)	Moderate Risk (6)

Risk Score Explanation:

1-3 represents acceptable risk (standard monitoring)

4-6 represents moderate risk (mitigation strategies recommended)

7-9 represents high/critical risk (urgent intervention required)

The risk scores in the matrix help teachers prioritize within their limited time. While urgent mitigation strategies are developed for tools in the critical risk category, standard monitoring may suffice for those in the minimal risk category (NIST, 2023). While this matrix provides general risk priority, teachers are advised to handle ethically critical risks like data privacy and equal opportunity with higher priority even if they appear in the "Moderate Risk" category in the matrix.

Likely probability and severe impact combination is critical risk, rare probability and low impact combination is minimal risk. Intermediate categories are classified as moderate risk. Five evaluation criteria are used in risk scoring but not all criteria are equally weighted. Data use and inequality creation risks are heavily weighted due to their pedagogical and ethical consequences. Error-making potential is dependent on system criticality; highly weighted in systems used for student admission decisions, lightly weighted in course material suggestions. Learning process contribution and irreplaceability criteria are used to assess risk-benefit balance; high-risk but pedagogically indispensable tools require different intervention strategies than low-risk but minimally contributing tools.

For example, an automated homework grading system may show this profile:

- Data use involves student name, homework content, past performance (moderate risk)
- Error potential has high likelihood of incorrectly grading original answers (high risk)
- Inequality has tendency to penalize non-standard language use (high risk)
- Learning contribution provides rapid feedback (moderate benefit)
- Irreplaceability allows manual grading (low criticality)

Overall assessment presents moderate-high risk requiring mitigation strategies

4.3 Step 3: Risk Mitigation Strategies

Risk mitigation strategies should be developed primarily for tools identified as high risk. Preventive measures are proactive approaches that prevent risk occurrence or reduce its probability. AI literacy training for students enables students to understand the functioning of tools they use, their potential risks and ethical use principles. These trainings should cover how AI can produce misleading information, importance of critical evaluation of its results, and academic integrity standards.

Creating transparent usage policies clearly defines what tools are used for what purpose, how student data is processed, and students' rights. These policies should be shared in writing, prepared in language understandable by students and parents, and regularly updated. Developing alternative assessment methods can reduce overdependence on AI tools. Oral exams, in-class applications, portfolio assessments and project-based assessments enable more reliable measurement of students' actual competencies.

Compensatory controls are reactive measures that limit harm when risk cannot be completely prevented. Preserving human oversight at every stage means that decisions made by AI are not automatically implemented and the teacher's professional judgment is the final decision authority. Using multiple assessment tools reduces dependence on a single AI tool and enables comparison of results from different tools. Regular stakeholder communication involves systematic collection and evaluation of feedback from students, parents and colleagues.

4.4 Step 4: Monitoring and Continuous Improvement

Risk assessment is not a static process but a dynamic and continuous cycle. Establishing performance indicators enables measurement of risk mitigation strategies' effectiveness. However, many AI risks cannot be directly measured. The effect of algorithmic bias on student motivation or the psychological harm of privacy breach cannot be expressed with quantitative metrics. Therefore, indicators should be both quantitative (system error rates, usage statistics) and qualitative (student feedback, teacher observations).

Complaints or concerns from students provide valuable information about system effectiveness. If a tool continuously produces erroneous results, leads to unfair outcomes among students, or negatively affects student motivation, this feedback should be taken seriously and necessary corrective measures implemented. Monitoring unexpected outcomes enables early detection of risks not initially foreseen. For example, if a personalized learning platform unexpectedly leads to low performance in a certain student group, this situation should be immediately investigated and platform use reviewed.

Systematic operation of feedback mechanisms enables continuous improvement. Regular surveys or focus group discussions with students provide direct information about tools' usability and effectiveness.

Design of student feedback mechanisms should be adapted according to age group and context. While visual scales and simplified questions are used at primary education level, structured surveys and focus group discussions can be preferred at secondary and higher education. What matters is ensuring students can safely express views not only about satisfaction but also about perceived risks and concerns. As suggested by Perkins and colleagues (2023), informing students about how AI tools work and what risks they carry enables obtaining more meaningful feedback.

Sharing experiences with colleagues enables learning about problems and solutions encountered in different contexts. Regular updating of risk assessment documentation, adding new tools, removing discontinued tools and reflecting changing risk profiles is necessary. This cyclical process supports teachers' responsible and effective use of AI tools.

4.5 Framework Implementation: Example Scenario

A high school mathematics teacher is considering using an automated homework assessment system.

- Step 1: Inventory. The system scans students' written solutions to mathematics problems, recognizes steps and assigns points to each step. Student name, class, homework content and past performance data are collected.
- Step 2: Risk analysis. Data risk is moderate (sensitive academic data but limited personal information). Error potential is high (non-standard solution paths may be incorrectly graded). Inequality risk is high (handwriting recognition accuracy may vary across different writing styles). Learning contribution is moderate (rapid feedback but superficial). Irreplaceability is low (manual grading is possible). Note that this system does not fall under the EU AI Act's high-risk category definition as it is used for daily homework assessment. However, it requires careful evaluation due to pedagogical and ethical risks. Overall risk assessment is moderate level.
- Step 3: Mitigation strategies. Preventive actions include explaining to students how the system works, encouraging them to write solutions clearly. The system is used only for low-impact homework (practice), not for high-impact homework (end-of-term project). Compensatory steps include all grades being reviewed by the teacher, solutions where the system shows low confidence scores being manually checked. Students are provided with a mechanism to challenge grades.
- Step 4: Monitoring. System performance is reviewed weekly in the first month, monthly thereafter. Mid-term feedback is collected from students. Accuracy rates are compared across different student groups (male-female, different writing styles). If systematic bias is detected, system use is re-evaluated.

5. CHALLENGES AND BARRIERS IN IMPLEMENTATION

The theoretical consistency of the risk assessment framework does not guarantee its practical applicability. Structural, cognitive and institutional barriers teachers face can make framework adoption difficult. This section examines five main barrier categories and realistic intervention strategies for each category.

5.1 Resource Constraints

The most fundamental barrier teachers face in implementing risk assessment processes is time and resource inadequacy. Given teachers' existing workload, curriculum requirements, administrative tasks and classroom management responsibilities, finding time for comprehensive risk assessments becomes difficult. Time constraint requires framework simplification. Short checklists focusing on critical risks and integration into existing planning routines reduce additional workload. For example, conducting a quick risk check of AI tools to be used during lesson plan preparation does not require a separate assessment session.

5.2 Digital Literacy Gaps

Differences in teachers' AI literacy levels directly affect the effectiveness of risk assessment processes. Lack of continuous professional development programs leads teachers to struggle in understanding rapidly changing AI technologies and conducting risk assessment. Teacher training should encompass algorithmic functioning, data flow and bias sources. UNESCO's AI Competency Framework structures this development in awareness, deepening and innovation stages (UNESCO, 2024). Peer learning enables benefiting from experienced colleagues' practical knowledge.

5.3 Legal Uncertainties and Liability Issues

How KVKK and GDPR apply to AI applications is unclear for most teachers. Does the EU AI Act's high-risk system definition cover an automated assessment tool a teacher uses? Is liability with the vendor, institution, or individual teacher? These questions remain unclear.

Liability is uncertain in cases of AI errors. Incorrect grading or false positive detection distributes legal and ethical responsibility among vendor, institution and teacher. Clear policies and legal consultation mechanisms are required.

5.4 Institutional Resistance and Change Management

Resistance to AI integration in educational institutions may stem from general skepticism toward technological change. Teachers, administrators and parents may carry concerns that AI will negatively affect educational processes, weaken the teacher-student relationship or threaten educational values. Institutional resistance may arise from concern that AI will weaken the teacher-student relationship. Pilot applications limit risks by testing on a small scale and produce evidence. When policy changes are developed with stakeholder participation, ownership increases. Top-down imposition increases resistance.

5.5 Cultural and Contextual Factors

AI access is limited in schools with low socioeconomic levels. Digital inequality stems from unequal distribution of physical infrastructure, teacher training and institutional resources. One-size-fits-all solutions fall short; context-specific adaptations are required. Age groups require different risk profiles. Primary school students require more supervision, high school students require critical evaluation skills. Cultural contexts affect privacy perceptions and technology attitudes. Universal frameworks should be open to local adaptation.

6. CONCLUSION AND RECOMMENDATIONS

This study aimed to develop a conceptual risk management model for teachers to evaluate AI tools. Findings were obtained through literature synthesis and comparative analysis of international standards, yielding the following answers to the four fundamental questions identified at the section's beginning.

Analysis for systematic classification of risk categories revealed four fundamental categories in educational context. In the ethical dimension, data privacy violations and lack of algorithmic transparency threaten student rights. Pedagogically, excessive AI interference with learning processes hinders development of critical thinking and metacognitive skills. At the technical level, model errors and algorithmic biases show varying performance across different student groups. From the institutional perspective, issues of legal compliance, financial resource allocation and reputation management are observed. This classification is based on synthesis of Zeng et al.'s (2024) general AI risk taxonomy with Holmes et al.'s (2022) education-specific framework.

The question of how international frameworks can be adapted to individual teacher practice constituted the study's second focus. UNESCO's Recommendation on the Ethics of Artificial Intelligence (2021), OECD's Classification Framework (2022), European Union Artificial Intelligence Act (2024) and NIST's Risk Management Framework (2023) were examined in detail. While these frameworks have different focal points, they are complementary. UNESCO offers ethical values as normative foundation, while OECD focuses on technical classification of systems. The EU AI Act brings legal obligations, while NIST presents operational methodology. All frameworks converge on protection of human rights, algorithmic transparency and accountability principles. The developed adaptation provides applicable guides to teachers by drawing from an integrated perspective of these frameworks. The EU AI Act's high-risk system definition provides teachers with concrete criteria in areas such as student admission, performance assessment, competence determination and surveillance.

Development of practical tools and methodologies constituted the study's third goal. NIST's cyclical risk management approach was transformed into a four-step model considering teachers' time constraints and technical expertise levels. In the first step, visible tools and embedded AI features are systematically inventoried. In the second step, risks are prioritized using a three-level probability and impact matrix based on qualitative assessment. In the third step, preventive and compensatory controls are developed for high-risk tools. In the fourth step, continuous monitoring is realized through performance indicators and feedback mechanisms. This methodology simplifies complex procedures in institutional risk management literature while maintaining conceptual consistency.

Identifying barriers teachers encounter when implementing risk assessment focused on the study's fourth question. Time and resource inadequacy is the most frequently encountered structural barrier. Digital literacy gaps make it difficult for teachers to understand algorithmic functioning and data flows. Legal uncertainties create confusion especially regarding application of regulations like GDPR and KVKK to AI tools. Institutional resistance stems from skepticism toward technological change and concern that the teacher-student relationship will be harmed. Socioeconomic inequalities create imbalance regarding tool access and teacher training in different schools. Intervention strategies developed for each barrier include short checklists, peer learning mechanisms, legal consultation channels, pilot applications and context-specific adaptations.

Three fundamental actions suffice for teachers to initiate risk assessment. Creating an inventory of AI tools used, identifying high-risk tools, and implementing preventive controls for these tools are the necessary steps for beginning. Assessment is beginning-focused rather than perfection-focused. The cyclical process provides improvement over time.

6.1 Directions for Future Research

This study presents a conceptual-theoretical model and does not involve empirical data collection. The proposed framework was developed through literature synthesis and comparative analysis of international standards, requiring field implementation and quantitative evaluation. As emphasized by Holmes et al. (2022), effectiveness of educational technology risk assessment models can only be validated through systematic applications in multiple contexts. Therefore, testing the presented framework through pilot applications at different educational levels, in cultural contexts and institutional structures should be the priority goal of future research.

On the other hand, examining teacher experiences in longitudinal studies is valuable for understanding how risk assessment processes change over time, which strategies are effective, and how encountered difficulties are overcome. Particularly, risk perceptions and assessment approaches of teachers at different career stages can be examined comparatively.

REFERENCES

Brundage, M., Avin, S., Wang, J., Belfield, H., Krueger, G., Hadfield, G., . . . Maharaj, T. (2020). Toward trustworthy AI development: Mechanisms for supporting verifiable claims. *arXiv preprint arXiv:2004.07213*. https://arxiv.org/abs/2004.07213

Chan, C. K. Y., & Hu, W. (2023). Students' voices on generative AI: Perceptions, benefits, and challenges in higher education. *International Journal of Educational Technology in Higher Education*, *20*(1), 43. DOI: 10.1186/s41239-023-00411-8

European Union. (2024). Regulation (EU) 2024/1689 of the European Parliament and of the Council laying down harmonised rules on artificial intelligence (Artificial Intelligence Act). *Official Journal of the European Union*. https://digital-strategy.ec.europa.eu/en/policies/regulatory-framework-ai

Floridi, L., & Cowls, J. (2019). A unified framework of five principles for AI in society. *Harvard Data Science Review*, *1*(1). Advance online publication. DOI: 10.1162/99608f92.8cd550d1

Hoel, T., Griffiths, D., & Chen, W. (2018). Privacy and data protection in learning analytics should be motivated by an educational maxim—Towards a proposal. *Research and Practice in Technology Enhanced Learning*, *13*(1), 20. Advance online publication. DOI: 10.1186/s41039-018-0086-8 PMID: 30595748

Holmes, W., Bialik, M., & Fadel, C. (2024). *Artificial intelligence in education: Promises and implications for teaching and learning*. Center for Curriculum Redesign.

Holmes, W., Persson, J., Chounta, I. A., Wasson, B., & Dimitrova, V. (2022). *Artificial intelligence and education: A critical view through the lens of human rights, democracy and the rule of law*. Council of Europe Publishing.

Hubbard, D. W., & Seiersen, R. (2016). *How to measure anything in cybersecurity risk*. John Wiley & Sons. DOI: 10.1002/9781119162315

Mittelstadt, B. D., Allo, P., Taddeo, M., Wachter, S., & Floridi, L. (2016). The ethics of algorithms: Mapping the debate. *Big Data & Society*, *3*(2), 1–25. DOI: 10.1177/2053951716679679

Mökander, J., & Floridi, L. (2021). Ethics-based auditing to develop trustworthy AI. *Minds and Machines*, *31*(2), 323–327. DOI: 10.1007/s11023-021-09557-8

NIST. (2023). *Artificial Intelligence Risk Management Framework (AI RMF 1.0)*. National Institute of Standards and Technology., DOI: 10.6028/NIST.AI.100-1

NIST. (2024). *Artificial Intelligence Risk Management Framework: Generative artificial intelligence profile (NIST AI 600-1).* National Institute of Standards and Technology., DOI: 10.6028/NIST.AI.600-1

OECD. (2022). *OECD framework for the classification of AI systems.* OECD Publishing., DOI: 10.1787/cb6d9eca-

Perkins, M., Roe, J., Postma, D., McGaughran, J., & Hickerson, D. (2023). Detection of GPT-4 generated text in higher education: Combining academic judgement and software to identify generative AI tool misuse. *Journal of Academic Ethics, 21*(4), 441–474. DOI: 10.1007/s10805-023-09492-6

Sullivan, M., Kelly, A., & McLaughlan, P. (2023). ChatGPT in higher education: Considerations for academic integrity and student learning. *Journal of Applied Learning & Teaching*, *6*(1), 1–10. DOI: 10.37074/jalt.2023.6.1.17

Trust, T., & Whalen, J. (2021). Emergency remote teaching with technology during the COVID-19 pandemic: Using the whole teacher lens to examine educator's experiences and insights. *Educational Media International*, *58*(2), 145–160. DOI: 10.1080/09523987.2021.1930479

Tyton Partners. (2023). *Time for class 2023: Demand, adoption, and efficacy in higher education.* Tyton Partners.

UNESCO. (2021). *Recommendation on the ethics of artificial intelligence.* UNESCO. https://unesdoc.unesco.org/ark:/48223/pf0000381137

UNESCO. (2024). *AI competency framework for teachers.* UNESCO. https://www.unesco.org/en/articles/ai-competency-framework-teachers

Weber-Wulff, D., Anohina-Naumeca, A., Bjelobaba, S., Foltýnek, T., Guerrero-Dib, J., Popoola, O., Šigut, P., & Waddington, L. (2023). Testing of detection tools for AI-generated text. *International Journal for Educational Integrity, 19*(1), 26. DOI: 10.1007/s40979-023-00146-z

Zeng, Y., Klyman, K., Zhou, A., Yang, Y., Pan, M., Jia, R., Song, D., Liang, P., & Li, B. (2024). AI risk categorization decoded (AIR 2024): From government regulations to corporate policies. *arXiv preprint arXiv:2406.17864.* https://arxiv.org/abs/2406.17864

Chapter 3
Digital Learning Environments and Tools:
Bridging the AI DIvide – A Developing Country Perspective

Willem Adolf Mostert
https://orcid.org/0000-0003-4072-9325
Two Oceans Graduate Institute, South Africa

Adrienne van As
https://orcid.org/0000-0003-0273-3868
Cape Peninsula University of Technology, South Africa

Amanda Jankowitz
https://orcid.org/0000-0002-8550-8107
University of Witwatersrand, South Africa

ABSTRACT

Educational institutes, with a special focus on higher education, have been increasingly flooded with a wide array of artificial intelligent (AI) tool such as such as ChatGPT, Claude, Gork and Jenny AI to assist students in academic output and performance. Through an intentional qualitative literature review, this chapter examines the impact of AI tools on students' academic performance, self-efficacy, creativity, and originality across different socio-economic groups in developed and developing countries. This chapter utilised Bandura's Self-Efficacy Theory, Constructivist Learning Theory and Van Dijk's Digital Divide Theory. The findings underscored three interrelated themes forming a reinforcing cyclical model. This chapter concludes with recommendations to bridge the AI divide in developing

DOI: 10.4018/979-8-3373-4521-5.ch003

countries, higher education institutes should prioritise infrastructural investments, AI literacy, and policies to ensure the integrity of creativity and originality of students' academic outputs.

1. INTRODUCTION

In recent years, higher education institutions have experienced a rapid influx of artificial intelligence (AI) tools, such as ChatGPT, Claude, Gork and Jenny AI designed to support students in enhancing academic performance and productivity (Lo, 2023), promising to revolutionise learning, personalised feedback, efficient information retrieval, and creative assistance (Sandu et al., 2024). However, the ethical implications of AI integration in education remain under continuous scrutiny, particularly regarding equitable access and its influence on academic outcomes (Khreisat et al., 2024).

Access to AI tools is not uniformly distributed (Valdivieso & González, 2025). Students from higher socio-economic backgrounds and urban centres often benefit from robust digital infrastructure and institutional support, while those in rural or under-resourced settings, especially in developing countries, face significant barriers (Kour et al., 2025)· This disparity raises critical questions about fairness, opportunity, and the construction of knowledge in digitally mediated learning environments. Students with consistent access to AI tools tend to exhibit different academic outcomes than their peers without such access, potentially widening existing educational gaps.

This chapter explores the intersection of AI access, academic performance, educational justice, and the construction of original thought through the comparative lenses of Bandura's Self-Efficacy Theory (SET) (Bandura, 1997), Constructivist Learning Theory (CLT) (Piaget, 1970) and Digital Divide Theory (DDT) (Van Dijk, 2006, 2012) investigating how students' belief in their academic capabilities are shaped by their interaction with AI tools. It examines how access can impact creativity, motivation, and meaningful engagement with academic tasks, without impeding the construction of knowledge.

A qualitative, intentional literature review with a focus on theory was used to analyse scholarly work from 2018 to 2025, to nuance the comparative experiences of students and higher education institutes (HEI) in developed countries and regions, and to highlight socio-economic and geographical factors influencing digital integration in developing regions, including South Africa. By foregrounding the lived experiences of students from under-resourced settings, this chapter aims to contribute to a more equitable understanding of AI integration in higher education.

The objectives of this chapter are to examine the relationship between access to AI tool in higher education and students' academic self-efficacy. In doing so, it seeks to address a critical gap in the literature and provide actionable insights for educators, policymakers, and technologists.

The chapter begins with a contextual background of AI tools in HEI followed by a theoretical overview. It then presents literature and findings from across developed and developing contexts. By critically examining the intersection of AI access and academic self-efficacy across diverse contexts, this chapter contributes to a more inclusive and justice-oriented understanding of digital learning in higher education. The key findings are synthesised through the lens of the selected theories. This chapter concludes with recommendations and directions for future research.

1.2 Background

The integration of artificial intelligence (AI) tools into higher education has sparked widespread debate regarding their potential to enhance learning outcomes and democratise access to academic support. With the rapid advancement of AI, critical voices have emerged, questioning the equity and inclusivity of these innovations. Farahani and Ghasemi (2024) argue that unequal access to AI tools can reinforce existing socio-economic disparities, particularly in low-resource educational contexts, raising concerns in developing countries, where digital infrastructure, affordability, and institutional support vary widely.

Globally, Selwyn (2022) cautions that without inclusive policy frameworks, AI may exacerbate digital privilege, benefiting students who already have access to high-quality educational resources while marginalising those who do not. Similarly, Maina and Kuria (2024) cite that resource constraints in African higher education institutes may contribute to the unsuccessful integration of AI tools and technologies, which may further widen the digital divide. In South Africa, Czerniewicz et al. (2020) highlight that students from rural and underfunded institutions face significant barriers to accessing digital tools. These disparities align with Van Dijk's (2006; 2012) DDT, which identifies three levels of inequality: access, skills, and outcomes.

The intersection of technology and equity provides a critical lens for understanding how generative AI tools shape educational experiences across socio-economic divides. In particular, the Global South presents a complex landscape in which digital innovation must be balanced against considerations of access and contextual relevance. As AI continues to evolve, higher education institutions must adopt inclusive approaches that prioritise equitable integration and support diverse student needs.

1.2.1 Access to AI Tools- Unequal Distribution

The integration of AI tools in education holds immense potential to transform learning experiences; however, access to these tools is far from uniform, resulting in significant disparities that reflect broader socio-economic and geographic inequalities. One of the most pressing concerns is the socioeconomic divide in access to AI. Students from lower-income backgrounds often rely on smartphones and free versions of AI tools, in contrast to their higher-income peers, who typically benefit from laptops, stable internet connections, and premium features of AI tools that enhance the learning experience (Farahani & Ghasemi, 2024).

This chapter's developing-country perspective acknowledges that everyday realities shape students' ability to participate in AI-enhanced learning. In many regions of the Global South, young people contend with persistent inequalities in income, infrastructure, connectivity, and institutional support, all of which affect their ability to meaningfully access digital tools (UNESCO, 2023; World Bank, 2023). These conditions affect far more than device ownership. They determine whether electricity is reliable enough for online learning, whether mobile data is affordable, and whether students can rely on a stable internet connection needed to interact with AI platforms. Historical inequalities, rural–urban divides, and uneven institutional capacity further intensify these challenges, particularly in South Africa and similar contexts where structural barriers continue to shape educational opportunity (Czerniewicz et al., 2020). Adopting a developing-country perspective, therefore, foregrounds students' lived experiences and highlights how socio-economic and geographical constraints directly mediate their engagement with AI in higher education.

In addition, the absence of institutional policies and support mechanisms limits students' ability to effectively leverage these technologies for academic success (Farahani & Ghasemi, 2024; Luckin et al., 2016). Beyond access and infrastructure, ethical and privacy concerns present additional challenges. The use of AI tools raises critical questions about data privacy and security, particularly in under-resourced institutions that may lack robust data protection frameworks (Schunk & DiBenedetto, 2021; Selwyn, 2022). Moreover, algorithmic bias embedded in AI systems can reinforce existing inequalities, disadvantaging certain student groups and perpetuating systemic discrimination (Czerniewicz et al., 2020). While access is critical, the ability to use AI meaningfully, known as AI literacy, emerges as a deeper layer of inequality that must be addressed through targeted educational interventions.

1.2.2 AI Literacy and Student Perspectives

AI literacy is increasingly recognised as a foundational skill in higher education. AI literacy is the ability to understand, critically evaluate and effectively use AI tools (Chen et al., 2025). Students who possess higher levels of AI literacy are more likely to engage confidently with digital platforms, enhancing their academic self-efficacy, or belief in their ability to succeed in academic tasks (Hussain & Anwar, 2025). This confidence fosters deeper engagement, creativity, and motivation, particularly when students can navigate AI tools to support original thought and problem-solving (Anghel et al., 2025). Conversely, limited AI literacy and overreliance can lead to frustration, disengagement, and reduced academic performance (Azeem & Abbas, 2025) especially in under-resourced contexts where support structures are minimal. Integrating AI literacy into curricula and institutional support systems is therefore essential for equitable and empowering educational experiences.

The disparities in AI access and AI literacy are not merely theoretical; they manifest in students' lived experiences. Research by Bećirović et al. (2025) confirm that students with higher AI literacy and access to practical applications of AI tools report greater academic self-efficacy and output quality. Similarly, Chun et al. (2025) found that AI literacy positively influences creativity and self-efficacy, which, in turn, enhance academic achievement.

From a student perspective, as reported in a study by Johnston et al. (2024) report that HEI should gear up to fully integrate AI, as banning it would be deemed unrealistic. Students hold the view that the full integration of AI and the necessity of AI literacy skills not only benefit and supplement their learning but also prepare them for future careers. Conversely, students without access to an AI tool and hands-on experience have reported that it can cause barriers that influence their academic motivation and hinder further development of AI literacy skills (Kong et al., 2025). Similarly, English et al. (2025) found that students from underprivileged backgrounds who lack access to AI tools may develop negative perceptions of these tools. In these under-resourced settings, students shared their concerns about their perceived inability to achieve the same level of academic success as their peers with access (Chen et al., 2025).

To address these disparities, targeted interventions are essential. Institutions must develop and implement policies that promote equitable access to AI tools, including structured guidance on responsible use and resource allocation (Farahani & Ghasemi, 2024; Luckin, et al., 2016). Comprehensive training programs for both students and lecturers can help mitigate technical barriers and enhance digital and AI literacy (Luckin, et al., 2016.; Schunk & DiBenedetto, 2021). Furthermore, establishing clear ethical frameworks and accountability mechanisms is crucial to ensuring that AI tools are used responsibly and inclusively (Selwyn, 2022; Williamson & Eynon, 2020).

The unequal distribution of AI tools in education underscores the urgent need for inclusive strategies that bridge socio-economic, geographic, and technical gaps. By prioritising equity and ethical integration, educational institutions can harness the full potential of AI to support diverse students and improve academic outcomes across contexts. This chapter argues for equitable distribution and access to AI tools, as well as the development of AI literacy among students in both developed and developing countries.

2. THEORETICAL FRAMEWORK

In a rapidly digitising educational landscape, access to AI tools is emerging as a critical determinant of student success. To understand how these disparities shape students' experiences, this chapter draws on three interrelated theoretical frameworks: Bandura's Self-Efficacy Theory (SET), Constructivist Learning Theory (CLT), and Digital Divide Theory (DDT) (figure 1). Together, these frameworks provide a comprehensive lens for exploring their cognitive, motivational, and structural implications. They help explain how students engage with AI tools, what shapes their confidence and learning, and why equitable digital inclusion remains elusive.

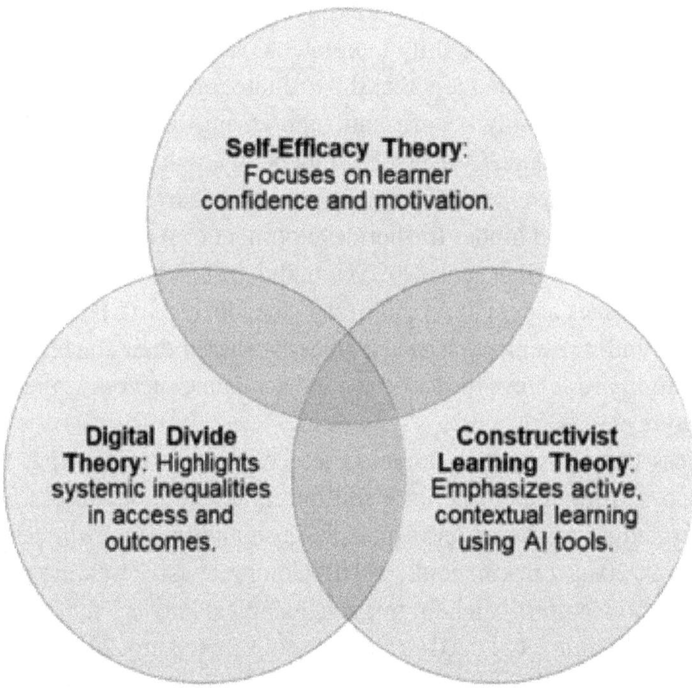

2.1 Bandura's Self-Efficacy Theory

Self-Efficacy Theory (SET) is a foundational concept in social cognitive theory, referring to a person's belief in their ability to organise and execute the actions required to achieve specific goals. Bandura argued that self-efficacy plays a significant role in how individuals approach challenges, persist in the face of difficulty, and regulate emotional responses. He defined it as: *"Perceived self-efficacy refers to beliefs in one's capabilities to organise and execute the courses of action required to produce given attainments"* (Bandura, 1997). Subsequent research extended Bandura's ideas to academic contexts, showing that students with strong self-efficacy beliefs are more motivated, more resilient, and more likely to achieve academically than those with low self-efficacy (Pajares, 1996; Schunk, 1991; Zimmerman, 2000).

At the heart of Bandura's theory are four primary sources of self-efficacy beliefs. Bandura identified four main sources of self-efficacy: mastery experiences, vicarious experiences, verbal persuasion, and emotional or physiological states (Maddux & Kleiman, 2021; Schunk, 1991; Zimmerman, 2000). An essential characteristic of self-efficacy is its task- and domain-specificity. Researchers such as Pajares (1996) and Zimmerman (2000) have explored academic self-efficacy, demonstrating that students' confidence in their academic skills often predicts performance more strongly than prior achievement, leading to the identification of multiple domain-specific constructs, including digital self-efficacy. Schunk and DiBenedetto (2021) emphasise that in technology-rich classrooms, fostering students' confidence in navigating digital platforms is essential for enhancing motivation and learning outcomes.

In the context of digital learning and AI tools, self-efficacy is an increasingly critical lens for understanding students' academic engagement. Students with high digital self-efficacy are more likely to explore and effectively use generative AI platforms (e.g. ChatGPT). In contrast, students with low self-efficacy may experience anxiety, avoid digital tasks, or rely passively on others. These perspectives position self-efficacy theory as both a psychological and social framework, illuminating how confidence, access, and opportunity intertwine to shape student success in a digitally divided world. From a constructivist perspective, however, such confidence and opportunity are not only individually determined but also shaped by the availability of tools that enable students to construct knowledge actively. While self-efficacy foregrounds individual belief systems and confidence, CLT extends this by showing how learning is socially mediated and context dependent.

2.2 Constructivist Learning Theory

Constructivist Learning Theory (CLT) posits that students actively construct their understanding and knowledge of the world through their lived experiences, reflection, and interactions with their environment. Rather than passively absorbing information, students interpret, question, and reorganise prior knowledge in response to new encounters. In digitally mediated contexts, especially where AI tools are involved, this theory emphasises the crucial role of access to technology in enabling meaningful, student-centred learning. According to Mensah (2015), knowledge is actively constructed through experience and dialogue; when learning tools such as AI are available, they can serve as cognitive partners that scaffold thinking, personalise feedback, and support creative exploration. Thus, CLT provides a powerful lens for critiquing both the potential and the inequalities of digital learning environments.

Piaget's cognitive constructivism (Piaget, 1970) foregrounds how knowledge is actively constructed through processes of assimilation and accommodation, highlighting learning as a continual restructuring of understanding. Contemporary applications of Piaget's cognitive constructivism highlight how digital and AI tools can act as stimuli for assimilation and accommodation. For students to reorganise their cognitive structures, they need sustained engagement with meaningful problems and opportunities to test their understanding. In the context of developing countries, Mensah (2015) advocates for a responsive, reflective pedagogy rooted in constructivist ideals, where lecturers facilitate learning that is contextual, participatory, and grounded in local realities. South African researchers such as Henning (2016), Sayed and Kanjee (2013), and Jansen (1990) have also engaged with constructivist principles in the domains of language learning, curriculum reform, and the decolonisation of education. Collectively, these perspectives reinforce that AI-supported learning is meaningful only if it is designed with awareness of students' contexts, histories, and opportunities for engagement. Nevertheless, even with strong motivation and student-centred pedagogy, systemic barriers remain, which DDT helps to explain.

2.3 Digital Divide Theory

Digital Divide Theory (DDT) offers a critical framework for understanding disparities in access to digital technologies, particularly in educational settings. Viewed through a constructivist lens, these disparities are not merely about having or lacking devices, but about whether students can participate in interactive, inquiry-based, and agency-rich learning that AI tools enable. Originating in the late 20th century, the DDT has since evolved into a multi-dimensional model encompassing access (first-level divide), skills and usage (second level), and outcomes (third level). Pioneered by Van Dijk (2006; 2012), this three-tiered approach recognises that simply providing devices or internet connections is insufficient. DDT critiques the assumption that the provision of technology alone ensures equity, highlighting that structural inequalities persist even when devices are available. In developing country contexts, unequal access to generative AI tools, such as ChatGPT or other digital learning platforms, can exacerbate broader socio-economic inequalities (Vassilakopoulou & Hustad, 2023).

Contemporary contributions to the theory highlight the growing complexity of digital inequalities. Vassilakopoulou and Hustad (2023) emphasise that digital divides are no longer closing but evolving in nuanced ways, particularly with the rise of algorithmic decision-making and AI-based learning. Selwyn (2004, 2022) offers a critical perspective by linking digital divides to structural injustices and warning against uncritical enthusiasm for educational technology. South African researchers such as Czerniewicz et al. (2020), Hodgkinson-Williams and Trotter (2018), and McKenna (2013) build on this work by contextualising the theory within African higher education. Their research reveals that students' academic participation is shaped not only by access but also by broader political, social, and institutional forces.

Together, the three theoretical lenses illuminate the layered complexities of digital learning in developing countries. They reveal that AI adoption in education is not solely a matter of infrastructure or policy but is also tied to students' confidence, pedagogical engagement, and socioeconomic realities. SET emphasises students' readiness to engage with digital tools, whereas CLT highlights the active, situated nature of learning. Additionally, DDT underscore how systemic inequities influence access to learning opportunities. By integrating these perspectives, we can better understand the enablers that must be cultivated to ensure meaningful, empowering, and equitable digital learning for all.

3. METHODOLOGY

This study adopts an intentional qualitative literature review (Creswell & Plano Clark, 2018) through the lenses of SET, CLT, and DDT, to examine the impact of generative AI in higher education. To ensure transparency and rigour, elements from systematic and scoping review methodologies were incorporated. A structured search strategy was applied across preselected databases, with predefined inclusion and exclusion criteria. The search strategy included peer-reviewed articles, journals, and policies that discuss the integration of AI-based tools in education, socioeconomic disparities, and academic performance outcomes. The analysis compared findings across developed and developing contexts to identify trends and gaps in the global educational response to AI. The review process involved identifying relevant studies, selecting them, charting and collating data, and summarising and reporting the results.

3.1 Methodological Approach

A well-structured and rigorous literature review extends beyond summarising current and relevant literature and knowledge to provide a robust foundation for enhancing educational practice and policy (Van Riel & Snyder, 2024). An intentional literature review can interrogate, synthesise, and interpret the literature through theoretical and conceptual lenses, making it especially suitable for emergent and ethically complex issues.

3.2 Data Collection and Identifying Relevant Studies

The search strategy included sources employing qualitative, quantitative, and mixed-methods methodologies. The search period covered January 2018 to August 2025, to account for the rise of generative AI and its applications in the academic output of higher education institutions globally and locally. This comprehensive search aimed to capture crucial and foundational discussions on AI in education, educational psychology, and the disparities in the distribution of educational resources across various socio-economic contexts.

Intentional searches were conducted using specific keywords and Boolean phrases. Only articles matching keywords in the title and or abstract were included. Manual searches of key studies were conducted to identify additional articles to supplement the research.

For this chapter, a comprehensive search was conducted across the following academic databases:

- Scopus
- ERIC (Education Resources Information Centre)
- EBSCOhost
- Web of Science
- PsycINFO
- Google Scholar (for grey literature and recent reprints)

3.2.1 Search Strings

Boolean search strings were developed by combining keywords aligned with the theoretical framework. These Boolean search strings included:

- "Artificial Intelligence" OR "AI tools"
- "Higher Education" OR "University"
- "Digital divide" OR "AI access"
- "Developed countries" OR "Developing countries."

3.2.2 Inclusion Criteria

The following inclusion criteria were used to search and identify relevant literature for this chapter:

- Peer-reviewed articles, book chapters, and grey literature (policy papers and reports)

- Literature published in English
- Relevant to higher education contexts, global trends in AI, benefits, and controversies of AI in higher education institutes (HEI), access to AI tools in high- and low socio-economic groups, support structures for the use of AI in HEI.
- Self-Efficacy Theory, Constructivist Learning Theory and Digital Divide Theory around the use of AI tools in HEI.

3.2.3 Exclusion Criteria

The following exclusion criteria were used during the search for relevant literature:

- Studies lacking in conceptual or empirical engagement with core constructs (AI tool, academic performance, equity, construction of knowledge, creativity, motivation)
- Articles focused on K-12 education and training.

Once studies were identified for the review, they were uploaded to Covidence and Mendeley. Duplicate sources were removed, and the remaining titles and abstracts were screened for relevance. Irrelevant articles were discarded, and the full text of eligible articles was selected.

3.3 Analysis and Discussion

Through an intentional literature review (Creswell & Plano Clark, 2018), this chapter analysed and compared the comparative insights from different socio-economic groups in developed and developing countries. The discussion was based on the impacts generative AI has on the construction of creative and original thought, and institutional factors that promote or hinder the inclusion of AI tool in HEI. The literature was examined thematically, using Bandura's SET, CLT, and DDT to interpret key trends and challenges.

3.4 Ethical Considerations

This study was solely based on the review of secondary sources and did not involve human participants. No ethical clearance or approval was required for this study. The researchers ensured to reference and credit all authors' work to avoid plagiarism.

4. FINDINGS AND DISCUSSION

This section presents a detailed discussion of the key themes that emerged from the literature review, offering a conceptual framework to understand the complex relationship between AI and the digital divide in higher education. Each theme is examined in depth, drawing on relevant literature and theoretical perspectives to highlight the critical factors shaping students' experiences with AI tools in academic contexts. To support this analysis, a conceptual diagram (figure 2) has been developed to visually represent the thematic structure of the findings. The diagram illustrates three interconnected themes that underpin the broader discourse on AI literacy, equity, and academic engagement.

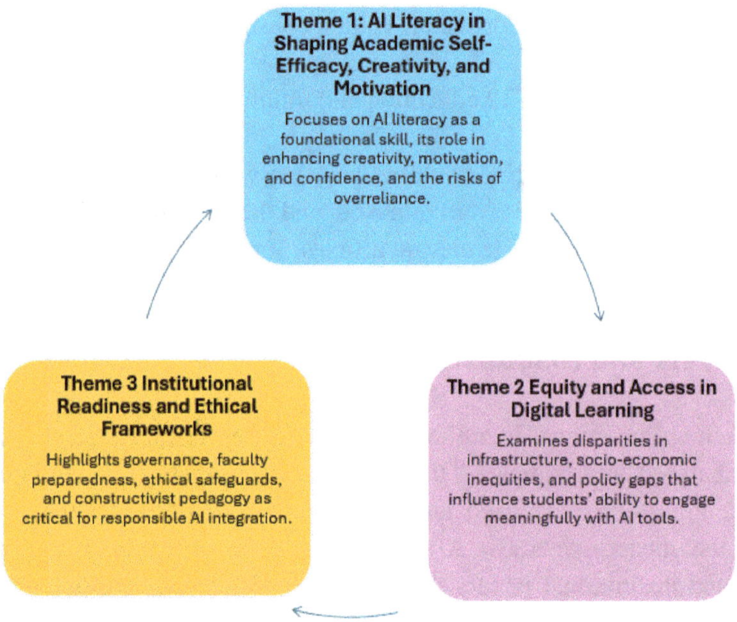

4.1 Theme 1: AI Literacy in shaping Academic Self-Efficacy, Creativity and Motivation

The discussion of theme 1 begins with Table 1, which summarises the concepts covered in this theme.

Table 1. Summary of Theme 1

Concepts	Description
AI Literacy as Foundational Skill	This refers to the ability to use AI tools ethically and effectively. This is an increasingly essential skill for academic success.
Creative Amplification	AI can support creative thinking by helping students explore a broader range of ideas and possibilities.
Equity of Access and Literacy	Students with better access to digital tools tend to develop stronger AI literacy, highlighting existing digital divides.
Ethical Use and Institutional Support	Institutions play a key role in promoting responsible AI use by integrating AI literacy into curricula and providing training.
AI Self-Efficacy	Student confidence in using AI tools enhances motivation, engagement, and academic performance.
Risks of Overreliance	Overuse of AI can lead to surface-level passive learning, plagiarism, and reduced critical thinking.

AI literacy, in shaping academic self-efficacy, creativity, and motivation, stands out as a foundational skill for navigating AI tools in higher education. According to Celik (2023) there is a need for students to appraise AI tools and technologies to use them effectively and to engage with them dynamically and constructively. Fully developed AI literacy skills underscore the potential to amplify students' creative thinking and widen the ideational search space by prompting recombination across sources and assisting in creative original contributions (Bai & Wang, 2025).

From the perspective of CTL, these cycles of assimilation and accommodation are exemplified by active engagement when students can reorganise prior knowledge through interaction with AI tools. Furthermore, these cycles of content generation rely on students' engagement to generate, evaluate, justify, and integrate results from AI tools (Bećirović et al., 2025). Such critical considerations are supported by Bandura's SET, in which successful experiences strengthen self-efficacy. Conversely, surface-level, or uncritical use can erode confidence and hinder motivational outcomes.

The uneven distribution of access exacerbates the divide in AI literacy, as students with access to ICT resources or prior exposure to digital tools are more likely to develop these competencies. In contrast, those without access may struggle, leading to uncritical use, overreliance, and plagiarism (Sydorenko et al., 2024). A study by Celik (2023) found that the digital divide accounted for 50% of cognitive absorption and 70% of the variance in computational thinking, emphasising the profound impact of access on learning outcomes and associated AI skills. Students in both developed and developing contexts lacking access are relegated to conventional learning methods, perpetuating cycles of poverty and limiting social mobility, which further diminishes the development of AI literacy skills (Szabó & Szoke, 2024). Demographic factors such as age, income, and education level influence students' attitudes toward AI, reflecting unequal access to and understanding of AI.

In ASEAN (Association of Southeast Asian Nations) countries, regional differences in AI adoption behaviour highlight the need for inclusive strategies that support diverse student populations (Bouteraa et al., 2024). CLT (Piaget, 1970) offers an insightful lens to understand these patterns. Without adequate scaffolding and opportunities to interact with digital tools, students are unable to construct new knowledge or participate in inquiry-driven learning.

Students across socio-economic backgrounds indicated a strong interest and need for professional training and development to become more AI literate, urging more comprehensive institutional guidance and support (Mah et al., 2025). To safeguard originality when engaging with AI tools, students are encouraged to provide process evidence to indicate transformative decisions (Alotaibi, 2023). Viewed through the lens of Bandura's SET, these practices emphasise verbal persuasion and feedback as reinforcing factors to build efficacy.

Higher levels of engagement with AI tools significantly increase levels of self-efficacy by acting as a 'personal assistant,' providing personal learning experiences and generating constructive feedback on assignments (Farmanesh et al., 2025). Thus, AI literacy and self-efficacy are reciprocally related: confidence builds literacy, and literacy strengthens confidence. However, the extent to which students can access and benefit from this cycle depends heavily on socio-economic and institutional conditions.

Psychological factors such as self-efficacy consistently emerge as mediators of AI outcomes. Chen et al. (2025) found that students with higher AI self-efficacy are better positioned to benefit from the moderating effect of AI self-efficacy on the relationship between AI learning anxiety and motivated learning. In other words, confident students can transform anxiety into motivation, while those without confidence experience paralysis. Huang et al. (2022) similarly shows that their AI learning frameworks had a marked effect on students' self-evaluation, self-efficacy, learning abilities, and satisfaction. Collectively, these findings affirm Bandura's theory that mastery experiences build confidence, which in turn strengthens persistence and achievement.

HEI has the responsibility to foster a positive and engaging relationship between AI literacy skills and learning outcomes, as this mediates and strengthens self-efficacy and cognitive engagement, further increasing student confidence when personalised learning environments are tailored for them (Liang et al., 2023). Increased academic self-efficacy indicates positive effects on student motivation to explore academic capabilities and proficiencies (Anghel et al., 2025). This indicates that enthusiasm and motivation to engage with learning material are driven by students' positive sentiments to use AI-based tools in their academic work and affords them the skills to enhance their understanding of concepts and their ability to learn (Amorin &

Gallaron, 2025). Thus, critical and ethical engagement with AI tools is paramount to academic success (Jai Lamimi et al., 2025).

The impact of AI on student engagement and motivation can have negative consequences, as overreliance on generative AI can lead to passive learning habits and a superficial approach to understanding course materials, further diminishing motivation and the active pursuit of academic success (Alotaibi, 2023). This is echoed by Azeem and Abbas (2025), who state that a lack of critical thinking, engagement, and overreliance on AI can result in students becoming passive learners, thereby further hindering academic self-efficacy, confidence, motivation, and student agency in completing academic tasks.

4.2 Theme 2: Equity and Access in Digital Learning

The discussion of theme 2 begins with Table 2, which summarises the concepts covered in this theme.

Table 2. Summary of Theme 2

Concept	Description
Infrastructure Disparities	The relationship between urban and rural, and public and private, institutions show stark differences in AI access.
Surface vs. Deep Engagement	There is a disparity between students with limited access who use AI for basic tasks and those with stable access who engage critically.
Socio-Economic Inequities	Wealthier students benefit from premium tools while low-income students face compounded barriers. This exacerbates the digital divide.
Psychological Mediators	Self-efficacy and trust influence how students engage and interact with AI tools.
Policy and Institutional Practices	Addressing access inequities demands zero-rated digital tools, multilingual scaffolding, and inclusive educational policies.

The integration of AI in higher education is increasingly framed through the lens of equity and access. In developed contexts, institutions often focus on refining ethical frameworks and pedagogical strategies, whereas developing regions (including South Africa, Sub-Saharan Africa, and parts of Latin America and Asia) grapple with structural barriers of infrastructure, affordability, and institutional readiness. In the Peruvian context, Arbulú Ballesteros et al. (2024) observe that higher access to digital infrastructure in urban areas has a marked effect on students' ability to succeed, in relation to students from under-resourced rural regions.

This mirrors challenges in South Africa, where high data costs, unstable electricity supply, and a mobile-first digital culture restrict students' ability to engage meaningfully with AI. These infrastructural inequalities constitute the "first-level divide," in which a lack of physical access determines who can participate (Van

Dijk, 2006, 2012). In South Africa, the digital divide in higher education is further shaped by historical, institutional, and socio-economic inequalities in access. Historically White Universities (HWUs) have made significant strides in AI integration due to better funding and international collaborations; however, Historically Black Universities (HBUs) still face systemic barriers to AI. COVID-19 worsened these gaps, revealing how disadvantaged students struggled with digital access (Azevedo et al., 2021; Ma, 2021). Many rural and township students continue to face challenges related to electricity, devices, and digital literacy.

By contrast, in developed contexts, the emphasis is less on access and more on ethical implications. Hussain and Anwar (2025) caution that, although AI chatbots have potential benefits for higher education institutions, there are reservations among the academic community about their potential to hinder students' critical thinking skills and their engagement with learning materials. Similarly, Anghel et al. (2025) report optimism in Romania, noting a strong alignment between the adoption of AI in higher education and the demands of the 21st-century digital age, to ensure academic success through enhanced student learning experiences.

In developing contexts, students are often limited to surface-level uses and utilitarian tasks, such as translation, summarisation, or task simplification, due to infrastructural and economic constraints. Liang et al. (2023) similarly demonstrate that learning achievement strongly relies on the positive interaction between students and AI. Students can only benefit from this vital synergy when they possess confidence in their ability to use AI, demonstrate sustained engagement, and have access to it.

CLT highlights that "deep engagement" is essential for meaning making, as students actively reorganise knowledge through critical inquiry (Piaget, 1970). SET explains why only students who are confident in their digital skills sustain this deeper engagement: belief in their ability enables them to persist and to explore AI tools as partners in learning. Where resources are stable, students can use AI to explore perspectives and refine arguments; where they are not, engagement becomes fragmented and superficial. This paradox is confirmed in the Philippines, where students acknowledged that AI has the potential to enhance their personal learning and promote critical thinking, but they continue to perceive limitations in their access to experiential learning (Capinding & Dumayas, 2024).

Socio-economic inequities reinforce these patterns. This reflects South African realities, in which wealthier students have access to premium AI accounts and private devices. In contrast, low-income students rely on shared facilities or mobile phones with limited capabilities. Altememy et al. (2023) found that in Iraqi HEI, due to existing and accessible digital infrastructure, students reported a positive correlation between their academic achievements and AI capabilities, suggesting that national or institutional investment can mitigate inequities by providing AI-enabled teaching and assessment tools. From a Digital Divide perspective, these are examples of both first level (infrastructure) and third level (outcome) divides, where socio-economic status determines who benefits academically.

This inequality in access creates a further divide to favour the more privileged student populations at HEI. Consequently, creative amplification from generative AI tools is unevenly distributed. Viewed through SET, low self-efficacy is not a reflection of personal deficit but can arise from barriers to opportunities for mastery (Bandura, 1997). This demonstrates how equity of access directly shapes literacy outcomes: without consistent infrastructure and opportunities for practice, students remain excluded from developing higher-order AI skills, thereby limiting their ability to benefit from AI tools.

Disadvantaged students are left with limited opportunities to construct new knowledge. SET explains that repeated exposure to inequities can erode low-income students' confidence in their academic capabilities, thereby further entrenching inequality. Similar insights come from Saudi Arabia, where Alotaibi (2023) observed that students' perceptions and technical capabilities shape adoption and lived experiences, which influence performance through the mediating role of trust. These findings underscore that socio-economic inequities manifest not only in material access but also in psychological confidence and trust, while motivation and habit may help some students compensate. As Sydorenko et al. (2024) explain, educated people in more financially secure positions are more likely to benefit from and have access to information technologies. In contrast, people living in more financially strained circumstances will not be in a position to develop the necessary digital skills to enhance their lives and navigate emerging technologies.

However, without structured support, students may face heightened anxiety or even dependency. Almaiah et al. (2022) confirm that high levels of digital- and AI anxiety may lead to students' negative perceptions of ITCs and AI tools. Such evidence demonstrates that access without confidence does not guarantee equitable outcomes. Here, SET is most visible: students' belief in their capability determines whether anxiety is transformed into persistence or withdrawal.

It was noted that lectures can further compound barriers to access; in Ghana, internal and external barriers were attributed to infrastructure and access to training, hindering full AI adoption and integration in higher education (Atuahene & XuSheng, 2024). Chu et al. (2022) note the critical role of administrators in understanding and supporting lecturers who face challenges in integrating AI at HEIs. This is echoed by Amorin and Gallaron (2025), who emphasise the importance of embedding ethics and integrity in higher education. Hussain and Anwar (2025) call for ethical guidelines, while Anghel et al. (2025) stress AI's role in preparing students for the digital world, and Leite (2025) warns against treating AI as a replacement for human creativity. Viewed through the three theoretical lenses, institutional practices that promote ethics, scaffolding, and equitable access both strengthen student confidence and create the participatory, inquiry-based learning environments necessary for meaningful AI adoption.

4.3 Theme 3: Institutional Readiness and Ethical Frameworks

The discussion of theme 3 begins with Table 3, which summarises the concepts covered in this theme.

Table 3. Summary of Theme 3

Concept	Description
Governance and Policy	Developed countries have well-structured AI policies, whereas developing countries often lack them.
Faculty and Student Preparedness	Readiness depends on training, exposure, and digital self-efficacy.
Ethical Safeguards	Developed contexts employ plagiarism-detection and data-privacy laws; developing contexts face cultural and epistemic biases.
Constructivist Pedagogy	Ethical use of AI should support inquiry, dialogue, and critical thinking.
Equity-Driven Strategies	Institutions must position AI as a learning partner rather than a replacement for human intelligence.

The integration of AI in higher education is not a neutral technological upgrade but a transformative shift that raises institutional, ethical, and pedagogical challenges. Whether AI enhances creativity, inclusivity, and efficiency, or deepens inequities and academic risks, depends on institutional readiness and the ethical frameworks guiding its adoption. Developed contexts approach readiness through structured governance and faculty development, while developing contexts, including South Africa, contend with fragmented policies, uneven infrastructure, and limited institutional support.

In developed regions readiness is underpinned by robust frameworks. The European Union AI Act classifies educational AI applications as "high risk" and mandates transparency, safety, and ethical compliance (Mah et al., 2025). Universities such as the University of Texas at Tyler embed AI in teaching with clear guidelines, training, and policies requiring students to cite AI-generated outputs, thereby promoting transparency and ethical literacy (Arbulú Ballesteros et al., 2024). Plagiarism detection tools, national strategies, and international frameworks such as UNESCO guidelines reinforce ethical safeguards (Selwyn, 2022).

By contrast, in developing contexts, institutional readiness is undermined by foundational inequities. Policies are often fragmented or absent, leaving regulation to individual faculties or lecturers (Capinding & Dumavas, 2024). In the Philippines, the use of AI is permitted or restricted at the discretion of teachers, whereas in Iraqi universities, the urgent need for governance frameworks is emphasised (Farmanesh et al., 2025). South Africa presents a dual reality: well-resourced urban universities can cautiously experiment with AI integration, but rural and historically disadvantaged institutions face unreliable connectivity, limited access to devices, and inadequate support (Czerniewicz et al., 2020). Readiness also hinges on the preparedness of faculty and students themselves. In developed contexts, professional development opportunities such as the Ethical AI Readiness Framework equip educators with both technical skills and ethical awareness (Mah et al., 2025).

Faculty self-efficacy is decisive: those who believe in their ability to integrate AI responsibly are more likely to persist, while sceptical or undertrained staff often resist adoption (Alotaibi, 2023). Students benefit from early exposure to AI tools, embedded training modules, and structured support, which together enhance digital self-efficacy (Schunk, 1991; Zimmerman, 2000). In developing contexts, resource limitations and training gaps undermine readiness. In Ghana, weak digital leadership reduces faculty confidence to adopt AI (Atuahene & XuSheng, 2024). In Pakistan, research indicates a negative association between AI use and academic self-efficacy, suggesting risks of overreliance and "learned helplessness" (Farmanesh et al., 2025). In South Africa, the divide is again evident: students at well-funded universities may attend AI literacy workshops and access online resources, while peers in underfunded institutions struggle with connectivity and lack exposure (Czerniewicz et al., 2020).

Ethical concerns further complicate readiness. In developed contexts, integrity and accountability are governed by established systems, including data privacy laws, plagiarism frameworks, and institutional policies that require students to evaluate AI critically. In developing contexts, ethical safeguards are weaker and imported AI systems often fail to represent local languages or epistemologies, raising concerns of cultural bias and epistemic exclusion (Williamson & Eynon, 2020). While some South African universities are beginning to integrate AI literacy into curricula, ethical frameworks remain less developed than in Europe or North America (Hodgkinson-Williams & Trotter, 2018).

Across contexts, institutions must therefore negotiate the paradox of AI: its promise of efficiency, personalisation, and enhanced learning versus its risks of plagiarism, bias, and dependency. In developed countries, this paradox is mediated by institutional frameworks that require students to interrogate AI outputs, compare perspectives, and apply critical thinking practices aligned with CLT principles of inquiry and dialogue. In developing contexts, including South Africa, the risks are magnified by systemic inequities: students without reliable access or training may use AI uncritically, undermining creativity and widening gaps. This underscores the need for equity-driven strategies that position AI as a partner in learning rather than a replacement for human intelligence (Walker, 2006).

Institutional readiness and ethical frameworks thus emerge as central mediators of AI's impact in higher education. In developed contexts, AI can enhance originality when supported by constructivist pedagogy and robust governance. In contrast, in developing contexts, the absence of policies and training risks passive dependence and inequitable outcomes. Socio-economic divides are exacerbated when institutions lack strategies to ensure equitable access, as seen in South Africa and other countries in the Global South (Selwyn, 2022).

4.4 Integrated Discussion of Themes: A Cyclical Model

Taken together, the findings of this chapter illustrate that the impact of AI tools on creativity, academic performance, self-efficacy, and knowledge construction is deeply contextual. The three themes are best interpreted as an interconnected cycle, hinging on psychological, pedagogical, and systemic influences, presented differently across developed and developing contexts. These dynamics are best analysed through the lens of the three theoretical frameworks.

The cycle begins with equity and access, highlighting students' need to engage with AI tools in academic work. Van Dijk's (2006, 2012) DDT exemplifies that access determines equity. In developing contexts, inequities manifest most visibly in access, whereas in developed contexts they centre on pedagogy, ethics, and critical use.

The cycle continues to flow into AI literacy. SET (Bandura, 1997) highlights the importance of students' confidence-driven beliefs and that literacy is not a standalone skill that determines success. In a well-resourced, developed context, students can leverage AI literacy to critically evaluate their claims (Liang et al., 2023).

Institutional readiness and ethical frameworks form the third link in the cycle. From the CLT perspective, the importance of scaffolding and inquiry-based pedagogy is evident. When institutional training is provided, ethical safeguards are enforced, and AI literacy is part of the curriculum, students can move toward deeper engagement and originality. Developed countries refine existing systems to integrate AI responsibly, while developing countries confront foundational gaps that shape equity, originality, and self-efficacy. The DDT completes this cycle, drawing on the intersection of access, AI literacy, and institutional readiness. This shows how inequities flow across all three levels of Van Dijk's (2006, 2012) theory.

Viewed together, the three themes from this chapter form a reinforcing cycle (Figure 3). The cycle reflects Van Dijk's three-tiered model: access (Theme 2), skills and literacy (Theme 1), and outcomes mediated by institutional readiness (Theme 3). When this cycle is viewed from a developed and well-resourced context, it is only hindered by ethical and pedagogical concerns. In a developing, under-resourced context, the cycle can be broken at the first and second stages. Without adequate access to digital technologies and AI tools, AI literacy development is hindered, with further implications for confidence and academic outcomes.

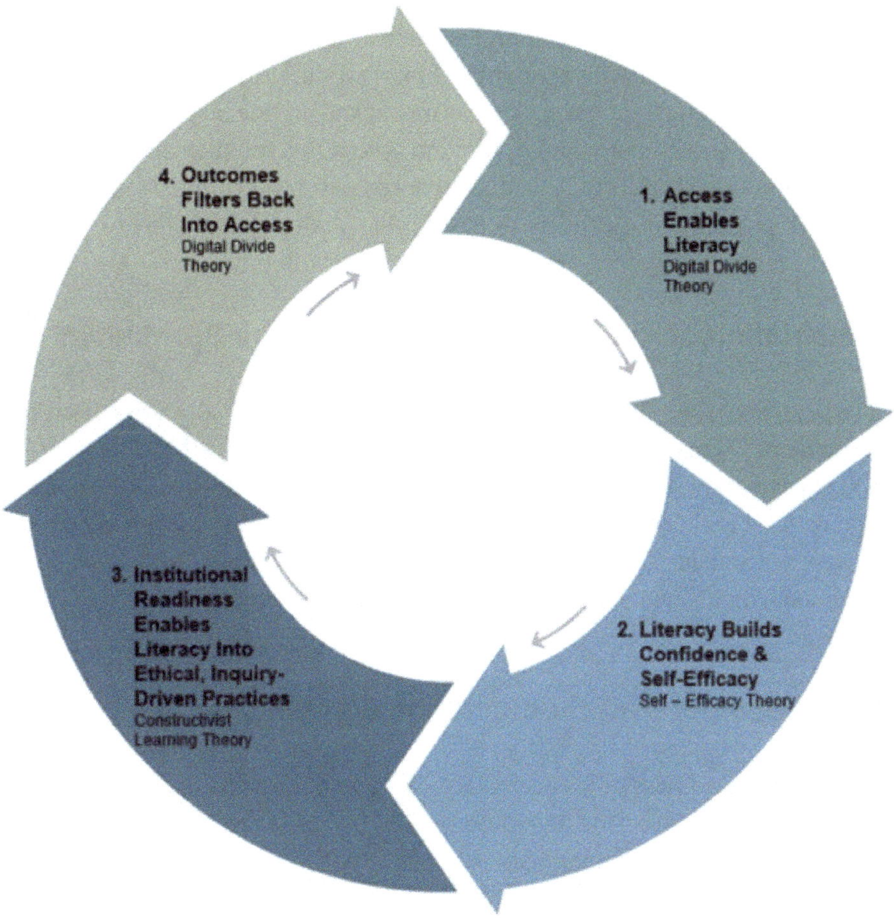

5. RECOMMENDATIONS

As AI advances in higher education, integrating it through equitable infrastructure is essential to ensure students can ethically and effectively use its potential in academic work. AI tools in higher education offer opportunities and risks for developing contexts. While students in well-resourced institutions benefit from enhanced academic support, those in under-resourced and rural areas continue to face persistent inequities. The following recommendations aim to address these gaps.

5.1 Investment in Infrastructure

This chapter recommends that higher education institutions invest in reliable digital infrastructure to ensure equitable AI integration. Institutes in more rural and under-resourced regions should seek government and private investment to upgrade existing digital infrastructure and to provide access to a reliable, stable electricity supply. Institutions with inefficient educational resources and limited internet access should seek government subsidies to ensure that students can compete with their more privileged peers in well-resourced areas and institutions.

5.2 Integration of AI Literacy to Strengthen the Curriculum

The inclusion and integration of AI literacy skills in curricula across disciplines are paramount to ensure that students are digitally competent, ethically aware, and able to engage critically with AI tools. Students and lecturers should be trained to engage with AI tools and to distinguish between surface-level uses and deep, constructive engagement. This training and embedded AI literacy instruction should be contextual, multilingual, and culturally responsive to serve students from diverse backgrounds.

5.3 Development of Clear Institutional AI Policies

Institutional readiness relies on the development of clear AI policies rather than ad hoc faculty decisions. This includes clear, equity-driven policies that can guide and promote responsible and inclusive use of AI tools. These policies must address ethical use and potential concerns regarding plagiarism. Students at higher education institutions should be guided in their engagement with AI tools to fully realise the potential AI offers for academic assignments and coursework.

5.4 Ethical Frameworks and Safeguards

To support the responsible use of AI in education, institutions should implement clear ethical measures, such as systems for detecting plagiarism, protecting student data, and ensuring that AI tools are culturally sensitive and inclusive. In low-resource settings, it is essential to strengthen ethical guidelines to guard against overreliance on AI, algorithmic bias, and the marginalisation of local knowledge systems.

5.5 Recommendations for Further Research

Building on the findings of this chapter, future research could examine how varying levels of AI literacy and access shape students' academic self-efficacy, particularly in contexts characterised by socioeconomic inequality. It would also be valuable to examine how prepared institutions are, in terms of both policy and infrastructure, for the ethical integration of AI into teaching and learning. Further studies might investigate practical ways to embed AI literacy into existing curricula and how different pedagogical approaches influence student engagement. Research should also consider the psychological aspects of AI use in education, such as learning anxiety and confidence, and assess how equity-focused strategies and educator training affect outcomes in under-resourced environments.

6. CONCLUSION

This chapter demonstrates that the advancement of AI in higher education is not only evolving but is also highly contextual across developed and developing contexts. It highlights the need to bridge gaps in access, equity, and skills development to level the playing field for students in developing contexts and enable them to compete academically with peers in developed, well-resourced contexts. This revealed that AI literacy among students is insufficient to bridge the AI gaps in developing countries. Students require access, supportive infrastructure, and institutional policies and frameworks to curtail inequities and socioeconomic divides and to enhance creativity and originality in academic assessments.

The three interrelated frameworks, SET, CLT, and DDT, provided key insights to interpret the findings of this chapter. Alongside the frameworks, the study identified three main themes that highlight the barriers to the full integration of AI in higher education in developing countries. From the analysis, a reinforcing cycle of embedded AI literacy across the curriculum will enable lecturers and students to engage ethically and effectively with AI tools, supported by institutional policies, ethical frameworks, and safeguards. Future scholars should examine practical ways for institutions and governments in developing countries to strengthen the AI adoption cycle in higher education.

AI Usage Statement

This chapter was developed using a combination of manual literature review and digital tools to support academic writing. Generative AI tools were not used to produce original content, conduct analysis, or interpret findings. Where AI-assisted tools (e.g., grammar or reference managers) were used, they served only to enhance clarity, formatting, and citation accuracy. All intellectual contributions, synthesis, and critical engagement with the literature reflect the authors' own work.

REFERENCES

Almaiah, M. A., Alfaisal, R., Salloum, S. A., Hajjej, F., Thabit, S., El-Qirem, F. A., Lutfi, A., Alrawad, M., Al Mulhem, A., Alkhdour, T., Awad, A. B., & Al-Maroof, R. S. (2022). Examining the impact of artificial intelligence and social and computer anxiety in e-learning settings: Students' perceptions at the university level. *Electronics (Basel)*, *11*(22), 3662. Advance online publication. DOI: 10.3390/electronics11223662

Alotaibi, M. S. (2023). Factors influencing early childhood educators' use of digital educational aids: A sequential explanatory study. *SAGE Open*, *13*(4), 21582440231217727. Advance online publication. DOI: 10.1177/21582440231217727

Altememy, H. A., Mohammed, B. A., Hsony, M. K., Hassan, A. Y., Mazhair, R., Dawood, I. I., Al Jouani, I. S. H., Zearah, S. A., & Sharif, H. R. (2023). The influence of the artificial intelligence capabilities of higher education institutions in Iraq on students' academic performance: The role of AI-based technology application as a mediator. *Eurasian Journal of Educational Research*, *104*, 267–282. DOI: 10.14689/ejer.2023.104.015

Amorin, R. B., & Gallaron, G. M. (2025). The mediating effect of learning motivation on Attitudes towards using ChatGPT (ATUC) as an educational resource and academic performance: Evidence from a state university in Iloilo, Philippines. *MIER Journal of Educational Studies Trends and Practices*, *15*(1), 214–239. DOI: 10.52634/mier/2025/v15/i1/2827

Anghel, G. A., Zanfir, C. M., Matei, F. L., Voicu, C. D., & Neac a, R. A. (2025). The integration of artificial intelligence in academic learning practices: A comprehensive approach. *Education Sciences*, *15*(5), 616. Advance online publication. DOI: 10.3390/educsci15050616

Arbulú Ballesteros, M. A., Acosta Enríquez, B. G., Ramos Farroñán, E. V., García Juárez, H. D., Cruz Salinas, L. E., Blas Sánchez, J. E., Arbulú Castillo, J. C., Licapa-Redolfo, G. S., & Farfán Chilicaus, G. C. (2024). The sustainable integration of AI in higher education: Analyzing ChatGPT acceptance factors through an extended UTAUT2 framework in Peruvian universities. *Sustainability (Basel)*, *16*(23), 10707. Advance online publication. DOI: 10.3390/su162310707

Atuahene, S. A., & XuSheng, Q. (. (2024). Overcoming e-learning hurdles: Strategies for enhancing STEM education in Africa through digital innovation. *Studies in Higher Education*. Advance online publication. DOI: 10.1080/03075079.2024.2413866

Azeem, S., & Abbas, M. (2025). Personality correlates of academic use of generative artificial intelligence and its outcomes: Does fairness matter? *Education and Information Technologies*, *30*(13), 18131–18155. Advance online publication. DOI: 10.1007/s10639-025-13489-6

Azevedo, J. P., Gutiérrez, M., De Hoyos, R., & Saavedra, J. (2021). The unequal impacts of COVID-19 on student learning. *Primary and secondary education during COVID-19: Disruptions to educational opportunity during a pandemic,* 421–459. DOI: 10.1007/978-3-030-81500-4_16

Bai, Y., & Wang, S. (2025). Impact of generative AI interaction and output quality on university students' learning outcomes: A technology-mediated and motivation-driven approach. *Scientific Reports*, *15*(1), 1367. DOI: 10.1038/s41598-025-08697-6 PMID: 40617950

Bandura, A. (1997). *Self-efficacy: The exercise of control.* W. H. Freeman.

Bećirović, S., Polz, E., & Tinkel, I. (2025). Exploring students' AI literacy and its effects on their AI output quality, self-efficacy, and academic performance. *Smart Learning Environments*, *12*(1), 29. Advance online publication. DOI: 10.1186/s40561-025-00384-3

Bouteraa, M., Bin-Nashwan, S. A., Al-Daihani, M., Dirie, K. A., Benlahcene, A., Sadallah, M., Zaki, H. O., Lada, S., Ansar, R., Fook, L. M., & Chekima, B. (2024). Understanding the diffusion of AI-generative (ChatGPT) in higher education: Does students' integrity matter? *Computers in Human Behavior Reports*, *14*, 100402. Advance online publication. DOI: 10.1016/j.chbr.2024.100402

Capinding, A. T., & Dumayas, F. T. (2024). Transformative pedagogy in the digital age: Unravelling the impact of artificial intelligence on higher education students. *Problems of Education in the 21st Century, 82*(5), 630–657. DOI: 10.33225/pec/24.82.630

Celik, I. (2023). Exploring the Determinants of Artificial Intelligence (AI) Literacy: Digital Divide, Computational Thinking, Cognitive Absorption. *Telematics and Informatics*, *83*, 102026. Advance online publication. DOI: 10.1016/j.tele.2023.102026

Chen, C., Hu, W., & Wei, X. (2025). From anxiety to action: Exploring the impact of artificial intelligence anxiety and artificial intelligence self-efficacy on motivated learning of undergraduate students. *Interactive Learning Environments*, *33*(4), 3162–3177. DOI: 10.1080/10494820.2024.2440877

Chu, H.-C., Hwang, G.-H., Tu, Y.-F., & Yang, K.-H. (2022). Roles and research trends of artificial intelligence in higher education: A systematic review of the top 50 most-cited articles. *Australasian Journal of Educational Technology, 38*(3). Advance online publication. DOI: 10.14742/ajet.7526

Chun, Z., Ning, Y., Chen, J., & Wijaya, T. T. (2025). Exploring the interplay among artificial intelligence literacy, creativity, self-efficacy, and academic achievement in college students: Findings from PLS-SEM and FsQCA. *Education and Information Technologies, 30*(15), 1–34. DOI: 10.1007/s10639-025-13617-2

Creswell, J. W., & Plano Clark, V. L. (2018). *Designing and conducting mixed methods research* (3rd ed.). Sage Publishers.

Czerniewicz, L., Agherdien, N., Badenhorst, J., Belluigi, D., Chambers, T., Chili, M., de Villiers, M., Felix, A., Gachago, D., Gokhale, C., Ivala, E., Kramm, N., Madiba, M., Mistri, G., Mgqwashu, E., Pallitt, N., Prinsloo, P., Solomon, K., Strydom, S., & Wissing, G. (2020). A wake-up call: Equity, inequality and COVID-19 emergency remote teaching and learning. *Postdigital Science and Education, 2*(3), 946–967. DOI: 10.1007/s42438-020-00187-4 PMID: 40477091

English, R., Nash, R., & Mackenzie, H. (2025). 'A rather stupid but always available brainstorming partner': Use and understanding of Generative AI by UK postgraduate researchers. *Innovations in Education and Teaching International.* Advance online publication. DOI: 10.1080/14703297.2024.2446236

Farahani, M. S., & Ghasemi, G. (2024). Artificial intelligence and inequality: Challenges and opportunities. *Qeios.* https://www.qeios.com/read/7HWUZ2

Farmanesh, P., Vehbi, A., & Solati Dehkordi, N. (2025). AI Literacy in Achieving Sustainable Development Goals: The Interplay of Student Engagement and Anxiety Reduction in Northern Cyprus Universities. *Sustainability (Basel), 17*(11), 4763. Advance online publication. DOI: 10.3390/su17114763

Henning, E. (2016). Reading as learning in the primary school. *South African Journal of Childhood Education, 6*(1), 6. DOI: 10.4102/sajce.v6i1.504

Hodgkinson-Williams, C., & Trotter, H. (2018). A social justice framework for understanding open educational resources and practices in the Global South. *Journal of Learning for Development, 5*(3), 204–224. https://jl4d.org/index.php/ejl4d/article/view/312. DOI: 10.56059/jl4d.v5i3.312

Huang, X., Dong, L., Chandru Vignesh, C., & Praveen Kumar, D.Chandru Vignesh C.Praveen Kumar D. (2022). Self-Regulated Learning and Scientific Research Using Artificial Intelligence for Higher Education Systems. *International Journal of Technology and Human Interaction, 18*(7), 1–15. DOI: 10.4018/IJTHI.306226

Hussain, F., & Anwar, M. A. (2025). Towards informed policy decisions: Assessing student perceptions and intentions to use ChatGPT for academic performance in higher education. *Journal of Asian Public Policy, 18*(2), 377–404. DOI: 10.1080/17516234.2024.2422917

Jai Lamimi, I., El Jemli, S., & Zeryouh, I. (2025). Enhancing Critical Thinking: Exploring Human-AI Synergy in Student Cognitive Development. *Arab World English Journal, 1*(1), 251–269. DOI: 10.24093/awej/AI.14

Jansen, J. D. (1990). Curriculum as a political phenomenon: Historical reflections on black South African education. *The Journal of Negro Education, 59*(2), 195–206. DOI: 10.2307/2295645

Johnston, H., Wells, R. F., Shanks, E. M., Boey, T., & Parsons, B. N. (2024). Student perspectives on the use of generative artificial intelligence technologies in higher education. *International Journal for Educational Integrity, 20*(1), 2. Advance online publication. DOI: 10.1007/s40979-024-00149-4

Khreisat, M. N., Khilani, D., Rusho, M. A., Ansah Karkkulainen, E., Cortezo Tabuena, A., & Diaz Uberas, A. (2024). Ethical implications of AI integration in educational decision making: Systematic review. *Educational Administration: Theory and Practice, 30*(5), 8521–8527. DOI: 10.53555/kuey.v30i5.4406

Kong, J., Liu, J., Chen, G., & Shang, W. (2025). Assessing AI literacy in college students: The mediating role of self-efficacy in motivational commitment pathways. *Education and Information Technologies, 30*(16), 23957–23979. Advance online publication. DOI: 10.1007/s10639-025-13753-9

Kour, J., Bhatia, R., & Joshi, R. (2025). Artificial intelligence in education: Insights from gender and locality-based perspectives. In *Impacts of AI on Students and Teachers in Education 5.0* (pp. 193–210). IGI Global., DOI: 10.4018/979-8-3693-8191-5.ch007

Leite, H. (2025). Artificial intelligence in higher education: Research notes from a longitudinal study. *Technological Forecasting and Social Change, 215*, 124115. Advance online publication. DOI: 10.1016/j.techfore.2025.124115

Liang, J., Wang, L., Luo, J., Yan, Y., & Fan, C. (2023). The relationship between student interaction with generative artificial intelligence and learning achievement: Serial mediating roles of self-efficacy and cognitive engagement. *Frontiers in Psychology*, *14*, 1285392. Advance online publication. DOI: 10.3389/fpsyg.2023.1285392 PMID: 38187430

Lo, C. K. (2023). What Is the Impact of ChatGPT on Education? A Rapid Review of the Literature. *Education Sciences*, *13*(4), 410. Advance online publication. DOI: 10.3390/educsci13040410

Luckin, R., Holmes, W., Griffiths, M., & Forcier, L. B. (2016). *Intelligence Unleashed: An Argument for AI in Education*. Pearson Education. https://static.googleusercontent.com/media/edu.google.com/en//pdfs/Intelligence-Unleashed-Publication.pdf

Ma, J. K. H. (2021). The digital divide at school and at home: A comparison between schools by socioeconomic level across 47 countries. *International Journal of Comparative Sociology*, *62*(2), 115–140. DOI: 10.1177/00207152211023540

Maddux, J. E., & Kleiman, E. M. (2021). Self-efficacy: The power of believing you can. DOI: 10.1093/oxfordhb/9780195187243.013.0035

Mah, D. K., Knoth, N., & Egloffstein, M. (2025). Perspectives of academic staff on artificial intelligence in higher education: Exploring areas of relevance. *Frontiers in Education*, *10*, 1484904. Advance online publication. DOI: 10.3389/feduc.2025.1484904

Maina, A. M., & Kuria, J. (2024). Building an AI future: Research and policy directions for Africa's higher education. *2024 IST-Africa Conference. IST-Africa*, *2024*, 01–09. Advance online publication. DOI: 10.23919/IST-Africa63983.2024.10569692

McKenna, S. (2013). The dangers of student-centred learning: A caution about blind spots in the scholarship. *Teaching in Higher Education*, *18*(3), 347–351. DOI: 10.1080/13562517.2012.744640

Mensah, E. (2015). Exploring constructivist perspectives in the college classroom. *SAGE Open*, *5*(3), 2158244015596208. Advance online publication. DOI: 10.1177/2158244015596208

Pajares, F. (1996). Self-efficacy beliefs in academic settings. *Review of Educational Research*, *66*(4), 543–578. DOI: 10.3102/00346543066004543

Piaget, J. (1970). *Science of education and the psychology of the child*. Viking Press. https://archive.org/details/scienceofeducati00piag

Sandu, R., Gide, E., & Elkhodr, M. (2024). The role and impact of ChatGPT in educational practices: Insights from an Australian higher education case study. *Discover Education, 3*(1), 71. Advance online publication. DOI: 10.1007/s44217-024-00126-6

Sayed, Y., & Kanjee, A. (2013). An overview of education policy change in post-apartheid South Africa. In Sayed, Y., & Kanjee, A. (Eds.), *The search for quality education in post-apartheid South Africa: Interventions to improve teaching and learning* (pp. 5–38). HSRC Press.

Schunk, D. H. (1991). Self-efficacy and academic motivation. *Educational Psychologist, 26*(3–4), 207–231. DOI: 10.1080/00461520.1991.9653133

Schunk, D. H., & DiBenedetto, M. K. (2021). *Motivation and social-emotional learning: Theory, research, and practice.* Springer Nature AG. https://link.springer.com/book/10.1007/978-3-030-70594-5

Selwyn, N. (2004). Reconsidering political and popular understandings of the digital divide. *New Media & Society, 6*(3), 341–362. DOI: 10.1177/1461444804042519

Selwyn, N. (2022). *Should robots replace teachers? AI and the future of education.* Polity Press. https://politybooks.com/bookdetail?book_slug=should-robots-replace-teachers-ai-and-the-future-of-education--9781509546146

Sydorenko, V. V., Akhnovska, I. O., Smirnov, S. V., Verbovskyi, I. A., & Melnychuk, O. V. (2024). Improvement of higher education: How to bridge the digital divide during the transformation? *Journal of Education and Learning, 18*(3), 1001–1014. DOI: 10.11591/edulearn.v18i3.21078

Szabó, F., & Szoke, J. (2024). How does generative AI promote autonomy and inclusivity in language teaching? *ELT Journal, 78*(4), 478–488. DOI: 10.1093/elt/ccae052

UNESCO. (2023). *Global Education Monitoring Report 2023: Technology in education.* UNESCO Publishing., DOI: 10.54676/UZQV8501

Valdivieso, T., & González, O. (2025). Generative AI tools in Salvadoran higher education: Balancing equity, ethics, and knowledge management in the global south. *Education Sciences, 15*(2), 214. Advance online publication. DOI: 10.3390/educsci15020214

Van Dijk, J. A. G. M. (2006). Digital divide research, achievements and shortcomings. *Poetics, 34*(4–5), 221–235. DOI: 10.1016/j.poetic.2006.05.004

Van Dijk, J. A. G. M. (2012). The evolution of the digital divide: The digital divide turns to inequality of skills and usage. In *Digital Enlightenment Yearbook 2012* (pp. 57–75). IOS Press., DOI: 10.3233/978-1-61499-057-4-57

Van Riel, A., & Snyder, H. (2024). Enhancing the impact of literature reviews: Guidelines for making meaningful contributions. *Spanish Journal of Marketing - ESIC*, *28*(3), 250–265. DOI: 10.1108/SJME-05-2024-0125

Vassilakopoulou, P., & Hustad, E. (2023). Bridging digital divides: A literature review and research agenda for Information Systems research. *Information Systems Frontiers*, *25*(3), 955–969. DOI: 10.1007/s10796-020-10096-3 PMID: 33424421

Walker, M. (2006). *Higher education pedagogies: A capabilities approach.* McGraw-Hill & Open University Press. https://doi.org/DOI: 10.4324/9780203966477

Williamson, B., & Eynon, R. (2020). Historical threads, missing links, and future directions in AI in education. *Learning, Media and Technology*, *45*(3), 223–235. DOI: 10.1080/17439884.2020.1798995

World Bank. (2023). *Digital dividends revisited: Leveraging technology for inclusive development.* World Bank., DOI: 10.1596/39555

Zimmerman, B. J. (2000). Self-efficacy: An essential motive to learn. *Contemporary Educational Psychology*, *25*(1), 82–91. DOI: 10.1006/ceps.1999.1016 PMID: 10620383

Chapter 4

Educators as Cognitive Architects in AI-Augmented Learning Environments:
Redefining Professional Agency and Pedagogical Co-Performance

Sónia Calado
https://orcid.org/0009-0004-6915-5438
University of Aveiro, Portugal

ABSTRACT

This chapter proposes a conceptual framework that redefines educators as cognitive architects in AI-augmented learning environments. It explores how the integration of artificial intelligence into instructional design, assessment, and learner engagement reshapes educators' roles, requiring new forms of agency, digital literacy, and ethical decision-making. Grounded in distributed cognition and the TPACK model, the chapter examines how pedagogical tasks are now co-performed between humans and intelligent systems. It introduces a model for understanding educator agency in technology-rich settings and provides strategic guidance for institutions aiming to support this shift. By analysing emerging competencies, ethical concerns, and institutional practices, the chapter contributes to ongoing efforts to position educators not as passive users of AI but as proactive designers of human-centred, data-informed, and ethically responsible educational experiences.

DOI: 10.4018/979-8-3373-4521-5.ch004

1. INTRODUCTION

Artificial intelligence (AI) has moved from peripheral tooling to a structural layer of the digital learning ecosystem. Beyond content retrieval and automated grading, contemporary AI now curates resources, diagnoses misconceptions, orchestrates adaptive practice, and mediates real-time feedback loops, altering, in substance, who does what in education (Roll & Wylie, 2016; Zawacki-Richter et al., 2019). Meta-analyses of intelligent tutoring and related Artificial Intelligence in Education (AIEd) applications report positive average effects on learning, with variation by context, discipline, and instructional design, which underscore the need to pair automation with sound pedagogy (Kulik & Fletcher, 2016; Ma et al., 2014). In this evolving division of labour, educators are not mere tool users but cognitive architects who design, govern, and ethically steer the interplay between human learning processes and machine intelligence.

This reframing is anchored in four complementary lenses. Distributed cognition conceptualises cognitive activity as stretched across people, artefacts and environments; performance does not reside solely in the individual mind but in a sociotechnical system, an idea that fits classrooms augmented by AI (Hutchins, 1995). Technological Pedagogical Content Knowledge (TPACK) articulates the interweaving of technological, pedagogical, and content knowledge required to design meaningful AI-enabled learning experiences (Mishra & Koehler, 2006). Activity theory helps map shifting goals, rules, mediating tools, and divisions of labour as AI becomes part of instructional practice (Engeström, 2001). Finally, professional identity research illuminates tensions between care-oriented teacher identities and pressures for data-driven governance (Beauchamp & Thomas, 2009). Together, these perspectives support this chapter's core claim: instructional, analytic, and affective tasks are increasingly co-performed by humans and intelligent systems, demanding expanded educator agency.

Human-centred AI scholarship translates these foundations into actionable design imperatives: set clear expectations, expose uncertainty, support human review and override, and learn from usage in situ (Amershi et al., 2019). A human-centred AI posture seeks high levels of both automation and human control, as a practical route to reliability, safety, and trustworthiness (Shneiderman, 2020). For educational contexts, this means workflows where models anticipate and assist while educators interpret, validate, and decide while also mindful of fairness, bias, and uncertainty in model behaviour (Drachsler & Greller, 2016; Mehrabi et al., 2022).

The regulatory and standards landscape reinforces a shift toward informed professional agency. The EU Artificial Intelligence Act, Regulation (EU, 2024) Official Journal 12 July 2024, designates several educational uses (e.g., determining access or placement, evaluating learning outcomes, monitoring behaviour during examinations) as high-risk, triggering duties around risk management, data governance, transparency, human oversight, logging, and robustness. In parallel, UNESCO's global guidance (UNESCO, 2023) advances a human-centred approach emphasising teacher capacity, equity, and academic integrity, while ISO/IEC 42001:2023 specifies requirements for an AI management system (AIMS) that institutions can adopt as a backbone for control, auditability, and continual improvement. In the UK, Department for Education guidance stresses workload reduction with retained human accountability, principles that travel well to other jurisdictions (EU, 2024; OBP, 2023; UNESCO, 2023).

Purpose and contribution of this chapter: This chapter (i) delineates the competencies and forms of agency that educators require to design AI-augmented learning (model literacy; pedagogical design with AI; assessment and analytics interpretation; ethical-legal judgment; data stewardship; change and communication) and (ii) propose an integrated Educator-as-Cognitive-Architect (ECA) framework that specifies roles, boundaries, and accountability across human and machine actors. The framework ties human oversight points to assurance mechanisms (data governance, documentation, sandboxing, incident response, bias/robustness checks) and to institution-level AIMS aligned with ISO/IEC 42001 and the EU AI Act (EU, 2024; OBP, 2023).

Scope and delimitations: This chapter focuses on higher education and post-compulsory training, with cautious extrapolations aimed at compulsory education when warranted by evidence. "AI" includes statistical and symbolic approaches, with emphasis on generative models and classifiers used for instructional design, feedback, assessment, and early-warning analytics. "Agency" is treated as situated capacity to set ends, choose means, and exercise meaningful human control at decision points affecting assessment, progression and equity, which are consistent with best practice and legal-ethical due diligence (Amershi et al., 2019; EU, 2024).

Despite the strategic appeal of AI in education, many classroom-level implementations fall short of expectations. Educators frequently report increased workload, ambiguity in responsibility for AI-generated outputs, and discomfort when required to interpret or justify algorithmic decisions. Even when technically sound, AI tools may undermine pedagogical trust by offering opaque feedback or triggering interventions without adequate human context.

These challenges are not primarily technical but institutional and epistemic. They reflect a broader failure to specify the agency of educators within human-AI collaboration. Current models often position instructors as passive end-users or procedural overseers rather than as active cognitive architects of AI-supported instruction. The result is friction, mistrust, and underutilisation of potentially beneficial systems.

At the classroom level, these gaps manifest in tangible tensions: Who decides whether feedback is accurate or fair? When does automation end, and educator judgment begin? How are equity, workload, and professional accountability balanced when AI systems generate decisions with knock-on effects on learners?

This chapter addresses those questions by positioning educators as cognitive architects, whose role is to specify concrete roles, competencies, and decisions that uphold both pedagogical integrity and regulatory compliance. The next section provides the theoretical grounding for this reframing.

2. THEORETICAL LENS

This chapter integrates four well-established perspectives; namely, distributed cognition, TPACK, activity theory, and professional identity, and enriches them with service/retail science constructs (perceived value, risk, trust, and brand signals). Together they ground this chapter's claim that, in AI-augmented learning, instructional, analytic, and affective work is co-performed by humans and intelligent systems and therefore requires appropriate professional agency.

2.1 Distributed Cognition: From Tool-Use to Cognitive Co-Performance

Distributed cognition treats cognition as stretched across people, artefacts and environments rather than contained within an individual mind (Hutchins, 1995). In classrooms augmented by AI, this means the unit of analysis is the human–AI assemblage: model prompts, dashboards, rubrics, and classroom norms jointly carry memory, inference, and control. Practically, the educator's task shifts from executing micro-operations (e.g., item-by-item feedback) to designing representational states and flows, determining what signals the model sees, when the human intervenes, and how uncertainty is surfaced for judgment. This lens legitimises the language of co-performance and makes interface design (e.g., confidence, provenance, rationales) a pedagogical variable, not an UX afterthought (Hutchins, 1995).

Implication 1: Treat prompts, policies and data schemas as instructional media: they shape what the joint system can perceive and remember, much like physical instruments in Hutchins' cockpit (Hutchins, 1995).

2.2 TPACK: Aligning Pedagogy, Content, and Models

The TPACK framework specifies how technological (TK), pedagogical (PK) and content knowledge (CK) interlock in design (Mishra & Koehler, 2006). With AI, TK expands from "how the tool works" to model literacy: limits, error modes, guardrails, token/temperature trade-offs, and evaluation. PK requires scaffold design that anticipates AI behaviour (e.g., when a generative model tends to hallucinate, when a classifier drifts). CK remains central: domain concepts, misconceptions, and representational forms that the model can reliably handle. The cognitive-architect role is precisely TPACK-centric, orchestrating the intersection so the model's affordances serve the intended learning mechanisms (Mishra & Koehler, 2006).

Implication 2: Task–model fit becomes an explicit design step: choose architecture and settings that match the learning objective (e.g., classification for risk alerts; constrained generation for rubric-aligned feedback) (Mishra & Koehler, 2006).

2.3 Activity Theory: Roles, Rules and CONTRADICTIONs in Transition

Activity theory conceptualises practice as an activity system (subjects, objects, tools, rules, community, division of labour). AI introductions reconfigure each element, often revealing productive contradictions that drive change (Engeström, 2001). Examples include rules about how assessment integrity meets generative feedback, how community expectations of care meet data governance, and how division of labour shifts as models draft, classify, or predict. Mapping these tensions enables deliberate supervision points (where humans must review/override), new rules (e.g., transparency to learners), and redistribution of roles (e.g., institutional AIMS teams) (Engeström, 2001).

Implication 3: Use activity-system mapping to place human-in-command checkpoints at consequential decisions (assessment, progression, risk flags) and to design feedback loops for iterative improvement (Engeström, 2001).

2.4 Professional Identity: Educator Agency Under Data-Fied Governance

Educator identity research highlights the dynamic, value-laden nature of professional selves, where care, judgment, and responsibility are central (Beauchamp & Thomas, 2009). AI may threaten or amplify this identity depending on whether systems defer to or displace judgment. The cognitive-architect stance preserves identity by reframing agency: instructors define ends, set boundaries, interpret uncertainty, and are accountable for decisions at the human-oversight points.

Implication 4: Make model outputs advisory and auditable, with transparent escalation paths that position educator judgment as the arbiter in high-stakes contexts (Beauchamp & Thomas, 2009).

2.5 Translational Insights From Service/ Retail Science: Value, Risk, Trust, Brand

Adoption of AI-supported practices in education depends on perceived usefulness, ease of use, and contextual trust, which are consistent with established technology acceptance frameworks (Davis, 1989; Venkatesh et al., 2003). Recent systematic reviews show that these constructs remain central in AI applications for higher education, particularly in shaping instructor and student agency (Zawacki-Richter et al., 2019). Retail branding clarifies trust transfer from institutional brand signals to novel offerings (Ailawadi & Keller, 2004), while private-label research details perceived-risk dimensions (performance, financial, social, psychological) that suppress adoption, and how value propositions mitigate them (Beneke & Carter, 2015; Bhukya & Singh, 2015; DelVecchio, 2001). Transposed to education, the literature suggests the following: articulate a clear value proposition ("what the AI co-teaching adds"), design for user control and explainability, and use institutional assurance (policy, auditing, ISO/IEC 42001 alignment) as brand-like trust signals for learners and staff.

Implication 5; Manage educator and learner acceptance with the same levers identified in technology acceptance research: opportunities for trialability and sandboxing, visible human oversight, clear risk communication, and institutional assurance that supports trust and accountability (Davis, 1989; Venkatesh et al., 2003; Zawacki-Richter et al., 2019).

2.6 Integrative Propositions for the ECA Framework

The synthesis of AI and pedagogy yields a set of integrative propositions that anchor the educator-as-cognitive-architect (ECA) framework. First, drawing on activity theory, this chapter proposes that educator agency is strengthened when AI integration is designed at the level of the activity system—encompassing roles, rules, and tools, rather than as the isolated adoption of discrete technologies (Engeström, 2001). Second, learning gains and ethical robustness are contingent on the degree of task–model fit and on the presence of TPACK-aligned scaffolds, which provide structure for effective human–AI collaboration (Mishra & Koehler, 2006). Third, this chapter argues that well-engineered representational states, prompts, rubrics, and dashboards enable human-AI co-performance that surpasses either one alone in routine diagnostics and feedback, while still reserving high-stakes judgment for educators (Hutchins, 1995). Fourth, educator and learner acceptance of AI-supported practices is mediated by perceptions of control, trust, and value clarity—elements that can be deliberately shaped through interface design and institutional assurance mechanisms (Davis, 1989; Venkatesh et al., 2003; Zawacki-Richter et al., 2019).

Finally, this chapter contends that framing AI as an advisory system with auditable oversight helps preserve professional identity and sustains meaningful educator agency (Beauchamp & Thomas, 2009).

3. METHODOLOGY

This chapter is conceptual and design oriented, aimed at theory building and the creation of an actionable artefact, namely the educator-as-cognitive-architect (ECA) framework. This chapter combines three complementary strands: (i) a structured, transparent literature synthesis spanning AIEd, human-computer interaction/human-centred artificial intelligence (HCI/HCAI) and teacher-agency research; (ii) a design-science logic to engineer and justify the framework; and (iii) a documentary/normative analysis of authoritative regulation and standards. Design-science provides criteria to link kernel theory, artefact, and utility claims (Gregor & Hevner, 2013; Hevner et al., 2004; Peffers et al., 2007; Whetten, 1989).

3.1 Data Extraction and Coding

This chapter's extraction schema captures for each item the study type, the educational context (level and discipline), the AI function involved (generation, classification, or analytics), the degree of task–model fit, the modality of human oversight, and the reported outcomes in terms of learning, workload, and equity. This chapter also documents how risks and biases are addressed and what institutional controls are in place, including policies and AIMS-like processes. The coding approach combines inductive and deductive thematic coding, guided by the theoretical lenses of distributed cognition, TPACK, activity theory, and professional identity. To ensure transparency and rigor, this chapter employs the Gioia methodology, distinguishing first-order terms, second-order themes, and aggregate dimensions, thereby making the process of concept emergence auditable (Gioia et al., 2013). The thematic analysis follows the six-phase protocol of Braun and Clarke, supplemented by reflexive memos, thick description, and audit trails to reinforce trustworthiness (Braun & Clarke, 2006; Nowell et al., 2017).

3.2 Synthesis Logic

This chapter adopts a two-layer synthesis. The first layer is a descriptive mapping, which organises frequencies by AI function, disciplinary domain, and oversight pattern, supported by evidence tables that connect specific use cases to their observed outcomes and associated risks. The second layer is an integrative synthesis, which derives design propositions and crystallises the ECA framework. In this phase, this chapter explicitly demonstrates how the artefact is grounded in kernel theories and articulates the utility claims it makes, including its boundary conditions and testable implications (Gregor & Hevner, 2013; Hevner et al., 2004; Peffers et al., 2007; Whetten, 1989).

3.3 Normative and Standards Link

This chapter constructs a link between EU AI Act obligations (risk management, data governance, transparency, meaningful human oversight, logging, accuracy/robustness) and major educational scenarios (assessment, early-warning analytics, proctoring, rubric-aligned generative feedback). In parallel, this chapter aligns relevant ISO/IEC 42001 clauses (roles, competencies, risk controls, monitoring, continuous improvement) with institution-level processes. The output is a matrix that, for each scenario, specifies risk class, human-oversight checkpoints, assurance mechanisms, and evidence requirements (EU, 2024; OBP, 2023).

3.4 Documentary Analytical Vignettes (No Human Subjects)

To demonstrate human–AI co-performance without fieldwork, this chapter includes three documentary vignettes, namely, adaptive practice with human coaching; feedback at scale with human validation; and early-warning analytics with tutorial action, using public documentation only (peer-reviewed studies, open model cards, institutional policies, and vendor white papers checked for credibility). Each vignette is stress-tested against ECA oversight points and governance controls, and rated for risk class, assurance evidence, and workload impact (Bowen, 2009).

Limitations of this study: Findings are shaped by publication bias, heterogeneous outcome measures, and the rapid evolution of AI capabilities; this chapter mitigates via triangulation, clear scope boundaries, and conservative interpretation (Mays, 2000; Nowell et al., 2017).

4. EDUCATOR-AS-COGNITIVE-ARCHITECT (ECA) FRAMEWORK

4.1 Overview

The ECA framework specifies how educators orchestrate human–AI co-performance across five interlocking layers: purpose and outcomes, task–model fit, human oversight points, assurance mechanisms, and feedback and improvement. It translates principles of human-centred AI (Amershi et al., 2019; Shneiderman, 2020) and duties set out in legal standards (EU, 2024; OBP, 2023) into classroom-level checkpoints that preserve professional agency and protect learner rights. Conceptually, Layer 1 anchors learning goals and values. Layer 2 aligns these goals with model capabilities and constraints. Layer 3 identifies the moments where meaningful human control must be exercised. Layer 4 operationalises assurance mechanisms, including data governance, transparency, robustness, and incident response. Layer 5 closes the loop with analytics and participatory feedback, allowing pedagogy and models to be iteratively improved.

4.2 Layer 1, Purpose & Outcomes

Layer 1 requires educators to define content-specific goals and to articulate the value proposition of AI in learning activities; for example, accelerating formative feedback without undermining instructor judgment. Success criteria must integrate learning outcomes with fairness and equity indicators, while also ensuring workload realism for staff (Black & Wiliam, 1998; Shute, 2008).

4.3 Layer 2, Task–Model Fit (TMF)

The second layer ensures that models are selected and configured to serve pedagogical aims rather than dictating them. A TMF rubric evaluates six criteria on a 0–3 scale: construct alignment, capability coverage, uncertainty legibility, bias and fairness risk, data protection footprint, and oversight cost–benefit. A score of 12 out of 18 or higher indicates acceptable fit, while lower scores trigger redesign, such as constraining generation or adopting rubric-guided templates (Amershi et al., 2019; Drachsler & Greller, 2016; EU, 2024; Mehrabi et al., 2022).

4.4 Layer 3, Human Oversight Points (HOPs)

Human oversight points (HOPs) designate mandatory checkpoints where educators must review or authorise AI outputs. In assessments, AI contributions remain advisory until verified by instructors (Shute, 2008). For early-warning alerts, human triage is required before student contact, with rationales documented. Outputs involving sensitive issues, such as ethics, harassment, or academic integrity, must be escalated to policy owners. Any changes to data inputs or retention require explicit educator approval and disclosure to students, in line with institutional policies.

4.5 Layer 4, Assurance Mechanisms

This layer operationalises the duties defined by the EU AI Act and ISO/IEC 42001. Risk management involves scenario-specific hazard analysis, mitigation, and acceptance of residual risks (EU, 2024). Data governance ensures minimisation, quality, and accurate representation, supported by DPIA-style documentation (Drachsler & Greller, 2016). Transparency obligations include learner-facing notices, tailored to the stakes of use (Amershi et al., 2019). Oversight protocols establish meaningful human review, such as double marking a sample of outputs. Logging and monitoring involve event records, exception registers, drift detection, and subgroup bias checks (Mehrabi et al., 2022). Robustness and accuracy are maintained through hold-out evaluation, service-level objectives, and incident response runbooks. Finally, an evidence kit supports audit readiness, consisting of model cards, dataset sheets, evaluation reports, oversight checklists, student disclosures, accessibility checks, and change logs (OBP, 2023).

4.6 Layer 5, Feedback & Improvement

After each instructional cycle, learning analytics are combined with teacher and student feedback to refine prompts, rubrics, and oversight thresholds. Changes in outcomes. including achievement, equity, and workload are tracked and practices that underperform or pose excessive risk are retired (Zawacki-Richter et al., 2019).

4.7 Design Principles (Actionable)

Across these layers, several principles guide implementation. Controls should be proportional to pedagogical stakes. Explicability requires that uncertainty and data sources are legible to non-experts. Minimum data principles demand that only data essential for pedagogy be collected. Human-in-command principles ensure educators retain the final say in consequential decisions. Assessment validity must be safeguarded against construct-irrelevant variance, and fairness across groups requires systematic monitoring and remediation of subgroup disparities. Finally, oversight must respect workload realism, ensuring that practices remain feasible for staff.

4.8 Worked Example (Thumbnail), Generative Feedback in "Writing 101"

To illustrate, consider a first-year writing course. The purpose is to deliver faster and more specific formative feedback to support student revision. The TMF assessment involves constrained text generation using rubric-linked prompts, with confidence levels and sources made visible. HOPs require instructor review before feedback release, with 10% of outputs double marked and weekly bias sampling. Assurance mechanisms include data minimisation (no full essays stored), event logging, drift checks, and student disclosure of AI-assisted feedback. The improvement cycle compares revision quality and time-on-task against prior cohorts, using results to adjust prompts and oversight.

4.9 Testable Implications

The framework generates testable implications. Courses with explicit HOPs are expected to report higher perceptions of fairness and fewer high-impact errors. TMF scores should predict the instructional validity of AI-supported feedback more effectively than average model quality measures. Finally, evidence-ready workflows are anticipated to reduce appeals and complaints without diminishing learning gains.

5. COMPETENCIES FOR THE COGNITIVE ARCHITECT

Educators acting as cognitive architects require competencies that integrate model-aware design with professional judgment, governance, and improvement. Eight competencies are specified below, each mapped to TPACK intersections, evidence artefacts that document practice, and regulatory/standards hooks to ensure auditability and alignment (Amershi et al., 2019; Drachsler & Greller, 2016; EU, 2024; Mehrabi et al., 2022; Mishra & Koehler, 2006; OBP, 2023).

5.1 Competency Matrix

Table 1 consolidates the eight core competencies required for educators to operate as cognitive architects in AI-augmented learning. The matrix formalises each competency as an operational construct, specified through (i) an observable practice description, (ii) its TPACK nexus, (iii) the evidence artefacts that render practice auditable (e.g., oversight checklists, bias-audit snapshots, sampling logs), and (iv) the regulatory/standards anchors that link classroom routines to system-level assurance (EU AI Act duties; ISO/IEC 42001 controls). Designed for both course-level enactment (e.g., defining human-oversight points, setting sampling thresholds, issuing learner disclosures) and programme/institutional capability-building within an AIMS, the matrix translates abstract principles from and human–AI interaction into actionable, evidence-ready behaviours. It also foregrounds task–model fit, bias/fairness vigilance, and workload realism as cross-cutting criteria, thereby coupling pedagogical validity with governance and equity requirements. The matrix should be read as a minimum viable competency architecture, adaptable to discipline and context, rather than an exhaustive taxonomy. (Amershi et al., 2019; Drachsler & Greller, 2016; EU, 2024; Mishra & Koehler, 2006; OBP, 2023).

Table 1. Competency matrix

Competency	What it looks like in practice	TPACK link	Evidence artefacts (for audit/ assurance)	AI Act / ISO 42001 hook
1. AI & Model Literacy	Reads model cards; anticipates error modes, hallucination, drift; calibrates prompts/policies; interprets confidence and provenance.	TK (+TPK)	Annotated prompts; model-limits summary; uncertainty glossary for students.	Transparency & accuracy/robustness; logging; monitoring (EU, 2024; OBP, 2023).
2. Pedagogical Design with AI	Aligns AI affordances to learning mechanisms (practice, elaboration, retrieval); designs scaffolds that anticipate AI behaviour.	PK+TK (TPK)	Task blueprints; alignment maps (objective → AI function); instructor notes on failure cases.	Risk management; human oversight (Amershi et al., 2019; EU, 2024).
3. Assessment & Analytics Interpretation	Triangulates AI outputs with rubrics; sets escalation thresholds; samples for double marking; checks subgroup parity.	CK+PK+TK (PCK+TPK)	Rubrics with AI-assistance notes; sampling logs; inter-rater checks; equity dashboards.	High-risk assessment contexts → human oversight, accuracy & bias checks (EU, 2024; Mehrabi et al., 2022).
4. Ethical-Legal Judgment	Applies purpose limitation, proportionality; decides what must be reviewed by humans; ensures student disclosures.	TPK	Oversight checklist; learner-facing notices; decision rationales on escalations.	Transparency; meaningful human oversight; fairness (EU, 2024).
5. Data Stewardship	Minimises data; documents data flows; sets retention; validates representativeness/quality.	TK	Data register; DPIA-style notes; dataset sheets; access controls.	Data governance (Drachsler & Greller, 2016; EU, 2024; OBP, 2023).
6. Bias, Fairness & Accessibility	Plans subgroup checks; mitigates linguistic/ cultural bias; aligns with accessibility/UDL principles.	TPK	Bias-audit snapshots; accommodation logs; error-parity reports.	Fairness & robustness; monitoring (EU, 2024; Mehrabi et al., 2022).

continued on following page

Table 1. Continued

Competency	What it looks like in practice	TPACK link	Evidence artefacts (for audit/ assurance)	AI Act / ISO 42001 hook
7. Change, Communication & Co-Design	Explains the value proposition of AI to students; invites feedback; sets norms for responsible use.	PK	Student brief; feedback surveys; changelog of course policies.	Transparency; post-market monitoring (EU, 2024; OBP, 2023).
8. Continuous Improvement & Incident Response	Uses analytics and incidents to refine prompts, rubrics, checkpoints; retires risky patterns.	TPK	Incident log; after-action reviews; prompt/ version history; improvement tickets.	Logging; incident response; continual improvement (OBP, 2023).

Source: Author's own elaboration

5.2 Behavioural Indicators (Succinct)

Educator competence in AI-augmented learning can be recognised through a set of observable behaviours. AI and model literacy is evident when instructors can explain in plain language when a generative model is likely to hallucinate and how such risks can be constrained, for instance, through rubric-conditioned prompting, while also recognising early signs of model drift (Amershi et al., 2019). Pedagogical design with AI is demonstrated when educators deliberately select the appropriate task–model fit, such as using classification models for risk flagging or constrained generation for formative feedback, and design "guardrails" that preserve the intended learning mechanisms (Mishra & Koehler, 2006). In the domain of assessment and analytics interpretation, educators treat AI outputs as advisory, sample at least ten percent for double review, and monitor parity of error rates across subgroups (Mehrabi et al., 2022; Shute, 2008).

Ethical–legal judgment is expressed by making AI contributions visible to learners, clarifying what the model produced, what the instructor decided, and how results can be contested, while also setting non-negotiable HOPs for consequential decisions (EU, 2024). Data stewardship is visible when educators collect only the data strictly required for pedagogy, document retention policies, justify each element of data collected, and avoid any hidden repurposing (Drachsler & Greller, 2016). Relatedly, competence in bias, fairness, and accessibility is reflected in the ability to plan reasonable bias spot-checks. For example, using small weekly samples, applying accommodations consistently, and avoiding construct-irrelevant penalties.

Further, change and communication skills involve framing the use of AI in terms of its added value and clear boundaries, while also inviting student agency through feedback loops. Finally, continuous improvement and incident responses are shown when educators run after-action reviews, update prompts and rubrics, record drift or bias incidents, and track the impact of these changes on learning, equity, and workload (OBP, 2023).

5.3 How Institutions Demonstrate Competence

Institutions can demonstrate competence in AI-supported education on multiple levels. At the course level, evidence includes the completion of an ECA oversight checklist for each assessment, the maintenance of sampling logs for AI-assisted feedback, the inclusion of student disclosure templates in syllabi, and the production of bias snapshots each term. At the programme level, competence is demonstrated through a portfolio of model-aware instructional designs, the preparation of periodic equity reports, and the documentation of incident summaries with corresponding corrective actions. At the institutional level, evidence takes the form of AIMS documentation that specifies roles, competencies, controls, and monitoring routines, all cross-referenced to concrete course artefacts (EU, 2024; OBP, 2023).

5.4 Barriers to Adoption: Practical and Contextual Constraints

While the ECA framework provides a structured approach to aligning pedagogy with AI and governance, several practical constraints may limit its adoption, particularly in under-resourced contexts.

First, workload ambiguity remains a core issue. The time and cognitive effort required to review AI outputs, maintain logs, and provide explainable oversight are often underestimated in institutional planning. Educators are expected to guarantee fairness and rigour without proportional time allocation or training.

Second, asymmetric AI literacy can undermine implementation. Educators may lack sufficient understanding of how models function, where they fail, and what constitutes responsible use. This gap contributes to either blind trust or blanket rejection, both of which reduce the pedagogical value of AI.

Third, role ambiguity increases risk aversion. Without clear lines of responsibility for decisions made in AI-supported settings, particularly in high-stakes contexts like grading or progression, educators may disengage entirely from the process.

Fourth, technical and institutional constraints, including lack of access to robust infrastructure, limited models configurability, and absence of institutional support for AIMS, inhibit meaningful implementation.

The ECA framework seeks to mitigate these constraints by specifying evidence-ready workflows, defining minimum oversight expectations, and supporting modular adoption even in low-capacity settings.

6. DOCUMENTARY ANALYTICAL VIGNETTES: HUMAN–AI PEDAGOGICAL CO-PERFORMANCE

This section operationalises the ECA framework through three documentary vignettes constructed from public sources (peer-reviewed literature, standards/policy texts, open model cards, or credible technical notes). Each vignette specifies purpose and outcomes, task–model fit considerations, HOPs, assurance mechanisms aligned to the EU AI Act and ISO/IEC 42001, demonstrates artefacts for auditability, and provides a concise evaluation plan. The vignettes are design exemplars rather than field cases; any scoring shown demonstrates how an institution could apply the framework (EU, 2024; OBP, 2023).

6.1 Vignette A, Adaptive Practice With Human Coaching (STEM Gateway Course)

The aim of vignette A is to accelerate mastery of threshold concepts by combining spaced, difficulty-adapted practice with targeted human coaching, thus reserving educator time for conceptual diagnosis and Socratic clarification. Intended outcomes include improved delayed retention, reduced persistence of misconception-related errors, and stable or reduced instructor workload (Cepeda et al., 2006; Shute, 2008). From a TMF perspective, the core functions are item selection/classification and scheduling, with optional succinct rationales. Construct alignment is ensured by targeting the same constructs later assessed as summative. Uncertainty is made legible through staff-facing displays of difficulty and mastery estimates, alongside confidence bands for at-risk indications. Fairness and drift are addressed by periodic re-estimation of item-response parameters and routine monitoring of subgroup performance (Kulik & Fletcher, 2016; Ma et al., 2014).

HOPs anchor consequential decisions to human judgment: instructors approve learning objectives, item taxonomies, and difficulty progressions prior to deployment; they review weekly analytics to adjust tasks and convene mini seminars around error clusters; and they validate any automated at-risk recommendations before outreach. Assurance mechanisms align with the EU AI Act and ISO/IEC 42001: the risk stance is typically non-high risk when systems are purely formative, but classification may be re-categorised as high risk if outputs directly affect grading or progression (EU, 2024). Controls include data minimisation, documented provenance for the item bank, event logging, drift monitoring, bias snapshots, and change management for content updates (Drachsler & Greller, 2016; OBP, 2023). Evidence artefacts comprise an objective-alignment map, an updated item bank, an oversight checklist, weekly analytics memos, and drift/bias snapshots. The evaluation plan combines pre–post and delayed-retention measures with analyses of instructor time, subgroup error parity, and student perceptions of usefulness and fairness (Black & Wiliam, 1998; Shute, 2008). Boundary conditions emphasise that gains depend on item construct validity and deliberate re-orchestration by instructors; superficial drilling without conceptual feedback yields diminishing returns.

6.2 Vignette B, Rubric-Aligned Generative Feedback at Scale (First-Year Writing)

Vignette B provides timely, specific formative feedback on drafts using a transparent rubric, with educator validation of tone, accuracy, and priorities. Expected outcomes are improved revision quality, faster turnaround, and stable perceived fairness (Shute, 2008). TMF considerations centre on constrained text generation tied to rubric criteria, claims, evidence, coherence, and style, so that feedback indexes rubric constructs rather than merely surface fluency. Uncertainty is made legible by exposing confidence and linking feedback to rubric anchors or exemplars; where sources or examples inform suggestions, these are referenced. Hallucination and accuracy risks are managed through guidelines, including citation requirements and refusals for unsupported claims, combined with sampling for double marking (Ji et al., 2023).

HOPs require educators to curate the rubric, exemplars, and style guide and to approve prompt templates; to perform a mandatory human check before release, editing for accuracy and affect while flagging anomalies; and to implement a weekly sample (≥10%) for double marking by a second instructor, logging exceptions to inform model/prompt refinement. Assurance mechanisms recognise that the risk stance becomes high where outputs influence grading or progression and is lower where the use remains purely formative under explicit human control (EU, 2024). Controls include student disclosures, conservative retention policies that avoid storing full essays where unnecessary, event logging, an incident-response playbook for hallucinations, and equity spot-checks by subgroup (Mehrabi et al., 2022; OBP, 2023). Evidence artefacts include updated "rubric and prompt pack" release checklists, sampling logs, exception registers, and learner notices. Evaluation focuses on changes in rubric-based revision quality, turnaround time, the rate of instructor edits per feedback segment, contestation/appeal rates, and subgroup parity. Boundary conditions note that benefits collapse if instructor validation is skipped or if the rubric under-specifies constructs, increasing the risk of construct-irrelevant variance.

6.3 Vignette C, Early-Warning Analytics With Tutorial Action (Multi-Section Course)

The objective of vignette C is early identification of students at risk of non-completion or failure to enable supportive intervention while preserving dignity and avoiding stigmatisation (Gašević et al., 2015; Slade & Prinsloo, 2013). TMF emphasises supervised classification to produce a risk score with interpretable factors and confidence bands. Construct alignment is safeguarded by using pedagogically justified predictors, engagement patterns, timely submissions, and low-stakes checks, while avoiding proxies that encode structural bias. Uncertainty is handled through actionable explanations rather than opaque scores and by providing clear off-ramps when risk diminishes.

HOPs are defined at three points: educators, together with the AIMS team, approve variables and thresholds and establish "do-no-harm" contact protocols; staff triage alerts before outreach, documenting rationales and actions; and teams review intervention outcomes to recalibrate thresholds or variables. Assurance mechanisms reflect the AI Act's treatment of profiling that influences educational decisions as typically high risk, requiring documented meaningful human oversight, logging, bias assessment, and post-deployment monitoring (EU, 2024). Controls further include data-protection notes on purpose limitation and minimisation, subgroup performance audits, periodic retraining and drift checks, and staff training on ethical contact (Drachsler & Greller, 2016; OBP, 2023). Evidence artefacts comprise a variable register with pedagogical justifications, oversight and contact playbooks, an alert-triage log, equity dashboards, and after-action reviews. The evaluation plan aligns positive, predictive value with resource capacity, measures time-to-intervention, tracks changes in completion rates, assesses perceived fairness, and monitors subgroup parity for false positives and negatives. Effectiveness ultimately depends on robust support pathways, tutoring and advising, and on careful messaging; poorly chosen variables risk amplifying inequities.

7. INSTITUTIONAL GUIDANCE: STANDING UP ECA WITH AN AI MANAGEMENT SYSTEM (AIMS)

This section translates the ECA framework into institution-level practice, aligning course-level design with assurance and governance requirements. The objective is a proportionate, evidence-ready operating model that satisfies legal/standards duties while protecting pedagogical validity, equity, and workload realism (Amershi et al., 2019; Drachsler & Greller, 2016; EU, 2024; OBP, 2023; Shneiderman, 2020).

7.1 Operating Model and Roles (RACI-style)

Institutions should establish a RACI-style operating model with clearly delineated responsibilities. The academic leader at the programme or course level oversees learning outcomes and HOPs and approves task–model fit decisions (accountable/responsible). The AIMS lead or AI governance officer operates the ISO/IEC 42001 management system and maintains the risk register, logs, and audits (Accountable/Responsible). The DPO or data steward assures data minimisation, purpose limitation, retention, and access controls (consulted/responsible). A Teaching and learning centres provide capacity-building and develop rubrics, prompt libraries, and sampling protocols (responsible). The IT/platform owner manages the model lifecycle, including drift and robustness monitoring and incident response (responsible). An accessibility and inclusion officer oversees bias checks, reasonable accommodation, and accessibility compliance (consulted/responsible). Students, treated as partners, supply feedback on clarity, fairness, and workload through established contestation channels (consulted).

7.2 Policy Architecture (Three-Tier)

A three-tier policy stack ensures coherence between guiding principles and classroom practice. Institutional principles state the baseline, human-in-command, proportionality, minimum data, fairness, and transparency. Process policies operationalise these principles in specific domains, AI-assisted assessment, early-warning analytics, generative feedback, and proctoring, each mapping HOPs, evidence requirements, and escalation paths to AI Act duties. Local SOPs at the course level specify TMF rubric scores, oversight checklists, sampling plans, and learner notices.

7.3 Lifecycle Controls (Plan–Do–Check–Act)

Governance follows a PDCA cadence. In the plan stage, teams define purpose and outcomes, conduct TMF assessment, and determine risk classification, noting that uses affecting grading/progression or profiling for decisions are typically high risk (EU, 2024). In the do stage, implementations include guidelines, uncertainty displays, and comprehensive event/exception logging (Amershi et al., 2019). In the check stage, staff sample outputs (e.g., ≥10% double-marked), audit subgroup bias, and review drift and error incidents (Mehrabi et al., 2022). In the act stage, prompts and rubrics are refined, thresholds adjusted, underperforming patterns retired, and all changes documented (OBP, 2023).

7.4 Capability-Building (Competency-Aligned)

Capacity is developed through short micro-credentials aligned with the Section 5 matrix, model literacy, TMF design, assessment and analytics interpretation, ethical–legal judgment, and data stewardship. Performance support includes prompt and policy libraries, oversight checklist templates, and example learner disclosures. Assessment of practice relies on a portfolio of artefacts such as rubrics with AI-assist notes, sampling logs, and equity snapshots.

7.5 Vendor and Procurement Assurance (When Using External Tools)

When procuring external tools, institutions should require a due-diligence pack containing a model card, data sheet, security and privacy posture, evidence of bias/robustness testing, logging/export capabilities, and accessibility conformance. Contracts should include purpose limitation, data location and retention terms, audit rights, incident-reporting SLAs, and termination/portability clauses. A sandbox-first approach pilots tools under constrained scope and captures workload and equity effects before scale-up.

7.6 Minimum Evidence Pack (Per AI-Supported Assessment)

For each assessment supported by AI, a minimum evidence pack should be maintained: a purpose and construct statement with the TMF rubric and score; an oversight checklist signed by the academic lead with HOPs identified; a sampling log (e.g., 10% double-marked) with inter-rater notes; a bias snapshot by subgroup with mitigation notes; a disclosure to learners explaining what the AI did, what the instructor decided, and how to contest; and a change/incident log recording hallucinations, drift, and appeals alongside corrective actions.

7.7 Maturity Model (Diagnostic)

Institutional capability can be staged diagnostically. Level 1 (ad-hoc) features tool-led experiments with no HOPs and limited logging. Level 2 (defined) establishes course-level TMF and oversight checklists, learner notices, and basic logs. Level 3 (managed) adds programme-level sampling plans, equity monitoring, incident response playbooks, and periodic audits. Level 4 (optimizing) institutionalises continuous improvement using outcome/equity/workload deltas, embeds procurement standards, and creates cross-course learning loops (ISO/IEC, 2023).

7.8 Monitoring & KPIs (Balanced)

A balanced scorecard tracks progress across five domains. Learning indicators cover effects on revision quality, retention, and on construct validity. Equity indicators monitor parity of error (FPR/FNR) across subgroups and the uptake of accommodations. Workload indicators compare time saved with oversight effort and measure feedback queue times. Governance indicators include the percentage of assessments with a complete evidence pack, time-to-resolve incidents, and completed audit findings. Trust indicators track student fairness and clarity scores and the rate of contestations upheld.

7.9 Learner Communication (Template, 90 Words)

AI-assisted tools were used to draft formative feedback aligned to the rubric for this study. An instructor reviews and may even edit all feedback before release. No grades are assigned by AI. Data are minimised and retained only for learning purposes. If feedback seems inaccurate or unfair, the course "Query Feedback" link should be used; a human will then review the case. A summary of model limits and oversight is available on the syllabus. (Aligns with transparency, human oversight, and data-governance duties (EU, 2024; OBP, 2023).

7.10 Accessibility and Inclusion

Universal design principles should be embedded in prompts and rubrics, with language support and alternative formats available as needed. Subgroup performance is routinely monitored, and materials are adapted to address disparities (Mehrabi et al., 2022).

7.11 Incident Response (Concise Playbook)

Concise playbook standardised response triggers include hallucinations affecting feedback, mis-flags in early-warning, accessibility failures, and privacy breaches. Immediate actions freeze the affected workflow, notify the AIMS lead/DPO as required, and log the incident. Triage classifies severity and identifies the root cause, prompt, data, model drift, or process. Remediation corrects outputs, notifies affected students, adjusts prompts/thresholds, and updates training. A post-incident report records a summary in the governance log and tracks corrective actions to achieve closure (OBP, 2023).

8. MEASUREMENT AND EVALUATION TOOLKIT

This section introduces an operational toolkit designed to evaluate the ECA framework. Its purpose is not to report empirical findings but to specify construct definitions, instruments, templates, and analysis guidance so that subsequent studies can generate auditable and comparable evidence across contexts.

8.1 Construct Definitions and Operationalisation

The toolkit begins by delineating key constructs and their operational indicators. Learning gains are assessed on rubric-anchored criteria directly tied to the target construct (e.g., argument quality rather than surface fluency). Validity is approached as an argument-based programme of evidence that spans content, internal structure, relations to other variables, and consequences (Kane, 2013; Messick, 1995). Perceived fairness and trust are captured through student and instructor judgments of procedural justice and the clarity of AI assistance, linked to disclosure quality and visible human oversight. Workload realism refers to instructor cognitive and temporal load, measured with short forms of the NASA-TLX and complemented by time-use logs with checks during peak periods (Braarud, 2021; Hart & Staveland, 1988). Equity and bias diagnostics are operationalised through error-rate parity (FPR/FNR), calibration by subgroup, and documentation of trade-offs where fairness criteria conflict (Saito & Rehmsmeier, 2015). Finally, fidelity of implementation concerns the degree to which TMF decisions, HOPs, and assurance steps are enacted as specified (O'Donnell, 2008).

8.2 Instruments and Short Forms

The toolkit includes rubric packs with construct maps, anchor exemplars, and inter-rater guidance, alongside double-marking subsamples with agreement statistics. Disclosure and oversight checklists capture student-facing notices, instructor confirmation of HOPs, and sampling and exception logs. A bias snapshot protocol enables small-N audits on a weekly or termly basis, with parity and calibration charts. Workload is measured with the NASA-TLX short form, accompanied by justification notes for weighting and aggregation. A codebook supports thematic memos, including explanatory rivalry and incident narratives.

8.3 Templates (Ready to Adapt)

To standardise evidence collection, the toolkit offers adaptable templates. T1 is a TMF scorecard covering construct alignment, capability coverage, uncertainty legibility, fairness risk, data footprint, and oversight cost–benefit. T2 is a HOPs register documenting the decision, reviewer, criteria, escalation path, and retained evidence. T3 is an evidence pack index cataloguing rubrics, prompt versions, sampling logs, bias snapshots, incident logs, and learner disclosures. T4 is an analysis pre-specification template identifying primary and secondary outcomes, the smallest effect of interest, and exclusion rules.

8.4 Sampling and Design Guidance

The toolkit is compatible with rigorous quasi-experimental designs such as stepped-wedge trials, staggered difference-in-differences, and regression discontinuity. Selection depends on institutional constraints and ethical feasibility. Researchers are expected to justify sample sizes using desired precision or the smallest effect of interest, and to pre-register analytic choices to ensure transparency and replicability (Callaway & Sant'Anna, 2021; Hemming et al., 2015; Imbens & Lemieux, 2008; Lakens, 2013, 2022; Nosek et al., 2018).

8.5 Analysis Notes

Analyses should prioritise precision–recall and threshold-sensitivity for imbalanced outcomes, reporting calibration alongside discrimination (Saito & Rehmsmeier, 2015). For learning outcomes, standardised effects with confidence intervals should be reported, and gains should be interpreted in relation to fidelity of implementation to avoid misattribution (Lakens, 2013; O'Donnell, 2008). For fairness, the primary criterion, such as calibration versus error-rate balance, must be declared and trade-offs justified in light of course stakes and resource limits. Workload analyses should triangulate subjective ratings with observed time-use data and incident rates.

8.6 Reporting and Transparency Package

To align with expectations for high-risk educational AI under the EU AI Act, studies should release a transparency package consisting of anonymised rubric anchors and prompts, code and analysis notebooks, fidelity and incident summaries, a pre-registration link, and a structured limitations statement specifying scope, bias risks, and generalisability bounds. This ensures transparency without disclosing personal data.

8.7 Boundary Conditions and Reuse

The toolkit is discipline-agnostic but rests on three assumptions: that constructs are clearly defined, that human oversight is feasible, and that institutions have capacity to perform basic bias snapshots. Deviations from these conditions should be documented and rationalised so that results contribute to cumulative synthesis across sites.

To synthesise the operational logic of the toolkit, Figure 1 illustrates its layered structure. It shows how construct definitions are translated into instruments, supported by standardised templates, and ultimately generate auditable outputs. This visual representation emphasises that the evaluation process is cumulative: each stage produces artefacts that enable transparency, comparability, and cross-site learning.

Figure 1. Measurement and Evaluation Toolkit

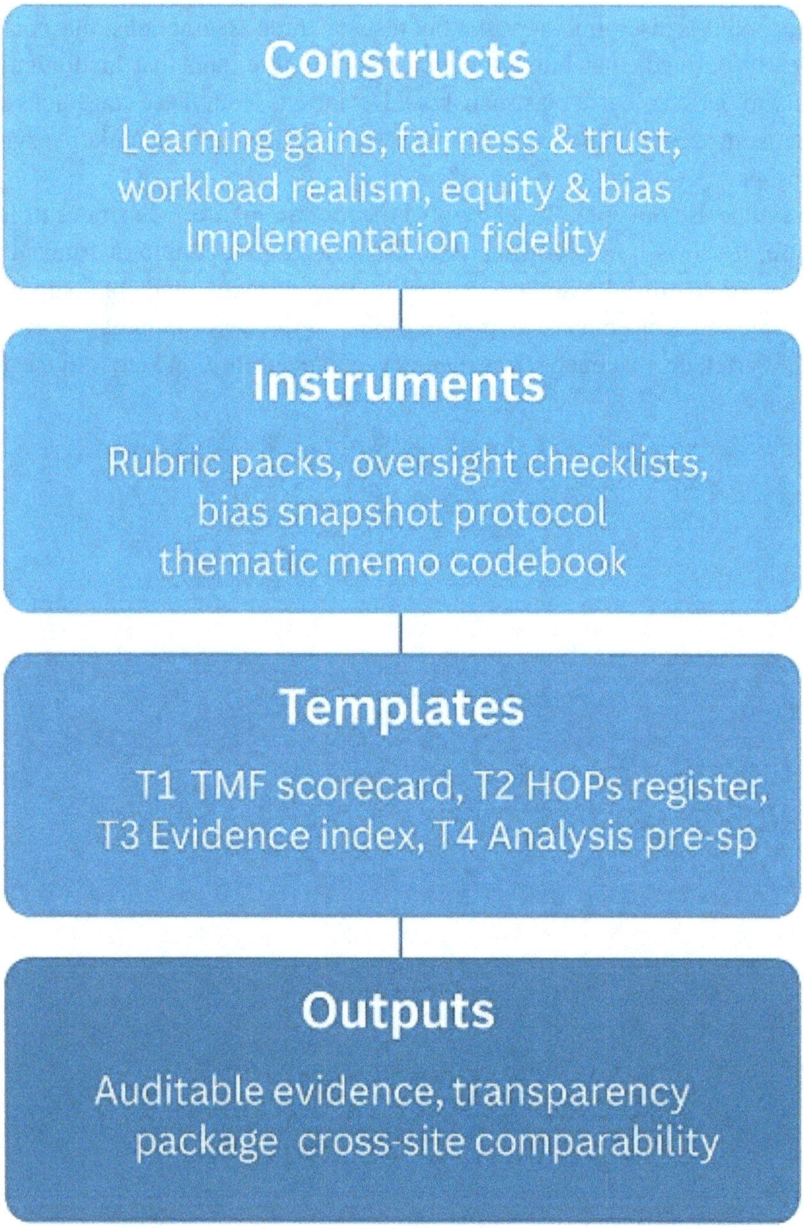

Source: Author's own elaboration

9. DISCUSSION AND IMPLICATIONS

This discussion consolidates the chapter's theoretical and practical contributions and provides decision rules for interpreting future empirical findings generated with the toolkit (Section 8). The goal is to ensure that subsequent studies can connect outcomes to pedagogical validity, equity, workload realism, and assurance under the EU AI Act and ISO/IEC 42001.

9.1 Contributions to Theory

This chapter advances three moves. First, it reframes educators as cognitive architects within human–AI co-performance, integrating distributed cognition with TPACK and foregrounding TMF as a first-class design construct (Hutchins, 1995; Mishra & Koehler, 2006). Second, it operationalises human-centred AI by converting principles into HOPs and evidence-ready workflows that specify when and how educator judgment constrains automation (Amershi et al., 2019; Shneiderman, 2020). Third, it couples pedagogy with governance through an AIMS-aligned architecture that links classroom routines to legal and standards-based duties (Drachsler & Greller, 2016; EU, 2024; OBP, 2023).

9.2 Implications for Research Design

The Section 8 measurement kit enables auditable, cross-site comparisons while respecting local contexts. Validity should be treated as an argument-based programme of evidence, not a single coefficient (Messick, 1995). Discrimination metrics should be paired with calibration and fairness diagnostics, and for imbalanced outcomes analyses should privilege precision–recall and threshold sensitivity (Mehrabi et al., 2022; Saito & Rehmsmeier, 2015).

9.3 Implications for Policy and Institutional Governance

ECA provides course-level mechanisms for meaningful human oversight and transparency, while aligning institutional practice with the EU AI Act and ISO/IEC 42001. The minimum evidence pack (Section 7.6) offers a practical audit basis that avoids over-collection, thereby protecting both rights and workload (EU, 2024; OBP, 2023).

9.4 Interpretive Decision Rules Mapped to the RQs

The following rules guide interpretation and action.

RQ1 (validity and learning). When rubric-aligned gains improve and inter-rater agreement rises on double-marked subsamples, the ECA workflow exhibits instructional validity and merits scale-up. When gains occur but agreement drops or construct drift is detected, TMF should be tightened and HOPs sampling increased until validity is restored.

RQ2 (explainability sufficiency). When minimal explanations (uncertainty combined with provenance) deliver equal or greater learning and higher perceived clarity, a lean explanation pattern is warranted. When learners or educators misinterpret outputs, explanation depth and/or training should be increased while monitoring workload.

RQ3 (equity and bias). When subgroup calibration is adequate and error-rate parity acceptable, current thresholds can be maintained. When disparities emerge, thresholds, variables, or prompts should be adjusted; fairness trade-offs must be documented and oversight escalated in high-risk contexts.

RQ4 (workload and identity). When time-to-feedback declines and NASA-TLX remains within bounds while instructors report preserved judgment and care, the workflow meets workload realism and professional identity criteria. When identity tension rises despite time savings, educator control should be increased (e.g., stricter HOPs) and communication refined to make human authorship and accountability visible.

RQ5 (governance at scale). When AIMS adoption reduces unresolved incidents and appeals without harming learning or equity, institutions should institutionalise the evidence pack and monitoring routines. When audit readiness improves but outcomes degrade, evidence requirements should be recalibrated to avoid assurance overreach.

9.5 Boundary Conditions and Transferability

ECA is most applicable where learning constructs are clearly specified, human oversight is feasible, and data can be minimised without undermining pedagogy. Transfer across disciplines requires re-scoring TMF and re-locating HOPs to discipline-specific decision points. Generative tasks with high lexical surface variance demand stronger construct mapping than classifier-based early-warning.

9.6 Limitations

This chapter is empirical in intent yet reports no practical results. Instruments and designs are proposed with citations but await implementation. Rapid model evolution may shift error modes; periodic re-validation of TMF and fidelity checks is therefore recommended (O'Donnell, 2008).

10. CONCLUSION

This chapter has reframed educators as cognitive architects in AI-augmented learning, advancing a practical synthesis that connects micro-level pedagogy to meso-level course design and macro-level governance. Conceptually, this chapter has integrated distributed cognition, TPACK, activity theory, and professional identity to argue that instructional, analytic and affective work is increasingly co-performed by human and intelligent systems. Practically, this chapter specified the ECA framework, centred on purpose and outcomes, TMF, HOPs, assurance mechanisms, and feedback and improvement, and aligned these with EU AI Act duties and ISO/IEC 42001 controls so that classroom routines are evidence-ready and auditable (Amershi et al., 2019; EU, 2024; OBP, 2023; Shneiderman, 2020).

This chapter's contributions are threefold. First, it operationalises human-centred AI principles by making meaningful human oversight concrete at the point of pedagogical decision (e.g., assessment, early-warning). Second, it embeds model-aware design into pedagogy via the TMF rubric, extending the TPACK conversation from tool familiarity to literacy about model limits, uncertainty, and bias (Mehrabi et al., 2022; Mishra & Koehler, 2006). Third, it links instructor agency to institutional assurance by specifying the minimum evidence pack (oversight checklists, sampling logs, bias snapshots, disclosures, incident records) that enables both improvement and compliance without excessive data capture (Drachsler & Greller, 2016).

This chapter was deliberately kept empirical in intent but non-reporting: Section 8 offered a measurement and evaluation toolkit, construct definitions, instruments, templates, and analysis guidance, so that future studies can test ECA's transparency claims across contexts. Section 9 provided interpretive decision rules to help institutions act on forthcoming evidence while balancing learning, equity, workload and assurance.

Two boundary conditions merit emphasis. ECA presupposes (a) clearly specified constructs and (b) feasible human oversight. Where either one is absent, the priority should be to strengthen construct clarity and slow the automation, particularly in high stakes uses. Finally, the value of ECA lies not in prescribing a single technology stack, but in offering a repeatable logic of design and accountability that can travel across disciplines and model families.

In sum, positioning educators as cognitive architects is not a rhetorical flourish; it is a design requirement for trustworthy, equitable, and pedagogically valid AI use in education. The framework, competencies, vignettes and toolkit together constitute a research and implementation programme. They specify what to build, how to demonstrate it, and how to decide when to scale or stop. The next step is empirical: deploy the toolkit, pre-register analyses, and report not only gains but also trade-offs, so that the sector learns, iterates, and governs with rigor commensurate to the stakes.

11. REFERENCES

Ailawadi, K. L., & Keller, K. L. (2004). Understanding retail branding: Conceptual insights and research priorities. *Journal of Retailing*, *80*(4), 331–342. DOI: 10.1016/j.jretai.2004.10.008

Amershi, S., Weld, D., Vorvoreanu, M., Fourney, A., Nushi, B., Collisson, P., Suh, J., Iqbal, S., Bennett, P. N., Inkpen, K., Teevan, J., Kikin-Gil, R., & Horvitz, E. (2019). Guidelines for Human-AI Interaction. *Proceedings of the 2019 CHI Conference on Human Factors in Computing Systems*, 1–13. DOI: 10.1145/3290605.3300233

Beauchamp, C., & Thomas, L. (2009). Understanding teacher identity: An overview of issues in the literature and implications for teacher education. *Cambridge Journal of Education*, *39*(2), 175–189. DOI: 10.1080/03057640902902252

Beneke, J., & Carter, S. (2015). The development of a consumer value proposition of private label brands and the application thereof in a South African retail context. *Journal of Retailing and Consumer Services*, *25*, 22–35. DOI: 10.1016/j.jretconser.2015.03.002

Bhukya, R., & Singh, S. (2015). The effect of perceived risk dimensions on purchase intention. *American Journal of Business*, *30*(4), 218–230. DOI: 10.1108/AJB-10-2014-0055

Black, P., & Wiliam, D. (1998). Assessment and Classroom Learning. *Assessment in Education: Principles, Policy & Practice*, *5*(1), 7–74. DOI: 10.1080/0969595980050102

Bowen, G. A. (2009). Document Analysis as a Qualitative Research Method. *Qualitative Research Journal*, *9*(2), 27–40. DOI: 10.3316/QRJ0902027

Braarud, P. Ø. (2021). Investigating the validity of subjective workload rating (NASA TLX) and subjective situation awareness rating (SART) for cognitively complex human–machine work. *International Journal of Industrial Ergonomics*, *86*, 103233. DOI: 10.1016/j.ergon.2021.103233

Braun, V., & Clarke, V. (2006). Using thematic analysis in psychology. *Qualitative Research in Psychology*, *3*(2), 77–101. DOI: 10.1191/1478088706qp063oa

Callaway, B., & Sant'Anna, P. H. C. (2021). Difference-in-Differences with multiple time periods. *Journal of Econometrics*, *225*(2), 200–230. DOI: 10.1016/j.jeconom.2020.12.001

Davis, F. D. (1989). Perceived Usefulness, Perceived Ease of Use, and User Acceptance of Information Technology. *Management Information Systems Quarterly*, *13*(3), 319–340. DOI: 10.2307/249008

DelVecchio, D. (2001). Consumer perceptions of private label quality: The role of product category characteristics and consumer use of heuristics. *Journal of Retailing and Consumer Services*, *8*(5), 239–249. DOI: 10.1016/S0969-6989(00)00030-8

Drachsler, H., & Greller, W. (2016). Privacy and analytics. *Proceedings of the Sixth International Conference on Learning Analytics & Knowledge - LAK '16*, 89–98. DOI: 10.1145/2883851.2883893

Engeström, Y. (2001). Expansive Learning at Work: Toward an activity theoretical reconceptualization. *Journal of Education and Work*, *14*(1), 133–156. DOI: 10.1080/13639080020028747

EU. E. U. (2024). *Regulation (EU) 2024/1689.* https://eur-lex.europa.eu/eli/reg/2024/1689/oj/eng

Gašević, D., Dawson, S., & Siemens, G. (2015). Let's not forget: Learning analytics are about learning. *TechTrends*, *59*(1), 64–71. DOI: 10.1007/s11528-014-0822-x

Gioia, D. A., Corley, K. G., & Hamilton, A. L. (2013). Seeking Qualitative Rigor in Inductive Research. *Organizational Research Methods*, *16*(1), 15–31. DOI: 10.1177/1094428112452151

Gregor, S., & Hevner, A. R. (2013). Positioning and Presenting Design Science Research for Maximum Impact1. *Management Information Systems Quarterly*, *37*(2), 337–355. DOI: 10.25300/MISQ/2013/37.2.01

Hart, S. G., & Staveland, L. E. (1988). *Development of NASA-TLX (Task Load Index): Results of Empirical and Theoretical Research* (pp. 139–183). DOI: 10.1016/S0166-4115(08)62386-9

Hemming, K., Haines, T. P., Chilton, P. J., Girling, A. J., & Lilford, R. J. (2015). The stepped wedge cluster randomised trial: rationale, design, analysis, and reporting. *BMJ*, *350*(feb06 1), h391–h391. DOI: 10.1136/bmj.h391

Hevner, M., March, S. T., Park, J., & Ram, S. (2004). Design Science in Information Systems Research. *Management Information Systems Quarterly*, *28*(1), 75–106. DOI: 10.2307/25148625

Hutchins, E. (1995). How a Cockpit Remembers Its Speeds. *Cognitive Science*, *19*(3), 265–288. DOI: 10.1207/s15516709cog1903_1

Imbens, G. W., & Lemieux, T. (2008). Regression discontinuity designs: A guide to practice. *Journal of Econometrics*, *142*(2), 615–635. DOI: 10.1016/j.jeconom.2007.05.001

Ji, Z., Lee, N., Frieske, R., Yu, T., Su, D., Xu, Y., Ishii, E., Bang, Y. J., Madotto, A., & Fung, P. (2023). Survey of Hallucination in Natural Language Generation. *ACM Computing Surveys*, *55*(12), 1–38. DOI: 10.1145/3571730

Kane, M. T. (2013). Validating the Interpretations and Uses of Test Scores. *Journal of Educational Measurement*, *50*(1), 1–73. DOI: 10.1111/jedm.12000

Kulik, J. A., & Fletcher, J. D. (2016). Effectiveness of Intelligent Tutoring Systems. *Review of Educational Research*, *86*(1), 42–78. DOI: 10.3102/0034654315581420

Lakens, D. (2013). Calculating and reporting effect sizes to facilitate cumulative science: A practical primer for t-tests and ANOVAs. *Frontiers in Psychology*, *4*. Advance online publication. DOI: 10.3389/fpsyg.2013.00863 PMID: 24324449

Lakens, D. (2022). Sample Size Justification. *Collabra. Psychology*, *8*(1), 33267. Advance online publication. DOI: 10.1525/collabra.33267

Ma, W., Adesope, O. O., Nesbit, J. C., & Liu, Q. (2014). Intelligent tutoring systems and learning outcomes: A meta-analysis. *Journal of Educational Psychology*, *106*(4), 901–918. DOI: 10.1037/a0037123

Mays, N. (2000). Qualitative research in health care: Assessing quality in qualitative research. *BMJ (Clinical Research Ed.)*, *320*(7226), 50–52. DOI: 10.1136/bmj.320.7226.50 PMID: 10617534

Mehrabi, N., Morstatter, F., Saxena, N., Lerman, K., & Galstyan, A. (2022). A Survey on Bias and Fairness in Machine Learning. *ACM Computing Surveys*, *54*(6), 1–35. DOI: 10.1145/3457607

Messick, S. (1995). Validity of psychological assessment: Validation of inferences from persons' responses and performances as scientific inquiry into score meaning. *The American Psychologist*, *50*(9), 741–749. DOI: 10.1037/0003-066X.50.9.741

Mishra, P., & Koehler, M. J. (2006). Technological Pedagogical Content Knowledge: A Framework for Teacher Knowledge. *Teachers College Record*, *108*(6), 1017–1054. DOI: 10.1111/j.1467-9620.2006.00684.x

Nosek, B. A., Ebersole, C. R., DeHaven, A. C., & Mellor, D. T. (2018). The preregistration revolution. *Proceedings of the National Academy of Sciences of the United States of America*, *115*(11), 2600–2606. DOI: 10.1073/pnas.1708274114 PMID: 29531091

Nowell, L. S., Norris, J. M., White, D. E., & Moules, N. J. (2017). Thematic Analysis. *International Journal of Qualitative Methods*, *16*(1), 1609406917733847. Advance online publication. DOI: 10.1177/1609406917733847

O'Donnell, C. L. (2008). Defining, Conceptualizing, and Measuring Fidelity of Implementation and Its Relationship to Outcomes in K–12 Curriculum Intervention Research. *Review of Educational Research*, *78*(1), 33–84. DOI: 10.3102/0034654307313793

OBP. O. B. P. (2023). *ISO/IEC 42001:2023*. https://www.iso.org/obp/ui/en/#iso:std:iso-iec:42001:ed-1:v1:en

Peffers, K., Tuunanen, T., Rothenberger, M. A., & Chatterjee, S. (2007). A Design Science Research Methodology for Information Systems Research. *Journal of Management Information Systems*, *24*(3), 45–77. DOI: 10.2753/MIS0742-1222240302

Roll, I., & Wylie, R. (2016). Evolution and Revolution in Artificial Intelligence in Education. *International Journal of Artificial Intelligence in Education*, *26*(2), 582–599. DOI: 10.1007/s40593-016-0110-3

Saito, T., & Rehmsmeier, M. (2015). The Precision-Recall Plot Is More Informative than the ROC Plot When Evaluating Binary Classifiers on Imbalanced Datasets. *PLoS One*, *10*(3), e0118432. DOI: 10.1371/journal.pone.0118432 PMID: 25738806

Shneiderman, B. (2020). Human-Centered Artificial Intelligence: Reliable, Safe & Trustworthy. *International Journal of Human-Computer Interaction*, *36*(6), 495–504. DOI: 10.1080/10447318.2020.1741118

Shute, V. J. (2008). Focus on Formative Feedback. *Review of Educational Research*, *78*(1), 153–189. DOI: 10.3102/0034654307313795

Slade, S., & Prinsloo, P. (2013). Learning Analytics. *The American Behavioral Scientist*, *57*(10), 1510–1529. DOI: 10.1177/0002764213479366

UNESCO. (2023). *Guidance for Generative AI in Education and Research*. https://cdn.table.media/assets/wp-content/uploads/2023/09/386693eng.pdf

Venkatesh, M., Morris, M. G., Davis, G. B., & Davis, F. D. (2003). User Acceptance of Information Technology: Toward a Unified View. *Management Information Systems Quarterly*, *27*(3), 425–478. DOI: 10.2307/30036540

Whetten, D. A. (1989). What Constitutes a Theoretical Contribution? *Academy of Management Review*, *14*(4), 490. DOI: 10.2307/258554

Zawacki-Richter, O., Marín, V. I., Bond, M., & Gouverneur, F. (2019). Systematic review of research on artificial intelligence applications in higher education – where are the educators? *International Journal of Educational Technology in Higher Education, 16*(1), 39. DOI: 10.1186/s41239-019-0171-0

12. KEY TERMS AND DEFINITIONS

AI Management System (AIMS): An institution-level system of policies, roles, and controls for AI lifecycle governance, risk management, data governance, logging/monitoring, incident response, and continual improvement specified in ISO/IEC 42001.

Algorithmic Bias and Fairness: Systematic performance differences across subgroups (e.g., error-rate disparities, miscalibration) arising from data, modelling, or deployment; monitored via subgroup audits and addressed through design and procedural mitigations.

Construct Validity (in educational assessment): The degree to which evidence and theory support the interpretations of scores for intended uses, covering content, internal structure, and relations to other variables and consequences.

Distributed cognition: A perspective that views cognitive activity as distributed across individuals, tools, and environments, rather than confined to individual minds.

Early-Warning Analytics: Predictive/diagnostic use of engagement and performance traces to flag at-risk learners, coupled with supportive human action plans; requires attention to variable justification, fairness, and consent.

Educator-as-Cognitive-Architect (ECA): A role conception in which instructors design, govern, and ethically steer human–AI co-performance in learning, linking micro-level pedagogy to course workflows and institutional assurance (e.g., oversight checkpoints, evidence packs). The construct operationalises human-centred AI principles under legal/standards duties.

Formative Feedback: Information provided to learners to close the gap between current and desired performance, emphasising specificity, timeliness and guidance for improvement; in AI-supported settings, it remains advisory pending instructor validation.

Human Oversight Points (HOPs): Explicit decision junctures where educator review/override is mandatory (e.g., grading-relevant feedback, risk alerts, sensitive content). HOPs instantiate "meaningful human oversight" at the classroom level.

Meaningful Human Oversight: A regulatory principle requiring that humans can understand, monitor, and effectively intervene in AI-assisted decisions, especially in high-risk contexts such as assessment or profiling.

Task–Model Fit (TMF): The alignment between a learning objective/construct and an AI system's capabilities, limits, and uncertainty affordances (e.g., when to use classification versus constrained generation). TMF extends TPACK by making model literacy a design criterion.

Transparency and Explainability: Making model limits, uncertainty, and provenance legible to non-experts at the point of use. In education, the aim is decision support that sustains pedagogical trust without cognitive overload.

Chapter 5
EFL Instructors' Digital Competencies and Their Perceptions of AI Integration in Language Teaching

Bora Demir
https://orcid.org/0000-0001-8187-3206
Çanakkale Onsekiz Mart University, Turkey

Hilal Alten
https://orcid.org/0009-0004-9591-0062
Çanakkale Onsekiz Mart University, Turkey

ABSTRACT

As a result of rapid technological advances and shifting expectations in education, integrating Artificial Intelligence (AI) has gained importance, particularly in English Language Teaching (ELT). This mixed-methods study explores the relationship between EFL instructors' digital competencies and their perceptions of using AI in instructional settings. Data were collected from 51 EFL instructors at preparatory schools of four state universities using the AI and English Language Teaching Scale (Edmett et al., 2023) and the Teachers' Digital Competencies Scale (Ergül & Taşar, 2023), along with semi-structured interviews. Quantitative findings revealed that instructors with higher digital competence held more positive views on AI use in teaching, while those with lower competence expressed reservations. Thematic analysis showed that AI integration presents both opportunities and challenges. The

DOI: 10.4018/979-8-3373-4521-5.ch005

study concludes that enhancing instructors' digital competencies may foster more positive attitudes and effective AI integration, emphasizing the need for targeted professional development.

1. INTRODUCTION

The development of AI technology has strongly influenced educational professionals by inspiring them to create and deliver instructional materials in more innovative and effective ways (Jafari & Keykha, 2024). As new generations have more opportunities to engage with digital tools and become familiar to technology-driven experiences starting from early ages, traditional teaching methods are now considered as less effective (Prensky, 2001). For that reason, teachers try to incorporate AI-powered tools into their curriculum, allowing for more interactive and personalized learning experiences (Almuhanna, 2024). Since AI has great potential in creating more engaging and interactive instructional settings, its utilization has become popular among language educators as they can generate speaking, listening, and writing exercises (Luckin et al., 2016). As a result of this, teachers who are capable of using AI and other technological innovations in their classes can better meet the evolving needs of students by creating more engaging learning sources (Baidoo-Anu & Owusu Ansah, 2023). For example, by using chatbots and AI-powered story creation tools, educators can develop customized reading passages, quizzes, and other materials that can meet the specific needs of their students (Abdulrahaman et al., 2020; Kamalov et al., 2023). However, while these technologies offer numerous advantages, they also present potential drawbacks for the educators.

First, many teachers believe that overreliance on AI technology bears the potential of fading students' critical thinking and problem-solving skills that are often nurtured through direct student-teacher interaction (Rahman & Watanobe, 2023). Second, technology may also become a source of distraction by the utilization of tools such as smartphones and laptops, as potential distractors for classroom management, and challenging for teachers to keep their learners engaged and focused on learning (Qi, 2019; Chiu et al., 2023). The third challenge for teachers might be the complexity of learning new technologies and acquire new skills associated with new tools since they require them to devote their time and effort to become proficient users of such technologies (Kim & Kwon, 2023).

The general expectation from educators is to be adaptive to new digital tools and their applications to boost their instructional practices and engage the digital generation. Although this integration offers potential for better instructional settings, it also creates a high responsibility for teachers to adopt novel technologies (Lee et al., 2023). Hence, the teachers with the intention of using these technologies should be proficient in integrating these tools meaningfully into their teaching strategies (Chen & Liu, 2023). This challenging task requires ongoing professional development and support to build confidence and competence in using new technologies effectively. In other words, teachers should leave their comfort zones and try hard to gain new skills of integrating cutting edge technology (Jafari & Keykha, 2024). In sum, while AI presents many opportunities and great potential, it is also challenging for language teachers to be able to adapt to this new technology by developing their digital competencies to use these tools effectively. Embracing technology and integrating it thoughtfully into the curriculum will enhance teaching practices and better support student learning outcomes in the digital age.

English as a Foreign Language (EFL) instructors play a crucial role in integrating digital technologies into language teaching, yet their digital competencies and perceptions significantly influence the extent and effectiveness of such integration (Benek, 2025). As AI-powered tools such as intelligent writing assistants, automated feedback systems, and speech recognition technologies become increasingly accessible, EFL instructors are expected to adapt their pedagogical approaches accordingly (Bower et al., 2024). However, research indicates that many instructors feel inadequately prepared to implement these technologies due to limited training opportunities, lack of institutional support, or uncertainty about pedagogical relevance (Arslan, 2025). While some educators view AI as a promising aid that can personalize instruction and enhance learner autonomy, others express concerns about over-reliance on automation, ethical implications, and the risk of diminishing the teacher's role in communicative language teaching (Hazaymeh et al., 2019; Demir & Aydın, 2026). Therefore, understanding EFL instructors' digital competencies and their nuanced perceptions of AI is essential for developing effective professional development programs and ensuring responsible, meaningful integration of AI into language education.

Despite the growing presence of AI tools in educational contexts, there remains a significant gap in research specifically addressing how English language teachers develop the digital competencies necessary to integrate these tools meaningfully into their practice (Arslan, 2025; Pham, 2025). While general discussions around AI in education are increasing, most studies tend to focus on technological affordances rather than teacher preparedness and pedagogical integration (Zawacki-Richter et al., 2019; Benek, 2025). In the field of English Language Teaching (ELT), the need is even more urgent, as AI applications such as automated feedback systems, intelligent tutoring, and natural language processing tools become more prevalent (Hazaymeh et al., 2019). However, many language teachers still report feeling unprepared to adopt these tools effectively, citing a lack of training, confidence, and institutional support (Bower et al., 2024; Koraishi, 2023). As such, there is a critical need for context-specific research and guidance that explores not only the benefits of AI but also the competencies ELT instructors need to navigate these technologies responsibly and pedagogically. This chapter addresses that gap by focusing on ELT instructors' perspectives, aiming to contribute to the growing body of literature on AI integration in language education through a lens of teacher readiness and digital competence development.

2. LITERATURE REVIEW

2.1 The Role of Technology in Foreign Language Education

With the astonishing improvement of the capabilities of technology, the integration of it into educational settings has gained significant importance in recent years, much like in other fields (Samala et al., 2024). As also claimed by Çelik and Baturay (2024), the current state of foreign language education has been significantly shaped by recent advancements in modern information and communication technologies. It is due to the fact that technology has become an inseparable part of our lives, and it also affects foreign language learning processes (Allman et al., 2024). Thinking and analysing processes of the students are shaped by the new technological devices, tools, software, or applications that are used almost all the time. According to Mollaei and Riasati, "No longer are students' experiences with new languages limited to their textbooks or immediate environment" (2013, p. 13). Since they easily access technology and the content they enjoy, they may get bored in the regular lessons if the activities are not interactive. It is because each generation is affected and shaped by the developments appearing at the time period they live in (Kesharwani, 2020).

Owing to its interactive nature, the field of foreign language education has increasingly adopted technology integration due to its interactive nature to enhance learner engagement and meeting the demands of a digitalized world. The transformative power of technology in foreign language education is crucial since it facilitates authentic language exposure by connecting learners to authentic learning experiences, multimedia content, and adaptive learning environments by bridging the gap between classroom instruction and practical use of the target language (Zhang & Dong, 2024). These adaptive and personalized learning opportunities allow language learners to progress at their own pace with unlimited chance of practicing through numerous tools (Godwin-Jones, 2018). Also, immersive technologies such as Virtual Reality (VR) and Augmented Reality (AR) proved their power in increasing learner engagement and reducing language learning anxiety by simulating real-life interactions in less stressful educational settings (Tai, 2022). Besides, mobile-assisted language learning (MALL) has made it possible for learners to further access to language resources, free from classroom hours (Kukulska-Hulme & Viberg, 2017). And finally, the increasing capabilities of AI has accelerated the integration of technology by navigating the educators and providing them a new role as content generators. By integrating AI into their courses, language teachers are now more confident in tailoring their own materials and activities for their own learners (Attard & Dingli, 2024).

2.2 Generational Differences in Technology Adaptation

Parallel with the increasing exposure of new generations to digital tools and software, educators had to adopt tools that prepare learners for multilingual, technology-mediated workplaces (Dooly & O'Dowd, 2018). However, research indicates that not all teachers are equally capable or eager to integrate technology due to several reasons. First, lack of training and professional development support from institutions makes teachers feel unprepared to effectively integrate digital tools in their teaching practices (Hockly, 2012). Owing to increased workload, time constraints and some other institutional responsibilities, teachers can hardly create free time to search for new technologies and their integration into the classroom (Hubbard, 2013). Another reason is to do with personality treats. While some teachers are eager to catch up with technology, others exhibit resistance to change and stay at their comfort zone preferring traditional methods due to negative attitudes towards technology's pedagogical value (Ertmer et al., 2012). Also, technostress has become an important factor for teachers, particularly in foreign language education where rapid technological integration demands constant adaptation (Willermark et al., 2023). As presented by empirical research, language teachers experience anxiety or psychological strain caused by frequent updates especially in AI and lack of training (Jena, 2015; Tarafdar et al., 2019). Teachers often report that they experience cognitive overload when managing multiple platforms such as Large Language Models (LLMs) or gamification applications alongside traditional pedagogy (Howard & Mozejko, 2015; Demir & Lüta, 2026). This increasing demand on the integration of technology into language learning has revealed generational divides, with older educators reporting higher technostress due to lower digital confidence compared to younger colleagues (Wang et al., 2020).

Today, most of the teachers can be refereed as digital immigrants by adopting technological developments in their life later on (Prensky, 2001) and may encounter certain difficulties while using these devices compared to the digital natives. Some empirical research has provided various evidence underlying this generational gap between digital natives and immigrants. For instance, Pongrac et al. (2025) argue that while digital natives possess an intuitive understanding of technology, due to their upbringing in digital-rich environments, digital immigrants often need to adapt and acquire these skills later in life, leading to distinct approaches to technology use. Similarly, David (2022) emphasize that these generational differences are not only embedded in access to technology but also in how individuals engage with it to support learning and problem-solving. Furthermore, Marzo (2024) explores the evolving roles of both groups in educational contexts, noting that digital natives often bring innovation and adaptability, whereas digital immigrants rely on structured strategies and experiential learning to bridge the technological gap. According to Merç (2015), EFL teachers mostly have positive attitudes toward the use of technology in their classrooms, however, they may have some difficulties in the integration of technology from time to time. On the contrary, in the study conducted by Yoon (2019), it was also concluded that the teachers mostly have positive attitudes towards AI, however, they do not prefer to use it in their classroom settings. Investigating university instructors' digital competencies and AI perceptions can demonstrate how this generational gap influences their ability to integrate AI into their teaching and what factors contribute to their reluctance or willingness to adopt AI-driven educational tools.

2.3 The Integration of AI into language education

As AI continues to transform educational environments, its incorporation into language instruction has become a promising innovation and a challenging pedagogical issue (Karataş et al., 2024). According to (Fakhar et al., 2024) the successful integration of AI in education hinges on the role of teachers, who must not only be adept at utilizing these technologies but also possess the pedagogical insight to guide students in leveraging AI tools effectively. Teachers play a crucial role in contextualizing AI's potential, ensuring that it complements traditional teaching methods, and fostering an environment where technology enhances rather than diminishes the human element of learning (Baskara, 2023). Their expertise is vital in adapting AI to meet the diverse needs of learners and in helping students navigate the complexities of these advanced tools.

Empirical research on AI awareness and digital competence have revealed several findings. In a mixed-method study conducted by Zengin Erbaş (2023) with 20 EFL teachers in Türkiye context, it has been pointed out that teachers mostly have positive attitudes toward AI integration into the lessons and they do not consider AI as a threatening technology for their professions. However, while some research emphasizes positive perspectives on technology, others point to a reluctance in adapting advanced innovations. For instance, in certain situations, especially the teachers who are digital immigrants may not welcome these sorts of tools due to the negative attitudes toward AI. Additionally, they may feel incompetent in using technology in their lessons (Sharma et al., 2024). Similarly, quantitative research conducted by Madu and Musa (2024) with 67 academic staff in the faculty of education in a university in Nigeria demonstrates that there is a positive correlation between digital competences and AI awareness. Their study concluded that promoting AI awareness is beneficial both for lecturers and students. Another systematic literature review research conducted by Basilotta-Gómez-Pablos et al., (2022), including 56 articles also emphasized the importance of digital competencies by suggesting that the successful integration of novel technologies can only be possible when teachers develop their digital competencies. Teachers who are competent enough to use AI can help their learners in enhancing their engagement and interactive learning experiences.

Besides, there are studies which attempt offer frameworks for teachers to integrate themselves into technologically enhanced language instruction. Muslimin et al. (2024) postulated that the integration of AI into EFL instruction can be better understood through established theoretical frameworks such as SAMR model, standing for Substitution, Augmentation, Modification, and Redefinition. The SAMR framework provides a solid foundation for transformative educational practices, highlighting the need for comprehensive training programs, supportive institutional policies, and ongoing research to address existing barriers (Krisbiantoro & Ashari, 2024). Additionally, TPACK, standing for Technological Pedagogical Content Knowledge emphasizes that effective technology integration requires not only technical skills, but also the ability to support technological tools with appropriate pedagogical strategies (Taopan et al., 2020).

As the main theoretical framework of this study, the TPACK framework, introduced by Mishra and Koehler (2006), provides a comprehensive lens for understanding how teachers integrate technology into their instructional practices by balancing three core knowledge domains: content knowledge (CK), pedagogical knowledge (PK), and technological knowledge (TK). In the context of English as a Foreign Language (EFL) instruction, TPACK has emerged as a valuable framework for examining how language teachers make informed decisions about the use of digital tools, including AI-powered technologies, in language learning environments. Recent studies have emphasized the relevance of TPACK in identifying EFL instructors' strengths and gaps in technology integration. For instance, Arslan (2025) found that EFL instructors with stronger TPACK competencies reported greater confidence and pedagogical flexibility when using AI-based tools. Similarly, Benek (2025) demonstrated that integrating TPACK-oriented professional development led to more meaningful use of digital resources in language classrooms. Hazaymeh et al., (2024) further argued that EFL instructors' technological knowledge must be supported by contextualized pedagogical practices to ensure successful AI integration. In line with this, Koraishi (2023) highlighted the importance of developing instructors' pedagogical content knowledge to navigate emerging challenges in digitally mediated language education. Pham (2025) also emphasized that a TPACK-informed approach allows instructors to reflect critically on the affordances and limitations of educational technologies within EFL contexts. Given these findings, this study adopts the TPACK framework as a theoretical lens to better understand the digital competencies of EFL instructors and to explore how these competencies shape their perceptions and use of AI in language teaching. The framework offers a robust foundation to examine not only the presence of technological skills but also how these skills intersect with pedagogical and content knowledge in practical instructional settings.

Together, these frameworks help explain the transition from traditional to technologically enhanced language instruction by offering insight into the evolving roles of educators and the challenges they face. Educators face numerous factors that distinguish their circumstances, making each teacher's situation unique and distinct from others by integrating technology into their practices (Devasena, 2024). Framing empirical findings within these models allows for a deeper understanding of how instructors' digital competencies and AI perceptions influence their readiness and capacity to implement AI tools effectively in the EFL classroom.

From this perspective, the current study is significant by exploring the impact of teachers' digital competencies on their perceptions and practices regarding the use of AI in EFL instruction. Apparently, the capacity of educators to effectively integrate AI tools into their teaching is increasingly dependent on their digital skills and knowledge (Uygun et al., 2024). Therefore, understanding how digital competencies influence teachers' attitudes towards AI and their ability to implement such technologies in the classroom is important in understanding the role of digital competencies in the successful implementation of AI for EFL instruction. In short, due to this increasing reliance on technology in language education, the reviewed studies collectively highlight the necessity of further exploration into the interplay between digital competencies and AI integration in EFL instruction. While existing research has demonstrated a positive correlation between teachers' digital competencies and their ability to incorporate AI tools effectively, it still needs to be investigated in a deeper way (Çiftçi, 2024). Additionally, as AI continues to evolve, understanding the specific challenges and training needs of EFL teachers, particularly digital immigrants, will be crucial for ensuring effective AI adoption in educational settings. To this end, the following research questions are addressed:

1. For what instructional purposes do EFL instructors employ artificial intelligence (AI) technologies in their teaching practices?
2. How do EFL instructors perceive the integration of AI technologies into language education?
3. What is the nature of the relationship between EFL instructors' digital competencies and their perceptions of AI integration in language teaching?

4. To what extent do EFL instructors' levels of digital competence influence their perceptions regarding the use of AI in language instruction?
5. What additional factors, beyond instructors' perceptions of AI, are identified through qualitative inquiry as contributing to their digital competencies?

3. METHOD

By analyzing both quantitative and qualitative data, the current study is based on mixed-methods design. Mixed methodology is often used by the researchers owing to its ability to combine both quantitative and qualitative approaches (Creswell & Plano Clark, 2018). While quantitative data allows for the measurement of statistical relationships and generalizability of findings, qualitative findings bear the potential deeper contextual understanding and explanations of these relationships (Tashakkori & Teddlie, 2020). This integrated approach not only enhances the validity of the research but also provides a richer, more holistic view of how digital competencies impact AI perceptions in language teaching (Johnson & Onwuegbuzie, 2004). Hence, mixed method design provided the researchers a comprehensive understanding of the complex relationship between EFL instructors' digital competencies and their perceptions of AI integration.

While this study provides valuable insights into the correlation between EFL instructors' digital competencies and their perceptions of AI, several limitations must be acknowledged. First, the study's reliance on self-reported data from the Artificial Intelligence and English Language Teaching Scale and the Teachers' Digital Competencies Scale may introduce response biases, as instructors might overestimate their digital skills or the benefits of AI. Sample size and the scope of the study appears as another limitation, so, the findings may not be generalized to diverse range of EFL instructors across different educational contexts and geographic locations.

3.1 Setting and Participants

In this research, the participants are experienced EFL instructors who are working at preparatory classes of 4 universities. 51 instructors participated in this study. Their age range is between 24 and 50 with the mean of 39,75. The number of female participants is 34 whereas the number of male participants is 17. A majority of the participants (N=32) graduated from English Language Teaching Department, 11 of them graduated from English Language and Literature, 5 of them from American Culture and Literature, 2 of them from Translation/Interpretation and 1 one of them from English Linguistics departments. The research has been conducted in preparatory classes at four state universities.

3.2 Instruments

With a mixed methods design, this study collects both quantitative and qualitative data from EFL instructors teaching at university. Firstly, two different quantitative measures were utilized. The first instrument, the "Artificial Intelligence and English Language Teaching Scale" (Edmett et al., 2023), is used to assess EFL teachers' perceptions and awareness of AI technologies in their instructional practices. The scale comprises two sections with different sets of items.

The first section contains six items as answers to the common question; "Which of the following do you use AI tools for?" A sample item reads as: "To correct your students' English or suggest improvements." "For each item on the questionnaire, participants were asked to indicate whether or not the item applied to them by ticking the corresponding box. If a participant ticked an item, it was assigned a value of '1,' indicating that the item was applicable. Conversely, if a participant did not tick an item, it was assigned a value of '0,' indicating that the item was not applicable. Thus, each item was effectively rated on a binary scale, with possible values of 0 or 1, reflecting whether or not the participant identified with the statement." The second section of the scale includes 13 items with a 5-point Likert type scale ranging from "strongly disagree" to "strongly agree". For all the items, the common statement was: "To what extent do you agree or disagree with the following statements?". A sample item is: "AI can help learners improve their English reading skills.

The second instrument, the "Teachers' Digital Competencies Scale" (Ergül & Taşar, 2023), evaluates teachers' proficiency in using digital tools and their overall digital competencies. The scale consists of 16 items with a 6-point Likert type (0= Not Suitable, 1= Never. 2= Rarely, 3= Sometimes, 4= Usually and 5= Always). A sample item reads as: "I create rich learning environments using digital technologies." These scales were selected to provide robust measures of both AI perceptions and digital skill levels among participants. Reliability analyses of the scales yielded Cronbach's Alpha values of .93 and .79, respectively. While the first scale focuses on AI perceptions and awareness of EFL teachers, the second one mostly focuses on evaluating the digital competencies of teachers by taking their proficiency in using these tools into consideration, indicating high internal consistency.

This study also utilized a question form to collect qualitative data. For this purpose, semi-structured interview questions developed by Edmett et al. (2023) were adapted. The original form included 12 questions about different aspects of AI. However, the researchers decided to use only seven of them since these questions were most relevant to the research objectives and aligned closely with the study's focus on exploring factors influencing EFL instructors' digital competencies. The selected questions were tailored to elicit in-depth insights into the instructors' experiences, attitudes, and challenges related to AI in education, thereby ensuring that the qualitative data would effectively complement the quantitative findings. As a result, the following semi-structured question form was developed to explore various dimensions of AI's role in ELT. The form was sent and received via email.

The questions addressed several key areas as:

3.2.1 Suitability for ELT vs. Other Subjects:

1. Do the current capabilities of AI make it better suited to the teaching and learning of language than some other subjects?
2. Do you think AI will impact English language teaching and learning more than other disciplines?

3.2.2 Potential/Ability of AI to Learn:

3. Will there come a time when AI has learned from a large enough sample of human interaction to mimic the more intangible elements of human teaching and learning (e.g., relationships, friendship, socialization, inspiration, culture, and ethnography)?

3.2.3 Influences on the Development of AI for ELT:

4. Are you worried that decisions made by AI tech companies will influence what happens in English language classrooms?

3.2.4 Increasing Impact on ELT Classrooms/Approach:

5. Will the ability of AI to create contextualized, immersive language learning experiences reduce the need for classroom-based language practice and learning?

3.2.5 Benefits and Downsides:

6. Where do you see the most benefits to be gained from AI in English language teaching and learning, and teacher development?
7. Do you see any downsides to English language teaching and/or learning being led by AI systems?

3.3 Procedures for Data Collection

The research has been conducted in two phases. In the first phase of the research, a quantitative data collection tool, including two scales about teachers' digital competencies and AI perceptions, were shared with the participants. The data has been collected voluntarily from 51 EFL instructors working at preparatory classes of 4 state universities from a target population of 175 instructors. All the participants signed a consent form before filling in the scales. The survey included demographic questions such as age, gender, and time of teaching experience and it was sent via Google Forms. As reported by the participants, the average time to complete the survey was 12 minutes. After collecting the quantitative data, five participants were randomly selected to participate in the semi-structured interviews. These interviews questions were sent to the selected participants via email, and they provided their responses through email as well.

The next step involves analyzing quantitative data using the SPSS software program. Initially, factors such as age and gender have been examined, followed by an assessment of the items in the scale based on these variables. Before conducting any inferential analysis, the dataset was analyzed in terms of normality assumption. The means of digital competences (Skewness = 0.29, Kurtosis = -0.48) and AI perceptions (Skewness = 0.29, Kurtosis = -0.48) are within the range of a normal distribution as also stated by Hair et al. (2013). Kolmogorov-Smirnov test results also revealed a normal distribution for digital competences (D(51) = 0.08, p >.05.) and AI perceptions (D(51) = 0.05, p >.05.

Figure 1. Digital Competencies Scale

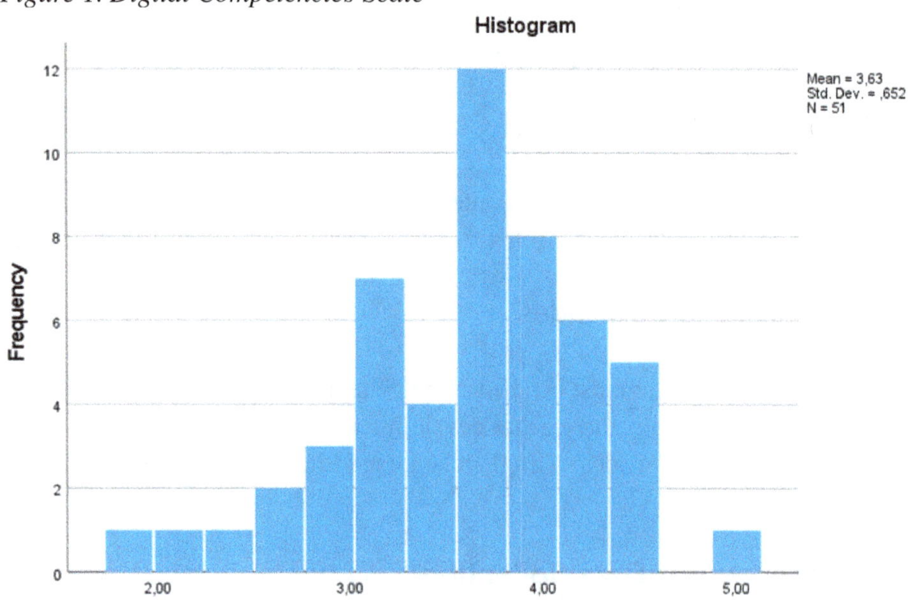

Figure 2. AI Perceptions Scale

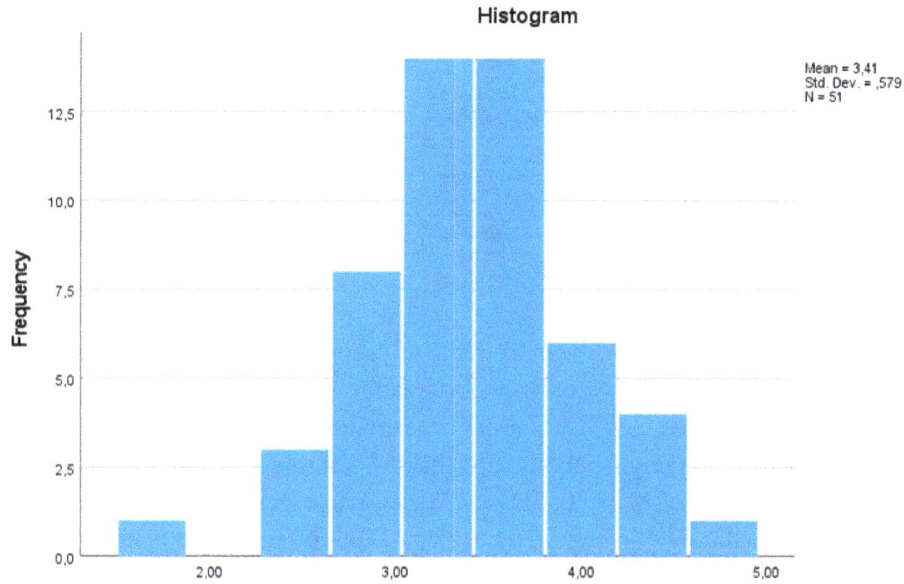

Figure 1 and Figure 2 visualize the distribution of the data obtained from both scales. Following that, correlational analysis (Pearson Correlation) has been conducted in order to demonstrate the relationship between the two variables.

4. FINDINGS AND DISCUSSION

According to the results of the study and in the light of the research questions below, the perceptions of EFL instructors on the integration of AI tools into language education is mostly positive and they tend to utilize this recent technology.

4.1 For What Instructional Purposes do EFL Instructors Employ Artificial Intelligence (AI) Technologies in Their Teaching Practices?

In order to analyze the reasons of AI use in teachers' teaching practices, descriptive statistics were calculated. Table 1 presents the descriptive analysis of the purposes for which EFL instructors utilize AI in their lessons.

Table 1. Descriptive analysis of the purposes of using AI

	Item	*M*	*SD*
4	To create materials for your English language classes (e.g. sample conversations, songs, reading texts)	,86	,348
1	To help your students' practice using English	,76	,428
2	To correct your students' English or suggest improvements	,73	,451
3	To create lesson plans for your English language classes	,35	,483
5	To grade or assess your learners' English language work	,31	,469
6	For administrative tasks (e.g. to manage and analyze student data)	,24	,428

N = 51

As can be seen in Table 1, the most frequently reported use of AI, with the highest mean score (M = .86, SD = .348), is for creating materials for English language classes. This indicates that instructors primarily use AI to enhance the resources available for teaching English. Following this, AI is commonly used to help students practice using English (M = .76, SD = .428), which suggests a focus on reinforcing language skills through practice. The use of AI for correcting students' English or suggesting improvements also ranks highly (M = .73, SD = .451), highlighting its role in providing immediate feedback and facilitating language learning. On the other hand, AI is less frequently used for creating lesson plans (M = .35, SD = .483) and grading or assessing learners' work (M = .31, SD = .469). These lower mean scores indicate that while AI is a valuable tool for material creation and practice, its application in planning and assessment may be more limited or supplementary. Lastly, the least reported use of AI is for administrative tasks, such as managing and analyzing student data (M = .24, SD = .428), which suggests that instructors may rely on other tools or methods for these purposes.

4.2 How do EFL Instructors Perceive the Integration of AI Technologies Into Language Education?

In order to analyze the instructors' perceptions of the integration of AI technologies into language teaching, descriptive statistics were calculated. Table 2 illustrates the descriptive analysis of the purposes for which EFL instructors utilize AI in their lessons.

Table 2. Descriptive analysis of the main perceptions

Item		*M*	*SD*
11	I worry about the impact AI will have on my role as an English language teacher	2,22	1,35
5	AI can have a negative impact on learners' ability to improve their English	2,43	1,20
4	AI can help learners improve their English reading skills	4,33	,71

**N = 51

In analyzing the data from Table 2, it is evident that EFL instructors have varied perceptions of the integration of AI technologies into language teaching. Among the lowest-rated items, the statement "I worry about the impact AI will have on my role as an English language teacher" (M = 2.22, SD = 1.35) indicates a relatively low level of concern among instructors about the potential negative effects of AI on their teaching roles. Similarly, the perception that "AI can have a negative impact on learners' ability to improve their English" also received a low rating (M = 2.43, SD = 1.20), suggesting that instructors generally do not believe AI will hinder students' English language acquisition.

On the other hand, the highest-rated item, "AI can help learners improve their English reading skills" (M = 4.33, SD = 0.71), shows strong agreement among instructors regarding the positive impact of AI on students' reading abilities. This significant difference in mean scores reflects a more optimistic view of AI's role in enhancing specific language skills, particularly reading, while concerns about AI negatively affecting teaching roles or overall language proficiency remain relatively low.

4.3 What is the nature of the relationship between EFL instructors' digital competencies and their perceptions of AI integration in language teaching?

To examine the relationship between EFL instructors' digital competencies and their perceptions of AI, a Pearson correlation analysis was conducted. This analysis was chosen to determine whether there is a statistically significant association between the instructors' proficiency in digital tools and their attitudes or beliefs regarding the integration of AI into their teaching practices.

Table 3. Pearson correlation analysis for digital competency and AI perceptions

		AI perceptions
Digital competency	Pearson Correlation	.507**
	Sig. (2-tailed)	<.001
	N	51

The Pearson correlation analysis, as shown in Table 3, reveals a statistically significant positive correlation between EFL instructors' digital competencies and their perceptions of AI, r(51) = .507, p<.001. This indicates that there is a moderate and significant relationship. As a widely recognized reference for the interpretation of effect sizes, including correlation coefficients, in the social sciences, Cohen indicated "values between 0.3 and 0.7 as a moderate positive (negative) linear relationship. This shows that as instructors' digital competencies increase, their perceptions of AI in education become more favorable.

4.4 To What Extent do EFL Instructors' Levels of Digital Competence Influence Their Perceptions Regarding the Use of AI in Language Instruction?

A linear regression analysis was conducted to examine the extent to which EFL instructors' perceptions of AI predict their digital competencies. The results of the analysis are presented in Table 4. The model was statistically significant, with AI perceptions significantly predicting digital competencies, B = 0.571, SE B = 0.139, β = 0.507, t(51) = 4.113, p < .001. This indicates that as EFL instructors' perceptions of AI become more favorable, their digital competencies tend to increase. The positive standardized beta coefficient (β = 0.507) suggests a moderate to strong effect size, indicating that AI perceptions account for a substantial portion of the variance in digital competencies.

Table 4. Regression analysis

	B	*SE B*	**B**	*t*	*P*
constant	1,680	,480		3,496	<, 001
AI perceptions	,571	,139	,507	4,113	

Dependent variable: Digital competencies

According to Cohen's benchmarks for interpreting effect sizes in social science research, a beta value around 0.5 is considered a large effect. This large effect size indicates that AI perceptions are a significant predictor of digital competencies and account for a considerable amount of variance in these competencies. To calculate the effect size for a regression analysis, we calculated R^2 as 0.257, which indicates the proportion of the variance in the dependent variable (digital competencies) that is explained by the independent variable (AI perceptions). This suggests that efforts to enhance AI perceptions among EFL instructors could potentially lead to meaningful improvements in their digital competencies. In practical terms, this suggests that how EFL instructors perceive AI plays a crucial role in determining their level of digital competency. Specifically, nearly a quarter of the variation in digital competencies among instructors is linked to differences in their perceptions of AI. While this is a substantial effect, it also implies that there are other factors (the remaining 74.3% of the variance) that contribute to digital competencies, which were not accounted for in this particular model.

In order to explore the remaining 74.3% of the variance in EFL instructors' perceptions of AI, qualitative data collected through a semi-structured question form has undergone content analysis. The following section presents the findings derived from the content analysis of the qualitative data addressing the last research question.

4.5 What Additional Factors, Beyond Instructors' Perceptions of AI, Are Identified Through Qualitative Inquiry as Contributing to Their Digital Competencies?

The qualitative analysis of the qualitative data focused on five key topics with reference to interview questions: *Suitability for ELT vs. Other Subjects*, *Potential/ Ability of AI to Learn, Influences on the Development of AI for ELT*, *Increasing Impact on ELT Classrooms/Approach,* and *Benefits and Downsides of AI.* The analysis of responses from five instructors revealed several insightful categories and themes across these topics. Specifically, for the *Suitability for ELT vs. Other Subjects* topic, two categories emerged: "Suitability for ELT" and "Impact on ELT vs. Other Disciplines," with three distinct themes. The *Potential/Ability of AI to Learn* topic yielded one category, "AI Learning Capacity," with two primary themes. The *Influences on the Development of AI for ELT* discussion revealed one category, "Influence of AI Tech Companies," comprising three themes. In the *Increasing Impact on ELT Classrooms/Approach* topic, one category, "Classroom Reduction," emerged, which contained three themes. Finally, the *Benefits and Downsides of AI* topic brought forward two categories, "Benefits of AI" and "Downsides of AI," with a total of five themes identified. The following section will present these findings in detail, providing a comprehensive understanding of the additional factors influencing EFL instructors' digital competencies.

As presented on Table 5, the thematic analysis of the category of "Suitability for ELT vs. Other Subjects" revealed that the instructors had mixed views on AI's suitability for different subjects, with the highest agreement (80%) being that AI would significantly impact English language teaching more than other disciplines. However, a smaller portion (40%) believed that AI's effectiveness could be comparable across various subjects, especially those involving data analysis. Among the written responses provided by the participants, Instructor B quoted as:

Instructor B: *"AI's capacity to adapt to linguistic nuances could revolutionize language education, setting it apart from other fields. Because learning a language requires interaction and this will be provided by the AI sooner or later."*

Table 5. Suitability for ELT vs. Other Subjects

Category	Theme	Description of the Theme	Count	%
Suitability for ELT	Language-specific advantages	AI is particularly well-suited for language learning due to its ability to process and analyze large linguistic data sets.	3	60
Suitability for Other Subjects	Broader application potential	AI can be equally effective in other subjects, especially those involving data analysis and pattern recognition.	2	40
Impact on ELT vs. Other Disciplines	Greater impact on ELT	AI is expected to have a more significant impact on ELT due to the unique challenges and opportunities in language acquisition.	4	80
	Equal impact across disciplines	AI will have a similar impact across different subjects, not just in ELT.	1	20

On the other hand, the participants were divided on the potential for AI to mimic human teaching elements as presented on Table 6.

Table 6. Potential/Ability of AI to Learn

Category	Theme	Description of the Theme	Count	F
AI Learning Capacity	Mimicking human interaction	AI may eventually learn to mimic complex human interactions, but significant limitations remain.	3	60%
	Limited by human elements	AI will struggle to replicate intangible human elements like relationships and culture.	2	40%
	Ethical concerns	Concerns about AI learning too much and the potential loss of human elements in teaching.	1	20%

The highest agreement (60%) was that AI might eventually learn to mimic complex human interactions, although with significant limitations. Conversely, 20% of the instructors expressed concerns about the ethical implications of AI learning too much, particularly when it comes to replacing human elements like relationships and culture. Instructor C mentioned:

Instructor C: "AI might get close to understanding and replicating certain aspects of human interaction like it might be able to simulate a conversation or provide feedback that feels somewhat personalized. But, let's be real, the emotional and cultural nuances that come with real human interactions, like empathy, inspiration, and even those little unspoken connections, they're just not something I see AI mastering anytime soon, if ever. And that's not just a technical challenge; it's a fundamental difference between machines and humans."

When it comes to the influence of AI tech companies on ELT (Table 7), a substantial 80% of the instructors expressed concern about corporate control over educational practices.

Table 7. Influences on the Development of AI for ELT

Category	Theme	Description of the Theme	Count	F
Influence of AI Tech Companies	Concerns about corporate control	Worry that tech companies' decisions could negatively influence ELT practices and educational priorities.	4	80%
	Need for educator involvement	Emphasis on the importance of involving educators in AI development to align with classroom needs.	3	60%
	Optimism about innovation	Belief that tech companies could positively innovate ELT with the right guidance.	2	40%

On the other hand, 40% were more optimistic, believing that with the right guidance, tech companies could positively innovate in the field of ELT. As one instructor remarked:

Instructor E: "... it's a bit worrisome to think that big tech companies could end up dictating how our classrooms operate, especially when their main goal is profit, not education. But honestly, if we, as educators, can find a way to collaborate with these companies, and ensure that the technology they're developing aligns with our pedagogical values and needs, then maybe we could harness that innovation in a way that genuinely enhances teaching and learning. It's all about striking that balance between caution and opportunity."

As can be seen on Table 8, the potential reduction of traditional classroom needs due to AI was seen as likely by 80% of the instructors, who felt that AI's immersive capabilities might lessen the need for classroom-based practice.

Table 8. Increasing Impact on ELT Classrooms/Approach

Category	Theme	Description of the Theme	N	F
Classroom Reduction	Decreased need for traditional classrooms	AI's ability to create immersive experiences might reduce the need for classroom-based practice.	4	80%
	Continued need for human interaction	Classroom-based learning remains essential for human interaction and cultural aspects of language learning.	3	60%
	Hybrid approach	A hybrid model that integrates AI with traditional classroom practices is preferred.	2	40%

Yet, 40% preferred a hybrid approach, blending AI with traditional methods to maintain the essential human interaction in learning. One instructor reflected as:

Instructor A: *"AI is great and all, and it's definitely going to change the way we teach, no doubt about that. But there's just something about face-to-face learning that we can't afford to lose; it's the human connection. You can't replicate the spontaneity of a classroom discussion, or the way a teacher can read the room and adjust on the fly. That's where a hybrid model comes in. Let's use AI to do what it does best like providing personalized practice or offering immersive experiences but let's keep the classroom as a space where students can interact, engage, and learn from each other and their teacher in real time."*

Regarding the benefits of AI in ELT as shown in Table 9, all instructors (f=100%) agreed that AI's ability to provide personalized learning experiences is a major advantage.

Table 9. Benefits and Downsides

Category	Theme	Description of the Theme	Count	F
Benefits of AI	Enhanced personalization	AI provides personalized learning experiences tailored to individual student needs.	5	100%
	Increased accessibility	AI makes language learning more accessible to a wider audience, including those with disabilities.	3	60%
	Efficient teacher development	AI offers new tools for teacher development, enabling continuous learning and improvement.	4	80%
Downsides of AI	Loss of human touch	Potential loss of human interaction and empathy in the learning process due to AI reliance.	3	60%
	Over-reliance on technology	Concerns about becoming too dependent on AI, potentially undermining traditional teaching methods.	2	40%

However, 40% raised concerns about an over-reliance on technology, fearing it might undermine traditional teaching methods. One instructor shared,

Instructor D: *"AI definitely makes learning more tailored, which is amazing. it's like having a personal tutor for every student, right? But we've got to be careful. If we start relying too much on AI, there's a real risk that we could lose some of the foundational aspects of teaching, like critical thinking, creativity, and even the basic human skills that come from interacting with a teacher and peers. We don't want to end up in a situation where students are technically proficient but lack the deeper understanding and social skills that come from a well-rounded education."*

In addition to quantitative findings, thematic analysis of the interview questions provided a deeper understanding of the relationship between teachers' technological competence and their perceptions for using AI in EFL in their teaching.

5. DISCUSSION

This study tried to explore the relationship between EFL instructors' digital skills and their attitudes toward incorporating AI in educational environments. Our first research question was to find out why EFL instructors use AI in their lessons. The results revealed that the participants use AI commonly to prepare teaching materials in English where as they do not prefer to use it for their administrative tasks. These findings are in line with the study conducted by Edmett, Ichaporia, Crompton and Crichton (2023). In the related research, it was also reported that EFL teachers utilize AI in terms of creating materials (%57), helping learners practice using English (%53) and creating lesson plans (%43) consecutively.

Our second research question was about exploring the main perceptions of EFL instructors regarding the integration of AI technologies into language teaching. The findings showed that the participants commonly have positive attitudes towards using AI applications and practices in their classes. Similar findings were presented in a study conducted by Merç (2015) as well. Additionally, the participants mostly agreed that AI can enhance learners' reading, speaking, writing, and listening skills. Moreover, they do not see AI as a threat to their future careers or as a negative influence on student learning. These findings are in line with the study conducted by Hazaymeh, Bouzenoun and Remache (2024). In the research, it was found out that teachers are mostly positive to use AI in their lessons and they believed that it helps learners improve their skills. On the contrary, in the study conducted by Yoon (2019), it was also found that the teachers mostly have positive attitudes towards AI, however, they do not prefer to use it in their classroom settings.

The third research question was asked to discover the relationship between EFL instructors' digital competencies and AI perceptions. The analysis of the quantitative data revealed a significant positive correlation between the two variables, indicating a moderate and meaningful relationship. Similarly, Madu and Musa (2024) also suggested that the teachers who are good at using digital tools tend to consider AI as a beneficial tool for educational purposes compared to the ones who are not good at benefiting from technology. Thus, it can be interpreted that digital competencies of the instructors affect their use of AI in EFL settings.

The fourth research question was about the correlation between instructors' digital competencies and their perceptions on use of AI in language teaching. We found that this correlation accounts for 25% of the total variability in the study. This suggested that the increase in teachers' digital competencies result in increased positive attitudes toward using AI in educational settings. In the research of Domínguez et al. (2024, p.1), it was also reported that "Regardless of educational stage, sex, age, years of experience or field of knowledge, higher teacher digital competence is associated with a more positive teacher attitude towards AI".

Finally, the last research question was about the additional factors that contribute to the digital competencies of EFL instructors. As identified through qualitative analysis, although instructors' opinions on the use of AI varied, 80% of them agreed that it would have a bigger impact on ELT than other subjects. Even so, 60% of the participants expressed their worries regarding AI's limitations in simulating complex human actions. Besides, 80% of respondents believed AI could eliminate the need for in-person instruction, while 40% preferred a hybrid model that combined AI and conventional teaching techniques. This indicates the potential of AI in effecting traditional classroom practices. Finally, while all instructors agreed that AI has the potential to provide personalized learning, they also expressed their concerns about an over reliance on technology and the potential loss of human interaction. 60% of instructors emphasized the necessity to maintain a balance between the use of AI tools and conventional teaching techniques.

6. CONCLUSION

The aim of this research was to explore the relationship between EFL instructors' digital competencies and their perceptions of using AI in educational settings. The data was collected by two different scales namely Artificial Intelligence and English Language Teaching Scale (Edmett et al., 2023) and Teachers' Digital Competencies Scale (Ergül & Taşar, 2023). After the analysis conducted to reveal the relationship between these two variables, it can be stated that there is a moderate correlation. The ones who are better in digital competencies tend to use AI more with different aims in the educational settings. It has also been revealed that the ones who have most of the digital competencies tend to consider artificial intelligence as a positive tool to enhance learning and teaching environments. Having digital competencies explains 25% of the factors affecting use of AI in EFL contexts. There are also other factors and variables that impact the utilization of AI in language teaching settings.

According to the findings of this study, EFL instructors utilize AI in their lessons mostly to prepare materials before and after the classes. Additionally, they benefit from AI to help their students practice the target language more. The integration of AI into material development assists them to create more engaging activities and tasks. This utilization underlines the importance of AI-based instructional tools and materials in enhancing the potential of language learners (Edmett et al., 2023) However, they do not prefer to benefit from it to conduct their administrative tasks mostly. When it comes to AI perceptions and practices, EFL instructors mostly agree on the fact that AI can help learners improve their reading, speaking, and writing skills consecutively. This finding is also related to the preferences of using AI to prepare language materials since EFL instructors also elaborated that they benefit from AI to create reading activities mostly. According to this relationship, it can easily be inferred that AI based materials improve students' language skills (Hazaymeh et al., 2024). Apart from these, EFL instructors do not mostly assume that AI will replace them in the near future. They believe that AI cannot act like a human teacher. They mostly have positive attitudes towards its use in language learning settings in order to create a more engaging and creative learning environment.

To conclude, the learning and teaching processes of a foreign language require lots of effort and practice. There is a quantity of titles and subtitles to be taken into consideration while teaching in an evolving world due to the development of technology and the other factors such as decreased attention spans of the students or distractions resulting from the impacts of excessive use of devices in early ages as well. Therefore, it is crucial to have certain digital competencies both for students and teachers in the educational fields (Lucas et al., 2021). For example, especially teachers should be more aware of the instructional tools, checking the reliability of the sources they get from the online platforms, choosing the most suitable digital materials for different age groups and so on. Apart from these, as among the most recent technologies, artificial intelligence should be integrated into language lessons to some extent. For instance, instructors can benefit from AI in developing materials, preparing more interactive language, assessment processes and creating engaging tasks or activities to be used in or outside of the classroom as also elaborated in the findings of this study. In this way, the learners are able to get engaged in the content and also have fun while learning, as digital natives. To be able to benefit from AI in language teaching contexts, instructors should have certain digital competencies as studied in this research.

6.1 Implications

Certain implications, both for theory and practice, in the English Language Teaching department can be asserted according to the results of the study conducted on the relationship between digital competencies and AI perceptions. Firstly, since the integration of modern technologies into language education is of quite importance, AI-based materials and applications should be used in the classrooms, especially in teaching language skills such as speaking and writing. To be able to improve more interactive instructional materials for students, new lessons such as preparing AI integrated materials and digital competencies can be implemented into the teacher training programs as well, to meet the evolving needs of the students who are mostly digital natives (Yoon, 2019). In addition to this, since the results of the study underline the fact that having digital competencies affects the use of AI to a certain degree, students should also be informed about different technological tools in order to gain more insight into their own learning at their own pace. In this way, they will be more aware of their expectations for the future in terms of personal and professional development. Lastly, among the factors affecting the use of AI in language education, only a minority of them were researched in this study. For further studies, other factors affecting AI use and perceptions of EFL instructors can also be implemented.

Moreover, the findings highlight the need for targeted professional development programs that address the specific needs of EFL instructors, particularly in relation to their level of teaching experience. While newer generation teachers may be more familiar with digital tools, more experienced instructors often face challenges in adapting to rapid technological changes due to limited prior exposure or lack of training opportunities (Bower et al., 2024). Therefore, differentiated professional development initiatives should be designed to support both novice and experienced EFL instructors in building their digital competencies and understanding the pedagogical affordances of AI tools. These programs should include hands-on workshops, mentorship models, and continuous in-service training that foster confidence and competence in integrating AI meaningfully into language instruction. Importantly, the implications discussed here are specific to EFL teacher education and should not be generalized to educators in other subject areas without further research, as the technological needs, instructional practices, and contextual realities may differ considerably.

6.2 Suggestions for Further Research

Based on the study's findings and limitations, several areas for future research are proposed. First, future research could use longitudinal designs to look into the causal relationships between digital competencies and attitudes toward AI over time, providing more information about how these factors change. Furthermore, increasing the sample size and incorporating a diverse range of educational contexts may improve the findings' generalizability and provide a more comprehensive understanding of AI integration in EFL settings. Finally, assessing the impact of various types of professional development programs designed to improve digital competencies may help identify best practices for assisting EFL instructors in incorporating AI into their teaching.

ETHICAL APPROVAL

This research (2024-YÖNP-0339) was approved by the decision number 06/25 taken in the Scientific Research and Publication Ethics Board of XXXXXX University. The research protocol rigorously ensured the confidentiality and anonymity of all participants.

INFORMED CONSENT

We confirm that written informed consent has been obtained from the participants.

REFERENCES

Abdulrahaman, M. D., Faruk, N., Oloyede, A. A., Surajudeen-Bakinde, N. T., Olawoyin, L. A., Mejabi, O. V., Imam-Fulani, Y. O., Fahm, A. O., & Azeez, A. L. (2020). Multimedia tools in the teaching and learning processes: A systematic review. *Heliyon*, *6*(11), e05312. DOI: 10.1016/j.heliyon.2020.e05312

Allman, B., Kimmons, R., Wang, W., Bao, H., Rosenberg, J. M., & Koehler, M. J. (2024). Trends and Topics in Educational Technology, 2024 Edition. *TechTrends*, *68*(3), 402–410. DOI: 10.1007/s11528-024-00950-5

Almuhanna, M. A. (2024). Teachers' perspectives of integrating AI-powered technologies in K-12 education for creating customized learning materials and resources. *Education and Information Technologies*, •••, 1–29. DOI: 10.1007/s10639-024-13257-y

Arslan, S. (2025). English-as-a-foreign language university instructors' perceptions of integrating artificial intelligence: A Turkish perspective. *System*, *131*, 103680. DOI: 10.1016/j.system.2025.103680

Attard, A., & Dingli, A. (2024). Empowering educators: Leveraging large language models to streamline content creation in education. In *ICERI2024 Proceedings* (pp. 1312-1321). IATED. https://doi.org/DOI: 10.21125/iceri.2024.0400

Baidoo-anu, D., & Owusu Ansah, L. (2023). Education in the Era of Generative Artificial Intelligence (AI): Understanding the Potential Benefits of ChatGPT in Promoting Teaching and Learning. *Journal of AI*, *7*(1), 52–62. DOI: 10.61969/jai.1337500

Basilotta-Gómez-Pablos, V., Matarranz, M., Casado-Aranda, L. A., & Otto, A. (2022). Teachers' digital competencies in higher education: A systematic literature review. *International Journal of Educational Technology in Higher Education*, *19*(1), 8. DOI: 10.1186/s41239-021-00312-8

Baskara, F. R. (2023). Ai-driven dynamics: ChatGPT transforming elt teacher-student interactions. *Lensa: Kajian Kebahasaan, Kesusastraan, dan Budaya*, 13(2), 261-275. DOI: 10.26714/lensa.13.2.2023.261-275

Benek, K. (2025). EFL learners' and teachers' perceptions of AI-powered language learning technologies: Benefits and challenges. *International Journal of Instruction*, *18*(2), 103–120. DOI: 10.29333/iji.2025.1827a

Bower, M., Torrington, J., Lai, J. W. M., Petocz, P., & Alfano, M. (2024). How should we change teaching and assessment in response to increasingly powerful generative Artificial Intelligence? Outcomes of the ChatGPT teacher survey. *Education and Information Technologies*, *29*, 15403–15439. DOI: 10.1007/s10639-023-12405-0

Çelik, F., & Baturay, M. H. (2024). Technology and innovation in shaping the future of education. *Smart Learning Environments*, *11*(1), 54. DOI: 10.1186/s40561-024-00339-0

Chen, W. H., & Liu, M. (2023). Integrating Multicultural Issues into Teaching and Learning: An English-Language Teacher's Experience with an International Baccalaureate Middle Years Program in Finland. *Educational Review*, (60), 1–49.

Chiu, T. K. F., Xia, Q., Zhou, X., Chai, C. S., & Cheng, M. (2023). Systematic literature review on opportunities, challenges, and future research recommendations of artificial intelligence in education. *Computers and Education: Artificial Intelligence*, *4*, 100118. DOI: 10.1016/j.caeai.2022.100118

Çiftçi, A. (2024). *AI Assisted Teaching: Practices and Perspectives of Instructors on Using AI Tools in ELT* (Master's thesis, Maltepe University (Turkey)).

Cohen, J. (1988). *Statistical power analysis for the behavioral sciences* (2nd ed.). Lawrence Erlbaum Associates., DOI: 10.4236/jwarp.2020.128041

Creswell, J. W., & Plano Clark, V. L. (2018). *Designing and conducting mixed methods research* (3rd ed.). Sage Publications.

David, H. (2022). Digital immigrants, digital natives and digital learners: Where are we now? *Journal for the Education of Gifted Young Scientists*, *10*(2), 159–172. DOI: 10.17478/jegys.1090172

Demir, B., & Aydin, S. (2026). The Ethics of Using Artificial Intelligence in Language Research. In Carlson, K. (Ed.), *Ethical, Legal, and Pedagogical Perspectives on AI in Education* (pp. 429–452). IGI Global Scientific Publishing., DOI: 10.4018/979-8-3373-3000-6.ch016

Demir, B., & Lüta, K. (2026). The Mediating Role of AI Literacy in the Relationship Between Technostress and Cognitive Load in Higher Education. In Demirdis, B. (Ed.), *Impacts of Artificial Intelligence on Educational Psychology and Cognitive Development* (pp. 157–182). IGI Global Scientific Publishing., DOI: 10.4018/979-8-3373-6375-2.ch007

Devasena, R. (2024). Artificial intelligence in education: An alternative to traditional learning. *Journal of English Language Teaching*, *66*(1), 13–21.

Edmett, A., Ichaporia, N., Crompton, H., & Crichton, R. (2023). *Artificial intelligence and English language teaching: Preparing for the future*. British Council., DOI: 10.57884/78EA-3C69

Erbaş, M. Z. (2023) Exploring the perspectives of EFL Teachers on the integration of Artificial Intelligence in Language Classrooms and the Perceived Impact of AI on the Future of Their Profession. In *9th International KTUDELL Conference: Language, Literature and Translation 25-26 September 2023, Trabzon, TÜRKİYE* (p. 181).

Ergül, D. Y., & Taşar, M. F. (2023). Development and validation of the teachers' digital competence scale (TDiCoS). *Journal of Learning and Teaching in Digital Age, 8*(1), 148-160. DOI: 10.53850/joltida.1204358

Fakhar, H., Lamrabet, M., Echantoufi, N., & Ajana, L. (2024). Towards a New Artificial Intelligence-based Framework for Teachers' Online Continuous Professional Development Programs: Systematic Review. *International Journal of Advanced Computer Science and Applications*, *15*(4). Advance online publication. DOI: 10.14569/IJACSA.2024.0150450

Hazaymeh, W. A., Bouzenoun, A., & Remache, A. (2024). EFL Instructors' Perspective on Using AI Applications in English as a Foreign Language Teaching and Learning. *Emerging Science Journal*, *8*, 73–87. DOI: 10.28991/ESJ-2024-SIED1-05

Jafari, F., & Keykha, A. (2024). Identifying the opportunities and challenges of artificial intelligence in higher education: A qualitative study. *Journal of Applied Research in Higher Education*, *16*(4), 1228–1245. DOI: 10.1108/JARHE-09-2023-0426

Johnson, R. B., & Onwuegbuzie, A. J. (2004). Mixed methods research: A research paradigm whose time has come. *Educational Researcher*, *33*(7), 14–26. DOI: 10.3102/0013189X033007014

Kamalov, F., Santandreu Calonge, D., & Gurrib, I. (2023). New era of Artificial Intelligence in education: Towards a sustainable multifaceted revolution. *Sustainability (Basel)*, *15*(16), 12451. DOI: 10.3390/su151612451

Karataş, F., Abedi, F. Y., Ozek Gunyel, F., Karadeniz, D., & Kuzgun, Y. (2024). Incorporating AI in foreign language education: An investigation into ChatGPT's effect on foreign language learners. *Education and Information Technologies*, *29*(15), 1–24. DOI: 10.1007/s10639-024-12574-6

Kesharwani, A. (2020). Do (how) digital natives adopt a new technology differently than digital immigrants? A longitudinal study. *Information & Management*, *57*(2), 103170. DOI: 10.1016/j.im.2019.103170

Kim, K., & Kwon, K. (2023). Exploring the AI competencies of elementary school teachers in South Korea. *Computers and Education: Artificial Intelligence*, *4*, 100137. DOI: 10.1016/j.caeai.2023.100137

Koraishi, O. (2023). Teaching English in the Age of AI: Embracing ChatGPT to Optimize EFL Materials and Assessment. [LET Journal]. *Language Education & Technology*, *3*(1), 55–72.

Krisbiantoro, B., & Ashari, I. A. (2024). Evaluating The SAMR Model For Enhancing Ict Integration In English Language Teaching At The Tertiary

Lee, J. H., Shin, D., & Noh, W. (2023). Artificial intelligence-based content generator technology for young English-as-a-foreign-language learners' reading enjoyment. *RELC Journal*, *54*(2), 508–516. DOI: 10.1177/00336882231165060

Lucas, M., Bem-Haja, P., Siddiq, F., Moreira, A., & Redecker, C. (2021). The relation between in-service teachers' digital competence and personal and contextual factors: What matters most? *Computers & Education*, *160*, 104052. DOI: 10.1016/j.compedu.2020.104052

Luckin, R., Holmes, W., Griffiths, M., & Forcier, L. B. (2016). *Intelligence Unleashed: An Argument for AI in Education.* Pearson. Retrieved from https://www.pearson.com/content/dam/one-dot-com/one-dot-com/global/Files/about-pearson/innovation/Intelligence-Unleashed-Publication.pdf

Madu, C. O., & Musa, A. (2024). Lecturers' level of awareness of artificial intelligence as correlate of their digital competence at Federal University Wukari, Nigeria. *Journal of Educational Research in Developing Areas*, *5*(1), 59–61. DOI: 10.47434/JEREDA.5.1.2024.59

Marzo, R. R. (2024). Bridging the Gap: Understanding and Fostering Intergenerational Communication in the Digital Age. In *Intergenerational Relations-Contemporary Theories, Studies and Policies*. IntechOpen. DOI: 10.5772/intechopen.1003205

Merç, A. (2015). Using technology in the classroom: A study with Turkish pre-service EFL teachers. *Turkish Online Journal of Educational Technology-TOJET*, *14*(2), 229–240. DOI: 10.17569/tojqi.41736

Mollaei, F., & Riasati, M. J. (2013). Teachers' perceptions of using technology in teaching EFL. *International Journal of Applied Linguistics and English Literature*, *2*(1), 13–22. DOI: 10.7575/ijalel.v.2n.1p.13

Muslimin, A. I., Mukminatien, N., & Ivone, F. M. (2024). Evaluating Cami AI across SAMR Stages: Students' Achievement and Perceptions in EFL https://doi.org/DOI: 10.24059/olj.v28i2.4246

Pham, N. K. L. (2025). "Are you on board?": University EFL instructors' readiness for integrating AI-powered tools in teaching. *VNU Journal of Foreign Studies*, *41*(3), 74–91. DOI: 10.63023/2525-2445/jfs.ulis.5524

Pongrac, D., Alić, M., & Cafuta, B. (2025, February). Digital Competences of Digital Natives: Measuring Skills in the Modern Technology Environment. In *Informatics* (Vol. 12, No. 1, p. 23). MDPI. https://doi.org/DOI: 10.3390/informatics12010023

Prensky, M. (2001). Digital natives, digital immigrants part 1. *On the Horizon*, *9*(5), 1–6. DOI: 10.1108/10748120110424816

Prensky, M. (2001). Digital natives, digital immigrants part 2: Do they really think differently? *On the Horizon*, *9*(6), 1–6. DOI: 10.1108/10748120110424843

Qi, C. (2019). A double-edged sword? Exploring the impact of students' academic usage of mobile devices on technostress and academic performance. *Behaviour & Information Technology*, *38*(12), 1337–1354. DOI: 10.1080/0144929X.2019.1585476

Rahman, M. M., & Watanobe, Y. (2023). Exploring the challenges of AI in programming education: The impact of ChatGPT on critical thinking and problem-solving skills. *Computers & Education*, *192*, 104687. DOI: 10.1016/j.compedu.2023.104687

Samala, A. D., Rawas, S., Criollo-C, S., Bojic, L., Prasetya, F., Ranuharja, F., & Marta, R. (2024). Emerging technologies for global education: A comprehensive exploration of trends, innovations, challenges, and future horizons. *SN Computer Science*, *5*(8), 1–24. DOI: 10.1007/s42979-024-03538-1

Sharma, S., Krishnamaraju, J. M. R., & Divakaran, P. (2024). Impact of artificial intelligence in English language teaching. *Migration Letters : An International Journal of Migration Studies*, *21*(S4), 1606–1612.

Taopan, L. L., Drajati, N. A., & Sumardi, S. (2020). TPACK Framework: Challenges and Opportunities in EFL classrooms. *Research and Innovation in Language Learning*, *3*(1), 1–22. DOI: 10.33603/rill.v3i1.2763

Tashakkori, A., & Teddlie, C. (2020). *Foundations of mixed methods research: Integrating quantitative and qualitative approaches in the social and behavioral sciences* (2nd ed.). Sage Publications., DOI: 10.4135/9781483348858.n9

Uygun, D., Aktaş, I., Duygulu, İ., & Köseer, N. (2024). Exploring teachers' artificial intelligence awareness. *Advances in Mobile Learning Educational Research*, *4*(2), 1093–1104. DOI: 10.25082/AMLER.2024.02.004

Willermark, S., Högberg, K., & Nilsson, P. (2023). Exploring technostress in disruptive teaching practices. *International Journal of Workplace Health Management*, *16*(4), 328–343. DOI: 10.1108/IJWHM-10-2022-0161

Yoon, S. Y. (2019). Student Readiness for AI Instruction: Perspectives on AI in University EFL Classrooms. *Multimedia-Assisted Language Learning*, *22*(4). Advance online publication. DOI: 10.15702/mall.2019.22.4.134

Zawacki-Richter, O., Marín, V. I., Bond, M., & Gouverneur, F. (2019). Systematic review of research on artificial intelligence applications in higher education – where are the educators? *International Journal of Educational Technology in Higher Education*, *16*(1), 39. DOI: 10.1186/s41239-019-0171-0

Zhang, Y., & Dong, C. (2024). Exploring the Digital Transformation of Generative AI-Assisted Foreign Language Education: A Socio-Technical Systems Perspective Based on Mixed-Methods. *Systems*, *12*(11), 462. DOI: 10.3390/systems12110462

Chapter 6
Examining the Impact of Human–Machine Collaboration in English–Arabic Translation

Mayada Nageeb Al-Maktary
https://orcid.org/0000-0002-5193-778X
Taiz University, Yemen

Marya Adel Al-Mareri
https://orcid.org/0009-0007-9022-1681
Al-Saeed University, Yemen

Hamas Samer Al-Qaisi
https://orcid.org/0009-0009-5121-7975
Al-Saeed University, Yemen

Somiaa Basheer Al-Kamel
https://orcid.org/0009-0002-8044-8093
Al-Saeed University, Yemen

ABSTRACT

The study investigated the impact of human-machine collaboration (HMC) in English-Arabic translation, examining both its benefits and challenges. A mixed-methods research design was employed, incorporating both quantitative and qualitative techniques. Sixty-four participants were involved, with four excluded due to a lack of experience with machine translation systems. Data was collected using a semi-structured questionnaire via the Google Forms platform. The findings indicated that HMC offers three major benefits: enhancing expertise in HMC, providing system

DOI: 10.4018/979-8-3373-4521-5.ch006

feedback and optimizing job satisfaction. Despite these benefits, the key accuracy challenges were primarily linked to fundamental linguistic differences, including grammatical, lexical, and contextual variations. Culture and technical differences also posed significant difficulties for collaboration in translation and post-editing processes.

1. INTRODUCTION

1.1 Background to the Study

Translation is crucial in our interconnected world. It is not merely about converting text from one language to another; it involves a multifaceted understanding of the complexities of language context and culture. For example, Arabic morphology is characterised by a root-and-pattern system, where words are formed by inserting vowels into a consonantal root. These rich inflectional and derivational forms in Arabic can create challenges in finding direct equivalents in English, resulting in potential loss of meaning. In addition, the phenomenon of diglossia in Arabic—where two dialects coexist: Modern Standard Arabic (MSA) and various colloquial forms—further complicates translation efforts. MSA is used in formal contexts, while colloquial Arabic varies greatly across regions. Cultural specificity also plays a critical role in translation, as language is deeply embedded in cultural contexts. For example, Arabic is rich in idiomatic expressions, proverbs, and references that may not have direct equivalents in English. These complexities corroborate the study of Al-khresheh and Almaaytah (2018), which said that since Arabic and English are unrelated languages, their differing linguistic structures can make translation work somewhat difficult at times.

The disparities between Arabic and English bring attention to the importance of the skills of human translators (HTs) in translation. HTs possess valuable skills, including linguistic proficiency, cultural awareness, and adaptability. However, they also encounter numerous challenges that can affect their work and the quality of the translations produced. They, for example, must explore ongoing linguistic and cultural changes that are constantly evolving in today's globalised world. They may also encounter texts outside their subject matter expertise, necessitating additional research. In addition, time constraints often force translators to sacrifice quality in favour of speed. The demands of the labour market further complicate their tasks, as professionals are required to work across various fields and adapt to the needs of different languages and societies. While these challenges highlight the inherent difficulties HTs face, a new era is dawning. This shift is largely driven by what's commonly known as artificial intelligence (AI) or computer intelligence (Cai et al., 2021)

Within the AI framework, machine translation (MT) serves a crucial role in developing automated translations. It showcases how AI, particularly in its narrow form, can be applied to complex linguistic, domain-specific, and cultural tasks. It is characterised by speed and the ability to process huge amounts of data. AI programmes are capable of producing translations that appear as though they were written by a native speaker, often drawing on vast datasets of human-translated text to learn natural phrasing and grammar. In spite of the machine's ability to perform translations, several studies (Al-Maktary et al., 2025; Alkhatib & Shaalan, 2018; Lihua, 2022; Nagi, 2023; Tahseen & Hussein, 2024; Wang, 2023) have demonstrated AI's limitations in accurately conveying complex meanings, cultural references, and linguistic and technical challenges. These shortcomings often result in translations that lack the depth and context needed for effective communication, highlighting the need for continual improvement in MT technologies.

Despite the flaws of HTs and MT, collaboration can lead to positive outcomes that address their challenges. This collaboration between HTs and MT systems has become increasingly significant in enhancing translation quality and efficiency (Adiel et al., 2023; Aragonés Lumeras & Way, 2017; ElBeheri, 2019; Muftah, 2022; Zhang et al., 2023). It reshapes the way HTs work and how content is produced from the source language into the target language. It represents a hybrid approach that utilises the strengths of both human expertise and technological efficiency. Regardless of the growing interest in human-machine interactions, there remains a significant gap in understanding the benefits and complexities of their collaboration. Therefore, the main objective of this study is to explore the impact of human-machine collaboration (HMC) in English-Arabic translation by addressing its benefits and challenges.

1.2 Research Questions

The primary aim of this chapter, stated earlier, is reached by exploring the following research questions:

1. What are the benefits that arise from the collaboration between HTs and MT systems in English-Arabic translation?
2. What are the challenges that arise from the collaboration between HTs and MT systems in English-Arabic translation?

2. LITERATURE REVIEW

This section summarises previous studies that have explored the challenges associated with MT and the strengths of human translation. It also discusses collaboration models between the two. Then, it identifies the research gap that the present study aims to address.

2.1 Machine Translation Challenges

Machine Translation (MT) is the process of using computer software to automatically convert text or speech from one language to another without human intervention. This technology relies on algorithms, linguistic rules, and large datasets to provide translations. Popular examples include Google Translate and DeepL. However, the effectiveness of MT is frequently hindered by its inability to capture the intricate cultural and linguistic subtleties inherent in human communication. These limitations reveal that MT frequently lacks the quality necessary for effective translation outcomes. Tahseen and Hussein (2024) analysed the translation of English literary texts into Arabic from a cultural perspective and identified the errors made by MT tools, emphasising the challenges faced by HTs when relying on these technologies. The method employed included the application of Newmark's translation model and Harris's linguistic model to assess the effectiveness of MTs in capturing the rhetorical impact of literary works. The findings revealed that MT programmes, such as Google Translate, Reverso Translation, and Bing Microsoft Translation produce poor quality translations that often lack meaning and clarity, highlighting the limitations of these tools in handling literary texts. The study recommended that it is necessary to prioritise HT over MT for literary works, as HTs can better understand and convey the nuances and rhetorical devices inherent in the original texts.

Linguistically, Alkhatib and Shaalan (2018) emphasised the key challenges faced in translating Arabic into other languages, particularly English, through MT. The method involved analysing the linguistic complexities of the Arabic language, including lexical, syntactic, and semantic issues that arise during translation. The findings indicated that Arabic's rich morphology and the presence of dialectal variations significantly complicate the translation process. For instance, the lack of resources for dialectal Arabic compared to Modern Standard Arabic presents a notable gap in effective MT systems. Alkhatib and Shaalan's study suggested that there is a need to enhance the development of resources and tools for dialectal Arabic, as well as to improve word sense disambiguation techniques to better handle the ambiguities inherent in the Arabic language.

In addition, Nagi (2023) conducted a study on an error analysis and evaluated the quality of neural machine translation (NMT). This study focused on how

Google Translate handles relative clauses in both Arabic and English. To achieve this goal, two test suites were developed: one consisting of 108 English sentences translated into Arabic, and the other comprising 72 Arabic sentences translated into English. The method involved error annotation performed by six professional annotators, who categorised the errors into accuracy and fluency errors based on the multidimensional quality metrics (MQM). Additionally, a manual evaluation was conducted alongside an automatic evaluation using the Bilingual Evaluation Understudy (BLEU) score on the Tilde Me platform. The findings revealed that fluency errors were more prevalent than accuracy errors, and the quality of MT from English to Arabic was notably lower compared to the reverse direction. The study concluded that there remains a significant gap between MT and professional HT, indicating a need for further improvements in NMT systems to enhance their performance in translating relative clauses.

Moghe et al. (2024) also introduced several accuracy challenges related to MT evaluation, particularly through the use of the Accuracy Challenge Evaluation Set (ACES). The study focused on 68 different translation accuracy errors, which ranged from simple word or character alterations to more complex issues, involving discourse and real-world knowledge. This diversity makes it challenging for metrics to consistently evaluate translation quality across various types of errors. The study concluded with recommendations for building better MT metrics.

2.2 Human Translation Strengths

HTs are specialists in converting texts or speech from one language to another. They rely on their linguistic skills and general cultural knowledge to understand deeper meanings and cultural symbols. As for the MT, it is a system that relies on AI and advanced algorithms to automatically convert texts between languages. However, some studies compared human and machine performance and showed the strengths of HTs. For example, Hasibuan (2020) determined some of the differences between HT and MT. The data sources for this article come from several references, books, journals, and articles related to the title of the discussion. The research found that HT is more effective and easier to understand when compared to MT which can only translate literal sentences or words without comprehending the intent and purpose of their meaning in the intended target language. The study focused on one aspect of both MT and HT. This proves the need to study the impact of cooperation between MT and HT in all respects.

Moreover, Ahrenberg's (2017) small case study conducted a close comparison of HT and MT issued from a state-of- the-art system using the same source text. The data collected from the source text (an opinion article published by the newspaper *Financial Times* entitled "Why I left my liberal London tribe". The article highlighted that the HT exhibited procedures beyond the capabilities of the MT system, emphasising the importance of considering translation procedures to understand the disparities between human and machine translation more accurately. Similarly, Alowedi and Al-Ahdal (2023) investigated the distinctions between MT and HT of Arabic poems into English. Two Arabic poems were used, namely: "Nothing of Note", and "One Day". The findings showed that HT is superior for poetry due to its ability to accurately capture cultural context, nuances, and lyrical elements, while MT often overlooks socio-cultural context, figurative language, historical references, and genre, usually producing a literal translation. Nevertheless, the study does not mention any collaboration between HTs and MT systems in the process of translating the Arabic poems into English.

Al-Maktary et al.'s (2025) study examined the translation effectiveness of HTs versus AI (such as ChatGPT) on 25 English legal terms within meaningful sentences. Analysing the outputs of 12 female translators and AI, the findings revealed that the latter generated correct, partially correct, and incorrect translations but struggled with contextually complex terms, often resulting in literal interpretations. In contrast, HTs produced correct, partially correct, incorrect translations and blank responses. Unlike MT, by leaving a space blank, HTs acknowledge the limitations of their understanding, demonstrating sensitivity to context and the importance of accuracy. This ability to recognise limitations is a key aspect of human creativity and critical thinking in translation.

2.3 Collaboration Models

Many studies, such as Wang (2023) and Al-Maktary et al. (2025), call for collaboration between humans and machines to achieve better outcomes. Interestingly, HMC integrates human cognitive capabilities with advanced machine learning algorithms. This partnership optimises efficiency, fosters innovation, and improves outcomes across diverse sectors. Studies also suggest that this cooperation enhances translation outcomes. For example, Alkodimi et al. (2024) studied the impact of AI translation tools on the translation and back translation of literary texts. 80 English-major students at Imam Mohammed Ibn Saud Islamic University in Saudi Arabia were randomly assigned into two experimental groups. Findings showed that students using AI tools produced better translations and back translations than those using traditional methods, with slightly better performance in back translation. Nevertheless, the study did not address the potential benefits and challenges of integrating human intuition with machine efficiency.

Remarkably, collaboration between HTs and MT systems is essential for enhancing translation accuracy and fluency. This partnership combines the efficiency of automated processes with the nuanced understanding that only human language experts can provide. Vieira (2019) analysed the evolutionary process of human post-editing of MT output over the years. A review of previous research was conducted, focusing on emerging issues and future directions for MT use in professional translation. The maturation of post-editing as a practice and service was highlighted, reflecting an encompassing understanding of post-editing tasks that reflect MT's changing role. The findings showed that post-editing significantly enhances translating productivity and target-text quality compared to translation performed from scratch. Furthermore, the evolution of post-editing from a basic step in MT development to a professional service with its own international standard was also highlighted, reflecting a shift towards more integrated and human-centred translation environments.

Thus, while there have been studies exploring the integration of both approaches, this review identifies a significant gap in research on the collaboration between HTs and MT technologies. Moreover, there is still a lack of research that examines the potential benefits and challenges of integrating human intuition with machine efficiency. Addressing this gap could lead to advancements in the translation field, benefiting professionals and everyday users alike.

3. METHODOLOGY

This section outlines the research methodology employed in this study. It begins by describing the population of interest and the approach used to select participants. Next, it details a single data gathering instrument: a questionnaire developed on the Google Forms platform, designed to gather both quantitative and qualitative data. Then, it discusses the data analysis instruments. Together, these methodological elements provide a robust and rigorous framework for addressing the research questions and achieving the stated objectives of the study.

3.1 Population and Sampling

The study population consisted of two key groups: professional translators and language learners proficient in both English and Arabic. It involved 60 participants after excluding four who were inexperienced with MT. The selected participants were specifically chosen for their familiarity with MT technologies, ensuring relevant insights. Demographically, the majority of participants (65%) fall into the 22-35 age group, followed by the 36-46 age group (26.7%). The sample also included smaller proportions of an older age group. In terms of gender, the sample is predominantly female, with 56.7% of participants being women and 43.3% being men. The educational background of the participants is diverse, with the largest group (46.7%) holding bachelor's degrees, followed by those with doctoral degrees (36.7%), and master's degrees (11.7%). The sample also included some university students and other educational levels, but in smaller percentages. Regarding translation experience, the majority of participants (45%) have an intermediate level, followed by those with advanced (20%) and beginner (20%) levels, while expert-level participants comprise 15% of the sample. In terms of preferred translation domains, the scientific field is the most common, with 33.3% of participants indicating this preference, followed by literary translation (21.7%) and religious translation (13.3%). The sample also includes participants with other translation specialisations, but in smaller proportions.

Participants were actively encouraged to engage with the study through the widespread promotion of the Google Forms questionnaire link. This included sharing posts, stories, and WhatsApp messages across various channels, extending an open invitation to their followers and contacts to take part in the survey.

3.2 Data Gathering Instrument

The data gathering instrument used in the present research was a questionnaire via Google Form platform. This questionnaire is semi-structured, comprising a combination of closed ended (multiple-choice) and open ended questions. Within the framework of closed ended questions, two different question formats were employed: standard single response questions, which require participants to select a single answer, and multiple response questions, which allow participants to provide more than one response. This variety of question types complements the research's exploratory, mixed method design. This approach allows certain aspects of the research to be quantified and also creates the opportunity to obtain more detailed, qualitative insights from the respondents.

The questionnaire begins with a welcome message that invites participants to take part in a translation research study. This message states that the purpose is to gather information about the participants' experiences, opinions, and projections related to translation, emphasising the importance of the participants' contribution to the research goals. Crucially, it highlights that participation is anonymous and voluntary, and ensures confidentiality. The estimated time for the questionnaire is approximately 15-20 minutes to complete. Participants are encouraged to reach out to the research team with any questions or concerns and are thanked in advance for their time and insights. Finally, participants are asked to proceed to the translation task and submit their responses.

The questionnaire is composed of three main sections:

- Section 1 (Demographic Information) collects data about the participants, including their age, gender, educational level (bachelor, master, PhD, or other), translation experience level (beginner, intermediate, advanced, or expert), preferred translation domains (religious, scientific, literary, or other), whether they have collaborated with MT systems, the types of collaboration they have experienced (post-editing, pre-editing, augmented translation, or other), and their level of experience with MT (beginner, intermediate, advanced, or expert). The purpose of including such elements in this section is to obtain an understanding of the participants' profiles and how these factors may influence the impact of collaboration between HTs and MT systems for the English-Arabic language pair.

- Section 2 (Benefits of HMC) addresses the first research question, "What are the specific benefits that arise from the collaboration between HTs and MT systems in English-Arabic translation?". This section consists of nine questions, which include both multiple-choice and open-ended questions.
- Section 3 (Challenges of HMC) addresses the second research question, "What are the specific challenges that arise from the collaboration between HTs and MT systems in English-Arabic translation?" The structure of this section is similar to the second section, with a mix of closed ended and open ended questions.

It is worth mentioning that the questionnaire was validated through a two phase review by national and international experts, ensuring strong content validity for English-Arabic translation constructs. Then, a pilot study with five participants was conducted to identify potential issues with the questionnaire's length and structure, prompting adjustments to improve its reliability before broader distribution.

3.3 Data Analysis Instruments

The present exploratory research employed two main data analysis instruments to analyse the collected data:

3.3.1 Statistical Data for Quantitative Analysis

As the submission of responses started, the data was monitored in real time, using the automatically generated statistical data and charts provided by the Google platform to quantitatively analyse the insights collected from the participants.

3.3.2 Thematic Analysis for Qualitative Data

The qualitative data was analysed using a thematic approach. This involved coding the transcripts and responses to identify recurring themes, patterns, and insights related to the impact of HMC in English-Arabic translation. The combination of quantitative and qualitative analyses provided a holistic understanding of the research findings, allowing the researchers to derive comprehensive, well-rounded insights from the data.

4. DATA ANALYSIS AND DISCUSSION

This section aims to explore the impact of HMC in English-Arabic translation. To set up the analysis of the current research data and address the research questions, the final three questions in the demographic section of the questionnaire were used to determine whether participants had prior experience using MT.

Findings showed that the majority of participants (93.8%) have experience working with MT, while only 6.2% do not have this experience, and they were therefore excluded from the present consideration. The high level of collaboration with MT systems suggested that translators are increasingly integrating these technologies into their workflows. The prevalence of augmented translation, where MT is used as a reference tool, indicates that translators are leveraging the capabilities of MT to enhance their productivity and efficiency. The sizeable proportion of pre-editing and post-editing activities also showed that translators are actively working to optimise MT output and improve its quality. This suggested a willingness to adapt their practices to take advantage of the benefits that MT can offer, while maintaining a high level of supervision and control over the translation process.

The relatively low percentage of advanced and expert-level users (26.7%, 5%, respectively) is not surprising, as the adoption and mastery of MT technology is still relatively new in the translation field. However, the significant presence of intermediate (41.8%) and beginner (26.7%) users suggests that there is a growing interest and uptake of MT, which may lead to a gradual increase in expertise over time as translators become more familiar with the technology. Overall, the sample indicates that MT is becoming an increasingly integral part of the translation workflow, with translators actively exploring and utilising its capabilities to enhance their work. This trend reflects the broader shift towards the integration of AI-based tools in the translation process. Thus, this study attempts to explore the impact of HMC in English-Arabic translation by addressing the following: the benefits and challenges of HMC in translation.

According to the questionnaire's responses, the present analysis falls under the category of single and multiple-response data analysis. Some of the questions utilise a multiple-response format, which allows participants to provide more than one answer, while other questions use a single-response format. The key characteristics that define multiple-response question classification are:

1. Deals with survey questions that allow respondents to select more than one answer. The goal is to understand the relative preferences for each option compared to the others.
2. Relative analysis, focusing on the individual percentage for each option rather than the total sum of percentages, which is expected to exceed 100% in such cases.
3. Exploratory analysis, aiming to discover the comparative popularity or selection frequency of the various options provided, without any prior hypotheses. The insights emerge directly from the data patterns.

Understanding this analytical approach sets the stage for deriving meaningful insights from the survey results, whether the data is collected through single response or multiple response questions.

4.1 Benefits of HMC in Translation

This section highlights the responses discussed in the second part of the questionnaire regarding the specific benefits that arise when HTs work with MT systems during English-Arabic translation. It aims to address the first research question:

1. What are the specific benefits that arise from the collaboration between HTs and MT systems in English-Arabic translation?

This section illustrates the various benefits that arise from the collaboration between HTs and MT technologies:

Figure 1. Complementary Capabilities in HMC

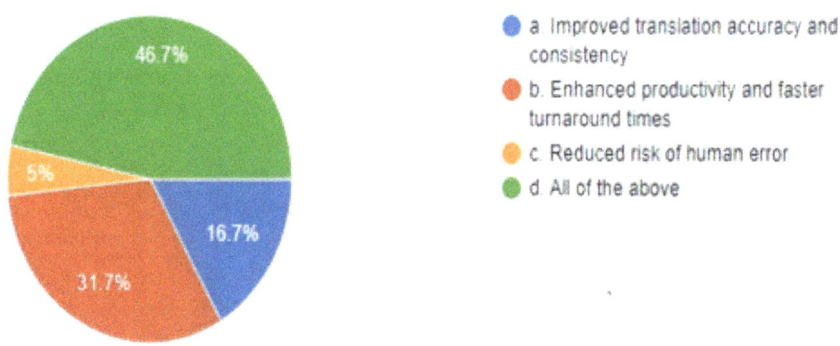

Figure 2. Translator Value to MT

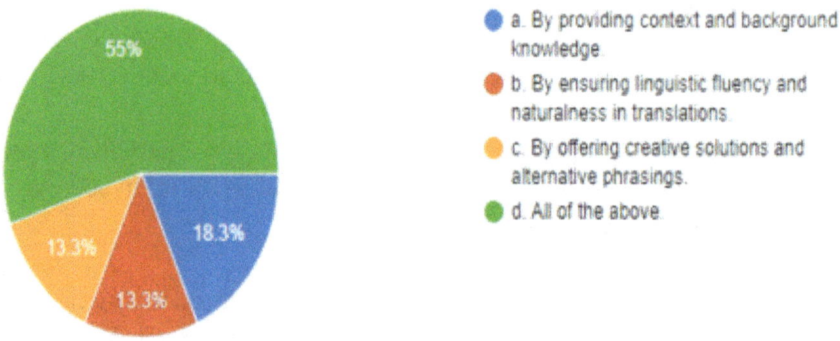

Figure 3. Machine Value to HT

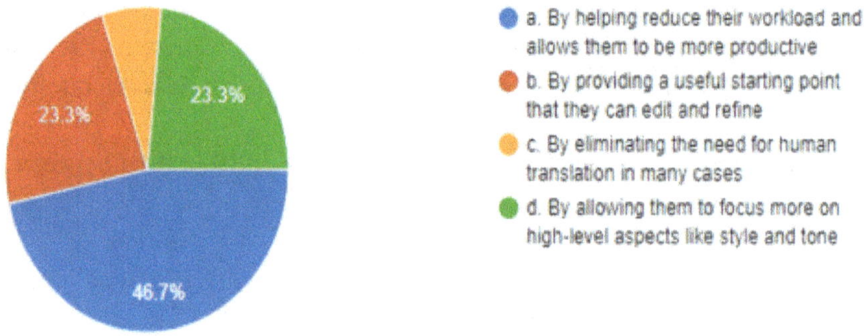

Figure 4. Increasing Translator Job Satisfaction

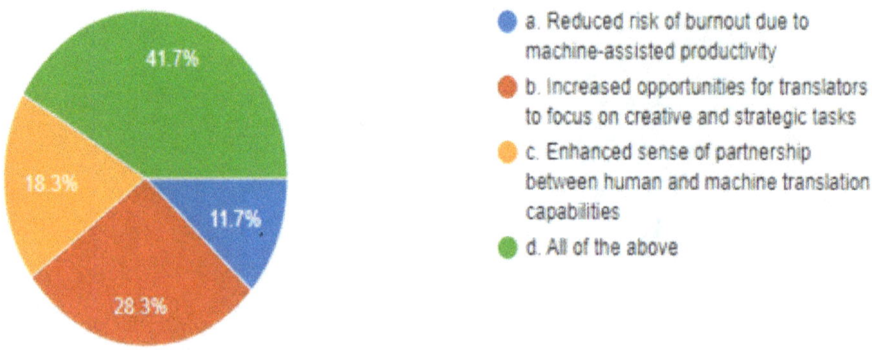

After investigating the four figures that illustrate the various aspects of collaboration between humans and machines in translation, the next step involves reviewing and discussing these results to bring attention to the benefits of this collaboration. This collaboration between HTs and MT systems offers several key benefits:

4.1.1 Enhancing Expertise in HMC

In terms of subject matter expertise, the most beneficial aspect of HMC is that both humans and machines contribute valuable and complementary forms of knowledge, as reported by 46.7% of participants (shown in Figure 1). This shared agreement on "all of the above" demonstrates a deep understanding of the interconnected benefits, such as improved translation accuracy, consistency, enhanced productivity, and reduced risk of human error. HTs are invaluable for improving the accuracy of MT outputs in various ways. First, HTs correct various errors in the machine-generated translations, identifying grammatical mistakes, mistranslated idioms, and inaccurate word choices. In addition, the cultural criterion is a crucial component of accuracy and represents a significant benefit of collaborative translation. HTs' grasp of cultural references and idiomatic expressions allows for more accurate alignment and consistent interpretation of nuanced elements in translation. Cultural knowledge enables HTs to more accurately convey intended connotations and implications, thereby minimising potential misunderstandings for the target audience. These findings have been highlighted by Sammer et al. (2006) whose paper emphasised the importance of human-computer collaboration in reducing ambiguity in MT, thereby enhancing the accuracy of translations in cross-domain applications.

Consistency is widely viewed as a crucial element in ensuring high-quality translations that effectively align the translated text with the original source material. It critically includes maintaining terminology, style, tone, and structural cohesion throughout the translation process. For example, machines can automatically suggest preferred terminology based on previously established term databases or machine learning models. Meanwhile, HTs can help maintain terminology consistency by reviewing translations and ensuring key terms are used correctly throughout a document. This collaborative approach allows the strengths of both MT and HTs systems to be utilised for optimal terminology control. This result aligns with a finding of Adiel et al.'s study (2023), which stated that while MT has its advantages in maintaining consistency in terminology, it does not replace the need for HTs. Instead, MT can serve as a tool that aids HTs by providing a first draft that can be refined, thus improving overall accuracy when combined with human expertise.

Collaboration between HTs and MT enhances productivity and enables faster turnaround times. It also reduces the risk of human error, as MT catches typos, inconsistencies, and other mistakes that a HTs may overlook, especially when working under tight deadlines. Referring to the data presented in Figure 3, the implementation of MT technology has led to a 46.7% reduction in overall workload, enabling translators to be more productive. This is because the machine can handle the initial translation of the text, significantly reducing the amount of work the HTs need to do, according to 23.3% of participants. This frees up the HTs' time and efforts. In addition, 23.3% of participants believe MT enables HTs to focus more on higher order aspects of translation, such as ensuring appropriate style, tone, and nuance, while relying on the machine to provide the basic translation. Alkodimi et al.'s (2024) study confirms the benefits of this collaboration, showing that students using AI tools produced better translations and back translations than those using traditional methods, with slightly better performance in back translation. According to Muftah (2022), the relationship between HTs and MTs is mutually beneficial, suggesting that while MT cannot not fully automate the translation process, it can enhance the work of HTs. Thus, by combining human expertise in language details and cultural context with machine speed and consistency, collaborative translation approaches can optimise accuracy and productivity (ElBeheri, 2019).

Nevertheless, the relatively low percentage (5%) highlighting the reduced risk of human error indicates that most participants may not view this as a significant advantage of collaboration. This could reflect the perception that human error, while important, is not the primary concern in their specific context. Alternatively, it may indicate confidence in human capabilities or an acknowledgment that errors can still occur despite machine assistance. A minority of participants (16.7%) believe that the primary benefit of HMC lies in enhancing translation accuracy and consistency. While this is a significant improvement, it indicates that many participants may not perceive this as the most critical advantage. This could reflect the belief that other aspects of collaboration are more impactful or that the translation process might already be sufficiently accurate without significant machine assistance.

4.1.2 Providing system feedback

A collaborative translation approach that combines HTs and MT systems is particularly advantageous when it comes to system feedback. Figure 2 revealed that the majority of participants (55%) indicated that the deep contextual knowledge of HTs play a vital role in collaborating with MT systems during the post-editing process, adding significant value despite the technological challenges. HTs' contextual knowledge derived from their training, experiences, and background understanding allows them to make more informed decisions about appropriate terminology, tone, and nuance that machines struggle to capture. HTs go beyond correcting errors by providing creative solutions and alternative phrasings that more accurately convey intended meaning and style. Moreover, HTs also bring their training and linguistic expertise to enhance the naturalness and fluency of translations by refining machine-generated output. The benefit of translator training is reflected in the findings of Guerberof-Arenas et al.'s study (2024), revealing that students became more open to creative shifts and gained confidence in handling MT issues. They also developed a better understanding of MT mechanics and error types, despite an increase in post-editing errors. Additionally, students demonstrated greater creativity in HT compared to post-editing (PE), with fewer errors in PE, particularly at the beginning of training. Numerous studies also emphasise the importance of the HT's intervention in automated translation in order to refine the translated text, such as the work of Adiel et al. (2023), Al-khresheh and Almaaytah (2018), El Yaâgoubi and El Biadi (2021), and ElBeheri (2019). For example, ElBeheri (2019) recommends that to simplify the analysis process and achieve natural translation, MT users can pre-edit their ST before submitting it to MT. This reduces post-editing workload and makes the ST easier to understand by MT.

HTs can utilise adaptive translation models that assimilate new information and incorporate updates, thereby avoiding the repetition of errors. Denkowski (2015) focused on enhancing the efficiency of HTs by developing MT systems specifically designed for post-editing tasks. The findings showed that error repetition could be effectively avoided by developing adaptive MT systems that take human feedback into account during post-editing. These systems update translation rules and feature scores after each sentence is edited, allowing for real-time improvements. They not only produce translations that require less mechanical effort to correct but are also preferred by HTs. In addition, HTs can also provide critical feedback to MT system developers. HTs can highlight recurrent problems and suggest terminology or stylistic improvements that can help the systems learn and enhance their performance over time.

4.1.3 Optimising job satisfaction

Beyond accuracy and consistency benefits, the collaborative translation model that combines HTs and MT systems offers several key advantages in terms of translators' job satisfaction and professional development. Figure 4 shows that respondents emphasised several key benefits, including a 41.7% reduction in professional burnout, an enhancement of creative output, and a greater appreciation for the collaborative partnership between human translators and technological resources. This acknowledgment of benefits indicates that a substantial proportion of translators perceive the advantages of collaborating with technology, particularly AI tools. It also indicates that collaboration allows translators to maintain their well-being and enthusiasm for their work. It enhances job satisfaction and provides more opportunities for professional growth. These findings confirm what Aragonés Lumeras and Way (2017) stated; that while many translators fear the impact of MT on their livelihoods, MT engines can improve productivity and ensure consistent output translations. However, the low percentage of those reporting reduced burnout (11.7%) indicates that many translators still feel overwhelmed, which could be due to high workloads or inadequate support from technology. The moderate belief in increased creativity (28.3%) suggests that while some translators find that collaboration enhances their creative processes, many do not experience this benefit, highlighting potential barriers in how tools are integrated into their workflows. The low appreciation of the partnership (18.3%) indicates that translators may still view technology as a tool rather than a collaborative partner. Therefore, to enhance job satisfaction, it is crucial for organisations to focus on integrating technology in ways that genuinely support translators, reduce stress, and foster a collaborative environment.

The varying percentages highlight the diversity of perspectives among participants regarding the benefits of HMC. This diversity suggests that different areas may prioritise different outcomes based on their unique challenges and contexts. The low percentage for some benefits could indicate a gap between expectations and reality. For example, if participants do not perceive a significant reduction in errors, this might lead to scepticism about the effectiveness of machine assistance, potentially hindering further adoption. Conversely, the high percentage for "all of the above" underscores the importance of a holistic approach to understanding the benefits of HMC. The emphasis on certain benefits aligns with current trends in many sectors where, for example, speed and efficiency are prioritised. However, it raises questions about whether this focus might overlook other important factors, such as quality and employee well-being. Organisations should consider multiple dimensions of impact rather than focusing solely on isolated benefits.

4.2 Challenges of HMC in translation

This section focuses on the responses discussed in the third part of the questionnaire regarding the specific challenges that arise when HTs work with MT systems for English-Arabic translation. It aims to address the second research question:

1. What are the specific challenges that arise from the collaboration between HTs and MT systems in English-Arabic translation?

The following illustrative figures highlight the diverse challenges that result from the collaboration between HTs and MT technologies.

Figure 5. Accuracy challenges of HMC

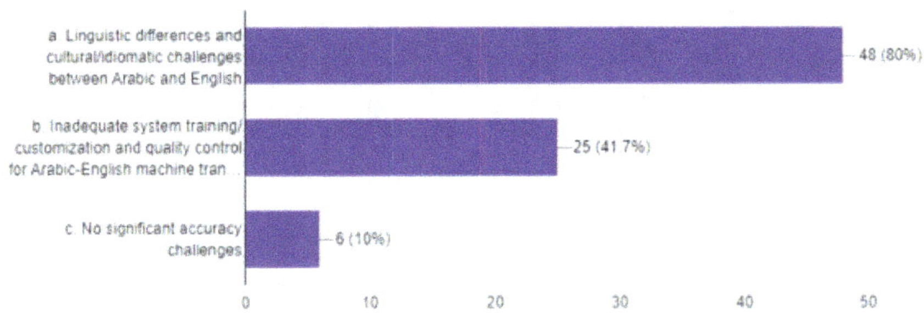

Figure 6. Structural challenges of HMT collaboration

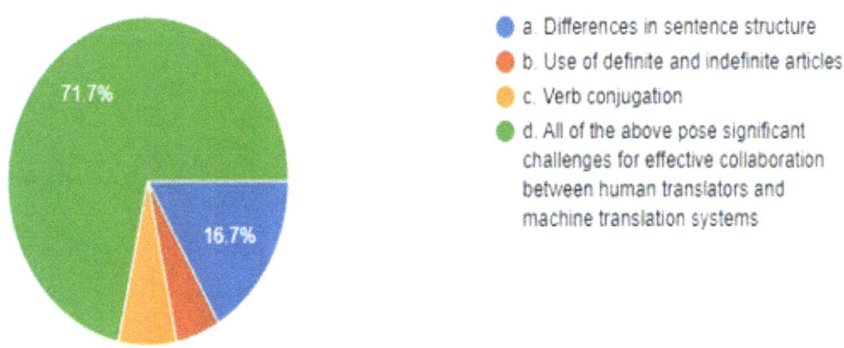

Figure 7. Contextual challenges of HMC

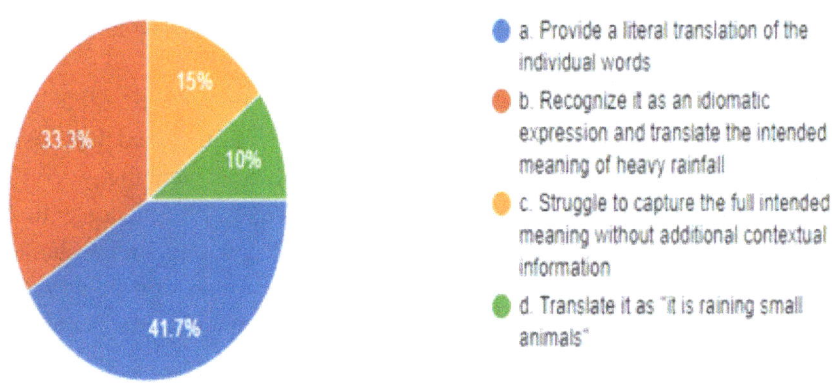

Figure 8. Lexical challenges of HMC

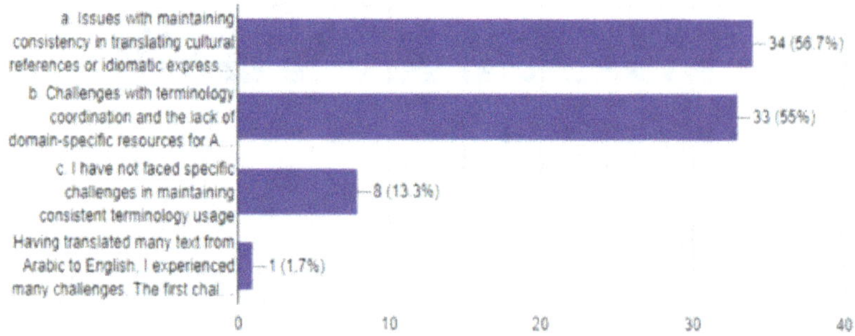

Figure 9. Technical challenges of HMT collaboration

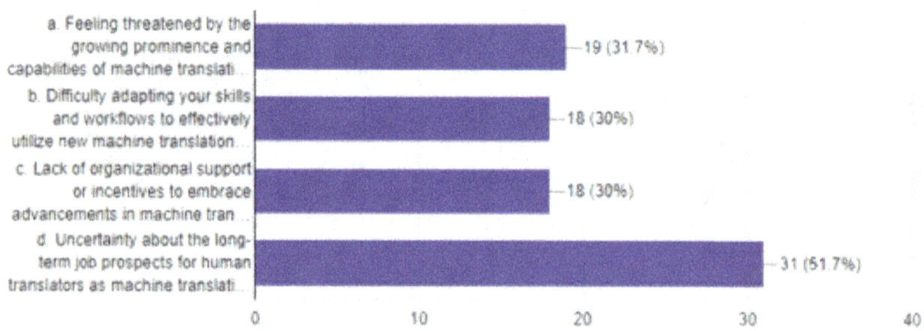

After examining the five figures that highlight the challenges of HMC in translation, the next step is to break down the data presented and discuss its implications to emphasise the difficulties inherent in this partnership:

In HMC in English-Arabic translation, the findings revealed that the accuracy challenge during the translation and post-editing stages is multifaceted. It necessitates precise, unambiguous language to accurately convey intended meaning. According to Figure 5, it includes 80% of linguistic challenges (such as structural, contextual, and lexical challenges) and cultural challenges, as well as 41.7% of technical challenges. However, only 10% of respondents indicated that there are no significant accuracy challenges. The following section outlines the different types of accuracy challenges.

4.2.1 Linguistic challenges of HMC in translation

Collaboration between humans and machines in translation shows linguistic challenges, including structural, contextual, and lexical challenges.

4.2.1.1 Structural challenges of HMC

Structurally, the survey revealed grammatical differences between English and Arabic as a challenging aspect for HMC in translation. For example, Figure 6 indicates that 71.7% identified sentence structure, article use, and verb conjugation as major challenges. This demonstrates the complexity involved in developing effective MT systems capable of handling the details of language pairs with significant structural and grammatical differences. This result confirms a finding from the study of Al-khresheh and Almaaytah (2018), which said that since Arabic and English are unrelated languages, their differing linguistic structures can make translation work somewhat difficult at times.

4.2.1.2 Contextual challenges of HMC

Contextually, understanding the appropriate usage of words and phrases based on the context is another type of accuracy challenge. For example, Figure 7 shows that most of the responses (41.7%) stated that a MT system would provide a literal translation of the individual words in the English idiom "it's raining cats and dogs", rather than recognising it as an idiomatic expression and translating the intended meaning of heavy rainfall. Another example comes from the responses to the open-ended question, which stated that many Arabic writers fail to use diacritical marks in their writing, resulting in incorrect translations of some words by machines, such as names, because the machines misinterpret the input. For example, the Arabic name 'رمزي' /Ramzī/ is a proper noun that is translated as 'symbolic'. Another response supports the contextual challenge by stating that the diversity of Arabic dialects presents challenges in accurate Arabic-English translation, as machines may misinterpret words with different meanings in various contexts. This suggests that MT systems may still face challenges in accurately handling idiomatic and contextual language, compared to HT.

Sabtan et al.'s study (2023) examined the impact of MT on translating English lexical collocations into Arabic. It surveyed 30 third-year translation students at an Omani university using an online MT system. Results showed that while students were able to generate accurate translations for some collocations, others had inaccuracies. The study highlighted the importance of not relying solely on MT, as it may reduce students' motivation to find the best translations independently. It recommends using MT in a balanced way while encouraging students to improve their translation skills.

4.2.1.3 **Lexical challenges of HMC**

Lexical translation faces challenges such as multiple meanings, cultural differences, and the lack of direct equivalents. Synonyms and morphological variations complicate the process, along with the need to consider tone and new terms. Lexically, the use of inconsistent terminology and the lack of specialised knowledge in MT also posed a significant barrier according to 55% of respondents, as shown in Figure 8. This challenge is reflected in the responses to the open-ended question.

MT faces difficulties in medical texts, legal terms, and technical domains. This indicates that the MT systems may not possess the necessary expertise in specific domains, which could result in inaccuracies. In contrast, HTs are indispensable for determining and interpreting specialised terminology, handling language differences, and retaining context. This finding has been highlighted by the study of El Yaâgoubi and El Biadi (2021), which discussed the limitations and failures of machine human-assisted translation in providing equivalences of terminologies across various domains. It highlighted the need for translators to choose the right terminology to match the source text's jargon, and the dichotomous notions of translatability and untranslatability in the translation field.

4.2.2 Cultural challenges of HMC in translation

In terms of culture, the survey indicates that 56.7% of participants (shown in Figure 8) cited challenges in translating cultural references and idioms. This is highlighted by the responses to the open-ended question, which generally indicated that the cultural challenges in Arabic-English translation are multifaceted. Firstly, the diverse Arabic dialects create difficulties in achieving accurate translations, as the details and cultural references can vary significantly across regions. This diversity complicates the translation process and requires skilled HTs to navigate these complexities. Secondly, the richness of the Arabic language in idioms, proverbs, and cultural allusions presents a unique challenge. These cultural details often lack direct equivalents in English, posing a barrier for MT. HTs must step in to provide the necessary context and cultural knowledge to ensure the intended meaning is conveyed. Ultimately, the cultural aspects of the source and target languages play a crucial role in the success of Arabic-English translation, requiring a deep understanding of both linguistic and cultural differences.

This result is supported by the findings of El-Saadany (2024), which indicated that MTs, particularly those generated by ChatGPT, often fail to capture cultural nuances and frequently make errors such as choosing incorrect lexical items and providing overly literal translations. These errors lead to a distortion of meanings and comprehension issues, especially when using strategies like paraphrasing. The study highlighted that comprehension errors and the misinterpretation of proverbs are common pitfalls in MT. As a recommendation, the study suggested that further research is needed to explore the limitations of MT tools like ChatGPT, particularly in the context of translating culturally rich content such as proverbs, to improve their effectiveness in language translation tasks.

Al-khresheh and Almaaytah's study (2018) likewise revealed limitations in translating proverbs via Google Translate. For example, the proverb "Once bitten, twice shy" was rendered in a syntactically incorrect manner, demonstrating the limitations of MT in capturing the essence of proverbs. The study emphasised the necessity of human intervention to enhance translation accuracy and suggests further research to explore a broader range of proverbs and compare different MT systems. Ultimately, the study underscores the cultural significance of proverbs and the importance of preserving their meanings across languages.

4.2.3 Technical challenges of HMC in translation

41.7% participants reported insufficient training data, lack of customisation, and inadequate quality control for English-Arabic MT, as illustrated in Figure 5. This percentage indicates a lack of adequate high-quality data available for training models. It also suggests that the models used may not be specifically designed to meet the needs of users or different cultural contexts. This technical challenge is corroborated by multiple studies, such as the work of Al-khresheh and Almaaytah (2018), which highlighted significant challenges when using systems like Google Translate. Key findings revealed that linguistic obstacles, including multiple meanings in English words and structural differences between English and Arabic, hinder accurate translations. This indicates significant room for improvement in the capabilities and deployment of these translation technologies.

The rapid advancement of MT capabilities can make HTs feel threatened according to 31.7% of participants (shown in Figure 9). Respondents expressed concerns about being replaced by automated tools. Additionally, a lack of organisational support and resources to adapt to emerging translation technologies poses a significant challenge. Translators may struggle to keep up with the industry's technological changes if their employers do not provide the necessary training, process changes, and investments to facilitate the adoption of new tools and workflows. Addressing these challenges around MT and organisational adaptation will likely be crucial for translation professionals to guide the ongoing changes in their field.

When combining HTs and MT systems in English-Arabic language pairs, several key accuracy challenges stem from fundamental linguistic differences, such as grammatical, lexical, and contextual. Additionally, these challenges include cultural and technical differences. Together, these factors pose difficulties for collaboration in translation and post-editing processes. The implications of these findings are multifaceted. There is a clear need for increased investment in research and technology development aimed at improving language processing systems. For example, there is a need to develop models that fit the diverse linguistic and cultural contexts of both Arabic and English speakers. This could involve collaboration with linguists and cultural experts to ensure that machine learning models reflect the complexities of both languages. Moreover, training programmes for users of MT tools could enhance their understanding of a given system's limitations, thereby improving user-machine interactions. Users should be equipped with knowledge of potential pitfalls in translation to facilitate better collaboration. As a further point, future studies could focus on developing hybrid models that integrate rule-based and statistical approaches to translation, aiming to capture the nuances of both Arabic and English more effectively. Additionally, exploring user feedback mechanisms could provide insights into real-world challenges faced by users, guiding the iterative improvement of translation systems. In conclusion, these findings highlight significant areas for improvement in HMC concerning Arabic-English interactions. Addressing the identified challenges could lead to more effective, accurate translations and collaboration in various applications, from business to education and beyond.

5. CONCLUSION

The main objective of this study is to explore the impact HMC in English-Arabic translation by addressing its benefits and challenges. Regarding the benefits, collaboration between HTs and MT systems presents three major advantages: enhancing expertise in HMC, providing system feedback, and optimising job satisfaction. Despite these benefits, the key accuracy challenges appeared to be related to fundamental linguistic (such as grammatical, lexical, and contextual), cultural, and technical differences, which pose difficulties for collaboration in translation and post-editing processes. Hence, the present study provides insights for multilingual education and guidelines for translation agencies. It provides insights for multilingual education and guidelines for translation agencies. It emphasises optimising MT and human post-editing integration and highlights metrics for assessing HMC.

On that basis, further studies could explore how the strengths and weaknesses of various MT systems influence the collaborative translation process and outcomes. Further studies could also be conducted to extend the study to a wider range of text types (e.g., technical, literary, legal) and domains to examine the generalisability of the findings. To enhance collaboration in translation, organisations are recommended to combine human oversight with machine suggestions. This approach creates a strong terminology management process. It ensures clear and consistent communication, especially for technical content. Additionally, organisations are encouraged to focus on technology that supports translators to improve job satisfaction, reduce stress, and foster a cooperative environment.

ACKNOWLEDGEMENT

We would like to extend our gratitude to Dr. Ramzi Al-Sharabi for his contributions during the data collection process and for his insightful review of the questionnaire. We would also like to thank Prof. Chokri Smaoui from Tunisia and Dr. Soumia Benyahia from Algeria for reviewing the questionnaire and expressing their satisfaction with its excellent coordination and alignment with the research questions.

REFERENCES

Adiel, M. A. E., Elsadig, M. A., Altigani, A., Mohamed, Y. A., Ahmed, B. E. S., & Elhassan, S. M. O. (2023). Accuracy and problems of machine-based translation in contrast to human-based translation when rendering health awareness texts versus poetry texts. *Academic J. Interdiscipl. Stud., 12*(4), 223-231. https://scholar.google.com/scholar?hl=ar&as_sdt=0%2C5&q=Accuracy+and+Problems+of+Machine-Based+Translation+in+Contrast+to+Human-Based+Translation+when+Rendering+Health+Awareness+Texts+Versus+Poetry+Texts&btnG=

Ahrenberg, L. (2017). Comparing machine translation and human translation: A case study. In I. Temnikova, C. Orasan, G. Corpas, & S. Vogel. *RANLP 2017: The First Workshop on Human-Informed Translation and Interpreting Technology (HiT-IT) Proceedings of the Workshop, September 7th, 2017; 2017, pp. 21-28.* https://www.diva-portal.org/smash/get/diva2:1148856/FULLTEXT02

Al-khresheh, M. H., & Almaaytah, S. A. (2018). English proverbs into Arabic through machine translation. *International Journal of Applied Linguistics and English Literature*, *7*(5), 158–166. https://scholar.google.com/scholar?hl=ar&as_sdt=0%2C5&q=English+Proverbs+into+Arabic+through+Machine+Translation&btnG=. DOI: 10.7575/aiac.ijalel.v.7n.5p.158

Al-Maktary, M. N., Mohammed, Z. A., Hassan, A. A., Almoughles, A. F., & Al-mekdad, A. I. (2025). Human Versus Artificial Intelligence (AI): Challenges in the Legal Translation of English to Arabic Terminology at Yemeni Universities, Taiz. *Al-Saeed Journal of Humanities and Applied Sciences, 8*(1), 177-212. https://journal.alsaeeduni.net/index.php/sjhas/article/view/257

Alkhatib, M., & Shaalan, K. (2018). The key challenges for Arabic machine translation. *Intelligent Natural Language Processing: Trends and Applications*, 139-156. https://www.researchgate.net/profile/Khaled-Shaalan-2/publication/321150077_The_Key_Challenges_for_Arabic_Machine_Translation/links/5a55f86f45851547b1bdec0d/The-Key-Challenges-for-Arabic-Machine-Translation.pdf

Alkodimi, K. A., Alqahtani, O. A., & Al-Wasy, B. Q. (2024). Human-AI collaboration in translation and back translation of literary texts. *The Journal of Social Studies, 30*(2), 173–192. https://scholar.google.com/scholar?hl=ar&as_sdt=0%2C5&q=Human-AI+collaboration+in+translation+and+back+translation+of+literary+texts&btnG=. DOI: 10.20428/jss.v30i2.2404

Alowedi, N. A., & Al-Ahdal, A. A. M. H. (2023). Artificial intelligence based Arabic-to-English machine versus human translation of poetry: An analytical study of outcomes. *Journal of Namibian Studies: History Politics Culture, 33*, 1523–1538. https://scholar.google.com/scholar?hl=ar&as_sdt=0%2C5&q=Artificial+Intelligence+based+Arabic-to-English+machine+versus+human+translation+of+poetry%3A+An+analytical+study+of+outcomes&btnG=

Aragonés Lumeras, M., & Way, A. (2017). On the complementarity between human translators and machine translation. *Hermes*, (56), 21–42. https://doras.dcu.ie/23313/1/On_the_Complementarity_between_Human_Translators_and_Machine_Translation%5B1%5D.pdf

Cai, Z., Liu, L., Chen, B., & Wang, Y. (2021). *Artificial intelligence: From beginning to date*. World Scientific. https://www.worldscientific.com/doi/pdf/10.1142/9789811223723_0001

Denkowski, M. (2015). *Machine translation for human translators. Unpublished doctoral dissertation*. Carnegie Mellon University., https://scholar.google.com/scholar?hl=ar&as_sdt=0%2C5&q=Machine+Translation+for+Human+Translators&btnG=

El-Saadany, M. (2024). A Comparative study between Chat GPT and human translation in translating English proverbs into Arabic. *Scientific Research in Literature, 25*(5), 24-54. https://scholar.google.com/scholar?hl=ar&as_sdt=0%2C5&q=A+Comparative+Study+between+Chat+GPT+and+Human+Translation+in+Translating+English+Proverbs+into+Arabic&btnG=

El Yaâgoubi, S., & El Biadi, M. (2021). Machine assisted human translation: The Dichotomy of translatability and untranslatability of terminology. *International Journal of Information Science and Technology*, *5*(1), 16–22. http://www.innove.org/ijist/index.php/ijist/article/download/167/135

ElBeheri, N. (2019). Collaboration between machine translation and human translation for higher quality and more production in translation. *Textual Turnings: An International Peer-Reviewed Journal in English Studies, 1(1), 446-473* https://scholar.google.com/scholar?hl=ar&as_sdt=0%2C5&q=Collaboration+between+Machine+Translation+and+Human+Translation+for+Higher+Quality+and+More+Production+in+Translation&btnG=

Guerberof-Arenas, A., Valdez, S., & Dorst, A. G. (2024). Does training in post-editing affect creativity? *JoSTrans The Journal of Specialized Translation*(41), 74-97. https://scholar.google.com/scholar?hl=en&as_sdt=0%2C5&q=Does+training+in+post-editing+affect+creativity%3F&btnG=

Hasibuan, Z. (2020). A comparative study between human translation and machine translation as an interdisciplinary research. *Journal of English Teaching and Learning Issues*, *3*(2), 115–130. DOI: 10.21043/jetli.v3i2.8545

Lihua, Z. (2022). The relationship between machine translation and human translation under the influence of Artificial Intelligence machine translation. *Mobile Information Systems, 2022*(1), 9121636. https://onlinelibrary.wiley.com/doi/pdf/10.1155/2022/9121636. DOI: 10.1155/2022/9121636

Moghe, N., Fazla, A., Amrhein, C., Kocmi, T., Steedman, M., Birch, A., . . . Guillou, L. (2024). Machine translation Meta evaluation through translation accuracy challenge sets. *arXiv preprint arXiv:2401.16313*. file:///C:/Users/dell/Desktop/2401.16313v1.pdf

Muftah, M. (2022). Machine vs human translation: A new reality or a threat to professional Arabic–English translators. *PSU Research Review*. https://www.emerald.com/insight/content/doi/10.1108/PRR-02-2022-0024/full/pdf

Nagi, K. A. (2023). Arabic and English relative clauses and machine translation challenges. *The Journal of Social Studies*, *29*(3), 145–165. https://scholar.google.com/scholar?hl=ar&as_sdt=0%2C5&q=Arabic+and+English+Relative+Clauses+and+Machine+Translation+Challenges&btnG=. DOI: 10.20428/jss.v29i3.2180

Sabtan, Y. M. N., Omar, A., & Hamouda, W. I. (2023). Exploring the role of machine translation in translating English collocations into Arabic: Insights from student translators. *World Journal of English Language*, *14*(2), 1–74. https://ideas.repec.org/a/jfr/wjel11/v14y2024i2p74.html. DOI: 10.5430/wjel.v14n2p74

Sammer, M., Reiter, K., Soderland, S., Kirchhoff, K., & Etzioni, O. (2006). Ambiguity reduction for machine translation: Human-computer collaboration. *Proceedings of the 7th Conference of the Association for Machine Translation in the Americas: Technical Papers*.

Tahseen, W. M., & Hussein, S. H. (2024). Investigating machine translation rrrors in rendering English literary texts into Arabic. *Integrated Journal for Research in Arts and Humanities, 4*(1), 68-81. https://scholar.google.com/scholar?hl=ar&as_sdt=0%2C5&q=Investigating+Machine+Translation+Errors+in+Rendering+English+Literary+Texts+into+Arabic&btnG=

Vieira, L. N. (2019). Post-editing of machine translation. In *The Routledge handbook of translation and technology* (pp. 319–336). Routledge. DOI: 10.4324/9781315311258-19

Wang, L. (2023). The impacts and challenges of artificial intelligence translation tool on translation professionals. SHS Web of Conferences. EDP Sciences.

Zhang, X., Yu, Z., Liu, J., Wang, H., Wang, L., & Guo, B. (2023). HMPT: a human–machine cooperative program translation method. *Automated Software Engineering*, *30*(2), 27. https://link.springer.com/content/pdf/10.1007/s10515-023-00395-9.pdf

APPENDIX: QUESTIONNAIRE

Dear participants,

We are pleased to invite you to participate in our translation research questionnaire. The purpose of this questionnaire is to gather information about your experiences, opinions, and projections. The questionnaire should take approximately 15-20 minutes to complete.

Your participation is greatly appreciated, as the information you provide will be invaluable in helping us achieve the goals of present research. It is both anonymous and voluntary. If you have any questions or concerns at any point during answering the questionnaire, please do not hesitate to reach out to the research team.

Your responses will be kept completely confidential, and only the researchers involved in this study will have access to data to be assessed based on predefined criteria. Thank you in advance for your time and contributions. We look forward to learning from your experiences.

If you agree to take part, please proceed to the translation task below. When you have completed the task, please click 'Submit' to finalise your responses.

Thank you for considering this request!

Section 1

Demographic Information

1. Age: Please specify the age category you belong to:
   a. 22-35 years
   b. 36-46 years
   c. 47-56 years
   d. 57 years and above
2. Gender:
   a. Male
   b. Female
3. Education Level:
   a. Bachelor
   b. Master
   c. PhD
   d. Other (please specify): ___________
4. Translation Experience:
   a. Beginner
   b. Intermediate
   c. Advanced
   d. Expert
5. Preferred Translation Domains:
   a. Religious
   b. Scientific

   c. Literary
   d. Other (please specify): __________
6. Have you collaborated with machine translation systems in your translation work?
   a. Yes
   b. No
7. If you have collaborated with machine translation systems, please indicate the type of collaboration you have experienced (Select all that apply).
   a. Post-editing: Reviewing and correcting machine-generated translations.
   b. Pre-editing: Preparing the source text to optimise machine translation output.
   c. Augmented Translation: Using machine translation as a reference tool during translation.
   d. Other (please specify): __________.
8. Experience with Machine Translation:
   a. Beginner
   b. Intermediate
   c. Advanced
   d. Expert

Section 2

1. In terms of subject matter expertise, the main benefit of human-machine collaboration is:
   a. Humans can provide deep domain knowledge.
   b. Machines can access a broader knowledge base.
   c. Both humans and machines contribute valuable expertise.
   d. Neither humans nor machines offer strong subject matter expertise.
2. In terms of capabilities, what are some potential benefits of the collaboration between. human translators and machine translation?
   a. Improved translation accuracy and consistency.
   b. Enhanced productivity and faster turnaround times.
   c. Reduced risk of human error.
   d. All of the above.
3. In a collaborative workflow, how do human translators typically benefit from the use of machine translation?
   a. By helping reduce their workload and allows them to be more productive.
   b. By providing a useful starting point that they can edit and refine.
   c. By eliminating the need for human translation in many cases.
   d. By allowing them to focus more on high-level aspects like style and tone.

4. How can human translators add value to the collaboration with machine translation systems despite the challenges?
   a. By providing context and background knowledge.
   b. By ensuring linguistic fluency and naturalness in translations.
   c. By offering creative solutions and alternative phrasings.
   d. All of the above.
5. How can human translators contribute to improving the accuracy of machine translation output?
   a. By correcting errors in the machine translation output.
   b. By providing feedback to machine translation systems.
   c. By ensuring cultural nuances are accurately conveyed.
   d. All of the above.
6. What specific benefits have you observed in terms of consistency when combining human translators and machine translation systems in Arabic-English language pairs? Please select the most applicable option(s):
   a. Promoting consistent terminology, style/tone, and structural coherence in translations.
   b. Better alignment of cultural references and idiomatic expressions for consistent interpretation.
   c. I have not observed specific benefits in terms of consistency.
   d. Other benefits (please specify): ___________.
7. When it comes to handling specialised terminology, a collaborative translation approach is advantageous because:
   a. Humans can maintain terminology consistency.
   b. Machines can automatically suggest preferred terms.
   c. Both human oversight and machine suggestions enhance terminology management.
   d. Terminology management is not improved in a collaborative model.
8. In terms of translators' job satisfaction and professional development, the main advantage of a collaborative model is:
   a. Reduced risk of burnout due to machine-assisted productivity.
   b. Increased opportunities for translators to focus on creative and strategic tasks.
   c. Enhanced sense of partnership between human and machine translation capabilities.
   d. All of the above.
9. Have you observed any other benefits that arise from the combination of human and machine translation in Arabic-English language pairs? Certain translation domains or industries? If yes, please provide examples.

Section 3

1. What do you see as the primary obstacles to achieving accurate and reliable translations when combining human translators and machine translation for Arabic-English language pairs? (Select all that apply)
    a. Differences in grammar and challenges in translating context, idioms, and culture between Arabic and English.
    b. Inconsistent terminology usage and lack of domain-specific knowledge in machine translation.
    c. Limitations in training data/models and inadequate quality assurance for Arabic-English machine translation.
    d. Other (please specify): ___________.
2. How have you personally struggled to maintain a positive and adaptive mindset towards the evolving role of machine translation in your work? Specifically, what challenges have you faced in terms of:
    a. Feeling threatened by the growing prominence and capabilities of machine translation.
    b. Difficulty adapting your skills and workflows to effectively utilise new machine translation tools and systems.
    c. Lack of organisational support or incentives to embrace advancements in machine translation.
    d. Uncertainty about the long-term job prospects for human translators as machine translation continues to improve.
3. When translating the English idiom “it's raining cats and dogs” into Arabic, a machine translation system would most likely:
    a. Provide a literal translation of the individual words.
    b. Recognise it as an idiomatic expression and translate the intended meaning of heavy rainfall.
    c. Struggle to capture the full intended meaning without additional contextual information.
    d. Translate it as “it is raining small animals”.
4. Which of the following grammatical differences between English and Arabic is the most challenging for human-machine collaboration in translation?
    a. Differences in sentence structure.
    b. Use of definite and indefinite articles.
    c. Verb conjugation.
    d. All of the above pose significant challenges for effective collaboration between human translators and machine translation systems.
5. When post-editing machine translated content for English-Arabic translation, which of the following challenges do you most often encounter?

a. Resolving grammatical and semantic issues.
b. Preserving cultural nuances and contextual references.
c. Maintaining consistency with the human translator's style.
d. All of the above.

6. In your opinion, what are the primary factors contributing to accuracy challenges when combining human translators and machine translation systems in Arabic-English language pairs? (Select all that apply)
   a. Linguistic differences and cultural/idiomatic challenges between Arabic and English.
   b. Inadequate system training/customisation and quality control for Arabic-English machine translation.
   c. Other (please specify): ___________.
   d. No significant accuracy challenges.
7. What challenges do you face in maintaining consistent terminology usage when combining human translators and machine translation systems in Arabic-English language pairs? Please select the most applicable option(s):
   a. Issues with maintaining consistency in translating cultural references or idiomatic expressions.
   b. Challenges with terminology coordination and the lack of domain-specific resources for Arabic-English machine translation.
   c. Other terminology-related challenges (please specify): ___________.
   d. I have not faced specific challenges in maintaining consistent terminology usage.
8. What strategies do you employ to overcome consistency challenges when working with machine translation systems in Arabic-English language pairs? Please select the most applicable option(s):
   a. Maintaining translation consistency through style guide updates, post-editing and quality checks.
   b. Utilising terminology resources and collaborating with machine translation developers to enhance consistency.
   c. Other measures or strategies (please specify): ___________.
   d. I do not employ specific strategies to overcome consistency challenges.
9. Have you observed any other challenges that arise from the collaboration of human and machine translation in Arabic-English language pairs? Certain translation domains or industries? If yes, please provide examples.

Chapter 7
From Exam Regulations to Prompt Literacy:
Generative AI as a Catalyst for an Epistemic Paradigm Shift in Higher Education

Silvio Andrae
https://orcid.org/0000-0002-8586-7812
Independent Researcher, Germany

ABSTRACT

The widespread adoption of generative artificial intelligence is fundamentally transforming academic knowledge practices and presents significant challenges for higher education institutions globally. This chapter investigates the impact of generative AI on the epistemic foundations of university teaching, advancing beyond perspectives that regard AI solely as a technical instrument or regulatory concern. Generative AI is conceptualized as a catalyst for an epistemic paradigm shift, with implications for didactics, assessment, and institutional governance. The chapter employs a conceptual and theory-driven methodology, drawing on Kuhn's paradigm theory, epistemic culture research, distributed cognition, and actor-network theory. The findings indicate that generative AI disrupts reproduction-oriented models of academic performance and shifts epistemic authority toward critical judgment within hybrid human machine contexts. Prompt literacy is identified as a crucial epistemic competence, while control-oriented assessment frameworks are increasingly invalid.

DOI: 10.4018/979-8-3373-4521-5.ch007

1. INTRODUCTION

The rapid diffusion of generative artificial intelligence (AI) represents a pivotal development that introduces significant epistemological, didactic, and organisational challenges for universities globally. Technologies once regarded as future-oriented have, in a brief period, become integral to daily academic practice. Generative models such as GPT-4, Claude 3.5, and Llama 3 now extend beyond auxiliary roles in information retrieval or processing and increasingly function as co-producers of texts, analyses, and argumentative structures (Kreps et al., 2020; Eloundou et al., 2023). This evolution influences not only the production and communication of knowledge but also how students and instructors conceptualise their academic roles.

From an epistemological standpoint, the integration of generative AI signals a transformation that surpasses incremental technological advancement. Established assumptions about individual authorship, linear reasoning, and text-based performance indicators are increasingly contested by hybrid forms of knowledge production, in which human judgment and algorithmic generation are closely intertwined. These dynamics prompt consideration of whether current developments constitute a paradigm shift in the Kuhnian sense, a perspective that will be elaborated in Section 2.

Economic disciplines such as controlling, marketing, and strategic management offer a particularly relevant context for analysing these developments. Knowledge production in these areas is highly model-based, text-intensive, and focused on interpretation amid uncertainty and decision making. Recent research demonstrates that generative AI not only automates routine tasks in these domains but also increasingly contributes to analytical framing, scenario construction, and strategic reasoning (Brynjolfsson et al., 2023; Mollick & Mollick, 2023). Consequently, AI attains epistemic significance not merely as a tool but as an actor that shapes problem definitions, heuristics, and evaluative processes.

These developments have direct implications for university teaching. Traditional conceptions of academic achievement are based on the premise that students independently produce texts, arguments, and analyses as demonstrations of individual cognitive performance. When generative AI systems undertake or support substantial portions of these activities, the epistemic significance of writing and analysis is altered. Learning objectives increasingly emphasise the ability to critically interpret, contextualise, and justify algorithmically generated content in accordance with scientific standards. In this context, hybrid learning arrangements, often referred to as human-in-the-loop configurations, gain importance by underscoring the ongoing responsibility of human judgment within AI-supported knowledge practices (Shneiderman, 2022). Competencies such as prompt literacy may thus become central elements of academic qualification, a proposition explored in subsequent sections.

In light of these considerations, this chapter addresses three guiding research questions:

(1) What epistemological changes does the integration of generative AI introduce into higher education teaching, particularly within economic disciplines?
(2) How do didactic concepts, competency models, and assessment formats evolve as generative AI becomes embedded within academic practice?
(3) What institutional and governance conditions are necessary for universities to integrate generative AI in a responsible, reflexive, and learning-oriented manner?

The objective of this chapter is to systematically analyse the impact of generative AI on the epistemic foundations of university teaching and to derive implications for didactic design, assessment practices, and institutional governance. This chapter contends that prevailing debates are incomplete if generative AI is primarily regarded as a regulatory or control issue. Instead, it conceptualises generative AI as a catalyst for epistemic reconfiguration, reshaping academic performance criteria, the roles of students and instructors, and the institutional structure of higher education. Methodologically, this contribution employs a conceptual-analytical approach and does not engage in technical evaluation of specific AI tools. The analysis centres on the epistemological, didactic, and organisational consequences of algorithmic knowledge production in higher education, with particular emphasis on economic disciplines.

This chapter is organised as follows. Section 2 develops the theoretical framework and interprets generative AI as a catalyst for an epistemic shift from knowledge reproduction to knowledge curation. Section 3 examines central epistemic risks associated with generative AI, including plausibility bias, epistemic homogenisation, and cognitive externalisation. Section 4 explores the didactic transformation of university teaching and discusses emerging competency requirements in hybrid learning environments. Section 5 addresses assessment practices and explains the diminishing epistemic validity of control-oriented examination approaches. Section 6 considers institutional and governance-related challenges, while Section 7 synthesises the findings into a future-oriented perspective on higher education. Section 8 concludes with the main implications of the analysis.

2. EPISTEMIC FOUNDATIONS: PARADIGM CHANGE AND HYBRID KNOWLEDGE PRODUCTION

A comprehensive analysis of generative AI in higher education necessitates moving beyond technological considerations to examine the epistemic frameworks that underpin academic knowledge production. Thomas S. Kuhn's concept of scientific paradigms, as articulated in *The Structure of Scientific Revolutions* (1962/2012), serves as a foundational theoretical lens for this inquiry. Kuhn posits that scientific progress is not a straightforward accumulation of knowledge, but rather a sequence of stable periods of "normal science" interrupted by paradigm shifts. In this context, paradigms consist of shared assumptions regarding legitimate problems, accepted methodologies, evaluation standards, and institutionalised practices that collectively determine what is recognised as valid knowledge within a scientific community.

When applied to higher education, this perspective reveals that teaching methods, assessment formats, and competency frameworks are not neutral pedagogical decisions, but rather manifestations of an underlying epistemic paradigm. Before the proliferation of generative AI, this paradigm was primarily based on the belief that knowledge production is an individual cognitive accomplishment, demonstrated through linear reasoning, written expression, and methodologically rigorous analysis. Textual production and analytical tasks were regarded as key indicators of epistemic autonomy, while technical tools occupied a secondary, supportive role.

The integration of generative AI challenges this epistemic order on multiple levels. In Kuhnian terms, the increasing presence of AI-supported academic practices can be interpreted as the emergence of epistemic anomalies—phenomena that cannot be adequately explained or managed within the existing paradigm. Examples include algorithmically generated texts that are largely indistinguishable from human writing, analytical outputs whose plausibility exceeds their epistemic grounding, and learning processes that unfold through iterative human–machine interaction rather than linear individual effort. Taken together, these developments suggest that the established epistemic framework of higher education is under growing strain.

Kuhn's theory has undergone significant refinement and critique within the philosophy and sociology of science (Hoyningen-Huene, 1993; Bird, 2000), yet its central insight remains salient: paradigms function not only as cognitive frameworks but also as social and institutional constructs. Consequently, shifts in epistemic order are intrinsically linked to changes in academic culture and practice. This perspective aligns with Ludwik Fleck's earlier assertion that knowledge arises within distinct "styles of thought" and "thought collectives" that determine what is regarded as meaningful, valid, and legitimate (Fleck, 1935/2023). Accordingly, generative AI does more than introduce new tools; it transforms the epistemic routines by which problems are defined, arguments are developed, and knowledge claims are validated.

A key aspect of this transformation is the transition from an epistemic culture centred on reproduction to one focused on curation. Historically, academic practices have emphasised the reproduction, synthesis, and articulation of knowledge through individual effort, especially in written form. Generative AI challenges this paradigm by undertaking significant portions of representational and preparatory tasks, such as literature synthesis, structural outlining, data interpretation, and textual formulation

(Bommasani et al., 2021). As a result, the epistemic emphasis shifts from the act of production to the evaluation, contextualisation, and justification of algorithmically generated outputs. The critical epistemic question is no longer who produces a text or analysis, but how its claims are evaluated, contextualised, and substantiated.

This reorientation is further elucidated by research on epistemic cultures. Knorr Cetina (1999) highlights that academic disciplines are defined by unique epistemic practices governing the generation and validation of knowledge. In environments supported by AI, these practices are being fundamentally reconfigured. Knowledge production is increasingly characterised by epistemic orchestration, involving the coordination, filtering, and critical integration of contributions from both human and algorithmic sources. Consequently, epistemic competence now centres on the ability to manage hybrid knowledge processes rather than on performing isolated acts of representation.

The hybridisation of knowledge practices brings the interplay between human cognition and algorithmic generation to the forefront as a central epistemic concern. The concept of human-in-the-loop learning refers to configurations in which humans and AI systems collaboratively shape cognitive processes, maintaining epistemic responsibility without defaulting to automation. This approach aligns with theories of distributed cognition, which view knowledge as emerging from networks of individuals, artefacts, and symbolic tools rather than from isolated minds (Hutchins, 1995). Generative AI introduces a qualitatively distinct element into these networks, as it actively generates hypotheses, interpretations, and argumentative structures that shape epistemic trajectories.

From this perspective, generative AI should be regarded as an epistemic actor. An epistemic actor is not simply a tool, but an active participant in the construction and organisation of knowledge (Collins & Evans, 2007). Generative AI assumes this role by shaping problem definitions, privileging specific heuristics, and structuring information environments. Actor-network theory supports this interpretation by asserting that epistemic orders arise from hybrid networks of human and non-human actors (Latour, 2005). The integration of generative AI into academic practice thus necessitates a reconfiguration of epistemic roles, responsibilities, and evaluation standards.

In summary, the epistemic foundations of higher education are experiencing a structural transformation. Generative AI functions not as an external disruption but as a catalyst that reveals the limitations of a paradigm focused on individual reproduction and linear knowledge production. Rather than eliminating academic standards, this transformation repositions them. Epistemic authority is now increasingly grounded in critical judgment, contextual reasoning, and reflexive justification within hybrid knowledge environments. The subsequent section will further explore the epistemic risks, biases, and limitations associated with this shift.

3. EPISTEMIC RISKS, BIASES, AND LIMITATIONS OF GENERATIVE AI

Generative AI catalyses epistemic transformation in higher education; however, its integration into academic knowledge practices introduces structural epistemic risks. These risks are not merely incidental consequences of immature technology, nor are they limited to misuse or misconduct. Instead, they originate from the fundamental characteristics of hybrid human–machine knowledge production and necessitate systematic analysis at the epistemic level.

A primary and widely recognised risk involves the distinction between plausibility and validity in knowledge representations. Generative AI systems are designed to produce outputs that are linguistically coherent, contextually appropriate, and statistically probable. Consequently, these systems often generate responses that are highly surface plausible, even when the underlying claims are factually incorrect, conceptually inconsistent, or methodologically unsound. This phenomenon, commonly termed hallucination, presents a distinct epistemic challenge in academic contexts, where coherence and argumentative fluency have traditionally indicated understanding. The central issue is not the mere presence of erroneous outputs, which also occur in human cognition, but the systematic separation of plausibility from epistemic grounding. In hybrid knowledge environments, plausibility may increasingly be mistaken for validity unless explicit practices of verification, justification, and methodological reflection are consistently applied.

A related concern is epistemic bias and homogenisation at the structural level of knowledge production. Generative AI systems are trained on extensive textual corpora that embody historically established patterns of language use, theoretical dominance, and institutional authority. As a result, their outputs tend to favour mainstream perspectives, established problem framings, and statistically prevalent argumentative patterns, while marginal, heterodox, or emerging viewpoints are systematically underrepresented. When these systems are integrated into academic workflows, epistemic diversity may be progressively diminished. Instead of promoting exploratory or disruptive thinking, algorithmic pattern recognition can reinforce existing knowledge regimes and perpetuate path-dependent reasoning. Over time, this process may result in a subtle convergence of thought and expression that undermines pluralism in scientific discourse, particularly in disciplines with strong paradigmatic foundations such as economics.

Another structural risk arises at the level of epistemic processes through cognitive externalisation. As generative AI systems increasingly undertake tasks such as outlining arguments, synthesising literature, generating hypotheses, and proposing interpretations, essential epistemic activities risk being transferred from human agents to algorithms. Although external cognitive aids have long been integral to scholarly practice, generative AI is distinct in its capacity to perform integrative and interpretive functions rather than solely instrumental ones. In the absence of intentional counterbalancing measures, this shift may erode reflexive competencies such as problem formulation, critical interpretation, and methodological judgment. The epistemic risk, therefore, is not inherent in delegation itself, but in the gradual reduction of active engagement when algorithmic suggestions are accepted without sustained scrutiny.

These developments also introduce challenges related to epistemic responsibility at the normative level of knowledge production. In hybrid human–machine practices, the attribution of agency, authorship, and accountability becomes increasingly ambiguous. When texts, analyses, or conceptual structures are co-produced by humans and machines, responsibility for errors, biases, or normative assumptions embedded in the outputs may be unclear. This diffusion of responsibility has significant epistemic implications, as academic knowledge production fundamentally depends on practices of justification, critique, and contestation. If epistemic agency is implicitly transferred to algorithmic systems, the capacity to defend, revise, or reject knowledge claims is diminished.

Collectively, these interconnected risks—plausibility bias in outputs, cognitive externalisation in processes, epistemic homogenisation at the structural level, and diffusion of responsibility at the normative level—demonstrate that the epistemic challenges associated with generative AI are systemic rather than incidental. These challenges stem from the very features that render generative AI appealing as a cognitive and epistemic resource: its ability to generate fluent representations, integrate diverse information, and provide heuristic guidance.

Recognising these limitations is therefore not an argument against integrating generative AI into higher education. Instead, it provides an essential analytical foundation for developing didactic models, assessment practices, and institutional frameworks that intentionally preserve epistemic judgment, pluralism, and responsibility in hybrid knowledge environments. The following section extends this analysis by exploring how these epistemic tensions inform new didactic requirements and competency configurations in university teaching.

4. DIDACTIC TRANSFORMATION: LEARNING IN HYBRID KNOWLEDGE ENVIRONMENTS

For decades, university teaching, particularly in economics, has operated within a stable didactic framework grounded in a specific epistemic understanding of learning and academic performance. Learning objectives have focused on enabling students to acquire, analyse, and articulate disciplinary knowledge independently.

Text production, model construction, and argumentative reasoning have been regarded as central indicators of individual cognitive achievement. At the same time, assessment formats such as written examinations, term papers, and oral exams have made these competencies visible and comparable (Biggs & Tang, 2011). In this context, writing has served not only as a means of representation but also as a heuristic process that generates understanding.

The integration of generative AI fundamentally challenges these didactic assumptions. When algorithmic systems contribute significantly to text generation, structuring, and preliminary analysis, writing can no longer be regarded as unequivocal evidence of individual epistemic performance. Rather than making writing obsolete, this development transforms its epistemic function. The didactic emphasis shifts from producing textual artefacts to fostering the capacity to critically engage with, contextualise, and justify AI-supported knowledge claims. Consequently, traditional learning objectives focused on individual reproduction are increasingly complemented, and sometimes replaced, by objectives that prioritise reflexive engagement with hybrid knowledge processes.

This transformation necessitates a reconfiguration of the division of labour between human learners and algorithmic systems. Generative AI can lower barriers to complex tasks by assisting with information retrieval, structural outlining, translation, and stylistic refinement, thereby making learning processes more iterative and exploratory. However, this support also introduces the risk of externalising core epistemic activities if students rely on algorithmic suggestions without sustained critical engagement. The didactic challenge, therefore, is not to prohibit AI use, but to intentionally design learning environments in which epistemic responsibility remains anchored in human judgment.

Generative AI also transforms the temporal and structural dynamics of learning. Traditional didactic models typically assume a linear progression from reception to processing to application. In contrast, AI-supported learning environments facilitate parallel and dialogical processes, enabling students to generate, evaluate, revise, and reflect simultaneously. Learning increasingly occurs through iterative interaction with algorithmic systems, creating a distributed cognitive process in which the machine becomes an integral component of the epistemic environment rather than a supplementary tool (Kasneci et al., 2023). This shift is especially significant in economics education, where learning is closely linked to modelling, scenario analysis, and interpretive reasoning under uncertainty.

In this context, new configurations of competency are emerging. Foremost among these is prompt literacy, which should be understood as an epistemic skill rather than a purely technical one. Prompt literacy involves the ability to formulate problems to elicit meaningful algorithmic responses, iteratively refine prompts, and critically interpret the resulting outputs. Importantly, it also includes understanding the limitations and biases of generative models and the ability to justify epistemic decisions made in interaction with AI (Bender et al., 2021; Zhai, 2024). Empirical studies demonstrate that these competencies are not intuitive but develop through guided practice, reflection, and iterative experimentation (Tzirides et al., 2024; Gurdil et al., 2024).

Prompt literacy is not an isolated skill. It is situated within a broader set of academic competencies, including critical thinking, methodological judgment, metacognitive reflection, and data-informed reasoning. Critical thinking remains essential in AI-augmented learning environments, as it enables students to differentiate between algorithmic plausibility and epistemic validity, identify biases and inconsistencies, and assess the normative implications of AI-supported analyses. Data literacy also becomes increasingly important, as students must understand how training data, probabilistic modelling, and statistical assumptions influence algorithmic outputs. Generative AI does not replace traditional academic skills but instead reconfigures their relative importance and the contexts in which they are applied. When competency requirements are incorporated into pedagogical practice, didactic design must be reoriented to structure epistemic processes rather than merely evaluate outcomes. Several interrelated design principles are particularly relevant in hybrid AI-supported learning environments. A first principle is epistemic transparency: students should be enabled and required to make visible how knowledge claims are produced, which algorithmic contributions are involved, and where human judgment intervenes. Transparency serves not as a mechanism of control, but as a condition for epistemic clarification and critique.

A second principle is iterative justification. Generative AI enables rapid cycles of variation, allowing students to explore multiple perspectives and alternative formulations within short periods. Didactic tasks should therefore prioritise the justification of epistemic decisions rather than the immediate presentation of optimal results. Students develop understanding not by producing perfect outputs initially, but by articulating the reasons for accepting, modifying, or rejecting specific algorithmic suggestions.

A third principle is structured epistemic friction. Since generative AI often optimises for coherence and plausibility, effective learning requires intentional moments of challenge and contrast. Didactic settings can introduce such friction through counter-prompts, by comparing outputs generated under different assumptions, or by confronting AI-generated arguments with empirical anomalies or theoretical counter-positions. These practices maintain epistemic tension as a catalyst for understanding and guarding against the uncritical acceptance of algorithmic suggestions.

A fourth principle highlights the importance of reflection before optimisation. In AI-supported contexts, there is a pronounced tendency to prioritise polished outputs. This tendency should be counteracted by incorporating explicit phases of reflection, during which students analyse problem framings, underlying assumptions, and the influence of algorithmic responses on their reasoning. Reflection thus serves as a prerequisite for meaningful optimisation rather than a supplementary step.

Finally, process visibility and metacognitive scaffolding are essential in hybrid learning environments. Students must navigate heightened epistemic complexity as they integrate disciplinary knowledge, algorithmic interaction, and self-reflection. Structured supports, including learning journals, reflective prompts, and peer discussion formats, facilitate the externalisation of epistemic strategies and help sustain epistemic autonomy over time.

Collectively, these developments foster hybrid learning environments defined by dialogical interaction, iterative knowledge construction, and collaborative engagement with AI systems. Learning shifts from the production of finalised artefacts to the documentation, justification of, and reflection on epistemic processes. Thus, didactic transformation in the era of generative AI involves rearticulating established educational aims within the context of hybrid knowledge production. University teaching increasingly prioritises cultivating students' ability to navigate complex epistemic environments where algorithmic systems play an active role. The following section explores how these didactic shifts present challenges for assessment practices and the validity of academic evaluation in AI-augmented contexts.

5. ASSESSMENT, EXAMINATION FORMATS, AND THE ILLUSION OF CONTROL

Assessment practices in higher education are never merely technical or organisational arrangements; they embody implicit epistemic assumptions about how knowledge is generated, validated, and attributed. In economics education, traditional examination formats—such as written exams, term papers, case study reports, and presentations—have long been grounded in the premise that academic performance manifests itself through individually produced texts, analyses, and arguments (McKeachie & Svinicki, 2013). These formats presuppose that writing and analytical reasoning reliably indicate epistemic autonomy and individual understanding.

The widespread adoption of generative AI fundamentally destabilises this epistemic foundation. The core challenge does not primarily arise from the risk of deception or misconduct, but from a more profound transformation of knowledge practices. Generative AI systems can produce texts, summarise literature, interpret models, and generate hypotheses that exhibit high coherence and disciplinary plausibility. As a result, written products increasingly lose their function as unambiguous indicators of individual epistemic performance. When academically styled texts can be generated with minimal effort, assessment formats that equate textual output with understanding become epistemically fragile. Attempts to preserve their validity by tightening formal requirements risk misdiagnosing the problem's nature.

Similar limitations apply to traditional written examinations. Exams focused on short-term knowledge retrieval reflect an epistemic ideal of isolated cognitive performance, increasingly disconnected from contemporary academic and professional practices. In environments where algorithmic systems routinely support analysis, interpretation, and decision-making, assessments centred on recall and reproduction measure competencies of diminishing relevance. The problem, therefore, is not one of declining integrity but of epistemic misalignment: examinations continue to test forms of knowledge practice that no longer correspond to the conditions under which knowledge is produced and used (Williamson, 2017).

Early institutional responses to generative AI have often relied on control-oriented strategies, including bans, AI-detection tools, and declarations of non-use. These measures are based on the assumption that academic integrity can be safeguarded by regulating the means of knowledge production rather than by rethinking epistemic criteria. Empirical evidence, however, suggests that this assumption is untenable. Studies consistently demonstrate that AI-detection systems generate substantial rates of false positives and false negatives and can be circumvented through paraphrasing, stylistic variation, or iterative prompting (Abdali et al., 2024; Fraser et al., 2025; Rafiq et al., 2025). More fundamentally, recent research questions the epistemic premise that human- and machine-generated texts can be reliably distinguished at all, particularly as model quality continues to improve.

Beyond technical unreliability, control-based approaches generate additional epistemic costs. In take-home exams, project-based assignments, and other non-supervised formats, the extent and nature of AI use are neither verifiable nor reconstructible in a robust manner. Efforts to monitor learning processes through declarations, metadata analysis, or surveillance-oriented software are easily bypassed, raising serious concerns about trust, data protection, and the pedagogical relationship between students and instructors. A regulatory environment grounded in suspicion risks transforming educators into enforcers rather than facilitators of learning and undermining the epistemic openness on which higher education depends.

Most importantly, a control-oriented logic fails to recognise the structural character of the epistemic transformation induced by generative AI. These technologies are not optional add-ons whose use can be excluded without consequence; they are embedded in evolving practices of problem formulation, interpretation, and textual articulation. Attempts to exclude AI from assessment artificially separate academic learning from the hybrid knowledge environments in which students already operate. Empirical findings indicate that assessment formats that integrate AI transparently into the learning process foster higher levels of AI literacy and more differentiated evaluative judgment than exclusionary models (Tzirides et al., 2024).

Assessment practices in higher education are often treated as neutral instruments for measuring learning outcomes. From an epistemic perspective, however, examinations perform a far more consequential function. They do not merely evaluate knowledge; they actively structure epistemic practices by defining what counts as legitimate knowledge, how it should be produced, and which forms of reasoning are institutionally rewarded. In this sense, exams function as epistemic interventions that shape learning behaviour, cognitive strategies, and normative expectations long before any formal assessment occurs.

In traditional higher education settings, examinations have reinforced an epistemic model centred on individual reproduction, linear reasoning, and text-based demonstration of competence. Written exams, term papers, and take-home assignments implicitly presuppose that knowledge production is a bounded, individual activity and that textual coherence reliably signals understanding. In the context of generative AI, this epistemic model becomes increasingly misaligned with actual knowledge practices. The resulting tension is not merely technical but epistemic: assessment formats continue to enforce norms that no longer align with how knowledge is generated, validated, and applied in hybrid human–machine environments.

Control-oriented responses to generative AI—such as bans, detection tools, or formal declarations of non-use—must therefore be understood not only as regulatory measures, but as epistemic interventions in their own right. By attempting to exclude AI from assessment contexts, such approaches implicitly reaffirm an epistemic ideal of isolated human cognition that has already been destabilised. At the same time, they incentivise strategic behaviour that runs counter to academic integrity: concealment rather than transparency, optimisation for detection avoidance rather than epistemic rigour, and surface compliance rather than reflective engagement. In this way, control-based assessment regimes risk producing precisely the epistemic practices they seek to prevent.

More fundamentally, examinations play a decisive role in shaping epistemic subjectivities. They signal to students which competencies are valued, and which forms of engagement are considered legitimate. Reproductive exam formats cultivate reproductive epistemic dispositions; control-heavy formats foster defensive and risk-averse strategies. Conversely, assessment designs that foreground justification, reflection, and accountability promote epistemic responsibility. From this perspective, the central question is no longer whether AI is used, but which epistemic practices examinations are designed to elicit and stabilise.

In hybrid knowledge environments, epistemically robust assessment must therefore shift its focus from authorship to justification, from outputs to processes, and from exclusion to transparency. The key object of evaluation is not the absence of algorithmic support, but the quality of human judgment exercised in interaction with generative systems. It includes the ability to assess algorithmic suggestions critically, contextualise them within disciplinary frameworks, identify limitations and biases, and justify epistemic decisions transparently. Assessment thus becomes a site where epistemic norms are not merely enforced, but actively enacted and learned.

Understanding assessment as an epistemic intervention also clarifies why validity cannot be secured through technical control alone. Exams that attempt to isolate human cognition from algorithmic environments lose ecological validity, as they no longer reflect the conditions under which knowledge is produced and applied in academic and professional contexts. Epistemic validity, by contrast, emerges when assessment formats align with the realities of hybrid knowledge production and evaluate precisely those competencies that enable responsible engagement with generative AI.

This reconceptualisation has far-reaching implications for examination design. Rather than asking how AI use can be detected or prevented, universities must determine which epistemic capacities they seek to cultivate and how assessment can support this goal. Exams become formative epistemic spaces in which students learn to assume responsibility for knowledge claims under conditions of algorithmic assistance. In this sense, assessment is not merely an endpoint of learning, but a central mechanism through which higher education shapes the epistemic order of the AI era.

These considerations lead to a central conclusion for assessment design: the more examinations are oriented toward excluding generative AI, the less epistemically valid they become. Valid assessment in hybrid knowledge environments does not hinge on the absence of algorithmic assistance, but rather on evaluating how students critically interpret, contextualise, and justify AI-supported outputs. Epistemic validity thus arises from assessing human judgment in interaction with generative systems rather than from attempting to isolate human cognition from its technological context.

In response to this shift, examination formats increasingly move toward reflective, curatorial, and dialogical models of assessment. Such formats include AI-supported written assignments that require transparent documentation of the prompting process and the critical evaluation of outputs; oral examinations that reconstruct epistemic decision making rather than merely reproducing texts; dialogical assessments in which students critique and refine AI-generated suggestions in real time; and process-oriented portfolios that document iterative reasoning, reflection, and justification. These formats do not abandon academic standards but recalibrate them toward competencies that remain epistemically meaningful under conditions of hybrid knowledge production.

Questions of quality assurance and fairness remain central in this transition. Ensuring epistemic fairness requires that assessments validly measure relevant competencies, apply transparent criteria, and provide comparable learning conditions for students with differing levels of AI-related expertise. At the same time, ethical and legal considerations—such as unequal access to advanced models, unresolved issues of authorship, and the handling of biased or erroneous outputs—underscore the need for institutional frameworks that accompany didactic innovation. These governance-related challenges are addressed in the following section.

6. GOVERNANCE AND ACADEMIC CULTURES IN TRANSITION

The integration of generative AI poses institutional challenges that go beyond mere adoption of new technologies. Universities exhibit pronounced path dependency; core structures such as examination regulations, curricula, committee procedures, and accreditation requirements are intentionally designed to ensure stability, predictability, and reproducibility (Clark, 1986). Consequently, change tends to occur incrementally, as entrenched routines, normative expectations, and legal frameworks constrain rapid adaptation. Generative AI disrupts this equilibrium by challenging foundational epistemic assumptions that underlie academic organisation, rather than simply necessitating new technological tools.

Within this context, institutional inertia is reflected less in resistance to technology itself and more in the difficulty of redefining legitimate academic performance. Faculty concerns, including apprehensions about declining learning outcomes or the erosion of individual achievement, are empirically substantiated (Bolívar-Cruz & Verano-Tacoronte, 2025). However, restrictive governance responses—especially those centred on prohibition or surveillance—tend to amplify rather than resolve these concerns. Governance frameworks that seek to stabilise traditional epistemic assumptions through control mechanisms risk increasing uncertainty rather than providing clear guidance.

A Kuhnian perspective helps to clarify the nature of this tension. Paradigm shifts do not simply involve the introduction of new instruments but require the reconfiguration of shared epistemic premises that guide problem definition, evaluation standards, and institutional routines (Kuhn, 1962/2012). In the context of generative AI, universities are increasingly confronted with questions that cannot be answered solely through existing regulatory logics: What constitutes individual academic achievement when knowledge production is hybrid? How should authorship and responsibility be defined in AI-supported work? Which competencies should institutional rules incentivise and protect? Governance thus shifts from rule enforcement toward epistemic orientation.

This challenge is intensified by universities' loosely coupled organisational structures (Weick, 1976). Faculties, departments, and degree programmes frequently operate with significant autonomy, leading to diverse responses to generative AI, ranging from strict prohibitions to open experimentation. Disciplinary epistemic cultures further accentuate this heterogeneity, as fields such as economics, literature, engineering, and the natural sciences differ fundamentally in their conceptions of valid knowledge, acceptable methodologies, and appropriate assessment forms. Consequently, effective AI governance cannot be uniformly imposed; it must align with discipline-specific epistemic norms while ensuring institution-wide coherence.

In light of these dynamics, three ideal-typical modes of AI governance can be identified. These modes serve as analytical frameworks rather than pure empirical descriptions, shaping how universities respond to epistemic transformation.

The first mode, control-oriented governance, conceptualises generative AI primarily as a threat to academic integrity. Standard instruments include bans on AI use, deployment of detection software, and formal declarations of non-use. Epistemically, this approach aims to preserve an ideal of isolated human cognition. Although such measures may provide short-term reassurance, they are structurally limited. Detection technologies are often unreliable, and control-based regimes tend to incentivise concealment rather than transparency. More fundamentally, these measures attempt to stabilise an epistemic order that no longer aligns with current knowledge practices.

A second mode, compliance-oriented governance, acknowledges AI use but manages it through procedural rules, documentation requirements, and differentiated permission regimes. This approach prioritises legal clarity, risk management, and organisational accountability. While compliance-oriented governance marks progress beyond outright prohibition, it remains epistemically limited if it treats AI primarily as an object of regulation rather than as a constitutive element of evolving knowledge practices. Procedural compliance may secure formal legitimacy without promoting epistemic adaptation.

A third, conceptually distinct mode is epistemic-enabling governance. This approach posits that generative AI catalyses rethinking the epistemic foundations of higher education, rather than merely presenting a governance problem. Instead of focusing on control or formalisation, epistemic-enabling governance aims to actively shape the conditions for the responsible development of hybrid knowledge practices. Its central objectives are the cultivation of epistemic judgment, transparency, and epistemic-enabling governance. Epistemic-enabling governance employs instruments such as integrating AI and prompt literacy into curricula, redesigning assessment formats to emphasise reflexive, process-oriented evaluation, providing institutional access to AI to promote fairness, and establishing competence centres that support both technical understanding and ethical reflection. In this model, academic rigour is redefined rather than diminished: transparency, documentation of AI use, and explicit justification of epistemic decisions become central governance mechanisms rather than surveillance tools.

Simultaneously, governance decisions directly affect academic freedom, creativity, and critical reflection. Generative AI can expand academic freedom by lowering participation barriers, reducing routine cognitive burdens, and enabling exploratory engagement with complex problems. It facilitates augmented creativity, where human imagination is stimulated rather than supplanted by algorithmic variation (Eapen et al., 2023; Mollick & Mollick, 2023). However, the widespread adoption of standardised models introduces the risk of epistemic homogenisation, as statistically dominant discourses and argumentation patterns are reinforced at the expense of heterodox perspectives (Anderson et al., 2024).

This tension highlights a central mission of higher education: cultivating critical distance rather than merely maximising efficiency. In AI-supported academic environments, this mission becomes increasingly essential. Universities must enhance students' and instructors' capacity to distinguish between algorithmic plausibility and epistemic validity, to interrogate underlying assumptions, and to reflect on the normative implications of AI-supported knowledge production. Governance frameworks that prioritise reflection over control are therefore essential for preserving academic freedom amid technological transformation.

Ethical considerations add further complexity to the governance landscape. As AI systems contribute substantively to academic outputs, questions of responsibility and authorship become increasingly prominent. Although prevailing norms appropriately exclude AI systems from authorship (COPE, 2023), the distinction between permissible assistance and impermissible delegation remains contested. Consequently, transparency requirements—such as disclosing AI use and documenting epistemic decisions—gain renewed significance as mechanisms for safeguarding academic integrity without resorting to exclusionary practices.

Bias and epistemic inequality constitute further governance challenges. Generative AI systems replicate biases present in their training data, including gendered, cultural, and ideological distortions. In economics education, this can reinforce dominant management narratives, Eurocentric perspectives, or normative assumptions about rationality and efficiency. Universities thus have an ethical responsibility to equip students with the analytical tools required to identify and critically engage with these biases (Buolamwini & Gebru, 2018).

Given these considerations, sustainable AI governance in higher education necessitates a multidimensional approach. At the programme level, discipline-specific guidelines should clarify permissible uses of AI, documentation requirements, and epistemic expectations. At the curricular level, competencies such as prompt literacy, data literacy, and ethical reflection must be integrated as core elements of academic education rather than treated as optional supplements. Institutionally, competence centres can function as epistemic infrastructures that support faculty development, curate best practices, and foster organisational learning. Finally, governance frameworks must address access and fairness to prevent unequal availability of AI tools from exacerbating existing social inequalities.

In summary, governance in the era of generative AI extends beyond compliance or control. It is an epistemic endeavour focused on shaping the conditions necessary for sustaining academic freedom, responsibility, and critical reflection within hybrid knowledge environments. Universities that adopt governance as an enabling, rather than a restrictive function are better equipped to integrate generative AI as a catalyst for institutional renewal rather than a source of fragmentation. The following section synthesises these insights into a future-oriented perspective on higher education in the context of algorithmic knowledge production.

7. TOWARD FUTURE-ORIENTED HIGHER EDUCATION

The preceding analysis demonstrates that generative AI functions not merely as an additional instructional technology but as a catalyst for a significant epistemic reconfiguration in higher education. Theoretical, didactic, assessment-related, and governance-oriented perspectives collectively indicate that the future of higher education will be defined by hybrid epistemic arrangements in which human judgment and algorithmic generativity are structurally interconnected. This transformation should be conceptualised as a paradigmatic shift from a culture of reproduction to an epistemic culture of curation, rather than as a disruption to be managed.

Theoretically, this shift can be synthesised according to three complementary dimensions. First, Kuhn's paradigm framework demonstrates that epistemic change occurs when established problem-solving strategies, methods, and evaluation standards lose coherence (Kuhn, 1962/2012). Generative AI simultaneously influences all three dimensions by transforming the framing of academic problems, the conduct of analytical and interpretive work, and the meaningful assessment of scholarly performance. Second, distributed cognition theories emphasise that learning and knowledge production arise from networks of human and non-human actors, rather than from isolated individuals (Hutchins, 1995). Within these networks, generative AI serves as a central epistemic artefact, actively shaping reasoning pathways. Third, actor-network theory affirms that epistemic orders are constituted through hybrid constellations of actors, practices, and technologies (Latour, 2005). Accordingly, generative AI should be regarded as an epistemic actor whose integration reconfigures academic roles, responsibilities, and evaluative standards.

From a didactic perspective, this synthesis indicates a need to reorient learning objectives. Future-oriented higher education should not be confined to equipping students with efficient AI tool usage; it must also foster the ability to exercise epistemic control within hybrid knowledge environments. Prompt literacy emerges as a key interface competency, enabling the connection between human problem formulation and algorithmic generation. However, prompt literacy attains epistemic significance only when integrated with broader academic competencies, such as critical thinking, methodological reasoning, metacognitive reflection, and data literacy. These competencies are not diminished by AI integration; instead, they become more demanding, as students must consistently distinguish between algorithmic plausibility and epistemic validity and transparently justify their epistemic decisions.

From an assessment perspective, this synthesis demonstrates that examination formats based on AI exclusion are becoming increasingly irrelevant. Valid assessment in hybrid knowledge-production contexts shifts the focus from products to processes, from authorship to justification, and from control to transparency. Examination formats that emphasise reflective engagement with AI, such as process documentation, dialogical examinations, and epistemic reconstruction, do not lower academic standards but instead realign them with current knowledge practices. Assessment thereby becomes an integral part of learning and epistemic development, rather than a mechanism of isolation.

At the organisational level, this synthesis underscores the necessity for institutional adaptation. Universities can realise the epistemic potential of generative AI only by conceptualising themselves as learning organisations capable of revising entrenched assumptions and institutional routines (Argyris & Schön, 1978). This requires curricular reconfiguration toward reflexive competencies, ongoing professional development for faculty, and governance structures that support experimentation while ensuring fairness, transparency, and academic freedom. In this context, governance serves as an enabling framework that aligns institutional rules with evolving epistemic realities.

Within this broader transformation, the economic disciplines serve as a particularly revealing stress test for epistemic change. Economics integrates formal modelling, narrative interpretation, and decision-oriented reasoning in ways that intensify the epistemic tensions associated with generative AI. Model-based reasoning benefits from AI-supported scenario generation and heuristic exploration but also risks reinforcing dominant paradigms and plausibility-driven shortcuts. Narrative coherence, which is central to applied economics and management studies, becomes easier to produce yet more challenging to validate epistemically. Decision-oriented reasoning raises significant questions of responsibility when algorithmic suggestions inform strategic or policy-relevant judgments. Thus, economics clearly demonstrates that generative AI cannot be regarded as a neutral efficiency-enhancing tool, but must be embedded within didactic, assessment, and governance frameworks that emphasise justification, critique, and accountability.

Collectively, these dimensions converge on a set of guiding principles for future-oriented higher education. Epistemic transparency becomes fundamental to academic integrity, necessitating the disclosure and justification of AI use in learning and assessment. Reflexive hybridity supplants the illusion of epistemic purity by recognising that knowledge is generated through human–machine interaction. Human judgment remains central to responsibility and meaning, even as algorithmic systems expand epistemic infrastructure. Fairness and equal access must be actively safeguarded to prevent AI from creating new forms of educational inequality. Ethical vigilance is essential to address biases, normative assumptions, and societal implications embedded in algorithmic knowledge production. Finally, governance should enable innovation rather than focus solely on control, supporting ongoing curricular and didactic development in response to rapid technological change.

In this context, higher education in the era of generative AI can be conceptualised as the cultivation of curatorial intelligence: the ability to orchestrate, evaluate, and responsibly integrate algorithmic contributions into human knowledge practices. Universities that adopt this role do not abandon their epistemic mission; instead, they renew it. By framing generative AI as a catalyst for epistemic reflexivity rather than as a threat to academic integrity, higher education can reaffirm its essential function as a space for critical judgment, intellectual autonomy, and societal responsibility.

8. CONCLUSION

This chapter examined the implications of generative AI for the epistemic foundations of higher education. Instead of framing generative AI solely as a technical tool or regulatory issue, the analysis positioned it as a catalyst for a broader paradigm shift in academic knowledge production. By drawing on Kuhn's theory of paradigms, as well as perspectives from epistemic culture research, distributed cognition, and actor-network theory, this chapter demonstrated that generative AI fundamentally reconfigures the production, evaluation, and attribution of knowledge within university contexts.

The preceding analysis revealed a coherent transformation in epistemic practices. Generative AI challenges an epistemic order historically centred on individual reproduction, linear reasoning, and text-based performance indicators. In hybrid human–machine environments, writing, analysis, and interpretation no longer serve as unequivocal proxies for individual understanding. Instead, epistemic authority increasingly depends on the ability to critically evaluate, contextualise, and justify algorithmically generated content. This shift does not undermine academic standards; instead, it relocates them toward reflexive judgment and epistemic accountability.

The analysis of epistemic risks demonstrated that generative AI introduces structural tensions that cannot be addressed solely through technical optimisation or control. Plausibility bias, epistemic homogenisation, cognitive externalisation, and ambiguous responsibility are not incidental but are constitutive features of hybrid knowledge production. These risks highlight the need to strengthen reflexive competencies and epistemic transparency, rather than attempting to maintain pre-AI epistemic ideals through exclusionary or surveillance-based measures.

From a didactic perspective, this chapter demonstrated that generative AI catalyses the re-evaluation of learning objectives and competency models. Prompt literacy emerged as a central epistemic interface skill, but only when integrated with broader capacities for critical thinking, methodological reasoning, data literacy, and metacognitive reflection. Learning in the AI era is becoming more demanding, as students are required to navigate complex epistemic environments, justify their decisions, and reflect on the interplay between human judgment and algorithmic suggestions.

The discussion of assessment practices further established that examination formats function not as neutral measurement instruments, but as epistemic interventions that shape learning behaviours and academic subjectivities. Traditional exams increasingly lose validity when designed to exclude generative AI. Control-oriented strategies, such as bans, detection tools, or declarations of non-use, are both technically unreliable and conceptually flawed. Epistemically robust assessment in hybrid knowledge environments shifts focus from products to processes, from authorship to justification, and from control to transparency. Examinations regain validity by evaluating the quality of human judgment exercised in conjunction with algorithmic systems, rather than by isolating human cognition.

At the institutional level, this chapter argued that governance in the era of generative AI should be conceptualised as an epistemic project rather than a compliance exercise. Universities must renegotiate fundamental assumptions about academic achievement, responsibility, and fairness amid institutional path dependency and disciplinary diversity. The comparison of governance modes indicated that only epistemic-enabling approaches—those aligning curricular design, assessment practices, and institutional support structures with hybrid knowledge realities—can simultaneously foster academic freedom, reflexivity, and epistemic responsibility.

Taken together, the findings collectively support a central conclusion: generative AI does not diminish the role of higher education but transforms it. University education's core mission shifts toward cultivating curatorial intelligence, defined as the ability to orchestrate, critically assess, and responsibly integrate algorithmic contributions into human knowledge practices. Consequently, higher education becomes less a site of isolated knowledge production and more a space of epistemic reflexivity, where judgment, interpretation, and responsibility are systematically developed. Rather than resisting or uncritically embracing generative AI, universities are called upon to shape its integration in ways that strengthen their epistemic foundations. By aligning didactics, assessment, and governance with the realities of hybrid knowledge production, higher education can reaffirm its societal role as a place where technological change is not merely adopted but critically understood, normatively guided, and institutionally shaped.

REFERENCES

Abdali, S., Anarfi, R., Barberan, C. J., & He, J. (2024). Decoding the AI pen: Techniques and challenges in detecting AI-generated text. *arXiv*. https://doi.org//arXiv.2403.05750DOI: 10.1145/3637528.3671463

Anderson, B. R., Shah, J. H., & Kreminski, M. (2024). Homogenization effects of large language models on human creative ideation. *arXiv*. /arXiv.2402.01536DOI: 10.1145/3635636.3656204

Argyris, C., & Schön, D. A. (1978). *Organizational learning: A theory of action perspective*. Addison-Wesley.

Bender, E. M., Gebru, T., McMillan-Major, A., & Shmitchell, S. (2021). On the dangers of stochastic parrots: Can language models be too big? *Proceedings of the ACM Conference on Fairness, Accountability, and Transparency*, 610–623. https://doi.org/DOI: 10.1145/3442188.3445922

Biggs, J., & Tang, C. (2011). *Teaching for quality learning at university. What the student does?* (4th ed.). Open University Press.

Bird, A. (2000). *Thomas Kuhn*. Princeton University Press. DOI: 10.1017/UPO9781844653065

Bolívar-Cruz, A., & Verano-Tacoronte, D. (2025). Is anxiety affecting the adoption of ChatGPT in university teaching? A gender perspective. *Technology. Knowledge and Learning*, *30*(4), 2373–2392. DOI: 10.1007/s10758-025-09830-0

Bommasani, R., Hudson, D. A., Adeli, E., Altman, R., Arora, S., & Arx, S. von et al. (2021). On the opportunities and risks of foundation models. *arXiv*. https://doi.org//arXiv.2108.07258DOI: 10.48550

Brynjolfsson, E., Li, Y., & Raymond, L. (2023). Generative AI at work. NBER Working Paper No. 31161. https://doi.org/DOI: 10.3386/w31161

Buolamwini, J., & Gebru, T. (2018). Gender shades: Intersectional accuracy disparities in commercial gender classification. Proceedings of the Conference on Fairness, Accountability, and Transparency, 77–91. https://proceedings.mlr.press/v81/buolamwini18a/buolamwini18a.pdf

Clark, B. R. (1986). *The higher education system: Academic organization in cross-national perspective*. University of California Press.

Collins, H., & Evans, R. (2007). *Rethinking expertise*. University of Chicago Press. DOI: 10.7208/chicago/9780226113623.001.0001

Committee on Publication Ethics (COPE). (2023). *Authorship and AI: COPE position statement.* COPE Council., DOI: 10.24318/cCVRZBms

Eapen, T. T., Finkenstadt, D. J., Folk, J., & Venkataswamy, L. (2023). How generative AI can augment human creativity. *SSRN, 10*(4), 56–64. DOI: 10.2139/ssrn.4759930

Eloundou, T., Manning, S., Mishkin, P., & Rock, D. (2023). GPTs are GPTs: An early look at the labor market impact potential of large language models. *arXiv*. https://doi.org//arXiv.2303.10130DOI: 10.48550

Fleck, L. (2023). *Entstehung und Entwicklung einer wissenschaftlichen Tatsache: Einführung in die Lehre vom Denkstil und Denkkollektiv*. Suhrkamp. (Original work published 1935)

Fraser, K. C., Dawkins, H., & Kiritchenko, S. (2025). Detecting AI-generated text: Factors influencing detectability with current methods. *Journal of Artificial Intelligence Research, 82*, 2233–2278. DOI: 10.1613/jair.1.16665

Gurdil, H., Soguksu, Y. B., Salihoglu, S., & Coskun, F. (2024). Integration of artificial intelligence in educational measurement: Efficacy of ChatGPT in data generation within the scope of item response theory. *arXiv*. https://doi.org//arXiv.2402.01731DOI: 10.48550

Hutchins, E. (1995). *Cognition in the wild.* MIT Press. DOI: 10.7551/mitpress/1881.001.0001

Kasneci, E., Sessler, K., Küchemann, S., Bannert, M., Dementieva, D., Fischer, F., Gasser, U., Groh, G., Günnemann, S., Hüllermeier, E., Krusche, S., Kutyniok, G., Michaeli, T., Nerdel, C., Pfeffer, J., Poquet, O., Sailer, M., Schmidt, A., Seidel, T., & Kasneci, G. (2023). ChatGPT for good? On opportunities and challenges of large language models for education. *Learning and Individual Differences, 103*, 102274. DOI: 10.1016/j.lindif.2023.102274

Kreps, S., McCain, R., & Brundage, M. (2020). All the news that's fit to fabricate: AI-Generated Text as a tool of media misinformation. http://dx.doi.org/DOI: 10.2139/ssrn.3525002

Kuhn, T. S. (1962/2012). The structure of scientific revolutions. 50th anniversary ed. University of Chicago Press.

Latour, B. (2005). *Reassembling the social: An introduction to actor-network-theory*. Oxford University Press. DOI: 10.1093/oso/9780199256044.001.0001

McKeachie, W. J., & Svinicki, M. (2013). *McKeachie's teaching tips: Strategies, research, and theory for college and university teachers*. Wadsworth Inc Fulfillment.

Mollick, E., & Mollick, L. (2023). Assigning AI: Seven ways to use Generative AI in the classroom. *arXiv*. https://doi.org//arXiv.2306.10052DOI: 10.48550

Rafiq, S. Qurat-ul-Ain, Afzal, A. (2025). The role of AI detection tools in upholding academic integrity: An evaluation of their effectiveness. *Contemporary Journal of Social Science Review, 3*(1), 901–915. https://contemporaryjournal.com/index.php/14/article/view/379

Shneiderman, B. (2022). *Human-centered AI*. Oxford University Press. DOI: 10.1093/oso/9780192845290.001.0001

Tzirides, A. O., Zapata, G., Kastania, N. P., Saini, A. K., Castro, V., Ismael, S. A., You, Y., Santos, T. A., Searsmith, D., O'Brien, C., Cope, B., & Kalantzis, M. (2024). Combining human and artificial intelligence for enhanced AI literacy in higher education. *Computers and Education Open*, *6*, 100184. DOI: 10.1016/j.caeo.2024.100184

Weick, K. E. (1976). Educational organizations as loosely coupled systems. *Administrative Science Quarterly*, *21*(1), 1–19. DOI: 10.2307/2391875

Williamson, B. (2017). Big data in education: The digital future of learning, policy and practice. *Sage (Atlanta, Ga.)*. Advance online publication. DOI: 10.4135/9781529714920

Zhai, X. (2024). Transforming teachers' roles and agencies in the era of generative AI: Perceptions, acceptance, knowledge, and practices. *arXiv*. https://doi.org//arXiv.2410.03018DOI: 10.2139/ssrn.4970687

Chapter 8
Gamification in Education for Educators and Policy Makers:
Gamification in Classrooms

Harika Rao
https://orcid.org/0000-0001-5443-1779
Lynn University, USA

ABSTRACT

Gamification, the strategic integration of game design elements into non-game contexts, has emerged as a powerful pedagogical approach aimed at enhancing motivation, engagement, and learning outcomes in educational environments. This chapter is designed to introduce educators to the fundamental concepts, theoretical foundations, and practical applications of gamification. It begins by defining key components such as points, badges, leaderboards, challenges, narratives, and feedback systems, illustrating how these elements can be tailored to support diverse learning objectives and student profiles.

INTRODUCTION

Gamification is the strategic incorporation of game elements, such as points, badges, leaderboards, challenges, and storytelling into non-game contexts to enhance motivation, engagement, and behavioral change (Groh, 2012). Gamification highlights psychological principles, including competition, achievement, and social connectedness, aiming to transform everyday activities into engaging and rewarding experiences. Its effectiveness lies in addressing intrinsic and extrinsic motivational

DOI: 10.4018/979-8-3373-4521-5.ch008

drivers, making complex or routine tasks more appealing and encouraging sustained engagement. As digital technology advances, the potential of Gamification to reshape how individuals learn, work, and interact continues to expand, positioning it as a powerful tool for fostering innovation and change across diverse domains.

Gamification has become an integral part of everyday life and business interactions. Examples include smartwatches tracking steps, Starbucks collecting and redeeming points or stars, and airline reward miles. Initially popularized in marketing and corporate training, Gamification has since gained significant traction in education, healthcare, and organizational contexts, where it is used to foster active participation and improve performance outcomes.

In recent years, the integration of Gamification into educational contexts has garnered considerable attention as a promising strategy to enhance student engagement and motivation. While initially popularized in marketing and corporate training, educators and researchers have increasingly recognized its potential to address longstanding challenges in learning environments, particularly in motivating students to participate actively and persist in their academic pursuits.

ARTIFICIAL INTELLIGENCE (AI) AND GAMIFICATION

AI and Gamification together form a powerful combination for enhancing education and engagement. Artificial intelligence can personalize gamified learning experiences by analyzing individual student data and adapting challenges, feedback, and rewards to match each learner's unique pace, preferences, and needs. This dynamic customization increases motivation and effectiveness by providing just-right difficulty levels and timely support. AI-powered analytics also help educators monitor progress, identify learning gaps, and refine gamification designs based on real-time insights.

Moreover, AI expands the possibilities of Gamification beyond traditional formats by enabling immersive, interactive environments such as virtual reality simulations, intelligent tutoring systems, and conversational agents. These technologies create rich, engaging experiences that motivate learners through storytelling, adaptive challenges, and social interaction. Together, AI and Gamification foster active, learner-centered environments that promote deeper engagement, personalized learning paths, and sustained motivation, ultimately improving educational outcomes in diverse settings.

UNDERSTANDING THE COMPONENTS OF GAMIFICATION

At its core, gamification leverages carefully curated game elements, design principles, and mechanics to motivate behavior, enhance user engagement, and foster a deeper connection to tasks and objectives. These components work synergistically to create immersive experiences that fulfill psychological needs such as autonomy, competence, and relatedness, thereby promoting sustained motivation. By systematically structuring how rewards, challenges, storytelling, and interaction are integrated, educators and designers can craft impactful systems that not only captivate their audiences but also achieve meaningful behavioral and learning outcomes. This overview provides a clear understanding of these fundamental building blocks, laying the groundwork for effective gamification strategies across diverse contexts.

Table 1. Different Components of Gamification

Concept	Definition	Key Components and Examples	Purpose and Impact
Game Elements	Fundamental building blocks or components used to create engaging and motivating gamified experiences.	Visual symbols, rules, rewards; examples include points, badges, leaderboards, levels, challenges, storytelling (Dicheva et al., 2015).	Satisfy psychological needs; promote motivation via recognition, competition, mastery, and narrative.
Game Design	Thoughtful planning and structuring of how game elements interact within a system to create cohesive experiences.	Objectives, rules, storylines, feedback mechanisms, and reward systems align with psychological theories, such as Self-Determination Theory (Kapp, 2012).	Supports autonomy, competence, and relatedness, maximizing motivation through a balance of challenge and meaningfulness.
Game Mechanics	Specific rules and systems governing how game elements function and interact to drive behavior.	Scoring algorithms, level progression, feedback loops, reward distribution, and social interactions (Salen Tekinbas & Zimmerman, 2003).	Structure motivation, flow, and sustained engagement; ensure fair and engaging activities are aligned with goals.

Note. The table provides detailed definitions of the different components of Gamification.

Game Elements and Their Functions

Game elements are the essential components that underpin any gamified experience. These elements, including points, badges, leaderboards, and narrative features, are carefully designed to engage learners, motivate participation, and guide behavior within educational environments. By utilizing visual symbols, rules, and rewards, game elements tap into fundamental psychological drivers such as the desire for recognition, mastery, and social connection. Understanding the distinct functions of these elements is key for educators and designers to create gamification systems that not only capture attention but also foster meaningful and sustained learning engagement. This section examines the primary game elements and how they interact to create motivating and interactive educational experiences.

Table 2. Different Game Elements

Game Elements	Functions
Points.	It is a fundamental gamification mechanic used to quantify achievement and progress. They serve as immediate reinforcers, rewarding users for completing tasks, reaching milestones, or participating actively (Hamari, Koivisto, & Sarsa, 2014). Points motivate continual engagement and help users track their progress within a system
Badges	They are visual symbols of achievement that recognize milestones, skills, or accomplishments (Seaborn & Fels, 2015). They satisfy users' needs for competence and recognition, serving as a form of social status within the community.
Leaderboards	Rank participants based on accumulated points or achievements, leveraging social comparison to stimulate competition and motivate improved performance (Hamari et al., 2014). They foster a sense of challenge and achievement when designed to emphasize personal and group progress.
Levels and Challenges	Structure the learning journey, providing staged goals that mark progression. They offer a tangible sense of mastery and growth, aligning with the desire for competence (Csikszentmihalyi, 1990). Challenges are activities or tasks designed to motivate users by presenting attainable yet meaningful objectives.
Quests and Storytelling	Involve narrative-driven, goal-oriented tasks that immerse users in a storyline, promoting engagement through context and purpose. Storytelling encourages emotional investment and personal connection to the content (Dicheva et al., 2015).
Feedback mechanisms	Such as instant feedback for actions or progress reports, provide learners with real-time reinforcement, guiding behavior, and promoting reflection. Feedback aligns with self-regulation and motivates sustained effort.
Collaboration and Competition	Foster social interaction: collaboration encourages teamwork and shared achievement, satisfying relatedness needs. Competition, when applied carefully, stimulates effort and excellence while fostering a sense of community.

Note. The table provides detailed definitions of the different game elements.

Design and Mechanics of Gamification Systems

- The design of Gamification involves careful consideration of how these elements function together to support specific behavioral goals. Practical gamification mechanics are grounded in psychological theories, such as Self-Determination Theory, and aim to satisfy users' basic needs for autonomy, competence, and relatedness. For example, enabling choices (autonomy), providing clear progress indicators (competence), and fostering social interaction (relatedness) are essential for meaningful engagement.

- Mechanics refer to the system's rules and processes that govern how game elements interact. They include achievement systems, reward cycles, adaptive difficulty, and social dynamics. Well-designed mechanics ensure a balance between challenge and skill, creating a state of flow (Csikszentmihalyi, 1990) and deep engagement.

Artificial intelligence (AI) has a significant influence on game design and game mechanics, enabling more dynamic, adaptive, and personalized gaming experiences. AI algorithms can analyze player behavior, preferences, and skill levels in real time, enabling games to adjust difficulty, offer tailored challenges, and deliver customized feedback. This adaptive design enhances player engagement by maintaining an optimal balance between challenge and skill, thereby preventing frustration or boredom. Additionally, AI can generate procedural content, such as levels, narratives, or quests, thereby expanding game variety and replayability without requiring exhaustive manual design.

In terms of game mechanics, AI enables more sophisticated interactions with non-player characters (NPCs) that exhibit realistic behaviors, strategic decision-making, and emotional responses, thereby enriching storytelling and immersion. AI-driven mechanics also support intelligent matchmaking, dynamic environments, and personalized reward systems that respond to player actions. These advancements allow game designers to create more complex, responsive, and immersive gameplay that caters to diverse player types and preferences, ultimately improving player satisfaction and the overall gaming experience.

THE EVOLUTION AND HISTORY OF GAMIFICATION IN EDUCATION AND INDUSTRY

The concept of Gamification, though relatively recent in scholarly discourse, has roots that trace back centuries, reflecting the enduring human tendency to engage with reward systems and competitive structures. Historically, elements of Gamification, such as reward systems and competitions, have been used across various cultural and social contexts to motivate individuals and shape behavior. For example, ancient civilizations employed reward and recognition mechanisms, such as medals and titles, to incentivize achievements and reinforce social hierarchies. However, as a formalized concept within the realm of behavioral and learning sciences, Gamification emerged prominently in the 21st century alongside advancements in psychology, particularly in reinforcement theory and motivation research.

The modern conceptualization of Gamification can be primarily attributed to the work of researchers and practitioners in marketing, corporate training, and education during the early 2000s. Its roots are often linked to the proliferation of digital game elements applied beyond entertainment, primarily to influence consumer behavior and employee performance. A pivotal moment in the history of Gamification occurred in 2010 when Yu-Kai Chou introduced the *Octalysis Framework*, which articulated the motivational core drives behind game design and formalized the strategic integration of incentives in non-game settings. This holistic framework helped shift the perspective from superficial point-scoring to a comprehensive approach rooted in behavioral psychology, emphasizing the importance of intrinsic motivation and engagement.

Simultaneously, the rise of digital technology and online platforms provided fertile ground for the implementation of gamified systems, especially in corporate, educational, and health domains. In education, the early 2010s saw a surge in pilot projects and experimental programs to integrate leaderboards, badges, and goal-oriented challenges into classroom activities—the pioneering work by practitioners such as Alfred and Kumar (2024). Moreover, Dicheva et al. (2015) have documented the successful application of Gamification to boost student motivation, participation, and retention rates. These early studies laid the foundation for a burgeoning body of research that consistently demonstrated the efficacy of gamified learning environments.

Throughout the decade, the adoption of Gamification expanded across industries, driven by the recognition of its capacity to enhance engagement, foster collaboration, and influence behaviors. Notably, organizations in healthcare, retail, and finance developed gamified platforms to promote health behaviors, increase customer loyalty, and motivate employees. The publication of systematic reviews and meta-analyses, such as those by Hamari et al. (2014), solidified their legitimacy as empirically supported strategies, underscoring the importance of well-designed mechanisms aligned with psychological needs.

Critics have argued that early implementations often relied on superficial game elements such as points and badges without fostering meaningful engagement or intrinsic motivation. This critique has led to a more nuanced understanding of Gamification's potential and limitations, prompting scholars to advocate for principles grounded in behavioral psychology, specifically Self-Determination Theory, and to develop more sophisticated, contextually sensitive frameworks (Dicheva et al., 2015; Kapp, 2012).

The history of Gamification is characterized by its evolution from primitive reward systems to a complex discipline informed by psychological theories, technological advances, and empirical research. Its journey reflects an ongoing quest to harness game design to motivate, educate, and influence behavior in diverse settings. As digital interfaces continue to evolve and research deepens, Gamification remains a vibrant and expanding field with profound implications for the future of education, industry, and society.

The evolution and history of Gamification in education and industry have seen significant advancements, driven by the integration of AI in recent years. Initially, Gamification involved the application of basic game elements such as points, badges, and leaderboards to motivate users in educational and industrial settings. Over time, these mechanics evolved to incorporate more sophisticated features, including narrative storytelling and social connectivity. The recent emergence of AI has revolutionized Gamification by enabling personalized, adaptive experiences that respond in real-time to user behavior and preferences. AI algorithms analyze vast amounts of data to tailor challenges, feedback, and rewards to individual learners or employees, enhancing motivation and engagement beyond traditional static game elements.

In education, AI-driven gamification supports differentiated instruction by adjusting difficulty levels and content to fit diverse learner needs, fostering deeper engagement, and promoting mastery learning (Deterding et al., 2011). In industry, AI facilitates dynamic training environments that simulate real-world tasks with intelligent virtual agents and adaptive scenarios, improving skill acquisition and performance (Hamari & Koivisto, 2015). Furthermore, AI-powered analytics provide educators and managers with actionable insights into user progress and engagement patterns, enabling continuous improvement of gamified systems. The synergy between AI and Gamification marks a new era where intelligent, data-informed design amplifies the motivational power of game-based strategies in both education and workforce development.

THE TRANSFORMATIVE POTENTIAL OF GAMIFICATION IN EDUCATION: ENHANCING MOTIVATION AND ENGAGEMENT

In recent years, educational stakeholders have increasingly recognized the limitations of traditional instructional methods, particularly in engaging contemporary learners. The rapid proliferation of digital technology, coupled with changing student expectations, has prompted a reevaluation of pedagogical strategies.

Numerous empirical studies underscore a pervasive issue: declining motivation and engagement among students in modern classrooms. Research by Finn (1989) and later by Fredricks et al. (2004) highlights alarming trends in which students exhibit decreased behavioral, emotional, and cognitive involvement in learning. This disengagement is more pronounced in higher education, where students often perceive coursework as disconnected from real-world applications, which can diminish intrinsic motivation. Furthermore, the rise of digital distractions, social media, and entertainment-oriented activities has exacerbated the challenge, making traditional pedagogical approaches less effective in captivating learners' attention (Thapa et al., 2025).

Research indicates that a significant proportion of students report feeling disconnected from classroom activities, citing boredom, lack of relevance, and perceived irrelevance of assessments as key factors. For instance, a study by the National Survey of Student Engagement (NSSE, 2019) revealed that over 50% of college students find their coursework unstimulating and disengaging, which correlates with lower academic achievement and increased dropout rates. The same research also emphasizes that motivation and engagement are vital determinants of deep learning, persistence, and overall academic success. Therefore, the educational community faces an urgent imperative to adopt innovative strategies that can rekindle students' intrinsic interest and foster a sense of purpose.

Since the advent of AI, motivation and engagement in educational and workplace settings have shifted toward more personalized and adaptive experiences. AI enables real-time analysis of individual behaviors, preferences, and performance, allowing motivational strategies to move beyond generic, one-size-fits-all approaches. This personalization helps sustain engagement by delivering challenges and rewards that align closely with each learner's or employee's current skill level, learning style, and interests, thereby enhancing intrinsic motivation. Additionally, AI can identify when motivation wanes and intervene with timely support or varied incentives to re-engage users (Deterding et al., 2011; Magomadov, 2020).

Engagement has also evolved with the introduction of immersive and interactive technologies powered by AI, such as intelligent tutoring systems, virtual coaches, and gamified simulations that dynamically respond to user input. These technologies create richer, more meaningful interactions that foster deeper cognitive and emotional involvement. As a result, motivation is not just driven by external rewards but by a continuous, responsive system that nurtures autonomy, competence, and relatedness, components central to self-determination theory. Overall, AI advances are shifting motivational paradigms from static incentives to fluid, learner-centered experiences that sustain long-term engagement and promote personalized growth (Ryan & Deci, 2020; Hamari & Koivisto, 2015).

THE ROLE OF GAMIFICATION IN REIMAGINING EDUCATION

Gamification offers a paradigm shift by leveraging motivational psychology and game design principles to enhance learner engagement. Unlike conventional didactic teaching, gamified learning environments seek to create an intrinsically rewarding experience where students feel competent, autonomous, and connected, the three fundamental needs delineated by Deci and Ryan (1985). By incorporating elements such as immediate feedback, achievement badges, competitive leaderboards, and narrative-driven challenges, Gamification energizes the learning process, making it more interactive, enjoyable, and meaningful.

One of the primary ways Gamification can revolutionize education is by transforming extrinsic motivation into a vehicle for fostering intrinsic interest. For instance, earning badges or unlocking levels can serve as symbols of mastery, fulfilling the need for competence and recognition. Real-time feedback provides students with immediate acknowledgment of their progress, reinforcing positive behavior and encouraging continued effort (Hamari et al., 2014). Leaderboards introduce a social dimension, instilling a healthy competitive spirit and promoting collaborative learning, which enhances relatedness and community-building (Antonaci et al., 2019). Moreover, narrative elements and storytelling can contextualize learning content, inspiring students by framing academic objectives within engaging, real-world scenarios.

EMPIRICAL EVIDENCE SUPPORTING GAMIFICATION IN EDUCATION

Empirical evidence supporting the Use of Gamification in education highlights its positive impact on student engagement, motivation, and learning outcomes across diverse contexts and disciplines. Numerous studies have demonstrated that incorporating game elements such as points, badges, leaderboards, and challenges can significantly enhance students' intrinsic and extrinsic motivation. For instance, research by Hamari, Koivisto, and Sarsa (2014) conducted a comprehensive review of gamification studies and found that Gamification consistently improved user engagement and participation, especially when the game elements were thoughtfully integrated into the learning objectives.

Experimental studies have shown that Gamification fosters active learning and improves knowledge retention. Domínguez et al. (2013) designed a gamified e-learning platform for university students and reported increased participation rates, higher grades, and improved long-term retention compared to traditional learning methods. Another randomized controlled trial by Asigigan & Samur (2021). found that gamified quizzes and interactive challenges significantly enhanced students' critical thinking and problem-solving abilities in STEM education. These findings suggest that gamified interventions encourage deeper cognitive processing by making learning enjoyable and relevant.

Social and collaborative aspects of Gamification have also been linked to improved learning experiences. Studies such as Sailer et al. (2017) emphasize how competitive and cooperative game mechanics foster social interaction, peer learning, and a sense of community among students, which are crucial for sustained engagement and academic success. Moreover, Gamification has been shown to benefit diverse learner populations by addressing different motivational profiles and learning preferences (Seaborn & Fels, 2015).

Despite promising results, empirical research also emphasizes the importance of carefully designed Gamification that aligns with pedagogical goals and avoids overreliance on extrinsic rewards, which can undermine intrinsic motivation. Overall, the body of evidence supports Gamification as a powerful pedagogical tool when implemented thoughtfully, with potential to enhance motivation, engagement, and educational achievement in various learning environments.

THEORETICAL FOUNDATIONS OF GAMIFICATION IN EDUCATION

In examining the transformative potential of Gamification within educational settings, it is essential to understand the psychological theories that underpin its effectiveness in fostering motivation and engagement. Central to this exploration is Self-Determination Theory (SDT), a comprehensive framework developed by Deci and Ryan (1985), which posits that human motivation is driven by the fulfillment of three fundamental psychological needs: autonomy, competence, and relatedness. When these needs are met, individuals are more likely to experience intrinsic motivation, an internal drive rooted in interest, enjoyment, and personal growth, which leads to sustained engagement and higher performance.

Self-Determination Theory (SDT) and Gamification

Within the context of education, Gamification supports SDT by providing learners with choices and autonomy in their learning pathways, which enhances their sense of ownership over their educational journey. For example, allowing students to select challenges, badges, or goals aligns with their preferences and interests, fostering a sense of control (Deci & Ryan, 1985). Competence is cultivated through clear objectives, immediate feedback, and opportunities for mastery, core elements embedded in gamified environments via progress bars, achievement badges, and levels. When students recognize their growth and mastery, their intrinsic motivation increases, encouraging persistence and deeper engagement (Kappen et al., 2017).

The need for relatedness, or social connection, is addressed through gamified features such as leaderboards, collaborative challenges, and social sharing platforms. These facilitate interaction, competition, and community building, which are critical for fostering a supportive learning environment. Research indicates that social engagement enhances motivation by satisfying the innate human desire to belong (Deci & Ryan, 2000; Ryan & Deci, 2017). Therefore, Gamification inherently appeals to these psychological needs, making learning more meaningful and engaging.

Motivational Constructs: Intrinsic and Extrinsic Motivation

A key aspect of the theoretical basis for Gamification involves understanding the distinction between intrinsic and extrinsic motivation. Intrinsic motivation is characterized by activities driven by interest, enjoyment, and personal challenge (Deci & Ryan, 1985). This form of motivation is associated with higher levels of engagement, creativity, and long-term persistence. On the other hand, extrinsic motivation occurs when external rewards, such as points, badges, or grades, drive behavior (Ryan & Deci, 2000). While extrinsic motivators can effectively initiate activity, their overuse may undermine intrinsic motivation, leading to superficial engagement (Elliot, 2013).

Effective gamification strategies, therefore, aim to balance these motivators by designing systems that reward achievement without overshadowing the natural desire for mastery and self-direction. For instance, when badges are linked to personal growth goals rather than only extrinsic rewards, students are more likely to internalize motivation and develop a genuine interest in learning (Deci & Ryan, 2000).

Motivational constructs, specifically intrinsic and extrinsic motivation, are fundamental concepts educators must consider when designing courses to foster meaningful and sustained student engagement. Intrinsic motivation refers to learners' internal drive to engage in an activity for its inherent satisfaction, curiosity, or personal growth. When courses are designed to tap into intrinsic motivation, students are more likely to experience deep learning, creativity, and persistence. This can be achieved by offering autonomy, challenging tasks that match skill levels, and opportunities for mastery and relevance, which help students find personal value in the learning process.

Extrinsic motivation, on the other hand, involves external rewards or recognition such as grades, badges, or praise. While extrinsic motivators can effectively encourage participation and goal achievement, they must be applied thoughtfully to avoid undermining intrinsic interest. A well-designed course strikes a balance between the two types by using extrinsic incentives to initially engage or guide students, while nurturing intrinsic motivation to promote long-term commitment and meaningful learning. Understanding how to leverage these motivational constructs enables educators to create more effective and engaging learning experiences that cater to diverse student needs.

The Four Gamer Personas: A Framework for Tailored Gamification

The Four Gamer Personas framework, developed by Andrzej Marczewski, offers a valuable approach to designing gamification systems that cater to diverse user motivations and preferences. This framework categorizes players into four primary personas, namely, Achievers, Explorers, Socializers, and Killers, each representing distinct motivations for engaging with games and gamified experiences. Achievers seek mastery and goal completion; Explorers enjoy discovery and learning; Socializers value connection and collaboration; while Killers thrive on competition and dominance. By recognizing these different player types, educators and designers can tailor gamification elements to address the unique needs and drives of each group, thereby enhancing motivation, engagement, and overall effectiveness (Marczewski, 2015).

The benefits of applying the Four Gamer Personas framework to educational Gamification are well documented. Tailored experiences that align with individual motivations help increase sustained engagement by providing relevant challenges, social opportunities, or exploratory tasks that resonate with learners. Research indicates that understanding player diversity leads to more inclusive and personalized gamified environments, which in turn promote better learning outcomes and user satisfaction (Seaborn & Fels, 2015). This framework also supports the creation of balanced systems that avoid alienating any group by ensuring a mix of competitive, cooperative, and achievement-oriented elements. Overall, the Four Gamer Personas provide a theory-driven foundation for crafting dynamic, motivating gamified experiences adaptable to varied educational contexts.

Figure 1. The Four Personas Defined

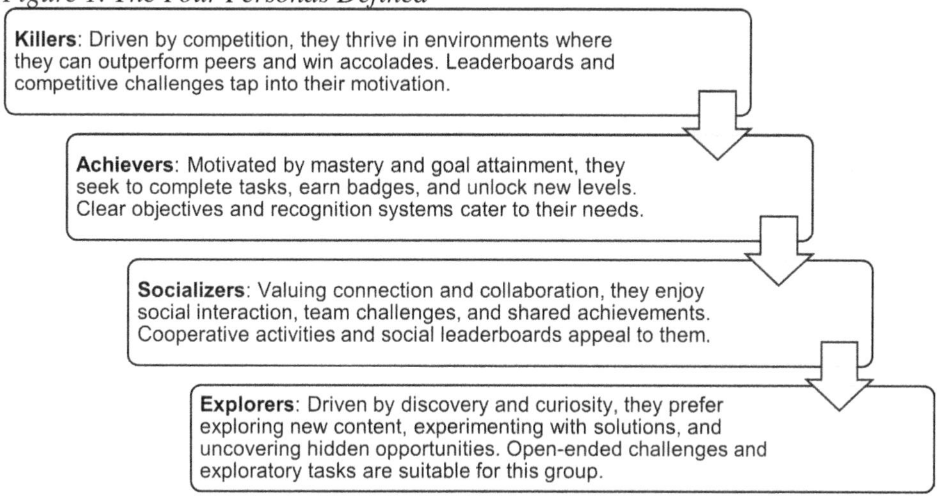

Note. The figure depicts the four personas: Killers, Achievers, Socializers, and Explorers.

Recognizing these diverse motivations enables educators to create multifaceted gamified environments that appeal to a broad spectrum of learners, thereby maximizing engagement and learning outcomes.

Educators can leverage the Four Gamer Personas framework to tailor gamification strategies that cater to diverse student motivations and preferences, thereby enhancing engagement and learning outcomes. This framework identifies four primary gamer types, namely, Achievers, Explorers, Socializers, and Killers; each driven by different intrinsic and extrinsic rewards. Achievers are motivated by mastering challenges and accumulating points or badges, so incorporating clear achievement goals and progress tracking can inspire their engagement. Explorers seek discovery and creativity, benefiting from open-ended tasks, puzzles, or opportunities for experimentation within gamified activities. By understanding these personas, educators can design course components that cater to varied needs, making the learning experience more personalized and engaging.

Moreover, the Socializers and Killers personas highlight the importance of social interaction and competition in motivating students. Socializers excel in collaborative environments where teamwork, effective communication, and peer recognition are valued. Educators can foster this by integrating group quests, discussion forums, or peer-review elements within their gamified courses. Killers, on the other hand, are driven by competition and influence, responding well to leaderboards, contests, and challenges that enable them to demonstrate their skills and impact. Using this framework enables educators to thoughtfully balance cooperative and competitive elements, creating a dynamic environment that maximizes motivation for all students by aligning game mechanics with diverse personality types.

LITERATURE REVIEW: SELF-DETERMINATION THEORY, MOTIVATION, AND ENGAGEMENT

Self-Determination Theory (SDT), developed by Deci and Ryan (1985), provides a powerful lens for understanding the factors that drive motivation and engagement in education, work, and health. At its core, SDT highlights three essential psychological needs: autonomy, competence, and relatedness. When these needs are met, people transition toward autonomous motivation, which fuels greater engagement, persistence, and overall well-being (Deci & Ryan, 2000). Motivation lies along a continuum from a lack of motivation to extrinsic incentives to deep intrinsic interest, which shifts depending on how well these needs are fulfilled.

Extensive research supports the relevance of SDT in educational settings. For example, Houlfort (2004) found that students thrive when classrooms nurture autonomy and social connection, showing stronger intrinsic motivation and more active participation. Similarly, when teachers adopt autonomy-supportive styles, motivation and persistence improve, resulting in better learning outcomes (Shernoff, 2013). Vansteenkiste et al. (2004) further revealed how autonomous motivation helps students engage deeply over time, especially when they internalize meaningful goals and feel a sense of competence. This connection extends to higher education, where intrinsic motivation correlates with academic persistence and self-regulation (Reeve, 2012).

Beyond education, SDT also influences workplace motivation. Deci and Ryan (2016) demonstrated that employee engagement and innovation thrive when jobs foster autonomy, mastery, and connection. Their meta-analysis showed that supportive organizational environments reduce burnout and inspire creativity. Crucially, the type of extrinsic motivation matters: external rewards can sometimes diminish intrinsic interest if they are perceived as controlling, but when activities align with personal values, motivation endures (Deci, Koestner, & Ryan, 1999).

Social context plays a vital role. Supportive relationships in faculty teams or peer groups satisfy relatedness needs, boosting engagement and fostering persistence in collaborative learning (Ryan & Deci, 2000; Houlfort, 2004). However, SDT also faces critiques, particularly regarding cultural variations in how autonomy and relatedness are valued, reminding us that motivation is shaped by context (Deci & Ryan, 2012).

Overall, a rich body of evidence confirms that when environments nurture autonomy, competence, and relatedness, individuals engage more earnestly and persistently. This makes SDT a cornerstone theory for crafting strategies that inspire meaningful and sustained motivation across diverse settings.

LITERATURE REVIEW OF GAMIFICATION

The growing body of literature on Gamification paints an exciting yet nuanced picture of its impact on student learning experiences. While many studies celebrate Gamification's ability to boost motivation and engagement, there is a cautionary side to this approach. Without careful alignment with course concepts, games risk becoming mere distractions, with students focusing on playing rather than learning. This delicate balance lies at the heart of recent research exploring how Gamification, when combined with summative assessments, can connect game elements meaningfully to educational content, transforming play into powerful learning.

Delving into recent studies reveals an overall positive trend, tempered by calls for thoughtful design and context-sensitivity. For example, Pelizzari (2023) emphasizes that the benefits of gamification hinge on selecting appropriate game elements and embedding them where students truly interact with the material. Thapa et al. (2025) highlight the potential of Gamification to spark enthusiasm, particularly in STEM fields, while also urging a deeper investigation into its long-term effects. Nadi-Ravandi & Batooli (2022) and Sailer & Homner (2020) offer a tempered view through their wide-reaching meta-analysis, finding only modest gains, often short-lived in low-stakes settings, and advocate for further exploration of lasting impacts. Similarly, Dicheva et al. (2015) underline how the right design conditions transform Gamification from a novelty into a meaningful motivator.

Other research echoes these themes with an emerging consensus. Mitchell (2023) reports the energizing effect of Gamification in programming courses, while Mekler et al. (2017) and Hew (2015) confirm improved motivation and learning across various contexts. Sailer et al. (2017) and Dicheva et al. (2015) further elaborate on the picture, emphasizing that the benefits of Gamification depend heavily on aligning its mechanics with educational goals and the learner's context. Together, these studies not only highlight the promise of Gamification but also guide educators in harnessing it thoughtfully, ensuring that games not only entertain but also fundamentally enhance learning journeys.

This literature review is crucial for the chapters that follow, as it establishes a solid foundation for understanding the current landscape of gamification research in education. It informs the theoretical framework by highlighting motivational theories, such as Self-Determination Theory, that underpin gamified learning. Moreover, it identifies critical design principles and challenges that the subsequent chapters address through practical strategies and policy recommendations. By critically examining both the benefits and limitations, this review sets the stage for a balanced approach that advocates thoughtful, evidence-based implementation of Gamification to maximize student engagement and learning outcomes.

LIMITATIONS AND CHALLENGES OF GAMIFICATION

Gamification holds great promise for transforming learning, but it is not without its challenges. While many studies confirm its ability to boost student motivation, engagement, and retention, Gamification must be implemented thoughtfully by faculty to avoid potential pitfalls. Here is an engaging exploration of the key limitations and challenges educators and administrators face and why addressing them is essential for success.

Table 3. Limitations of Gamification

Limitation	Description	Impact
Short-term Effects	Engagement gains may fade, and long-term retention remains unclear (Çınar et al., 2022; Rodrigues et al., 2021; Hamari & Koivisto, 2015).	Motivation wanes after gamification activities end.
Over-reliance on Extrinsic Motivation	Emphasis on rewards can overshadow intrinsic interest, reducing genuine engagement in learning (Deci & Ryan, 1985; Ryan & Deci, 2000).	Risks discouraging deep, meaningful learning.
Limited Generalizability	Effectiveness varies by context (subject, learners, environment) (Kapp, 2012).	Results are situational, not universally applicable.
Misalignment with Learning Objectives	Gamification may create superficial engagement if not aligned with goals (Kapp, 2012).	Engagement without meaningful knowledge gain.
Design Challenges	Creating effective, tailored Gamification requires expertise and time (Faiella & Ricciardi, 2015).	Poor design can undermine motivation and learning.
Unintended Consequences	Competition-focused Gamification may harm collaboration (Deterding et al., 2011).	May disrupt positive team dynamics.
Cultural Considerations	Designs failing to consider cultural differences can reduce engagement (Kaya & Ercag, 2023).	Unequal motivational impact across diverse groups.

Note. The table outlines the various limitations associated with implementing Gamification.

Understanding these limitations and challenges is crucial for anyone seeking to implement Gamification meaningfully. Without addressing issues such as short-lived motivation, overemphasis on extrinsic rewards, and technical and behavioral hurdles, even the most exciting gamified programs risk falling short. An informed, strategic approach that incorporates customization, cultural sensitivity, and ongoing assessment enables sustainable and impactful Gamification, truly enhancing learning and engagement.

Table 4. Challenges of Gamification

Challenge Type	Key Issues	Possible Solutions
Technical	Need for robust hardware and infrastructure (Lin et al., 2017)	Careful infrastructure evaluation
	Complex gamification software integration with LMS (Bourgonjon et al., 2010)	Engage skilled developers and IT teams.
	Compatibility issues across devices, browsers, and platforms (Thapa et al., 2019)	Ensure cross-platform compatibility
	Requirement for intuitive user experience design to avoid frustration (Hart, 2015)	Design user-friendly interfaces
Administrative	Time-intensive content creation aligned with curriculum and learning goals (Yildirim, 2017).	Develop dedicated content development teams.
	Faculty and staff training on gamification tools (Dicheva et al., 2015)	Provide ongoing professional development
	Continuous assessment and management of gamification systems (Hamari et al., 2014)	Implement feedback loops and monitoring processes
Financial	High initial and ongoing costs for technology and training (Freeman et al., 2024; Nylén-Eriksen et al., 2025)	Budget planning with a sustainability focus
	Need for cost-benefit justification to secure stakeholder support (Project Management Institute, 2021)	Conduct thorough cost-benefit analyses
Behavioral	Resistance to change and limited staff motivation (Castillo-Parra et al., 2022)	Identify and empower change champions.
	Balancing engaging, fun experiences with meaningful learning outcomes (Bonsignore et al., 2022)	Align incentives with institutional priorities.
	Encouraging student adoption and overcoming resistance (Pelizzari, 2023)	Develop engaging and rewarding gamified content.

Note. The table outlines the various challenges associated with implementing Gamification.

By recognizing potential pitfalls upfront and planning thoughtfully across technical, administrative, financial, and behavioral dimensions, universities can unlock the full potential of Gamification to create vibrant, motivating educational experiences that resonate deeply with students and faculty alike.

Leveraging Gamification in education offers an exciting pathway for educators to ignite student motivation and deepen engagement, both through Learning Management Systems (LMS) and dynamic in-class strategies. By thoughtfully blending technology with face-to-face interaction, educators can create immersive, learner-centered environments that spark curiosity, foster collaboration, and support meaningful achievement.

GAMIFICATION IN LEARNING MANAGEMENT SYSTEMS: MAKING EVERY CLICK COUNT

LMS platforms like Canvas, Moodle, or Blackboard serve as rich canvases where game elements transform routine tasks into rewarding experiences. Educators can award points and badges for completing quizzes, participating in discussions, or submitting assignments. These tokens of progress provide immediate recognition, encouraging students to stay motivated and track their growth. For example, using Canvas's Badges plugin, instructors can design custom badges that students proudly showcase, reinforcing a sense of accomplishment.

Leaderboards and competitive challenges add a social spark, igniting friendly competition that motivates students to improve consistently. Private or team-based leaderboards can encourage collaboration while maintaining a healthy and supportive competitive environment. Weekly challenges or quizzes tied to rankings inspire ongoing engagement without overshadowing individual progress.

With levels, quests, and narrative structures, educators can design a journey of mastery. Unlocking advanced content or missions that require problem-solving contextualizes learning, making abstract theories more vivid and applicable. Storytelling weaves these tasks into a compelling adventure, captivating students, and connecting lessons to real-world scenarios.

Instant feedback and reflective prompts delivered through quizzes or gamified surveys empower students to build confidence and develop self-awareness. This continuous loop deepens understanding while keeping learners invested in their pathway.

Moreover, LMS platforms often support external integrations, such as Badgr or Classcraft, enabling personalized badge systems, virtual currencies, or story-driven experiences that seamlessly bridge classroom and online learning.

ACTIVE IN-CLASS GAMIFICATION: ENERGIZING LEARNING THROUGH INTERACTION

In the physical classroom, gamified tactics spark collaboration and creativity. Group challenges, whether problem-solving, case studies, or concept mapping, encourage students to rely on one another, strengthening social bonds and boosting motivation through peer recognition. This approach nurtures relatedness, a vital psychological need for engagement.

Physical rewards and public recognition, such as certificates, "Student of the Week" honors, or small prizes, celebrate effort and achievement, fostering a culture of appreciation. These cues affirm competence and encourage continuous participation.

Organizing competitive team challenges, such as quiz bees or debate battles, cultivates excitement and active participation. When aligned with course objectives and balanced to highlight growth over winning, these contests motivate students to strategize, collaborate, and engage deeply.

Gamified self-assessment and reflection empower learners to take ownership of their progress. Through badges for setting goals, tracking achievements, or journal reflections, students develop metacognitive skills that fuel intrinsic motivation and self-regulation.

Scenario-based role-plays and simulations immerse students in real-world challenges, rewarding creativity, teamwork, and strategic decision-making. These experiential activities link theory to practice, making learning dynamic and memorable. Consistent feedback loops and classroom incentives reinforce behaviors and guide improvement, blending extrinsic rewards with intrinsic satisfaction for sustained motivation.

For the most significant impact, educators must align gamification methods with clear learning goals while respecting diverse motivations and backgrounds. Combining LMS features with in-class practices builds a vibrant ecosystem where motivation flourishes intrinsically and extrinsically. This synergy energizes students to actively participate, meaningfully collaborate, and take initiative in their learning journeys, leading not only to improved academic performance but also to lasting engagement and mastery. By leveraging Gamification thoughtfully, educators craft educational experiences that are not only instructive but also inspiring.

Understanding and addressing individual differences in Gamification is a game-changer for educators aiming to maximize motivation and engagement in their classrooms. While Gamification offers powerful tools, such as points, badges, leaderboards, and narrative challenges, to make learning more stimulating, students do not all respond to these elements in the same way. Recognizing factors such as prior gaming experience, personality traits, cognitive styles, and motivational orientations enables educators to design flexible, inclusive gamified environments that genuinely resonate with every learner. This insight is essential—not only for boosting engagement but for sustaining meaningful learning over time.

Table 5. Factors Impacting Gamification

Factor	Impact on Gamification Response	Educator Strategies
Prior Gaming Experience	Experienced gamers tend to engage more readily due to familiarity and intrinsic enjoyment; novices, on the other hand, may feel overwhelmed or frustrated.	Provide tutorials, scaffolding, and optional simplified pathways to ease access and build confidence for learners with less experience.
Personality Traits & Motivation	Competitive and extroverted students thrive on leaderboards and rankings, whereas introverts or collaborative learners prefer group challenges and storytelling.	Offer varied game modes: competitive, collaborative, personal achievement, and diverse feedback styles to match different personalities.
Cognitive Styles & Learning Preferences	Visual learners respond well to graphical badges and storylines; kinesthetic learners benefit from physical or simulation tasks.	Incorporate multimedia elements, multiple feedback forms, and activity choices to cater to different learning preferences and enhance autonomy.
Developmental & Motivational Factors	Younger students seek novelty and immediate rewards; older learners value relevance, mastery, and self-directed goals.	Tailor gamification with real-world scenarios and meaningful rewards; balance intrinsic and extrinsic motivators through choice and social recognition.

Note. The table highlights the factors that influence Gamification response and offers strategies for educators to design their courses.

How Educators Can Harness This Knowledge? By embracing individual differences, educators can shift from a one-size-fits-all gamification model to a more personalized, engaging experience that motivates each student uniquely. For instance, scaffolding game mechanics ensures novice gamers are not left behind, while enabling competitive leaderboards can energize more extroverted students. Collaborative quests and storytelling appeal to social learners, helping build community and shared purpose. Multimedia-rich designs and diverse activity formats cater to a range of cognitive styles, making learning accessible and appealing to learners with visual, auditory, and kinesthetic preferences alike.

Additionally, understanding the nuances of developmental and motivational factors helps educators craft experiences that foster long-term engagement. Incorporating practical, real-world challenges supports mature learners' mastery goals, while varied reward systems strike the right balance between intrinsic joy and extrinsic incentives for all. This tailored approach to Gamification not only fosters greater motivation but cultivates a stronger sense of autonomy, competence, and relatedness, the key psychological needs that underpin sustained engagement and deep learning.

Why This Matters for Educators? For educators, integrating these insights into gamified learning is crucial for creating inclusive and effective environments where every student can thrive. It moves Gamification from being a mere novelty or competition tool to a powerful, evidence-based strategy that honors diversity in learning styles, personalities, and motivations. By attentively designing Gamification that welcomes all learners, educators foster deeper engagement, persistent motivation, and enriched educational outcomes that resonate far beyond the classroom walls.

Implications for Design and Implementation

Considering individual differences requires educators to adopt a flexible, inclusive approach to Gamification. Strategies include:

1. **Offering Multiple Pathways:** Provide options for competition, collaboration, or personal achievement, allowing students to select the approach that aligns with their preferences. This not only caters to diverse personality types but also promotes a sense of autonomy, which is crucial for fostering intrinsic motivation (Deci & Ryan, 2000).
2. **Customizable Goals and Rewards:** Enable learners to set their own goals or choose from a variety of reward systems, thereby increasing relevance and engagement. Personalized pathways enable students to take ownership of their learning, leading to increased motivation and persistence.
3. **Differentiated Feedback and Support:** Use adaptive feedback mechanisms tailored to individual learning progress and motivational needs. For instance, some students may benefit from encouraging messages, while others prefer detailed progress reports or peer recognition.
4. **Flexible Content Delivery:** Incorporate multimedia elements, such as videos, simulations, and interactive activities, that cater to different learning styles and cognitive preferences. Providing multiple formats ensures accessibility and engagement for all learners.
5. **Progressive Complexity:** Design gamified systems that adjust challenge levels based on individual performance, avoiding boredom for high-achievers and frustration for those who need more support. This adaptive difficulty promotes flow and sustained engagement across diverse learner profiles (Csikszentmihalyi, 1990).
6. **Fostering Inclusivity and Equity:** Ensure that gamification elements are culturally sensitive and accessible to students with varying backgrounds and abilities. This promotes fairness and encourages participation from all students.

7. **Continuous Evaluation and Feedback:** Regularly gather student input and analyze engagement data to refine gamification strategies, ensuring they remain responsive to individual needs and preferences.

POLICY AND SYSTEM-LEVEL CONSIDERATIONS FOR SCALING AND SUPPORTING GAMIFICATION IN EDUCATION

The integration of Gamification into education holds tremendous promise to transform how students learn by boosting engagement and motivation on a large scale. While gamified strategies can enrich individual classrooms, their full potential lies in education systems and policymakers adopting these approaches broadly and integrating them into the fabric of schooling. Achieving this requires thoughtful policy decisions, infrastructure investments, and a strong focus on inclusivity and sustainability. This section explores the key policy and system-level considerations for successfully scaling Gamification, drawing on public policy examples, civic engagement platforms, and technological infrastructure.

Scaling Gamification means creating a policy environment that encourages broad adoption without sacrificing quality or equity. Policymakers must view Gamification not just as a teaching tool, but as a powerful systemic strategy capable of transforming school culture, instructional quality, and student success. This calls for frameworks that support pilot programs, evaluate their effectiveness, and allow for continuous improvement as Gamification expands.

An example from public policy is the use of gamified government websites that engage citizens by awarding points and badges for participation in surveys or community events (Hassan, 2017). Such platforms illustrate how Gamification can scale to promote broader engagement and accountability. Similarly, education systems can develop gamified portals that bring together students, parents, and teachers, encouraging involvement in school activities, professional development, and community projects.

Building a strong technological foundation is critical for scaling Gamification effectively. Schools and districts need reliable internet access, modern devices, and flexible learning platforms that support gamified features. Without these elements, the digital divide risks widening, significantly limiting access and undermining equity goals. Equally important is investing in professional development for educators and administrators. Training should extend beyond technical skills to include aligning gamified mechanics with learning objectives and developing inclusive strategies that cater to diverse learners. Policies should fund ongoing training, foster communities of practice, and provide resources to support educators as they integrate Gamification into their classrooms.

Ensuring equitable access to gamified learning experiences is vital. Policymakers must focus on inclusive design that accounts for the needs of all students, regardless of their socioeconomic status, ability, or location. This means subsidizing devices, expanding broadband coverage, and developing accessible platforms tailored for learners with disabilities or language differences. Adapting content and mechanics to different cultures and learning preferences promotes a universal design approach that benefits every student (Majdoub, 2022).

A research-driven approach underpins the responsible scaling of Gamification. Governments and educational authorities should invest in rigorous evaluation of pilot projects to identify what works best, for whom, and under what conditions. Long-term studies can reveal how Gamification sustains engagement and learning, while ongoing assessments support continuous refinement.

Ultimately, collaboration among educators, researchers, game developers, and policymakers is crucial for creating gamification solutions that are pedagogically sound, technologically robust, and culturally relevant. Open dialogue between policymakers and frontline educators ensures that systemic efforts reflect real classroom challenges and effectively meet students' needs. By addressing these policy and system-level factors, educational institutions can unlock the full power of Gamification, creating motivating, inclusive, and scalable learning environments that prepare students for success in today's dynamic world.

PROMOTING ETHICAL AND RESPONSIBLE USE

Promoting ethical and responsible use in Gamification involves several key principles to ensure positive, fair, and meaningful engagement. These include respecting user autonomy, fostering intrinsic motivation over coercion, ensuring transparency about game mechanics and data use, and prioritizing equity and inclusion. Ethical Gamification avoids manipulative tactics that exploit psychological triggers unfairly and ensures participants have choice and control over their engagement. Incorporating ongoing evaluation and adaptation to identify and address unintended consequences is also crucial.

For example, frameworks for ethical Gamification emphasize designing systems that empower users to make informed decisions aligned with their values, promote fairness, protect privacy in accordance with regulations such as GDPR, and encourage genuine learning and behavior change rather than superficial compliance (Pong et al., 2021; Sustainability Directory, 2025). In education, ethical Gamification supports collaboration, provides meaningful feedback, and incorporates culturally sensitive design to respect diverse learner backgrounds and needs (Sardi et al., 2020).

At the system level, policies should also address ethical considerations in Gamification, such as data privacy, user consent, and the potential for manipulation. Clear guidelines must be established to protect student data, especially when gamified platforms collect personal information or behavioral data. Transparency about how data is used, coupled with consent procedures, is essential for ethical practice.

CULTURAL SENSITIVITY AND DEMOGRAPHIC DIFFERENCES IN PERCEIVED BENEFITS FROM GAMIFICATION

The impact of Gamification varies significantly across different cultural contexts, reflecting diverse values and social dynamics. In collectivist cultures such as many East Asian societies, gamified elements that emphasize group achievements and cooperative rewards tend to foster greater engagement and motivation. For instance, collective badges or team leaderboards align with the values of harmony and shared success. Conversely, in more individualistic cultures prevalent in North America and Western Europe, competitive leaderboards and personalized achievement badges resonate strongly with learners who prioritize individual recognition and autonomy. Studies from the African and Latin American regions suggest that access to technology and socioeconomic conditions influence the gamified learning experience (Farinha & de Fatima Pina, 2025).

Neglecting these cultural nuances can limit the inclusiveness and effectiveness of gamification strategies. From the author's experiential perspective, pilot initiatives implementing identical competitive leaderboards across culturally diverse classrooms produced mixed outcomes. While North American students thrived, some collectivist learners reported feelings of exclusion or heightened pressure. This underscores the importance of culturally adaptive gamification designs that honor local norms and learner identities, ensuring equitable engagement.

Demographic differences, such as age and gender, can influence how individuals perceive the benefits of Gamification. Research generally indicates:

- Age: Younger users tend to exhibit higher engagement and motivation from gamified elements than older users, partly because of their greater familiarity with digital games and technology. However, well-designed Gamification can appeal to people of all ages if adapted to varied preferences and cognitive styles. Older adults may prioritize meaningful learning and social connectedness over competitive features (Koivisto & Hamari, 2014).
- Gender: Studies frequently find gender differences in responses to Gamification, with males typically showing a stronger preference for competitive and achievement-based features, such as leaderboards and points.

Females respond more positively to collaborative, narrative-driven, or socially interactive game elements. These tendencies are not absolute, and cultural context and individual differences also play important roles (Koivisto & Hamari, 2014).

Understanding these demographic nuances enables the design of gamified systems that are inclusive and effective across diverse populations by tailoring game mechanics and rewards to user preferences.

POLICY RECOMMENDATIONS

Universities are increasingly adopting Gamification to enhance student engagement, motivation, and learning outcomes. However, to maximize its benefits while minimizing potential risks, institutions need to establish clear policies governing the ethical and practical use of Gamification. Such policies provide guidelines for transparency, data privacy, inclusivity, and responsible design to ensure gamified elements support diverse learners fairly and meaningfully.

Several universities, including Utica University, Oklahoma State University, the University of Michigan-Dearborn, the University of Chicago, Dakota State University, and Air University, have integrated Gamification into their institutional policies and educational practices to enhance student engagement and learning outcomes. These institutions not only implement gamified systems such as points for campus involvement, coursework quests and challenges, interactive quizzes, and virtual reality simulations, but also support faculty and students through clear frameworks, training, and resources. By embedding Gamification within policy and practice, these universities promote inclusive, motivating, and innovative learning environments. Their proactive approaches serve as exemplars for other higher education administrations, highlighting the importance of developing or updating policies that address ethical considerations, accessibility, and effectiveness in gamified learning initiatives. These models encourage a strategic, responsible adoption of Gamification that aligns educational goals with student needs across diverse contexts.

Table 6. Universities Implementing Gamification

University Name	Program
Utica University	Uses a platform called Modern Campus Involve to award points for attending campus events, which has significantly boosted student engagement and retention. The program is integrated into their student culture to promote lifelong engagement (Modern Campus, 2025).
Oklahoma State University	Incorporates Gamification in courses, using quests and challenges to increase student participation and motivation, demonstrating measurable increases in engagement (Okstate.edu, 2025).
University of Michigan-Dearborn	Launched a "Talent Gateway" gamification program allowing students to earn points for a variety of achievements, cultivating soft skills and lifelong learning habits amid a vast student population (Schwartz, 2019).
University of Chicago	Employs gamified activities at varying levels of complexity, such as Poll Everywhere for interactive quizzes and escape room activities, to maintain student interest and enhance knowledge retention (Deng, 2025).
Dakota State University	Utilizes the Modern Campus platform to integrate gamified engagement tools, encouraging participation in campus activities and enhancing retention rates (Leichner, 2023).
Air University	Has explored Gamification in military education settings to modernize teaching and learning, including card-based games and virtual reality tools to develop discussion facilitation skills and conceptual understanding (Furstenau, 2022).

Note. The table lists the institutions that have implemented Gamification in their coursework to increase motivation and engagement.

It is important to establish clear ethical guidelines that respect student autonomy and privacy while promoting transparency about how gamified elements function. Policies should emphasize inclusivity by ensuring game mechanics accommodate diverse cultural backgrounds, learning styles, and accessibility needs. Administrators should also define criteria for evaluating the effectiveness and long-term impact of gamification initiatives. Providing faculty with training and resources to design and implement gamified activities responsibly is essential. Finally, involving students in the co-creation process can help tailor Gamification to their interests and foster a sense of ownership and engagement. Below are some key considerations for administrators when developing a gamification policy.

- **Supporting Research and Evaluation:** Allocate funding and resources to study gamification programs to assess their effectiveness and scalability systematically.
- **Fostering Collaboration:** Facilitate partnerships among educators, researchers, technology firms, and policymakers to develop sustainable and pedagogically sound gamified systems that promote learning.
- **Ensuring Inclusive Design:** Mandate that all gamification initiatives adhere to universal design principles, addressing accessibility, cultural relevance, and diverse learning needs.

- **Investing in Infrastructure:** Prioritize equitable access to devices, high-speed internet, and scalable platforms necessary for effective system-wide Gamification.
- **Building Capacity:** Provide ongoing professional development and resources for educators to implement and adapt gamification strategies effectively

CHALLENGES, LIMITATIONS, AND FUTURE DIRECTIONS IN GAMIFICATION FOR EDUCATION

While Gamification has emerged as a promising approach to enhance motivation, engagement, and learning outcomes, it is not devoid of challenges and limitations that warrant careful consideration. Recognizing and addressing these limitations is essential to harnessing the full potential of Gamification in educational contexts. Additionally, identifying key areas for future research can guide the development of more effective, equitable, and sustainable gamified learning environments.

Challenges and Limitations of Gamification

1. Overemphasis on Extrinsic Rewards and Its Impact on Intrinsic Motivation

One of the most extensively discussed concerns in gamification literature pertains to the potential erosion of intrinsic motivation, defined as motivation driven by internal interest, enjoyment, and personal fulfillment, when extrinsic rewards are overemphasized. Deci and Ryan's (1985) Self-Determination Theory emphasizes that extrinsic incentives, such as points or badges, can undermine intrinsic motivation if perceived as controlling or if they diminish learners' sense of autonomy. Early gamification implementations often relied heavily on extrinsic motivators, leading to superficial engagement that diminishes once rewards are removed (Deci & Ryan, 1985; Elliot, 2013). For instance, students motivated solely by badges might focus narrowly on earning rewards rather than engaging deeply with the learning process, which can reduce long-term motivation and the transferability of skills.

2. Poorly Designed Game Elements and Misalignment with Learning Objectives

The success of Gamification heavily depends on meticulous design that aligns game mechanics with pedagogical goals. Poorly designed game elements may fail to foster meaningful engagement or can even disengage students altogether. If game mechanics do not correspond with learning objectives, such as rewarding only effort rather than mastery or understanding, they risk fostering superficial participation rather than deep learning (Dicheva et al., 2015). For example, awarding badges for completion regardless of quality or understanding can incentivize rote participation rather than critical thinking. Furthermore, superficial use of game elements, such as points and leaderboards, without meaningful narratives or challenges, can lead to boredom or cynicism, undermining the entire purpose of Gamification (Kapp, 2012). Therefore, the design process must be pedagogically driven, ensuring that game mechanics support genuine learning engagement.

3. Equity and Access Concerns

Another significant challenge relates to equity. Gamification strategies often rely on technology, such as online platforms, mobile apps, or gamified learning management systems, that may not be accessible or equitable across all student populations. Students from disadvantaged backgrounds, rural areas, or those with limited digital literacy may face barriers to accessing gamified tools, thus widening the digital divide (Gottschalk & Weise, 2023). Additionally, prior gaming experience can influence how students respond to Gamification, with some students preemptively disengaging due to unfamiliarity or discomfort with game-like environments. This raises concerns about inclusivity: if not carefully designed, Gamification can unintentionally marginalize certain groups, counteracting the very goal of equitable educational access (Bates, 2015). To mitigate these issues, policy interventions and inclusive design principles are critical.

FUTURE DIRECTIONS AND RESEARCH OPPORTUNITIES

The future of Gamification in education holds exciting potential as researchers and practitioners strive to overcome today's challenges and unlock deeper, more sustained impacts on learning. By pushing the boundaries of current knowledge, future studies can shape Gamification into an even more powerful tool for motivation and engagement across a broad spectrum of learners.

1. Longitudinal Studies: Unlocking Sustainable Impact. While most current research highlights the immediate benefits of Gamification, the real test lies in its long-term effectiveness. Future research should prioritize longitudinal studies that track learners' motivation, engagement, and achievement over months or years, rather than just weeks. These studies can reveal whether Gamification fosters lasting behavioral change, deep understanding, and enduring enthusiasm or if initial excitement fades once novelty wears off (Seaborn & Fels, 2015). Furthermore, they can uncover hidden risks, such as overreliance on extrinsic

rewards or diminished responsiveness to game elements, and offer guidance on maintaining a healthy balance that sustains intrinsic motivation.

2. Co-Design with Learners: Fostering Ownership and Relevance: Integrating students as active collaborators in the creation of gamified learning environments, known as co-design or participatory design, promises to make Gamification far more personalized, inclusive, and engaging (El Shemy et al., 2025). When students share their insights on preferences, challenges, and motivations, educators and developers gain invaluable input that shapes more meaningful, culturally relevant experiences. Research exploring co-design can illuminate how this collaborative process enhances learner agency, sense of ownership, and motivation. Tailoring Gamification collaboratively not only enriches engagement but also aligns learning more closely with student goals, strengthening internalization and persistence.
3. Intelligent, Adaptive Gamification: The Power of Personalization. Recognizing the vast individual differences among learners requires adaptive gamification systems powered by artificial intelligence and machine learning (Chiotaki et al., 2023; Manoharan & Nagulapally, 2024). These innovative systems dynamically tailor difficulty, rewards, feedback, and social interactions based on real-time learner data. For instance, adaptive platforms can calibrate task complexity to challenge students just enough to keep them engaged without overwhelming or tiring them. They can also offer personalized content formats, whether simulations, quizzes, or team projects, that resonate with learners' unique strengths and interests (Ristianto et al., 2025). This learner-centered customization fosters autonomy and self-regulation, core drivers of lasting intrinsic motivation (Deci & Ryan, 2000).

Future exploration should focus on how adaptive Gamification influences long-term motivation, persistence, and knowledge transfer across varied educational contexts. Simultaneously, challenges such as scalability, cost, equity, and ensuring pedagogical soundness must be addressed collaboratively by educators, technologists, and policymakers. Developing accessible, affordable, adaptive platforms that serve diverse populations will be pivotal to broadening the transformative impact of Gamification.

For educators, these future directions are more than academic curiosities; they are blueprints for evolving Gamification into a finely tuned educational instrument. Understanding the need for sustained engagement encourages designing beyond flash-in-the-pan rewards to cultivate deep, motivational roots. Embracing co-design reinforces the importance of student voice, making learners partners rather than passive recipients. Finally, harnessing AI-driven personalization offers an unprecedented opportunity to meet each student where they are, nurturing their unique learning journeys with precision and care. By engaging with these forward-looking insights, educators can lead the way in creating motivating, adaptive, and inclusive gamified experiences that empower all learners to thrive now and in the future.

CONCLUSION

Gamification stands as one of the most promising strategies poised to revolutionize education by transforming learning into an engaging, motivating, and interactive journey. In an era where traditional teaching methods struggle to sustain student motivation amid rapid digital transformation, Gamification offers an innovative pathway to deepen involvement and maintain long-term engagement. When thoughtfully crafted, gamified environments tap into learners' intrinsic needs of autonomy, competence, and relatedness, empowering students to participate meaningfully and cultivate a genuine passion for academic content.

Extensive research confirms the power of Gamification across varied educational settings, showing that carefully designed gamified systems boost motivation, improve retention, and elevate academic performance (Dicheva et al., 2015; Hamari, Koivisto, & Sarsa, 2014). However, the magic lies in intentional design. Superficial or misaligned Gamification can backfire, causing shallow engagement or even disengagement. Here, educational theory, especially Self-Determination Theory (Deci & Ryan, 1985), plays a pivotal role. Grounding gamification in theory ensures that it fosters autonomous motivation, nurturing sustained, self-regulated learning that extends beyond short-term excitement.

AI significantly amplifies these efforts by enabling personalized, adaptive gamification experiences. AI-powered systems analyze learner behaviors in real time, tailoring challenges and feedback to match individual needs and preferences. This intelligent customization increases relevance and engagement while supporting students' autonomy and competence. As digital landscapes evolve, integrating AI ensures gamified learning remains responsive, meaningful, and accessible for diverse learners.

This chapter is crucial for educators and policymakers because it provides a comprehensive roadmap to harness Gamification's transformative potential. It highlights best practices rooted in sound theory, enriched by practical case studies and innovative solutions. By emphasizing data-driven approaches, establishing clear metrics, and ongoing evaluations, stakeholders can measure impact, refine strategies, and make informed decisions that sustain success. Equally important is the call for inclusive policy frameworks that prioritize infrastructure, educator training, and equitable access to education. Ensuring that all learners, regardless of their background or digital literacy, benefit from gamified education is essential to narrowing gaps rather than widening them.

Looking forward, collaboration among educators, researchers, game developers, and policymakers is key. Initiatives such as co-design, where learners shape their own gamified experiences, and the creation of adaptive platforms tailored by AI promise to deepen engagement and empower students as active agents in their learning journeys.

In essence, when executed with rigor, inclusivity, and the thoughtful integration of emerging technologies, Gamification becomes a potent catalyst for educational reform, equipping learners with the motivation, skills, and adaptability needed to thrive in an ever-changing world. This chapter highlights the crucial importance of engagement and motivation, shedding light on the path toward vibrant, equitable, and future-ready learning environments.

REFERENCES

Alfred, R., & Kumar, T. (2024). Reinventing Design Education with the Power of Innovative Game Design. *Procedia CIRP, 128*, 752–757. DOI: 10.1016/j.procir.2024.04.022

Antonaci, A., Klemke, R., & Specht, M. (2019, August). The effects of Gamification in online learning environments: A systematic literature review. [). MDPI.]. *Informatics (MDPI), 6*(3), 32. DOI: 10.3390/informatics6030032

Asigigan, S. İ., & Samur, Y. (2021). The Effect of Gamified STEM Practices on Students' Intrinsic Motivation, Critical Thinking Disposition Levels, and Perception of Problem-Solving Skills. *International Journal of Education in Mathematics. Science and Technology, 9*(2), 332–352.

Bates, A. W. (2015). Teaching in a digital age.

Bonsignore, E., Hansen, D., Hickey, D., Piety, P., Chartrand, G., Gedris, K., & Kartchner, K. (2022, June). The Playable Case Study Authoring and Simulation Platform. In *General Proceedings of the 2nd Annual Meeting of the International Society of the Learning Sciences 2022* (Vol. 1, No. 1).

Bourgonjon, J., Valcke, M., Soetaert, R., & Schellens, T. (2010). Students' perceptions about the use of video games in the classroom. *Computers & Education, 54*(4), 1145–1156. DOI: 10.1016/j.compedu.2009.10.022

Castillo-Parra, B., Hidalgo-Cajo, B. G., Vásconez-Barrera, M., & Oleas-López, J. (2022). Gamification in Higher Education: A Review of the Literature. *World Journal on Educational Technology: Current Issues, 14*(3), 797–816. DOI: 10.18844/wjet.v14i3.7341

Castillo-Parra, B., Hidalgo-Cajo, B. G., Vásconez-Barrera, M., & Oleas-López, J. (2022). Gamification in Higher Education: A Review of the Literature. *World Journal on Educational Technology: Current Issues, 14*(3), 797–816. DOI: 10.18844/wjet.v14i3.7341

Chiotaki, D., Poulopoulos, V., & Karpouzis, K. (2023). Adaptive game-based learning in education: Systematic review. *Frontiers of Computer Science, 5*, 1062350. DOI: 10.3389/fcomp.2023.1062350

Çınar, A., Erişen, Y., & Çeliköz, M. (2022). A mixed-method research on the effectiveness of using gamification elements in an online English course. *International Journal of Educational Research Review, 7*(4), 280–291. DOI: 10.24331/ijere.1140960

Csikszentmihalyi, M. (1990). *Flow: The Psychology of Optimal Experience*. Harper & Row.

Deci, E. L., Koestner, R., & Ryan, R. M. (1999). A meta-analytic review of experiments examining the effects of extrinsic rewards on intrinsic motivation. *Psychological Bulletin, 125*(6), 627–668. DOI: 10.1037/0033-2909.125.6.627 PMID: 10589297

Deci, E. L., & Ryan, R. M. (1985). *Intrinsic Motivation and Self-Determination in Human Behavior*. Springer. DOI: 10.1007/978-1-4899-2271-7

Deci, E. L., & Ryan, R. M. (2000). The "what" and "why" of goal pursuits: Human needs and the self-determination of behavior. *Psychological Inquiry, 11*(4), 227–268. DOI: 10.1207/S15327965PLI1104_01

Deci, E. L., & Ryan, R. M. (2012). Self-determination theory. *Handbook of theories of social psychology, 1*(20), 416-436.

Deng, Y. (2025). Enhance Student Learning with Poll Everywhere: Faculty Perspectives. https://academictech.uchicago.edu/2025/07/30/enhance-student-learning-with-poll-everywhere-faculty-perspectives/

Deterding, S., Dixon, D., Khaled, R., & Nacke, L. (2011, September). From game design elements to gamefulness: defining" gamification". In *Proceedings of the 15th International Academic MindTrek Conference: Envisioning Future Media Environments* (pp. 9–15). DOI: 10.1145/2181037.2181040

Dicheva, D., Dichev, C., Agre, G., & Angelova, G. (2015). Gamification in education: A systematic mapping study. *Journal of Educational Technology & Society, 18*(3), 75–88.

Domínguez, A., Saenz-de-Navarrete, J., De-Marcos, L., Fernández-Sanz, L., Pagés, C., & Martínez-Herráiz, J. J. (2013). Gamifying learning experiences: Practical implications and outcomes. *Computers & Education, 63*, 380–392. DOI: 10.1016/j.compedu.2012.12.020

El Shemy, I., Jaccheri, L., Giannakos, M., & Vulchanova, M. (2025). Participatory design of augmented reality games for word learning in autistic children: The parental perspective. *Entertainment Computing, 52*, 100756. DOI: 10.1016/j.entcom.2024.100756

El Shemy, I., Jaccheri, L., Giannakos, M., & Vulchanova, M. (2025). Participatory design of augmented reality games for word learning in autistic children: The parental perspective. *Entertainment Computing, 52*, 100756. DOI: 10.1016/j.entcom.2024.100756

Elliot, A. J. (2013). *Handbook of approach and avoidance motivation*. Psychology Press. DOI: 10.4324/9780203888148

Faiella, F., & Ricciardi, M. (2015). Gamification and learning: a review of issues and research. *Journal of e-learning and knowledge society, 11*(3).

Farinha, J., & de Fatima Pina, M. (2025). Cross-Cultural Perspectives on Gamification in Business Environments: How Cultural Differences Influence Design and Reception. In *Evolving Strategies for Organizational Management and Performance Evaluation* (pp. 77-88). IGI Global Scientific Publishing.

Finn, J. D. (1989). Withdrawing from school. *Review of Educational Research, 59*(2), 117–142. DOI: 10.3102/00346543059002117

Fredricks, J. A., Blumenfeld, P. C., & Paris, A. H. (2004). School engagement: Potential of the concept, state of the evidence. *Review of Educational Research, 74*(1), 59–109. DOI: 10.3102/00346543074001059

Freeman, S., Fletcher, J., Clouston, K., & Higson, A. (2024). Gamifying simulated nursing education: A digital technology approach to enhancing pedagogy and student experience. *British Journal of Nursing (Mark Allen Publishing), 33*(4), 206–214. DOI: 10.12968/bjon.2024.33.4.206 PMID: 38386519

Furstenau, G. (2022). Air University exploring gamification teaching model. https://www.maxwell.af.mil/News/Display/Article/3066369/air-university-exploring-gamification-teaching-model/

Gottschalk, F., & Weise, C. (2023). Digital equity and inclusion in education: An overview of practice and policy in OECD countries. *OECD Education Working Papers*, (299), 0_1-75.

Groh, F. (2012). Gamification: State of the art definition and utilization. *Institute of Media Informatics Ulm University, 39*, 31.

Hamari, J., & Koivisto, J. (2015). "Working out for likes": An empirical study on social influence in exercise gamification. *Computers in Human Behavior, 50*, 333–347. DOI: 10.1016/j.chb.2015.04.018

Hamari, J., & Koivisto, J. (2015). Why do people use gamification services? *International Journal of Information Management, 35*(4), 419–431. DOI: 10.1016/j.ijinfomgt.2015.04.006

Hamari, J., Koivisto, J., & Sarsa, H. (2014). Does Gamification work? A literature review of empirical studies on Gamification. *2014 47th Hawaii International Conference on System Sciences*, 3025–3034. https://www.computer.org/csdl/proceedings-article/hicss/2014/2504d025/12OmNzE54xe

Hart, J. (2015). *Investigating user experience and user engagement for design*. The University of Manchester.

Hassan, L. (2017). Governments should play games: Towards a framework for the Gamification of civic engagement platforms. *Simulation & Gaming*, *48*(2), 249–267. DOI: 10.1177/1046878116683581

Hew, K. F. T. (2015). Towards a model of engaging online students: Lessons from MOOCs and four policy documents. *International Journal of Information and Education Technology (IJIET)*, *5*(6), 425–431. DOI: 10.7763/IJIET.2015.V5.543

Houlfort, N. (2004). The impact of performance-contingent rewards on perceived autonomy and intrinsic motivation.

Houlfort, N. (2004). The impact of performance-contingent rewards on perceived autonomy and intrinsic motivation.

Kapp, K. M. (2012). *The Gamification of learning and instruction: game-based methods and strategies for training and education*. John Wiley & Sons.

Kappen, D. L., Mirza-Babaei, P., & Nacke, L. E. (2017, October). Gamification through the application of motivational affordances for physical activity technology. In *Proceedings of the Annual Symposium on Computer-Human Interaction in Play* (pp. 5–18). DOI: 10.1145/3116595.3116604

Kaya, O. S., & Ercag, E. (2023). The impact of applying a challenge-based gamification program on students' learning outcomes: Academic achievement, motivation, and flow. *Education and Information Technologies*, *28*(8), 10053–10078. DOI: 10.1007/s10639-023-11585-z PMID: 36691635

Koivisto, J., & Hamari, J. (2014). Demographic differences in perceived benefits from Gamification. *Computers in Human Behavior*, *35*, 179–188. DOI: 10.1016/j.chb.2014.03.007

Leichner, B. (2023). Gamification in Education. https://dsu.edu/news/2023/05/gamification-in-education.html

Lin, J., Yu, W., Zhang, N., Yang, X., Zhang, H., & Zhao, W. (2017). A survey on Internet of Things: Architecture, enabling technologies, security and privacy, and applications. *IEEE Internet of Things Journal*, *4*(5), 1125–1142. DOI: 10.1109/JIOT.2017.2683200

Magomadov, V. S. (2020, November). The application of artificial intelligence and Big Data analytics in personalized learning. [). IOP Publishing.]. *Journal of Physics: Conference Series*, *1691*(1), 012169. DOI: 10.1088/1742-6596/1691/1/012169

Majdoub, M. (2022). Applying Gamification to enhance the Universal Design for Learning Framework. *Handbook of research on transformative and innovative pedagogies in education*, 233-256.

Manoharan, A., & Nagulapally, S. (2024). Adaptive gamification algorithms for personalized learning experiences in educational platforms. *International Research Journal of Modernization in Engineering Technology and Science*, *6*(3), 2582–5208.

Marczewski, A. (2015). Even Ninja Monkeys like to play. *London. Blurb Inc*, *1*(1), 28.

Mekler, E. D., Brühlmann, F., Tuch, A. N., & Opwis, K. (2017). Towards understanding the effects of individual gamification elements on intrinsic motivation and performance. *Computers in Human Behavior*, *71*, 525–534. DOI: 10.1016/j.chb.2015.08.048

Mitchell, B. (2023). Can Gamification improve student engagement and learning? A proposed quasi-experiment. In *Annual Conference of the Australasian Society for Computers in Learning in Tertiary Education 2023* (pp. 1–6). Australasian Society for Computers in Learning in Tertiary Education.

Modern Campus. (2025). Utica University Increases Engagement Through Gamification. https://moderncampus.com/success-story/utica-university-gamification-with-presence.html

Nadi-Ravandi, S., & Batooli, Z. (2022). Gamification in education: A scientometric, content, and co-occurrence analysis of systematic review and meta-analysis articles. *Education and Information Technologies*, *27*(7), 10207–10238. DOI: 10.1007/s10639-022-11048-x PMID: 35431599

Nadi-Ravandi, S., & Batooli, Z. (2022). Gamification in education: A scientometric, content, and co-occurrence analysis of systematic review and meta-analysis articles. *Education and Information Technologies*, *27*(7), 10207–10238. DOI: 10.1007/s10639-022-11048-x PMID: 35431599

NSSE. (2019). Academic Advising: Quality Matters More Than Quantity. https://nsse.indiana.edu/research/annual-results/2019/academic-advising.html#:~:text=Conclusion,promote%20high%2Dquality%20academic%20advising

Nylén-Eriksen, M., Stojiljkovic, M., Lillekroken, D., Lindeflaten, K., Hessevaagbakke, E., Flølo, T. N., & Tørris, C. (2025). Game-thinking: Utilizing serious games and Gamification in nursing education–a systematic review and meta-analysis. *BMC Medical Education, 25*(1), 140. DOI: 10.1186/s12909-024-06531-7 PMID: 39881301

Okstate.edu. (2025). Gamification. https://itle.okstate.edu/tnl/gamification.html

Pelizzari, F. (2023). Gamification in higher education. A systematic literature review. *Italian Journal of Educational Technology*, (31 (3)), 21–43.

Pelizzari, F. (2023). Gamification in higher education. A systematic literature review. *Italian Journal of Educational Technology*, (31 (3)), 21–43.

Pong, J., Pilat, D., & Chudleigh, S. (2021). Design is becoming behavioral: here's how to ethically implement Gamification. https://thedecisionlab.com/insights/technology/design-is-becoming-behavioral-heres-how-to-ethically-implement-gamification

Project Management Institute. (2021). *A guide to the Project Management Body of Knowledge (PMBOK Guide)* (7th ed.). Project Management Institute.

Reeve, J. (2012). A self-determination theory perspective on student engagement. In *Handbook of research on student engagement* (pp. 149–172). Springer US. DOI: 10.1007/978-1-4614-2018-7_7

Ristianto, S. D., Putri, A., & Rosmansyah, Y. (2025). Personalized Gamification for Student Education: A Systematic Literature Review. *IEEE Access : Practical Innovations, Open Solutions*. Advance online publication. DOI: 10.1109/ACCESS.2025.3552826

Rodrigues, L., Palomino, P. T., Toda, A. M., Klock, A. C., Oliveira, W., Avila-Santos, A. P., & Isotani, S. (2021). Personalization improves Gamification: Evidence from a mixed-methods study. *Proceedings of the ACM on Human-Computer Interaction, 5*(CHI PLAY), 1–25. DOI: 10.1145/3474714

Ryan, R. M., & Deci, E. L. (2000). Self-determination theory and the facilitation of intrinsic motivation, social development, and well-being. *The American Psychologist, 55*(1), 68–78. DOI: 10.1037/0003-066X.55.1.68 PMID: 11392867

Ryan, R. M., & Deci, E. L. (2020). Intrinsic and extrinsic motivation from a self-determination theory perspective: Definitions, theory, practices, and future directions. *Contemporary Educational Psychology*, *61*, 101860. DOI: 10.1016/j.cedpsych.2020.101860

Sailer, M., Hense, J. U., Mayr, S. K., & Mandl, H. (2017). How Gamification motivates: An experimental study of the effects of specific game design elements on psychological need satisfaction. *Computers in Human Behavior*, *69*, 371–380. DOI: 10.1016/j.chb.2016.12.033

Sailer, M., & Homner, L. (2020). The Gamification of learning: A meta-analysis. *Educational Psychology Review*, *32*(1), 77–112. DOI: 10.1007/s10648-019-09498-w

Salen Tekinbas, K., & Zimmerman, E. (2003). Rules of play: Game design fundamentals.

Sardi, L., Idri, A., & Fernández-Alemán, J. L. (2020). Assessing Ethoshunt as a gamification-based mobile app in ethics education: A pilot study. *JMIR Serious Games*, *8*(3), e18247. DOI: 10.2196/18247 PMID: 32663153

Schwartz, N. (2019). Gen Z Takeover: How colleges are using Gamification to engage students. https://www.highereddive.com/news/gen-z-takeover-how-colleges-are-using-gamification-to-engage-students/549722/

Seaborn, K., & Fels, D. I. (2015). Gamification in theory and action: A survey. *International Journal of Human-Computer Studies*, *74*, 14–31. DOI: 10.1016/j.ijhcs.2014.09.006

Shernoff, D. J. (2013). Optimal learning environments to promote student engagement.

Sustainability Directory. (2025). Ethical gamification frameworks. Retrieved November 22, 2025, from https://prism.sustainability-directory.com/term/ethical-gamification-frameworks/

Thapa, P., Sharma, P., Goundar, S., Tsirkas, P., Valamontes, A., & Adamopoulos, I. (2025). Digital Distractions in the Classroom Among Students: A Cross-Sectional Study.

Vansteenkiste, M., Simons, J., Lens, W., Sheldon, K. M., & Deci, E. L. (2004). Motivating learning, performance, and persistence: The synergistic effects of intrinsic goal contents and autonomy-supportive contexts. *Journal of Personality and Social Psychology*, *87*(2), 246–260. DOI: 10.1037/0022-3514.87.2.246 PMID: 15301630

Yildirim, I. (2017). The effects of gamification-based teaching practices on student achievement and students' attitudes toward lessons. *The Internet and Higher Education*, *33*, 86–92. DOI: 10.1016/j.iheduc.2017.02.002

Yu-Kai, C. (2010). The Octalysis Framework: Seven Core Drives for Motivating Engagement.

Chapter 9
Generative AI and Redefining Scope of Language Curriculum: TESOL Educators' Voices

Rashad Ahmed
Jacksonville State University, USA

Abdu Al-kadi
https://orcid.org/0000-0003-3805-7507
Bergen University, Norway

Beatricce Namusiginyi
Makerere University, Uganda

ABSTRACT

This chapter is based on an argument that while AI offers opportunities for adaptive and on-demand learning, it tends to reduce the scope of the curriculum. A dataset collected through semi-structured interviews with twenty university-level TESOL educators from fifteen countries was analyzed qualitatively. Three interconnected themes surfaced from this analysis: bias in content selection, reduced critical engagement, and teacher mediation. As AI tools work on measurable skills rather than critical thinking and cultural depth, they risk narrowing language curricula to quantifiable features, underscoring the importance of pedagogical strategies for holistic development. Positioning educators as active agents helps in shaping inclusive and reflective language learning, preserving cultural depth, critical engagement, and holistic learning outcomes in AI-enhanced environments.

DOI: 10.4018/979-8-3373-4521-5.ch009

1. INTRODUCTION

The rise of artificial intelligence (AI) and its sweeping changes continue to reshape education. AI-enabled tools such as ChatGPT and adaptive learning platforms (e.g., Duolingo) have transformed how language learners access and engage with linguistic content. Tools such as ChatGPT (Wang & Fan, 2025) and DeepSeek (Al-Obaydi & Pikhart, 2025) represent the latest phase in a long trajectory of technological evolution in language education, from early computer-assisted language learning (CALL) in the 1980s to mobile-assisted language learning (MALL) in the early 2000s (Chapelle & Sauro, 2017; Hasumi & Chiu, 2024; Lee, 2022). These tools were not initially developed for language instruction, though (Al-Kadi, 2017), they enable flexible and on-demand engagement with language outside of traditional classroom settings (Pikhart & Al-Obaydi, 2025). Educators also adopt them to support learner-centred instruction. According to recent estimates, AI accounts for nearly half of language learning and teaching tasks (Cardona et al., 2023; Pikhart & Al-Obaydi, 2025).

AI tools generate content for individual needs and proficiency levels (Bayly-Castaneda et al., 2024; Giray, 2025). However, this personalised language learning (PLL) mode challenges the breadth and depth of formal curricula. Beyond curricular narrowing, GenAI introduces cognitive offloading (Gerlich, 2025). The term refers to learning situations wherein learners delegate memory, reasoning, and problem-solving tasks to AI systems (Moqbel, 2025). Arguably, it reduces cognitive load and accelerates performance on discrete skills, and thereby limits opportunities for deep processing, interpretive reasoning, and autonomous knowledge construction.

A growing body of literature highlights concerns that AI-driven education prioritises efficiency and discrete skills at the expense of cultural literacy and critical engagement (Castro et al., 2025; Gokcearslan et al., 2024). While many educators welcome the autonomy and accessibility AI offers, others assert that overreliance on AI narrows the scope of the language learning experience (Moqbel, 2025). Rather than expanding learners' exposure to diverse texts and perspectives, GenAI may reinforce patterns that limit engagement with broader social, cultural, and linguistic contexts. These concerns are pressing in contexts where curriculum design emphasises intercultural competence, dialogic learning, and critical pedagogy.

Research on AI-driven instruction has explored immediate gains and user satisfaction. There remains a lack of understanding as to how PLL influences learners' cultural competence, interpretive sophistication, and critical thinking skills over time (Gonsalves, 2024). It is unclear whether learners eventually compensate for any deficiencies in cultural or critical thinking components, or whether these gaps persist and widen at advanced proficiency levels. Questions regarding sociolinguistic biases in AI systems are food for thought. Learners whose cultural or linguistic backgrounds differ from the normative datasets used to train AI systems may get AI-generated content that misaligns with their contextual needs (Meniado, 2023).

The aim of this chapter is to showcase how TESOL educators across a range of institutional contexts perceive the influence of GenAI on TESOL programmes. Building on prior research in technology-mediated language education (Hasumi & Chiu, 2024; Modhish & Al-Kadi, 2016; Wang & Fan, 2025), this chapter illuminates educators' perceptions about content diversity, critical engagement, and language instructors' evolving role in maintaining the depth and breadth of language curricula and how they have been affected by ongoing AI advances. It is structured around two central research questions: How do TESOL educators perceive the impact of GenAI-driven tools on the structure and objectives of formal English language curricula? How do educators perceive their role in AI-enhanced language education?

2. THEORETICAL BACKGROUND

Early digital technologies in language education operated using behaviourist and communicative approaches to second language learning. However, AI has facilitated a significant shift toward connectivist learning theories that emphasise knowledge generation through technological networks (Sen, 2021; Wang & Fan, 2025). Theoretical evolution from CALL, to MALL (Al-Kadi, 2017), to AI-enhanced learning (Laak & Aru, 2024) has improved accessibility and flexibility of English language learning, allowing learners to engage with content regardless of time or location constraints (Lee, 2022).

The notion of critical pedagogy provides an essential theoretical lens for examining AI's role in language education. Originating from Paulo Freire's seminal work on the subject the theory maintains that authentic education transcends mere knowledge transfer; it is a way of empowering learners in questioning and transforming social conditions (Freire, 2020). This has extended to technology-enhanced learning with the argument that digital tools can reinforce existing inequities unless guided by critical pedagogical principles (Giroux, 2021; Modhish & Al-Kadi, 2016). Selwyn (2023) noted that AI systems generally reproduce systemic biases embedded in their training data. Knox (2020) observed that AI-based platforms, when integrated into large-scale educational systems, may perpetuate unequal power relations and constrain learner agency. Through this theoretical lens, AI-driven strategies prioritise instrumental skills (e.g., grammar exercises, test preparation) over broader sociocultural engagement. It transforms language education into a transactional process rather than a dialogical (Laak & Aru, 2024; Shemshack & Spector, 2020), human-centred experience (Al-Kadi, 2018).

Constructivist learning theory, associated with Jean Piaget, offers another valuable framework for understanding AI's impact (Wang & Fan, 2025). This theory posits that learners actively construct knowledge through interactions, integrating new information into existing cognitive frameworks (Piaget & Inhelder, 2008). A central element of this theory is the idea of 'cognitive conflict,' wherein learners encounter information that challenges their current understanding, which in turn stimulates deeper cognitive engagement. Recent empirical studies have investigated how digital tools create constructivist learning opportunities that promote such cognitive conflicts. Arici et al. (2019) analysed research trends in augmented reality apps for science education. Findings showed that immersive learning experiences effectively challenge students' preconceptions and facilitate cognitive conflict and deeper understanding. In the context of AI-driven learning, it is crucial to consider how AI might either promote or inhibit these productive cognitive conflicts (Lee, 2022). Positioning development as a social process mediated by language (Vygotsky 1978), AI personalisation may reduce cognitive conflict by encouraging cognitive offloading (Gerlich, 2025). That is, with the assistance of AI students rely on automated feedback rather than actively grappling with challenging content.

Sociocultural theory emphasises the collaborative and culturally embedded nature of learning. Lantolf and Poehner (2014) highlighted that to maintain social interactivity, educational technologies must balance individualised feedback with collaborative opportunities. Educational tools should enhance, rather than replace, meaningful interactions among peers and educators. In this regard, AI-based platforms present potential risks if they isolate students from collaborative activities such as group projects, debates, or discussions in favour of machine-guided exercises. While AI-driven PLL benefits skill reinforcement (Giray, 2025), learners still need opportunities to engage with diverse perspectives, cultural artifacts, and collective problem-solving experiences that develop both linguistic competence and social awareness. Excessive PLL may isolate learners from these social dimensions, potentially undermining motivation and cultural understanding.

Curriculum theory illuminates the tension between easily measurable skills and the more nuanced objectives central to holistic education. As AI operates through data-driven metrics, it may direct learners toward discrete language skills or test preparation activities that overshadow intangible yet vital aspects of language study. Essential components of a comprehensive curriculum, such as engagement with diverse literary traditions or interpretive capacities, may be marginalised in favour of quantifiable outcomes. Recent research, including Laak and Aru (2024), demonstrated how data-driven approaches sideline holistic development goals. Baillifard et al. (2023) emphasised the importance of ensuring that such tools support comprehensive educational goals rather than focusing exclusively on easily quantifiable outcomes.

3. PRIOR RESEARCH FINDINGS

AI-driven tools and platforms offer obvious advantages in language education (Bayly-Castaneda et al., 2024), from adaptive language software like Duolingo to sophisticated tools like ChatGPT. These technologies have demonstrated the capacity to generate individualised study plans, provide immediate feedback on grammar and vocabulary, and offer tailored reading and listening materials (Sol & Heng, 2024). Educational policymakers and practitioners increasingly view these technologies as essential tools for improving learning outcomes and addressing disparities in language proficiency (UNESCO, 2019). Researchers have documented how AI can customise content according to learners' proficiency levels, interests, and pace, often resulting in more efficient skill acquisition (Sol & Heng, 2024). For instance, the natural language processing capabilities of software like ChatGPT enable immediate feedback on grammatical and stylistic elements, allowing learners to progress individually (Meniado, 2023). Additionally, features such as adaptive assessments, gamified learning activities, and analytics dashboards empower both students and instructors to identify areas requiring remediation, potentially reducing cognitive load and enhancing motivation (Crompton et al., 2024).

Despite these benefits, concerns about the potential unintended consequences of AI in language education cannot be ignored. Studies have reported decreased student engagement with authentic reading materials in programmes heavily dependent on AI-based systems. They potentially limit exposure to literary diversity and advanced reasoning tasks (Ali, 2023). Gokcearslan et al. (2024) reveal that learners in AI-driven contexts excel in discrete measurable skills, but may struggle with interpretive or context-rich assignments. This discrepancy aligns with warnings that excessive focus on efficiency may compromise integrative competencies such as critical thinking (Gonsalves, 2024) and intercultural awareness (Crompton et al., 2024). Gokcearslan et al. (2024) documented instances where students in AI-driven programmes excelled in grammar assessments and short-answer exercises but encountered significant difficulties interpreting metaphorical language or analysing passages with strong cultural or contextual elements. These challenges illuminate the complexities of language proficiency, which extends beyond mechanical aptitudes to encompass engagement with layered meanings, subtext, and cross-cultural references. This discrepancy echoes concerns raised by Crompton et al. (2024) about excessive focus on operational language skills, which are the most easily measured, and as such may inadvertently overshadow integrative competencies like critical thinking, cultural literacy, and nuanced textual interpretation.

Educators have consequently been encouraged to carefully monitor and supplement AI outcomes to ensure learners develop comprehensive linguistic competencies (Ali, 2023). According to Gokcearslan et al. (2024), when AI prioritises short-term performance gains, such as improved quiz scores or accelerated grammar mastery, broader language objectives, including cultural literacy, critical thinking (Gonsalves, 2024), and exposure to diverse textual genres may be marginalised. Shemshack and Spector (2020) found that AI-based language learning tools and a few platforms successfully integrate rich cultural content or promote higher-order thinking tasks. Most excel at providing adaptive quizzes and vocabulary building exercises, but few successfully integrate rich cultural content or promote higher order thinking tasks. Similarly, Mariyono et al. (2024) highlighted ethical challenges associated with AI-driven course designs that may inadvertently perpetuate biased content or cultural stereotypes.

Gokcearslan et al. (2024) and Mariyono et al. (2024) posited that while AI enables more autonomous learning, it may restrict the scope of students' language engagement. Excessive reliance on bite-sized PLL features has been associated with decreased exposure to diverse cultural contexts and literary genres. It also potentially impedes the holistic development of language competencies (Ali, 2023). This phenomenon is sometimes described as 'learning in a nutshell'. It raises important questions about how AI systems select and filter educational content, particularly when students interact with these systems outside formal classroom structures (Meniado, 2023). Laak and Aru (2024) identified salient gaps between AI-driven learning and the broader objectives of modern education, including collaboration, cognitive engagement, and general competencies. According to the study, AI tools fail to address nuanced aspects of language learning that require human interaction and cultural context. Likewise, Baillifard et al. (2023) found that careful design is necessary for integrating AI tutors into university coursework. This care ensures that the technology supports comprehensive educational goals rather than merely focusing on easily measurable competencies.

While AI can tailor instruction to individual needs and enhance efficiency, it risks creating 'learning silos' that limit exposure to diverse content. In the existing body of literature, insufficient attention has been given to PLL, which might influence curriculum breadth and depth over time. A central debate in this discourse concerns whether PLL enhances or restricts learning opportunities. Proponents argue that AI technology democratises access to quality resources, making language practice more inclusive and efficient (Luckin et al., 2016; Modhish & Al-Kadi, 2016). Critics, however, emphasise the risk of algorithmic tunnel vision (ATV), wherein generated content consistently reinforces existing skill profiles with little exploring beyond immediate learning requirements (UNESCO, 2019). This narrow focus potentially limits exposure to literature from diverse cultures and genres, thereby constraining learners' broader engagement with language.

4. METHOD

This chapter is part of a larger project about AI in language learning. For this chapter, a qualitative research design was employed to examine the implications of using AI for PLL from the perspectives of TESOL educators.

4.1 Participants

The sample comprised twenty university-level TESOL educators in fifteen countries across Africa, Asia, Europe, North America, South America, and the Middle East. They were selected through a purposive sampling technique from professional networks, academic listservs, including *myTESOL,* and targeted email outreach to faculty listed on public university websites. Two criteria guided participant selection: (1) at least four years of teaching experience in English language instruction at the tertiary level, and (2) familiarity with GenAI tools. Their familiarity with GenAI ranged from beginners to advanced AI users. Their teaching spanned from 4 to 15 years. All participants were provided with an overview of the study and informed that their participation was voluntary. They could withdraw at any time during the data collection without consequence.

4.2 Data Collection and Analysis

Data for this study were gathered through Zoom-based interviews to accommodate the international distribution of the participants. Each interview lasted between twenty and thirty minutes. For this purpose, a protocol was prepared beforehand to elicit detailed insights into participants' experiences with GenAI tools in English education. The protocol included both closed-ended and open-ended questions about using GenAI tools, observed changes in curricula scope, student engagement, and challenges related to cultural content and critical thinking that stem from reliance on PLL tools. Such questions solicited responses on the perceived effects of AI on language curricula scope and strategies for preserving cultural and critical engagement. Participants were encouraged to provide examples from their teaching contexts. The protocol was piloted and refined in consultation with experts in qualitative research to improve clarity, focus, and relevance.

4.3 Data Analysis

The interviews were recorded and transcribed using Otter.ai. This AI-powered transcription tool generated time-stamped transcripts with speaker identification, which were reviewed and manually corrected for accuracy. The transcripts were then anonymised and stored securely for analysis. Five of the participants were later invited to review the thematic interpretations and confirm that their perspectives remained unchanged. This approach enabled an understanding of how TESOL educators negotiate the pedagogical possibilities and constraints introduced by GenAI in curriculum design. Thematic analysis was employed, following Braun and Clarke's (2014) six-phase methodological framework. The process began with a close reading of the transcripts to ensure deep familiarity with the data. Codes were generated inductively, allowing key ideas and patterns to emerge from participants' responses, rather than imposing pre-established categories. These codes were refined through a recursive process, culminating in the identification of three overarching themes (Figure 1). The analysis linked qualitative findings to patterns identified in participants' structured responses to draw meaningful connections between individual narratives and broader pedagogical trends. It resulted in an integrated understanding of how educators adapt both the benefits and limitations of GenAI in curriculum design and classroom practice.

Figure 1. A Flowchart of Thematic Analysis in the Study

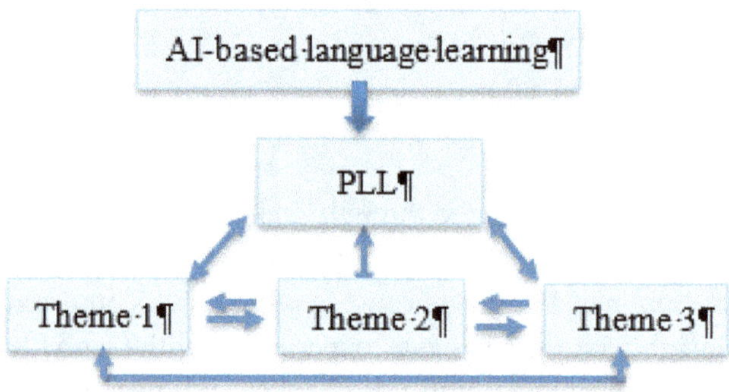

5. RESULTS

The overarching themes (Table 1) emerged consistently across participant responses. They provide insight into both the challenges and potential solutions for maintaining supervised AI in TESOL programmes. In this section, the participants are represented as numbers (e.g., TESOLer 1, 2, etc.) when presenting illustrative quotations.

Table 1. TESOL Educators' Perspectives on Curriculum Change in TESOL Under GenAI

Bias in Content Selection	AI presents tasks similar to learners' previous usage patterns. It reinforces a narrow range of material.	"The platform notices my students gravitate toward short grammar exercises, and it keeps giving them more of the same." - TESOLer 6
Reduced Critical Engagement	AI prioritises performance metrics (e.g., quiz accuracy, user retention) over exposure to cultural or thematic diversity.	"Our primary metrics for 'success' are user retention and quiz accuracy, not whether learners explore global perspectives." - TESOLer 11
Teacher Mediation	Active oversight (by educators) can offset PLL biases and introduce broader cultural and analytical content.	"I monitor the platform's data to see where students improve, but I also assign curated readings. AI is just one part of our curriculum." - TESOLer 17

5.1 Bias in Content Selection

The respondents expressed concerns that AI tools offer content based on past usage patterns rather than encouraging students to explore new forms of text. One interviewee (TESOLer 6) remarked:

The platform notices my students gravitate toward short grammar exercises, and it keeps giving them more of the same. It rarely suggests they try reading a news article or analysing poetry.

These observations align with what UNESCO (2019) termed ATV, wherein software optimises user retention and performance on discrete tasks rather than broadening subject matter exposure. The respondents also noted that the AI systems appeared to prioritise content that yielded immediate, measurable outcomes. TESOLer 5 explained:

AI seems to prefer activities where progress is easily quantified, such as vocabulary quizzes, gap-filling exercises, and multiple-choice questions. It's much less likely to involve critical analysis or cultural exploration, which are harder to score automatically. TESOLer 5.

As students are repeatedly directed toward similar types of content and tasks, this tendency creates a feedback loop that narrows the curriculum over time. AI preference for easily measurable competencies reflects broader concerns about how data-driven education may constrain learning experiences by prioritising metrics over meaningful educational objectives. Participants also observed that AI systems' reliance on historical usage data creates a self-reinforcing cycle where learners become increasingly confined to familiar content types. This pattern emerged as problematic for advanced learners who might benefit from exposure to more challenging or diverse materials but instead receive content that maintains their comfort zones.

5.2 Reduced Critical Engagement

The second theme relates to how AI-based PLL often misses opportunities to cultivate critical thinking or cultural awareness. The participants were aware that AI platforms generally prioritise user retention metrics, such as quick quiz completions, over more exploration or critical engagements with language. TESOLer 11 explained:

My learners use AI *not* to explore global perspectives or engage with complex texts but to answer their immediate questions.

TESOLer 14 noted:

AI seems to prefer activities where progress is easily quantified, such as vocabulary quizzes and gap-filling exercises. It rarely suggests tasks involving critical analysis or cultural exploration.

TESOLers also noted an increasing dependence on AI-driven tasks, with fewer students independently seeking out extracurricular readings or sociocultural discussions. To illustrate, TESOLer 8 commented that:

Many [students] seem content to take whatever the platform suggests for granted, which rarely includes rich cultural content.

TESOLer 11 also stated:

Our primary metrics for 'success' are user retention and quiz accuracy, not whether learners explore global perspectives.

This mirrors Freire's (1970) warnings against commodified forms of education that undermine transformative learning. The reduction in student-initiated exploration suggests that AI systems may inadvertently discourage autonomous intellectual curiosity that leads to deeper cultural understanding and critical thinking development. Participants reported that AI systems tend to recommend materials that align with dominant cultural narratives or mainstream content, potentially limiting students' exposure to diverse voices and perspectives.

5.3 Teachers' Role as Mediators

Educators who actively monitor AI analytics can offset AI limitations highlighted in Theme 1 and Theme 2 by supplementing lessons with culturally rich texts and interactive discussions. TESOLer 20 reported:

I look at where students are excelling in AI, but also bring in readings from global news outlets. AI is just a part of our curriculum, not all of it.

TESOLer 17 also explained monitoring the AI platform data to see where students are improving by assigning curated readings.

This approach aligns with Vygotsky's (1978) sociocultural view of learning as an interactive process. It suggests that human facilitation is crucial for breadth and depth in language instruction. The prevalence of the theme of mediation reveals the critical role that educators play in maintaining curriculum comprehensiveness while leveraging AI's PLL benefits. Participants described three strategies: curating additional materials, group discussions about cultural topics, and explicitly addressing gaps in AI-generated content. These strategies reflect TESOLers' insights on how thoughtful human interventions can counteract the narrowing tendencies of AI-based PLL while preserving the efficiency benefits that AI systems provide. However, the success of instructor mediation strategies depends on educators' capacity to understand both the capabilities and limitations of AI while maintaining focus on comprehensive language education goals. On this issue, TESOLer 13 contends that

Educators should ensure that AI tools serve broader educational objectives. This requires not only pedagogical expertise but also technological literacy.

Taken together, the three themes illustrate the complex dynamics involved in AI-driven language education. They reveal both significant challenges and strategies for addressing curricula narrowing concerns. While AI bias and reduced critical engagement present real risks to language curricula breadth, instructor mediation emerges as a crucial mechanism for maintaining comprehensive language education in AI-enhanced environments. Findings suggest that cognitive offloading amplifies these concerns when learners depend on AI for immediate answers, which may bypass interpretive processes essential for higher order thinking.

6. DISCUSSION

The first theme of bias in content selection reveals how AI systems tend to generate content based on learners' previous usage patterns. It creates feedback on familiar tasks rather than encouraging new explorations. This reflects UNESCO's concept of algorithmic tunnel vision (ATV), where PLL optimises for engagement metrics rather than educational breadth. This narrows curricula over time (Moqbel, 2025), as it limits exposure to diverse genres and perspectives. Similarly, the second theme of reduced critical engagement highlighted how AI-enabled PLL often misses opportunities to cultivate critical thinking or cultural awareness. These findings resonate with Freire's (1970) critique of commodified education, suggesting that AI-driven PLL may discourage autonomous intellectual curiosity. The reduction in student-initiated exploration underscores the need for deliberate pedagogical interventions to maintain cultural engagement and critical thinking opportunities. It aligns with Shemshack and Spector's (2020) systematic review, in which most AI-based language learning tools excel at adaptive quizzes and vocabulary building but incorporate fewer opportunities for cultural engagement or higher order thinking. The reduction in student-initiated exploration of cultural content represents a significant concern, as it suggests that AI systems may discourage autonomous intellectual curiosity that leads to deeper understanding and critical thinking.

Despite these pitfalls, this study demonstrates that AI's impact on curricula breadth is not uniform across educational contexts. The third theme of instructor mediation emerged as a critical factor in mitigating the potential narrowing effects of AI-based PLL. In settings where instructors deliberately supplemented AI-driven instruction with expansive cultural content reported balanced outcomes. TESOLers in these contexts encourage additional reading. Still, there remains a great deal of potential for peer discussions and project-based activities to broaden students' linguistic and cultural exposure beyond the AI's immediate responses. Such purposeful additions resonate with Freire's (2020) call for dialogical, transformative education, emphasising the importance of teacher agency in shaping how technological tools are integrated.

These hybrid approaches also align with Vygotsky's (1978) sociocultural theory and Pinar's (2019) curriculum theory. The former emphasises that meaningful social interactions, such as peer discussions, instructor feedback, and group projects are integral to promoting linguistic competence and cultural understanding. The latter advocates for educational frameworks that prioritise empathy, global awareness, and creativity alongside technical proficiency. They are also in congruence with Meniado's (2023) argument that platforms like ChatGPT function best when educators use them as supplements rather than replacements, ensuring that authentic texts and human-led guidance remain central to the curriculum. The three strategies mentioned under the third theme align with Vygotsky's sociocultural theory, which underscores the importance of human interaction in learning. By supplementing AI-driven tasks with collaborative activities and culturally rich materials, educators ensure that technology serves as a tool rather than a substitute for comprehensive education.

Figure 2 illustrates the conceptual relationship between AI-driven PLL and curriculum design in TESOL. It emphasises how PLL, while efficient, can narrow curricular scope (Moqbel, 2025) unless actively mediated by educators. The figure reinforces the study's central argument that teacher intervention is essential to preserve cultural depth, critical engagement, and holistic learning outcomes in AI-enhanced environments. By integrating teacher mediation, AI technology becomes a supplemental tool rather than a singular driver of curricular experiences. Teacher mediation serves as a critical counterbalance to the narrowing tendencies of AI personalisation (Moqbel, 2025), ensuring that cultural depth and critical thinking remain integral to language education. In contexts where teachers actively blend AI-driven tasks with culturally rich materials and collaborative activities, learners reported more balanced and enriching experiences.

Figure 2. Interplay between PLL, AI, and Curriculum Scope

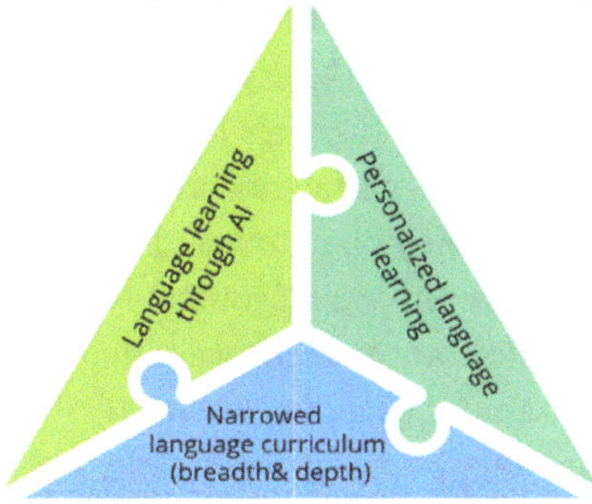

According to the Pinar's curriculum theory (Pinar, 2019), education cannot be reduced to discrete competencies or test scores. Instead, a robust educational framework should encompass intangible yet essential elements like empathy, global awareness, and creative thinking. The hybrid approaches observed in public high school and university settings demonstrate that these elements can be sustained when educators actively embed AI within a broader pedagogical vision. From a constructivist perspective (Piaget, 2008), the results suggest that AI personalisation may not consistently provide the cognitive conflict necessary for deeper learning, particularly for advanced students. For constructivist learning to occur, learners need exposure to novel and challenging content that prompts cognitive restructuring, something that highly personalised systems may fail to provide if they primarily recommend familiar content types. From a critical pedagogy standpoint (Freire, 2020; Giroux, 2021), the findings highlight how AI-driven PLL can reinforce a transactional view of education focused on discrete skills rather than transformative learning. The sociocultural perspective (Lantolf & Poehner, 2014; Vygotsky, 1978) is relevant to understanding the importance of teachers' roles in AI-enhanced environments. The finding that educators who actively supplement AI tools with collaborative activities and cultural content achieve more balanced outcomes emphasises the social nature of language learning. This suggests that effective AI integration must preserve opportunities for meaningful social interaction and cultural engagement rather than isolating learners in bite-sized learning pathways.

Overall, the results emphasise the importance of active oversight and supplementation when integrating AI tools into language curricula. However, there are challenges for educators that may go beyond their capacities and need broader intervention. A major challenge is maintaining curricula breadth in the face of AI's tendency to prioritise efficiency and measurable skills. This shift also introduces cognitive offloading (Gerlich, 2025), where learners delegate complex reasoning and memory tasks to AI. It potentially diminishes opportunities for deep cognitive engagement. As several participants noted, PLL often narrows content exposure, requiring teachers to actively supplement AI-driven tasks with culturally rich materials and critical thinking activities (Mariyono, Akmal, & Kamila, 2024; Pikhart & Al-Obaydi, 2025). Another challenge lies in addressing algorithmic bias, which can perpetuate dominant cultural narratives and limit inclusivity. Educators also face the risk of learner dependency on automated feedback, which may undermine autonomy and higher order cognitive engagement (Wang & Fan, 2025; Gonsalves, 2024). These challenges underscore the need for continuous professional development and institutional support to enhance language educators' digital literacy for effective AI-driven language education (Tenberga & Daniela, 2024; UNESCO, 2019).

7. IMPLICATIONS

The chapter explores some of the ongoing discussions about controlled AI integration in language education. It highlights the need for guidelines that align technological tools with broader educational standards. Educational policies should encourage the development and adoption of AI systems that support comprehensive language education rather than focusing exclusively on efficiency metrics. In addition, professional development programmes should be built around digital literacy skills that effectively help teachers to integrate and supplement AI tools in ways that maintain curricular breadth and depth. For AI developers, the results reveal opportunities to enhance PLL to include broader educational objectives beyond immediate skill mastery. By collaborating with curriculum theorists and language education specialists, developers could create systems that recommend diverse content types, incorporate cultural contexts, and promote critical thinking alongside discrete skill practice. Collaborations between AI developers and curriculum theorists could facilitate the creation of adaptive systems that incorporate reflective, collaborative, and culturally diverse learning pathways. Such initiatives are vital to ensure that AI enriches rather than restricts educational experiences.

8. CONCLUSION

This chapter examines the ways GenAI both limits and redefines language curricula, along with the implications for educators navigating this evolving landscape. While AI-based PLL can accelerate discrete language skill acquisition, it often narrows curricular scope by emphasising easily measurable, bite-sized content. Such narrowing risks limit learners' exposure to cultural diversity and critical thinking opportunities. The findings illustrate that effective AI integration in TESOL is not a technical fix but a pedagogical challenge. It requires active instructor mediation to counterbalance AI tendencies. The findings highlight the need for intentional and collaborative curricula design to ensure AI supports inclusive language education. Design strategies should counterbalance cognitive offloading by incorporating tasks that require independent reasoning and collaborative problem solving. However, these pedagogical insights also reveal critical gaps in the current evidence base, raising important questions for future investigation. The rapidly evolving nature of AI means that findings based on current systems may not fully apply to future iterations. Although the current findings provide useful insights, they rely on self-reported perceptions from a limited sample and lack longitudinal scope. Broader research that integrates learner perspectives, classroom observations, and long-term tracking is needed to evaluate how AI influences critical thinking, intercultural competence, and the breadth of language curricula over time. While interviews bring depth to the research problem, the self-reported data from interviews may be subject to social desirability bias. Other agencies, including learners, course developers, and parents, would enrich an understanding of how GenAI affects learners' linguistic repertoire and learning performance in the sense of formal curricula. Future studies could also develop objective measures, such as standardised assessments, to examine the scope and depth of AI-mediated learning.

REFERENCES

Al-Kadi, A. (2017). *Some aspects of ICT uses in the teaching of EFL at the tertiary level in Yemen* (PhD dissertation), Carthage University, Tunisia.

Al-Kadi, A. (2018). Towards humanizing ELT: Revisiting the need for English in the medical context in Yemen. *Language Teaching and Educational Research, 1*(2), 121–138.

Al-Obaydi, L., & Pikhart, M. (2025). DeepSeek as an AI-powered learning tool: Uncovering EFL college students' preferences and satisfaction. *SAGE Open, 15*(4), 21582440251381683. Advance online publication. DOI: 10.1177/21582440251381683

Ali, J. K. M. (2023). Benefits and challenges of using ChatGPT: An exploratory study on English language programs. *University of Bisha Journal for Humanities, 2*(2), 629–641.

Arici, F., Yildirim, P., Caliklar, Ş., & Yilmaz, R. M. (2019). Research trends in the use of augmented reality in science education: Content and bibliometric mapping analysis. *Computers & Education, 142*, 103647. DOI: 10.1016/j.compedu.2019.103647

Baillifard, A., Gabella, M., Lavenex, P. B., & Martarelli, C. S. (2023). *Implementing Learning Principles with a Personal AI Tutor: A Case Study*. arXiv preprint arXiv:2309.13060.

Bayly-Castaneda, K., Ramirez-Montoya, M.-S., & Morita-Alexander, A. (2024). Crafting personalized learning paths with AI for lifelong learning: A systematic literature review. *Frontiers in Education, 9*, 1424386. Advance online publication. DOI: 10.3389/feduc.2024.1424386

Braun, V., & Clarke, V. (2014). *Successful qualitative research: A practical guide for beginners* (1st ed.). SAGE.

Cardona, M. A., Rodríguez, R. J., & Ishmael, K. (2023). Artificial intelligence and the future of teaching and learning: Insights and recommendations. U.S. Department of Education, Office of Educational Technology. https://tech.ed.gov/files/2023/05/AI-Future-Teaching-Learning.pdf

Castro, G. P., Chiappe, A., Ramírez-Montoya, M. S., & Alcántar Nieblas, C. (2025). Key barriers to personalized learning in times of artificial intelligence: A literature review. *Applied Sciences (Basel, Switzerland), 15*(6), 3103. DOI: 10.3390/app15063103

Chapelle, C. A., & Sauro, S. (2017). TELL, CALL, and MALL. In Chapelle, C. A., & Sauro, S. (Eds.), *The Handbook of Technology and Second Language Teaching and Learning* (pp. 1–20). IGI Global., https://www.igi-global.com/chapter/tell-call-and-mall/242301 DOI: 10.1002/9781118914069.ch1

Crompton, H., Edmett, A., Ichaporia, N., & Burke, D. (2024). AI and English language teaching: Affordances and challenges. *British Journal of Educational Technology*, *55*(6), 2503–2529. DOI: 10.1111/bjet.13460

Freire, P. (1970). *Pedagogy of the oppressed.* Continuum.

Freire, P. (2020). Pedagogy of the oppressed. In *Toward a sociology of education* (pp. 374–386). Routledge.

Gerlich, M. (2025). AI tools in society: Impacts on cognitive offloading and the future of critical thinking. *Societies (Basel, Switzerland)*, *15*(1), 6. DOI: 10.3390/soc15010006

Giray, L. (2025). Unlocking learners' potential in English language learning: the synergy of artificial intelligence, cognitive science, and ChatGPT, Learning: Research and Practice, DOI: DOI: 10.1080/23735082.2025.2501037

Giroux, H. A. (2021). *Race, politics, and pandemic pedagogy: Education in a time of crisis*. Bloomsbury Publishing. DOI: 10.5040/9781350184466

Giroux, H. A., & Bosio, E. (2021). Critical pedagogy and global citizenship education. In *Conversations on global citizenship education* (pp. 3–12). Routledge. DOI: 10.4324/9780429346897-1

Gokcearslan, S., Tosun, C., & Erdemir, Z. G. (2024). Benefits, challenges, and methods of Artificial Intelligence (AI) chatbots in education: A systematic literature review. [IJTE]. *International Journal of Technology in Education*, *7*(1), 19–39. https:////ijte.net/index.php/ijte/article/view/600. DOI: 10.46328/ijte.600

Gonsalves, C. (2024). Generative AI's impact on critical thinking: Revisiting Bloom's Taxonomy. *Journal of Marketing Education*, *1*, 02734753241305980. Advance online publication. DOI: 10.1177/02734753241305980

Hasumi, T., & Chiu, M. S. (2024). Technology-enhanced language learning in English language education: Performance analysis, core publications, and emerging trends. *Cogent Education*, *11*(1), 2346044. Advance online publication. DOI: 10.1080/2331186X.2024.2346044

Knox, J. (2020). Artificial intelligence and education in China. *Learning, Media and Technology*, *45*(3), 298–311. DOI: 10.1080/17439884.2020.1754236

Laak, K. J., & Aru, J. (2024). *AI and personalized learning: bridging the gap with modern educational goals*. arXiv preprint arXiv:2404.02798.

Lantolf, J. P., & Poehner, M. E. (2014). *Sociocultural theory and the pedagogical imperative in L2 education*. Routledge. DOI: 10.4324/9780203813850

Lee, J. S. (2022). *Informal digital learning of English: Research to practice*. Routledge.

Luckin, R., Holmes, W., Griffiths, M., & Forcier, L. B. (2016). *Intelligence unleashed: An argument for AI in education*. Pearson.

Mariyono, D., Akmal, A. N. A., & Kamila, A. N. A. (2024). *Navigating ethical dilemmas in AI-enhanced language education: Addressing bias and ensuring inclusivity*. Universitas Islam Malang, Universitas Bwawijaya Malang, University of Brawijaya.

Meniado, J. C. (2023). The impact of ChatGPT on English language teaching, learning, and assessment: A rapid review of literature. *Arab World English Journal, 14*(4), 3–18. DOI: 10.24093/awej/vol14no4.1

Modhish, A., & Al-Kadi, A. (2016). Internet integration in EFL college instruction: Attitudes and perspectives. [IJSELL]. *International Journal on Studies in English Language and Literature*, *4*(6), 52–62.

Moqbel, M. S. S. (2025). Impact of AI-based personalized English learning on cognitive offloading and breadth of formal curriculum. *Journal of English Studies in Arabia Felix*, *4*(2), 50–64. DOI: 10.56540/jesaf.v4i2.127

Piaget, J., & Inhelder, B. (2008). *The psychology of the child*. Basic books.

Pikhart, M., & Al-Obaydi, L. H. (2025). Reporting the potential risk of using AI in higher education: Subjective perspectives of educators. *Computers in Human Behavior Reports*, *18*, 100693. DOI: 10.1016/j.chbr.2025.100693

Pinar, W. F. (2019). W*hat is curriculum theory?* Routledge.

Selwyn, N. (2023). *The critique of digital education. Rethinking Sociological Critique in Contemporary Education: Reflexive Dialogue and Prospective Inquiry*.

Sen, M. (2021). Mobile-assisted language learning (MALL): A comprehensive review. *International Journal of English Language Teaching and Studies*, *3*(2), 165–180.

Shemshack, A., & Spector, J. M. (2020). A systematic literature review of personalized learning terms. *Smart Learning Environments*, *7*(1), 1–20. DOI: 10.1186/s40561-020-00140-9

Sol, K., & Heng, K. (2024). AI-powered chatbots as personalized academic writing assistants for non-native English speakers. In Peters, M. A., & Heraud, R. (Eds.), *Encyclopedia of educational innovation* (pp. 1–5). Springer. DOI: 10.1007/978-981-13-2262-4_313-1

Tenberga, I., & Daniela, L. (2024). Artificial intelligence literacy competencies for teachers through self-assessment tools. *Sustainability (Basel)*, *16*(23), 10386. DOI: 10.3390/su162310386

UNESCO. (2019). *Artificial intelligence in education: Challenges and opportunities for sustainable development.*

Vygotsky, L. S. (1978). *Mind in society: The development of higher psychological processes.* Harvard University Press.

Wang, J., & Fan, W. (2025). The effect of ChatGPT on students' learning performance, learning perception, and higher-order thinking: Insights from a meta-analysis. *Humanities & Social Sciences Communications*, *12*(1), 621. DOI: 10.1057/s41599-025-04787-y

Chapter 10

Integrating Digital Humanities in Teaching Research Methodologies for Postgraduate Students in Arabic and Islamic Studies

Tawffeek Mohammed
https://orcid.org/0000-0002-7314-9688
University of the Western Cape, South Africa

Mohamed Faraj Saleh Raheel
https://orcid.org/0000-0002-8219-9695
Qatar University, Qatar

Muhammad Ashraf Ebrahim Dockrat
LanCSAL University of Johannesburg, South Africa

ABSTRACT

The integration of Digital Humanities (DH) into postgraduate education offers transformative possibilities for advancing research methodologies in Arabic and Islamic Studies. This chapter investigates how digital tools, computational approaches, and interactive platforms can enrich traditional modes of scholarly inquiry. By examining applications such as text mining, digital manuscript preservation, corpus-based linguistic analysis, and data visualization, the study highlights how DH fosters interdisciplinary exploration and critical engagement with classical and

DOI: 10.4018/979-8-3373-4521-5.ch010

contemporary sources. In addition, the chapter proposes a technology-enhanced learning (TEL) prototype designed specifically to support research methodology training in Arabic and Islamic Studies. The prototype integrates digital research environments, collaborative annotation tools, and multilingual data resources to cultivate students' digital literacy and methodological innovation.

1. INTRODUCTION

Postgraduate research is a vital phase in academic development. It marks the transition of scholars from knowledge consumers to knowledge creators. Consequently, mastering research methodologies is essential to this shift. In other words, research methods provide both a foundation for rigorous investigation and a connection to disciplinary innovation (Stein & Galliers, 2018). Training in research methods not only enhances the quality of academic output but also equips students with the analytical and conceptual tools essential for meaningful contributions to their respective fields (Creswell & Poth, 2016). In particular, research methodologies in social sciences and humanities are widely diverse. They include qualitative, quantitative, and interpretive approaches, and each of these approaches requires systematic instruction and contextual awareness (Given, 2008).

Nevertheless, due to rapid technological progress and changing epistemological frameworks, traditional research training methods are being scrutinised. Scholars assert that methodological education needs to be redefined to include digital tools and interdisciplinary perspectives (Borgman, 2010). In fact, the digital transformation of scholarly practices, including data collection, analysis, visualisation, and dissemination, requires recalibrating postgraduate curricula to remain relevant and future-focused. This is especially important for disciplines such as Arabic and Islamic Studies, where big data, extensive textual corpora, and historical archives offer significant opportunities for digital research.

In line with the above, integrating digital humanities (DH) and research methods offers considerable transformative potential for postgraduate education. This chapter examines the instructional design and pedagogical strategies of a technology-enhanced module centred on research methods in Arabic and Islamic Studies, but still relevant to all other disciplines in the Social Sciences and Humanities. The module can be delivered via the *Moodle* or *Sakai* Learning Management System (LMS), either fully online or in a hybrid mode. It employs a range of DH tools to help students develop the skills and knowledge necessary for conducting rigorous academic research and producing high-quality outputs.

This chapter is situated at the intersection of several interrelated issues and trends shaping contemporary postgraduate education in the humanities. These include the increasing digitalisation of research practices, the growing influence of AI-assisted tools, persistent disparities in digital access and preparedness, and the need to reconcile technological innovation with disciplinary epistemologies and ethical responsibility. In Arabic and Islamic Studies, these challenges are further intensified by the scale and complexity of textual corpora, the cultural and religious sensitivity of sources, and the demand for methodological transparency. Responding to these dynamics, the chapter positions digital humanities not as a technical add-on but as a pedagogical framework through which emerging problems—such as skills gaps, ethical uncertainty, and methodological fragmentation—can be addressed in a structured and context-sensitive manner.

While the chapter is grounded in Arabic and Islamic Studies, its contribution extends beyond disciplinary boundaries by illustrating how human–AI collaboration is enacted through pedagogical design, supervisory practice, and ethical mediation in postgraduate research training. Rather than advancing a general theory of human–AI interaction, the chapter presents a context-specific case that demonstrates how educators engage with AI-enabled digital tools as curriculum designers, methodological guides, and critical evaluators of research practice. In this way, the chapter complements broader discussions in the volume by showing how evolving educator roles and human–AI collaboration materialise within a concrete disciplinary and institutional setting.

2. CONTEXT AND RATIONALE

There is a growing focus in higher education institutions worldwide on rethinking postgraduate curricula to keep pace with the digital shift in research and scholarship. As digital infrastructures become vital to the creation and dissemination of knowledge, postgraduate education must develop by equipping students with both traditional scholarly skills and digital literacy. This dual competence is particularly important in social sciences and humanities, where new research questions often demand a blend of computational techniques and humanistic inquiry (Hayles, 2012; Svensson, 2016). Institutions must ensure that their students possess these skills to be prepared for interdisciplinary, collaborative, and digitally mediated academic settings.

In South Africa, especially at institutions such as the University of the Western Cape, this need is even more pressing due to the strong push to decolonise and democratise knowledge. Integrating digital humanities (DH) into research training offers methodological innovation and a way to recover, preserve, and reinterpret African and Islamic intellectual traditions through digital methods. For example, the digitisation of manuscripts, computational analysis of religious texts, and digital archiving of oral histories enable scholars to generate new knowledge relevant both locally and globally (Risam, 2018). Therefore, DH acts as a strategic avenue to improve epistemic access and make the curriculum more pertinent.

In line with the above, many departments at the Faculty of Arts and Humanities at the University of the Western Cape have recognised the need to update their research methodology curriculum to better prepare students for modern academic and professional environments. While traditional research methods in Arabic and Islamic Studies are still fundamental, they often lack digital tools that can improve research efficiency, breadth, and interdisciplinarity. Students and researchers are required to master advanced tools that can enable them to process, analyse and interpret extensive collections of texts or corpora and historical data (Schreibman et al., 2015).

In addition to infrastructural and technical considerations, integrating digital humanities into Arabic and Islamic Studies may encounter epistemological resistance within segments of traditional scholarship. Concerns may centre on the digitisation of sacred texts, the perceived dilution of oral authority systems (such as *ijāzah*), or the legitimacy of computational analysis in religious interpretation. Acknowledging these tensions is pedagogically important, as it prepares students to engage respectfully with conservative objections while articulating the scholarly value of digital methods as complementary—rather than oppositional—to classical modes of knowledge transmission.

3. INTEGRATING DH INTO POSTGRADUATE RESEARCH TRAINING

In the evolving world of higher education, it is becoming increasingly important to integrate Digital Humanities (DH) into postgraduate research training. As humanities disciplines face the challenges and opportunities of digital transformation, there is a growing consensus that digital humanities methodologies should be incorporated directly into research curricula (Gold & Klein, 2019). The adoption of this approach in postgraduate programmes will enable students to grasp essential skills in digital literacy and analytical reasoning. These skills are highly valued both within academia and beyond, as they help students stay abreast of emerging technologies.

Digital Humanities can be broadly defined as the use of computational tools and digital methods in humanistic research. It is not a single discipline but a methodological approach that encompasses text mining, data visualization, geographic information systems (GIS), topic modelling, digital editing, and social network analysis, among others (Schreibman et al., 2015). The field fosters the creation of novel digital artefacts such as online databases, annotated corpora, or digital exhibitions while also critically examining digital culture and its epistemological implications (Burdick et al., 2016). Consequently, DH encourages both technical skill and conceptual understanding, offering a versatile toolkit for research across various disciplines.

Integrating DH into postgraduate education fosters not only individual skills development but also collaborative learning environments. Students can participate in project-based assignments or workshops to learn how to use digital tools while engaging in collaborative problem-solving and knowledge production, often across disciplinary boundaries. For example, a student studying Islamic Studies might utilise optical character recognition (OCR) and natural language processing (NLP) to examine old Arabic manuscripts. At the same time, another might use Geographic Information System (GIS) software to produce a digital map of early Islamic trade routes. These experiences improve research outcomes and also develop professional qualities such as teamwork, project management, and adaptability (Siemens et al., 2010).

Undoubtedly, the use of such a framework may promote a comprehensive and inclusive pedagogical approach. It familiarizes students with the affordances of digital tools and their potential in enhancing their disciplinary perspectives. The approach is also in line with current calls for higher education to produce graduates who are not only knowledgeable in a particular discipline but also adaptable, tech-savvy, and prepared for evolving knowledge economies (Knight & Yorke, 2004).

4. INSTITUTIONAL BEST PRACTICES AND CASE STUDIES

Institutions like the University of Sheffield have made significant progress in integrating DH into their postgraduate programmes. The university has embedded digital methods into core curricula and promoted interdisciplinary research projects that link computing with arts, culture, and society by establishing specialised research centres such as the Digital Humanities Institute (DHI)[1]. The postgraduate programmes at the university offer practical training for students in several areas such as text encoding, data visualisation, and digital archiving. This ensures students graduate with both theoretical understanding and practical skills (University of Sheffield, 2020)[2].

In the South African context, national and regional collaborations have taken the initiative to institutionalise DH. In this regard, the South African Centre for Digital Language Resources (SADiLaR), based at North-West University, plays a vital role, especially in the development of DH and language resources. SADiLaR's focus on digitising and preserving indigenous languages aligns well with the objectives of many humanities disciplines. It provides linguistic corpora, computational tools, and language technologies to support both teaching and research. This infrastructure enables postgraduate students and researchers in linguistics, history, literature, and cultural studies to utilise digital tools in their work, particularly when working in multilingual or under-resourced settings (SADiLaR, n.d.)[3]. Moreover, the South African Digital Humanities Network (DHASA) is another significant initiative in the field of digital humanities in South Africa. It acts as a centre for scholars, institutions, and digital humanities projects across the country. It plays a vital role in promoting best practices, sharing pedagogical resources, and fostering collaboration between universities and research organisations. Conferences, workshops, and advocacy are among its activities that have helped build capacity for DH in South African higher education. DHASA supports overcoming barriers to adoption and advocates for fair access to digital infrastructure and expertise by cultivating a supportive community of practice (DHASA, n.d.)[4].

Given the significance of DH in today's research programmes, we do believe that the integration of digital humanities (DH) into Arabic and Islamic Studies at the University of the Western Cape (UWC) serves as a model for parallel departments at other faculties and universities. It seeks to develop research training that is both locally relevant and globally informed. Using DH tools to analyse classical texts, map intellectual networks, and visualise historical developments not only improves the academic rigour of student projects but also supports the university's broader goals of decolonising the curriculum and encouraging innovation.

However, any integration of digital humanities should be approached very carefully rather than in an ad hoc manner. The DEAR framework (Diversity, Employability, Application, Reflection) offers a possible model for integration. It emphasises developing a broad range of technical and methodological skills, understanding how they can be applied across different research disciplines, and employing digital tools in a critical and reflective manner (Benatti et al., 2021).

The successful integration of digital humanities into postgraduate research training also depends on faculty preparedness and institutional support. Lecturers and supervisors need opportunities for professional development in DH methodologies, digital pedagogy, and the ethical use of AI to ensure effective teaching and supervision. In addition, institutional infrastructure, such as access to licensed software, digital repositories, learning management systems, and technical support, is essential for the sustainable implementation. While this chapter focuses on curriculum design, it assumes parallel institutional investment in staff capacity building and digital infrastructure to support long-term adoption.

In addition, while the chapter highlights examples from South Africa and the United Kingdom, the integration of digital humanities in postgraduate education is also advancing across North America, Europe, and parts of Asia and the Middle East. International initiatives increasingly emphasise interdisciplinarity, open-access infrastructures, and culturally responsive DH practices. A detailed comparative analysis is beyond the scope of this chapter; however, the proposed module aligns with global trends that position DH as a flexible, context-sensitive framework adaptable to diverse institutional and regional settings.

5. MODULE DESIGN AND STRUCTURE

The module proposed in this chapter takes a tangible step towards integrating Digital Humanities (DH) into postgraduate research training. It is based on the institutional rationale, pedagogical principles, and theoretical framework discussed in the previous sections. The module specifically targets students in Arabic and Islamic Studies. It combines traditional research methodology teaching with digital tools and computational methods. Its structure responds to the needs of a digitally evolving academic landscape while remaining attentive to the field's distinctive cultural and epistemological dimensions (Chavanayarn, 2024; Ferreira & Borges, 2022; Hayles, 2012).

The module is in line with emerging best practices in DH pedagogy, which highlight a deliberate blend of conceptual inquiry and practical skill development (Tiedau et al., 2014; Tracy & Hoiem, 2017). This dual approach is vital for fostering digitally literate scholars who are also critically reflective about the tools and methods they use. Furthermore, by integrating practical digital training, such as text analysis, data visualisation, and reference management, into the research curriculum, the module fosters a constructivist learning environment where students develop skills through active experimentation and collaboration. The following outline highlights the key components of this module. Each component is designed to support students' progression from basic research theoretical concepts to advanced research skills, with special focus on digital skills that are likely to enhance the quality and productivity of their projects. This approach guarantees that each part of the module aligns purposefully with learners' needs, disciplinary aims, and current digital research methods. The module's structure is presented as a matrix model that visually displays content areas, tools, and methodological frameworks throughout the module.

Table 1. Research Methods in Arabic and Islamic Studies

Component	Method	Tools
Intro to Research Methodologies	Theoretical	Paradigms, DH
Literature Review & Reference Management	Qualitative	Zotero, NVivo, LitMap
Theoretical & Conceptual Frameworks in Arabic and Islamic Studies	Theoretical/Interpretive	Paradigms, Classical Approaches

continued on following page

Table 1. Continued

Component	Method	Tools
Textual Analysis & Visualization	Digital/Textual	Voyant Tools, AntConc
Quantitative Analysis	Quantitative	SPSS
Qualitative Analysis	Qualitative	NVivo, ATLAS.ti
Digital Humanities in Arabic and Islamic Studies	Digital/Textual/Computational	Voyant Tools, AI-assisted tools
Research Ethics & Responsible Use of DH Tools	Ethics/AI	ChatGPT, AI Tools
Workshops & Peer-Review	Collaborative	Discussion Forums

The structure is also guided by a circular model that emphasises iterative learning, as shown in Figure 1.

Figure 1. Circular module layout: Research methods in Arabic and Islamic Studies

The design of this postgraduate research methods module is guided by the ADDIE instructional design model, which provides a structured yet adaptable approach to course development. ADDIE represents Analysis, Design, Development, Implementation, and Evaluation. It facilitates systematic planning and ongoing improvement based on learner needs and feedback (Branch, 2009). The model is particularly suitable for curriculum design in a higher education context because it accommodates diverse student backgrounds and complex learning aims through a responsive, iterative teaching approach.

While no primary data have been collected from participants at the Analysis stage, a cursory look at available literature in Arabic and Islamic Studies shows clearly that few studies utilise digital humanities tools such as corpora tools, quantitative and qualitative analysis tools in this discipline.

An important consideration at the Analysis stage is students' prior digital literacy and readiness for technology-enhanced learning. Postgraduate cohorts in Arabic and Islamic Studies often show uneven exposure to digital research tools, ranging from advanced familiarity to minimal prior engagement. The module therefore adopts a scaffolded approach, beginning with accessible, low-threshold tools (e.g., reference management and basic textual analysis) and progressing to more advanced digital humanities and AI-assisted methods. This graduated design aims to minimise cognitive overload, support inclusive participation, and accommodate diverse technological competencies.

In the Design and Development phases, the focus was on ensuring that the module content matched the intended learning outcomes, utilised digital tools, and selected the most effective teaching methods, such as blended learning and peer-based approaches. During the Implementation phase, the module is initially made available through *Moodle* and *Sakai* Learning Management System (LMS). The use of these widely adopted learning management systems ensures accessibility and facilitates asynchronous participation. The Evaluation stage includes both formative (ongoing) and summative (final) feedback to ensure that the module remains effective and relevant (Mohammed et al., 2021). A snapshot of the module is given in Figure 2.

Figure 2. Snapshot of the module

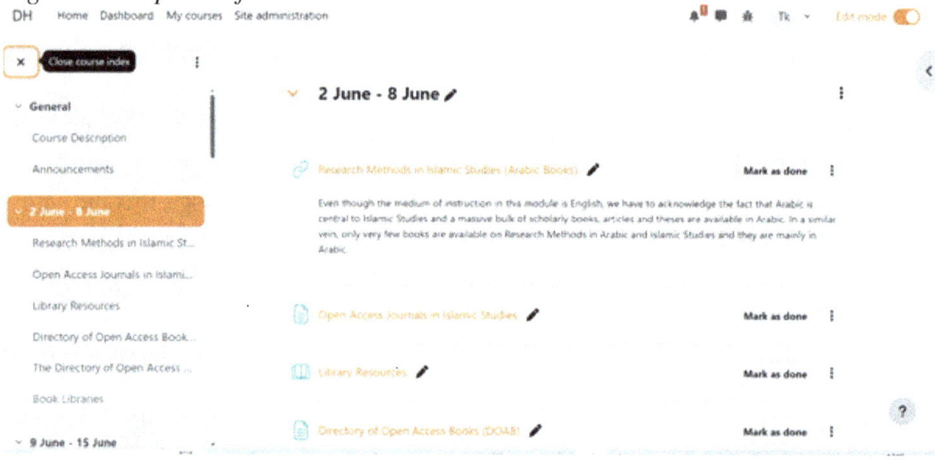

6. MODULE COMPONENTS

As previously shown in the matrix and circular models, the module is arranged in a weekly format comprising three main components: theory, peer-review workshops and a practical capstone project as follows:

6.1. Theory

6.1.1. Introduction to Research Methodologies

This unit introduces the module and provides an overview of research methodology, including definitions of research, methodology, methods, and related concepts. It presents the conceptual foundations of research methodology, emphasising the structured, question-oriented nature of scholarly inquiry. In addition, it provides an overview of research paradigms in Arabic and Islamic Studies (i.e., interpretive, historical, and empirical). In Arabic and Islamic Studies, research involves a dynamic interplay between traditional epistemologies such as *isnād* (chain of transmission), *tafsīr* (exegesis), and *ijtihad* (reasoning), *qiyās* (analogical reasoning), among others. It also involves modern research protocols such as hypothesis testing, source evaluation, and methodological transparency (Adiyono et al., 2024a; Ritonga & Saputra, 2025).

To help students navigate this complexity, the unit uses the "Five Ws" (What, Why, Who, Where, and When) as a heuristic framework (Repko & Szostak, 2020).

For example, a student exploring *maqā id al-sharī ah* in modern legal discourse must refine their topic (What), justify its importance (Why), identify relevant sources (Who), specify the geographic and historical context (Where and When), and ultimately develop a feasible research question. This structure not only aligns with Islamic intellectual traditions but also fosters transferable academic skills. Lastly, the unit also involves a critical reflection on decolonial perspectives in Islamic and area studies.

6.1.2. Literature Review and Reference Management

Unit 2 of the module focuses on constructing literature reviews, synthesising information, and positioning scholarly work. In doing so, the unit covers one of the most critical and often misunderstood aspects of research: the literature review. In Arabic and Islamic Studies, literature reviews are not merely background summaries; they serve as strategic tools for defining research territory, establishing a scholarly niche, and articulating the purpose of the research (Nurhasnawati et al., 2020).

Students are guided to refine and narrow their research topics. They are encouraged to systematically search for classical sources such as *tafsīr* texts, *hadith* collections, or philosophical treatises, as well as modern scholarship, including peer-reviewed articles and interdisciplinary critiques. Digital databases, manuscript archives, and online corpora expand access and improve the review's thoroughness.

Once sources are identified, learners must evaluate methodologies, synthesize key themes, and organize findings. The presentation and synthesis can be thematic, chronological, or analytical (Xiao & Watson, 2019). A literature review on Islamic bioethics, for example, might compare traditional juristic rulings with emerging ethical frameworks in medical technology. It may end with a clear purpose statement that identifies a gap or unresolved tension. This process encourages analytical rigour and ensures that the review becomes a key element of the overall research design.

Regarding this week's practical session, training in citation and reference tools such as *Zotero* and *EndNote* is provided. Students are also introduced to some practical and user-friendly bibliometric and scientometric tools that can help them find their literature, such as *Publish or Perish* and *Elicit.org* (Mohammed, 2024). The peer-review workshop for the week focuses on using bibliometric tools to gather relevant studies on their topics, as well as summarising and synthesising these studies with proper citations and generating a bibliography using Zotero or similar tools.

If time permits, students can be introduced to the use of *ATLAS.ti*, *NVivo* and *LitMap* for mapping and synthesising literature across disciplines. These tools will be covered in detail later in the module, especially in the analysis section.

6.1.3. Theoretical and Conceptual Frameworks in Arabic and Islamic Studies

This unit deals with the theoretical and conceptual foundations that underpin research in Arabic and Islamic Studies. Frameworks serve as the scaffolding through which scholars define research problems, engage with texts and communities, and position their inquiries within broader intellectual traditions. In this context, the unit introduces classical Islamic frameworks such as *u ūl al-fiqh* 'Principles of Islamic Jurisprudence', *ilm al-kalām* 'Islamic Theology', *tafsīr* 'Qur'anic Exegesis' and *mu ala al- adīth* 'Science of Hadith Classification' alongside modern conceptual tools drawn from the humanities and social sciences.

The unit covers a range of theoretical approaches that shape the interpretive dimensions of research. Hermeneutics, for example, is commonly used in the textual analysis of sacred texts not only as an interpretive approach but also as a tool for examining linguistic nuance, historical context, and the contemporary relevance of these texts (Thomas, 2003; Wodak, 2011). For instance, hermeneutical analysis in Qur'anic studies enables deep engagement with context, semantics, and theological intent, while ethnography supports contemporary inquiries into lived Islam (Abenante & Cantini, 2014; Dorroll & Dorroll, 2017). Critical discourse analysis can be used to investigate texts in contexts (Van Dijk, 2001). It offers a conceptual toolkit for the examination of the use of language in religious contexts, such as sermons, *fatwas*, or online platforms, which reflect and reinforce power relations and social norms (Mohammed, 2023, 2025). Grounded theory, while commonly seen as a methodology, also functions as a conceptual strategy for allowing themes and patterns to emerge inductively (Charmaz, 2008; Glaser et al., 2010). This is particularly applicable to studies of Islamic education or to the applications of *maqā id al-sharī ah* in educational, legal, business, or medical contexts. Action research, on the other hand, introduces a participatory, transformative framework that links scholarly inquiry to social engagement in Muslim communities (Chevalier, 2019) .

By engaging with these frameworks, students will learn to critically position their research within both the classical Islamic intellectual tradition and relevant contemporary theoretical paradigms.

6.1.4. Qualitative, Quantitative, and Mixed Methods

This unit is devoted to methodological frameworks, including qualitative, quantitative and mixed methodologies, with particular attention to their adaptation and application in Arabic and Islamic Studies (Adiyono et al., 2024b; Trimulyaningsih et al., 2017). Qualitative approaches such as ethnography (Ahmed, 2014), hermeneutics (Zulfa, 2024), and critical discourse analysis (Fattahizadeh & Langeroudi,

2022) are widely common in Arabic and Islamic Studies as they match the field's textual and interpretive legacy.

Although Quantitative methods are less common in religious studies (Løøv, 2016; Slife & Melling, 2012) and in Arabic and Islamic Studies, in particular, they are increasingly used in demographic, historical, and sociological research. The availability of survey tools and statistical software has spurred the use of quantitative research. They have not only facilitated the analysis of patterns in religious education, jurisprudential diffusion, or charitable practices but have also enabled researchers to analyse sacred text and big data more scientifically. The unit also familiarised students with triangulation and mixed method approaches, which involve combining both qualitative and quantitative data. A study on Qur'anic memorisation, for instance, might include participant observation in *madāris* alongside statistical analysis of memorisation outcomes. Such a triangulation approach may yield a more comprehensive and dependable dataset.

This unit highlights that the selection of methodology should match research goals and sources, urging scholars to cultivate epistemological reflexivity, a characteristic of advanced Islamic inquiry and contemporary social science alike (Kapinga et al., 2022).

Data collection is also an integral part of research methodology. In this sense, this unit deals with data collection, especially primary data that can be collected directly from participants. Like any other discipline in the Social Sciences and Humanities, the choice of data collection methods in Arabic and Islamic Studies should take into account research goals, cultural context, and the nature of the sources or participants involved. The unit focuses in particular on interviews, questionnaires, and observations as sources of data collection.

The unit introduces students to different types of interviewees. Unstructured interviews, which often resemble life histories, are helpful in collecting oral narratives from scholars, *imams*, or community elders about religious practices or historical events. In this type of interview, the conversation can flow naturally, capturing the unique insights and lived experiences of participants (Zhang & Wildemuth, 2016). Semi-structured interviews are especially compelling for exploring interpretative themes in Qur'anic exegesis, Islamic law, or contemporary Islamic thought (Ismail, 2020; Rohmah, 2024). The third type, structured interviews, may be employed for comparative studies across institutions or regions (Foulds et al., 2023). They are well-suited for applied linguistics (e.g., sociolinguistics) or pedagogical research (Mann, 2011).

In a similar vein, focus groups can promote collective reflection on topics such as Islamic education, gender roles within Muslim communities, or responses to contemporary ethical debates (Ibrahim et al., 2024). Questionnaires, both closed and open-ended, are useful in large-scale surveys of language use (Reja et al., 2003;

Wilson & Dewaele, 2010)(e.g., dialect variation in Qur'anic recitation or Arabic teaching methods), or in gathering attitudes towards religious practices (Wilt et al., 2020). Participant observation is valuable in ethnographic studies of Islamic rituals, such as mosque activities, Ramadan celebrations, or Sufi gatherings (Abo-Zena & Hassan, 2024; Dupret, 2012). They enable the researcher to gain a detailed understanding of embodied and communal religious life.

Furthermore, the unit pays attention to sampling techniques, which are especially important when studying an entire population is impractical. It highlights the key difference between probability sampling, where each individual has a known chance of being selected, and non-probability sampling, which relies on accessibility or the researcher's judgment (Shamsudin et al., 2024). Probability methods (simple random, systematic, stratified, and cluster sampling) are essential for generating statistically generalisable results in quantitative research (Rahman et al., 2022). Each method has particular advantages: for instance, stratified sampling guarantees subgroup representation, while cluster sampling is suitable for geographically dispersed populations.

Non-probability methods (i.e., convenience, voluntary response, purposive, and snowball sampling) are commonly utilised in qualitative or exploratory research, where depth and contextual understanding are more critical than representativeness (Pace, 2021). These techniques are more straightforward and cost-effective but come with a higher risk of bias. The unit stresses the importance of defining the target population and a clear sampling frame, considering sample size, and justifying choices in the research methodology. It emphasises that combining sampling methods can be practical and strategic to balance rigour, feasibility, and research objectives.

6.1.5. Digital Humanities Tools in Arabic and Islamic Studies

The tools discussed in this section are revisited across module components and workshops to reinforce iterative learning, linking conceptual instruction with practical application rather than presenting them as a standalone catalogue. As indicated earlier, the proposed module adopts a practical approach to integrating digital humanities into research methods. This unit, therefore, provides a detailed overview of digital tools and platforms that are likely to support all research activities in Arabic and Islamic Studies. These tools include reference management systems, literature analysis tools, bibliometric tools, corpus linguistics software, and emerging artificial intelligence (AI) tools, among others. These tools are discussed in relation to their methodological use, and ethical considerations are elaborated.

Examples are given to demonstrate how these tools enhance scholarly rigour while adhering to the values and intellectual traditions of Islamic inquiry.

It is worth noting that applying digital humanities methods to Arabic texts presents specific technical challenges that students must be prepared to navigate. Arabic's right-to-left script, rich morphology, and orthographic variation can affect the accuracy of optical character recognition, tokenisation, lemmatisation, and frequency analysis in tools originally developed for Western languages. Pre-processing steps such as text normalisation, diacritic handling, and morphological disambiguation are therefore essential to rigorous digital research in Arabic and Islamic Studies. Explicitly addressing these challenges within the module helps students develop realistic expectations of error rates and reinforces critical engagement with algorithmic outputs rather than uncritical reliance on automated results.

6.1.5.1 Reference Management tools and Bibliographic Organization

One of the fundamental requirements in research consists in effective bibliographic management, especially in textually expansive disciplines such as Arabic and Islamic Studies. It is therefore necessary to familiarize students with reference management tools the like of *Zotero*, *EndNote*, and *Mendeley* (Butros & Taylor, 2010). These tools can support scholars in categorizing primary and secondary sources across historical periods and intellectual schools; generating accurate citations in styles such as Chicago, APA, or MLA and even annotating entries with interpretive notes or links to digital archives. For example, a researcher in Qur'anic studies can use *Zotero* to build separate libraries for classical *tafsīr* works (e.g., *al- abarī*, *al-Rāzī*) and contemporary commentaries, with AI-suggested related readings based on existing entries.

6.1.5.2 Literature Synthesis and Thematic Mapping

A key challenge for researchers in Arabic and Islamic Studies is finding relevant literature, so they need to be introduced to practical and user-friendly bibliometric and scientometric tools that can assist them, such as *Publish or Perish* and *Elicit.org* (Mohammed, 2024). Similarly, synthesising diverse and conflicting sources is equally difficult. In this regard, digital humanities tools, including *ATLAS.ti*, *NVivo*, *MAXQDA*, and *LitMap* can help them to overcome this challenge. These tools not only enable researchers to process big data but also to code and visualise thematic patterns across large textual corpora (Kayyali, 2025). In addition, *ATLAS.ti*, *NVivo* and *MAXQDA* apply AI-enhanced coding to qualitative data (e.g., interviews, legal texts), surfacing recurring discourses or anomalies. In a similar vein, *LitMap* creates visualizations of scholarly relationships. This type of visualization can show thematic patterns or bibliographic gaps. A researcher interested in modern Islamic educational discourse, for instance, might use *NVivo* to process literature related to the topic. The tool is ideal for coding *fatwas*, interviews, and curricula. AI-assisted analysis may be employed to detect recurring themes like *tarbiya* (i.e., moral education) or *tajdīd* (i.e., renewal).

6.1.5.3. Manuscript Digitization and Corpus Linguistics

Access to classical texts is a cornerstone of Arabic and Islamic Studies, and digitization tools have vastly expanded what is possible in textual research. *Transkribus* enables palaeographic transcription of Arabic manuscripts using AI-trained handwriting recognition models (Boroş et al., 2024; Muehlberger et al., 2019). *Google Cloud Vision* facilitates the conversion of printed Arabic sources into editable digital formats (Mulfari et al., 2016). *OpenITI* offers machine-readable classical Arabic texts for high-volume linguistic research (Bednarkiewicz et al., 2023; Padillo-Saoud, 2019). Lastly, *Sketch Engine* and *AntConc* allow detailed corpus-level analysis of lexical frequency, collocations, and semantic shifts. For example, a researcher who is conducting research on comparative analysis of Qur'ānic concepts of *adl* (justice) across *tafsīr* traditions can use Sketch Engine to identify wordlists, collocations, frequency, context, and translation variance.

6.1.5.4. Field-Based Qualitative Data Collection

Digital tools can also assist Arabic and Islamic Studies researchers who use ethnographic and interview-based methods as data collection tools. Two of these tools are *Otter.ai* and *Trint,* which use AI to transcribe Arabic interviews automatically (Chia et al., 2020) . Advanced tools and packages such as *ATLAS.ti, NVivo,* and *MAXQDA* allow data coding and theme extraction as well as pattern recognition (Sankar et al., 2025). For example, a researcher in a study of *Sufi* ritual practices can record ceremonies, annotate video and textual reflections in *ATLAS.ti*, and identify recurring motifs of unity, *dhikr*, and symbolism.

6.1.5.5. Survey Design and Quantitative Analysis

Quantitative research in Arabic and Islamic Studies often involves collecting large-scale data on attitudes towards religious practices, education, or social issues. There are many digital humanities tools that can assist researchers in the collection and processing of data. *Qualtrics* and *Google Forms*, for example, can be used in the creation of bilingual surveys and their digital dissemination (Hellman et al., 2021). Processing big quantitative data can be done using *Social Packages for Social Sciences* (SPSS) and *R* (Singh, 2022). The two statistical software programs can handle quantitative data analysis. They enable researchers to test their hypotheses based on a myriad of statistical tests, such as correlation, regression, and trend identification.

For instance, a researcher who attempts to examine views on *ijāb* legislation can use either *Qualtrics* or *Google Forms* for data collection. Afterwards, data from these survey tools can be exported to *SPSS* or *R* for statistical analysis.

6.1.5.6 Mixed Methods and Triangulation

Many Arabic and Islamic Studies projects employ triangulating multiple data types to ensure methodological robustness. Tools that support this integration include *ATLAS.ti, MAXQDA* and *Tableau* (Kuckartz & Rädiker, 2022). The first two can be used for linking qualitative coding with survey data. *Tableau*, on the other hand, is useful for visualising complex datasets geographically and temporally (Murray, 2013). For example, a study on the spread of the *Mālikī* school from North Africa to Andalusia might visualize legal influences over time. *Tableau*'s interactive maps, based on bibliometric and textual metadata, is ideal for this task.

6.1.5.7 Discourse and Hermeneutic Analysis

AI-enhanced platforms enable researchers to interrogate classical and modern Islamic discourses with greater nuance. *Voyant Tools* is a free tool that can support visual textual analysis (e.g., word clouds, frequency graphs). *Sketch Engine* is ideal for advanced lexico-semantic searches, morphological analysis, and collocation analysis across many languages, including Arabic (Mohammed, 2025). For example, a comparative hermeneutic study on *ijtihād* in classical and contemporary texts can use *Sketch Engine* to analyze how semantic ranges and usage contexts have shifted.

6.1.5.8 Collaborative Platforms and Scholarly Communication

Collaborative authorship and international research projects are increasingly supported today. *Mendeley*, for example, is widely used to share citation libraries and annotations. *Overleaf*, which includes Arabic support, is also popular for LaTeX-based collaborative writing (Wang et al., 2025). For example, a collaborative project on Islamic environmental ethics can coordinate text analysis through shared *NVivo* projects and co-author findings using *Overleaf*.

However, the integration of digital humanities tools must also consider economic accessibility, particularly in Global South contexts. Many widely used platforms, such as *NVivo*, *ATLAS.ti*, and *SPSS*, require costly institutional licences that may restrict student access outside formal university settings. To align with the goal of democratising knowledge, the module encourages a critical comparison between proprietary tools and open-source or low-cost alternatives (e.g., *AntConc*, V*oyant Tools*, *R*, Python-based NLP libraries). This comparative approach enables students to make informed methodological choices that balance analytical suitability with resource constraints.

6.1.6. Research Ethics and Responsible Use of DH Tools

This unit focuses on ethical supervision and institutional compliance in Arabic and Islamic Studies Research. Ethical research in Arabic and Islamic Studies extends beyond compliance. In fact, it is a moral imperative which is deeply connected to the sacredness of sources, the sensitivity of topics, and the diversity of cultural settings (Adiyono et al., 2024c; Rahman et al., 2024). Therefore, this unit synthesizes institutional training insights from the Humanities and Social Sciences Research Ethics Committee (HSSREC) with a view to offering guidance on ethical procedures and supervisory responsibilities critical to research integrity.

Trust must be cultivated across all levels between students and supervisors, researchers and participants, and departments and ethics committees (Guillemin et al., 2016; Khodyakov et al., 2017). Ethics is part and parcel of the entire research process, from the initial proposal stage to data dissemination.

Researchers who work with primary data (e.g., interviews, fieldwork) must strictly adhere to ethical standards, including obtaining informed consent, maintaining confidentiality, and, above all, protecting participants' safety. Supporting documents must meet Protection of Personal Information Act (POPIA) standards. Insofar as secondary data (e.g., classical texts, manuscripts) is concerned, ethical use involves proper attribution, accurate contextualization, and critical interpretation.

Part of this unit focuses on the ethical and responsible use of digital humanities tools. While the potential of AI tools is significant, incorporating them into Arabic and Islamic Studies research requires ethical vigilance and disciplinary sensitivity. Given the deeply contextual, theological, and normative facets of Islamic knowledge, researchers must balance technological efficiency with scholarly integrity. Digital Humanities tools, especially AI-enabled research tools, are expanding rapidly. These include AI-driven text analysis and generative AI models (e.g., ChatGPT). Such models are used to summarise documents, paraphrase historical content, or brainstorm research structures. However, it remains crucial to verify content against scholarly standards. In other words, AI should be used with great care and transparency across all disciplines, and particularly in Islamic studies, where theological depth and cultural specificity are paramount.

Key ethical concerns include ensuring accuracy and contextual sensitivity (Tampubolon & Nadeak, 2024). AI models may lack the nuanced understanding needed to interpret religious texts, such as the Qur'an or Hadith. They may also be trained on biased or Western-centric data that can misrepresent Islamic teachings. It is therefore incumbent to evaluate datasets critically. Scholars must also guard against overreliance on AI (Zhai et al., 2024), with the aim of safeguarding the central role of human interpretation rooted in classical methods.

Furthermore, students should be taught that generative AI models may have some issues of plagiarism and attribution, as these models can produce content that closely matches existing scholarly work. Proper disclosure and citation of AI-generated material are therefore essential (Avery et al., 2024). Moreover, researchers must approach sacred texts and theological themes with cultural and religious sensitivity. That is, researchers must avoid reductive analyses that could distort meanings or offend beliefs.

Transparency in methodology by disclosing the tools and processes used is essential for academic integrity and peer review (Kishan & Gupta, n.d.). Best practices include integrating AI with human expertise, obtaining training in relevant tools, adhering to ethical guidelines, and treating AI outputs as starting points for critical inquiry rather than final conclusions.

Ultimately, AI should complement traditional scholarship, not replace it. Its responsible application can enhance research in Arabic and Islamic Studies while maintaining the integrity, depth, and diversity of the Islamic intellectual tradition.

Beyond the ethical use of AI, digital humanities research in Arabic and Islamic Studies raises broader concerns about copyright, data privacy, and intellectual property. The digitisation and reuse of manuscripts, archival materials, and interview data require careful attention to ownership rights, licensing terms, and community sensitivities. Researchers must ensure compliance with copyright regulations, respect the custodianship of cultural heritage, and adhere to data protection frameworks, particularly when working with digitised religious texts or community-generated data.

Beyond student-facing ethical considerations, the integration of AI tools also necessitates reflection on instructional roles and responsibilities. The use of AI-assisted digital humanities tools in postgraduate research training also has implications for instructional practice. Rather than replacing pedagogical roles, AI reconfigures the educator's function towards curriculum design, ethical supervision, methodological guidance, and critical evaluation of AI-generated outputs. While a full analysis of educator–AI collaboration and institutional role transformation is beyond the scope of this chapter, the proposed module implicitly foregrounds the educator as an active mediator between disciplinary knowledge, digital tools, and scholarly integrity.

Thus, ethical training in Arabic and Islamic Studies research aims to foster a culture of accountability and methodological integrity. By embedding ethics into digital and traditional methods, the highest academic standards will be upheld, and at the same time, the epistemological and cultural richness of the Islamic intellectual tradition will be respected.

6.2. Workshops

The proposed module comprises both theoretical and practical workshops. There are six workshops, each linked to the module's theoretical units. A snapshot of one of these workshops is given in Figure 3.

Figure 3. Self and peer-assessment workshops

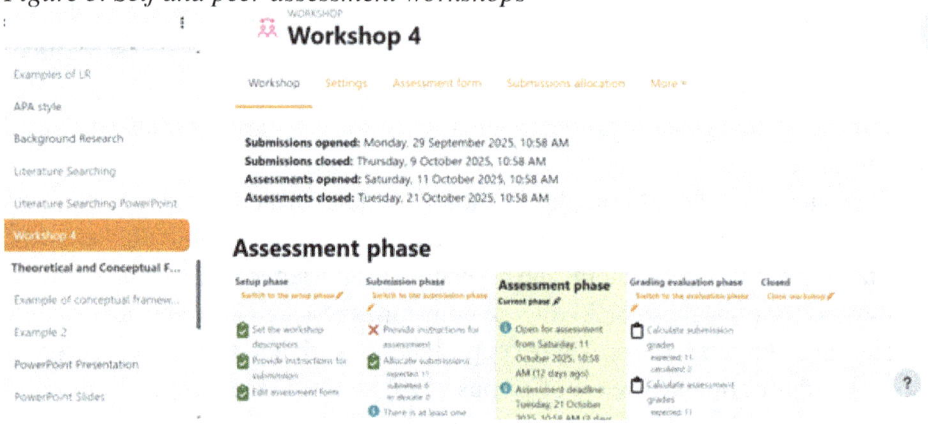

In these sessions, students are expected to evaluate their own submissions as well as those of their peers. Ultimately, the lecturer assesses all submissions. These workshops aim to develop students' research skills across various components of a research thesis. The theoretical workshops focus on topics such as identifying research topics, writing introductions, synthesising literature, developing theoretical and conceptual frameworks, and selecting suitable methods. A brief overview of these workshops is provided below.

Workshop 1 relates to the topic identification. In this workshop, students are encouraged to select a research topic in Arabic and Islamic studies. The workshop aligns with week 1, during which students are introduced to research methods in Arabic and Islamic studies, as well as the field's scope. At this stage, students are not expected to provide their final, refined title; it may be general or broad. Students are required to self-assess their submissions using a rubric. Additionally, students are given four other assessments of their peers and should complete them, providing constructive feedback on these topics.

Workshop 2 encourages students to use the five Ws to refine and narrow down their research topic. The objective of this workshop is to enable students to refine and narrow their research focus. The five Ws will help them identify their topic, the participants, where the study will be conducted, when it will take place, and why the chosen topic is significant. A rubric is also provided to help students assess their submissions and those of their peers.

Workshop 3 introduces the research process. Students must submit a 1000-word essay covering the research background, problem statement, objectives and aims, questions and/or hypotheses, rationale, as well as scope and limitations. Since the rubric for this workshop is more detailed, students are expected to evaluate two of their peers instead of five.

Workshop 4 is associated with the literature review. Here, students are required to search their literature across databases, the internet, and library sources, and to provide a list of 10 to 15 studies relevant to their topic. A brief write-up and synthesis are required. As with other workshops, self-assessment and peer-assessment are needed.

Workshop 5 centres on the theoretical and conceptual framework. Here, students must submit an essay of 500-1000 words that describes the theories, concepts, and analytical frameworks they intend to use in their proposed research. It is necessary to demonstrate the application or integration of theories. Students are encouraged to visualise the frameworks where possible.

Workshop 6 focuses on research methods, and students must describe their methodology in 500-1000 words. Students should indicate whether their methodology is qualitative, quantitative, or mixed. They must also illustrate whether their study is textual or empirical. If empirical, they need to describe their participants, the study population, the sampling techniques, and the data collection tools (e.g., questionnaires, interviews, focus groups, observation). A section on ethics and ethical considerations is required.

The use of self- and peer-assessment in these collaborative workshops is an effective pedagogical tool; it enhances students' critical thinking and their ability to assess themselves more objectively. Self-assessment fosters deeper engagement and metacognition (Andrade & Du, 2007). In a similar vein, peer assessment enhances evaluative judgement, a crucial skill for lifelong learning. It also encourages academic dialogue and provides a better understanding of the principles of academic quality (Boud & Molloy, 2013). Studies have also shown that peer assessments, due to their interactive and collaborative nature, may be more valuable than traditional teacher feedback (Nicol et al., 2014; Topping, 2009).

To further professionalise collaborative digital research practices, students may be introduced to the Contributor Roles Taxonomy (CRediT), a standardised framework for defining and acknowledging specific contributions, including data curation, visualisation, software use, and writing. Familiarity with such taxonomies prepares postgraduate students for interdisciplinary and team-based research environments by promoting transparency, accountability, and fair attribution in digital humanities projects.

6.3. Project Capstone

The module culminates with a capstone in which students are required to submit a 12-page proposal covering all aspects of research, including the introduction, problem statement, questions and/or hypotheses, aims and objectives, rationale, scope, literature review, theoretical framework, and methodology (Figure 4).

Figure 4. Snapshot of the capstone project

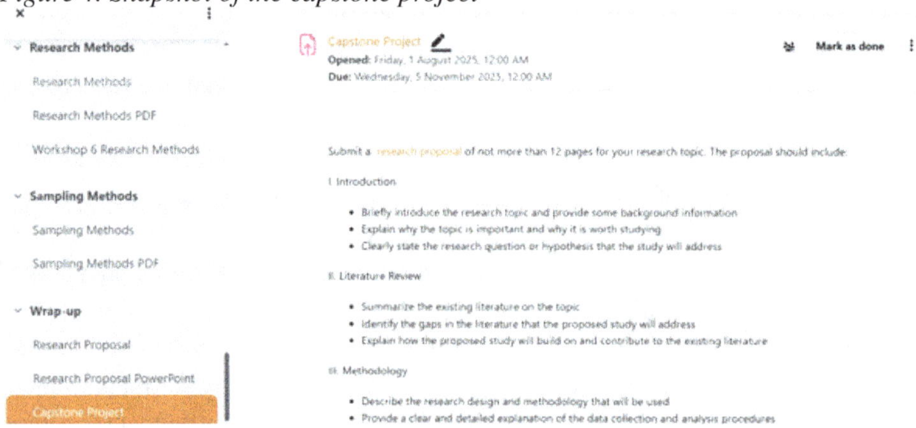

Students are also expected to disclose any ethical considerations in their project. Furthermore, the project should demonstrate the students' ability to utilise digital humanities tools they have studied in the module.

A key feature of the proposal is the integration of digital humanities tools. Students should demonstrate how these tools can improve and transform their research in Arabic and Islamic studies. The project must show the student's ability to select, justify, and apply suitable digital methodologies and technologies, reflecting their engagement with the module's practical training. Examples include, but are not limited to corpora and textual analysis tools, reference management and bibliographic tools, codification, annotation and visualization tools, data management and coding environments, data collaboration and publication platforms. In their proposals, students should clearly justify their choice of tools, outlining how each supports their research questions and methodological approach. They are encouraged to critically reflect on the epistemological implications of digital methods in Islamic and Arabic scholarship, such as issues of representation, translation, and digitisation ethics.

Beyond methodological design, the long-term preservation and sustainability of student-generated digital research outputs is a critical consideration. Students are encouraged to adopt best practices in digital preservation, including clear file organisation, use of open and non-proprietary formats, documentation of workflows, and, where possible, deposition of outputs in institutional repositories or trusted digital archives. Embedding preservation awareness into the capstone project reinforces responsible scholarship and ensures that digital research products remain accessible and reusable beyond the duration of the module.

7. CONCLUSIONS

The chapter proposes the integration of digital humanities into postgraduate research in Arabic and Islamic studies. While its main focus is on this discipline, the proposed module acts as a miniature example for including DH in other areas of the humanities. The module is organised around various theoretical units covering all aspects of research methodology, some practical sessions, and many peer-review workshops. It is also based on best practices in digital humanities and instructional design.

However, this design, in its initial phase, requires implementation and evaluation, preferably with more than one student cohort. Student feedback on the content, opportunities, and challenges of integrating digital humanities can be valuable. An empirical study investigating students' attitudes towards the design will help in a more professional revision and refinement of the content. Additionally, feedback from experts in the field can also be gathered through a dedicated research project.

Evaluating students' capstone projects to determine how they plan to use digital humanities tools in their theses and dissertations may be necessary to assess the impact of the design on their performance.

Future evaluation of the module's effectiveness may combine qualitative and quantitative indicators. These could include analysis of students' capstone proposals, reflective feedback on tool use, peer-review outcomes, and supervisory assessments of methodological rigour. Pre- and post-module self-assessments of digital research confidence may also provide insight into skills development. Such multi-layered evaluation would allow iterative refinement of content, pedagogy, and tool selection.

REFERENCES

Abenante, P., & Cantini, D. (2014). Introduction. Life-worlds and religious commitment: Ethnographic perspectives on subjectivity and Islam. *La Ricerca Folklorica*, •••, 3–19.

Abo-Zena, M. M., & Hassan, A. (2024). Reflecting personal, family, and community ethnographies to understand how fasting Ramadan fuels the religious development of Muslim youth. *Journal of Islamic Faith and Practice*, *5*(1), 53–83. DOI: 10.18060/28094

Adiyono, A., Ni'am, S., & Akhyak, A. (2024a). Methodology of Islamic Studies: Islam as Religion (A Perspective Epistemology, Paradigm, and Methodology). *Analisis: Jurnal Studi Keislaman*, *24*(1), 169–200. DOI: 10.24042/ajsk.v24i1.22636

Adiyono, A., Ni'am, S., & Akhyak, A. (2024b). Methodology of Islamic Studies: Islam as Religion (A Perspective Epistemology, Paradigm, and Methodology). *Analisis: Jurnal Studi Keislaman*, *24*(1), 169–200. DOI: 10.24042/ajsk.v24i1.22636

Adiyono, A., Ni'am, S., & Akhyak, A. (2024c). Methodology of Islamic Studies: Islam as Religion (A Perspective Epistemology, Paradigm, and Methodology). *Analisis: Jurnal Studi Keislaman*, *24*(1), 169–200. DOI: 10.24042/ajsk.v24i1.22636

Ahmed, F. (2014). Exploring *halaqah* as research method: A tentative approach to developing Islamic research principles within a critical 'indigenous' framework. *International Journal of Qualitative Studies in Education : QSE*, *27*(5), 561–583. DOI: 10.1080/09518398.2013.805852

Andrade, H., & Du, Y. (2007). Student responses to criteria-referenced self-assessment. *Assessment & Evaluation in Higher Education*, *32*(2), 159–181. DOI: 10.1080/02602930600801928

Avery, J. J., Abril, P. S., & del Riego, A. (2024). Attributing AI Authorship: Towards a System of Icons for Legal and Ethical Disclosure. *Nw. J. Tech. & Intell. Prop.*, *22*, 1.

Bednarkiewicz, M., Qurboniev, A., Van Den Bossche, G., Blecher, J., & Brinkmann, S. (2023). Studying Hadith Commentaries in the digital age. *Edinburgh Studies in Islamic Scripture and Theology*, 263–280.

Benatti, F., Gooding, P., & Sillence, M. (2021). Learning digital humanities in a community of practice: The DEAR model of postgraduate research training. *Digital Humanities Quarterly, 15*(3). https://oro.open.ac.uk/79455/

Borgman, C. L. (2010). *Scholarship in the digital age: Information, infrastructure, and the Internet*. MIT press.

Boroş, E., Ehrmann, M., Romanello, M., Najem-Meyer, S., & Kaplan, F. (2024). Post-correction of historical text transcripts with large language models: An exploratory study. *Proceedings of the 8th Joint SIGHUM Workshop on Computational Linguistics for Cultural Heritage, Social Sciences, Humanities and Literature (LaTeCH-CLfL 2024)*, 133–159. https://aclanthology.org/2024.latechclfl-1.14/

Boud, D., & Molloy, E. (2013). *Feedback in higher and professional education*. https://api.taylorfrancis.com/content/books/mono/download?identifierName=doi&identifierValue=10.4324/9780203074336&type=googlepdf

Branch, R. M. (2009). *Instructional Design: The ADDIE Approach*. Springer US., DOI: 10.1007/978-0-387-09506-6

Burdick, A., Drucker, J., Lunenfeld, P., Presner, T., & Schnapp, J. (2016). *Digital_Humanities*. mit Press.

Butros, A., & Taylor, S. (2010). Managing information: Evaluating and selecting citation management software, a look at EndNote, RefWorks, Mendeley and Zotero. *Netting Knowledge: Two Hemispheres/One World: Proceedings of the 36th IAMSLIC Annual Conference*, 17–21.

Charmaz, K. (2008). Grounded theory as an emergent method. *Handbook of Emergent Methods, 155*, 172.

Chavanayarn, S. (2024). 'Anti-essentialism and digital humanities: A defense of the field against epistemological challenges'. *Cogent Arts & Humanities, 11*(1), 2439158. DOI: 10.1080/23311983.2024.2439158

Chevalier, J. M. (2019). *Participatory action research: Theory and methods for engaged inquiry*. Routledge. DOI: 10.4324/9781351033268

Chia, C. K., Ghavifekr, S., & Razak, A. Z. A. (2020). Online interview tools for qualitative data collection during Covid-19 pandemic; Riview of web conferencing platforms' functionality. *Malaysian Journal of Qualitative Research, 7*(1), 95–106.

Creswell, J. W., & Poth, C. N. (2016). *Qualitative inquiry and research design: Choosing among five approaches*. Sage publications.

DHASA. (n.d.). *South African Digital Humanities Network*. https://digitalhumanities.org.za/

Dorroll, C., & Dorroll, P. (2017). Teaching Islam in contemporary America: Digital ethnography and the affective challenges of Islamic studies pedagogy. *Teaching Theology and Religion*, *20*(4), 304–313. DOI: 10.1111/teth.12410

Dupret, B. (2012). *Ethnographies of Islam: Ritual performances and everyday practices*. Edinburgh University Press.

Fattahizadeh, F., & Langeroudi, M. (2022). Investigate the Qur'anic Verses of Hypocrisy Using Fairclough's Critical Discourse Analysis Model. *MISHKAT*, *40*(4), 110–133.

Ferreira, B. B., & Borges, M. M. (2022). The Epistemic Cultures of the Digital Humanities and Their Relation to Open Science: Contributions to the Open Humanities Discourse. *Central European Journal of Educational Research*, *4*(2), 1–7. DOI: 10.37441/cejer/2022/4/2/11388

Foulds, C., Khalid, R., Jensen, E. A., Sule, O., & Lorenz, L. (2023). Social responsibility in research and innovation practice and policy across global regions, institutional types, and fields: Interview data and qualitative content analysis outputs revealing the perspectives and experiences of professionals. *Open Research Europe*, *3*, 65. DOI: 10.12688/openreseurope.15688.1 PMID: 37645483

Given, L. M. (2008). *The Sage encyclopedia of qualitative research methods*. Sage publications. DOI: 10.4135/9781412963909

Glaser, B. G., Strauss, A. L., Paul, A. T., Kaufmann, S., & Hildenbrand, B. (2010). *Grounded Theory-Strategien qualitativer Forschung*. Verlag Hans Huber. https://ixtheo.de/Record/160438008X

Gold, M. K., & Klein, L. F. (2019). *15 Zonas de Contacto: A Digital Humanities Ecology of Knowledges*. https://muse.jhu.edu/pub/23/edited_volume/chapter/2293537

Guillemin, M., Gillam, L., Barnard, E., Stewart, P., Walker, H., & Rosenthal, D. (2016). "Doing Trust": How Researchers Conceptualize and Enact Trust in Their Research Practice. *Journal of Empirical Research on Human Research Ethics; JERHRE*, *11*(4), 370–381. DOI: 10.1177/1556264616668975 PMID: 27638866

Hayles, N. K. (2012). *How we think: Digital media and contemporary technogenesis*. University of Chicago Press. DOI: 10.7208/chicago/9780226321370.001.0001

Hellman, A. B., Uribe-Zarain, X., Bell, A. B., & González, A. (2021). Surveying multilingual families in schools. *MIDTESOL Journal*, *4*, 28–52.

Ibrahim, M., Islam, S., Zohriah, O., & Azid, M. (2024). Addressing contemporary ethical and moral issues through islamic education. *Journal of Islamic Studies*, *1*(1), 36–51. DOI: 10.35335/kbbzar83

Ismail, M. (2020). *A comparative study of methods used in the exegesis of the Qur'an and the Bible* [PhD Thesis, Middlesex University]. https://repository.mdx.ac.uk/item/89788

Kapinga, L., Huizinga, R., & Shaker, R. (2022). Reflexivity through *positionality meetings*: Religion, muslims and 'non-religious' researchers. *International Journal of Social Research Methodology*, *25*(1), 103–117. DOI: 10.1080/13645579.2020.1853876

Kayyali, M. (2025). The Role of Technology in Modern Qualitative Research: Tools, Software, and Emerging Trends. *Evolving Designs, Applications, Technological Advances, and the Future of Qualitative Research*, 71–106.

Khodyakov, D., Mikesell, L., & Bromley, E. (2017). Trust and the ethical conduct of community-engaged research. *European Journal for Person Centered Healthcare*, *5*(4), 522. DOI: 10.5750/ejpch.v5i4.1263 PMID: 29375883

Kishan, S., & Gupta, U. (n.d.). Research Publication Ethics: Ensuring Integrity, Transparency, and Responsible Scholarship. *JOURNAL OF TECHNICAL EDUCATION*, 128.

Knight, P., & Yorke, M. (2004). *Learning, curriculum and employability in higher education*. Routledge.

Kuckartz, U., & Rädiker, S. (2022). Using Maxqda for integration in mixed methods research. In *The Routledge handbook for advancing integration in mixed methods research* (pp. 540–562). Routledge. DOI: 10.4324/9780429432828-41

Løøv, M. (2016). *Quantitative Approaches to New Religions* (Vol. II). The Oxford Handbook of New Religious Movements.

Mann, S. (2011). A critical review of qualitative interviews in applied linguistics. *Applied Linguistics*, *32*(1), 6–24. DOI: 10.1093/applin/amq043

Mohammed, T., Saidi, M., Assam, B. N., & Eldokali, E. M. (2021). Towards a Blended Programme for Arabic and Other Less Commonly Taught Languages (LCTLs) in the South African Higher Education Context. *Education Research International*, *2021*, 1–12. DOI: 10.1155/2021/1455705

Mohammed, T. A. (2023). *From eco-jihad to politicization: A corpus-based eco-linguistic discourse analysis of the arab media coverage of the safer floating oil tanke.*

Mohammed, T. A. (2024). A scientometric study of Maqasid al-shariah research: Trending issues, hotspot research, and co-citation analysis. *Frontiers in Research Metrics and Analytics*, *9*, 1439407. DOI: 10.3389/frma.2024.1439407 PMID: 39664104

Mohammed, T. A. (2025). Exploring child marriage in Yemen: A critical analysis of an Arab media corpus. *Qualitative Research Journal*, *25*(2), 125–146. DOI: 10.1108/QRJ-02-2024-0036

Muehlberger, G., Seaward, L., Terras, M., Ares Oliveira, S., Bosch, V., Bryan, M., Colutto, S., Déjean, H., Diem, M., Fiel, S., Gatos, B., Greinoecker, A., Grüning, T., Hackl, G., Haukkovaara, V., Heyer, G., Hirvonen, L., Hodel, T., Jokinen, M., & Zagoris, K. (2019). Transforming scholarship in the archives through handwritten text recognition: Transkribus as a case study. *The Journal of Documentation*, *75*(5), 954–976. DOI: 10.1108/JD-07-2018-0114

Mulfari, D., Celesti, A., Fazio, M., Villari, M., & Puliafito, A. (2016). Using Google Cloud Vision in assistive technology scenarios. *2016 IEEE Symposium on Computers and Communication (ISCC)*, 214–219. https://ieeexplore.ieee.org/abstract/document/7543742/

Murray, D. G. (2013). *Tableau your data!: Fast and easy visual analysis with tableau software*. John Wiley & Sons.

Nicol, D., Thomson, A., & Breslin, C. (2014). Rethinking feedback practices in higher education: A peer review perspective. *Assessment & Evaluation in Higher Education*, *39*(1), 102–122. DOI: 10.1080/02602938.2013.795518

Nurhasnawati, N., Alwizar, A., Syafaruddin, S., Darmawati, D., MFZ, M. F. Z., HKM, H. W., & ISQ, I. (2020). Systematic review of the literature on islamic religious education design in indonesia: The role of parents in islamic religious education. *COUNS-EDU: The International Journal of Counseling and Education*, *5*(4), 216–223.

Pace, D. S. (2021). Probability and non-probability sampling-an entry point for undergraduate researchers. *International Journal of Quantitative and Qualitative Research Methods*, *9*(2), 1–15.

Padillo-Saoud, A. (2019). *Open Islamicate Texts Initiative (OpenITI), 2016 [Reseña]*. https://digital.csic.es/handle/10261/214111

Rahman, Md. M., Tabash, M. I., Salamzadeh, A., Abduli, S., & Rahaman, Md. S. (2022). Sampling Techniques (Probability) for Quantitative Social Science Researchers: A Conceptual Guidelines with Examples. *SEEU Review, 17*(1), 42–51. DOI: 10.2478/seeur-2022-0023

Rahman, M. M., Razimi, M. S. A., Ariffin, A. S., & Hashim, N. (2024). Navigating moral landscape: Islamic ethical choices and sustainability in Halal meat production and consumption. *Discover Sustainability*, *5*(1), 225. DOI: 10.1007/s43621-024-00388-y

Reja, U., Manfreda, K. L., Hlebec, V., & Vehovar, V. (2003). Open-ended vs. Close-ended questions in web questionnaires. *Developments in Applied Statistics*, *19*(1), 159–177.

Repko, A. F., & Szostak, R. (2020). *Interdisciplinary research: Process and theory*. Sage publications.

Risam, R. (2018). *New digital worlds: Postcolonial digital humanities in theory, praxis, and pedagogy*. Northwestern University Press. DOI: 10.2307/j.ctv7tq4hg

Ritonga, M., & Saputra, R. (2025). Epistemology of Knowledge: Bridging Western and Islamic Thought. *Solo International Collaboration and Publication of Social Sciences and Humanities*, *3*(01), 95–110.

Rohmah, S. (2024). The Effect of the Qur'anic Interpretation Method on Students' Understanding of the Concept of Ethics in High Schools in West Java: A Case Study on Islamic Religious Education Subjects. *West Science Islamic Studies*, *2*(02), 143–148. DOI: 10.58812/wsiss.v2i02.828

SADiLaR. (n.d.). *About SADiLaR*. South African Centre for Digital Language Resources. https://sadilar.org/en/about/

Sankar, J. G., Darwish, D., & Valan, P. (2025). Evaluating Qualitative Data Analysis Tools: A Comparative Study of NVivo and ATLAS. ti. In *Evolving Designs, Applications, Technological Advances, and the Future of Qualitative Research* (pp. 107–136). IGI Global Scientific Publishing.

Schreibman, S., Siemens, R., & Unsworth, J. (2015). *A new companion to digital humanities*. John Wiley & Sons. DOI: 10.1002/9781118680605

Shamsudin, M. F., Hassim, A. A., & Abd Manaf, S. (2024). Mastering probability and non-probability methods for accurate research insights. *Journal of Postgraduate Current Business Research*, *9*(1), 38–53.

Siemens, L., Cunningham, R., Duff, W., & Warwick, C. (2010). "More Minds are Brought to Bear on a Problem": Methods of Interaction and Collaboration within Digital Humanities Research Teams. *Digital Studies / Le Champ Numérique, 2*(2). DOI: 10.16995/dscn.80

Singh, A. (2022). Use of Statistical Analysis Supporting Tools in Libraries: An overview of statistical package for social science. *World Digital Libraries-An International Journal, 15*(2), 91–104.

Slife, B. D., & Melling, B. S. (2012). Method Decisions: Quantitative and Qualitative Inquiry in the Study of Religious Phenomena. *Pastoral Psychology, 61*(5–6), 721–734. DOI: 10.1007/s11089-011-0366-3

Stein, M.-K., & Galliers, R. (2018). *The Routledge companion to management information systems*. Routledge Taylor & Francis Group.

Svensson, P. (2016). *Big digital humanities: Imagining a meeting place for the humanities and the digital*. University of Michigan Press.

Tampubolon, M., & Nadeak, B. (2024). Artificial intelligence and understanding of religion: A moral perspective. *International Journal of Multicultural and Multireligious Understanding, 11*(8), 903–914.

Thomas, R. L. (2003). Modern linguistics versus traditional hermeneutics. *The Master's Seminary Journal, 14*(1), 23–45.

Tiedau, U., Mahony, S., & Terras, M. (2014). *Digital Humanities Pedagogy: Integrative Learning and New Ways of Thinking About Studying the Humanities*. The Digital Humanities Institute., https://discovery.ucl.ac.uk/id/eprint/1472816/

Topping, K. J. (2009). Peer Assessment. *Theory into Practice, 48*(1), 20–27. DOI: 10.1080/00405840802577569

Tracy, D. G., & Hoiem, E. M. (2017). Scaffolding and play approaches to digital humanities pedagogy: Assessment and iteration in topically-driven courses. *Digital Humanities Quarterly, 11*(4).

Trimulyaningsih, N., Wulandari, E., & Sofia, N. (2017). *Qualitative research on Islamic psychotherapy: A meta synthesis study in Indonesian culture*.

University of Sheffield. (2020). *Digital Humanities Institute*. https://www.dhi.ac.uk/

Van Dijk, T. A. (2001). *Critical discourse analysis. The Handbook of discourse analysis*. Blackwell Publishers Ltd.

Wang, L., Lee, M., Volkov, R., Tuyen Chau, L., & Kang, D. (2025). ScholaWrite: A Dataset of End-to-End Scholarly Writing Process. *arXiv E-Prints*, arXiv-2502.

Wilson, R., & Dewaele, J.-M. (2010). The use of web questionnaires in second language acquisition and bilingualism research. *Second Language Research*, *26*(1), 103–123. DOI: 10.1177/0267658309337640

Wilt, J. A., Takahashi, J. T., Jeong, P., Exline, J. J., & Pargament, K. I. (2020). Open-ended and closed-ended measures of religious/spiritual struggles: A mixed-methods study. *Religions*, *11*(10), 505. DOI: 10.3390/rel11100505

Wodak, R. (2011). Complex texts: Analysing, understanding, explaining and interpreting meanings. *Discourse Studies*, *13*(5), 623–633. DOI: 10.1177/1461445611412745

Xiao, Y., & Watson, M. (2019). Guidance on Conducting a Systematic Literature Review. *Journal of Planning Education and Research*, *39*(1), 93–112. DOI: 10.1177/0739456X17723971

Zhai, C., Wibowo, S., & Li, L. D. (2024). The effects of over-reliance on AI dialogue systems on students' cognitive abilities: A systematic review. *Smart Learning Environments*, *11*(1), 28. DOI: 10.1186/s40561-024-00316-7

Zhang, Y., & Wildemuth, B. M. (2016). Unstructured interviews. In Wildemuth, B. M. (Ed.), *Applications of social research methods to questions in information and library science* (2nd ed., pp. 222–231). Bloomsbury Publishing USA.

Zulfa, I. (2024). The Application of Hermeneutics in Indonesia as a Koranic interpretation Method. *Journal of Islamic Scriptures in Non-Arabic Societies*, *1*(1), 18–38.

ENDNOTES

1 https://www.dhi.ac.uk/

2 https://sheffield.ac.uk/hpdh/postgraduate/phd-study/digital-humanities

3 https://sadilar.org/en/

4 https://digitalhumanities.org.za/

Chapter 11

Intelligent Learning: The AI Revolution in Digital Education

Prerna Agrawal
https://orcid.org/0000-0003-3097-639X
GLS University, India

Savita Gandhi
https://orcid.org/0000-0002-6581-2814
GLS University, India

ABSTRACT

The integration of Artificial Intelligence (AI) into digital education marks a major shift in pedagogy, learner engagement, and institutional functions. AI-driven systems such as intelligent tutoring, adaptive learning, and learning analytics are transforming how knowledge is delivered and assessed. This chapter explores AI's role in creating adaptive learning environments, supporting both cognitive and emotional assessment, and improving institutional efficiency through automation. Global platforms including Squirrel AI, Carnegie Learning, Duolingo, and DIKSHA are examined. The chapter also addresses ethical, technical, and infrastructural challenges, including privacy, algorithmic bias, and the digital divide. It synthesizes current literature and promotes comparative perspectives to support ethical, equitable, and learner-centered AI integration, while outlining key AI tools for education, research, paraphrasing, and collaboration.

DOI: 10.4018/979-8-3373-4521-5.ch011

1. INTRODUCTION

Artificial Intelligence (AI) is rapidly transforming the global education landscape, particularly within digital and online learning environments. The accelerated shift toward remote and hybrid education models following the COVID-19 pandemic highlighted the limitations of traditional pedagogical approaches in addressing scalability, personalization, and learner engagement (Zawacki-Richter et al., 2019; Holmes et al., 2019). AI-driven technologies such as intelligent tutoring systems, natural language processing (NLP), automated assessment, and learning analytics have emerged as powerful enablers of adaptive and learner-centered education (Chen et al., 2020).

AI systems can analyze large volumes of learner data to identify learning patterns, predict performance outcomes, and provide personalized feedback in real time, thereby enhancing both teaching effectiveness and student learning outcomes (Luckin et al., 2016; Baker & Inventado, 2014). By automating routine instructional and administrative tasks, AI also allows educators to focus more on higher-order pedagogical activities such as mentoring, curriculum design, and learner support (Holmes et al., 2019).

This chapter examines the role of AI in enhancing digital education with a focus on access, equity, engagement, and learning efficacy. Drawing on global case studies and recent academic literature, it explores the opportunities, challenges, and ethical implications associated with AI-enabled e-learning systems (Zhang & Aslan, 2021; Wang et al., 2024).

2. MOTIVATION FOR INCLUDING AI IN EDUCATION

Artificial Intelligence has gained significant attention in education due to its potential to transform how knowledge is delivered, accessed, and personalized across diverse learning contexts. Traditional education systems often struggle with large class sizes, standardized curricula, and limited capacity to address individual learner needs (Ayeni et al., 2024). AI-based adaptive learning systems offer solutions by dynamically adjusting content, pace, and instructional strategies based on learners' cognitive profiles, preferences, and performance data (Gligorea et al., 2023).

Personalized learning enabled by AI has been shown to improve knowledge retention, learner motivation, and academic performance by promoting self-directed and mastery-based learning approaches (VanLehn, 2011; Baker & Inventado, 2014). Technologies such as NLP, speech-to-text, and predictive analytics further enhance inclusivity by supporting learners with disabilities, multilingual backgrounds, and socioeconomically disadvantaged contexts (Lee, 2017; Holmes et al., 2022).

AI-powered tools such as intelligent tutoring systems, educational games, and immersive virtual environments foster active learning by shifting students from passive content consumption to interactive knowledge construction (Fryer et al., 2019; Burton, 2024). Immediate and personalized feedback provided by AI systems helps learners identify misconceptions, reflect on their understanding, and improve learning outcomes more effectively than delayed traditional feedback mechanisms (Chen et al., 2020).

From an instructional perspective, AI reduces educators' administrative workload by automating attendance tracking, grading, course recommendations, and early identification of at-risk students (Arnold & Pistilli, 2012; Luckin et al., 2016). This enables teachers to devote more time to pedagogical innovation, student mentoring, and emotional support—elements that remain uniquely human and essential to quality education (Holmes et al., 2019).

As labor markets evolve rapidly, lifelong learning has become a necessity. AI-supported education systems provide flexible, on-demand, and scalable learning opportunities aligned with changing industry needs (Jordan & Mitchell, 2015; Strielkowski et al., 2025). Thus, the integration of AI in education is not merely a technological advancement but a strategic imperative for creating equitable, inclusive, and future-ready learning ecosystems (Onyebuchi et al., 2024).

3. UNDERSTANDING AI IN EDUCATION

The way people are being taught and the method by which new knowledge is gained has become different now, thanks to AI. Instructional technology that uses natural language processing, data analysis and machine learning in smart systems allows for this change to occur. These technologies allow teachers to examine student data, learn patterns in learning, predict how students will do and deliver personalized feedback. Thus, AI is making learning more flexible and accessible for everybody while also increasing its engagement.

Intelligent Tutoring System (ITS) — great example of AI in Education ITS helps by customizing the content based on how and when each child learns. And, these technologies track students progress as human teachers do and provide customized exercise explanation feedback. Teaching becomes more effective for students overall, especially the struggling student.

Another major development has emerged in adaptive learning systems with the help of AI. This is the ability to immediately change the type of information, format or level of difficulty according to how a student performs. One example is the system feeding more challenging assignments to students that are performing above average. It can make the content simpler or provide extra help if a student is experiencing difficulties. This flexible method lets each student learn at their own pace and helps them understand further by using mastery based learning.

From an assessment perspective, automated assessment tools utilizing AI have changed the game for grading and evaluating student performance. These tools are capable of quickly and precisely grade objective tests like multiple choice tests. Advanced systems can also grade essays, written assignments, and programming exercises. Grading student artifacts utilizing AI will in turn save educators time, quicken the assessment at a possibly, lower the cost in comparison to human evaluation and provide reliability for consistency in grading that humans struggle to maintain, thus allowing educators to spend more time instructing and mentoring students.

Conversational agents, including chatbots and virtual agents, mimic human conversation, functioning in a 24/7 capacity to assist students. They can respond to frequently asked course related questions, guide students regarding course expectations, and even engage students in conversations related to specific subject matter to emphasize learning. By utilizing natural language processing, a conversational agent can behave in a responsive and human-like manner, in order to provide better support and interactivity for students learning experiences.

Finally, predictive analytics is an additional powerful AI tool that users can take advantage of due to the ability to examine patterns in student behavior, performance, and engagement, to predict future outcomes. These tools can often find possible difficult academic areas, students who might drop out or fail, and propose immediate action. With the proper identification of warning aspects in behavior models, educators and administrators can act on these findings, making a faculty or an institution to enhance retention, improve learning outcomes, and proactively support student success.

Together, these AI enabled tools are transforming education by providing scaled, personalized, and data informed learning experiences that drive learners and instructors. As education evolves with the incorporation of Artificial Intelligence, the opportunity to democratize quality education and connect learning gaps can become a reality.

4. GLOBAL LEADERS USING AI IN E-LEARNING

AI is being used extensively by a lot of countries in the e-learning sector. Figure 1 shows the top 10 global leading countries data in percentage that use AI in e-learning as per the data of 2023 (Indian Express, 2025).This figure shows the global concentration of AI development and the size of AI utilization in e-learning by country.

Figure 1. Top 10 Countries using AI in e-learning

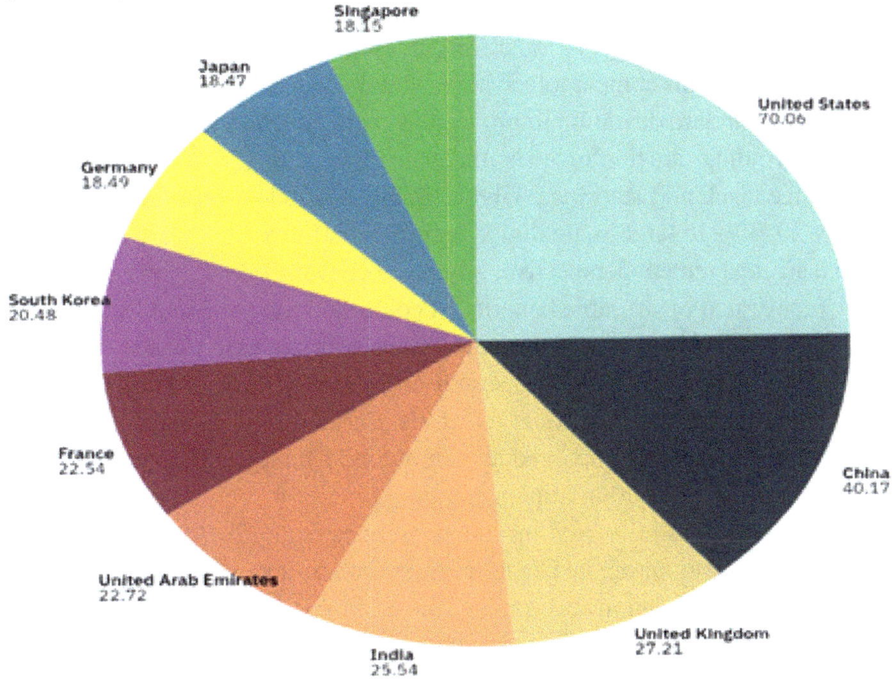

Source: (Indian Express, 2025)

Developed nations like China and the United States hold a leading position in the education industry, with rising powers like India and the United Arab Emirates following closely behind. It is clear that the global AI scene is highly competitive, since the percentages indicate the proportional size of AI activity or financing in different countries.

5. QUANTITATIVE EVIDENCE SUPPORTING AI IN DIGITAL EDUCATION

Recent empirical studies provide strong quantitative evidence demonstrating the effectiveness of Artificial Intelligence (AI) in improving learning outcomes, engagement, and institutional efficiency in digital education environments. A large-scale systematic review by Wang et al. (2024), analyzing over 2,000 AI-in-education research papers, reported that AI-enabled adaptive learning systems led to learning performance improvements of up to 62% compared to traditional static e-learning approaches. The study further highlighted that predictive analytics and intelligent feedback mechanisms significantly reduced learner dropout rates in online courses.

Similarly, VanLehn (2011) found that Intelligent Tutoring Systems (ITS) can achieve learning gains comparable to human tutors, with students using ITS demonstrating 0.76 standard deviation improvement over conventional classroom instruction. These findings are reinforced by Baker and Inventado (2014), who showed that real-time feedback and learning analytics improved student retention and mastery levels by 20–30% in large-scale digital learning platforms.

From an engagement perspective, AI-driven conversational agents and chatbots have demonstrated measurable benefits. A controlled experimental study by Fryer et al. (2019) revealed that students interacting with AI-based chatbots exhibited significantly higher task persistence and engagement levels compared to those interacting with static instructional materials. Furthermore, Labadze et al. (2023) reported that AI chatbots improved learner autonomy and confidence in over 70% of reviewed higher education implementations.

In terms of accessibility and inclusion, Holmes et al. (2019) reported that AI-assisted tools such as automated captioning, speech-to-text, and adaptive interfaces improved course completion rates among learners with disabilities by 15–25%. These tools also enhanced participation among non-native language learners, particularly in multilingual digital education environments.

Institutional efficiency gains have also been quantitatively documented. According to Luckin et al. (2016), AI-based automation of administrative and assessment tasks reduced educators' grading and administrative workload by approximately 40–50%, enabling greater focus on instructional design and student mentoring. Additionally, early-warning systems based on learning analytics, such as Purdue University's Course Signals, increased student retention rates by up to 21% (Arnold & Pistilli, 2012).

Collectively, these quantitative findings validate the pedagogical and operational value of AI in digital education. They demonstrate that when implemented responsibly, AI-driven systems not only enhance learning outcomes and engagement but also contribute to equity, accessibility, and sustainability in education systems worldwide.

6. APPLICATIONS OF AI IN E-LEARNING

Artificial Intelligence (AI) is changing the game in e-learning by providing increasingly powerful tools to improve what is taught and how it is learned. AI is capable of personalized, scalable, and interactive digital education by utilizing data, adaptive systems, and automation. Below are some of the most meaningful applications of AI in e-learning:

6.1 Customized Educational Pathways

A major advantage of AI in e-learning environments is the ability to create personalized learning paths. In contrast to institutional learning, where one curriculum is provided to all learners, AI can take a variety of factors into consideration including a student's learning style, speed, strengths, weaknesses, and past performance to build a unique learning experience for that student.

Several AI platforms such as DreamBox and Squirrel AI utilize adaptive learning algorithms to change the difficulty and type of content as the learner works, automatically in the real time. For example, if a learner is struggling with a particular mathematical concept, the system will automatically backtrack and present the learner with easier problems, hints, or associated foundational content to help the learner's understanding before moving to a more advanced task. The ability to receive continuous feedback ensures that each learner is receiving content that is appropriately difficult and provides an opportunity for greater engagement and mastery (Chen et al., 2020). Such systems allow for self paced learning, limit cognitive overload when learning is individualized, and promote differentiated instruction, particularly when there are ranges of abilities in diverse classrooms or in scaled learning environments (i.e. a MOOC), where the teacher cannot provide individual attention.

6.2 Cognitive Evaluation and Appraisal

Assessment is a major part of education, and AI enhances assessment through the use of timely assessment tools, automated for objectivity, and real-time assessments. Cognitive assessment refers to AI's ability to assess traditional learning outcomes, knowledge-based learning and skill-based learning assessments.

There are platforms like Gradescope which use machine learning to automate grading for mathematical or programming assignments through pattern recognition. To assess a student's work and identify their task, its patterns are matched with rubric. Pattern recognition not only helps in grading on time but it also maintains consistency and fairness of the evaluations.

Tools like Grammarly use technology to determine the readability, tone and grammar style of your particular article as you type it. More advanced NLP models rank legitimacy of the citation, veracity in writing and argument strength. AI-based tests frees the teachers of the tedious task of grading and allows them to concentrate more on qualitative feedback and teaching strategies. They additionally assist in creating evaluation loops of ongoing development by offering students instantaneous responses.

6.3 Digital Teaching Assistants

Digital Teaching Assistants (DTAs) are like chatbots or voice assistants that use artificial intelligence (AI) to talk with students. They're designed to help students learn at their own speed. Powered by tech like Natural Language Processing (NLP) and Machine Learning (ML), these DTAs can respond in a way that sounds human. They can answer questions, explain tough ideas, and guide students through different subjects or activities.

One of the best parts is that DTAs are available all the time. Students can get help whenever they need it, no matter where they are. This is super useful for students in different time zones or those who prefer to study at odd hours. DTAs can handle common questions about what's being taught, when things are due, and how to fix tech issues. Moreover, they can give answers that fit each student's learning style and speed. Research has shown that DTAs can really make a difference in learning. For teachers, DTAs take over those boring tasks like setting up appointments, sending reminders, and answering the same questions over and over. This gives teachers more time to plan interesting lessons and work closely with students. The DTAs help students feel more connected while learning online. They offer support that feels like a conversation, which makes the whole online learning experience better. Some fancy DTAs can even tell when a student is confused or annoyed. They use emotional intelligence to figure this out and then either offer help or pass the student on to a real person for more assistance.

6.4 Content Generation and Curation

AI-powered content creation and curation has changed the way assessments are given to educational content. AI systems scan algorithms to create quizzes, summarize long texts, create flashcards, and compile video content tailored speedily and easily to meet the learner's needs. Companies such as Quizlet and ScribeSense use machine learning to recommend the best study strategies and resources to individual students. Machine learning uses existing data to determine the best way for getting important content to students. AI systems can analyze huge educational content and extract key information and represent that information in easy-to-read and understandable formats. Furthermore, AI systems can also curate content, leverage the information from different sources about the same subject, and organize the content that meets the expectations of the curriculum learning, by the proficiency of the student or an intended learning outcome. This adaptive personalization allows learners to work with the most relevant material for their knowledge and understanding capability, thus reducing cognitive overload and increasing retention. Additionally, for educators, AI based content tools can save considerable time in creating learning materials, redirecting time, and planning the learning pedagogies. As the learners have access to on demand assessments, adaptive content, and communication with instructors in real time, the learner receives timely feedback regarding their level of learning, irrelevant of their current knowledge and understanding stage of learners is always improving.

6.5 Educational Learning Analytics

Artificial Intelligence powered education learning analytics provides educators with extensive knowledge of student behavior, performance and engagement patterns. Educational analytics helps to utilize data from a multitude of sources including learning management systems, quizzes, discussion groups and biometric feedback in order to create dashboards and reports that help educators and institutions understand and interrogate performance data in meaningful ways. By delving into the data, educators can identify underperforming students, verify student progression, monitor student engagement and also perform early identification of students likely to withdraw or dropout. In addition, AI algorithms can identify learning gaps and predict precisely what students are likely to achieve based on past student data, allowing for proactive intervention. For example, if a student is consistently performing poorly in formative assessments and regularly missing interactive modules, the analytics system can alert educators about this behavior and recommend methods of intervention which can provide added support. This responsive feedback loop enables educators to make informed decisions about the pedagogical direction of the course, and adaptively adjust their methods to meet the needs of the students in the class. Moreover, learning analytics promotes a student culture of accountability, as students are provided with visual feedback on their performance trends. In online courses or MOOCs, where individual students are difficult to monitor and support, AI learning analytics helps carry the weight of providing quality education and personalized learning experiences.

7. CASE STUDIES AND EXAMPLES OF AI IN E-LEARNING

Several applications in the real world that demonstrate the potential of artificial intelligence to revolutionize online education are discussed below.

7.1 Squirrel AI (China) – Adaptive Learning Systems

Squirrel AI is a China - based flagship in the adaptive learning space and has begun to make waves globally due to its prominent use of artificial intelligence. AI powered platform for K-12 focused around cutting edge AI techniques like machine learning, knowledge graphs and NLP to deliver super personalized learning. Squirrel AI has the ability to simulate a one-to-one tutoring experience as a result of its constant and comprehensive analysis of student behavior, strengths, weaknesses, and knowledge gaps, and the platform uses this exposure and performance information to adapt and adjust to a student's preferred learning complexity, performance and pace. Hence, when a student encounters difficulty in a mathematical topic, the system can not only identify this but also determine related pre-requisite knowledge and suggest specific exercises to strengthen or fortify background knowledge of each learner. Moreover, Squirrel AI has also been deployed to enhance the process of how students learn. It also helps in supporting teachers by providing them with analytics and real time decision making moments so they are more informed in their teaching practices. Squirrel AI has become one of the most iconic and proven successful cases on how an intelligent system can go beyond conventional educational or learning zones, to make them personalized & data responsive.

7.2 Carnegie Learning (USA) – Intelligent Tutoring System (ITS)

Carnegie Learning is well-known in educational tech and has done great work to improve intelligent tutoring systems (ITS), especially for teaching math. Coming from decades of work in cognitive science and AI at Carnegie Mellon University, their main platform, MATHia, tries to act like a human tutor by being adaptive and responsive.

The MATHia system watches how students work on problems in real-time using machine learning and data analysis. It doesn't just look at the answers students give; it also considers how they try to solve the problem. Because it watches how students engage with problems, the ITS can figure out what misconceptions, knowledge gaps, and learning patterns students have. The software gives personalized hints, step-by-step help, and feedback that matches each student's way of learning based on what it sees and analyzes. The ITS can change things up based on how well each person is doing, giving extra practice when needed and moving forward when students show they understand the material. Lots of studies have shown that students who use Carnegie Learning's MATHia do better on tests and become better at solving problems than those who learn in the usual ways. It gives teachers dashboards that can be accessed online or offline to give instructions and provide timely help. Carnegie Learning's programs show how AI can change a classroom into a smart, student-focused space that takes care of each student's learning needs.

7.3 Duolingo – Language Learning with AI

Duolingo and its application are among the most prevalent techniques for learning a new language globally. Individuals appreciate their entertaining and game-like nature, along with their use of AI to generate personalized learning experiences. Machine learning and natural language processing (NLP) are fundamental components that enable Duolingo's functionality. The program adapts according to each user's performance and areas of difficulty. As learners engage in activities, the system continuously collects data regarding their responses, including the types of errors they frequently commit and the duration spent on specific tasks. Duolingo can utilize this information to adapt in several ways, like adjusting the difficulty of subsequent lessons, reviewing vocabulary or grammar rules, or providing a tailored practice session that focuses on the user's areas of weakness. The AI driven smart review in Duolingo employs spacing theory to facilitate users re-engagement with information at ideal intervals for memory retention. Moreover, NLP is responsible for many speech recognition aspects that assess a learner's pronunciation and fluency, providing instant feedback to learners. The application also provides a chatbot feature that simulates real life conversation scenarios that push learners to practice speaking. Through intelligent and adaptive design, Duolingo continues to inspire interest and staying power in learning, user learning outcomes, therefore, it is a great opportunity to illustrate that AI can personalize language education, improve the learner's practical skills, and understand the depth of engagement it provides to millions of users around the world (Settles & Meeder, 2016).

7.4 Coursera – AI-Powered Course Recommendations

Coursera, one of the world's largest online course platforms, employs artificial intelligence in a highly strategic manner. Coursera's course recommendation application is one of its most successful AI applications. Coursera employs a course recommendation engine that integrates fundamental machine learning techniques and algorithms to suggest pertinent courses to a learner in accordance with their preferred learning style, objectives, and behavioral patterns. For example, Coursera analyzes a variety of behavioral and preference-based data points (search history, courses taken, courses completed, course ratings, time spent on content, peer group comparisons) after a user signs up for a course to predict the type of course material that user would most likely find valuable and to interact with. Coursera's AI models can suggest not only courses, but also entire learning paths, specializations, based on their educational interests or career aspirations, as result of this analysis. Additionally, Coursera employs natural language processing (NLP) technology to evaluate overviews and reviews submitted by users. Coursera is capable of offering users even more refined recommendations by taking into account the sentiment of all users. Coursera's personalized recommendations assist learners in efficiently utilizing their time to identify high quality content that is pertinent to them from a vast catalog of thousands of courses offered by prestigious universities and companies. Subsequently, users experience enhanced learning outcomes, engagement, and enjoyment. Coursera's intelligent recommendation engine is a substantial illustration of how artificial intelligence can enhance an online learning platform and render education more user-friendly, goal-oriented, and accessible.

7.5 DIKSHA - India's digital school education platform

The DIKSHA platform has been developed by the National Council for Educational Research and Training (NCERT) and is India's flagship initiative for digital school education countrywide. DIKSHA is a platform designed to provide equitable access to quality educational resources, that contains interactive content, textbooks, assessments, and teacher training in multiple Indian languages. In the past three years, the Ministry of Education has also identified some potential for Artificial Intelligence (AI) to improve learning outcomes, and has taken significant steps to integrate AI into DIKSHA beginning with the development of Personalised Adaptive Learning (PAL) systems. PAL systems that use AI can provide individual learning experiences, with the potential to assess students existing level of knowledge, speed of learning and gaps in knowledge and skills. PAL technologies constantly check how engaged learners have been and how effective they are to systematically tailor the delivery of content by providing simpler, alternative exercises or more challenging material as needed. PAL technologies constantly check how engaged learners have been and how effectively they are learning so that they can adjust how they present the material by giving students easier, different exercises or harder material as needed. This will help keep students from falling behind, especially in India's diverse educational landscape, where students come from very different social, economic, and language backgrounds. It will also help keep disruptions to a minimum that come from being inadequately academically prepared or having gaps in knowledge. The government's plan to add AI to DIKSHA is a step toward a bigger goal of making learning more student-centered and getting the education system ready for the future and for everyone. The Government of India has stated that this change is necessary to modernize how courses are delivered in classrooms. It will also make digital learning interfaces more effective around the world.

8. BENEFITS OF AI IN E-LEARNING

This chapter examines the most significant advantages of implementing Artificial Intelligence (AI) in online education with extensive reference to the academic literature and current technological developments. This deep exploration of AI in a global context has attempted to explore how each benefit is taking shape, how they are being practically demonstrated, and the impact they are likely to have on the overall ecosystem of education.

8.1 Improved Outcomes From Learning

Perhaps the most innovative aspect of AI in online education is its potential to maximize individual learning outcomes through personalization. Unlike traditional instructional strategies, where pacing, content, and assessment are determined by the instructor, AI systems can modify all of these features based on the learners cognitive profile. Through ongoing analysis of learners interactions, behavioral data, and knowledge deficiencies, AI algorithms can also provide immediate feedback and individualized content to reinforce concepts precisely in time (Baker & Inventado, 2014). For example, if a learner struggles with mathematical word problems, an AI could assign assisted tasks to help the learner process mathematical word problems by scaffolding their cognitive load, provide alternative pedagogical materials, or explain material in smaller portions to help learners overcome their weakness. In summary, the adaptive learning that could come with AI has been shown to increase knowledge retention, reduce cognitive load and frustration, and increase learning time, especially in larger diverse virtual environments where teachers may have difficulty providing individual and unique attention.

8.2 Increased Participation and Engagement

Traditional online learning environments often exhibit poor engagement levels and are distinguished by passive learning experiences. AI can provide solutions to the limitations of traditional environments by providing gamified experiences, simulations, and interactive storytelling which can make learning more immersive and empowering. AI powered gamification provides opportunities to reward students by obtaining points, badges, or level advancements upon demonstrating mastery of the content, fostering persistence and a growth mentality. Furthermore, AI powered simulation tools and virtual labs can replicate real world situations, whether it is conducting chemical experiments, or exploring historical incidents by associating real world situations with learning which helps the students to learn by performing on such tools and virtual labs. These experiences activate the curiosity, emotional involvement, and intrinsic motivation necessary for students to learn effectively, and also have fun while learning. Numerous studies demonstrate that when experiential and game based learning is driven through AI personalization, learners have dramatically higher levels of cognitive engagement and conceptual understanding.

8.3 Better Usability

AI technologies can eliminate educational barriers for students with disabilities and create a more inclusive and equitable educational context. Streams of potential, such as AI generated real time captions, text-to-speech (TTS), speech-to-text (STT), and personalization of UI and UX, create possibilities for students with visual, auditory, or impaired mobility. For example, AI based natural language processing (NLP) tools convert spoken lectures to written text or reduce complex content into easy straightforward segments for students with hearing impairments or focus difficulties. Other examples could include predictive text input, voice-controlled navigation, or adaptive screen readers that can provide more usable interfaces for students who have physical disabilities or cognitive challenges. These features promote an equitable situation and they ultimately may decrease dropout rates for physically challenged learners through an accessible learning ecosystem (Holmes et al., 2022).

8.4 Improving Management Effectiveness

AI is changing the way educational administrations function by removing the repetitive and laborious tasks that are common occurrences in education and providing more time for educators and support staff to spend on teaching and supporting students. Tasks such as grading quizzes and assignments, scheduling classes dependent on student schedules, sending personalized reminders to students, and curating content based on syllabus changes can now be captured by intelligent systems. Thus, as an example, AI chatbots can manage frequently asked questions asked by students 24 hours a day, 7 days a week, which will help reduce the burden on administrative teams. Moreover, Learning Management Systems (LMS) powered by AI can assess course completion rates, flag at-risk students, and even make recommendations based on those assessments before they become problematic. This is a highly efficient way to not only reduce operational costs, but also ensure educational institutions become more responsive and flexible in their ability to manage a greater number of larger and more diverse students (Luckin et al, 2016).

9. CHALLENGES AND ETHICAL CONSIDERATIONS

The implications of Artificial Intelligence (AI) on education and the concerns raised about integrity are very important topics that need to be explored in more detail and clarity. Some of the challenges and ethical considerations are listed below:

9.1 Protecting Personal Information

AI tools in educational environments require vast amounts of data that always includes sensitive student data such as academic performance, behavioral information, biometrics, and learning styles. Due to sensitivity of the data in more recent AI systems, concerns surrounding data security and privacy arose. Introducing AI tools without a sound data governance framework comes with risks of hacking, accessing sensitive information surrounding students, surveillance of student behavior, and potential misuse of student data collected. Educational institutions are then forced to implement data security measures, some of which should include cybersecurity policies with end-to-end encryptions, proper data anonymization of students, adequate data protection for storage, and explaining and outlining data collection and student data. Furthermore, for data generated with the full consent of students, guardians need to have an absolute understanding of what data is generated and why it was being collected, and how it is likely to be used. If appropriate cybersecurity protections are not taken for the AI tools being developed for the use in education that violate rights and student privacy, many educational institutions may increase mistrust around educational systems.

9.2 Systematic Inaccuracy

Another significant challenge is the systemic bias embedded in AI algorithms. Biases can result from biased training data such as using historical educational data with inequities. If historical educational data contains disparities, such as missed minority students, non-native language learners, or students with disabilities and an AI system uses this data to train itself, the likely outcome would be to create and accelerate the biases. For example, adaptive learning technologies could under-challenge minority students or if the linguistic pattern deviates from the expected pattern, such deviations will be categorized as error resulting in lowering student expectations. Holmes et al. (2021) examined this in their article on AI and the need for fairness in its use. Authors recommend our approaches must change to include datasets that represent inclusion, be algorithmically transparent, and regularly monitor AI algorithm decision making processes.

9.3 Dependence on Robots Too Much

The rising automation of educational functions (tutoring, assessing), can lead to unintended consequences in dependence on AI and robotic systems that can result in inhibiting a student's social and emotional development. AI tutors offer personalized features that can be scaled up and down, but they don't have the emotional intelligence or social skills of a person to build sensitivity, persistence, and relationships. The too much dependence on this automation, ultimately will lead to decreased human interaction among students themselves, which is an integral component of education that encourages collaborative learning and contributes to the development of critical thinking and moral reasoning skills. If robots are left alone, they act differently than teachers and will lead students to a learning experience where information is less personalized and students are less socially and emotionally involved.

9.4 Digital Divide

That difference between people who have access to and know how to use computers, the internet, and other ICTs well and people who don't is called the digital divide. There are many things that can cause this divide, such as age, education level, socioeconomic position, and geographical location. One of the apparent solutions is to overcome the issue of the digital divide, which refers to the disparity in access to technology and digital literacy skills across socioeconomic groups. AI designed for education assumes access to devices, internet, and minimal level of digital fluency. In certain low-income or rural contexts, those assumptions cannot be confirmed. This imbalance may worsen educational gaps, causing the most underprivileged students to lag even further behind than previously. If AI based tools are produced with little regard to accessible policies, we build exclusionary gates instead of platforms for empowerment. In response to this "digital divide," important parties such as those in government and post-secondary education need to provide the funding to create infrastructure, subsidized devices, internet plans and provide learning on the part of students and educators in order to level the playing field for access to AI enriched education.

10. RELEVANT WORK

Ting Zhao (2023) offers a broad overview of AI's function in educational technology, contextualizing EdTech as an area of interdisciplinary research that is influenced primarily by computer science and cognitive psychology. Zhao discusses AI applications in EdTech as involving personalized learning, adaptive systems, automated grading systems, and virtual tutors that respond to learners needs at varying times and rates. AI infused personalized learning creates the potential for real-time feedback loops and individualized instruction that mimics human tutors, with the potential for instruction to accommodate diverse learner needs (Zhao, 2023).

Sarnato et al. (2024) build on Zhao's conceptual overview from a traced journey from ubiquitous learning to AI based adaptive platforms. Their thematic analysis shows how early e-learning spaces tended to focus on providing access to materials, content, and experiences, while today's adaptive platforms personalize learning pathways, provide immersive relational engagement through simulations and VR, and increase efficiency and effectiveness through real-time analytics, although they are also critical of AI enhanced educational tools and their disconnectedness to ethical data privacy issues and responsiveness to culturally situated adaptations of quality education access (Sarnato et al., 2024).

Radif and Hameed (2024) examine some additional effects of AI in teaching and learning, explaining that AI can disrupt learning experiences and combine different methods of content delivery, tailor instruction, and promote engagement through immersive experiences. They found that AI content delivery via intelligent tutoring systems (ITS) or natural language processing (NLP) applications personalize learning while allowing real-time assessment, while reminding us about the importance of human-centered teaching, not just letting AI take over (Radif & Hameed, 2024). The authors also encouraged the ethical implementation of AI to avoid issues like algorithm-based bias and improper use of data, which connect to broader conversations occurring in education and AI.

Strielkowski et al. (2025) offer a bibliometric analysis of more than 3,500 publications and identify some of the most significant research clusters related to adaptive learning with AI. They argue that AI technologies hold promise for and have proven to be effective in helping instructional designers think about how to tailor curriculum and assessment for learner profiles, however, the utilization of adaptive learning systems is uneven in terms of scalability, accessibility, and equitable use of AI developments. Finally, they stress the importance of organizational readiness and facilitating professional development for teachers to optimize their use of these technologies and methods for teaching (Strielkowski et al., 2025).

Onyebuchi et al. (2024) consolidate the empirical insights with a critical review of personalized learning facilitated by AI. The study categorizes AI's contributions into adaptive content delivery, intelligent feedback mechanisms, and administrative automation. Importantly, it flags digital equity and the "algorithmic divide" as persistent barriers to effective AI integration. The authors argue for strategic collaboration among educators, technologists, and policymakers to align AI systems with pedagogical goals and ethical standards (Onyebuchi et al., 2024).

Gligorea et al. (2023) provide a strong overview of adaptive learning approaches that use a combination of AI and machine learning technologies to achieve learning outcomes. Their systematic review of 63 studies indicates the importance of varying content and pacing based on learner proficiencies. The adaptive learning systems use data-analytics to track learner profiles (e.g., learner strengths, gaps, preferences etc.) and use their data to shift and adapt learning content, in real time, to promote student retention, interest and engagement. While there are still technical and ethical issues such as data privacy and complexity of systems, the study showed the potential effectiveness of adaptive AI in providing better learning outcomes in an e-learning environment (Gligorea et al., 2023).

Zhang and Aslan (2021) build from this work with a comprehensive empirical analysis of 40 studies over nearly three decades. Their findings depict persistent difficulties with actualizing technology adoption at the classroom level versus the potential found in technological advancements. Using a mixed methods approach, Zhang and Aslan's evaluation of AI systems like intelligent tutoring systems or dynamic assessment shows the benefits for learners. However, use of AI at the classroom-level is incongruous with enhanced knowledge of educational theory and interdisciplinary approaches among stakeholders. The authors assert that developers and educators need to build stronger bridges to ameliorate both the educational and practical complexities of using AI tools (Zhang & Aslan, 2021).

Investigating AI chatbot research, Labadze, et al. (2023) outline several potential applications including virtual assistants, tutors, and engagement tools in academic learning contexts. The authors review 67 studies, noting that chatbots offer significant affordances such as 24/7 availability, on-demand personalized feedback and guidance for learner autonomy. The popular platforms ChatGPT, Google Bard, Ada were noted to improve study habits, assist with committing concepts to memory, and increase learner confidence in their abilities. The paper also raised serious concerns around over-reliance, costs in terms of accuracy, and ethical issues including data privacy and bias (Labadze, et al., 2023).

In a large scale bibliometric and content analysis study, Wang, et al. (2024) surveyed more than 2,000 AIED research papers mapping four key AI applications areas: adaptive and personalized learning, intelligent assessment and feedback, profiling and predictive analytics, and new AI products. The authors found a clear bias toward system design and adoption studies guided by constructivist and cognitive learning theories. Importantly, the authors noted that the use of AI in adaptive learning tools led to test improvements of up to 62%, further validating its pedagogical role. They observed that there were many potential areas that remain unexplored including emotional AI, and culturally adaptive systems (Wang, et al., 2024).

Ultimately, Burton (2024) provides a theoretical and practical articulation of what AI means for higher education. Based on constructivist learning theory, Burton states that AI technologies can support experiential and immersive learning through the use of intelligent tutoring systems, decision-tree models, and modules that integrated VR. Additionally, her research is leading to larger institutional support for learner-centricity and adaptive approaches to instruction in higher education, which she says will be supported by AI. Nevertheless, Burton has also stated the importance of ethical governance, recognizing that successful deployment of AI requires that learning with the use of AI operates through equity in education and privacy and digital inclusion standards (Burton, 2024).

Recent academic literature likewise acknowledges that Artificial Intelligence (AI) will change the world of education through personalized learning and smart e-learning systems. Ayeni et al. (2024) review the current scholarship and acknowledge that AI is at the forefront of new pedagogy, in large part because it can personalize learning for students. The authors state that personalized learning through AI has a lot of tailoring learning experiences, content and forms of assessment upon a student's learning history, cognitive profile, and student's preferences. AI-enabled intelligent tutoring systems and real time feedback mechanisms help to maximize student engagement, understanding, and decrease retention ratio. Changing the interactivity, accessibility, and safety of curriculum design and development in order to meet student-centered ecology can be accomplished through the use of educational technology tools such as simulations generated using artificial intelligence, virtual reality puppet shows generated through AI, such as natural language software. The above corpus of literature represents a newly emerging area of scholarship on ethical concerns regarding artificial intelligence technologies such as privacy, automated discrimination, inequality of access to digital and digital precarity; and calls for governance structures around responsible AI in order to ensure that educators from working-class and low-income backgrounds, as well as their students, have comparable access to equitable educational education opportunities.

The IJNRD work (2024) provides a practical assessment of how artificial intelligence especially deep learning models such as Long Short Term Memory (LSTM), could be integrated into personalized e-learning. The article provides a definition of an intelligent system that provides the user with not only personalized delivery of content, adaptive placement testing but also the support features of internship recommendations, connections with alumni, and college updates. By utilizing AI to track user performance and user preferences, the system provided personalized course recommendations, and helped the learner advance professionally in the real world. The proposed model created a link between education and employment by combining personalized teaching and learning with alumni mentorship and job readiness tools. Additionally, the literature analysis identified key areas of past AI usage in learner modeling, knowledge tracing, and the feedback loop, giving a sense of the scope of AI's contribution to adaptive e-learning. The study likewise recognizes areas of importance where gaps remain, such as the need for data privacy, behavioral transparency that commands a level of ethical competence, and the pervasive challenges associated with system redundancy and complexity. The study proposes that future studies will center on scalable and equitable models that maintain personalization without sacrificing data integrity or creating user mistrust (IJNRD, 2024). Table 1 shows the comparative analysis of different AI methodologies in Digital Learning. Table 2 describes the listing of AI Tools for Education, Research, Paraphrasing, and Collaboration.

Table 1. Comparison of different AI methodologies in Digital Learning

Paper Name	Focus Area	Methods Used	Key Contribution	Target Audience	AI Techniques	Challenges Addressed
Ayeni et al. (2024)	AI in Personalized Learning and Educational Technology	Review	Real-time feedback, intelligent tutoring systems, ethical issues	K-12 and Higher Education	Adaptive algorithms, NLP	Privacy, algorithmic bias, digital divide
IJNRD (2024)	AI-driven Personalized e-learning System	Survey, System Design	LSTM-based personalization, alumni engagement, placement support	College Students	LSTM, Recommendation Systems	Personalization, alumni interaction, data privacy
Gligorea et al. (2023)	AI in Adaptive e-learning	Systematic Literature Review	Personalized learning, LSTM, user modeling	General e-learning Users	Machine Learning, User Modeling	System complexity, data security
Zhang & Aslan (2021)	AI Technologies in Education	Mixed Methods	Bibliometric analysis, gaps in adoption and practice	Researchers, Educators	Bibliometrics, Content Analysis	Interdisciplinary gap, lack of educational theory
Labadze et al. (2023)	AI Chatbots in Education	Systematic Review	Chatbot impact on engagement and self-directed learning	Higher Education	Chatbots, NLP	Overdependence, ethical use
Wang et al. (2024)	AI in Education	Systematic Literature Review	Research trends, dominant application areas, gaps	Researchers, Policy Makers	Machine Learning, Analytics	Empirical gaps, theoretical underpinnings
Burton (2024)	AI in Higher Education	Conceptual/ Theoretical Review	Constructivist learning, VR tools, ethical policies	Higher Education	VR, Intelligent Agents	Policy gaps, ethical governance
Radif & Hameed (2024)	AI in e-learning	Narrative Review	ITS, NLP, predictive analytics, human-AI synergy	Online Learners	Intelligent Tutoring, NLP	Bias, infrastructure gaps
Strielkowski et al. (2025)	AI-driven Adaptive Learning	Bibliometric & Content Analysis	Institutional readiness, teacher training	Institutions	Adaptive Systems	Scalability, teacher preparedness

continued on following page

Table 1. Continued

Paper Name	Focus Area	Methods Used	Key Contribution	Target Audience	AI Techniques	Challenges Addressed
Onyebuchi et al. (2024)	Personalized Learning and Tech Integration	Critical Review	Algorithmic divide, ethical integration	Students and Educators	Predictive Analytics	Digital equity, trust in algorithms
Sarnato et al. (2024)	e-learning Evolution	Thematic Analysis	Transition from u-learning to adaptive AI systems	e-learning Developers	Adaptive Algorithms	Effectiveness, cultural adaptation
Zhao (2023)	AI in Educational Technology	Review	Personalized instruction, virtual tutors, adaptive systems	Educational Technologists	Personalized AI Systems	Scalability, implementation gaps

Table 2. AI Tools for Education, Research, Paraphrasing, and Collaboration

Tool Name	Category	Function	Website
Curipod	Education & Presentation	AI-powered slide generation for interactive lessons	https://curipod.com/
NearPod	Education & Presentation	Interactive quizzes, polls, and slides for classrooms	https://nearpod.com/
ChatPDF	Research Assistance	Ask questions based on uploaded research papers	https://www.chatpdf.com/
PopAI	Research Assistance	AI-based Q&A for academic documents	https://www.popai.pro/
Wordtune	Research Assistance	Summarizes academic content and papers	https://www.wordtune.com/
Consensus	Research Assistance	Finds literature reviews in scientific research	https://consensus.app/
SciSpace	Research Assistance	AI for extracting insights and literature reviews from papers	https://typeset.io/
PNAS	Research Assistance	Journal platform for accessing literature reviews	https://www.pnas.org/
Writefull	Research Assistance	Helps in writing abstracts and improving academic texts	https://writefull.com/
MyBib	Research Assistance	Generates citations in multiple formats	https://www.mybib.com/
PlagiarismDetector.net	Research Assistance	Checks academic content for plagiarism	https://plagiarismdetector.net/
GPTZero	Research Assistance	Detects AI-generated text	https://gptzero.me/

continued on following page

Table 2. Continued

Tool Name	Category	Function	Website
HIX.AI	Research Assistance	Humanizes AI-generated content	https://hix.ai/
Trinka	Research Assistance	Grammar checker for academic writing	https://www.trinka.ai/
HyperWrite	Research Assistance	AI tool for title generation	https://www.hyperwriteai.com/
Custom Writing	Research Assistance	Generates keywords and topic suggestions	https://custom-writing.org/
SpinBot	Paraphrasing	Rewrites and rephrases content	https://www.spinbot.com/
QuillBot	Paraphrasing	Paraphrases and checks grammar	https://quillbot.com/
GPT-Minus1	Paraphrasing	Paraphrases to reduce AI-detection likelihood	https://gptminus1.com/
Padlet	Collaboration	Collaborative whiteboard and idea-sharing platform	https://padlet.com/
Coggle	Collaboration	Mind-mapping and brainstorming tool	https://coggle.it/

11. FUTURE DIRECTIONS

The prospects of AI in e-learning are exceedingly promising in future as listed below:

11.1 Affective Computing (SSEmotion AI): Emotion-Aware Learning Environments

The most recent trend to support AI powered e-learning is the field called affective computing, or SSEmotion AI. This enables systems to observe and not only measure, but also respond to, learners' emotional states through inputs like facial expressions, voice tone, and physical indicators (Calvo & D'Mello, 2010). AI systems can evaluate the emotional signals of students in real time, via facial recognition and voice analytics, and then update instructional strategies accordingly. For example, if a student looks confused or bored, then the delivery of content could slow down or find some way of encouraging them, or switch to a different modality such as a video or game principles.

The evaluation of the student's complete learning experience, covering not only what they know but also how they feel while they are learning, is based on this degree of emotional intelligence, enabling a higher level of customisation than simply knowing cognitive metrics. When it comes to assisting kids who are struggling with anxiety, learning difficulties, or a lack of desire, effective computing has proven to be very helpful. Emotional feedback that is based on artificial intelligence has the potential to be more empathic, attentive, and sensitive than a human instructor.

11.2 Explainable AI (XAI): Transparency and Trust in Educational Decisions

Traditional AI systems, though powerful, are often "black boxes" making decisions without offering reason. For example an automated decision making process offers no explanation which could be a significant drawback in high stakes educational contexts. An approach known as explainable artificial intelligence (XAI) is a method that helps reduce cases of low-level, poorly directed scientific agency. This is accomplished by rendering the reasoning behind AI decisions interpretable to both educators and students. Holstein et al. (2020) explained that XAI leads to higher trust and acceptance for users, especially when AI decisions impact learners grades, adaptive path or resources.

The transparency of this feature contains clear benefits: the learner can act with information and the educator may better describe the logic behind the automated intervention, should it be necessary to intervene or override. Academic institutions that are seriously considering the deployment of AI should clearly think about responsible, ethical uses of AI, particularly in relation to bias, equity, and access. For example, XAI is being considered as an ethical AI in view of fairness, accountability and explainability.

11.3 AI-Powered Peer Learning: Intelligent Matching for Collaborative Education

Older online environments are unable to properly match students with one another for the purpose of peer learning, despite the fact that collaboration is a hallmark of deeper learning. Through the utilization of natural language processing (NLP), learning analytics, and profile modeling, a peer learning environment that is enabled by an artificial intelligence (AI) system is able to effectively resolve this issue. This environment then matches and/or groups students together based on complementary skill levels, learning styles, and interests.

For example, a student who is a strong problem solver but a weak theoretical thinker, could be matched with another student who exhibited the opposite pattern; the two can gain key learning insights and experiences through the student supporting, tutoring, discussing, or engaging in collaborative assignments with each other. In this way, students can be intelligently matched or grouped not just within a class, but across a global learning community, create ubiquitous peer learning experiences and broaden both funding exposure, diversity, and networked knowledge.

AI systems are also capable of tracking group based interaction, and through metrics associated with peer engagement and final evaluation of outcomes, modify groupings over time. The development of a peer assessment system enabled by AIs, as well as peer group projects, study situations and discussion boards, have the potential to make peer-to-peer learning much more equitable and productive for all students while releasing further time for educators who provide manual cohorts for student grouping.

12. CONCLUSION

AI is not only a technological advance but it has become an essential component in the process of reimagining the structure of digital education. In this chapter, we have discussed the several applications of artificial intelligence (AI) in the field of education, as well as the benefits and drawbacks associated with each of these applications. A few examples of these are intelligent tutoring systems, tailored learning pathways, administrative automation, and predictive analytics. The application of artificial intelligence in online learning settings has caused a shift in the way education is seen. Through its implementation, it has produced a place that is more learner-centered, inclusive, and flexible, surpassing the limitations of traditional education.

This chapter describes how global initiatives are reshaping education through practical examples such as Squirrel AI, Carnegie Learning, Duolingo, Coursera, and DIKSHA. These platforms illustrate that artificial intelligence (AI) isn't just a future concept, it's a day to day tool that widens access to learning, narrows equity gaps, and delivers instruction matched to each person's needs on a scale never before imagined. Technologies that adapt to a student allow for approaches that cater to different learning styles, provide immediate support when students struggle, and adjust the material in response to a student's performance and behavior.

This transformation clarifies how AI is reshaping the role of teachers. By taking over routine tasks, providing quick performance reviews, and giving useful data through learning analytics, AI frees teachers to put effort into mentorship, creative teaching methods, and emotional support. These human elements remain essential and are beyond the ability of AI to replicate. As AI becomes more common in education, it promotes lifelong learning by giving students from all backgrounds learning opportunities suited to their individual needs that can be adjusted and expanded as needed.

These opportunities also come with real challenges. People still have ethical issues to face regarding data privacy, bias in algorithms, excessive automation, and unequal access to technology. It's important to quickly work to lessen the chances of leaving out already disadvantaged groups due to money problems and infrastructure gaps. If people are not careful, too much dependence on automated systems could cause learners to lose important social skills, emotional intelligence, and critical thinking abilities. AI should supplement human potential, not take its place.

Looking ahead, advancements in areas like emotional AI, easily understanding AI, and AI-supported peer learning could make educational interactions more emotionally aware, open, and cooperative. These improvements can change how information can be converted from boring to exciting, making learning more emotionally and mentally engaging. For teachers, gaining the trust of students and policymakers is the key and requires improving AI by making it easier to understand and fairer. Ethical and practical governance should guide how AI is added to education, and its integration needs to be fair, open, and with accountability at the forefront.

The rise of AI in education isn't just about making machines smarter; it's also about teaching with more humanity, using technology to help people reach their best potential, narrow gaps, and foster a worldwide learning community that is empowered, curious, and well-prepared for what's ahead. This calls for combining technology, ethical responsibility, and experience in teaching thoughtfully.

The use of artificial intelligence in the future of education does not involve doing away with instructors. The focus should instead be on modifying the way in which learning and teaching are approached. Students are not only getting information in learning settings that are compassionate, but they are also engaging in the creation of knowledge inside digital spaces that are intelligent, open, and fair. In the event that we move forward with a strategy and remain vigilant while incorporating AI, it will transform education while simultaneously making it increasingly human.

REFERENCES

Arnold, K. E., & Pistilli, M. D. (2012). Course Signals at Purdue. *Proceedings of the 2nd International Conference on Learning Analytics and Knowledge*, 267–270. DOI: 10.1145/2330601.2330666

Arnold, K. E., & Pistilli, M. D. (2012). Course Signals at Purdue: Using learning analytics to increase student success. *Proceedings of the 2nd International Conference on Learning Analytics and Knowledge*, 267–270. DOI: 10.1145/2330601.2330666

Ayeni, O. O., Al Hamad, N. M., Onyebuchi, N. C., Osawaru, B., & Adewusi, O. E. (2024). AI in education: A review of personalized learning and educational technology. *GSC Advanced Research and Reviews, 18*(2), 261–271. DOI: 10.30574/gscarr.2024.18.2.0062

Baker, R. S., & Inventado, P. S. (2014). Educational data mining and learning analytics. In Larusson, J. A., & White, B. (Eds.), *Learning analytics: From research to practice* (pp. 61–75). Springer., DOI: 10.1007/978-1-4614-3305-7_4

Baker, R. S., & Inventado, P. S. (2014). Educational data mining and learning analytics. In Larusson, J. A., & White, B. (Eds.), *Learning analytics: From research to practice* (pp. 61–75). Springer., DOI: 10.1007/978-1-4614-3305-7_4

Burton, S. L. (2024). Advancements in AI-driven education: Transforming learning and training with intelligent technologies. World Journal of Business Research, 4(1). https://commons.erau.edu/publication/2267

Calvo, R. A., & D'Mello, S. (2010). Affect detection: An interdisciplinary review. *IEEE Transactions on Affective Computing*, *1*(1), 18–37. DOI: 10.1109/T-AFFC.2010.1

Chen, L., Chen, P., & Lin, Z. (2020). Artificial intelligence in education: A review. *IEEE Access : Practical Innovations, Open Solutions*, *8*, 75264–75278. DOI: 10.1109/ACCESS.2020.2988510

Fryer, L. K., Ainley, M., Thompson, A., Gibson, A., & Sherlock, Z. (2019). Stimulating and sustaining interest in a language course. *Computers in Human Behavior*, *95*, 136–145. DOI: 10.1016/j.chb.2018.08.045

Fryer, L. K., Ainley, M., Thompson, A., Gibson, A., & Sherlock, Z. (2019). Stimulating and sustaining interest in a language course: An experimental comparison of chatbot and human task partners. *Computers in Human Behavior*, *95*, 136–145. DOI: 10.1016/j.chb.2018.08.045

Gligorea, I., Cioca, M., Oancea, R., Gorski, A.-T., Gorski, H., & Tudorache, P. (2023). Adaptive learning using artificial intelligence in e-learning: A literature review. *Education Sciences*, *13*(12), 1216. DOI: 10.3390/educsci13121216

Government of India. (n.d.). DIKSHA – Digital Infrastructure for Knowledge Sharing. https://services.india.gov.in/service/detail/diksha-digital-infrastructure-for-knowledge-sharing

Holmes, W., Bialik, M., & Fadel, C. (2019). *Artificial intelligence in education: Promises and implications for teaching and learning*. Center for Curriculum Redesign.
Holmes, W., Bialik, M., & Fadel, C. (2019). *Artificial intelligence in education: Promises and implications for teaching and learning*. Center for Curriculum Redesign.
Holstein, K., Wortman Vaughan, J., Daumé, H., Dudík, M., & Wallach, H. (2020). Improving fairness in machine learning systems: What do industry practitioners need? *Proceedings of the 2020 CHI Conference on Human Factors in Computing Systems*, 1–16. DOI: 10.1145/3313831.3376727

IJNRD. (2024). Revolutionizing education through AI-driven personalized e-learning systems. *International Journal of Novel Research and Development*, *9*(4), 877–889. https://www.ijnrd.org/

Indian Express. (2025, May 17). Top 10 countries leading in artificial intelligence (AI): India ranks 4th globally. https://indianexpress.com/article/trending/top-10-listing/top-10-countries-leading-in-artificial-intelligence-ai-india-rank-9820641/

Jordan, M. I., & Mitchell, T. M. (2015). Machine learning: Trends, perspectives, and prospects. *Science*, *349*(6245), 255–260. DOI: 10.1126/science.aaa8415 PMID: 26185243

Labadze, L., Sadriev, R., Khasanov, M., & Usmanova, G. (2023). Chatbots in education: A systematic review. *International Journal of Educational Technology in Higher Education*, *20*(56). Advance online publication. DOI: 10.1186/s41239-023-00471-5
Labadze, L., Sadriev, R., Khasanov, M., & Usmanova, G. (2023). Chatbots in education: A systematic review. *International Journal of Educational Technology in Higher Education*, *20*(56). Advance online publication. DOI: 10.1186/s41239-023-00471-5
Lee, K. (2017). Rethinking the accessibility of online higher education. *The Internet and Higher Education*, *33*, 15–23. DOI: 10.1016/j.iheduc.2017.01.001

Luckin, R., Holmes, W., Griffiths, M., & Forcier, L. B. (2016). *Intelligence unleashed: An argument for AI in education*. Pearson Education.

Luckin, R., Holmes, W., Griffiths, M., & Forcier, L. B. (2016). *Intelligence unleashed: An argument for AI in education*. Pearson Education.

Onyebuchi, N. C., Ayeni, O. O., Adewusi, O. E., & Osawaru, B. (2024). AI in education: A review of personalized learning (Preprint). ResearchGate. https://www.researchgate.net/publication/390163119

Radif, M., & Hameed, O. M. (2024). AI-driven innovations in e-learning: Transforming educational paradigms for enhanced learning outcomes. *ArtsEduca, 38*, 404–414. DOI: 10.58262/ArtsEduca.3830

Sarnato, A. Z., Sari, W. D., Rahmawati, S. T., Hidayat, R., & Patry, H. (2024). The evolution of e-learning platforms: From U-learning to AI-driven adaptive learning systems. *Journal of Social Science Utilizing Technology*, *2*(2), 289–300. DOI: 10.70177/jssut.v2i2.1131

Settles, B., & Meeder, B. (2016). A trainable spaced repetition model for language learning. *Proceedings of the 54th Annual Meeting of the Association for Computational Linguistics*, 1848–1858. DOI: 10.18653/v1/P16-1174

Strielkowski, W., Grebennikova, V., Lisovskiy, A., Rakhimova, G., & Vasileva, T. (2025). AI-driven adaptive learning for sustainable educational transformation. *Sustainable Development (Bradford)*, *33*(2), 1921–1947. DOI: 10.1002/sd.3221

VanLehn, K. (2011). The relative effectiveness of human tutoring and intelligent tutoring systems. *Educational Psychologist*, *46*(4), 197–221. DOI: 10.1080/00461520.2011.611369

VanLehn, K. (2011). The relative effectiveness of human tutoring, intelligent tutoring systems, and other tutoring systems. *Educational Psychologist*, *46*(4), 197–221. DOI: 10.1080/00461520.2011.611369

Wang, S., Wang, F., Zhu, Z., Wang, J., Tran, T., & Du, Z. (2024). Artificial intelligence in education: A systematic literature review. *Expert Systems with Applications*, *252*, 124167. DOI: 10.1016/j.eswa.2024.124167

Wang, S., Wang, F., Zhu, Z., Wang, J., Tran, T., & Du, Z. (2024). Artificial intelligence in education: A systematic literature review. *Expert Systems with Applications*, *252*, 124167. DOI: 10.1016/j.eswa.2024.124167

Zawacki-Richter, O., Marín, V. I., Bond, M., & Gouverneur, F. (2019). Systematic review of research on artificial intelligence applications in higher education. *International Journal of Educational Technology in Higher Education*, *16*(1), 1–27. DOI: 10.1186/s41239-019-0171-0

Zhang, K., & Aslan, A. B. (2021). AI technologies for education: Recent research and future directions. *Computers and Education: Artificial Intelligence*, *2*, 100025. DOI: 10.1016/j.caeai.2021.100025

Zhao, T. (2023). AI in educational technology (Preprint). DOI: 10.20944/preprints202311.0106.v1

Chapter 12
Policy by Design:
Regulating Human-AI Collaboration in Higher Education

Yasien Ryklief
https://orcid.org/0000-0003-3012-1834
Two Oceans Graduate Institute, South Africa

Mariette Fourie Jardin
https://orcid.org/0000-0001-8283-775X
University of the Western Cape, South Africa

ABSTRACT

The accelerating integration of generative artificial intelligence (GenAI) technologies such as ChatGPT, Claude, and other large language models has rapidly altered the landscape of higher education (HE). These tools are transforming how teaching, learning, and research are conceptualised and practised. However, while GenAI presents opportunities for innovation and expanded access, it also exposes deep ethical, social, and governance challenges. Questions of academic integrity, authorship, digital inclusion, and institutional accountability have become increasingly urgent. This study argues that higher education institutions (HEIs) can no longer rely on reactive or fragmented approaches to AI governance. Instead, they require a proactive and anticipatory model of policymaking that embeds ethical and pedagogical foresight into institutional design. To address this need, the research introduces policy-by-design as a conceptual and practical framework for regulating human–AI collaboration in higher education.

DOI: 10.4018/979-8-3373-4521-5.ch012

1. INTRODUCTION AND BACKGROUND

Generative artificial intelligence (GenAI) holds transformative potential and pedagogical value for education, particularly in navigating the complex terrain of academic integrity, student success, and institutional innovation. As higher education institutions (HEIs) grapple with the rapid integration of GenAI tools such as ChatGPT, Claude, and other large language models (LLMs), the need for coherent, context-sensitive, and ethically grounded policy frameworks becomes increasingly urgent (Gupta, 2024; Johnston,Wells, Shanks, Boey & Parsons. 2024).

To realise a higher education (HE) environment that flourishes in the context of GenAI, institutions must move beyond reactive measures and adopt a proactive, design-oriented approach to policy development. Research consistently indicates that clear, transparent, and inclusive institutional policies are essential to establish consistent standards and practices around GenAI use (Kruger-Roux & Alberts, 2024; Hill & Hargis, 2024). These policies must be informed by interdisciplinary perspectives, drawing from education, ethics, law, computer science, and social justice to ensure they are both comprehensive and adaptable.

This chapter deliberately engages both South African contexts and international developments, offering an analytical exploration of current policy paradigms in educational systems across both developed and developing countries. In South Africa, where HEIs operate within a landscape marked by historical inequalities and ongoing socio-economic disparities, the integration of GenAI presents both opportunities and challenges. While GenAI can support personalised learning, automate administrative tasks, and enhance research capabilities, it also risks exacerbating existing digital divides if not implemented with care and foresight (Universities South Africa, 2024).

Internationally, policy responses to GenAI in education vary widely. In countries such as the United Kingdom, Australia, and Canada, universities have begun to issue institutional guidelines that define acceptable uses of GenAI in teaching, learning, and assessment. These guidelines often emphasise academic integrity, transparency, and student agency, while also encouraging experimentation and innovation (Higher Education Policy Institute, 2024; Gupta, 2024). Much of the prevailing global discourse on AI in HE is dominated by Northern perspectives, which often inadvertently overlook the structural inequities that shape digital participation in the Global South. Bridging the digital divide extends beyond merely providing infrastructure; it necessitates equitable access to devices, reliable connectivity, and comprehensive digital literacies. In South Africa, persistent socio- economic disparities significantly mediate access to higher education, making context- sensitive, inclusive strategies absolutely crucial for democratising AI access and ensuring that all staff and students can genuinely benefit from its transformative potential.

Illustrative examples from South African institutions, such as North-West University (NWU), provide practical insights into the integration of GenAI. NWU has successfully implemented the MindJoy tutor bot, supporting approximately 4,000 engineering students, 1,000 accounting students, and 20 psychology master's students across various disciplines [Verhoef, 2025]. These initiatives highlight AI's profound potential to enhance comprehension, simulate real-world scenarios, generate training datasets, and support pedagogical innovation, particularly when combined with robust assessment and curriculum design. Despite these emerging applications, there remains a notable lack of explicit integration of Global North experiences within the broader discourse, underscoring the urgent need for a comprehensive, context-sensitive policy-by-design framework that can effectively guide institutions internationally. This framework emphasizes ethical AI use, pedagogical innovation, digital inclusion, institutional culture, and governance, ultimately aiming to balance the promises and perils of AI in HE while steadfastly ensuring academic integrity, equity, and transformative learning outcomes (Horings, 2024).

The chapter further explores the tension between innovation and regulation, emphasising that policy frameworks must be adaptive and enabling, supporting responsible AI use without becoming mere red tape. Overly rigid or punitive policies risk stifling creativity and discouraging the exploration of GenAI's pedagogical potential.

Conversely, the absence of clear guidelines can lead to inconsistent practices, ethical breaches, and reputational risks (Hill & Hargis, 2024). Striking the right balance requires a nuanced understanding of the educational ecosystem, the capabilities and limitations of GenAI, and the diverse needs of stakeholders.

Effective AI policies should be clearly defined, context-sensitive, ethically grounded, and co-created through collaboration. Co-creation is particularly important in ensuring that policies are not imposed top-down but are instead developed through inclusive dialogue with students, staff, administrators, and external partners. This participatory approach enhances legitimacy, fosters buy-in, and ensures that policies are responsive to the lived realities of those they affect (Johnston et al., 2024; Kortext, 2024).

Scholarly literature emphasises that effective guidelines must be flexible enough to accommodate rapidly evolving technologies while providing clear ethical boundaries and practical implementation strategies. These guidelines must also address the unique challenges posed by AI, including issues of attribution, verification, and appropriate use cases. For instance, how should institutions handle student submissions that incorporate GenAI-generated content? What constitutes original work in an era of AI-assisted creativity? How can educators verify the authenticity of student outputs without resorting to surveillance or punitive measures? (Gupta, 2024; Hill & Hargis, 2024).

Against this backdrop, it becomes critical to establish mechanisms for regular policy review and updates as technologies evolve. Static policies quickly become obsolete in the face of rapid technological change.

Institutions must therefore adopt a dynamic policy cycle that includes horizon scanning, stakeholder consultation, pilot testing, and iterative refinement. This approach ensures that policies remain relevant, effective, and aligned with institutional values and strategic goals (Kruger-Roux & Alberts, 2024; HEPI, 2024). Transparency and accountability are also central to effective policy design. Institutions must clearly communicate AI policies to all stakeholders, using accessible language and multiple channels.

This includes not only formal policy documents but also workshops, training sessions, and digital resources that help students and staff understand their rights and responsibilities. Open dialogue should be encouraged, creating safe spaces for questions, concerns, and feedback (Kortext, 2024; Johnston et al., 2024).

In addition, regular AI audits can help institutions assess the impact of GenAI tools, identify unintended consequences, and make evidence-based adjustments. The chapter therefore recommends that advisory councils be established with intersectoral representation, including educators, representatives from the private and public sectors, as well as civil society, to guide AI integration in education nationally and internationally. Such structures would ensure the effective and efficient integration of GenAI while safeguarding the rights and agency of all stakeholders. These councils could also serve as platforms for knowledge exchange, capacity building, and policy harmonisation across institutions and regions (University of Pretoria, 2024).

Drawing from practical policy examples, the chapter underscores the importance of regulations that promote digital inclusion and equitable access. Bridging the digital divide is fundamental not merely providing access to technology, but ensuring equity in digital literacy, devices, and connectivity across students and staff. In the South African context, this means addressing infrastructural gaps, supporting under-resourced institutions, and developing targeted interventions for marginalised communities (Universities South Africa, 2024; Horings, 2024).

Without such efforts, the benefits of GenAI risk being concentrated among the already privileged, further entrenching educational inequalities. Inclusive, context-sensitive strategies are needed to empower users with meaningful digital participation. This includes integrating digital literacy into curricula, offering professional development for educators, and creating support structures for students navigating new technologies.

Central to this is the cultivation of lifelong digital skills for all stakeholders, students and staff as GenAI and other emerging technologies rapidly reshape educational practices and the labour market (HEPI, 2024; Hill & Hargis, 2024).

These skills include not only technical competencies but also critical thinking, ethical reasoning, and the ability to evaluate and interpret AI-generated content.

At the same time, higher education institutions must proactively navigate the opportunities and risks of generative AI, embedding ethical and responsible use, critical digital literacies, and ethical awareness into both teaching, learning, and institutional practice. This requires a shift in institutional culture one that embraces innovation while remaining grounded in core academic values. Leadership plays a crucial role in this transformation, setting the tone for responsible AI use and fostering a shared vision of digital transformation (University of Pretoria, 2024; Gupta, 2024).

These shifts demand more than technology; they require fostering an enabling organisational culture rooted in leadership, shared vision, and a digital mind-set capable of driving change at all levels. Institutions must invest in change management, support experimentation, and celebrate successes while learning from failures. They must also remain vigilant to the broader societal implications of AI, including issues of surveillance, bias, and algorithmic discrimination.

The purpose of this chapter is to clarify why thoughtful, contextually grounded policy design is essential for higher education institutions as they confront the rapid rise of generative artificial intelligence. While GenAI tools are already reshaping teaching, learning, assessment, and administrative practices, the speed and scale of this shift have outpaced the capacity of many institutions to respond with coherent and ethically sound policies. This chapter therefore seeks to establish a strong conceptual foundation for understanding how higher education particularly within the South African context can navigate this moment with foresight, integrity, and a commitment to equity.

Situated at the intersection of global developments and local realities, the chapter aims to examine how institutions can build policy frameworks that both protect and enable. It explores the tensions between innovation and regulation, showing why policies that are too rigid risk stifling pedagogical creativity, while policies that are too vague leave institutions exposed to ethical breaches, inconsistency, and reputational harm. By drawing from emerging examples, such as GenAI implementations at North-West University, the chapter also illustrates the practical possibilities of AI-enabled learning when supported by intentional governance structures and curriculum design.

A central purpose of the chapter is to highlight the significance of context. Global North institutions have begun to articulate guidelines on acceptable AI use, yet these frameworks often overlook the structural inequalities, infrastructural disparities, and digital divides that shape educational participation in countries like South Africa. In response, the chapter positions policy not as a bureaucratic exercise, but as a mechanism for promoting digital inclusion, safeguarding academic integrity, and ensuring that the benefits of GenAI can be experienced equitably by all staff and students.

Finally, the chapter seeks to offer a policy-by-design framework that institutions can use to develop responsive, ethical, and future-oriented GenAI strategies. This includes emphasising co-creation with stakeholders, transparent communication, ongoing review, and the cultivation of an institutional culture capable of adapting to technological change. By foregrounding these elements early in the chapter, the discussion aims to support readers in recognising policy development as an active, continuous, and collaborative process that is fundamental to shaping a just and educationally meaningful AI future.

2. RESEARCH METHODOLOGY

This chapter employs a qualitative, conceptual research methodology grounded in policy analysis and an interpretive framework. A qualitative, conceptual research methodology is well suited to this chapter because the aim is not to generate empirical findings but to interpret, synthesise, and theorise the rapidly expanding body of knowledge on generative AI in higher education. Conceptual research enables the critical analysis of existing policies, frameworks, and scholarly debates in order to clarify key ideas and develop new theoretical insights (Jabareen, 2009; Grant & Osanloo, 2014). Given that GenAI policy is still emerging and that institutional responses are uneven across contexts this methodology provides an appropriate lens for examining how policy discourses take shape, what assumptions they embed, and how they may be reframed to support ethical, equitable, and context-sensitive implementation in South African and international settings. A qualitative orientation further allows for close attention to meaning, interpretation, and the social realities that frame policy development, aligning with established qualitative traditions that foreground context, complexity, and human experience (Creswell & Poth, 2018; Merriam & Tisdell, 2016).

Within the scope of this chapter, therefore, the conceptual approach is not merely a methodological choice but a necessity. Policy texts, institutional guidelines, and scholarly arguments must be read interpretively, as they reflect underlying concerns about academic integrity, digital divides, governance, and innovation. By drawing on this methodology, the chapter is able to identify gaps in current policy thinking particularly the dominance of Global North narratives while proposing a more inclusive and forward-looking policy-by-design framework. This approach strengthens the analytical depth of the chapter and supports the development of a theoretically informed, contextually grounded contribution to emerging scholarship on AI governance in higher education.

The objective is to critically examine how higher education institutions (HEIs) are responding to the emergence of generative artificial intelligence (GenAI) through policy development, with particular attention to both South African and international contexts.

The research is based exclusively on the analysis of secondary sources, including:

- Published institutional policy documents;
- National and international guidelines on AI in education;
- Peer-reviewed academic literature from the fields of education, ethics, law, and technology;
- Reports from professional bodies, think tanks, and government agencies concerned with the integration of AI in higher education.

A comparative approach is adopted to explore how institutions in both the Global North and Global South are addressing GenAI through regulatory frameworks.

Case examples from countries such as the United Kingdom, Australia, Canada, and South Africa are used to highlight differences and similarities in policy design, institutional readiness, and ethical considerations.

This methodology allows for a synthesised, interdisciplinary perspective that informs the development of a theoretically robust and context-sensitive understanding of AI policy in higher education. The interpretive nature of the study facilitates critical reflection on the underlying values, assumptions, and socio-political factors that shape policy responses.

The study does not involve primary data collection or empirical fieldwork. Instead, it focuses on constructing a conceptual and analytical framework to inform policy-makers, educators, and institutional leaders about the principles and practices needed to govern GenAI in an equitable, ethical, and sustainable manner.

As the chapter now shifts toward the practical implications of governing generative AI within higher education, it becomes essential to interrogate the limitations of traditional policy formation. Conventional reactive or ad hoc approaches often triggered by crises or technological disruption are increasingly inadequate in a landscape characterised by rapid innovation, epistemic uncertainty, and evolving ethical demands. The section that follows therefore introduces *policy-by-design* as a proactive, future-oriented alternative. By defining this paradigm and contrasting it with historically reactive policy practices, the discussion demonstrates why the unprecedented pace, complexity, and socio-institutional impact of GenAI necessitate a deliberate, design-oriented methodology. Establishing this conceptual distinction provides a foundation for understanding how higher education institutions can cultivate more agile, participatory, and ethically robust governance frameworks capable not only of addressing immediate challenges but also of anticipating those yet to emerge.

3. MAPPING THE GLOBAL POLICY LANDSCAPE: NAVIGATING THE AI FRONTIER IN HIGHER EDUCATION

The rapid emergence of GenAI in HE necessitates the urgent development of robust, ethically grounded, and adaptive institutional policies. In the absence of clear frameworks, individual instructors often resort to fragmented, ad hoc strategies, which can lead to widespread confusion and jeopardise academic integrity. It is crucial to recognize that AI is not a neutral tool; it actively reshapes pedagogical possibilities, personalizes learning experiences, and challenges traditional notions of authorship, knowledge production, and professional identity. To better understand this the chapter will explore the current development context of both the global north as well as that of the global south [CIGI Online, 2024].

3.1 Developed Contexts (Global North)

Higher education systems in the Global North, encompassing regions such as the UK, Australia, Canada, and the European Union, are actively engaged in developing formal responses to GenAI. While institutional guidelines are still evolving, international policy instruments provide crucial guiding frameworks that inform institutional strategies [CIGI Online, 2024].

At a global level, UNESCO's Recommendation on the Ethics of Artificial Intelligence (2021) stands as a foundational normative framework for AI governance. It emphasizes core principles such as human rights, transparency, fairness, and accountability, offering sector- specific guidance for education and research [UNESCO, 2021]. Complementary publications, including AI and Education: Guidance for Policy-Makers and the AI Competency Frameworks for Students and Teachers (UNESCO, 2023, 2024), operationalise these principles for higher education through curriculum design, digital literacy initiatives, and the promotion of responsible AI use.

Within the European Union (EU), the Artificial Intelligence Act (Regulation EU 2024/1689) introduces a risk-based approach to AI regulation. This landmark legislation differentiates obligations based on the assessed risk level of AI systems, imposing requirements for transparency, labelling, and copyright compliance for AI models deployed within EU jurisdictions [European Union, 2024]. The EU Code of Practice on AI further provides voluntary guidelines that underscore safety, transparency, and responsible AI development [European Commission, 2025]. Despite these efforts, critiques persist, particularly concerning copyright protections, with scholars cautioning that existing loopholes may inadvertently undermine fair use principles and traditional notions of authorship [Rankin, 2025].

Individual institutions in the Global North are also pioneering innovative approaches. For instance, the European University Institute (EUI) has implemented comprehensive AI literacy workshops, pedagogical training programs, accessible resources for non-native speakers, and detailed FAQs to guide AI use within its community [European University Institute, 2024]. Similarly, the European Commission's Guidelines on Responsible Use of Generative AI in Research highlight the paramount importance of reliability, honesty, respect, and accountability, emphasizing the critical need for contextualized local adaptation [European Commission, 2024]. Collectively, these multi-layered global and institutional measures illustrate a dynamic policy ecosystem that integrates ethical considerations, legal frameworks, and pedagogical strategies to guide the responsible adoption of AI. This practice portrays the roadmap for South African universities to employ to ensure a dynamic policy development and implementation ecosystem.

3.2 Developing Contexts (Global South)

In developing contexts, including regions such as South Africa, Nigeria and Brazil the discourse surrounding GenAI integration is profoundly shaped by pre-existing socio-economic disparities that fundamentally structure participation in higher education. The digital divide remains a critical and pervasive challenge, extending beyond mere access to devices and connectivity to encompass the equitable provision of digital literacy, AI literacy, and the cultivation of lifelong learning dispositions [Fourie-Jardim, 2025; Horings, 2024]. Without targeted interventions to address these foundational issues, infrastructural access alone risks perpetuating and even exacerbating existing exclusions [Universities South Africa, 2024].

Structural constraints in these regions often include significant infrastructural limitations, persistent gaps in digital literacy, and a notable policy lag, as existing academic integrity policies are frequently ill-equipped to effectively manage AI-generated content [Fourie- Jardim, 2025]. Moreover, there is a limited body of empirical research on the specific competencies required for responsible GenAI use in these contexts, underscoring the urgent need for ongoing experimentation, adaptive strategies, and robust capacity building initiatives [Fourie-Jardim, 2025].

Despite these formidable challenges, GenAI offers unique opportunities for "leapfrogging" traditional developmental stages. Students in these regions often perceive AI as a powerful catalyst for intellectual growth, a means to democratize knowledge access, a pathway to personalized learning experiences, and a tool for enhanced cognitive engagement. Institutional responses in the Global South include the formation of dedicated task teams to draft ethical AI guidelines, the implementation of capacity-building programs for both faculty and students, and the development of frameworks that clearly define permissible AI use while simultaneously mitigating potential misconduct (Fourie-Jardim, 2025).

Together, these developments illustrate how institutions are beginning to transform the disruptive pressures of GenAI into structured opportunities for capacity building, ethical governance, and equitable access.

The next section therefore outlines the proposed frameworks and guidelines that can support higher education institutions in operationalising these strategic responses.

3.3 Proposed Frameworks and Guidelines

The AI^2 Competency Framework (From Artificial Intelligence to Academic Integrity) provides a structured and comprehensive approach for the ethical and responsible adoption of AI in HE, emphasising several key pillars [Fourie- Jardim, 2025]:

Relevance: This involves the proactive development of clear AI policies, comprehensive guidelines, and accessible resources. Responsiveness: This mandates the adaptation of curriculum, pedagogy, and assessment (AIAS) strategies to integrate AI effectively. Capacity Building: This focuses on fostering digital [AI] inclusion, enhancing AI readiness, and developing foundational AI literacy across the academic community. Integrated Approach: This pillar emphasizes the seamless integration of ethics, morality, academic integrity, intrinsic motivation, and a learning-first culture into all AI- related initiatives.

The "New Rules for Student Success in an Age of AI," outlined at the Siyaphumelela Network Student Success Conference 2025 (Verhoef et., al), further recommend practical institutional strategies for navigating the AI era:

- Engagement and Training: Institutions should provide comprehensive engagement and training in AI technologies through dedicated literacy courses and continuous integration within existing curricula.
- Development of Critical Skills: Emphasis should be placed on cultivating essential human skills, including discernment, creativity, adaptability, ethical reasoning, and critical thinking, which are augmented rather than replaced by AI.
- Promotion of Integrity: Clear guidelines for ethical AI use must be established, fostering a culture of honesty and academic integrity.
- Redesigning Outcomes and Assessments: Assessment methods should be redesigned to appropriately leverage AI while maintaining robust human oversight and evaluation.

The following section outlines the key challenges and provides comprehensive insights pertaining AI higher education institutions to consider.

3.4 Key Challenges and Comparative Insights

Several critical challenges universally confront higher education institutions in the age of AI:

- Academic Integrity: The ease with which AI can facilitate misconduct necessitates the development of robust and adaptable policy frameworks that redefine plagiarism, authorship, and attribution in the context of AI-generated content.
- Digital and AI Literacy: Comprehensive capacity-building initiatives are essential to ensure equitable participation and to equip all stakeholders with the necessary skills to engage effectively and ethically with AI technologies.
- Policy Lag and Institutional Adaptation: The rapid pace of AI development continually challenges established professional identities and institutional structures, often revealing the "illusion of control" maintained by traditional frameworks [Fourie- Jardim, 2025].

While the South African case provides invaluable practical insights, broader issues such as national-level policy development (e.g., via Universities South Africa) and persistent resource inequality remain underexplored in much of the global discourse.

Comparatively, developed contexts primarily focus on issues of compliance, governance, and the refinement of existing ethical frameworks for AI. In stark contrast, developing contexts grapple with more foundational challenges related to access, equity, and literacy. Despite these divergent starting points, both regions share common concerns regarding academic integrity. Consequently, the ethical integration of AI in HE must be inherently context-sensitive, embedding universal principles such as transparency and accountability within the unique socio-economic realities of each local environment.

4. THE CASE FOR POLICY-BY-DESIGN IN HIGHER EDUCATION

4.1 Define "Policy-By-Design" in Contrast to Reactive or Ad Hoc Policies

In the rapidly changing environment of systems and the introduction and use of technology within sectors such as higher education, the need for an equally agile approach to policy development has become a necessity. Erratic shifts in technology now calls for a drastic shift in the mind-set and approach of policy makers from a reactive or ad hoc approach to a more structured pre-emptive and proactive approach.

This paradigm shift will allow for the production of new interventions and governance foresight and not merely the formulation of a response to or reformulation of current policies.

Policy-by-design can therefore be interpreted as an agile pre-emptive methodology to policy development that is cognisant of regulatory and ethical requirements as well as forecasted and structured designs of developments within the institution and the higher education sector holistically (Mortati, Mullagh & Schmidt, 2022).

This approach allows policy makers to view policy design and amendments as an enabling and developmental approach rather that an approach brought about by disruption or unexpected developments to the policy environment. Policy-by-design is therefore considered to be an epistemological reorientation detailing the functionality of policies within the various systems and sectors (Brownsword & Goodwin, 2012).

At this point it is important to understand the contrast to the historical reactive and ad hoc approach to policy development, which was often a response to very specific events or crises. Reactive policy development may be deemed as necessary or urgent based on a particular context, often lack rationality with the broader objectives and may result in poor implementation as well as unintended outcomes. An example of this would be the formulation of a policy on the acceptability and usage of Artificial Intelligence (AI) tools. It should therefore be noted that the full scale of AI should first be understood before these considerations can be made for policy development (Hallsworth, 2011).

According to Gurumurthy and Chami (2014) the concept of Policy-by-design is therefore distinguished via specific qualities namely: Pre-emptive as it allows for the identification of current and future potential risk, ethical conflict, inefficiencies and by doing so and through proper planning allows for reduced future ramification. Entrenched which allows for the development of policy that is geared toward tackling the root course of the matter instead creating policy that is superimposed on current systems. Policy objectives and goals are therefore embedded into the core of an organisation's workflows. **Iterative** as is the case with design thinking, this approach acknowledges that for policies to be effective it requires constant feedback and input from its intended stakeholders.

A vital component of the concept of policy by design is its requirement for a transdisciplinary approach. For effective implementation it requires collaboration between all role players in the process such as but not limited to policy makers, ethicist, affected communities and educators. By adopting this bottom up approach to policy making the "top down" imposition can be resisted and the co-production model (where everyone feels valued and included) can be embraced (Jasanoff, 2004).

4.2 Why GenAI Requires a Design-Oriented Approach

GenAI is now no longer a niche but has become the norm in every working environment and classroom. It has become the universally accepted method for content creation and if used effectively and ethically could enhance teaching and learning experiences. However, it should be noted that the technology itself does not guarantee the production of useful outcomes. To effectively utilise the potential of GenAI one has to transition from an engineering (building and deploying) mind-set to one that is more design-orientated that is moulded by the frame of reference of stakeholders. This chapter explains why GenAI calls for design as a primary discipline, not an afterthought, and illustrates the argument with concrete examples drawn from one private higher education institute in the Western Cape, South Africa's teaching and research contexts. The value of and the integration of real world challenges as well as the adoption of GenAI into workflows are increased if institutions adopt a design approach instead of the standard static approach to policy making. This process also promotes innovation and reduces transformation fatigue (Davenport & Mittal, 2022). The added benefit of the design- oriented approach over the standard static approach is that it focusses on frame of reference of the human aspect and their experience that in essence makes technology advantageous and not simply technically impressive. In the South African higher education context, empirical analyses corroborate this practical logic: recent work documents uneven AI readiness across institutions but also identifies pockets of institutional innovation where anticipatory governance and structured experimentation have helped reconcile institutional transformation goals (including decolonisation and equity) with rapid AI adoption, suggesting that policy-by-design can support contextually anchored, ethically attentive roll-outs of AI tools on campus (Maimela & Mbonde 2025; Mogoale, Pretorius, Mogase & Segooa, 2025).

5. ILLUSTRATIVE CASE EXAMPLES

While the existing literature by (Taeihagh, 2025; Mochan, Farinha, Bailey, Rodríguez, Zanca, & Pólvora, 2024; Reuel & Undheim, 2024) extensively addresses the key dimensions of effective GenAI policy and theoretical frameworks outlining general strategies for the ethical integration of AI in HE, it falls short of providing concrete examples of how these principles are implemented at specific universities.

Several relevant points are noted in the sources:

- The International Association of University Presidents (IAUP) conference in 2024 highlighted discussions among thought leaders on harnessing AI to promote equitable access to quality education. While informative, this represents a broad sectoral dialogue rather than a detailed university-level case study (International Association of University Presidents [IAUP], 2024).

- Research from Stanford University indicates that the introduction of ChatGPT did not lead to a statistical increase in academic dishonesty; in many cases, students used the tool to enhance their learning. Although this study offers valuable insight into student behaviour, it does not provide evidence of institutional policy responses or the operationalization of GenAI strategies (Lee and Pope, 2023).
- The literature emphasizes the critical importance of bridging the digital divide, ensuring equitable access to devices, connectivity, and digital literacy, particularly in South Africa, where socio-economic disparities are pronounced. While this underscores a key regional challenge, the sources do not document specific institutional policies or concrete examples of how South African universities are addressing these issues in practice (Kafile, Ninana and Makhetha-Kosi, 2025).

In sum, while the literature provides a strong conceptual and theoretical foundation for GenAI policy development, there is a clear gap in practical, university-specific case examples that demonstrate how these policies are applied, tested, and adapted in real-world higher education contexts.

To address this gap, the following illustrative vignettes present plausible examples of how universities in the UK, Australia, and South Africa might operationalize GenAI policy principles. These vignettes are informed by broader research, sectoral reports, and policy discussions, providing concrete scenarios that highlight potential strategies, challenges, and innovations. While hypothetical, they offer comparative touchpoints for understanding how institutions could translate theoretical frameworks such as the AI^2 Competency Framework and the "Embrace and Disclose" approach into practical policy and practice. These examples help to contextualize the key dimensions of effective GenAI policy and illustrate how universities might balance ethical integration, pedagogical innovation, digital inclusion, and governance in real-world settings.

5.1 Case 1: United Kingdom – Balancing Innovation and Integrity

At a mid-sized UK university, the adoption of GenAI prompted the creation of a working group on "Assessment Futures." The group piloted new forms of assessment designed to minimize over-reliance on AI, such as oral vivas, collaborative projects, and reflective portfolios. While students appreciated the transparency of the "Embrace and Disclose" policy requiring them to note when AI tools were used, staff raised concerns about increased workload and uneven digital literacies among students. The policy's success was mixed: it fostered innovation but also highlighted the challenge of supporting both staff and students through rapid change (Universities UK, 2023).

5.2 Case 2: Australia – Embedding AI Literacy Across the Curriculum

An Australian research-intensive university introduced a cross-disciplinary "AI Literacy Framework" that embedded GenAI training into first-year curricula across faculties. The framework emphasised metacognitive skills, ethical decision-making, and practical awareness of AI limitations. Early evaluations found that students gained confidence in using GenAI responsibly, but faculty reported uncertainty about assessment standards and grading consistency. The initiative showed promise as a scalable model yet underscored the importance of institutional coherence and continuous professional development for educators (Tertiary Education Quality and Standards Agency, 2023; Selwyn,2024).

5.3 Case 3: South Africa – Bridging the Digital Divide

At a South African university serving a diverse student body, a task team was established to draft a GenAI policy with a focus on equity and inclusion. Recognising connectivity and device disparities, the institution partnered with telecom providers to offer subsidized data and piloted low-bandwidth AI tools accessible via mobile phones. While these measures improved access, faculty noted gaps in digital literacy and the lack of clear disciplinary guidelines for AI use in research and coursework. The case illustrates both the potential for AI to act as a catalyst for democratizing access to information and the persistent challenges posed by socio-economic disparities (Czerniewicz, Deacon & Smallwood, 2020; Hodges et al., 2020; UNESCO, 2023, 2024).

6. KEY DIMENSIONS OF EffECTIVE GENAI POLICY: A BLUEPRINT FOR RESPONSIBLE INTEGRATION

Developing effective policies for GenAI in HE demands a multi-faceted approach that meticulously addresses technological, ethical, pedagogical, social, and governance considerations. This section presents a thematic blueprint designed to guide institutions in designing or refining GenAI policies that are human-centered, ethically grounded, and contextually responsive.

6.1 Ethical and Legal Foundations: Redefining Integrity in the AI Era

The ethical and legal foundations of GenAI policy are paramount, particularly given the "Great Revelation" that AI is ubiquitous and inevitably used in HE [Fourie-Jardim, 2025]. This pervasive reality necessitates clear institutional frameworks that redefine traditional concepts of plagiarism, authorship, and attribution in the context of AI-generated content. Unlike conventional plagiarism, AI outputs are not directly copied from existing human- authored sources, rendering many traditional policies inadequate and often obsolete [European Commission, 2024; UNESCO, 2024].

Effective policies in this domain must be clear, ethically anchored, collaboratively created, and inherently adaptable. They should serve as guiding principles for both individual behaviour and the broader institutional culture. The AI² Competency Framework explicitly emphasizes ethics, morality, and academic integrity as core components of an Integrated Approach, fostering principled use while actively mitigating potential misconduct [Fourie- Jardim, 2025; UNESCO, 2021, 2023].

The "Embrace and Disclose" approach offers practical and pragmatic guidance, acknowledging the inevitability of AI's presence while vigorously promoting transparent and ethical use [European University Institute, 2024]. Policies must clearly delineate ethical applications such as enhancing learning, supporting inquiry, safeguarding data privacy, and verifying outputs, from unethical uses, which include misrepresentation of authorship, academic dishonesty, or the propagation of bias. By foregrounding integrity, institutions can ensure that AI serves to augment human decision-making and creativity rather than replacing it.

6.2 Pedagogical Integration: Fostering Human-AI Synergy

GenAI acts as an active agent in reshaping learning and teaching paradigms, thereby requiring policies that actively foster human–AI synergy [UNESCO, 2023]. In this evolving landscape, educators' roles are transforming from mere content experts to sophisticated ecosystem stewards, facilitating inquiry, critical thinking, and meaning making while strategically leveraging AI to enhance, not replace, human judgment.

Key policy imperatives for pedagogical integration include:

- Prioritising Process Over Product: Policies should promote metacognitive awareness among learners regarding when and how to appropriately use AI tools, emphasizing the learning process rather than solely the final output.
- AI Literacy for All: Comprehensive AI literacy programs for both learners and educators are crucial to demystify AI use, enable informed engagement, and build confidence in navigating AI-powered environments.
- Cultivating Human Skills: Policies must explicitly encourage the development of uniquely human skills such as creativity, discernment, adaptability, critical thinking, ethical reasoning, and curiosity, recognizing that these are augmented by AI, not diminished.
- Assessment Redesign: Assessment methodologies need to be re-evaluated and redesigned to incorporate AI appropriately into marking schemes and rubrics, with a strong emphasis on formative, process-oriented evaluation that assesses critical engagement with AI.
- Curriculum Responsiveness: Curricula must be responsive to AI's capabilities, identifying tasks that are well-suited for AI assistance, those that unequivocally require human expertise, and opportunities for innovative hybrid approaches.

AI presents significant opportunities for personalized learning, enhanced comprehension, sophisticated problem-solving, efficient content creation, streamlined academic writing, and improved feedback mechanisms. Simultaneously, institutions must address potential risks such as over-reliance on AI, superficial learning outcomes, and the erosion of critical human creativity. Policies should therefore guide educators in curriculum redesign efforts that emphasize knowledge creation, proper attribution, and critical engagement with AI- generated content [Fourie-Jardim, 2025].

6.3 Digital Inclusion and Equity: Bridging the Divide

In diverse contexts, particularly in regions like South Africa, digital inclusion and equity are central policy concerns. It is widely recognized that access to devices and connectivity alone is insufficient; meaningful participation in the AI era necessitates inclusive digital literacy, the cultivation of lifelong learning dispositions, and cultural adaptation to new technologies [Fourie-Jardim, 2025].

Policies in this dimension should ensure:

- Equitable Access: Guaranteeing access to essential tools, robust infrastructure, and AI platforms for all students and educators, irrespective of their socio-economic background.

- Capacity Building: Implementing comprehensive programs for digital [AI] inclusion, enhancing AI readiness, and building foundational literacy in AI across the entire academic community [UNESCO, 2024].
- Inclusive Participation: Ensuring that no learner is left behind, and that all individuals can engage safely, ethically, and effectively with AI technologies.

By proactively addressing these critical dimensions, institutions can strategically leverage AI to democratize knowledge, enhance cognitive capacities across the student body, and actively bridge systemic inequalities that have historically marginalized certain populations.

6.4 Institutional Culture and Change Management: Embracing Transformation

The advent of GenAI necessitates a profound cultural shift within higher education institutions. Recognizing that students are increasingly co-authors of their own educational journeys, challenges traditional teacher-centered models and prior “illusions of control” [Freire, 1970; 2005; Fourie-Jardim, 2025].

Policy in this area should actively promote a human-centered approach, fostering an enabling organizational culture rooted in strong leadership, a shared vision for digital transformation, and a proactive digital mindset capable of driving change at all levels. Institutions must invest strategically in change management initiatives, support-controlled experimentation, and celebrate successes while learning constructively from failures.

Furthermore, they must remain vigilant to the broader societal implications of AI, including critical issues of surveillance, algorithmic bias, and potential discrimination.

6.5 Governance, Accountability, and Transparency

Robust governance ensures sustained, responsible integration of GenAI. Policies must be dynamic, adaptable, and ethically anchored (European Commission, 2024).

Key components include:

- Establishing AI task teams/advisory councils: Draft frameworks, train stakeholders, and manage misconduct.
- Risk and security assessments: Applying Confidentiality, Integrity, and Availability (CIA) principles in AI selection.
- Dialogical design: Engaging learners in co-creation and critical AI literacy.
- Iterative review: Continuous audits, feedback loops, and policy evaluation.

- Institutional coherence: Ensuring consistent application across faculties and departments.
- Transparency: Mitigating bias and commodification risks while fostering trust.

The AI^2 Competency Framework provides a foundation through its Integrated Approach, ensuring that ethical, pedagogical, and operational pillars work cohesively to advance innovation, inclusivity, and academic integrity (Fourie-Jardim, 2025).

7. THE POLICY CYCLE: A DYNAMIC GOVERNANCE MODEL

At the rate in which Generative Artificial Intelligence (GenAI) is rapidly progressing higher education institutions would need to adopt innovative approaches to policy making that are both flexible and forward thinking. Generic and direct policy models, which envisages stability over lengthy periods, are often not suitable for the application to these agile technological landscapes (Bryson & Winfield, 2022).

Therefore, a cyclical approach needs to be adopted to allow institutions to forecast changes, involve key stakeholders in decision making and adapt policies to market related feedback and requirements.

The formulation of the proposed GenAI Policy Development Cycle is informed by intersecting strands of scholarship in anticipatory governance, participatory policy design, experimental policymaking, and adaptive governance. Research on anticipatory governance emphasises the importance of horizon scanning as a means of institutional sense-making in contexts characterised by technological uncertainty, rapid innovation, and systemic risk, positioning foresight as a prerequisite for responsible governance rather than a predictive exercise (Taeihagh, 2025; Mochan, Farinha, Bailey, Rodríguez, Zanca, & Pólvora, 2024). The inclusion of co-design with stakeholders draws on participatory and socio-technical policy literature, which demonstrates that policies governing complex technologies achieve greater legitimacy, contextual relevance, and practical effectiveness when those affected by them are meaningfully involved in their development, particularly within higher education settings marked by disciplinary diversity and normative contestation (Chan, 2023; UNESCO, 2021). The pilot implementation phase is grounded in experimental and adaptive policymaking research, which advocates for controlled, small-scale experimentation as a response to the inherent unpredictability of emerging technologies, allowing regulatory assumptions and operational arrangements to be empirically tested prior to institutionalisation (Taeihagh, 2025). Finally, the emphasis on continuous review and revision reflects adaptive governance and policy learning theories, which reject static regulatory models in favour of iterative, feedback-driven approaches capable of responding to ongoing technological, organisational, and regulatory change, thereby ensuring sustained policy relevance and institutional reflexivity in the governance of generative AI (Reuel & Undheim, 2024).

In light of the above, the following GenAI Policy Development Cycle is proposed. This cycle consists of four interlinked phases namely: *Horizon Scanning*, *Co-design with Stakeholders*, *Pilot Implementation*, and *Continuous Review and Revision*. Collectively, these phases create a loop that ensures policies are adaptable and evidence based.

Figure 1. GenAI Policy Development Cycle

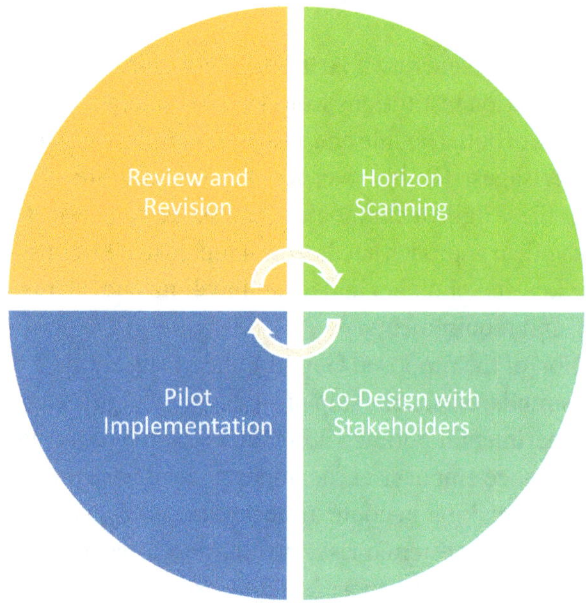

7.1 Horizon Scanning

The concept of horizon scanning encompasses the active process of determining and monitoring trends, opportunities and potential risk within the GenAI environment. This process is an intricate exercise which draws on various categories of data collection ranging from screening research publications to determining regulatory developments and looking at what the general industry is forecasting. This process cannot be dealt with in isolation form engagement with the various ethical reports and pedagogical content pertaining to policy development for GenAI (Sutherland & Beach, 2023).

When looking specifically at the context of higher education, the above may include:

- Incorporating considerations of intellectual property
- Forecasting implications for assessment and the general integrity of teaching and learning
- Through the adoption of a horizon scanning approach into ones policy cycle, an institution can be proactive instead of reactive when formulating responses to crises.

7.2 Co-design with Stakeholders

Policy design as a tool can benefit from the involvement of its intended audience and affected stakeholders. The implantation of policy and its design often fails due to institution adopting a top-down approach to policy making. By co-designing the policy with its affected stakeholders, you ensure their buy in and create a sense of ownership which enables a positive environment for the implementation process. Co-designing policy is a medium used to ensure that the diverse perspectives of all effected parties are tabled. These include advice from industry experts, academic advisors, technical teams, students as well as external partners. By doing so the development team can effectively inform the general scope, landscape, language as well as the operational principles of the policy. There are various ways in which data can be collected for this process which include stakeholder workshops, open dialogues and collective drafting sessions. At this juncture it should be noted that co-designing policies brings about strengthened legitimacy, ensures the buy in by affected stakeholders and most importantly reflects and addresses actual and real-world requirements (Bryson and Winfield, 2022).

7.3 Pilot Implementation

As is the case with any new development, institutions should consider a phased implementation approach. The general practice is to incorporate pilot implementation which allows for controlled experimentation. This includes:

- Creating a testing environment for regulated use; and
- Restricting the application of the policy to a limited audience or a particular department or faculty.

7.4 Continuous Review and Revision

With the rapid development and agile ability of GenAI advancement, policies cannot be static and its developers should therefore be willing to continuously review and adapt policy documents to ensure relevance to market demands. These reviews could involve:

- Monitoring and evaluation (annual audits);
- Tracking technological developments; and
- Encouraging and incorporating user feedback.

This phase of the development cycle ensures that policies remain relevant, transparent, informed and aligned with institutional norms and market needs (Sutherland and Beach, 2023).

This GenAI Policy Development Cycle proposes a governance model that combines both strategic foresight as well as responsive agility. By integrating the four above phases higher education institutions can proactively navigate the uncertainties and probabilities of AI integration.

8. POLICY RECOMMENDATIONS

To effectively integrate GenAI into higher education institutions would have to consider the multi-layered response to policy. A silo or fragmented approach to responding to policy may increase risk and create inequalities as well as limit innovation. Policy design and transformation should therefore operate across all applicable levels including institutional, national and global levels.

8.1 Global Level

The governance and agility of GenAI spans international boundaries. The rapid integration of AI requires presence within international forums.

Recommendations include:

- Contributing to the formulation of international ethical frameworks
- Encouraging international collaboration to foster research capacity, technology transfer, and comprehensive curriculum design.

Through these efforts higher education institutions ensure that they are meeting local standards while adhering to international trends.

8.2 National Level: Department of Higher Education and Training (DHET) and the Council on Higher Education (CHE)

National authorities provide the regulatory and strategic backbone for AI in higher education.

Key recommendations include:

- Commenting on and assist through consultation with formulating national strategic guidelines on the pedagogical and administrative uses of GenAI.
- Highlighting the gap and addressing the need for resources when implementing GenAI nationally across all economic spectrums of society; and
- Contribute to the establishment of potential funding streams for AI-related infrastructure.

By introducing such measures, national regulatory bodies are able to create an ecosystem for institutions to experiment safely without compromising common standards.

8.3 Institutional Level: Higher Education Institutions (HEIs)

The first point of departure is at institutional level. Universities and colleges are at the frontline of GenAI adoption, especially regarding matters of teaching and learning as well as research. Policy development at this level should prioritise and encourage an inclusive governance approach. In order to achieve this, institutions would need to adopt a co-design method which involves various stakeholders such as students, academic and administrative personnel as well as external contributors' thus embedding legitimacy and ownership in AI policies (Floridi, 2021).

According to Zawacki-Richter et al (2019) HEIs should for effective implementation:

- Establish **AI literacy and training programmes** for staff and students;
- Conduct **regular technological audits** to evaluate the alignment of AI tools
- Develop **context-sensitive ethical guidelines** for plagiarism detection, and authorship in research outputs.

8.4 Ethical Imperative of GenAI Policy

The ethical dimension of GenAI policy is paramount. AI is widely available, and its use by students and educators is inevitable, making it critical to harness benefits while mitigating risks. The key challenge is not simply how AI transforms learning but how individuals engage with it responsibly.

Ethical applications of AI include enhancing learning, fostering critical inquiry, and supporting knowledge creation, positioning AI as a complementary tool rather than a replacement for human learning. Ethical use also encompasses proper attribution, maintenance of academic integrity, data privacy and security, verification of outputs, recognition of AI's limitations, and promotion of inclusive practices. Conversely, unethical use undermines trust and fairness, encompassing academic dishonesty, misrepresentation of authorship, privacy violations, and reinforcement of bias.

The AI^2 Competency Framework explicitly integrates ethics and morality as foundational components, guiding both individual behaviour and institutional culture while reinforcing academic integrity (Fourie-Jardim, 2025). It promotes a Human-Centered Approach and an Integrated Nature, ensuring that academic work remains principled and trustworthy. The "Embrace and Disclose" approach offers practical guidance, acknowledging AI's inevitability while establishing norms for ethical implementation. Cultivating a learning-first culture, prioritising deep understanding, critical inquiry, and intellectual growth naturally supports integrity over mere performance metrics.

8.5 Emphasising Balance: Innovation and Regulation

Achieving ethical and inclusive AI futures requires balancing innovation with regulation (Fourie-Jardim, 2025). The AI^2 Competency Framework promotes a Balanced Approach and Critical Engagement, encouraging HE communities to avoid both uncritical acceptance and reactionary rejection of AI. This perspective recognises that AI can simultaneously challenge and enhance academic integrity, making robust ethical frameworks essential.

AI policies should foster human-AI synergy, where AI augments human judgment, emotional intelligence, and ethical reasoning rather than replacing human effort. The future of teaching is envisioned as a partnership between human educators and AI, embracing Intelligence Augmentation (IA) to enhance teacher and student capacities. Policies must be clearly defined, ethically anchored, collaboratively developed, and adaptable to evolving AI capabilities. Given the limited research on competencies for responsible GenAI use, ongoing experimentation, reflection, and iteration are essential.

8.6 Call for Long-Term Vision, Collaborative Leadership, and Global Solidarity

Forward-thinking policy requires long-term vision, collaborative leadership, and global solidarity. The metaphor of "a rising tide lifts all boats" underscores the collective nature of learning, emphasizing shared responsibility within HE communities. Leveraging AI to achieve equitable access to quality education has been identified as a priority, envisioning personalized, lifelong, and in-demand learning enabled by AI technologies. Educators are called to become ecosystem stewards, curating learning environments, facilitating ethical reflection, and designing for diversity and complexity. Collaborative governance, including student involvement in AI policy development, fosters agency and shared responsibility. Task teams play a pivotal role in structuring ethical frameworks, capacitating faculty and students, defining AI use parameters, and sharing best practices.

Global solidarity is particularly critical in addressing the digital divide, ensuring equitable access to technology, digital literacy, devices, and connectivity for all students and staff. Inclusive, context-sensitive strategies empower meaningful digital participation worldwide, while the "Confluence Delta" metaphor illustrates the merging of human-centered pedagogy with AI to co-create new, ethically grounded educational terrain (Fourie-Jardim, 2025).

8.7 Cultivating a Humanizing and Life-Affirming Education

AI integration represents a "Great Revelation", challenging traditional notions of control and exposing the limitations of the banking model. Recognising that students have always been co-authors of their educational journeys encourages a more honest, humanizing model. Rather than policing the boundary between human and AI-generated content, educators should cultivate students' deeper relationship with knowledge, emphasizing discovery, critical evaluation, and meaning-making over mere content production. As noted, "AI won't take educators' jobs; someone using AI effectively will" (Fourie-Jardim, 2025). Proficiency in ethical and effective AI use is therefore crucial, positioning AI as a tool that augments human decision-making rather than replacing human expertise).

This perspective calls educators to embrace new roles as "stewards of complexity, curators of agency, and co-authors of pedagogical futures," guiding HE toward a humanizing, life-affirming education in the age of AI.

9. CONCLUSION

In conclusion, regulating human-AI collaboration in HE is far more than a mere technical or administrative task; it represents a deeply ethical and strategic endeavour. Policies must be meticulously designed not only to effectively manage the inherent risks associated with AI but, more importantly, to unlock its transformative potential in ways that are inclusive, equitable, and sustainable. By proactively adopting a "policy-by-design" approach - one that is firmly grounded in collaboration, adaptability, and ethical foresight - HEIs are uniquely positioned to lead the way in shaping a future where humans and AI work synergistically to advance knowledge, foster creativity, and promote social justice. Regulating human-AI collaboration in HE is not merely a technical or administrative task it is a deeply ethical and strategic endeavour. Policies must be designed not only to manage risks but to unlock the transformative potential of GenAI in ways that are inclusive, equitable, and sustainable. By adopting a policy-by-design approach, grounded in collaboration, adaptability, and ethical foresight, HEIs can lead the way in shaping a future where humans and AI work together to advance knowledge, creativity, and social justice. The emergence of GenAI in HE demands a forward-thinking, values-driven orientation that prioritises ethical, inclusive, and human-centered AI futures. This orientation is essential for navigating the transformative "tides" of technological advancement, diverse student populations, and evolving knowledge systems.

This chapter has underscored the critical need for HEIs to move beyond reactive measures and embrace a proactive, comprehensive strategy for integrating GenAI. This strategy must acknowledge the diverse contexts of the Global North and Global South, addressing both universal challenges like academic integrity and context-specific issues such as digital inclusion and resource disparities. The proposed framework, built upon ethical foundations, pedagogical integration, digital equity, and cultural transformation, offers a roadmap for institutions to navigate this complex landscape.

Ultimately, the successful integration of AI in higher education hinges on a collective commitment to fostering an environment where innovation thrives within a robust ethical perimeter. This requires ongoing dialogue, continuous policy refinement, and a shared vision that prioritizes human flourishing and the core values of education in an increasingly AI-driven world. The future of HE, enriched by the responsible and thoughtful application of AI, promises to be one of unprecedented learning opportunities and societal advancement.

REFERENCES

Brownsword, R., & Goodwin, M. (2012). *Law and the technologies of the twenty-first century: Text and materials*. Cambridge University Press. DOI: 10.1017/CBO9781139047609

Bryson, J. J., & Winfield, A. F. T. (2022). *Ethics and governance of artificial intelligence*. Oxford University Press.

Chan, C. K. Y. (2023). A comprehensive AI policy education framework for university teaching and learning. *International Journal of Educational Technology in Higher Education*, *20*(1), 38. Advance online publication. DOI: 10.1186/s41239-023-00408-3

Creswell, J. W., & Poth, C. N. (2018). *Qualitative inquiry and research design: Choosing among five approaches* (4th ed.). SAGE.

Czerniewicz, L., Deacon, A., & Smallwood, H. (2020). A wake-up call: Equity, inequality and COVID-19 emergency remote teaching and learning. *Higher Education Research & Development*, *39*(1), 1–4. DOI: 10.1007/s42438-020-00187-4 PMID: 40477091

Davenport, T. H., & Mittal, N. (2022). How generative AI is changing creative work. *Harvard Business Review*, •••, 14.

European Commission. (2024). *Guidelines on the responsible use of generative AI in research*. https://research-and-innovation.ec.europa.eu

European Union. (2024). *Regulation (EU) 2024/1689 laying down harmonised rules on artificial intelligence*. https://eur-lex.europa.eu

Floridi, L. (Ed.). (2021). *Ethics, governance, and policies in artificial intelligence*. Springer., DOI: 10.1007/978-3-030-81907-1

Fourie-Jardim, M. (2025). *Reimagining student success and expanding opportunity for all* [Conference presentation]. Siyaphumelela Network Student Success Conference, South Africa.

Freire, P. (1970). Cultural action and conscientization. *Harvard Educational Review*, *40*(3), 452–477. DOI: 10.17763/haer.40.3.h76250x720j43175

Grant, C., & Osanloo, A. (2014). Understanding, selecting, and integrating a theoretical framework in dissertation research. *Administrative Issues Journal*, *4*(2), 12–26.

Gupta, R. (2024). Governing academic integrity: Ensuring the authenticity of higher thinking in the era of generative artificial intelligence. *Journal of Academic Ethics*. Advance online publication. DOI: 10.1007/s10805-025-09639-7

Hallsworth, M. (2011). Policy-making in the real world. *Political Insight*, *2*(1), 10–12. DOI: 10.1111/j.2041-9066.2011.00051.x

Higher Education Policy Institute. (2024, November 8). *Generative AI in higher education: Navigating policy, ethics, and skills development*. https://www.hepi.ac.uk

Hill, C., & Hargis, J. (2024). An ethics module on academic integrity and generative AI. *New Directions for Teaching and Learning*. Advance online publication. DOI: 10.1002/tl.20626

Jabareen, Y. (2009). Building a conceptual framework: Philosophy, definitions, and procedure. *International Journal of Qualitative Methods*, *8*(4), 49–62. DOI: 10.1177/160940690900800406

Jasanoff, S. (2004). *States of knowledge: The co-production of science and social order*. Routledge. DOI: 10.4324/9780203413845

Johnston, H., Wells, R. F., Shanks, E. M., Boey, T., & Parsons, B. N. (2024). Student perspectives on the use of generative artificial intelligence technologies in higher education. *International Journal for Educational Integrity*, *20*(2), 2. Advance online publication. DOI: 10.1007/s40979-024-00149-4

Kafile, M., Ninana, A., & Makhetha-Kosi, P. (2025). The digital divide and e-learning participation: A mixed-methods study of Extended Curriculum Programme students in South Africa. *International Journal of Learning. Teaching and Educational Research*, *24*(9), 769–784. DOI: 10.26803/ijlter.24.9.37

Kortext. (2024). *Ensuring academic integrity amidst the rise of generative AI*. https://kortext.com

Kruger-Roux, H., & Alberts, R. (2024). Generative artificial intelligence policy for academic literacy in South African higher education. In *AI Approaches to Literacy in Higher Education* (pp. 1–22). IGI Global Scientific Publishing. DOI: 10.4018/979-8-3693-1054-0.ch001

Lee, V. R., & Pope, D. (2023). *What do AI chatbots really mean for students and cheating?* Stanford Graduate School of Education. https://ed.stanford.edu

Maimela, C., & Mbonde, P. (2025). Artificial intelligence in South African universities: Curriculum transformation and decolonisation—Aid or obstacle? *Frontiers in Sociology*, *10*, 1543471. Advance online publication. DOI: 10.3389/fsoc.2025.1543471 PMID: 40697567

Merriam, S. B., & Tisdell, E. J. (2016). *Qualitative research: A guide to design and implementation* (4th ed.). Jossey-Bass.

Mochan, A., Farinha, J., Bailey, G., Rodríguez, L., Zanca, F., & Pólvora, A. (2024). *Horizon scanning for emerging technologies and AI governance*. Publications Office of the European Union., DOI: 10.2760/1426669

Mogoale, P. D., Pretorius, A., Mogase, R. C., & Segooa, M. A. (2025). Integrating artificial intelligence within South African higher learning institutions. *South African Journal of Information Management*, *27*(1), a1939. Advance online publication. DOI: 10.4102/sajim.v27i1.1939

Mortati, M., Mullagh, L., & Schmidt, S. (2022). Design-led policy and governance in practice: A global perspective. *Policy Design and Practice*, *5*(4), 1–11. DOI: 10.1080/25741292.2022.2152592

Online, C. I. G. I. (2024). *Generative AI policy in higher education: A preliminary survey*. Centre for International Governance Innovation. https://www.cigionline.org/publications/generative-ai-policy-in-higher-education-a-preliminary-survey/

Reuel, A., & Undheim, T. (2024). Why generative AI requires adaptive governance. *arXiv*. https://doi.org//arXiv.2406.04554DOI: 10.48550

Selwyn, N. (2024). On the limits of artificial intelligence (AI) in education. *Nordisk Tidsskrift for Pedagogikk og Kritikk*, *10*(1), 3–14. DOI: 10.23865/ntpk.v10.6062

Taeihagh, A. (2025). Governance of generative artificial intelligence. *Policy and Society*, *44*(1), 1–22. DOI: 10.1093/polsoc/puaf001

Tertiary Education Quality and Standards Agency. (2023). *Guidance note: Artificial intelligence in higher education*. https://www.teqsa.gov.au

UNESCO. (2021). *AI and education: Guidance for policy-makers*. DOI: 10.54675/PCSP7350

UNESCO. (2021). *Recommendation on the ethics of artificial intelligence*. https://www.unesco.org

UNESCO. (2024). *AI competency frameworks for students and teachers*. https://www.unesco.org

Universities South Africa. (2024). *Adapt or perish: A call for academics to embrace artificial intelligence*. https://usaf.ac.za

Verhoef, A. H. (2025). *AI in higher education: Rethinking student success* [Conference presentation]. Siyaphumelela Network Student Success Conference, South Africa.

Zawacki-Richter, O., Marín, V. I., Bond, M., & Gouverneur, F. (2019). Systematic review of research on artificial intelligence applications in higher education—Where are the educators? *International Journal of Educational Technology in Higher Education, 16*(1), 39. DOI: 10.1186/s41239-019-0171-0

Chapter 13

Re-Tooling Research Pedagogy in Higher Education Contexts:
A Systemic Analysis of Human-AI Practices

Belqes Al-Sowaidi
https://orcid.org/0000-0002-3752-2684
Two Oceans Graduate Institute, South Africa

Masnoenah Kamalie
Two Oceans Graduate Institute, South Africa

Huda Saif
Prince Sattam Bin Abdulaziz University, Saudi Arabia

ABSTRACT

This chapter examines how final-year undergraduate and postgraduate students at four Global South universities use digital and AI-enhanced research tools in research modules. Employing a convergent-parallel mixed-methods design, the study integrates survey data, TOPOI-coded supervisor feedback, and structural and discourse metrics from student research proposals. Analyses conducted in SPSS, JASP, and MAXQDA reveal distinct institutional profiles: Taiz University and TOGI demonstrate methodological strength but lower readability; IPSA shows reliance on generative tools with weak referencing; and PSAU exhibits high lexical diversity with limited methodological depth. Cross-stream triangulation shows that proposal

DOI: 10.4018/979-8-3373-4521-5.ch013

quality emerges from the interaction of tool use, feedback practices, and institutional conditions. The chapter concludes with equity-focused pedagogical interventions to strengthen research training.

1. INTRODUCTION

Recent developments in educational technology, including cloud-based reference managers, digital libraries, automated writing tools, and AI applications, have improved support for student researchers throughout all stages of the academic writing process. Empirical evidence demonstrates that such tools enhance student work organisation, clarity, and correctness (Mohammed, 2025; Ramadhan et al., 2024). Citation managers and plagiarism detectors enable novices to adhere to scholarly conventions, while AI-driven grammar checkers and large language models reduce mechanical errors and provide stylistic suggestions (Knight et al., 2020; Ramadhan et al., 2024). Despite these advances, adoption remains uneven across disciplines, academic levels, and cultural contexts (Shahzad et al., 2024; Xu et al., 2024). Students at well-resourced universities typically enjoy seamless access to advanced tools, whereas students in lower-resource settings face infrastructural and training barriers (Van Dijk & Van Deursen, 2019). Disciplinary norms further shape uptake: in translation studies, students frequently exploit machine translation engines, whereas Islamic studies cohorts often rely on specialised textual corpora (Bassnett, 2002; O'Hagan, 2013). As a result, comparative, multi-site evidence on how diverse student populations navigate and benefit from digitally mediated research environments remains limited (Venkatesh et al., 2003).

Responding to this gap, the present study examines how postgraduate and final-year undergraduate students in the Global South integrate digital research-support tools into their research practices and proposal development processes with particular attention to supervisory feedback and document-level structural quality. To achieve this, the study employs a convergent-parallel mixed-methods design (Creswell & Plano Clark, 2018),enabling the integration of quantitative and qualitative perspectives on tool adoption and research development. The research is conducted across four institutions in the Global South: Taiz University (TU, Yemen), International Peace College South Africa (IPSA, South Africa), Two Oceans Graduate Institute (TOGI, South Africa), and Prince Sattam bin Abdulaziz University (PSAU, Saudi Arabia). These institutions represent contrasting research infrastructures and supervisory contexts. Taiz University offers a BA in English Language and Translation that exposes students to multilingual tasks under resource-constrained conditions, with intermittent electricity and unstable internet access. TOGI delivers research-intensive capstone modules through a fully online Bachelor of Education programme. PSAU integrates multiple digital tools and bilingual corpora within a resourced BA Translation programme. Each site reflects distinct infrastructural and epistemic affordances, offering comparative insights into digitally mediated research support. Combining cohort-specific surveys, supervisor-tracked revision analyses, and proposal-structure metrics paints a layered portrait of how postgraduate and final-year undergraduate students adopt, value, and benefit from digital research-support tools.

1.2 Objectives and Research Questions

The objectives of this study are threefold. First, it evaluates which research-support tools students adopt and how they perceive their usefulness. Second, it examines how students respond to supervisor feedback and how revisions are reflected in the structural and discourse features of their proposals, such as sectioning, readability, and citation density. Third, this study investigates how thematic feedback patterns, particularly those classified through the TOPOI framework, align with students' self-reported tool usage and the quality of their final proposals. Three guiding research questions are derived from these objectives: [Q1] Which digital research-support tools do students adopt most frequently, and how useful do they find them in the context of proposal writing? [Q2] How do students respond to supervisor feedback, and how do their proposals' structural and discourse features differ across institutions and academic levels? [Q3] Finally, what do thematic feedback patterns reveal about students' educational development needs, and how do these patterns align with survey-reported tool usefulness and observed proposal quality?

1.1 Hypotheses

Two hypotheses underpin the investigation of this study, linked to differences between undergraduate and postgraduate cohorts. For the undergraduate group, it is hypothesised that higher perceived usefulness of digital research-support tools will be positively associated with improved structural quality in their proposals, particularly in clearer sectioning and increased citation density. For the postgraduate group, it is hypothesised that higher adoption of digital tools and stronger engagement with supervisor feedback, reflected in insertions, deletions, and comment resolution, will be associated with greater structural and rhetorical sophistication in final submissions.

1.3 Rationale and Significance

Although digital research support tools are increasingly embedded in higher education workflows, much existing research remains limited to single-site studies or relies primarily on self-reported data. This narrow scope restricts the generalisability of findings across institutions and cultural contexts (Ramadhan et al., 2024; Venkatesh et al., 2003). Moreover, despite their growing reliance on digital tools, fields such as translation studies, Islamic studies, and Arabic language research are underrepresented in the broader literature on AI integration and pedagogy. This study addresses these gaps by combining three complementary streams of data: survey responses, supervisor-tracked revisions, and proposal-structure metrics. Including institutions from Yemen, South Africa, and Saudi Arabia enables cross-contextual comparisons that account for distinct infrastructural realities, supervisory cultures, and writing norms. Focusing on text-based and supervisor-embedded academic interventions, this study adopts a novel approach that improves the relevance of validity for individual institutions and aligns with educational theory, research, pedagogy, and revision literacy frameworks.

2. LITERATURE REVIEW

Research on artificial intelligence in higher education has expanded rapidly, spanning studies on academic writing support, feedback systems, translation technologies, and digital equity. However, this literature remains fragmented across disciplinary, methodological, and regional boundaries. To situate the present study clearly, the review is organised around three intersecting strands: (a) AI-supported academic writing and research tools, (b) human-AI collaboration and feedback literacy in higher education, and (c) institutional and equity-related dimensions of AI adoption in Global South contexts. This thematic structure clarifies how prior work informs the study's design, analysis, and interpretation.

Digital tools now permeate higher-education research workflows, from cloud reference managers and digital libraries to AI writing assistants. Many empirical studies confirm that these technologies enhance students' organisation and adherence to academic conventions (Ajabshir & Ebadi, 2023). Citation managers, for instance, help novice researchers maintain accurate referencing, while grammar checkers and automated writing evaluation (AWE) systems have been shown to effectively reduce mechanical errors such as punctuation, sentence structure, and word form issues (Fan & Ma, 2023). Nevertheless, uptake remains uneven across disciplines and programmes (Qu et al., 2024; Shahzad et al., 2024). In Global South and Arab contexts, infrastructure gaps and cultural factors further mediate use (Al-Ansari, 2010). Alsadika et al. (2024) show that e-learning platforms and mobile apps can significantly boost Arabic-language learners' motivation and comprehension, but the digital divide and limited teacher training often limit these gains. This reflects a broader digital-literacy challenge: access alone is insufficient without structured pedagogical support (Al-Sabbagh, 2023; Al-Sowaidi & Clarke, 2025).

Recent studies on AI-supported language tools continue to underscore the importance of human-AI collaboration. Klimova et al. (2023), for example, synthesise 46 empirical studies on neural machine-translation (NMT) in the educational context. Their analysis shows that services such as Google Translate and ChatGPT can accelerate comprehension and support critical literacy, yet they frequently mishandle cultural nuance and idiomatic expressions. Their review therefore recommends explicit post-editing training so learners can critique and refine machine output, a "human–machine collaboration" strategy that deepens learning. Evidence from real tasks supports this view. Yang et al. (2023) show that novice translators find NMT post-editing faster than manual translation, yet are still dependent on human revision for semantic and cultural accuracy. Complementing these findings, Shin & Chon (2023) analyse second-language learners' post-editing moves and report that success hinges on metalinguistic reflection and guided feedback skills, which are absent when AI is used uncritically. Al Sawi & Allam (2024) provide parallel evidence in the context of audiovisual translation. Their analysis of Arabic subtitles for the film Birdman shows that only the human translator uses contextual notes and flexible reformulations for culturally loaded phrases, whereas ChatGPT relies on more literal renderings. These studies highlight AI's limitations with nuanced content and reinforce the consensus that AI should complement, not replace, human insight. Notably, Chiu & Rospigliosi (2025) build on this argument by demonstrating that successful human-AI collaboration in education relies on developing metacognitive skills. When students are trained to reflect on AI suggestions and revise critically, they better understand feedback and develop transferable writing skills competence. This aligns closely with tracked-change analyses of supervisor feedback, in which the challenge is not access to tools but the ability to interpret and act on feedback signals.

Other domain-specific reviews reach parallel conclusions. Alwazna et al. (2025), in their review of technology in Arabic legal translation, note that computer-assisted translation (CAT) and neural machine translation systems are now indispensable for drafting and localising legal statutes, yet human post-editing remains critical. Legal Arabic has specialised terminology and culturally embedded concepts, so automated outputs demand careful expert revision. Omar & Salih (2024) echo this in their systematic review of English-Arabic MT post-editing, noting that most studies focus on software optimisation while largely overlooking translators' skill development. They argue that post-editing is an essential skill of digital literacy that still receives scant curricular attention. They call for programmes that cultivate cultural insight, critical thinking, and evaluative competence. Extending the critique, Nguyen et al. (2025) synthesise 20 empirical AI-translation studies and show that efficiency gains can erode pedagogical depth and equity unless educators embed structured instructional frameworks. One proposed solution is to embed AI directly into curriculum design itself. Padovano & Cardamone (2024) argue that human-AI collaboration in curriculum development can strengthen competency-based education when implemented as a scaffolded, locally adapted framework. Drawing on case evidence from engineering and management education, they demonstrate how AI-assisted semantic analysis, natural language processing, and data-informed curricular design can support educators in drafting content and aligning competencies. At the same time, human instructors ensure contextual relevance, disciplinary rigour, and equitable access. This approach resonates with institutional contrasts found in Global-South contexts, where infrastructural gaps demand tailored toolkits rather than one-size-fits-all adoption. The same warning appears in (Zubaidi et al. (2025), who evaluate a ChatGPT-supported writing model for Arabic learners. Although 88% of participants exceeded baseline proficiency, the system produced frequent contextual and lexical miscues. Their tri-dimensional human-AI collaboration framework, therefore, assigns drafting and brainstorming to the AI, while human instructors validate, edit, and ensure situational appropriateness. A meta-analysis by Wang & Fan (2025) of 51 experiments across 13 countries corroborates the same pattern. Generative AI tools yield significant gains in surface accuracy (g = 0.87) but only modest improvements in higher-order thinking unless instructor scaffolds and discipline-specific rubrics are in place. Classroom studies further echo this mediation effect. Kurt & Kurt (2024) find that Turkish pre-service teachers welcomed ChatGPT's rapid feedback on structure and vocabulary, yet still rely on instructor guidance to resolve genre conventions and discourse cohesion. Likewise, Gu et al. (2025) show that embedding explicit digital-literacy modules into Arabic teacher training significantly boosted student engagement and technical skill, but only when activities were carefully scaffolded. (Nguyen (2025) further observes that ChatGPT's benefits taper off without structured human feedback, and (Tran, 2023) reports that while AI comments trigger more surface-level revisions than instructor feedback, deeper content issues are better addressed by the latter. These findings reinforce the consensus that AI should augment, not replace, expert guidance, and they underscore the importance of pedagogical frameworks that cultivate critical post-editing, reflective revision, and adaptive digital literacy.

While prior research has explored digital and AI-supported tools in higher education, much of it has been limited to single contexts, narrow disciplinary foci, or tool-specific evaluations (e.g., grammar checkers, machine translation, or feedback systems). The present study extends this scholarship by adopting a comparative, multi-site design across four Global-South institutions, triangulating student surveys, supervisor feedback analysis, and structural discourse metrics. Unlike previous studies that rely on self-reported data, this work systematically integrates tracked revisions, coded supervisor comments, and Coh-Metrix[1] indices, offering a more holistic account of how digital tools shape research development. This layered approach not only situates tool adoption within pedagogical practices but also generates actionable, curriculum-oriented recommendations tailored to diverse institutional realities.

In summary, while prior research has explored isolated aspects of AI tool use, feedback practices, and proposal development, this study uniquely triangulates multiple data streams to investigate how these elements interact across four Global-South institutions. This integrated approach addresses gaps in comparative digital pedagogy research and directly informs the study's research questions regarding adoption patterns, feedback integration, and writing outcomes.

3. METHODOLOGY

This study adopts a parallel mixed-methods design to capture the layered dimensions of student research practices across four Global South institutions. Quantitative and qualitative data were collected concurrently. Each dataset was analysed independently. The findings were then merged during interpretation to generate a multidimensional account of how students adopt digital and AI research tools, how supervisors provide feedback, and how research writing quality develops (Creswell & Plano Clark, 2018).The study maintained cogency and prevented premature cross-contamination by keeping data streams analytically independent while allowing triangulation of findings.

3.1 Research Context and Participants

Data were collected between July 2024 and July 2025 from four institutions representing diverse educational ecosystems: Taiz University (TU), International Peace College South Africa (IPSA), Two Oceans Graduate Institute (TOGI), and Prince Sattam bin Abdulaziz University (PSAU). These sites were chosen purposefully to reflect linguistic, infrastructural, and curricular contrasts (Wadasinghe, 2025). Participants included postgraduate students (MA/PhD in Translation; Honours/MA in Islamic Studies) and final-year undergraduates (capstone modules in Education and Translation). Ethical approval and informed consent were secured at all sites. Demographic variables such as age, gender, programme level, and prior experience with digital tools were recorded to contextualise results and allow for stratified comparative analyses (Al-Ansari, 2010).

3.2 Data Collection Streams

3.2.1 Stream 1: Student Survey on Tool Use and Perceptions

A structured survey was administered using Microsoft Forms, selected for its institutional integration, mobile compatibility, and secure data management features (the full questionnaire is provided in Appendix A). The survey investigated the frequency and perceived usefulness of a wide range of digital and artificial-intelligence-assisted research tools, including writing assistants such as ChatGPT and Grammarly, reference managers like Zotero and Mendeley, and collaborative platforms such as Google Docs. In addition, items addressed barriers to adoption, including limited access to premium tools and insufficient training opportunities. Anonymised responses were exported to Excel and CSV file formats, then analysed using both JASP and SPSS statistics software. Descriptive statistics were used to determine baseline patterns of tool usage, while chi-square and independent sample t-tests were employed to highlight significant differences across institutions and levels of study. This survey provided the quantitative foundation for understanding how students position digital tools within their research practices (Zawacki-Richter et al., 2019).

3.2.2 Stream 2: Supervisor Feedback and Revision Analysis

Students submitted paired proposal drafts (original and supervisor-annotated) in Microsoft Word. Revision metadata were extracted using a custom VBA macro informed by established revision-analysis frameworks for tracking writing changes, capturing insertions, deletions, and margin comments (Conijn et al., 2022), and were complemented by a Python pipeline (zipfile + lxml) for batch processing and XML validation of edit markers (w:ins, w:del, w:comment).[2]

To interpret supervisor comments beyond surface-level edits, a stratified 20% sample of margin comments was qualitatively coded using MAXQDA software into categories such as grammar, style, structure, citation, and clarification (Ajabshir & Ebadi, 2023). Reliability ($\kappa > 0.80$) was achieved through double coding. MAXQDA's joint displays integrated these thematic codes with edit frequencies, highlighting patterns of supervisory emphasis on methodological rigor, citation practice, or argument clarity. Building on this, the TOPOI model-originally developed in the field of intercultural communication (Hermans, 2018; Hoffman & Verdooren, 2018), was adapted as a diagnostic coding scaffold for supervisor feedback. The model was restructured into eight analytical categories (T1–T8): methodology, planning, literature, organisation, referencing, argumentation, intentions/alignment, and surface issues. Supervisor margin comments were re-coded into these categories, then normalised per 1,000 words and aggregated by institution. This allowed for the generation of comparable feedback profiles and the application of BH-FDR-adjusted inferential contrasts (Benjamini-Hochberg False Discovery Rate correction).

In this study, TOPOI serves as a functional analytic framework (distinct from the classical rhetorical term *topoi*), enabling cross-stream linkage with discourse analysis in Stream 3-for example, aligning T5 (referencing) with citation density, or T3 (literature engagement) with MTLD[3] via MAXQDA joint displays and shared file identifiers.

Table 1. Mapping of TOPOI Framework to Study-Specific Categories

Original TOPOI Domain	Adapted Feedback Category (T1–T8)	Application in This Study
Language	T8 – Surface-level issues	Grammar, phrasing, and formatting.
Structure	T4 – Organisation T6 – Argumentation	Logical sequencing, coherence, and argumentative flow.
Persons	T7 – Intentions/Alignment	Fit between aims, research questions, and methods.
Organisation	T1 – Methodology T2 – Planning	Research design detail, sampling, procedural clarity, and planning.
Intentions	T3 – Literature Engagement T5 – Referencing	Integration of prior scholarship, citation accuracy, and bibliographic consistency.

3.2.3 Stream 3: Proposal Structure and Discourse Analysis

Ten anonymised final proposals from each institution were analysed to assess both structural and discourse-level qualities of academic writing. Structural metrics-including total word count, number of sections, citation counts, and citation density per 1,000 words-were extracted from the DOCX files using python-DOCX and cross-validated by parsing the corresponding PDF renderings via ChatPDF API[4] to ensure consistency across formats. Text complexity and cohesion were assessed with Coh-Metrix (Graesser et al., 2004), which provided indices of syntactic complexity, referential cohesion, and deep cohesion. Lexical diversity was assessed using the measure of textual lexical diversity (MTLD) to quantify the breadth of vocabulary use across proposals.

To capture rhetorical organisation, proposal introductions were coded using Swales' (1990) CARS[5] model (move 1: establishing a territory; move 2: establishing a niche; move 3: occupying the niche), supplemented by extended genre-analysis frameworks (Permyakova et al., 2024) to operationalise steps within each component (e.g., gap signalling, purpose statements, methodological announcements). Alignment with the study design was ensured by linking CARS move/step scores to discourse and feedback metrics: correlations were computed with TOPOI categories (e.g., T3 literature engagement, T6 argumentation), structural measures (citation density, sections per proposal), and quality indicators (Flesch readability, MTLD). This dual-layered approach enabled the mapping of quantitative text-quality indicators (e.g., readability and MTLD lexical diversity) alongside qualitative rhetorical features (e.g., gap signalling, argumentation strength, organisational coherence) across institutions.

3.3 Ethical Considerations

Ethical approval was obtained from the institutional review boards (IRBs) or ethics committees at all four participating institutions: Taiz University, IPSA, TOGI, and Prince Sattam University. Participation was voluntary, with informed consent secured from all students and supervisors involved. Anonymity and confidentiality were strictly maintained across all data streams-surveys, supervisor feedback and final proposals. Identifiable information was removed, and all data were stored on secure, institutionally approved platforms.

Examining AI-assisted research tools alongside supervisory feedback practices raises distinct ethical considerations that extend beyond standard research protocols. Students' use of generative-AI platforms such as ChatGPT and Grammarly raised concerns about authorship attribution, academic integrity, and the potential for uncritical over-reliance. These were addressed by framing AI as a drafting and support tool, with students guided to reflect on, revise, and appropriately cite its use. The study also recognised the risk of algorithmic bias in AI-generated feedback and language suggestions, which may privilege dominant linguistic norms and misrepresent intent in multilingual or culturally situated academic writing. As a safeguard, AI outputs were always mediated through human review and critical post-editing, ensuring that evaluative decisions remained context-sensitive and pedagogically grounded. A further ethical consideration concerned the analysis of supervisor comments and revision trails, which was conducted with full awareness of power asymmetries in supervisory relationships. Coded feedback was anonymised and interpreted within the institutional context to prevent individual attribution or evaluative judgment. This ethical framing ensured alignment with global best practices for responsible AI integration, student rights, and intercultural sensitivity in higher-education research.

3.4 Integration and Triangulation

Following independent analysis, datasets were anonymised and merged using a shared student ID schema to enable cross-stream triangulation. Integration was achieved through multiple strategies. Statistical testing examined correlations and regression analyses linking tool adoption, supervisor comments, and proposal indicators. MAXQDA joint displays were used to align thematic codes with revision counts and cohesion indices, enabling a mixed-method synthesis. Visualisation outputs, including principal component analysis (PCA)[6] clustering, heatmaps, and scatterplots, were generated to reveal institutional contrasts and developmental patterns.

Tool selection across streams was grounded in their analytical affordances: Microsoft Forms for survey deployment; Word VBA and Python for revision metadata extraction; MAXQDA for qualitative coding and mixed method integration; Python-DOCX and ChatPDF for structural parsing and validation; Coh-Metrix for automated discourse metrics; SPSS and JASP for robust statistical testing; and rhetorical move coding for genre-sensitive proposal analysis. This layered methodology ensured rigor, transparency, and pedagogical relevance. This study established a coherent evidence base for designing targeted research-writing interventions at both undergraduate and postgraduate levels by linking survey insights, supervisor interventions, and discourse outcomes.

4. DATA ANALYSIS AND RESULTS

4.1. Reliability and Validity

Internal consistency, reliability, and construct validity were assessed to ensure the soundness of the survey scales prior to conducting any inferential tests. Cronbach's alpha was used to evaluate reliability across the nine extracted factors, yielding excellent internal consistency for the first factor ($\alpha = .98$), good reliability for factors 2–7 ($\alpha = .73–.82$), and marginal yet acceptable reliability for factors 8–9 ($\alpha = .60–.69$). These results support the internal coherence of the scales and suggest that the survey sufficiently captured students' use of digital and AI tools. Targeted item refinement, such as revising low-loading or cross-loading items, may further improve the reliability of factors 8 and 9. Moreover, construct validity was examined using a two-stage process: exploratory factor analysis (EFA) followed by confirmatory factor analysis (CFA). Sampling adequacy and factorability were confirmed (KMO = .797; Bartlett's $\chi^2(903) = 3775.37$, $p < .001$). The EFA, conducted on the full survey dataset ($N = 87$) using principal axis factoring with oblimin rotation, revealed a nine-factor structure representing distinct domains, including AI-assisted writing, advanced research, collaborative tools, and traditional validation practices. Factors were retained based on parallel analysis, eigenvalues > 1, and the scree-plot criterion.

The CFA yielded an acceptable to good model fit ($\chi^2/df = 2.01$; CFI = .93; TLI = .92; RMSEA = .056; SRMR = .045), with most standardised loadings exceeding .50, indicating convergent validity. To assess cross-site comparability, a multi-group confirmatory factor analysis (MGCFA) was conducted across the four participating institutions (TU, IPSA, TOGI, and PSAU) and demonstrated configural, metric, and scalar invariance (ΔCFI $\leq$ .01; ΔRMSEA $\leq$ .015). These findings indicate that students across contexts interpreted survey items consistently, thus supporting measurement equivalence and enabling robust cross-institutional comparisons.

4.2 Section 1: Survey of Digital & AI Tools Usage (Stream 1)

This section presents the results of the survey administered to the full participant cohort (N = 87), which included both undergraduate and postgraduate students from four institutions. The purpose of the analysis is to understand how students across different institutional contexts adopt and use digital and AI-supported tools within research pedagogy. Analysis of the survey responses shows that students rely on a wide range of tools in their research activities, using an average of approximately five digital or AI tools each. At the same time, clear differences emerge across institutions in terms of which tools are preferred and how frequently they are used. These patterns are visualised in Figure 1, which compares the most commonly used tools across the four sites. The cleaned survey data, exported from Microsoft Forms as a CSV file, were analysed using JASP and Python (Matplotlib[7]). A chi-square test was applied to examine whether tool usage patterns differed significantly by institutional context. The results confirm that institutional affiliation plays a significant role in shaping students' tool preferences. For example, students at one institution show stronger use of specialised data-analysis software such as SPSS, whereas students at other institutions rely more heavily on general-purpose AI assistants, including ChatGPT and Gemini.

Overall, the most widely adopted tools across all institutions are generative AI platforms (ChatGPT), collaborative writing tools (Google Docs), and Grammarly. Among these, ChatGPT consistently ranks as the most frequently used tool across sites, followed by Google Docs and Grammarly. These findings suggest that differences in local infrastructure, curricular design, and supervisory practices strongly influence how students engage with digital and AI-supported research tools.

Figure 1. High-frequency digital research tools reported by students across four institutions.

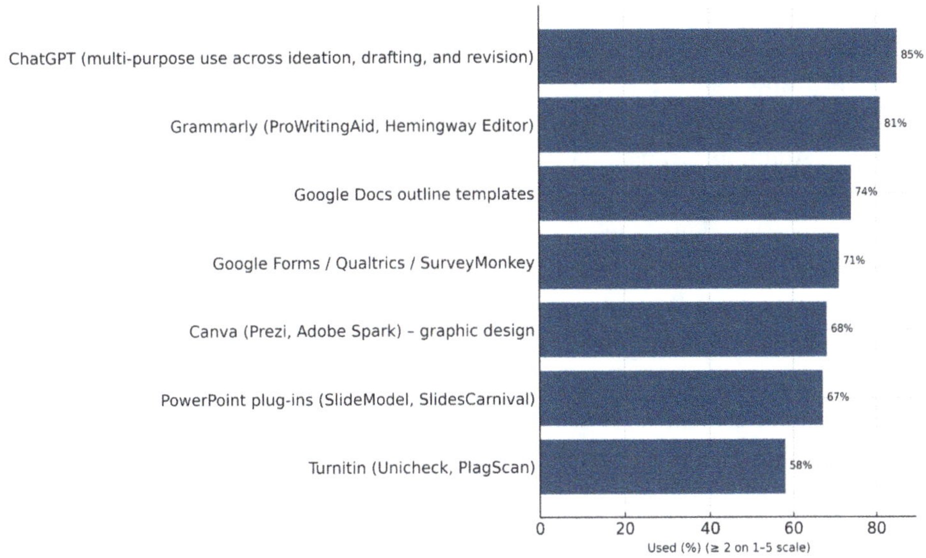

Note. *Percentages represent respondents reporting use ≥ 2 on a 1–5 scale (N = 87).*

Building on the usage patterns established in the preceding section, the aggregated survey findings indicate that a limited set of digital tools now structures students' research practices across institutions. Collaboration platforms, most notably Google Docs, were consistently valued for drafting, shared revision, and supervisor interaction, while reference managers such as Zotero and Mendeley were widely adopted to support citation organisation and bibliographic accuracy. Generative AI tools were most strongly embedded in early research activities, including idea generation, outlining, and framing, underscoring their growing role in the preparatory and cognitive stages of research. This concentration on a small set of tools suggests that students' digital research practices are shaped more by institutional guidance and supervisory norms than by the full range of available tools.

By contrast, specialised literature mapping and synthesis tools, including Litmaps, Rayyan, and ResearchRabbit, showed markedly lower uptake. This disparity suggests that students' engagement with digital research support remains concentrated on general-purpose tools, with limited exposure to advanced evidence synthesis workflows. The uneven adoption pattern indicates a training and curriculum-alignment gap rather than resistance to digital tools themselves. The pattern points to a pedagogical gap rather than a technological one, highlighting the need for structured instruction and supervisory guidance that extend beyond drafting support to encompass systematic literature exploration and critical synthesis.

Alongside reported usage patterns, the survey also captured structural and pedagogical barriers that shape students' adoption of digital and AI-supported tools. The most frequently reported barrier was limited access to premium or institutional versions of tools (66.7%), followed by lack of training or tutorials (62.5%). Nearly half of respondents cited low confidence in using digital tools (45.8%), while technical complexity (37.5%) and time constraints (37.5%) were also prominent concerns. Additional constraints included unreliable internet access (20.8%) and language-related challenges (8.3%).

Taken together, these barriers point to systemic constraints rather than individual reluctance, reinforcing the conclusion that uneven adoption is driven primarily by access, training, and institutional support structures. While students demonstrate strong willingness to engage with generative and collaborative tools, structural limitations restrict their ability to use a broader range of research-support technologies consistently and critically. These findings underscore the need for institutional strategies that expand access to premium tools, embed AI-literacy and digital research skills into curricula, and support supervisor-led modelling of ethical, reflective, and effective tool use. The results from this stream emphasise that balanced integration is required not only for ideation and writing, but also for research organisation, analysis, and synthesis. Figure 2 visualises these constraints by summarising the most frequently reported barriers to digital and AI-supported tool adoption across the full participant cohort.

Figure 2. Reported barriers to digital and AI-supported tool adoption (percentage of respondents; multiple responses allowed).

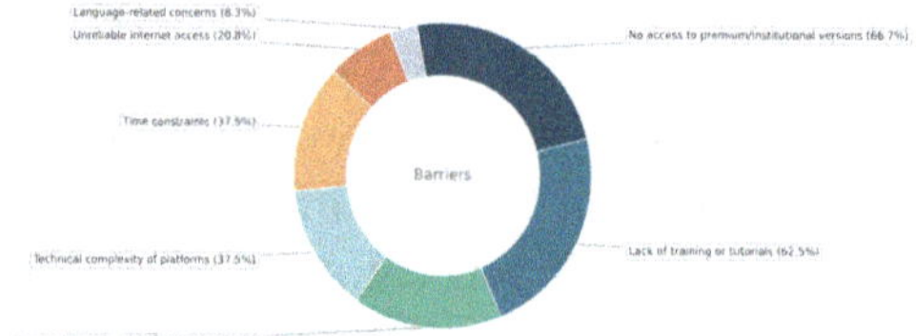

4.3 Section 2: Supervisor Feedback Analysis (TOPOI - Stream 2)

This analysis covers the same participant subset aligned with streams 1 and 3. Feedback rates are normalised per 1,000 words to control for document length and allow meaningful comparison across institutions. Coding followed the adapted TOPOI scheme noted in the methodology.

Analytic frame: Supervisor annotations on proposals were coded into eight categories to capture feedback emphases beyond surface edits and to align with feedback-literacy constructs:

- T1 – Methodology: design, sampling, instruments, and procedural clarity.
- T2 – Planning: staging of tasks, timelines, feasibility, and sequencing.
- T3 – Literature engagement: integration, critique, and synthesis of sources; identifying gaps.
- T4 – Organisation: overall structure, section order, headings, and logical flow.
- T5 – Referencing: citation style, accuracy, completeness, and consistency.
- T6 – Argumentation: logic, evidentiary support, development of claims, and coherence of reasoning.
- T7 – Intentions/alignment: fit between aims, research questions, and chosen methods.
- T8 – Surface-level issues: grammar, phrasing, punctuation, formatting, and style.

Although all eight TOPOI categories were used in the coding process, only categories with non-trivial frequencies across institutions are reported in the descriptive table for interpretive clarity.

4.3.1 Descriptive Profile (Institutional Patterns)

Clear institutional tendencies emerge (see Table 2). TOGI exhibits the strongest methodology-oriented supervision, combining higher methodology/planning signalling with elevated literature engagement and comparatively more surface/formal signalling. TU shows substantial literature engagement, with a strong emphasis on methodology and planning, indicating concurrent pressure for theoretical integration and design clarity. IPSA presents a balanced profile with moderate methodology/planning, relatively stronger support for argument development, and routine attention to referencing, consistent with stream 1 evidence of heavier AI-assistant usage and a supervisory push toward consolidating scholarship and citation practice. PSAU remains an outlier with very low annotation density across categories, consistent with a low-feedback environment. Overall, TU and TOGI align with methodology-oriented feedback cultures, IPSA leans toward literature/referencing consolidation with argumentation support, and PSAU shows minimal supervisory intervention.

These distinctions corroborate stream 1 and set up the cross-stream links in stream 3 (e.g., T5 with citation density; T3 with MTLD).

Table 2. TOPOI feedback rates by institution (signals per 1,000 words)

TOPOI Category[8]	TU	IPSA	PSAU	TOGI
T1 – Methodology	1.68	1.44	0.05	**3.86**
T2 – Planning	1.10	0.85	0.04	**2.95**
T3 – Literature	**2.25**	1.40	0.01	2.56
T5 – Referencing	**0.41**	0.28	0.04	0.33
T6 – Argumentation	0.15	**0.20**	0.02	0.18
T8 – Surface-level	0.12	0.04	0.00	**0.61**

Note. Values represent normalised feedback signals per 1,000 words. TOPOI categories T4 (Organisation) and T7 (Intentions/Alignment) occurred at very low frequencies and are therefore excluded from the table for readability.

These institutional feedback profiles provide the basis for the cross-stream analysis in Stream 3, where feedback categories are examined in relation to proposal-level textual and structural outcomes.

4.4 Inferential Analysis and Interpretation of BH–FDR-Adjusted Pairwise Contrasts

4.4.1 Inferential Contrasts (BH–FDR)

To test whether the descriptive differences in supervisor feedback were statistically meaningful, pairwise institutional contrasts were conducted for the focal TOPOI categories, adjusting all p-values using the Benjamini-Hochberg False Discovery Rate (BH–FDR, $q = .05$). This correction controls the expected proportion of false positives across multiple comparisons while retaining good power. Results reported in Table 3 reveal clear and robust institutional differences in supervisor feedback patterns. TOGI registers significantly higher methodology feedback (T1) than both IPSA and PSAU. In the domain of literature engagement (T3), both TU and TOGI exceed PSAU. TU also provides significantly more referencing feedback (T5) than PSAU. In addition, TOGI shows significantly higher levels of surface-level feedback (T8) than IPSA. These effects remain statistically significant after BH–FDR adjustment and corroborate the institutional profiles identified in the descriptive analysis.

Table 3. Pairwise institutional contrasts in TOPOI categories (rates per 1,000 words; p values BH–FDR adjusted, q = .05)[9]

TOPOI	Institution A	Rate A/1k	Institution B	Rate B/1k	p (BH–FDR)
T1	PSAU	0.05	TOGI	3.86	**0.0000**
T1	IPSA	1.44	TOGI	3.86	**0.0000**
T3	PSAU	0.01	TOGI	2.56	**0.0000**
T3	PSAU	0.01	TU	2.25	**0.0000**
T5	PSAU	0.04	TU	0.41	**0.0002**
T8	IPSA	0.04	TOGI	0.61	**0.0000**

4.4.2 Interpretation of BH–FDR–Adjusted Pairwise Contrasts (Table 3)

All four institutions (TOGI, TU, IPSA, PSAU) are included in the inferential analysis. Table 3, reported in Section 4.4.1, presents only those pairwise differences in TOPOI feedback categories that remain statistically significant after Benjamini-Hochberg False Discovery Rate (BH–FDR) adjustment for multiple comparisons. Each row reflects a case where the second institution (Institution B) recorded a significantly higher frequency of feedback than the first (Institution A) in the specified TOPOI category, with values normalised per 1,000 words. For example, in T1 (Methodology), TOGI supervisors gave substantially more feedback (3.86 per 1,000 words) than those at PSAU (0.05), with the difference statistically significant at $p = 0.0000$ after BH-FDR correction.

These contrasts together show:

(i) TOGI supervisors provided significantly more feedback on methodology (T1) than both IPSA and PSAU;
(ii) TOGI and TU provided more literature engagement (T3) feedback than PSAU;
(iii) TU exceeded PSAU on referencing (T5); and
(iv) TOGI gave more surface-level feedback (T8) than IPSA.

The absence of a particular institutional pairing in Table 3 (e.g., TU vs IPSA on T1) indicates that no statistically significant difference was found between them in that category after adjustment, not that the institutions were excluded from analysis.

Figure 3. Distribution of TOPOI categories by institution (signals per 1,000 words, combined subset)

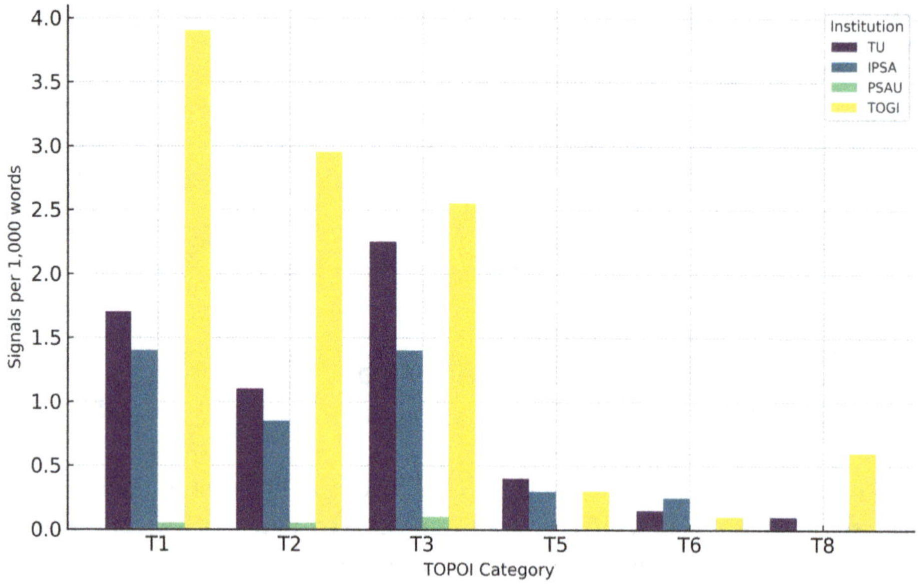

Figure 3 provides a visual summary of the descriptive patterns reported in Table 2, enabling rapid comparison of supervisor feedback emphasis across TOPOI categories and institutions. This chart displays institutional differences across six TOPOI feedback categories. Bar heights reflect average signal density. TOGI stands out in methodology (T1) and planning (T2). TU shows a strong emphasis on literature engagement (T3). IPSA appears moderate in referencing (T5) and argumentation (T6). PSAU remains consistently low across all categories. T4 (Organisation) and T7 (Intentions/Alignment) were omitted due to minimal presence across all institutions, enabling more explicit visual focus on the dominant patterns.

Complementing this comparative view, Figure 4 presents a heatmap that captures the full distribution of TOPOI feedback categories (T1–T8) across all four institutions using combined undergraduate and postgraduate data. Each cell represents the rate of supervisor comments per 1,000 words, with darker shading indicating higher prevalence. This visualisation reinforces the patterns observed in Figure 3 by highlighting TOGI's strong emphasis on methodology (T1) and planning (T2), TU's concentration on literature engagement (T3), IPSA's moderate feedback density, and PSAU's consistently low supervisory intervention. These two figures support rapid pattern recognition while illustrating both the magnitude and the distribution of institutional feedback styles.

Figure 4. Heatmap of Institutional TOPOI Profiles (signals per 1,000 words)

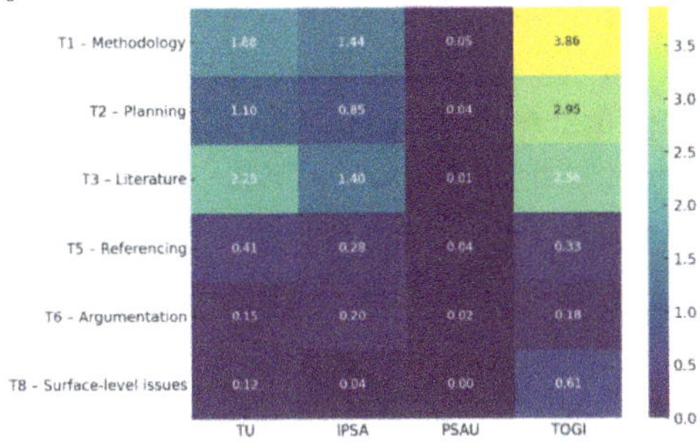

4.5 Section 3: Proposal Structure & Discourse Quality (Stream 3)

Stream 3 analyses final-year undergraduate and postgraduate research proposals from TU, IPSA, PSAU, and TOGI using automated structural and discourse metrics. These align with the same subset examined in streams 1 and 2. Structural indicators were extracted from DOCX files (word count, number of sections, in-text citations, citation density per 1,000 words) and cross-validated against PDF versions for consistency. Cohesion was computed via Coh-Metrix (referential and deep cohesion), and lexical diversity via MTLD. In line with the convergent-parallel design, stream 3 computations were conducted independently and integrated only at the interpretation stage. To assess whether supervisory emphasis (stream 2) translates into textual outcomes, institutional means for selected TOPOI categories-T5 (referencing) and T3 (literature engagement) are paired with citation density and MTLD, respectively. While planning feedback (T2) is central to the supervisory profiles identified in Stream 2, it is treated here as an indirect influence expressed through proposal length, sectioning, and structural density rather than as a separate analytic variable. This approach allows supervisory feedback to be traced as a latent influence on final output structure without re-analysing the feedback itself.

4.5.1 Structural Indicators

As summarised in Table 4, the structural indicators reveal clear institutional differences in proposal length, organisation, readability, and lexical diversity, which provide the empirical basis for the patterns discussed in this section. Two structural patterns emerge. The TU and TOGI proposals are longer and have more developed methodological sections, which correlate with lower Flesch readability, indicating more complex and technical language. PSAU proposals are shorter but contain more sections and achieve the highest readability and lexical diversity (MTLD), suggesting accessible structure and surface fluency. IPSA occupies a mid-range position: shorter than TU/TOGI but less fragmented than PSAU, and with citation density on par with TU. These structural tendencies align with stream 2's supervision profiles: high-feedback institutions tend to produce more elaborate but denser proposals, whereas lower-feedback environments favour brevity and surface coherence.

Table 4. Structural Indicators by Institution (Final Proposal Subset)

Institution	Word Count	Sections	Citation Density (/1,000 words)	Flesch	MTLD
TU	13,148.3	11.5	9.14	35.3	76.1
IPSA	7,862.2	16.2	9.24	43.0	74.8
PSAU	5,221.8	26.9	6.33	46.9	86.1
TOGI	11,450.0	14.8	8.02	41.2	79.4

4.5.2 Cohesion Indicators

Building on the structural patterns identified in the previous subsection, this section examines textual cohesion to clarify how proposal organisation and discourse flow vary across institutions. As shown in Table 5, PSAU exhibits the strongest deep cohesion and the highest readability scores, a pattern consistent with its shorter proposals, higher section counts, and explicit use of connective devices. These features support surface clarity and facilitate reader navigation. By contrast, TU and IPSA display lower deep cohesion values alongside reduced readability, reflecting theory-dense prose in which logical relationships are more frequently implicit and rely on disciplinary inference rather than overt cohesive markers. TOGI occupies an intermediate position, with moderate cohesion and readability levels that mirror its balanced proposal length and sectioning profile. Referential cohesion remains relatively stable across institutions, indicating that differences are driven primarily by discourse organisation rather than lexical overlap.

Overall, the cohesion metrics in Table 5 reinforce and expand upon the structural differences identified in Table 4. They indicate that readability and cohesion are shaped jointly by proposal design and supervisory expectations, rather than by length or lexical diversity alone. These findings provide a necessary foundation for the following subsection, which examines whether supervisory feedback patterns identified in Stream 2 are systematically associated with the cohesion and structural outcomes observed in Stream 3.

Table 5. Cohesion Metrics from Coh-Metrix by Institution

Institution	Referential Cohesion	Deep Cohesion	Flesch	MTLD
TU	0.04	8.9	35.3	76.1
IPSA	0.04	9.2	43.0	74.8
PSAU	0.03	11.4	46.9	86.1
TOGI	0.04	9.7	41.2	79.4

4.5.3 Cross-Stream Associations with TOPOI Feedback

Extending the structural and cohesion analyses presented in Sections 4.5.1 and 4.5.2, this subsection examines whether supervisory feedback patterns identified in Stream 2 leave measurable traces in Stream 3 proposal outputs. Specifically, it aligns referencing feedback (T5) with citation density and literature-engagement feedback (T3) with lexical diversity (MTLD) to trace feedback effects as latent influences on academic writing practices rather than as direct revisions.

4.5.3.1 T5 Feedback vs. Citation Density

Table 6 reports institutional means for referencing-related supervisory feedback (T5) alongside citation density in final proposals. A clear correspondence emerges. Institutions with stronger T5 feedback-most notably TU (0.41 signals per 1,000 words) and IPSA (0.28)-also exhibit the highest citation densities (9.14 and 9.24 citations per 1,000 words, respectively). This pattern suggests that sustained supervisory attention to referencing fosters habitual source anchoring and systematic citation practices in student writing. By contrast, PSAU records minimal T5 feedback (0.04), accompanied by substantially lower citation density (6.33), indicating weaker institutional reinforcement of referencing norms. TOGI occupies an intermediate position, with moderate T5 signalling (0.33) and proportionate citation density (8.02), reflecting a balanced but less intensive emphasis on referencing supervision. These trends indicate that referencing feedback functions not merely as corrective intervention but as a mechanism for shaping enduring academic attribution habits.

Table 6. Supervisor Referencing Feedback (T5) vs. Citation Density (Institutional Means)

Institution	T5 – Referencing (/1,000 words)	Citation Density (/1,000 words)
TU	0.41	9.14
IPSA	0.28	9.24
PSAU	0.04	6.33
TOGI	0.33	8.02

To support visual interpretation of this relationship, Figure 5 plots institutional averages with a fitted linear trendline. The scatterplot corroborates the tabulated results by showing a clear positive association between T5 feedback intensity and citation density. TU and IPSA cluster in the upper range on both axes, while PSAU appears in the lower-left quadrant, and TOGI aligns with the overall trend at a moderate level. The fitted trendline visually consolidates the relationship already evident in Table 6.

Figure 5. Relationship between T5 referencing feedback and citation density by institution

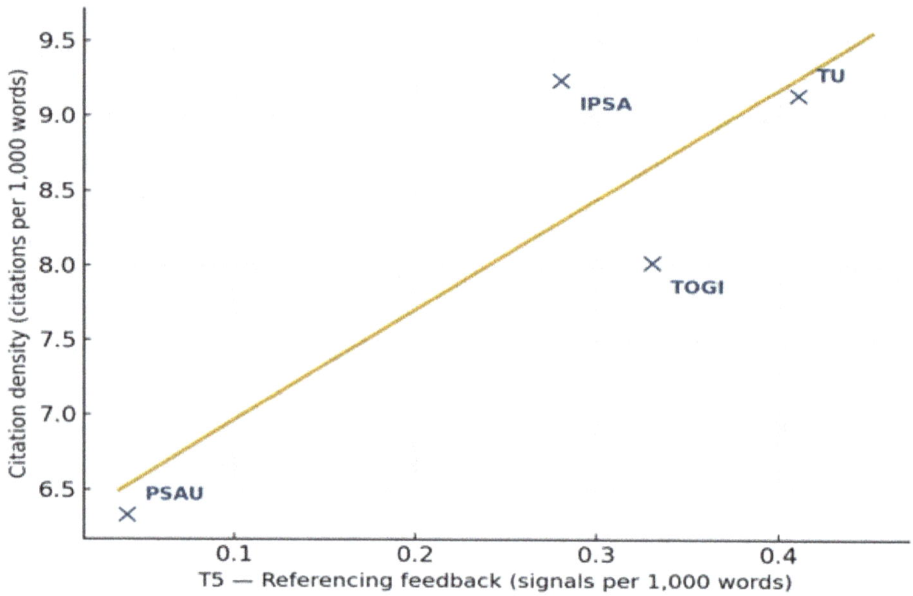

4.5.3.2 T3 Feedback vs. Lexical Diversity (MTLD)

Having established the association between referencing feedback (T5) and citation density in the previous subsection, this section turns to literature-engagement feedback (T3) to examine how supervisory emphasis on "closing the literature gap" is reflected in students' lexical diversity. Higher T3 feedback frequencies, observed most clearly at TOGI and TU, correlate with lower MTLD values. This pattern likely reflects the additive nature of "close the gap" literature feedback, which encourages students to incorporate additional sources without necessarily engaging in integrative synthesis. As a result, lexical variation may be compressed as source accumulation takes precedence over evaluative integration. PSAU, by contrast, records negligible T3 feedback and exhibits the highest MTLD, suggesting greater freedom of expression or reduced editorial intervention in student writing. IPSA occupies a mid-range position on both variables, indicating a balance between supervisory guidance and lexical flexibility. From a pedagogical perspective, these findings suggest that T3 feedback should be explicitly scaffolded to promote synthesis and evaluative citation practices, rather than relying on increased source volume alone.

Table 7. Supervisor Literature-Gap Feedback (T3) vs. Lexical Diversity (MTLD) (Institutional Means)

Institution	T3 – Literature (/1,000 words)	MTLD
TU	2.25	76.1
IPSA	1.40	74.8
PSAU	0.01	86.1
TOGI	2.56	79.4

The relationships evident in Tables 6 and 7 demonstrate that institutional feedback emphasis, particularly on referencing (T5) and literature engagement (T3), correlates with distinct textual outcomes in student proposals. To integrate these relationships across streams, Figure 6 synthesises both pairings into a comparative heatmap, illustrating how supervisory feedback practices align with output metrics across institutions. The heatmap presents each institution's average scores for two key feedback categories, T5 (referencing) and T3 (literature engagement), alongside the corresponding textual indicators of citation density and lexical diversity (MTLD). Rows represent institutions, while columns represent feedback and output variables. Colour shading enables rapid visual comparison of feedback intensity and its potential impact on writing outcomes. For example, TU and IPSA combine stronger T5 feedback with higher citation density, whereas PSAU exhibits weaker feedback emphasis alongside higher MTLD. TOGI occupies a mid-range position across both dimensions. In this way, the figure condenses the principal cross-stream patterns and reinforces the institutional profiles described above.

Figure 6. Cross-Stream Heatmap: T5/T3 vs. Citation Density/MTLD (Institutional Means)

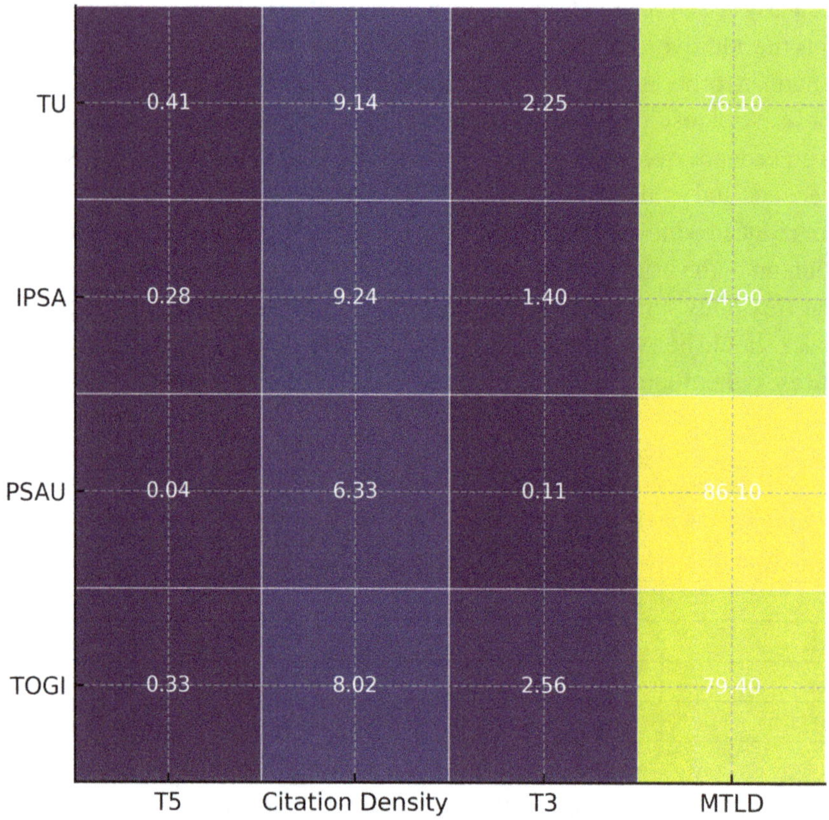

This heatmap displays each institution's average scores for the supervisory feedback categories T5 (referencing) and T3 (literature engagement), alongside the associated output metrics of citation density and lexical diversity (MTLD). Darker shading indicates higher values, supporting visual comparison of feedback intensity and writing outcomes. The figure highlights how feedback practices are systematically reflected in proposal-level textual features across institutions.

In summary, the data indicate that, across institutions, product-level indicators closely reflect the supervisory signatures identified in Stream 2 and the adoption patterns documented in Stream 1. Methodology-intensive environments such as TU and TOGI tend to produce longer, denser proposals with moderate to lower readability. In contrast, low-feedback settings, such as PSAU, yield more readable, highly segmented texts with broader lexical diversity but reduced evidentiary depth and lower citation density. IPSA occupies an intermediate position, characterised by mid-length proposals with concentrated citation practices. Collectively, these cross-stream patterns indicate that supervisory emphasis on referencing and engagement with the literature is reflected in the textual features of students' final proposals.

4.5.4 Statistical Power and Effect Size (Full Survey, N = 87)

This subsection evaluates the adequacy of statistical power and effect sizes underlying the institutional contrasts, cohort comparisons, and feedback-pattern analyses reported across Streams 1–3. All power and effect-size estimates were computed on the full survey cohort (N = 87) across all four institutions: TU, IPSA, TOGI, and PSAU. The survey results were consistent with the reliability and validity analyses presented earlier. A post hoc statistical power analysis was conducted using the full study cohort (N = 87), following conventional benchmarks (Cohen, 1988). Statistical power ($1-\beta$) was estimated for all major inferential tests, including ANOVA, t-tests, and chi-square analyses. The results indicated adequate power to detect medium-sized effects across all tests. Specifically:

- For institutional contrasts (ANOVA), power reached .81 with an effect size of $\eta^2 = .09$, reflecting a medium effect.
- For comparisons between graduate and undergraduate students (independent-samples t-tests), power was .84 with Cohen's d = .52, again reflecting a medium effect.
- For chi-square tests examining differences in supervisor comment distributions across TOPOI categories, the association measured Cramer's V = .28, representing a moderate relationship.

These findings confirm that the study attained sufficient statistical power ($\geq$ .80) to detect meaningful differences across institutions and academic levels. The observed effect sizes further indicate that the institutional patterns identified in tool adoption (Stream 1), supervisory feedback profiles (Stream 2), and proposal structure and discourse outcomes (Stream 3) reflect substantive pedagogical differences rather than artefacts of sample size or statistical noise. This confirmation of adequate power strengthens the validity of the cross-stream interpretations advanced in the following conclusion chapter, where these empirical patterns are integrated to address the study's research questions and hypotheses.

Table 8. Statistical Power and Effect Sizes (Full Cohort, N = 87)

Test	Power (1–β)	Effect Size	Interpretation
ANOVA (institutions)	.81	$\eta^2 = .09$	Medium effect, adequate power
t-test (postgraduate vs undergraduate)	.84	Cohen's d = .52	Medium effect, adequate power
Chi-square (TOPOI categories)	—	Cramer's V = .28	Moderate association

5. PEDAGOGICAL AND POLICY IMPLICATIONS

This section synthesises findings from the three analytical streams and translates them into actionable implications for research pedagogy in higher education in the Global South. Rather than treating students, supervisors, institutions, and policy as isolated domains, the discussion is organised around three interlocking levels of intervention: learner development, supervisory practice, and institutional–policy alignment. Together, these levels reflect how tool access, feedback practices, and writing development interact to shape research competence over time.

5.1 Learner Development and Research Writing Support

The findings indicate that differentiated learner support is essential, given the distinct institutional writing profiles identified across Streams 1-3. At TU and TOGI, students produced methodologically ambitious but linguistically dense proposals. These learners would benefit from targeted instruction in readability, cohesion, and lexical control, particularly through explicit teaching of signposting, connective devices, and genre-modelled paragraphing. Such interventions would enhance communicative clarity without undermining existing strengths in research design.

At IPSA, student writing reflected weaker integration of literature and inconsistent citation practices, corresponding to lower engagement with T3 (literature engagement) and T5 (referencing) in supervisory feedback. The data further suggest that unstructured reliance on generative AI tools contributed to surface-level paraphrasing rather than critical synthesis. This points to the need for structured academic literacy support that foregrounds evaluative reading, synthesis strategies, and responsible AI-assisted revision. By contrast, PSAU students produced readable and lexically rich texts but demonstrated limited methodological depth. Here, learner support should prioritise alignment with research, sampling logic, and design coherence to prevent superficial execution. These patterns underscore that student-level interventions must be context-responsive, addressing not only writing quality but also the interaction between tool use, feedback, and disciplinary expectations.

5.2 Supervisory Practice and Feedback Literacy

Stream 2 highlights the central role of supervision in shaping the development of research writing. Across institutions, corrective or generic feedback was less effective than targeted, dialogic, and developmentally sequenced feedback. At IPSA, supervisory practice would benefit from a stronger emphasis on modelling synthesis, aligning feedback explicitly with assessment criteria, and reinforcing deeper engagement with literature, particularly in areas corresponding to T3 and T5.

At TU and TOGI, supervisors demonstrated strong attention to methodological rigour (T1 and T2), but the findings suggest scope for expanding feedback to include audience awareness, coherence, and rhetorical structuring. Coaching students in how arguments unfold across problem statements, literature reviews, and design sections would help translate methodological strength into clearer scholarly communication.

These findings align with research showing that content-specific, scaffolded feedback supports autonomy, metacognitive awareness, and transfer of learning more effectively than evaluative commentary alone (Bitchener & Storch, 2022; Zhang & Hyland, 2023). Integrating TOPOI-informed feedback training into institutional development programs can enhance supervision as a formative process. This is especially effective when combined with staged drafting, peer review, and ethical AI-assisted revision practices, like those demonstrated in the Proposal Rehearsal Pipeline.

5.3 Institutional and Policy Alignment: Equity, Agency, and Ethical AI Use

Beyond individual learners and supervisors, the study reveals a clear institutional and policy mandate. Stream 1 data show substantial inequities in access to premium AI and research tools, with over two-thirds of students reporting limited access and inadequate training. Without institutional intervention, such disparities risk entrenching inequalities in research productivity and academic progression. Institutions should therefore prioritise equitable access to core platforms (e.g., reference managers, cohesion analysis tools, and qualitative analysis software) and embed AI literacy within undergraduate and postgraduate research curricula. Crucially, staff development must accompany these initiatives so that supervisors can model responsible, reflective, and pedagogically grounded tool use.

At a broader level, the findings demonstrate that learner agency in AI-supported research does not emerge from tool access alone. Instead, agency develops through structured interaction with feedback systems, where students learn to interpret, evaluate, and revise their work in relation to disciplinary norms. In this sense, AI operates as a cognitive amplifier only when embedded within ethically grounded pedagogical frameworks.

These conclusions align with international policy guidance on human-centred educational technology. UNESCO (2018, 2021) emphasises autonomy, transparency, and accountability in digitally mediated and AI-supported learning. The present study reinforces these principles by demonstrating that ethically scaffolded AI use supports critical thinking and sustained research competence rather than diminishing them.

6. CONCLUSION

This conclusion synthesises the chapter's findings by explicitly linking the study's research questions and hypotheses to the integrated evidence generated across the three analytical streams. In doing so, it demonstrates how patterns of digital and AI tool adoption, supervisory feedback practices, and proposal-level textual outcomes jointly shape research development across institutional contexts. The chapter addresses three interrelated research questions: (RQ1) students' adoption and perceived usefulness of digital and AI research-support tools; (RQ2) students' responses to supervisor feedback and institutional variation in the structural and discourse features of research proposals; and (RQ3) the extent to which thematic feedback patterns, operationalised through the TOPOI framework, align with observed differences in proposal quality.

Interpretation of these findings was guided by two hypotheses. For undergraduate students, H1 proposed that higher perceived usefulness of digital research-support tools would be associated with stronger structural features, particularly more evident sectioning and higher citation density. For postgraduate students, H2 proposed that greater tool adoption combined with more intensive engagement with supervisor feedback would be associated with higher levels of rhetorical and structural sophistication in final submissions. Evidence across streams converges in support of both hypotheses and reveals important moderating effects of institutional culture and feedback intensity.

Stream 1 confirmed enthusiastic uptake of generative AI and collaboration platforms. Adoption, however, was uneven and shaped by access, training, and institutional culture. This pattern is consistent with H1. Weaker undergraduate proposal structures coincided with limited engagement with advanced tools. Perceived usefulness translated into structural gains only when supported by adequate access and training. Stream 2 revealed distinct supervisory profiles: TU/TOGI emphasised methodology (T1/T2), IPSA prioritised referencing and literature integration (T3/

T5), and PSAU exhibited sparse intervention. This supports H2, as cohorts exposed to more intensive feedback and stronger tool use (e.g., TU/TOGI) produced more structurally ambitious, though less readable, proposals. Stream 3 showed systematic output differences: TU/TOGI produced long, dense texts with lower readability; IPSA sat in the mid-range, with persistent integration issues; PSAU excelled in readability and lexical breadth but lacked methodological depth. Cross-stream links reinforced these patterns: a stronger T5 emphasis was associated with denser citation practices, whereas stronger T3 signalling was associated with reduced lexical diversity, highlighting the need for synthesis scaffolds that go beyond citation accumulation.

The findings illustrate a systemic ecology in which student outcomes are determined by digital access, supervisory practices, and institutional infrastructure, rather than by effort alone. TU and TOGI exemplify methodology-heavy cultures that risk gaps in readability and cohesion; IPSA demonstrates how unscaffolded reliance on AI can weaken integration; PSAU highlights the vulnerabilities of low-feedback environments despite surface clarity.

The practical implications of these findings are therefore clear. Advancing research pedagogy in Global South contexts necessitates differentiated training for students, particularly in readability, lexical development, and scholarly integration, to enhance coherence and academic voice. Equally important is capacity-building for supervisors, equipping them with the feedback literacy needed to balance rigour with formative guidance. At an institutional level, investment in equitable access to research tools and structured AI literacy is essential to mitigate infrastructural disparities. Finally, at the policy level, there is an urgent need to align curricula with a spiral progression model, supported by a Proposal Rehearsal Pipeline that embeds iterative drafting, peer feedback, and supervisor commentary. Through their collective integration, these elements establish a feedback-rich, equity-focused, and systematically scaffolded framework that enables meaningful research development for students across levels.

This study is subject to several limitations. The sample size (N = 87), while diverse across four institutions, may not capture the full variability of Global South higher education contexts. Furthermore, the study draws primarily from final-year undergraduate and postgraduate cohorts, which may limit generalisability to earlier years of study. The design focuses on tool adoption and feedback practices within a short post-intervention window, without capturing longitudinal learning outcomes. While the analysis triangulates multiple data streams, the absence of supervisor interviews restricts the interpretive depth of institutional practices.

Future research may adopt longitudinal or cross-regional approaches to investigate how human-AI collaboration in research pedagogy evolves over time. Further studies could explore supervisor development, institutional uptake of AI policy, and ethical dilemmas surrounding authorship and automated feedback. Including additional voices across the academic support ecosystem would provide a more comprehensive view of the development of digitally mediated academic writing.

REFERENCES

Ajabshir, Z. F., & Ebadi, S. (2023). The effects of automatic writing evaluation and teacher-focused feedback on CALF measures and overall quality of L2 writing across different genres. *Asian Journal of Second and Foreign Language Education*, *8*(1), 26. DOI: 10.1186/s40862-023-00201-9

Al-Ansari, H. (2010). Internet use by the faculty members of Kuwait University. *The Electronic Library*, *28*(4), 512–523.

Al-Sabbagh, A. A. G. (2023). Impact of different multimedia modalities on vocabulary acquisition among second-language English learners: An empirical investigation. *Studies in Educational Sciences Journal*, *27*(1), 1–24. DOI: 10.21608/ssj.2023.323795

Al Sawi, I., & Allam, R. (2024). Exploring challenges in audiovisual translation: A comparative analysis of human- and AI-generated Arabic subtitles in Birdman. *PLoS One*, *19*(10), e0311020. DOI: 10.1371/journal.pone.0311020

Al-Sowaidi, B., & Clarke, A. (2025). AI-digital divide in Yemeni and South African higher education: Towards an inclusive policy-oriented approach. In S. Mistretta (Ed.), *Comparative Education – A Global Perspective*. IntechOpen. https://www.intechopen.com/online-first/1228359

Alsadika, Z. H., Akmansyah, M., Alkhodri, E. A., & Koderi, K. (2024). Technology integration in Arabic language learning: A literature review on the effectiveness of e-learning and mobile applications. *Journal of Research in Instructional*, *4*(2), 481–494.

Alwazna, R. Y., Hurley, Z., & Elyas, T. (2025). Integrating technology in translating laws from and into Arabic: Benefits, implications and limitations. *International Journal for the Semiotics of Law*, *38*(6), 1851–1862. Advance online publication. DOI: 10.1007/s11196-025-10295-8

Bassnett, S. (2002). *Translation Studies* (3rd ed.). Routledge.

Bitchener, J., & Storch, N. (2022). Written corrective feedback for L2 development: Current knowledge and future research. *Language Teaching*, *55*(1), 1–18.

Chiu, T. K. F., & Rospigliosi, P. A. (2025). Encouraging human-AI collaboration in interactive learning environments. *Interactive Learning Environments*, *33*(2), 921–924. DOI: 10.1080/10494820.2025.2471199

Cohen, J. (1988). *Statistical Power Analysis for the Behavioral Sciences* (2nd ed.). Lawrence Erlbaum Associates.

Conijn, R., van Zaanen, M., & Dux, E. (2022). Development and validation of a product- and process-oriented tagset for revisions in writing. *Written Communication, 39*(3), 304–334. DOI: 10.1177/07410883211052104

Creswell, J. W., & Plano Clark, V. L. (2018). *Designing and Conducting Mixed Methods Research* (3rd ed.). SAGE Publications.

Fan, N., & Ma, Y. (2023). The effects of automated writing evaluation (AWE) feedback on students' English writing quality: A systematic literature review. *Theory and Practice in Language Studies, 13*(12), 2729–2738.

Graesser, A. C., McNamara, D. S., Louwerse, M. M., & Cai, Z. (2004). Coh-Metrix: Analysis of text on cohesion and language. *Behavior Research Methods, Instruments, & Computers, 36*(2), 193–202. DOI: 10.3758/BF03195564

Gu, B., Siraj, S. B., & Ismail, Z. (2025). The effectiveness of a digital literacy-integrated syllabus for Arabic-speaking courses in teacher-education universities in China. *Journal of Curriculum and Teaching, 14*(1), 202–214. DOI: 10.5430/jct.v14n1p202

Hermans, H. (2018). The dialogical self in education: Introduction. *Learning, Culture and Social Interaction, 16*, 1–4. DOI: 10.1080/10720537.2013.759018

Hoffman, E., & Verdooren, A. (2018). *Diversity Competence: Cultures Don't Meet, People Do*. Coutinho Publishers.

Klimova, B., Pikhart, M., Delorme Benites, A., Lehr, C., & Sanchez-Stockhammer, C. (2023). Neural machine translation in foreign-language teaching and learning: A systematic review. *Education and Information Technologies, 28*(1), 663–682. DOI: 10.1007/s10639-022-11194-2

Knight, S., Shibani, A., Abel, S., Gibson, A., Ryan, P., Sutton, N., Wight, R., Lucas, C., Sándor, Á., Kitto, K., Liu, M., Mogarkar, V. R., & Buckingham Shum, S. (2020). AcaWriter: A learning analytics tool for formative feedback on academic writing. *Journal of Writing Research, 12*(1), 141–186. DOI: 10.17239/jowr-2020.12.01.06

Kurt, G., & Kurt, Y. (2024). Enhancing L2 writing skills: ChatGPT as an automated feedback tool. *Journal of Information Technology Education, 23*, 24–45. DOI: 10.28945/5370

Nguyen, H. (2025). Integrating ChatGPT in translation learning. *SEAAIR Conference Proceedings, 4*, 157–167.

Nguyen, T. N. N., Tran, T. T., Nguyen, N. H. A., Lam, H. P., Nguyen, H. M. S., & Tran, N. A. T. (2025). The benefits and challenges of AI translation tools in translation education at the tertiary level: A systematic review. *International Journal of TESOL and Education*, *5*(2), 132–148. DOI: 10.54855/ijte.25527

O'Hagan, M. (2013). The impact of new technologies on translation studies: A corpus-based perspective. *Perspectives*, *21*(4), 1–18.

Omar, L. I., & Salih, A. A. (2024). Systematic review of English–Arabic machine-translation post-editing: Implications for AI application in translation research and pedagogy. *Informatics (MDPI)*, *11*(2), 23. DOI: 10.3390/informatics11020023

Padovano, A., & Cardamone, M. (2024). Towards human AI collaboration in the competency-based curriculum development process: The case of industrial engineering and management education. *Computers and Education: Artificial Intelligence*, *7*, 100256. DOI: 10.1016/j.caeai.2024.100256

Permyakova, M., Tynkkynen, S., & Koskimaa, R. (2024). Mapping rhetorical moves in student research writing across disciplines: A genre-based corpus study. *English for Specific Purposes*, *72*, 102167. DOI: 10.1177/232949062312060

Qu, Y., Tan, M. X. Y., & Wang, J. (2024). Disciplinary differences in undergraduate students' engagement with generative AI. *Smart Learning Environments*, *11*, 51. DOI: 10.1186/s40561-024-00341-6

Ramadhan, R. A., Abdul Rahim, A., Darmanto, D., & Paris, A. S. (2024). Enhancing academic writing through digital tools: A systematic review. *Journal of Language and Literature Studies*, *4*(4), 758–770. DOI: 10.36312/jolls.v4i4.2342

Shahzad, M. F., Xu, S., & Javed, I. (2024). ChatGPT awareness, acceptance, and adoption in higher education: The role of trust as a cornerstone. *International Journal of Educational Technology in Higher Education*, *21*(1), 46. DOI: 10.1186/s41239-024-00478-x

Shin, D., & Chon, Y. V. (2023). Second language learners' post-editing strategies for machine-translation errors. *Language Learning & Technology*, *27*(1), 1–25. DOI: 10.64152/10125/73523

Swales, J. M. (1990). *Genre Analysis: English in Academic and Research Settings*. Cambridge University Press.

Tran, T. T. T. (2023). Enhancing EFL writing revision practices: The impact of AI- and teacher-generated feedback and their sequences. *Education Sciences*, *15*(2), 232. DOI: 10.3390/educsci15020232

UNESCO. (2018). *ICT Competency Framework for Teachers (Version 3)*. UNESCO. https://unesdoc.unesco.org/ark:/48223/pf0000265721

UNESCO. (2021). *Recommendation on the Ethics of Artificial Intelligence*. UNESCO. https://unesdoc.unesco.org/ark:/48223/pf0000381137

van Dijk, J., & van Deursen, A. (2019). The first-level digital divide shifts. *New Media & Society*, *21*(3), 352–353. DOI: 10.1177/1461444818797082

Venkatesh, V., Morris, M. G., Davis, G. B., & Davis, F. D. (2003). User acceptance of information technology: Toward a unified view. *Management Information Systems Quarterly*, *27*(3), 425–478. DOI: 10.2307/30036540

Wadasinghe, C. (2025). Adoption of Reference Management Software in Academic Writing among Postgraduate Medical Professionals at the Postgraduate Institute of Medicine in Sri Lanka. *KLISC Journal of Information Science & Knowledge Management*, *3*(1), 37–50. DOI: 10.61735/1cb27747

Wang, J., & Fan, W. (2025). The effect of ChatGPT on students' learning performance, learning perception, and higher-order thinking: Insights from a meta-analysis. *Humanities & Social Sciences Communications*, *12*(1), 621. DOI: 10.1057/s41599-025-04787-y

Xu, X., Wang, X., Zhang, Y., & Zheng, R. (2024). Applying ChatGPT to tackle the side effects of personal learning environments from learner and learning perspective: An interview of experts in higher education. *PLoS One*, *19*(1), e0295646. Advance online publication. DOI: 10.1371/journal.pone.0295646

Yang, Y., Liu, R., Qian, X., & Ni, J. (2023). Performance and perception: Machine-translation post-editing in Chinese–English news translation by novice translators. *Humanities & Social Sciences Communications*, *10*(1), 798. DOI: 10.1057/s41599-023-02285-7

Zawacki-Richter, O., Marín, V. I., Bond, M., & Gouverneur, F. (2019). Systematic review of research on artificial intelligence applications in higher education – where are the educators? *International Journal of Educational Technology in Higher Education*, *16*(1), 39. DOI: 10.1186/s41239-019-0171-0

Zhang, Z., & Hyland, K. (2023). Feedback in academic writing: Contexts, practices, and implications. *Journal of Second Language Writing*, *62*, 101017.

Zubaidi, A., Munip, A., Widodo, S. A., & Zerrouki, T. (2025). Enhancing Arabic writing skills using ChatGPT-based AI learning models: A tridimensional human–AI collaboration framework. *Indonesian Journal of Applied Linguistics*, *15*(1), 127–141. DOI: 10.17509/ijal.v15i1.75378

ENDNOTES

1 A computational text-analysis tool that reports multi-level cohesion and complexity indices (e.g., referential/deep cohesion, syntactic complexity) for discourse-level assessment.

2 w:ins- A WordprocessingML element that marks an insertion (i.e., a segment added via tracked changes). w:del-A WordprocessingML element that marks a deletion (i.e., a segment removed via tracked changes).

3 MTLD (Measure of Textual Lexical Diversity) is a computational metric used to assess how varied a writer's vocabulary is within a text.

4 ChatPDF AI is an automated PDF-parsing service (API available) that extracts structured text and metadata (e.g., sections, headings, citations, tables) for computational analysis.

5 CARS (Create-A-Research-Space): A genre model for introductions with three moves: *establishing the territory* (context), *identifying the niche* (gap), and *occupying the niche* (purpose/methods/claims). Used here to code rhetorical organisation and compare how proposals frame problems and aims.

6 Principal component analysis (PCA): A dimensionality-reduction method that converts correlated indicators into a few orthogonal components ranked by explained variance, enabling 2-D visualisations of complex profiles. Used here to depict institutional similarities and differences across structure, readability, cohesion, and citation metrics; descriptive, not causal.

7 Matplotlib: A Python plotting library used to generate publication-quality static charts (e.g., bar plots, scatter plots, heatmaps) directly from data, with high-resolution export for academic use.

8 Given that T4 (organisation) and T7 (intentions/alignment) are near zero across all institutions, they have been omitted from the figures to avoid visual clutter while preserving interpretive clarity

9 P values are BH–FDR adjusted ($q = .05$) across all pairwise comparisons. Rates are normalised per 1,000 words to control for proposal length.

APPENDIX A

A: Student Survey on "Research Pedagogy in Higher Education Contexts"

Section 1: Participation Confirmation (Survey Consent)

I confirm that I have read and understood the study information and voluntarily consent to participate.

- **Yes, No**

Section 2: Extended Research Consent (Academic Data Consent)

I give permission for my anonymised academic data (research proposal and supervisor feedback) to be included in this study.

- **Yes, No**

Response Scale

For all tool-related items, respondents rated perceived usefulness on a 5-point Likert scale:

1 = Not useful 2 = Slightly useful 3 = Moderately useful 4 = Very useful 5 = Extremely useful

Section 3: Participant Profile

3. Current programme of study
   - Bachelor's
   - Honours
   - Master's
   - Doctoral
4. Current year of study
   - Year 1
   - Year 2
   - Year 3
   - Year 4
   - Year 5

Section 4: Ideation and Planning Tools

Rate the usefulness of the following tools:

- ChatGPT / Generative AI
- Google Docs (outlining and drafting)
- Miro / Trello / Notion
- MindMeister / XMind / Markmap
- Evernote / OneNote / Notion Notes
- Zooniverse

- DeepResearch
- GenSpark

Section 5: Literature Discovery and Synthesis Tools

- Scholarcy
- Elicit
- Publish or Perish
- Litmaps / Connected Papers
- ResearchRabbit
- Rayyan

Section 6: Theoretical and Conceptual Framework Tools

- SAGE Research Methods
- ChatGPT (theory clarification)
- Lucidchart / Kumu / Creately
- Connected Papers
- CmapTools

Section 7: Data Collection, Analysis, and Management Tools

- Google Forms / Qualtrics / SurveyMonkey
- Otter / Trint
- DataRobot / RapidMiner
- ObservableHQ / GitHub
- OmegaT / SDL Trados / MemoQ
- Grammarly

Section 8: Methodological Analysis Tools

- SPSS / PSPP
- NVivo / MAXQDA / Dedoose
- AntConc / Sketch Engine / Voyant Tools
- Rayyan / RevMan / QDA Miner
- VOSviewer / Bibliometrix / CiteSpace

Section 9: Reference and Resource Management Tools

- Zotero / EndNote / Mendeley / Paperpile
- Institutional repositories (Figshare, OSF, DSpace, Zenodo)

- ReadCube Papers / EndNote Click / RefWorks
- Hypothes.is / Perusall
- Scite Assistant

Section 10: AI-Assisted Writing, Editing, and Translation Tools

- ChatGPT / Bard / Claude
- Grammarly / ProWritingAid / Hemingway
- Writefull
- Turnitin / Unicheck / PlagScan
- OmegaT / SDL Trados / Memsource
- Word Track Changes / Google Docs revision history

Section 11: Visualisation and Dissemination Tools

- Tableau Public / Power BI / Google Data Studio
- Gephi / Cytoscape
- Canva / Prezi / Adobe Spark
- ArcGIS Online / QGIS
- Beautiful.ai
- PowerPoint plug-ins

Section 12: Barriers to Tool Use
Select all that apply:

- Lack of training or tutorials
- Unreliable internet access
- No access to premium or institutional versions
- Complex interfaces or technical language
- Tools available only in other languages
- Low confidence in new technologies
- Time constraints
- Other

Chapter 14
Revolutionizing Education:
Evaluating the Impact of AI and Ed Tech Tools on Learning Outcomes

Ansella Anna Thomas
https://orcid.org/0009-0008-4999-3409
Christ University, India

Riya Baby
Christ University, India

Benny Godwin J. Davidson
https://orcid.org/0000-0001-5755-2920
University of Fraser Valley, Canada

Jossy P. George
https://orcid.org/0000-0003-3285-5081
Christ University, India

ABSTRACT

The rapid evolution of artificial intelligence (AI) and educational technology (EdTech) tools is significantly transforming teaching and learning processes across the globe. This chapter seeks to critically examine the impact of AI-driven platforms and digital learning tools on educational outcomes, learner engagement, and pedagogical practices. By exploring empirical evidence, theoretical frameworks, and real-world implementations, this chapter aims to provide a comprehensive understanding of how AI and EdTech tools are reshaping personalized learning, assessment, student support, and teacher facilitation. Particular emphasis will be given to the effectiveness of these tools in diverse educational contexts, including challenges related to

DOI: 10.4018/979-8-3373-4521-5.ch014

accessibility, ethical considerations, and the digital divide. The chapter will also present recommendations for integrating AI and EdTech in ways that are pedagogically sound, inclusive, and outcome-focused.

1. INTRODUCTION

1.1 Evolution of EdTech and AI in Education

The journey of educational technology unfolded over six decades ago, progressing from early computer-assisted instruction to sophisticated AI-enabled systems. Sidney Pressey's mechanical teaching machine of the 1920s allowed students to respond and receive immediate feedback; feedback was the precursor to computer-mediated instruction (Benjamin, 1988). Mid-century, B.F. Skinner's teaching machines and Norman Crowder's branching instruction models incorporated reinforcement and subjective paths (Pappas, 2025).

In the 1960s, Computer-Assisted Instruction through Patrick Suppes's mathematics and reading programs introduced systematic analysis of curricula, allowing feedback, branching logic, and progress tracking (Suppes et al., 1971). Becker's meta-analysis showed that students using computer-assisted instruction improved their examination percentile ranks from the 50th to the 63rd, indicative of the notable efficacy. (Hasselbring, 1984).

The intelligent tutoring system emerged in the 1990s, personalizing instructions based on cross-disciplinary approaches combining computer science, psychology, and education to model cognition, predict learner performance, and personalize instruction. Unlike computer-assisted instruction's stagnant replies, intelligent tutoring focuses on real-time student modelling (Eberts & Brock, 1988).

Corbett and Anderson's knowledge-tracing model (1994) used Markov processes to capture students' evolving knowledge states. Applications like AutoTutor demonstrated comparable effectiveness to human tutors in fostering deep comprehension through conversational engagement. (Guo et al., 2021). Meta-analyses validated ITS educational impact; ITS nearly matched human tutoring, confirming effectiveness across domains and settings (Ma et al., 2014; Kulik & Fletcher, 2015).

From 2000 to 2010, adaptive educational tools integrated richer media and learning analytics. Text-based drill and practice shifted to more engaging graphical and video-rich representations across disciplines such as mathematics and science, leveraging perpetual, intelligent interfaces to respond flexibly to learner behaviours and preferences (Hamilton, 2021).

1.2 Defining Key Terms: AI, EdTech, and Learning Outcomes

The integration of technology in education has given rise to a range of concepts that shape contemporary discussions on teaching and learning, including Artificial Intelligence and Education technology. It is essential to understand both the opportunities and challenges of digital transformation in education.

Artificial Intelligence in education refers to computational systems designed to perform tasks that typically require human intelligence, including adaptive decision-making, natural language processing, and predictive analytics. In educational contexts, AI applications often include intelligent tutoring systems, automated grading, learning analytics, and chatbots that personalize learning experiences (Holmes et al., 2019). These systems not only process vast amounts of data but also generate feedback loops that can adjust instructional delivery to student needs. AI thus functions as both a tool for efficiency and a catalyst for rethinking pedagogy.

Educational Technology encompasses a broader spectrum, referring to a range of technology-based innovations and tools used to support teaching, learning, and administrative functions in education. EdTech includes learning management systems, online platforms, digital content, collaborative tools, and, more recently, immersive technologies such as virtual and augmented reality (Selwyn, 2022). While AI is a subset within the EdTech ecosystem, EdTech itself represents the larger infrastructural and pedagogical shift toward digitalization. Scholars argue that EdTech is not neutral but embedded with pedagogical, cultural, and social assumptions that shape learning environments.

Learning outcomes are indicators of educational effectiveness; learning outcomes need to be assessed to measure the impact of AI and EdTech. The learning outcomes have been classified into three domains: cognitive, affective, and behavioural domains. The domains were said to work together as indicators of assessing what students learn, how they implement the knowledge in practice, and how they feel about learning. Cognitive outcomes refer to the intellectual skills, such as knowledge acquisition, problem-solving, and critical thinking. Meanwhile, the visible actions, application of skills, collaboration, and participation in real settings are the behavioural component. Lastly, a student's attitude, motivation, emotional engagement, and educational values are the affective outcomes.

Linking these concepts highlights the interdependence between technology and pedagogy. While AI tools can enhance personalization and efficiency, and EdTech infrastructure broadens access, their ultimate value should be assessed by their impact on learner cognitive, affective, and behavioural growth. This framing underscores the need to critically evaluate emerging technologies in education, ensuring that their implementation promotes meaningful, equitable, and sustainable learning outcomes.

1.3 Educators' Role in AI Adoption

Educators transform from knowledge transmitters to facilitators, ethical guides, and co-learners who leverage AI to personalize education. Teachers leverage AI tools for adaptive instruction; student data is analyzed in real-time to adapt lessons based on real-time feedback, implementing student-centred pedagogies. The teacher's strong TPACK Knowledge enables them to integrate AI into education effectively; AI tools can function as adaptive platforms, achieving curriculum goals. Educators address biases and equity issues by demonstrating responsible use and emphasizing human-AI collaboration. Emotional affection is cultivated to balance efficiency perception and dehumanization with ethical training (Kashif et al., 2025).

Collaborative AI co-designs enable educators to exercise agency, e.g. lesson planning, etc., which enhances ownership and innovation amid limited resources; this builds confidence. The educators mentor students in AI ethics and responsible use, transforming educators from assistants to leaders (Gentile et al., 2023). When using an AI teacher, ensure to prioritize soft skills such as creativity and problem-solving (Tan et al., 2024).

2. AI AND ED-TECH TOOLS

2.1 AI in Personalized Learning

Artificial intelligence profoundly transforms education by enabling personalized learning experiences and enhancing academic performance and engagement, via machine learning algorithms for learner profiling and data analytics. Contrary to the traditional approach of "one size fits all", AI and EdTech customize experiences by analyzing students' learning style, their prior and current knowledge, and their progress (Saleem et al., 2025). To make digital platforms' responses to students' interactions increasingly accurate, algorithms constantly refine profiles by assessing educational data and identifying strengths and challenges to make accurate predictions (Song et al., 2024).

AI tutors and Intelligent tutoring systems provide step-by-step guidance, error correction, and adapt the difficulty of the problem based on real-time performance, mimicking human tutoring. ITS achieves learning outcomes comparable to one-on-one human tutoring, often considered the gold standard for individualized instruction (Farhood et al., 2025; Vanlehn, 2011). Predictive metrics maintain the optimal level of challenge to sustain motivation (Shute & Rahimi, 2017).

Predictive models assist administrators identify at-risk students through the analysis of interaction data, enabling targeted interventions that improve retention and success (Romero & Ventura, 2024). Despite the innovations, algorithmic bias, over-reliance, and the narrowing of the learning experiences raise ethical and pedagogical concerns (Holmes et al., 2021). AI tools cannot replace the relational and emotional dimensions of teaching, which are essential for holistic development.

In conclusion, AI-driven personalization offers transformative potential through intelligent tutors, adaptive assessments, and predictive analytics. However, its success hinges on careful integration into pedagogical frameworks that balance technological efficiency with human connection; evidence-based evaluations are essential to ensure AI supports equitable, meaningful, and inclusive educational experiences.

2.2 EdTech Platforms: The Spectrum of Digital Learning Environments

EdTech platforms transform education by enhancing teaching, learning, and collaboration through tools such as LMSs, VR/AR, gamification and MOOCs, widening access and engagement.

LMS such as Moodle, Blackboard, and Canvas incorporate forums, assignments, and multimedia for course delivery and assessments (Dahlstrom et al., 2014). They streamlined administration, blended modalities, and eased COVID-19 transitions to digital instruction (Rapanta et al., 2020).

When implemented effectively in education, gamified elements are found to sustain learners' motivation by enhancing engagement. Elements such as badges, scores, and leaderboards, utilized in software such as Kahoot and Classcraft, have been found to enhance knowledge retention, academic engagement, and performance, particularly in K-12 and higher education (Subhash & Cudney, 2018). The poor implementation of the gamification can also cause the students to be distracted from the learning objectives

AR overlays digital content on the real world, VR immerses in simulations. Ideal for medicine, engineering, and history, they enable visualization, simulations, and storytelling (Latif et al., 2024). Immersive learning enhances spatial skills, critical thinking, and empathy by offering unattainable real-world experiences (Liu et al., 2025; Samala et al., 2025).

Massive Open Online Courses (MOOCs) mark another significant milestone in digital education, amid high dropout rates. Coursera, edX, and FutureLearn provide free or affordable access to MOOC courses from top institutions (Reich & Ruipérez-Valiente, 2019). These courses are particularly beneficial for self-motivated learners seeking to acquire new skills to develop their careers. MOOCs democratize learning by widening their access to global audiences, including those outside traditional higher education (Kizilcec et al., 2016).

Offering structure, engagement, and experiential learning, LMS, immersive technologies, and MOOCs make knowledge accessible to a global audience. This showcases how the implementation of EdTech platforms in education transcends the traditional educational boundaries, while also emphasizing the importance of improving and evaluating their pedagogical and societal impacts.

2.3 Automated Essay Scoring: Benefits and Challenges

AI is fundamentally reshaping education, specifically assessment through automated essay scoring, by leveraging large language models (Singh, 2025). LLMs benefit from formative assessments through automated scoring by providing improvements during learning in the form of instant feedback. Personalized suggestions and real-time feedback support ongoing skill development and substantially increase task accuracy (Tang et al., 2024b). Regarding summative assessment efficiency, automated scoring can be used to evaluate a large number of essays using a rubric derived from human-scored datasets. It reduces the work hours, minimizing fatigue and subjectivity. Research has shown fairly similar scoring to an expert's scoring (Aydın et al., 2025).

Automating scoring risks academic integrity and compromises the ethical implementation of AI. Students can exploit LLMs to generate essays that undermine the validity of evaluation by evading detection. Compromised automated scoring often assigns inflated scores to AI-generated work, indicating weak correlation with human assessments. It can lead to erosion of trust and credibility in AI, demanding advanced plagiarism detection, and raising equity issues. To overcome these challenges, the tasks need to be redesigned, placing greater emphasis on critical thinking over rote learning (Dwivedi et al., 2023; Uyar & Büyükahıska, 2025).

2.4 Critical Perspectives

Although AI and EdTech promise personalization and efficiency, various studies reveal profound risks requiring further exploration. A systematic review by Wang et al. (2024) explored more than 2000 AI and EdTech studies, revealing that, along with efficiency in personalized tutoring, around 40% of implementations resulted in increased inequities due to the biased algorithms developed on underrepresentative data, putting the marginalized groups at a disadvantage. Al-Zahrani (2024) indicates that untransparent models and the opacity of AI impact teacher autonomy, requiring them to supervise the automated processes rather than empowering them. Additionally, critics tend to quote the inadequate 70-85% reliability of automated essay scoring across diverse styles, raising questions about authenticity amid the current trend of plagiarism surges, indicating that policy triumphs over hype (Quah et al., 2024).

Costa and Murphy (2025) reveal the risk of over-reliance by replacing the human relational teaching, at times, oversimplification prioritizes efficiency over holistic development. These perspectives are highly indicative of human-centred regulation and safeguards to sustain the benefits without increasing the chances of inequities.

3. THEORETICAL FOUNDATIONS AND PEDAGOGICAL ALIGNMENT

3.1 Constructivism, Connectivism, and Personalized Learning Theories

The integration of AI and EdTech in modern education is drawn from constructivism, connectivism, and personalized, learner-centred approaches. These tools embody pedagogical principles that prioritize active engagement, knowledge creation, and tailored learning experiences.

Constructivism views learners as active participants who develop understanding through authentic tasks and reflection. EdTech supports this through interactive environments like simulation tools and virtual labs, enabling experimentation without real-world risks (Dalgarno & Lee, 2009). AI tools like adaptive quizzes and intelligent tutoring systems provide scaffolding in Vygotsky's concept of the Zone of Proximal Development, tailoring challenges promoting exploration and problem-solving (Tan et al., 2025).

Connectivism emphasizes that knowledge emerges from networks of people, tools, and resources (Goldie, 2016). LMS facilitate this through discussion forums, peer feedback tools, and collaborative workspaces for co-creating knowledge. AI analytics personalize these by linking learners' interests and resources (Chen et al., 2017), as seen in collaborative MOOCs blending human and machine-mediated networks

AI's defining characteristic in education lies in enabling personalized, learner-centred approaches, aligning with constructivist meaning-making and adaptive pathways responsive to behaviours and preferences. These environments predict challenges and recommend interventions to boost engagement (Tapalova & Zhiyenbayeva, 2022), shifting from teacher- to learner-centred models, emphasizing autonomy and self-regulation. Platforms like Duolingo exemplify this through reinforcement learning by providing real-time feedback and adjusting difficulty.

Together, AI and EdTech create a learning ecosystem supporting experiential, networked, and personalized education. Constructivism shines in interactive, exploratory nature of digital environments; connectivism in peer-expert connections; and learner-centredness in adaptive trajectories. The effectiveness of these technologies depends on pedagogical integration, educator training, and equitable access (Pawar, 2023), alongside ethical and contextual factors.

3.2 Bloom's Taxonomy and Learning Outcome Categorization

Bloom's Taxonomy provides a hierarchical framework for educational objectives, from basic remembering and understanding to advanced evaluating and creating (Ajayi, 2024). EdTech and AI enable innovative, interactive, and adaptive support across these cognitive domains

At foundational levels of remembering and understanding, digital tools like flash-card apps, AI retrieval systems, and adaptive quizzes enhance recall through spaced repetition (Selvi & K, 2024). Intelligent tutoring systems, like Carnegie Learning, offer step-by-step guidance to solidify concepts (Bhushan et al., 2023). Platforms like Khan Academy reinforce comprehension through revisitable multimodal videos.

Middle levels, application and analysis, involve applying knowledge in new contexts and deconstructing concepts. Simulation software and virtual labs offer safe real-world scenarios (Khokhar, 2025). VR assists medical students build clinical decision-making without risk (Pottle, 2019). AI-integrated LMS detects performance trends to aid deeper analysis.

Upper levels: evaluating and creating foster critical thinking. MOOCs, discussion forums, and peer assessments enable critiquing arguments and reflective judgement (Ekahitanond, 2013). Design software and project tools support idea generation and artifact creation. Problem-solving games promote collaborative strategy design (Adipat et al., 2021), with AI feedback refining creativity beyond mere accuracy. AI and EdTech personalize pathways, adjusting task difficulty through real-time performance and interactive loops in intelligent tutoring systems, impersonating human tutors to transition students from rote memorization to evaluation, creation (Y. Luo et al., 2025).

Bloom's framework adapts to digital tools for diverse outcomes, balancing lower-order skills with AI-driven higher-order development. Effectiveness relies on proper integration, training, and viewing technology as a complement to human tutoring, not a replacement (Naseer et al., 2025).

3.3 SAMR Model and TPACK Framework for Technology Integration

Effective technology integration in education requires alignment of content, pedagogy, and technology, guided by the SAMR Model and TPACK model.

SAMR model, developed by Puentedura, outlines four levels: Substitution, which is replacing traditional tools with digital counterparts without functional change;

Augmentation is adding enhancement to functionality; Modification is redesigning tasks for significant changes in practice; and Redefinition is creating previously impossible tasks for transformative learning (Jenkins et al., 2022).

Researchers found that teachers often reach only augmentation or modification level, especially in remote emergency teaching, with full redesign rare (De Morais Bicalho et al., 2022). In Pakistan, higher education teachers are stuck at substitution/augmentation due to infrastructure deficits, limited support, and training gaps (Rehman et al., 2022).

TPACK extends Shulman's pedagogical content knowledge by incorporating technology, helping educators blend content, pedagogy, and technology for optimal tool selection and curricular goals (Tunjera & Chigona, 2019). While TPACK assesses integration depth, SAMR measures task transformation. A study of Indonesian English lectures using TPACK- SAMR found strong competencies but mostly substitution/augmentation, with limited modification/redefinition (Ahmada & Rizkiyah, 2024).

Combining models reveals teaching practices: SAMR gauges transformation extent, TPACK model evaluates teachers' preparedness and decision-making. High TPACK enables higher SAMR levels for transformative tasks, like in mathematics education, and helps identify the scope of upskilling themselves. Although capable educators face contextual barriers like training gaps, inequities, and institutional support shortages hinder the advancement.

3.4 Real-World Examples Across Educational Contexts

EdTech and AI applications vary across K-120, higher education, and vocational training, tailored to each sector's goals, revealing benefits and challenges.

In K-12 schools, adaptive platforms like DreamBox Learning adjust math problems in real-time for mastery, yielding proficiency gains over traditional methods (Mirea et al., 2025; Gibbs, 2025). Tools like Knewton and Carnegie Learning deliver feedback and scaffolding, aiding diverse student needs in linear models.

In universities, Ed Tech adoption emphasizes scalability, flexibility, and personalized learning. Arizona State University's Global Freshman Academy, offered via edX, exemplifies the integration of MOOCs into formal degree programs. By providing open-access, credit-bearing courses, ASU has expanded educational access for underserved communities while maintaining academic standards (edX, n.d.). Another example is the Open University (UK), which utilizes analytics dashboards to identify at-risk students and enhance student retention and engagement, of first-generation learners (Rienties et al., 2016).

Vocational training leverages immersive tech for real-world simulation. VR-wielding simulators in U.S. community colleges cut costs and risks while accelerating proficiency (Onum & Agama, 2025). AR aids nursing students in practicing diagnostics safely, enhancing skills and workplace confidence (Radianti et al., 2019). These cases show EdTech and AI boosting outcomes, access, and skills development, but success requires contextual implementation, training, and equity evaluation.

Beyond tutoring systems, adaptive assessments dynamically adjust difficulty for precise ability measurement and reduce fatigue. Platforms like ALEKS and GRE exams pinpoint and identify gaps for personalized paths. Yet, careful design is essential to avoid amplifying data baises, promoting equitable personalization.

Figure 1. Theoretical and Pedagogical Foundations of AI and EdTech

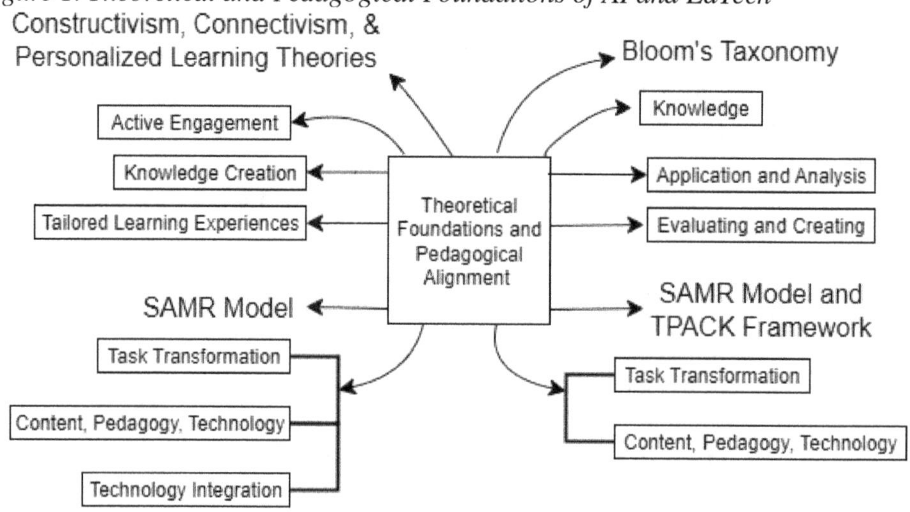

4. IMPACT ON LEARNING OUTCOMES

4.1 Academic Performance and Achievement

The integration of EdTech and AI into learning sparked debate on whether they truly boost student performance, through test scores, retention, and mastery, or merely act as a supplement.

Research affirms positive impacts on standardized scores when paired with evidence-based methods. A meta-analysis of 74 rigorous studies showed computer-assisted instruction (CAI) in mathematics yielded modest achievement gains (Cheung & Slavin, 2013). Adaptive systems improved math and reading outcomes by adjusting to performance (Major et al., 2021). Gains are strongest in structured settings with strategic educator use rather than as a mere add-on.

EdTech excels in long-term retention, retrieval-based digital platforms like adaptive quizzes and spaced repetition, outperform conventional study for better memory consolidation (Karpicke et al., 2011). Virtual laboratories and simulations foster deeper understanding through active experimentation, shifting learners from surface to durable mastery (De Jong et al., 2013).

AI fosters sustained subject mastery through intelligent tutoring with step-by-step feedback, yielding gains in complex skills (Zerkouk et al., 2025). In STEM disciplines, these platforms narrow problem-solving gaps for struggling students. Effectiveness depends on implementation quality, resource access, and curricular alignment (Joseph & Uzondu, 2024).

However, not all evidence is positive. Technology alone doesn't guarantee improvement; success relies on instructional design, teacher preparation, and support (Carter et al., 2016; Arrington, 2022). Poor integration can yield minimal or negative effects, often from over–automation eroding human interaction (Zhai et al., 2024). Thus, EdTech must complement, not replace, effective teaching.

4.2 Student Motivation and Engagement

Student motivation and engagement are central to effective learning, and recent advances in educational technology (EdTech) have introduced new approaches for fostering these outcomes. Due to an increase in engagement and active participation from the implementation of gamification and real-time feedback, the technologies are now more widely acknowledged.

Incorporating typical game-like elements into educational settings is referred to as Gamification. Different elements like badges, leaderboard, and points are incorporated. The elements help educators establish clear objectives, provide immediate rewards, and a sense of progress, leading to intrinsic motivation (Dichev & Dicheva, 2017). For instance, Different studies emphasize the role of gamification, enhancing involvement and perseverance in the long term, as they highlight that greater engagement and enhanced practical application are displayed by the students who participate in a gamified learning experience (Waluyo & Balazon, 2024).

Motivation levels are found to be elevated in students as a result of real-time feedback. It is seen that students are able to monitor their performance and adjust their progress and strategies accordingly, based on the immediate feedback they receive on digital platforms. Self-regulated learning is encouraged, and engagement and confidence levels are also enhanced by real-time feedback, as it creates a motivational environment, where learners are empowered to take charge of their success (Qadir et al., 2025; Mejeh et al., 2024).

Collaborative platforms and immersive technologies are the interactive tools that are vital in enhancing engagement. Sung et al. (2015) conducted a meta-analysis revealing that motivation and achievement were found to be positively influenced by the interactive learning environments. These technologies encourage active participation, peer collaboration, and experiential learning, perfectly aligning with pedagogical approaches that emphasize hands-on involvement.

4.3 Development of Skills

The incorporation of digital tools into education has gained widespread recognition for promoting essential twenty-first-century skills, including critical thinking, creativity, collaboration, and communication. These abilities are crucial for learners navigating ever-evolving social and professional landscapes.

Digital environments stimulate critical thinking by engaging learners in activities that demand analysis, evaluation, and problem-solving. For instance, Mejia and Sargent (2023) found that online inquiry-based learning platforms improved students' capacity to critically assess information sources and develop evidence-based arguments. By providing access to varied resources and perspectives, deeper engagement is promoted through digital tools.

Platforms that empower the learner to create, refine, and design solutions are more likely to nurture creativity. Students generate legitimate and novel outcomes by designing, creating, and refining solutions effectively, integrating project-based learning and digital tools, as they are found to enhance creativity in the context of problem-solving scenarios. Indicative of technology as a lever in the real-world complexities. (Baziukė et al., 2025)

Lavanya et al. (2024) in their research indicated that Wikis, forums, and cloud-based tools are interactive and networked technologies that create a platform for peer-to-peer learning, helping students engage in meaningful dialogue, co-create knowledge, and strengthen communication and teamwork.

As AI ensures adaptability, equitable participation, and collaboration, it has opened new possibilities for skill development through its expanding role of AI in education. The study observed that AI-assisted feedback in collaborative settings helps students refine their reasoning and sustain productive group interactions. Kim et al. (2025) observed that Teacher guidance is complemented by AI, in turn developing higher-order skills by enhancing the potential of peer learning environments. Technological tools, in conjuction with Project-based learning and peer collaboration, enable educational systems to create atmospheres where the learners construct, communicate, and innovate actively. Skill acquisition can be further enhanced by digital and AI-enhanced pedagogies.

In conclusion, AI and EdTech enhance learning outcomes across cognitive, affective, and behavioural domains. Mastery, improved retention, and problem-solving are the indicators of advanced learning outcomes in the cognitive domain. Similarly, advancement in affective learning outcomes is shown by increased motivation and self-efficacy, and greater engagement. Meanwhile, behavioural results are evident in collaboration, creativity, and communication skills. The impact of AI and EdTech on learning outcomes, whether positive or negative, varies across contexts, i.e., accessibility to supportive bodies and the effectiveness of implementation. As an adverse impact, gamification might undermine intrinsic motivation and put some students at a disadvantage due to limited reliable resources and low digital literacy. Additionally, the long-term sustainability of the impact and equitable access across a diverse range of learners needs to be considered.

4.4 Transformative Impact of LLMs: ChatGPT and Gemini

Large Language Models drive profound changes due to the widespread adoption of across sectors, boosting productivity, education and healthcare through advanced NLP (Zhang et al., 2024). Writing tasks saw 40% productivity gains and 18% quality improvements, narrowing performance gaps; multi-LLM exposure doubles workplace adoption (Noy & Zhang, 2023).

In education, LLMs transform medical training by generating patient materials, interpreting data, reducing cognitive load, and enabling personalized learning. Prompt engineering overhauls teaching; multimodal processing aids diagnosis, treatment, and research toward personalized medicine, despite bias/privacy challenges (Aydin et al., 2024; Khan et al., 2024). ChatGPT excels in healthcare queries and treatment recommendations (Ahn, 2024; Fattah et al., 2025).

Along with advancements come certain challenges: the possibility that inequalities may widen, biases, authorship issues, and job displacement, all of which require a human-AI balance. Given widespread adoption across disciplines, it also urges safeguards (Liang et al., 2025).

Generative AI powered by GPT-4o and Gemini 2.0; reshapes education via dynamic creation and hyper-personalization. Multimodal systems (images, texts, videos) outperform unimodal systems in tutoring, prediction and diagnostics (Yuan et al., 2024). Agentic AI eases teachers workloads in planning/adapting lessons, enhancing student agency. Retrieval-augmented generation (RAG), grounds outputs in verified sources for accuracy. Edge AI enables low-latency, privacy-preserving personalization, in resource-limited settings (Li et al., 2025).

Explainable AI ensures transparent grading/bias detection; hybrid models align 92% with experts. Federated learning supports collaborative training without data sharing, addressing privacy concerns under GDPR-like regulations. Risk of cognitive offloading and critical thinking decline from over-reliance, though Gen AI aids curriculum co-creation.

Figure 2. AI and EdTech Impact on Learning Outcomes

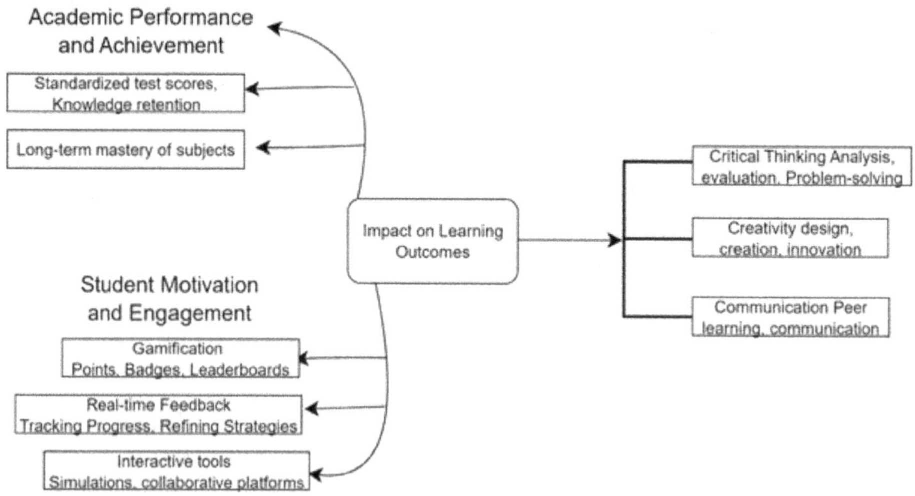

5. CHALLENGES AND ETHICAL CONSIDERATIONS

5.1 Data Privacy, Algorithmic Bias, and Transparency

The swift incorporation of artificial intelligence (AI) and educational technologies (EdTech) has heightened concerns about the collection of student data, algorithmic bias, and transparency in decision-making. The widespread use of digital platforms necessitates that students generate substantial amounts of personal and behavioural data, leading to significant privacy and ethical concerns. Slade et al. (2019) emphasize that learning analytics frequently involve the collection of sensitive information without students being fully aware or in control, posing potential risks of surveillance and misuse.

Another urgent issue pertains to biased AI algorithms. Since AI models are trained on pre-existing datasets, they often replicate and even amplify the systemic inequalities present in the datasets. Boateng and Boateng (2025) warn that predictive algorithms in education, used to evaluate performance or identify at-risk students, might inadvertently disadvantage marginalized groups if they depend on biased historical records. There is a possibility that, instead of reducing educational disparities, they might get reinforced.

Equally troubling is the lack of transparency in decision-making systems. Many AI-driven platforms function as "black boxes", where educators and students have limited understanding of how outputs, such as risk scores or recommendations, are produced (Xi, 2024). Trust in AI is undermined, and accountability gets limited, as it becomes difficult to question or comprehend algorithmic decisions that impact learning paths.

There always lies a risk of content fabrication and intellectual property violations with Generative AI. LLMs can produce outputs that sound plausible but contain faulty information, heavily impacting educational trust. AI contents are often found to have subtle biases or errors, amplifying misinformation, also heavily risking cognitive offloading, reducing critical thinking capacity (Lai et al., 2023). Individuals can evade detectors, blurring authorship lines and plagiarism, indicative of unprecedented threats to academic integrity.

These challenges highlight the need for stronger ethical frameworks, regulatory guidelines, and participatory approaches to AI adoption in education. Ensuring transparency, accountability, and equity is crucial to prevent technological innovation from worsening the very disparities it seeks to address.

5.2 Teacher Roles and Techno-Pedagogical Readiness

Incorporating technology into educational settings holds great potential, but also poses significant obstacles for teachers. A major hurdle is the reluctance to embrace change. Educators who are used to conventional teaching methods might view digital tools as disruptive or unnecessary, especially if they doubt the impact of technology on enhancing educational outcomes. According to Ertmer et al. (2012), teachers' ingrained beliefs about education influence their readiness to embrace new methods, with resistance often tied to fears of losing control over classroom dynamics or reducing face-to-face interactions.

Another issue is the lack of adequate training and professional development. Merely providing technological resources does not ensure their effective use in teaching. Tondeur et al. (2019) in their study note that many teachers receive insufficient training in digital pedagogy during their education, leaving them unprepared to integrate technology in ways that align with curriculum objectives. Without ongoing, structured professional development, educators might use technology merely as a substitute rather than as a means to transform learning activities.

Additionally, gaps in digital pedagogy skills remain a critical concern. Beyond technical skills, teachers need to develop the ability to create technology-enhanced lessons, facilitating online collaboration, and evaluating digital learning outcomes. Rahmawati et al. (2025) note that digital competence is multifaceted, encompassing not only operational skills but also ethical awareness, critical assessment, and pedagogical integration. When these skills are lacking, the potential of educational technologies to drive innovation and engagement is limited.

Tackling these challenges requires systemic support that includes capacity-building, leadership encouragement, and fostering a professional culture that values innovation. Without such efforts, technological adoption risks reinforcing, rather than transforming, existing inequities and inefficiencies in education.

5.3 Equity and the Digital Divide in AI/EdTech Access

Although educational technology holds the promise of making learning more accessible to all, differences in access to devices, internet connectivity, and high-quality digital content continue to widen existing inequalities. Students from rural, low-income, or marginalized backgrounds are particularly impacted by these disparities, which hinder their full participation in digital learning settings. The study by Shamsudinova et al. (2025) highlights that the "digital divide" extends beyond mere physical access to devices, encompassing disparities in skills, usage, and opportunities.

A significant obstacle is the lack of internet connectivity, especially in rural areas where broadband infrastructure is lacking. According to UNESCO, nearly half of the world's students were left out of online education during pandemic-related school closures, with rural and low-income families being the hardest hit. Even when devices are available, unstable or expensive internet connections prevent consistent engagement with digital platforms, leading to uneven educational outcomes (*When Schools Shut: Gendered Impacts of COVID-19 School Closures*, 2021).

Another aspect of disparity is the quality of digital content. Many resources are tailored for well-funded, urban settings and often overlook linguistic, cultural, or contextual diversity. The study contends that digital education frequently perpetuates rather than alleviates inequity, as the content often mirrors dominant cultural narratives while sidelining alternative knowledge systems. For students from disadvantaged groups, this creates further obstacles to meaningful engagement and knowledge-building.

To tackle these inequities, efforts must extend beyond merely distributing devices and include sustainable investments in connectivity, localized digital content, and teacher support. Without such comprehensive approaches, EdTech risks reinforcing systemic inequalities instead of promoting educational equity.

Another significant ethical concern is the well-being of students in technology-mediated learning environments. Research indicates that excessive reliance on digital platforms can lead to screen fatigue, reduced social interaction, and increased stress, especially when online systems prioritize performance monitoring rather than holistic growth (Ibrahim et al., 2025). This highlights the necessity for balanced integration where technology complements, rather than replaces, human-centred teaching. Equally important are strong governance and policy frameworks that regulate data use, ensure accountability, and protect equity in digital learning ecosystems. Without such coordinated efforts, the integration of AI and EdTech risks worsening educational inequities and psychosocial challenges for learners.

6. FUTURE DIRECTIONS AND RECOMMENDATIONS

6.1 Designing Inclusive AI-Enhanced Learning Systems

Creating educational technologies that cater to the diverse needs of learners, including those with disabilities, language differences, and various learning preferences, necessitates a focused approach on equity, accessibility, and adaptability. The Universal Design for learning (UDL) framework is widely acknowledged as a best practice because it advocates for multiple methods of representation, engagement, and expression, allowing learners to access content and demonstrate understanding in different ways (Doyle et al., 2025).

For students with disabilities, features like screen readers, captioning, voice recognition, and customizable interfaces are essential. Bucheli et al. (2024) found that digital platforms based on UDL enhance participation and achievement for learners with physical, sensory, or cognitive challenges. Likewise, flexible navigation and assistive technologies enable students to customize their learning environments.

Language diversity poses another challenge. Inclusive systems incorporate multilingual support and scaffolding tools such as translation features, glossaries, and visual aids, which have been shown to improve comprehension for non-native speakers (Zafar et al., 2025). By addressing linguistic differences, these tools promote equitable access to content and lower barriers for immigrant and minority students. Recognizing different learning styles is equally crucial. Adaptive systems that employ analytics and machine learning can offer personalized pathways based on students' preferences, whether they learn best through visual, auditory, or kinesthetic methods. Studies suggest that adaptive learning platforms boost engagement and achievement by aligning instruction with learner needs (Balasubramanian, 2022).

Ultimately, inclusive design must extend beyond technical solutions. It involves engaging learners and educators in the design process to ensure cultural relevance and usability. Such participatory approaches build trust and ensure that EdTech systems function as tools for empowerment rather than exclusion.

6.2 Capacity-Building for Educators and Institutions

The successful integration of AI and EdTech in education hinges on educators' readiness to weave these tools into teaching practices in a meaningful way. Continuous professional development (CPD) programs and digital literacy training are key to equipping teachers with the skills, confidence, and teaching strategies they need to effectively use technology. Research shows that one-off workshops just don't cut it; CPD needs to be ongoing, collaborative, and tied to real classroom situations to make a lasting difference (Fakhar et al., 2024).

In today's world, digital literacy training is more important than ever. Teachers are expected not just to use tools but also to assess their educational value critically. The study conducted by Uzorka et al. (2023) discovered that training that combines technical skills with teaching strategies boosts confidence and leads to better implementation. This connection helps educators avoid treating technology as just an extra layer and instead integrate it in ways that genuinely enhance learning outcomes.

Institutional support is equally crucial. Without the right infrastructure, technical support, and leadership support, even the best-trained educators might find it tough to use these tools effectively. Research emphasizes that a supportive school culture, clear technology visions, and strong administrative support are essential for overcoming resistance to change and fostering ongoing innovation. Schools that focus on mentoring peer collaboration and reflective practices in their CPD frameworks further empower teachers to adapt to the ever-changing digital landscape (Ertmer & Ottenbreit-Leftwich, 2010).

When it comes to effective technology integration, it is a collective effort. Strong CPD programmes, digital literacy initiatives, and supportive institutional structures all work together to create an environment where technology can be used responsibly and effectively, ultimately benefiting both teachers and students.

6.3 Insights and Implications

The blend of AI and educational technology (EdTech) has opened up a world of possibilities and challenges for how we learn. On the bright side, research shows that adaptive platforms, smart tutoring systems, and instant feedback tools can really boost student success and engagement by tailoring lessons to individual needs (N. P. M. Banerjee et al., 2020). Gamification, interactive settings, and data-driven learning insights have been proven to enhance motivation and retention. These innovative tools can cater to a variety of learners by providing flexible pathways and support that match their unique requirements (Capatina et al., 2024).

On the contrary, the swift rise of AI and Edtech comes with its own challenges. Studies emphasize that depending excessively on algorithm-based systems might reinforce existing biases, jeopardize student privacy, and deepen the divide in access to quality digital resources. Differences in infrastructure and digital skills can further widen the performance gap between the privileged and the underprivileged (Farheen et al., 2025).

To navigate this landscape responsibly, educators, developers, and policymakers need to take a comprehensive approach. This means incorporating ethical considerations into design, investing in teacher training for digital teaching methods, and ensuring everyone has fair access to the necessary infrastructure and resources. Most importantly, policies should promote the inclusive and transparent use of AI, with active involvement from students, families, and communities to help create trustworthy systems. When used wisely, AI and EdTech can serve not as substitutes for human teachers but as powerful allies that broaden opportunities and make learning more accessible, engaging, and equitable.

REFERENCES

Adipat, S., Laksana, K., Busayanon, K., Ausawasowan, A., & Adipat, B. (2021). Engaging Students in the Learning Process with Game-Based Learning: The Fundamental Concepts. *International Journal of Technology in Education, 4*(3), 542–552. DOI: 10.46328/ijte.169

Ahmada, A., & Rizkiyah, F. (2024, December 30). Technology Integration in English Language Learning Based on the TPACK-SAMR Framework at Three Indonesian Universities. Ahmada | *IJEE (Indonesian Journal of English Education).* https://journal.uinjkt.ac.id/index.php/ijee/article/view/37996/0?

Ahn, S. (2024). The transformative impact of large language models on medical writing and publishing: Current applications, challenges and future directions. *The Korean Journal of Physiology & Pharmacology; Official Journal of the Korean Physiological Society and the Korean Society of Pharmacology, 28*(5), 393–401. DOI: 10.4196/kjpp.2024.28.5.393 PMID: 39198220

Ajayi, J. (2024). Bloom's taxonomy. *ResearchGate.* https://www.researchgate.net/publication/380814622_Blooms_taxonomy

Al-Zahrani, A. M. (2024). Unveiling the shadows: Beyond the hype of AI in education. *Heliyon, 10*(9), e30696. DOI: 10.1016/j.heliyon.2024.e30696 PMID: 38737255

Arrington, Q. (2022). The impact of modern technology on education. *MDSK 6691: Seminar in Professional Development.* https://files.eric.ed.gov/fulltext/ED619067.pdf

Aydın, B., Kışla, T., Elmas, N. T., & Bulut, O. (2025). Automated scoring in the era of artificial intelligence: An empirical study with Turkish essays. *System, 133*, 103784. DOI: 10.1016/j.system.2025.103784

Aydin, S., Karabacak, M., Vlachos, V., & Margetis, K. (2024). Large language models in patient education: A scoping review of applications in medicine. *Frontiers in Medicine, 11*, 1477898. DOI: 10.3389/fmed.2024.1477898 PMID: 39534227

Balasubramanian, A. (2022). Personalized learning style detection and pathway optimization using hybrid machine learning approaches. *International Journal of Scientific Research in Engineering and Management, 08*(12), 1–6. DOI: 10.55041/IJSREM6557

Banerjee, N. P. M., Sinha, N. P. S., & Pandey, N. D. P.Prof. (Dr.) Mita BanerjeeProf. (Dr.) Sridipa SinhaDr. Pranay Pandey. (2020). Artificial Intelligence in Education: Revolutionizing. *Learning and Teaching.* Advance online publication. DOI: 10.25215/9358094575

Baziukė, D., Rupšienė, I., Kesylė, K., & Norvilienė, A. (2025). How E-Learning Platforms are Addressing Project-Based Learning: An assessment of Digital learning tools in Primary education. *Applied Sciences (Basel, Switzerland)*, *15*(23), 12422. DOI: 10.3390/app152312422

Benjamin, L. T. (1988). A history of teaching machines. *The American Psychologist*, *43*(9), 703–712. DOI: 10.1037/0003-066X.43.9.703

Bhushan, M., Shingate, R., Shah, T., & Vyas, N. (2023). Intelligent Tutoring System: Personalized Learning Plans with AI. *ResearchGate*. DOI: 10.13140/RG.2.2.36573.59369

Boateng, N. O., & Boateng, N. B. (2025). Algorithmic bias in educational systems: Examining the impact of AI-driven decision making in modern education. *World Journal of Advanced Research and Reviews*, *25*(1), 2012–2017. DOI: 10.30574/wjarr.2025.25.1.0253

Bucheli, M. G. V., Gómez-Galán, J., Mesa, M. L. C., & Catalán, L. L. (2024). Digital technologies as enablers of universal design for learning: Higher education students' perceptions in the context of SDG4. *Discover Sustainability*, *5*(1), 473. Advance online publication. DOI: 10.1007/s43621-024-00699-0

Capatina, A., Juarez-Varon, D., Micu, A., & Micu, A. E. (2024). Levelling up in corporate training: Unveiling the power of gamification to enhance knowledge retention, knowledge sharing, and job performance. *Journal of Innovation & Knowledge*, *9*(3), 100530. DOI: 10.1016/j.jik.2024.100530

Carter, S. P., Greenberg, K., & Walker, M. S. (2016). The impact of computer usage on academic performance: Evidence from a randomized trial at the United States Military Academy. *Economics of Education Review*, *56*, 118–132. DOI: 10.1016/j.econedurev.2016.12.005

Chen, X., Breslow, L., & DeBoer, J. (2017). Analyzing productive learning behaviours for students using immediate corrective feedback in a blended learning environment. *Computers & Education*, *117*, 59–74. DOI: 10.1016/j.compedu.2017.09.013

Cheung, A. C., & Slavin, R. E. (2013). The effectiveness of educational technology applications for enhancing mathematics achievement in K-12 classrooms: A meta-analysis. *Educational Research Review*, *9*, 88–113. DOI: 10.1016/j.edurev.2013.01.001

Costa, C., & Murphy, M. (2025). Generative artificial intelligence in education: (what) are we thinking? *Learning, Media and Technology*, •••, 1–12. DOI: 10.1080/17439884.2025.2518258

Dahlstrom, E., Brooks, D. C., & Bichsel, J. (2014). The Current Ecosystem of Learning Management Systems in Higher Education: Student, Faculty, and IT Perspectives. In *EDUCAUSE*. Retrieved September 20, 2025, from https://library.educause.edu/resources/2014/9/the-current-ecosystem-of-learning-management-systems-in-higher-education-student-faculty-and-it-perspectives

Dalgarno, B., & Lee, M. J. W. (2009). What are the learning affordances of 3-D virtual environments? *British Journal of Educational Technology*, *41*(1), 10–32. DOI: 10.1111/j.1467-8535.2009.01038.x

De Jong, T., Linn, M. C., & Zacharia, Z. C. (2013). Physical and virtual laboratories in science and engineering education. *Science*, *340*(6130), 305–308. DOI: 10.1126/science.1230579 PMID: 23599479

De Morais Bicalho, R. N., Coll, C., Engel, A., & De Oliveira, M. C. S. L. (2022). Integration of ICTs in teaching practices: Propositions to the SAMR model. *Educational Technology Research and Development*, *71*(2), 563–578. DOI: 10.1007/s11423-022-10169-x PMID: 36533221

Dichev, C., & Dicheva, D. (2017). Gamifying education: what is known, what is believed, and what remains uncertain: a critical review. *International Journal of Educational Technology in Higher Education*, *14*(1), 9. Advance online publication. DOI: 10.1186/s41239-017-0042-5

Doyle, A. J., O'Toole, M., Cassidy, D., & Condron, C. M. (2025). Universal Design for Learning (UDL) in simulation-based health professions education. *Advances in Simulation (London, England)*, *10*(1), 33. Advance online publication. DOI: 10.1186/s41077-025-00361-3 PMID: 40506788

Dwivedi, Y. K., Kshetri, N., Hughes, L., Slade, E. L., Jeyaraj, A., Kar, A. K., Baabdullah, A. M., Koohang, A., Raghavan, V., Ahuja, M., Albanna, H., Albashrawi, M. A., Al-Busaidi, A. S., Balakrishnan, J., Barlette, Y., Basu, S., Bose, I., Brooks, L., Buhalis, D., & Wright, R. (2023). Opinion Paper: "So what if ChatGPT wrote it?" Multidisciplinary perspectives on opportunities, challenges and implications of generative conversational AI for research, practice and policy. *International Journal of Information Management*, *71*, 102642. DOI: 10.1016/j.ijinfomgt.2023.102642

Eberts, R. E., & Brock, J. F. (1988). Computer-Based instruction. In *Elsevier eBooks* (pp. 599–627). DOI: 10.1016/B978-0-444-70536-5.50032-4

edX. (n.d.). *EDX and Arizona State University Reimagine the first Year of College, offering an alternative entry into higher education*. https://press.edx.org/edx-arizona-state-university-reimagine

Ekahitanond, V. (2013). Promoting university students' critical thinking skills through a peer feedback activity in an online discussion forum. *The Alberta Journal of Educational Research*, *59*(2), 247–265. DOI: 10.55016/ojs/ajer.v59i2.55617

Ertmer, P. A., & Ottenbreit-Leftwich, A. T. (2010). Teacher technology change. *Journal of Research on Technology in Education*, *42*(3), 255–284. DOI: 10.1080/15391523.2010.10782551

Ertmer, P. A., Ottenbreit-Leftwich, A. T., Sadik, O., Sendurur, E., & Sendurur, P. (2012). Teacher beliefs and technology integration practices: A critical relationship. *Computers & Education*, *59*(2), 423–435. DOI: 10.1016/j.compedu.2012.02.001

Fakhar, H., Lamrabet, M., Echantoufi, N., Khattabi, K. E., & Ajana, L. (2024). Towards a New Artificial Intelligence-based Framework for Teachers' Online Continuous Professional Development Programs: Systematic Review. *International Journal of Advanced Computer Science and Applications*, *15*(4). Advance online publication. DOI: 10.14569/IJACSA.2024.0150450

Farheen, N. S., Cheema, N. A. A., Ullah, N. R. S., & Bandeali, N. D. M. M. (2025). Equity and Bias in AI Educational Tools: A Critical Examination of Algorithmic Decision-Making in Classrooms. *the Critical Review of Social Sciences Studies*, *3*(3), 67–85. DOI: 10.59075/zqmnpa62

Farhood, H., Nyden, M., Beheshti, A., & Muller, S. (2025). Artificial intelligence-based personalized learning in education: A systematic literature review. *Discover Artificial Intelligence*, *5*(1), 331. Advance online publication. DOI: 10.1007/s44163-025-00598-x

Gentile, M., Città, G., Perna, S., & Allegra, M. (2023). Do we still need teachers? Navigating the paradigm shift of the teacher's role in the AI era. *Frontiers in Education*, *8*, 1161777. DOI: 10.3389/feduc.2023.1161777

Gibbs, H. (2025, January 28). *Evidence for ESSA: DreamBox Math*. DreamBox by Discovery Education. https://www.dreambox.com/family/essa-study-page-dreambox

Goldie, J. G. S. (2016). Connectivism: A knowledge learning theory for the digital age? *Medical Teacher*, *38*(10), 1064–1069. DOI: 10.3109/0142159X.2016.1173661 PMID: 27128290

Guo, L., Wang, D., Gu, F., Li, Y., Wang, Y., & Zhou, R. (2021). Evolution and trends in intelligent tutoring systems research: A multidisciplinary and scientometric view. *Asia Pacific Education Review*, *22*(3), 441–461. DOI: 10.1007/s12564-021-09697-7

Hamilton, E. (2021). *Computer-Assisted Instruction*. EBSCO. Retrieved September 15, 2025, from https://www.ebsco.com/research-starters/computer-science/computer-assisted-instruction?

Hasselbring, T. (1984). Research on the Effectiveness of Computer-Based Instruction: A Review. In George Peabody College. for Teachers, Nashville, TN. Learning Technology Center, *Technical Report No. 84.1.3* (Information Analyses ED 262 754) [PDF]. https://files.eric.ed.gov/fulltext/ED262754.pdf

Holmes, W., Bialik, M., & Fadel, C. (2019). Artificial Intelligence in Education. Promise and implications for teaching and Learning. *Center for Curriculum Redesign* [Book]. https://curriculumredesign.org/wp-content/uploads/AIED-Book-Excerpt-CCR.pdf

Holmes, W., Porayska-Pomsta, K., Holstein, K., Sutherland, E., Baker, T., Shum, S. B., Santos, O. C., Rodrigo, M. T., Cukurova, M., Bittencourt, I. I., & Koedinger, K. R. (2021). Ethics of AI in Education: Towards a Community-Wide Framework. *International Journal of Artificial Intelligence in Education*, *32*(3), 504–526. DOI: 10.1007/s40593-021-00239-1

Ibrahim, R. K., Marar, Y. A. A., Salman, M., Jehad, S., Hamza, M. G., Abouelnasr, A. S., Abdelaliem, S. M. F., Alahmedi, S. H., & Hendy, A. (2025). Impact of multiple educational technologies on well-being: The mediating role of digital cognitive load. *BMC Nursing*, *24*(1), 1028. Advance online publication. DOI: 10.1186/s12912-025-03655-z PMID: 40764954

Jenkins, C., Cale, C., Panesar-Aguilar, S., & McCraney, M. (2022). A critical examination of implementing the substitution, augmentation, modification, and redefinition model in elementary school instruction. *International Journal of Multidisciplinary Research and Growth Evaluation*, *3*(4), 206–212.

Joseph, N. O. B., & Uzondu, N. N. C.Olatunbosun Bartholomew JosephNwankwo Charles Uzondu. (2024). Integrating AI and Machine Learning in STEM education: Challenges and opportunities. *Computer Science & IT Research Journal*, *5*(8), 1732–1750. DOI: 10.51594/csitrj.v5i8.1379

Karpicke, J. D., Blunt, J. R., & Nick Buttrick, A. Gampa, Lilian Hummer, & Brian Nosek. (2011). Replication of Retrieval Practice Produces More Learning than Elaborative Studying with Concept Mapping. In *Science* (Vol. 331, pp. 772–775). http://www.socialsciencesreplicationproject.com/src/pre-reports/Karpicke%20and%20Blunt%20(2011)%20-%20Pre-Data%20Collection%20Replication%20Report.pdf

Kashif, M., Ammar, M., Sellami, A., Chiu, T. K., Abbasi, S. A., & Ahmad, Z. (2025). Teachers' perspectives on AI integration in K-12 education: Challenges, opportunities, and preliminary assessment model – a systematic review. *Computers in the Schools*, •••, 1–27. DOI: 10.1080/07380569.2025.2602507

Khan, N., Khan, Z., Koubaa, A., Khan, M. K., & Salleh, R. B. (2024). Global insights and the impact of generative AI-ChatGPT on multidisciplinary: A systematic review and bibliometric analysis. *Connection Science*, *36*(1), 2353630. Advance online publication. DOI: 10.1080/09540091.2024.2353630

Khokhar, Y. (2025). BLOOM'S TAXONOMY AND ITS DIGITAL EVOLUTION: A FRAMEWORK FOR SCHOOL EDUCATION. *e-ISSN: 2582-5208International Research Journal of Modernization in Engineering Technology and Science, 7*(2). DOI: 10.13140/rg.2.2.21309.52969

Kim, J., Detrick, R., Yu, S., Song, Y., Bol, L., & Li, N. (2025). Socially shared regulation of learning and artificial intelligence: Opportunities to support socially shared regulation. *Education and Information Technologies*, *30*(9), 11483–11521. Advance online publication. DOI: 10.1007/s10639-024-13187-9

Kizilcec, R. F., Pérez-Sanagustín, M., & Maldonado, J. J. (2016). Self-regulated learning strategies predict learner behaviour and goal attainment in Massive Open Online Courses. *Computers & Education*, *104*, 18–33. DOI: 10.1016/j.compedu.2016.10.001

Kulik, J. A., & Fletcher, J. D. (2015). Effectiveness of intelligent tutoring systems. *Review of Educational Research*, *86*(1), 42–78. DOI: 10.3102/0034654315581420

Latif, W. B., Ph, D., Yasin, I. M. Y., Ph, D., Rahaman, M. A., Ph, D., Forid, M. S., Islam, M. N., & Hossain, M. Z. (2024). Impact of augmented reality (AR) and virtual reality (VR) on interactive learning systems. *Pacific Journal of Advanced Engineering Innovations*, *1*(1), 23–32. DOI: 10.70818/pjaei.2024.v01i01.016

Lavanya, P., Kumari, B. S. S., & Padmambika, P. (2024). Collaborative learning and group dynamics in digital environments. *International Journal of Social Science and Education Research*, *6*(2), 105–108. DOI: 10.33545/26649845.2024.v6.i2b.131

Li, Z., Wang, Z., Wang, W., Hung, K., Xie, H., & Wang, F. L. (2025). Retrieval-augmented generation for educational application: A systematic survey. *Computers and Education Artificial Intelligence*, *8*, 100417. DOI: 10.1016/j.caeai.2025.100417

Liang, W., Zhang, Y., Codreanu, M., Wang, J., Cao, H., & Zou, J. (2025). The widespread adoption of large language model-assisted writing across society. *Patterns (New York, N.Y.)*, *6*(12), 101366. DOI: 10.1016/j.patter.2025.101366 PMID: 41472824

Liu, C., Meng, S., Zheng, W., & Zhou, Z. (2025). Research on the impact of immersive virtual reality classrooms on student experience and concentration. *Virtual Reality (Waltham Cross), 29*(2), 82. Advance online publication. DOI: 10.1007/s10055-025-01153-w

Luo, Y., Liu, T., Cheong-Iao Pang, P., McKay, D., Chen, Z., Buchanan, G., & Chang, S. (2025). Enhanced Bloom's Educational Taxonomy for Fostering Information Literacy in the Era of Large Language Models. *arXiv*. https://arxiv.org/pdf/2503.19434

Ma, W., Adesope, O. O., Nesbit, J. C., & Liu, Q. (2014). Intelligent tutoring systems and learning outcomes: A meta-analysis. *Journal of Educational Psychology, 106*(4), 901–918. DOI: 10.1037/a0037123

Major, L., Francis, G. A., & Tsapali, M. (2021). The effectiveness of technology-supported personalized learning in low- and middle-income countries: A meta-analysis. *British Journal of Educational Technology, 52*(5), 1935–1964. DOI: 10.1111/bjet.13116

Mejeh, M., Sarbach, L., & Hascher, T. (2024). Effects of adaptive feedback through a digital tool – a mixed-methods study on the course of self-regulated learning. *Education and Information Technologies, 29*(14), 1–43. DOI: 10.1007/s10639-024-12510-8 PMID: 39464525

Mejia, M., & Sargent, J. M. (2023). Leveraging technology to develop students' critical thinking skills. *Journal of Educational Technology Systems, 51*(4), 393–418. DOI: 10.1177/00472395231166613

Mirea, C., Bologa, R., Toma, A., Clim, A., Plăcintă, D., & Bobocea, A. (2025). Transforming Learning with Generative AI: From Student Perceptions to the Design of an Educational Solution. *Applied Sciences (Basel, Switzerland), 15*(10), 5785. DOI: 10.3390/app15105785

Naseer, M. A., Saeed, S., Afzal, A., Ali, S., & Malik, M. G. R. (2025). Navigating the integration of artificial intelligence in the medical education curriculum: A mixed-methods study exploring the perspectives of medical students and faculty in Pakistan. *BMC Medical Education, 25*(1), 273. Advance online publication. DOI: 10.1186/s12909-024-06552-2 PMID: 39979912

Noy, S., & Zhang, W. (2023). Experimental evidence on the productivity effects of generative artificial intelligence. *Science, 381*(6654), 187–192. DOI: 10.1126/science.adh2586 PMID: 37440646

Onum, F. O., & Agama, O. (2025). *Evaluating the Impact of Virtual Reality Training on Workforce Skill Development in Emerging Economies. Malaysian E Commerce Journal*. MECJ., DOI: 10.26480/mecj.01.2025.26.34

Pappas, C. (2025, April 28). *Instructional Design Models and Theories: Programmed Instruction Educational Model*. eLearning Industry. https://elearningindustry.com/programmed-instruction-educational-model

Pawar, P. (2023). *AI-Enhanced education: personalized learning and educational technology*. ResearchGate., DOI: 10.25215/9358791152.0

Pottle, J. (2019). Virtual reality and the transformation of medical education. *Future Healthcare Journal*, *6*(3), 181–185. DOI: 10.7861/fhj.2019-0036 PMID: 31660522

Qadir, H. M., Khan, R. A., Rasool, M., Sohaib, M., Shah, M. A., & Hasan, M. J. (2025). An adaptive feedback system for the improvement of learners. *Scientific Reports*, *15*(1), 17242. Advance online publication. DOI: 10.1038/s41598-025-01429-w PMID: 40383780

Quah, B., Zheng, L., Sng, T. J. H., Yong, C. W., & Islam, I. (2024). Reliability of ChatGPT in automated essay scoring for dental undergraduate examinations. *BMC Medical Education*, *24*(1), 962. DOI: 10.1186/s12909-024-05881-6 PMID: 39227811

Radianti, J., Majchrzak, T. A., Fromm, J., & Wohlgenannt, I. (2019). A systematic review of immersive virtual reality applications for higher education: Design elements, lessons learned, and research agenda. *Computers & Education*, *147*, 103778. DOI: 10.1016/j.compedu.2019.103778

Rahmawati, S., Prestridge, S., Abdullah, A. G., & Widiaty, I. (2025). Unpacking the digital competence challenge in vocational education: A case from Indonesia. *Social Sciences & Humanities Open*, *12*, 101803. DOI: 10.1016/j.ssaho.2025.101803

Rapanta, C., Botturi, L., Goodyear, P., Guàrdia, L., & Koole, M. (2020). Online university teaching during and after the COVID-19 crisis: Refocusing teacher presence and learning activity. *Postdigital Science and Education*, *2*(3), 923–945. DOI: 10.1007/s42438-020-00155-y PMID: 40477148

Rehman, Z. U., Aurangzeb, W., & Saeed, R. (2022). Reflections on adopting the SAMR model for technology integration at the University level: A phenomenological study from Pakistan. *Journal of Social Sciences Advancement*, *3*(3), 117–129. DOI: 10.52223/JSSA22-030303-39

Reich, J., & Ruipérez-Valiente, J. A. (2019). The MOOC pivot. *Science*, *363*(6423), 130–131. DOI: 10.1126/science.aav7958 PMID: 30630920

Rienties, B., Cross, S., & Zdrahal, Z. (2016). Implementing a Learning Analytics Intervention and Evaluation Framework: What works? In *Springer eBooks* (pp. 147–166). DOI: 10.1007/978-3-319-06520-5_10

Romero, C., & Ventura, S. (2024). Educational data mining and learning analytics: An updated survey. *Wiley Interdisciplinary Reviews: Data Mining and Knowledge Discovery;2020; 10(3): E1355.*

Saleem, N. D. S., Aziz, N. M. U., Iqbal, N. D. M. J., & Abbas, N. S. (2025). AI in Education. *Personalized Learning Systems and Their Impact on Student Performance and Engagement. the Critical Review of Social Sciences Studies, 3*(1), 2445–2459. DOI: 10.59075/c35qa453

Samala, A. D., Rawas, S., Rahmadika, S., Criollo-C, S., Fikri, R., & Sandra, R. P. (2025). Virtual reality in education: Global trends, challenges, and impacts—game changer or passing trend? *Discover Education, 4*(1), 229. Advance online publication. DOI: 10.1007/s44217-025-00650-z

Selvi, V. T., & K, T. K. (2024). Applications and Analyses of Artificial Intelligence in Enhancing English Vocabulary. *IRO Journals*. DOI: 10.36548/rrrj.2024.2.002

Selwyn, N. (2022). *Education and Technology* (3rd ed.). Bloomsbury Publishing Plc., https://books.google.co.in/books?id=dMZKEAAAQBAJ&lpg=PR1&ots=wnSTKO1ECs&dq=Selwyn%2C%20N.%20(2016).%20Education%20and%20technology%3A%20Key%20issues%20and%20debates.%20Bloomsbury%20Publishing.&lr&pg=PR4#v=onepage&q=Selwyn,%20N.%20(2016).%20Education%20and%20technology:%20Key%20issues%20and%20debates.%20Bloomsbury%20Publishing.&f=true DOI: 10.5040/9781350145573

Shamsudinova, I., Karimov, N., Umarova, M., Mustafaqulova, D., Almuratova, G., Qodirov, S., Istamova, D., & Matniyoz, S. (2025). Educational disparities in the digital era and the impact of information access on learning achievements. *Indian Journal of Information Sources and Services, 15*(1), 6–11. DOI: 10.51983/ijiss-2025.IJISS.15.1.02

Shute, V., & Rahimi, S. (2017). Review of computer-based assessment for learning in elementary and secondary education. *Journal of Computer Assisted Learning, 33*(1), 1–19. DOI: 10.1111/jcal.12172

Singh, A. (2025). Generative AI-powered Automated Essay Scoring System. *Social Science Research Network*. https://papers.ssrn.com/sol3/papers.cfm?abstract_id=5203163

Slade, S., Prinsloo, P., & Khalil, M. (2019). Learning analytics at the intersections of student trust, disclosure, and benefit. *The 9th International Conference*, 235–244. DOI: 10.1145/3303772.3303796

Song, R., Pang, F., Jiang, H., & Zhu, H. (2024). A machine learning based method for constructing group profiles of university students. *Heliyon*, *10*(7), e29181. DOI: 10.1016/j.heliyon.2024.e29181 PMID: 38601658

Subhash, S., & Cudney, E. A. (2018). Gamified learning in higher education: A systematic review of the literature. *Computers in Human Behavior*, *87*, 192–206. DOI: 10.1016/j.chb.2018.05.028

Sung, Y., Chang, K., & Liu, T. (2015). The effects of integrating mobile devices with teaching and learning on students' learning performance: A meta-analysis and research synthesis. *Computers & Education*, *94*, 252–275. DOI: 10.1016/j.compedu.2015.11.008

Suppes, P. Institute for Mathematical Studies in the Social Sciences, Stanford University, National Science Foundation, United States Office of Education, Carnegie Corporation of New York, Atkinson, R. C., & McCarthy, J. (1971). *Computer-Assisted Instruction at Stanford*. https://web.stanford.edu/group/csli-suppes/techreports/IMSSS_174.pdf

Tan, L. Y., Hu, S., Yeo, D. J., & Cheong, K. H. (2025). Artificial Intelligence-Enabled Adaptive Learning Platforms: A Review. *Computers and Education Artificial Intelligence*, *100429*, 100429. Advance online publication. DOI: 10.1016/j.caeai.2025.100429

Tan, X., Cheng, G., & Ling, M. H. (2024). Artificial intelligence in teaching and teacher professional development: A systematic review. *Computers and Education Artificial Intelligence*, *8*, 100355. DOI: 10.1016/j.caeai.2024.100355

Tang, X., Chen, H., Lin, D., & Li, K. (2024b). Harnessing LLMs for multi-dimensional writing assessment: Reliability and alignment with human judgments. *Heliyon*, *10*(14), e34262. DOI: 10.1016/j.heliyon.2024.e34262 PMID: 39113951

Tapalova, O., & Zhiyenbayeva, N. (2022). Artificial Intelligence in Education: AIED for Personalized Learning Pathways. *Electronic Journal of e-Learning*, *20*(5), 639–653. DOI: 10.34190/ejel.20.5.2597

Tondeur, J., Scherer, R., Baran, E., Siddiq, F., Valtonen, T., & Sointu, E. (2019). Teacher educators as gatekeepers: Preparing the next generation of teachers for technology integration in education. *British Journal of Educational Technology*, *50*(3), 1189–1209. DOI: 10.1111/bjet.12748

Tunjera, N., & Chigona, A. (2019). Teacher educators' appropriation of TPACK-SAMR models for 21st-century pre-service teacher preparation. *International Journal of Information and Communication Technology Education, 16*(3), 126–140. DOI: 10.4018/IJICTE.2020070110

Uyar, A. C., & Büyükahıska, D. (2025). Artificial intelligence as an automated essay scoring tool: A focus on ChatGPT. *International Journal of Assessment Tools in Education, 12*(1), 20–32. DOI: 10.21449/ijate.1517994

Uzorka, A., Namara, S., & Olaniyan, A. O. (2023). Modern technology adoption and professional development of lecturers. *Education and Information Technologies, 28*(11), 14693–14719. DOI: 10.1007/s10639-023-11790-w PMID: 37361776

Vanlehn, K. (2011). The relative effectiveness of human tutoring, intelligent tutoring systems, and other tutoring systems. *Educational Psychologist, 46*(4), 197–221. DOI: 10.1080/00461520.2011.611369

Waluyo, B., & Balazon, F. G. (2024). Exploring the impact of gamified learning on positive psychology in CALL environments: A mixed-methods study with Thai university students. *Acta Psychologica, 251*, 104638. DOI: 10.1016/j.actpsy.2024.104638 PMID: 39647452

Wang, S., Wang, F., Zhu, Z., Wang, J., Tran, T., & Du, Z. (2024). Artificial intelligence in education: A systematic literature review. *Expert Systems with Applications, 252*, 124167. DOI: 10.1016/j.eswa.2024.124167

When schools shut: gendered impacts of COVID-19 school closures. (2021). United Nations Educational, Scientific, and Cultural Organization. https://unesdoc.unesco.org/ark:/48223/pf0000379270

Xi, R. (2024). A Systems Approach to Shedding Sunlight on AI Black Boxes. *SSRN, 53*(3). Advance online publication. DOI: 10.2139/ssrn.4966957

Yuan, M., Bao, P., Yuan, J., Shen, Y., Chen, Z., Xie, Y., Zhao, J., Li, Q., Chen, Y., Zhang, L., Shen, L., & Dong, B. (2024). Large language models illuminate a progressive pathway to artificial intelligent healthcare assistant. *Medicine Plus, 1*(2), 100030. DOI: 10.1016/j.medp.2024.100030

Zafar, N. D. N., Saira, N. D., & Afzal, N. S. (2025). AI-Powered Reading Support for Multilingual Learners in Higher Education: A Critical Review. *Journal for Social Science Archives, 3*(1), 776–786. DOI: 10.59075/jssa.v3i1.158

Zerkouk, M., Mihoubi, M., & Chikhaoui, B. (2025). A Comprehensive Review of AI-based Intelligent Tutoring Systems: Applications and Challenges. *Journal of Computers in Education*. https://doi.org//arXiv.2507.18882DOI: 10.48550

Zhai, C., Wibowo, S., & Li, L. D. (2024). The effects of over-reliance on AI dialogue systems on students' cognitive abilities: A systematic review. *Smart Learning Environments, 11*(1), 28. Advance online publication. DOI: 10.1186/s40561-024-00316-7

Zhang, K., Meng, X., Yan, X., Ji, J., Liu, J., Xu, H., Zhang, H., Liu, D., Wang, J., Wang, X., Gao, J., Wang, Y., Shao, C., Wang, W., Li, J., Zheng, M., Yang, Y., & Tang, Y. (2024). Revolutionizing Health Care: The Transformative Impact of large language models in medicine. *Journal of Medical Internet Research, 27*, e59069. DOI: 10.2196/59069 PMID: 39773666

KEY TERMS AND DEFINITIONS

Academic performance: Measurable learning outcomes, such as test scores, knowledge retention, and subject mastery. Aadaptive quizzes, intelligent tutoring systems, and virtual labs, can enhance these outcomes by personalizing instruction and feedback.

Artificial Intelligence: AI is a computer system mimicking human intelligence, such as decision-making, problem-solving, and language processing, to personalize learning. Examples include intelligent tutors, chatbots, automated grading, and predictive analytics.

Bloom's Taxonomy: Hierarchical framework of cognitive skills, from basic recall to higher-order skills, i.e., remembering to creating, used to design learning goals.

Connectivism: Learning is a process occurring through networks of people, digital tools, and shared resources. LMS, MOOCs, and AI-driven analytics enable learners to access distributed knowledge and engage in peer discussions.

Constructivism: Learners actively build their understanding through authentic, active experiences, problem-solving, and reflection. Using interactive simulations, virtual labs, etc., learners experiment and progress at their own pace according to their individual learning needs.

Educational Technology: is the broad use of digital tools and platforms to support teaching, learning, and administration. It includes learning management systems, online platforms, digital resources, and immersive technologies.

Personalized Learning: Learning experiences tailored to individual needs, preferences, and behaviours. Systems dynamically adjust content, difficulty, and feedback, promoting autonomy, engagement, and self-regulated learning.

SAMR Model: The SAMR model includes stages like Substitution, Augmentation, Modification, and Redefinition, illustrating the depth of technology use in teaching, rfrom simple replacement of traditional tools to creation of transformative tasks that were previously impossible.

TPACK Model: The TPACK model emphasizes the intersection of teachers' content expertise, pedagogical strategies, and technological skills, guiding them in selecting tools that align with both subject matter and learning goals, highlights teachers' capacity to transform classroom practices effectively.

Chapter 15
Smart Learning With Educational Robotics

Sunil Sankathala
https://orcid.org/0009-0004-7809-7647
Ajeenkya D.Y. Patil University, India

Susanta Das
https://orcid.org/0000-0002-9314-3988
Ajeenkya D.Y. Patil University, India

ABSTRACT

Driven by rapid technological advancements in the 21st century, Education 4.0 emphasizes innovation, customization, and digital integration in education. Incorporation of robots into educational environments and its increasing importance in contemporary pedagogy are examined in this chapter. They improve STEM/STEAM education by encouraging teamwork, creativity, critical thinking, and problem-solving abilities. They have demonstrated promises particularly for kids with autism spectrum disorder. They provide an interesting means for pupils to connect theoretical ideas with real-world applications. Their many functions as peers, instructors, and learning partners are changing the dynamics of classrooms. The necessity of pedagogically sound applications and teacher readiness for robotics use are emphasized. This chapter also examines instructional ideas including constructivism and constructionism, curriculum design issues, programming tools, and international case studies. It also emphasizes the significance of inclusion, usefulness, and accessibility.

DOI: 10.4018/979-8-3373-4521-5.ch015

1. INTRODUCTION

The fourth industrial revolution (Industry 4.0) has been associated with Education 4.0 where advanced technologies including robotics, augmented reality, and the internet of things have been integrated to revolutionise learning. Education 4.0 is aimed at delivering personalised, interactive learning experiences tailored to the specific needs of each student. The use of educational robots has been central to this change, connecting students, helping those with disabilities, and maximising learning outcomes (Umbara, 2024).

Robotics has developed into a useful, experiential learning tool in education in recent years, combining technology, science, and mathematics. Effective learning requires integrating robots with sound teaching ideas and philosophies like constructivism and constructionism. Pedagogy, curriculum design, and positive learning settings ought to be the main priorities. Following the initiation of the European project known as Teacher Education in Robotics Enhanced Constructivist Pedagogical Methods (TERECoP) (2006–2009), a new way to teach instructors how to use robots as a learning tool emerged. This paved the way for other ongoing initiatives which have undertaken TERECoP's process (Alimisis, 2012).

Robotics in Education (R-in-E) similarly seeks to improve students' learning. Curto and Moreno (2015) mentioned in their paper about how robots help in science, technology, engineering, and mathematics (STEM) learning while Kalaitzidou and Pachidis' (2023) study analysed robots in science, technology, engineering, arts, and mathematics disciplines. Robots have the potential to make the learning process more interesting and engaging for students, whether at school, college, or university. Learning activities that integrate the use of robots can motivate students to pursue STEM careers by providing hands-on experiences that help bridge the gap between theory and practice. This field draws on the contributions of educators, researchers, software developers, and robotics specialists, whose collaboration enables the effective application of robotics across a wide range of learning environments.

As learners increasingly demand curricula that integrate social and emotional learning, research has shifted focus towards "social robots" that can react to individual differences, detect emotions, and perform a given role in the learning process. Nevertheless, regardless of which robotic platforms are used, educators should ensure that they are directly related to educational goals, student groups, and real classroom scenarios (Lampropoulos, 2025).

Robots are increasingly used as educational aids for students with autism spectrum disorder (ASD), a developmental disorder that frequently manifests in early childhood, and impacts behaviour, social interaction, and communication. Language, social-emotional abilities, and behavioural flexibility are often challenging for students with ASD. Since there is still no known medical treatment for ASD, education remains the most successful strategy for coping with these conditions (Yavuz & Nuri, 2024).

Current studies emphasise the increased role played by robots in teaching. Educational theorists, as mentioned by Kubilinskiene et al. (2017) in their paper are convinced that learning facilitated by robots increases student participation and intellectual abilities. Research indicates that using robots in teaching assists with connecting experiments to scientific knowledge.

This chapter seeks to examine the advantages of using teaching robots in schools, analyse their effect on student learning in various subjects, investigate teaching approaches, and determine potential areas of future research. This chapter considers studies from various cultures, ages, and subjects in order to provide a broader investigation.

2. A BIBLIOMETRIC REVIEW

The figure from PubMed (Figure 1) clearly shows a detailed, intricate landscape of research related to smart learning and educational robotics. The term "humans" appears most often and is the main focus in the network. PubMed-based analyses often include this term, since research in biomedicine and health care tends to include "humans" as the main subject, giving this term priority in semantic networks. Although it has central importance in the network, it also indicates that human involvement remains a main connection linking a variety of technical and educational terms.

Surrounding "humans", various topics such as artificial intelligence, deep learning, algorithms, and wearable electronic devices are found. They are closely bunched, proving that many studies are being carried out on blending Artificial Intelligence (AI) and wearable devices for human use. "Artificial intelligence" links the development of smart learning with tools used in medicine and health, meaning that an increasing number of learning tools are working alongside health-monitoring and cognitive improvement systems. Among the themes in educational robotics are attention, cognition, and computer-assisted teaching. In addition to these terms, robotics and AI tutors are mentioned as examples of tools being used in various teaching contexts to promote focused learning and improved development in students. The presence of the phrase "adolescent behaviour" shows that many studies in this area look at how education affects young people. Healthcare education appears as a significant topic when considering clinical competence, medical education, and distance learning. The main goal of this study was to train students by using robotics, simulators, and deep learning tools in medical education. Both the mention of "laparoscopy" and "virtual reality" confirm that surgical training and simulations with robots are also part of remote or mixed learning methods.

Figure 1. Bibliometric Co-occurrence Network Based on PubMed Data Related to "Smart Learning with Educational Robotics"

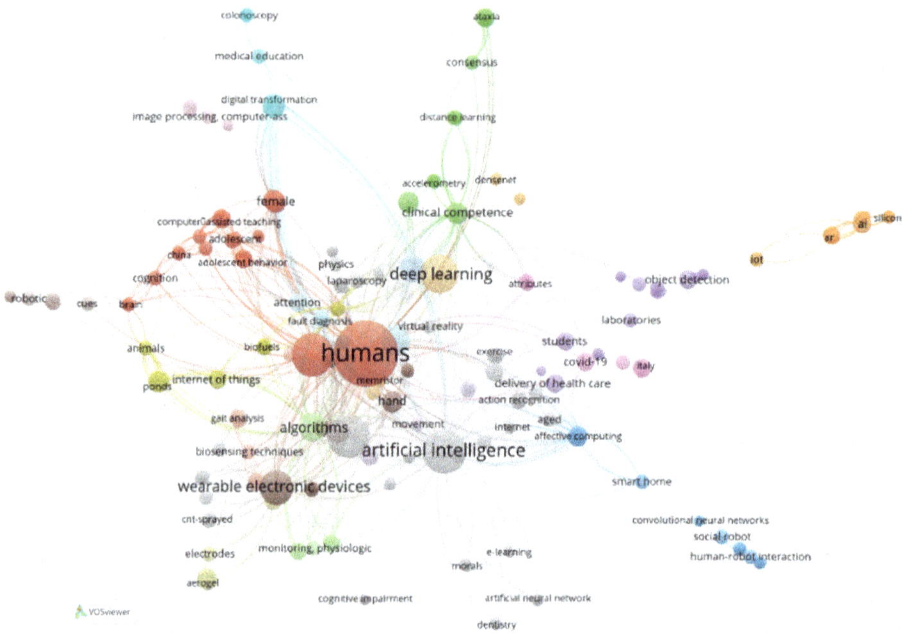

A notable point is that "image processing," "computer-assisted," and "object detection" are software phrases that show up in educational robotics related to visual systems. This set of key phrases focuses on computer vision which is commonly used in interactive robotics to help machines step in and react to image information. This aligns with educational robotics activities where robots are guided by vision or by hand movements.

In addition, "students", "e-learning" and "affective computing" are not strongly linked to the main groups and are found towards the edges of the network. Since they are located farther from the central concept of "AI-healthcare" than other subjects, it appears that emotionally aware machines and digital learning are emerging fields within this domain. At the same time, this group is valuable for its "smart learning" idea mentioned in the here (Figure 1), since it demonstrates how affective and cognitive feedback loops are being integrated into intelligent tutoring and educational robotics.

Specialised areas of robotics research associated with the abovementioned terms indicate that robotics is increasingly being applied in domestic and social contexts. These findings support the view that educational robotics extends beyond schools and traditional learning environments. The cluster including the terms "IoT," "AI," "silicon," and "AR," located in the upper-right orange region of the network, appears to represent research focused on industrial technologies, hardware development, and AI-enabled applications that can be adapted for educational purposes. Although this cluster is not explicitly education-focused, its presence reflects the technological foundations that enable the broader development of educational robotics. The integration of multiple clusters in Figure 1 clearly demonstrates that smart learning through educational robotics is inherently interdisciplinary. Fields such as biomedical sciences, engineering, educational theory, and cognitive psychology intersect to shape contemporary educational practices, particularly those that incorporate advanced technological systems.

VOSviewer generated another visualisation using data from Lens.org, showing keyword co-occurrence associated with "Industry 4.0". The term "Industry 4.0" stands out in the middle of the map, showing that it is the most commonly discussed topic. Thus, Industry 4.0 is the main theme that characterises the organisation of research topics in this area. Since this node is linked to many different areas, it shows how Industry 4.0 is related in many ways to technology, industry, and education. There are several groups of other keywords for unique themes. "Digitalisation", "automation," "cloud computing," "digital twin," and "the internet" are the main elements of the Industry 4.0 ecosystem, indicated by the red cluster. This cluster stresses the key points related to the rise of smart technology. Beside it is the blue cluster, which is concerned with intelligent automation and robotics, with phrases including "smart factories", "industrial internet of things", "the future of industry", and "human–robot interaction". This indicates that industrial organisations need to familiarise themselves with the main cyber-physical systems guiding Industry 4.0.

The applications of Industry 4.0 involving life and ethics are highlighted in the yellow cluster, including words and phrases like "animals", "animal husbandry", "care 4.0", "engineering", and "trust." The cluster also illustrates how new technology is used in various sectors like agriculture and healthcare, and the concerns that are brought up regarding ethics and trust in the hands of the user. The green cluster stands out because it includes words that are not explicitly connected, like "durapatite" and "chemistry". This could give the impression that the field of manufacturing is not strongly linked to Industry 4.0, as the former seems to concentrate on niche research in the field of biomedical engineering that does not intersect with other dominant areas of Industry 4.0. Such keywords and phrases appear in the purple group, which include "circular economy", "recycling", "pharma 4.0", and "sustainable development". This group illustrates the emergence of more studies dedicated to sustainability in Industry 4.0, in particular, to green innovation and the implementation of digital solutions in pharmaceuticals. The brown cluster (Figure 1) groups studies related to education, implementation processes, skills development, critical policy research, and survey-based investigations.The cluster also highlights the implications of Industry 4.0 on society, politics, and education as aspects of setting up policies, arranging workforce training, and ensuring that institutions are ready for the digital industry's evolution.

The presence of peripheral keywords and phrases including "COVID-19", "company perception", "data space", "simulation", and "dentistry" points to more specific or developing research subjects. For this reason, the topic COVID-19 may be discussed in studies focusing on the role of the pandemic in boosting digital changes in industrial industries. Likewise, the terms "simulation" and "digital twin" point to easy access to virtual training and learning that are currently relevant. Because they are important but show up less often in several studies, it is clear that these subjects are still on the rise. On the whole, the map shows a dense, well-connected core and a less organised, less crowded outer surrounds. Such an arrangement confirms that Industry 4.0 is the primary focus, with multiple new applications and perspectives comprising its core. The diagram also demonstrates that Industry 4.0 involves a lot of study on technology and industry, but smart learning, applications for people, and ethics are combined important factors that are quickly being recognised and researched.

An analysis of publishing data from PubMed and Lens provides contrasting and yet compatible views on the place of educational robotics in the wider domain of intelligent learning. PubMed and Lens reflect different ideas about how knowledge is constructed in biomedical sciences, cognitive sciences, and industrial-technological systems (Figure 2). In this type of visualisation, the term "humans" appears in the middle, surrounded by clusters on "artificial intelligence", "deep learning", "algorithms", and "wearable electronic devices." Most of the research in this area is concentrated on educational robotics that affect cognitive skills, interest in education, and medicine-related teaching. Especially in the medical and health sciences fields, robotics is seen as helpful for stimulating thinking and changing behaviours by using terms like "clinical competence", "attention", "affective computing", "cognition", and "computer-assisted teaching" (Rathore & Afridi, 2021). Additionally, the presence of students, using distance learning, and applying virtual reality in education points to an increased use of robots in remote courses and virtual reality, possibly encouraged by the challenges faced throughout the education sector due to the COVID-19 pandemic (Yuan et al., 2021). Thus, the dataset in this study illustrates the view that educational robotics is specially designed to benefit individuals, enhance learning, and improve both clinical and cognitive skills.

In the Lens data, Industry 4.0 is the main focus for bibliometric mapping, implying that social and technological aspects are increasingly included in the role of educational robotics in changing industrial systems. "Cloud computing", "digital twin", "automation", "cyber-physical systems", and "internet of things" (IoT) are the main themes found, suggesting that there is an aim to use the latest technology, train workers, and update skills (Augello et al., 2020). Terms such as "skills", "simulation", and "human–robot interaction" are included in the literature, even though they are mostly discussed in relation to industrial or operational topics such as smart factories, pharma 4.0, and data-driven automation, among others. Unlike what is found in the PubMed network, which mainly highlights psychological and cognitive aspects, the Lens map reveals that educational robotics serves functions in industry systems and helps enhance productivity, integration, and sustainability approaches, as shown by Huang et al. (2021). Other important issues such as trust, human factors, and smart factories illustrate how human-machine relationships play a key role in preparing people for future jobs.

Figure 2. Keyword co-occurrence network of "Industry 4.0" research visualised using VOSviewer from Lens.org data.

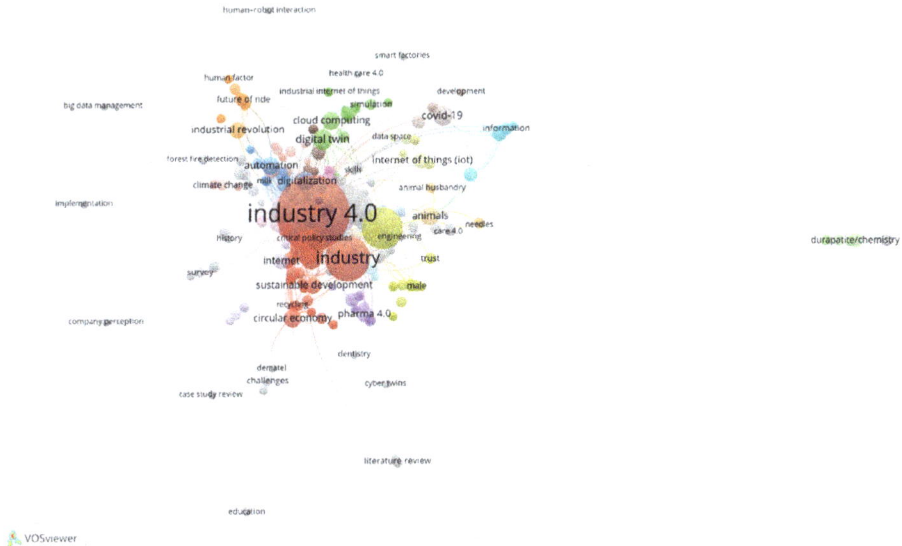

Together, these visualisations show that educational robotics has many dimensions. The database emphasises the use of educational technology to help people learn, adjust to new situations, and receive feedback during their training with the aid of AI. Alternatively, the Lens database depicts the use of robotics at an extensive level in industry and as a main part of digitalisation, showing how robotics shapes vocational education, industrial automation, and sustainable industry activities (Flatebo et al., 2024). Humanistic and health-related dimensions are emphasised in the PubMed-based visualisation, whereas the Lens-based visualisation focuses more on large-scale technological implementation, industrial integration, and operational scalability. Together, these perspectives provide a more comprehensive understanding of educational robotics that supports individual learning while contributing to the development of a skilled and adaptable workforce for industry.

3. LITERATURE REVIEW

3.1. Education

A new category of educational technology that extends beyond the conventional educational robots is the social robots. In contrast to conventional robots, social robots are able to interpret and react to emotions, communicate in a natural manner, and even replicate human-like behaviour. Their capacity to build social relationships makes them very effective instruments in the classroom, particularly as learners increasingly demand personalised, emotional methods of learning (Lampropoulos, 2025).

Robots have grown in sophistication in that they are able to recognise and even generate subjective feelings, make choices, and converse with human beings. These innovations have seen the popular use of pedagogic robots in schools as a way of enhancing student education. It is proven that the application of robots in the classroom can increase the level of digital literacy in students, improve their engagement, and support the development of their verbal, social, and cognitive skills. They promote teamwork, creativity, and practice. Students tend to be more inspired to learn when they are exposed to technology that they already know and are interested in (Yavuz and Nuri, 2024).

One of the most significant objectives of introducing robotics into the educational process is to change the way of teaching and learning using real-life, practical experience, rather than simply introducing high-tech devices in the classroom. By focusing on active learning and exploration during the learning process, and at the same time attaching importance to what students already know and are interested in learning, students will be able to develop relatable, concrete models in the form of projects that the students will want to explore, and which will challenge them to solve some problems. Students are included in the construction and programming of the robots, as opposed to being provided with ready-made and ready-programmed devices that hide their inner mechanisms. This shift from "black-box" to "white-box" technology empowers students, encourages experimentation, and increases innovation (Alimisis, 2012).

Under this strategy, students work in groups to find solutions to open-ended problems, which require building, configuring, and programming robotic systems to perform real-life activities. These projects often incorporate concepts from mathematics, science, technology, and engineering and may span multiple fields.

As part of the planning, construction, testing, and presentation of their robotic creations, students engage in critical reflection. This reflection enhances teamwork, communication skills, and strengthens learning (Alimisis, 2012).

To assist students with creating real products, it is common to introduce cheap, printable robots in engineering programmes. Such applied projects promote project-based learning and encompass a variety of practical aspects, from conception to commercialisation and beyond (Curto and Moreno, 2015).

The primary role of the educator, in this case, is to encourage and direct. The instructor prepares the classroom, provides the required equipment, asks thought-provoking questions, and assists the learners throughout the entire learning process. Evaluation is performed in collaboration with students in order to support the learning objectives and assess individual and team contributions (Alimisis, 2012).

In some cases, learners play around with the design, assembly, and programming of humanoid robots and underwater vehicles (ROVs). As a result of such exercises, students developed and enhanced their problem-solving and team-building skills, and became acquainted with the educational and practical aspects of engineering (Curto & Moreno, 2015).

One of the more effective exercises was to utilise smartphones in programming the robots. This enabled vocational students to more effectively identify with and easily access the learning process. To create robotics education which can be operated and accessed remotely, another initiative created an online system that allows students to remotely write, test, and run programmes on real robots (Curto & Moreno, 2015).

Robots are programmed for social interactions, including the use of speech, facial expressions, and body language, in such a way that they can act as tutors, classmates, or study companions. They have been promising both in formal (schools) and informal (after-school programmes) learning settings. In certain cases, social robots are even able to teach students approximately as well as human tutors, which is why they become especially beneficial in areas such as special education, where students require unique or more personalised forms of attention (Lampropoulos, 2025).

3.2. Science, Technology, Engineering, & Mathematics (STEM)

Learning robots have shown impressive effectiveness in STEM education as they encourage student interest, creativity, collaboration, and problem-solving. The International Organization for Standardization (ISO) identifies three critical factors for the use of educational robots. These include effectiveness, efficiency, and satisfaction. Instructional robots in a STEM curriculum were tested in research conducted at South-West University Neofit Rilski in Bulgaria by the Department of Applied Sciences. The study's participants were students who had previously completed a course titled "Technical Modelling" that includes education on robotics (Tosheva, 2024).

Instructors generally welcome social robots and appreciate the value they bring to the classroom. Rather than envisioning them as substitutes for instructors, attention should be given to how they can expand and assist in teaching and learning when used wisely (Lampropoulos, 2025).

3.3. Science, Technology, Engineering, Arts, & Mathematics (STEAM)

STEAM education promotes hands-on, project-based learning in which students work together and discover through science, technology, engineering, arts, and mathematics. Robotics has an increasingly important role to play in this method, assisting students in grasping difficult ideas in subjects such as mathematics, physics, and art. Robots serve as learning aids, taking abstract concepts and making them concrete and interactive. There are various types of educational robots; for example, Lego Mindstorms EV3, which is commonly used for its modularity, sensors, and easy-to-use programming interface (Kalaitzidou & Pachidis, 2023).

Several educational robots facilitate STEAM learning, each appropriate for various age ranges and budgets. The Nao robot (~€12,300) is a sophisticated humanoid with numerous sensors, encouraging emotional and social growth but is complicated and expensive, and thus more appropriate for universities. Beebot (~€100) is perfect for young children (ages 3–5), providing easy programming via buttons, assisting in the development of memory and spatial abilities. Another innovation is printbots, which are affordable, open-source robots that can be 3D printed and easily assembled. These DIY robots offer a budget-friendly and customisable way for students and educators to explore robotics and STEAM concepts (Kalaitzidou & Pachidis, 2023).

In educational robotics, programming languages are important for allowing students to communicate with and operate robots. There are two broad categories of languages: traditional scripting languages and visual programming languages (Kalaitzidou & Pachidis, 2023).

Traditional scripting languages include popular and general-purpose programming languages like Python, Java, JavaScript C, and C++. They are robust and generally form the building blocks for more complex robotics applications. Python specifically is extremely popular in educational robotics because of its easy syntax and large libraries supporting robotics and AI (Kalaitzidou & Pachidis, 2023).

3.4. Visual Programming Languages

To simplify robotics, particularly for elementary school children, visual programming languages have emerged. They are easy-to-use, block-based spaces where users drag and drop graphical code blocks (puzzles, icons, or shapes) to build programmes. This approach obviates the memorisation of arcane syntax and enables learners to concentrate on the logical foundations of programming (Kalaitzidou & Pachidis, 2023).

Some of the more well-known visual programming environments utilised in schools are:

1. Scratch: Enables students to develop interactive stories, animations, and games, and makes programming fun and interactive. It is particularly favoured in primary and secondary education. Evidence indicates that Scratch is utilised in nearly 50% of projects in STEAM education and provides an excellent introduction to more powerful languages such as Python (Kalaitzidou & Pachidis, 2023).
2. Google Blockly: Similar to Scratch, this visual language programme is based on a drag-and-drop model whereby blocks are code equal. Blockly can be used to write standard code in JavaScript, Python, PHP, Lua or Dart. Blockly is open-source and web-based and is easy to set up and use in classrooms (Kalaitzidou and Pachidis, 2023).
3. Snap: An online block programmer platform which builds upon the principles of Scratch but adds more functionalities like the possibility to create one's own blocks of the programme. It is flexible and creative, enabling students to experiment and share their work online. Snap does not require installation and is very easy for beginners to use (Kalaitzidou and Pachidis, 2023).

These visual programming languages not only excel at teaching core programming logic but also assist students in acquiring computational thinking, problem-solving skills, and creativity. They provide tangible representation of abstract concepts, raise engagement levels, and can be especially useful for assisting students in their migration to textual programming languages such as Python (Kalaitzidou & Pachidis, 2023).

3.5. Robot Categories

Robotic studies in education can be categorised according to three key dimensions: what, when, and how something is being studied (Mubin et al., 2013). Learning domain is one fundamental requirement when identifying the way in which robots are applied to learning. There are two major classifications: technical learning and non-technical learning. Technical learning entails learning about fields such as computer science and programming, raising the level of consciousness, and technological/robotic skill acquisition by learners. For instance, students who are engaged in designing and coding robots often exhibit increased enthusiasm and participation. Non-technical education employs robots as instruments to supplement instruction on topics such as mathematics, science, and language. For example, robots can be utilised to instruct students in geometry through movement or in assisting with language instruction by offering an unintimidating audience where one can practice speaking in the target language (Mubin et al., 2013).

Non-technical learning revolves around the site of the learning activity: intra-curricular or extra-curricular. Intra-curricular activities are incorporated into the formal school syllabus, whereas extra-curricular activities are undertaken outside formal classroom settings, like workshops or parent-guided learning at home. Extra-curricular activities are generally less formal and more flexible, offering greater opportunities for innovative and diverse learning experiences. Because of their typically less formal structure, extra-curricular activities are generally easier to set up, but perhaps more challenging to evaluate in the long term (Mubin et al., 2013).

3.6. Role of the Robot

Robots are able to adopt various roles as they learn; for example, as a passive tool, an active co-learner, or even a tutor. A robot may exist as a simple teaching tool for courses like robotics, where pupils construct and develop robots. Otherwise, a robot is able to become more interactive as it works cooperatively with students in group learning or, to some extent, as a mentor. However, the latter requires technological innovations for the robot to be independently used in this way (Mubin et al., 2013).

3.7. Pedagogical Theories

Constructionism theory, as advocated by Seymour Papert, is prominent in robotics teaching. This states that students learn best by building physical artifacts and thinking about their problem-solving journeys. Robotics teaching is suitably aligned with this, providing interactive experiences that foster creativity and problem-solving. Other theories such as active learning and social constructivism, based on learning through interaction and collaboration, are also applicable (Mubin et al., 2013).

1. Collaborative learning: Are robots as effective as peers in collaborative learning? Experiments to compare the effectiveness of learning individually, with robots, or with peers assess how impactful robots can be in collaborative learning (Mubin et al., 2013).

2. Roles of teachers: Incorporating robots into formal instruction requires explicit curricula development and training for teachers. Teachers should perceive robots as supplements, not substitutes (Mubin et al., 2013).
3. Conformity to learners: Robots should be capable of conforming to various types of learners based on such aspects as age, gender, and prior knowledge (Mubin et al., 2013).
4. Designing socially acceptable robots: For robots to be effective and fun, they require ongoing enhancements in behaviour and communication, e.g., improved speech recognition and natural human-like interaction (Mubin et al., 2013).

Fabiane Barreto Vavassori Benitti (2012) of the Italian Univali University conducted a detailed systematic review of robotics in education. Benitti analysed peer-reviewed publications published between 2000 and 2009, which outlined the introductory features of robotics in education and preconditioned the continuation of this field (Kubilinskiene et al., 2017).

Alimisis (2012) in his practical study demonstrated that robots can be successfully incorporated into regular classroom instruction and confirmed the efficacy of the training methods to achieve this. The study emphasised how crucial teacher preparation is and how project-based learning affects students' creativity, engagement, and comprehension of challenging subjects like programming.

3.8. Robots for Autism Spectrum Disorder (ASD) Students

Teaching people with ASD is one prominent area where robots are increasingly used. Children with ASD frequently struggle with social communication, adaptability in behaviour, and comprehension of intricate human relationships. Many children with ASD react more positively to robots than to people. For many with ASD, the repeated and predictable activities of robots are reassuring and simpler to comprehend. According to several studies, when these children interact with robots, they typically exhibit higher levels of attention, social feedback, and engagement (Yavuz & Nuri, 2024).

The intricacies of human contact and the comfort level that children with ASD have with machines can be reconciled through the use of robots. When it comes to improving social, emotional, and communication skills, robots can be useful tools. Even while a large number of studies reveal favourable results, some have produced contradictory findings, indicating that individual effectiveness can differ. However, a number of children with ASD have demonstrated that robotic interventions are a viable way to increase their learning engagement and maybe even transfer their robot-based interaction abilities to human situations. The potential for robots to contribute significantly to inclusive and supportive education is growing along with technology (Yavuz & Nuri, 2024).

3.9. Case Studies, Learning Gains, and Student Engagement in Educational Robotics

Robotics in education is increasingly used in many countries, and has been proven to help students perform better, be more engaged, and grow socially and mentally. Countries such as the United States and several European nations now include LEGO Mindstorms in their learning activities from K–12 to university levels. Children learn computational thinking, cooperation, and problem-solving with the help of these educational platforms. Based on 147 studies, robotics-based education increases student engagement, raises academic performance, and boosts interest in STEM subjects in multiple settings (Anwar et al., 2019; Ching & Hsu, 2023). An example is from the US, where after-school programmes in robotics for children between ages 6 and 8 noticeably improved their visuospatial memory, logic, and attention as seen in cognitive and eye-tracking tests after six months (Liu et al., 2023).

Greece is also using robotics in primary school classrooms thanks to the CODESKILLS4ROBOTICS Erasmus+ project, helping children with special needs including ASD, ADHD and other learning disabilities. Robotics has also fostered the growth of digital abilities, increased student involvement, and promoted inclusivity in schools. Reports from educators suggest that students became more social and behaved positively after interacting with robots. For instance, an intervention using robotics and Arduino for 12 weeks with middle schoolers in Turkey raised their academic performance and helped them solve more problems than students studying with traditional ICT. Because of e-learning, students indicated stronger interest and desire to study STEM-related subjects (Erol et al., 2023; Koray & Uzuncelebi, 2023).

Modernising education in developing countries has in many cases relied on using robotics. As part of the move to more engaging lessons, Nao and hexapod robots were delivered to several Mexican schools and universities. The use of these technologies helped students pay more attention, feel more motivated, and increased their comprehension in physics and programming as confirmed by both behaviour studies and surveys (Hamidu, 2022). Robotics is taught in basic education in Brazil in an effort to get students more involved, allow them to think creatively, and improve their problem-solving abilities. As a result, there was an increase in students' motivation, and they considered science and technology with wider perspectives (Aliyu, 2022). Although using robotics in schools is limited in Nigeria, many acknowledge that it helps close the digital gap and brightens the future for engineering and computer science students. Some of the main problems in several contexts are a lack of infrastructure, inadequate funding for education, and insufficient training for teachers (Aliyu, 2022).

The application of robotics-based STEM learning resources in Nigeria has shown positive effects on academic performance and student learning activities. Students who were engaged in practical robotics projects registered quantifiable changes in their academic performance whereby the average assessment scores rose by a margin of 85 out of 100 to 90 out of 100. In addition to academic performance, research by (Chaidi et al. 2021) found that students were more motivated, interested, and enjoyed learning via robotics-driven exercises. The respondents rated the effectiveness of robotics to support their knowledge of STEM concepts as 4.2 out of five (On a scale of 0-5) and gave even a higher rating of 4.5 for motivation, which suggests high levels of enthusiasm and engagement in learners. These results indicate that robotics education enhances active learning through promoting problem-solving, creativity, and teamwork that consequently enhance conceptual knowledge of students in STEM subjects. In general, the findings indicate that robotics-based learning is not only an effective means of enhancing academic performance but also developing a positive attitude towards STEM education, which makes robotics-based learning a strong instrument for improving both the cognitive and affective learning outcomes in school environments (Chaidi et al. 2021).

Investigations of both statistics and personal observations confirm the benefits of educational robotics for students' academics. There was a noticeable difference in results from robotics-based versus conventional science teaching in Turkey; the gain was significant for multiple-choice and open-ended tests (Koray & Uzuncelebi, 2023).

Other similar studies have indicated that students in the United States who attend underserved middle schools and who have been exposed to robotics-based learning exhibit increased achievement in science and mathematics over the long term compared to students with similar backgrounds who do not receive robotics-enhanced learning. Research has also found a positive correlation between knowledge acquisition and use of robotics assignments among students, indicated by their enhanced cognitive abilities, such as the visuospatial working memory, logical reasoning, abstract thinking, and computational competence (Liu et al., 2023; Ching and Hsu, 2023). It has also been discovered that robotics-based learning outperforms tablet-based learning when it comes to the development of important 21st-century skills, including adaptability, self-directed learning, and competitive thinking, specifically in mathematics, language studies, and computer programming (Trapero-Gonzalez et al., 2024). Moreover, robotics work usually involves long-term cooperation, which contributes to the formation of teamwork and improved communication among learners. Notably, robotics-based learning environments prove especially helpful for students with unique learning or other educational needs since such settings offer practical, interactive, and inclusive learning that can support various students with different learning requirements.

Students' positive views of robotics programmes strengthen the reasons why they are important in education. Many learners consider robotics activities to be both fun and interesting which typically improves their involvement in class activities. Students find they are more interested in STEM after using robots in class and many become more confident and eager to participate in STEM competitions and other similar activities (Liu et al., 2023; Erol et al., 2023; Rahman et al., 2025; Chaidi et al., 2021). In Indonesia, one study reported that both the motivation and usefulness of robotics programmes were appreciated by students and most indicated a wish to pursue STEM careers. It seems that students in robotics-related programmes also tend to perform well academically and many become more interested in technology-related careers.

Robotics helps make education inclusive since it works with different abilities and helps students to collaborate with their peers. Programmes that support special educational needs have shown that robotics helps students socialise and become involved with their peers, proving that robotics should be included in every student's education. A summary of above discussed topics is given in Table 1. People who promote educational robotics largely agree that robotics helps people better understand technology. It makes difficult subjects easier and more enjoyable to learn by relating them to real life. Involvement in robotics gives students an opportunity to learn how advanced technology works by performing tasks independently.

Table 1. Key Impacts of Educational Robotics Across Countries

Country/Region	Education Level	Main Outcomes	Student Perceptions	References
United States / Europe	K–12, university	Enhanced STEM scores, computational thinking, problem-solving, teamwork.	High engagement, greater interest in STEM.	Anwar et al., 2019; Ching & Hsu, 2023; Liu et al., 2023
Greece	Primary	Improved digital skills, inclusion, socialisation for special needs students.	Positive feedback, increased classroom participation.	Erol et al., 2023
Turkey	Middle school	Higher academic achievement, problem-solving, positive STEM attitudes.	Described as fun, interesting, and motivating.	Erol et al., 2023; Koray & Uzuncelebi, 2023
Mexico	Elementary, university	Improved attention, motivation, and knowledge retention	Stronger focus, increased interest in physics and coding.	Aliyu, 2022

continued on following page

Table 1. Continued

Country/Region	Education Level	Main Outcomes	Student Perceptions	References
Brazil	K–12	Creativity, problem-solving, hands-on engagement.	Broadened perspectives on science and technology.	Aliyu, 2022
Nigeria	Secondary (projected)	Potential STEM gains, improved digital inclusion, academic performance.	Anticipated positive results if implemented.	Aliyu, 2022
Indonesia	High school	Academic score increase (85 → 90), higher motivation and teamwork.	Rated 4.2/5 for effectiveness, 4.5/5 for motivation.	Chaidi et al., 2021

Overall, educational robotics is already being used in many schools worldwide and has led to improved grades, enhanced learning skills, and increased motivation among students in various socio-economic contexts. Those studying in higher education accomplish both technology- and analysis-based tasks and show improvements in working, sharing, and handling practical matters. Examples from across the world illustrate that educational robotics is a suitable and sustainable way to address the needs of 21st-century education.

4. CONCLUSION

The way in which students inquire, learn, and acquire knowledge have been transformed with the use of robots in the classroom. The integration of robotics in educational innovation is not a novel concept, particularly in STEM as well as STEAM subjects. Its use encourages inquiry-based and project-driven learning, enabling students an opportunity to work closely with real world problems and master critical thinking, creativity, and collaborative working. This chapter has demonstrated that instructional robots are effective in diverse fields and learning contexts. They transform abstract ideas into practical understanding through the use of practical learning. Together with a thoughtful instructional approach using the constructivist and constructionist theories, robots have demonstrated the potential to enhance student motivation and autonomy in addition to academic performance. Moreover, robots have much potential in the field of special education, particularly in children with ASD. As per research, foreseeable, steady exchanges that are offered by robots are more likely to elicit a positive reaction in children with ASD as compared to human interactions. Robots may act as bridges, helping children to work on their social and communication skills which can be applied in human situations in the real world. One should also consider individual differences, since not all children will respond to robotic treatments in a similar manner. The success of the introduction of robotics in the classroom is determined by the presence of an instructor. Educators as facilitators guide learning activities, promote inclusive learning environments, and integrate robot-based activities with curriculum objectives. Therefore, educational robotics require adequate instructor support and training in order to maximise the use of robotics in education. The importance of usability as a measure of the effectiveness of robotics in education as a result of efficiency and user satisfaction is reaffirmed in this chapter as well. Moreover, the exploration of both visual (Scratch, Blockly) and textual (Python, Java) programming languages focuses on the flexibility which robotics provides in terms of coding and teaching computer-related thinking. Students who begin with less complex, block-based platforms and progressively advance to more complicated languages may build confidence and mastery.

In conclusion, educational robots have the potential to transform education, making it more accessible, participatory, and responsive to the needs of a diverse population of students. With the ongoing progress of the technology, the opportunities in the field of education are unlimited. Future research should consider the development of versatile robots, curricula that are inclusive, and evaluate the long-term effects of the use of robotics in the classroom on students. The future increasingly depends on robotics in education, and increased implementation is one of the options that could be used to continue offering captivating, meaningful learning experiences.

REFERENCES

Alimisis, D. (2012). Robotics in Education & Education in Robotics: Shifting Focus from Technology to Pedagogy. In Obdrzálek, D. (Ed.), *Proceedings of the 3rd International Conference on Robotics in Education* (pp. 7–14). Charles University in Prague, Faculty of Mathematics and Physics., https://roboesl.eu/wp-content/uploads/2017/08/Robotics-in-Education-Education-in-Robotics.pdf

Aliyu, H. (2022). Robotics education in developing countries: where do we start? *Sokotostateuni*. https://www.academia.edu/105780303/Robotics_education_in_developing_countries_where_do_we_start

Anwar, S., Bascou, N. A., Menekse, M., & Kardgar, A. (2019). A Systematic review of studies on educational Robotics. *Journal of Pre-College Engineering Education Research (J-PEER), 9*(2). DOI: 10.7771/2157-9288.1223

Augello, A., Daniela, L., Gentile, M., Ifenthaler, D., & Pilato, G. (2020). Editorial: Robot-Assisted Learning and Education. *Frontiers in Robotics and AI, 7* (Article 591319), 1. DOI: 10.3389/frobt.2020.591319

Chaidi, E., Kefalis, C., Papagerasimou, Y., & Drigas, A. (2021). Educational robotics in Primary Education. A case in Greece. *Research Society and Development, 10*(9), e17110916371. DOI: 10.33448/rsd-v10i9.16371

Ching, Y., & Hsu, Y. (2023). Educational Robotics for Developing Computational Thinking in Young Learners: A Systematic review. *TechTrends, 68*(3), 423–434. DOI: 10.1007/s11528-023-00841-1 PMID: 37362587

Curto, B., & Moreno, V. (2015). Robotics in education. *Journal of Intelligent & Robotic Systems, 81*(1), 3–4. DOI: 10.1007/s10846-015-0314-z

Erol, O., Sevim-Cirak, N., & Gulsoy, V. G. B. (2023). The Effects of Educational Robotics Activities on Students' Attitudes towards STEM and ICT Courses. *International Journal of Technology in Education, 6*(2), 203–223. DOI: 10.46328/ijte.365

Flatebo, S., Tran, V. N., Wang, C. E. A., & Bongo, L. A. (2024). Social robots in research on social and cognitive development in infants and toddlers: A scoping review. *PLoS ONE, 19*(5), 1, e0303704. DOI: 10.1371/journal.pone.0303704

Huang, Z., Shen, Y., Li, J., Fey, M., & Brecher, C. (2021). A survey on AI-Driven digital twins in Industry 4.0: Smart manufacturing and Advanced Robotics. *Sensors (Basel), 21*(19), 6340. DOI: 10.3390/s21196340 PMID: 34640660

Kalaitzidou, M., & Pachidis, T. P. (2023). Recent robots in STEAM education. *Education Sciences, 13*(3), 272. DOI: 10.3390/educsci13030272

Koray, A., & Uzuncelebi, B. H. (2023). The Effect of Educational Robotics Applications on Students; Academic Achievement and Problem-Solving Skills in Science Education. *Journal of Education in Science, Environment and Health, 9(4)*, 317–329. DOI: 10.55549/jeseh.1381251

Kubilinskiene, S., Zilinskiene, I., Dagiene, V., & Sinkevičius, V. (2017). Applying Robotics in School Education: A Systematic Review. *Baltic Journal of Modern Computing*, *5*(1), 50–69. DOI: 10.22364/bjmc.2017.5.1.04

Lampropoulos, G. (2025). Social robots in Education: Current trends and future perspectives. *Information (Basel)*, *16*(1), 29. DOI: 10.3390/info16010029

Lens, (2025). *Scholar search: Smart Learning with Educational Robotics* https://www.lens.org/lens/search/scholar/list?q=Smart%20Learning%20with%20Educational%20Robotics

Liu, Y., Odic, D., Tang, X., Ma, A., Laricheva, M., Chen, G., Wu, S., Niu, M., Guo, Y., & Milner-Bolotin, M. (2023). Effects of Robotics Education on Young Children's Cognitive Development: A Pilot Study with Eye-Tracking. *Journal of Science Education and Technology*, *32*(3), 295–308. DOI: 10.1007/s10956-023-10028-1 PMID: 37113265

Mubin, O., Stevens, C. J., Shahid, S., Mahmud, A. A., & Dong, J. (2013). A review of the applicability of robots in education. *Technology for Education and Learning*, *1*(1). Advance online publication. DOI: 10.2316/Journal.209.2013.1.209-0015

PubMed. (2025). *Scholar Search: Smart Learning with Educational Robotics* https://pubmed.ncbi.nlm.nih.gov/?term=Smart+Learning+with+Educational+Robotics&sort_order=asc

Rahman, T. F. A., Zakariah, Z. B., Anuar, N. B., Noh, Z. B., & Razak, N. B. A. (2025). The impact of STEM activities on students' knowledge and project development skills. *International Journal of Research and Innovation in Social Science*, *IX*(I), 3172–3182. DOI: 10.47772/IJRISS.2025.9010257

Rathore, F. A., & Afridi, A. (2021). Is exercise training effective within 12 months of lung resection for non-small cell lung cancer? A Cochrane Review summary with commentary. *PM & R*, *13*(3), 336–338. DOI: 10.1002/pmrj.12564 PMID: 33527624

The International Organization for Standardization (ISO) https://www.iso.org/standard/63500.html

Tosheva, E. (2024). Usability of educational robots in STEM education. *International Journal for Research in Applied Science and Engineering Technology, 12*(3), 59–64. DOI: 10.22214/ijraset.2024.58725

Trapero-González, I., Hinojo-Lucena, F. J., Romero-Rodríguez, J., & Martínez-Menéndez, A. (2024). Didactic impact of educational robotics on the development of STEM competence in primary education: A systematic review and meta-analysis. *Frontiers in Education, 9*, 1. DOI: 10.3389/feduc.2024.1480908

Umbara, D. M. A. (2024). Revolutionizing Education 4.0: Evaluating the role of robots in learning effectiveness. *E3S Web of Conferences, 482*, 05011. DOI: 10.1051/e3sconf/202448205011

VOSviewer. https://www.vosviewer.com/

Yavuz, N. M., & Nuri, N. H. (2024). Use of robot in the education of individuals with autism spectrum disorder. *Trakia Journal of Sciences, 22*(Supplement 1), 58. DOI: 10.15547/tjs.2024.s.01.009

Yuan, F., Klavon, E., Liu, Z., Lopez, R. P., & Zhao, X. (2021). A Systematic Review of Robotic Rehabilitation for Cognitive Training. *Frontiers in Robotics and AI, 8*, 605715. Advance online publication. DOI: 10.3389/frobt.2021.605715 PMID: 34046433

ADDITIONAL READING

Evripidou, S., Georgiou, K., Doitsidis, L., Amanatiadis, A. A., Zinonos, Z., & Chatzichristofis, S. A. (2020). Educational Robotics: Platforms, competitions and expected learning outcomes. *IEEE Access : Practical Innovations, Open Solutions, 8*, 219534–219562. DOI: 10.1109/ACCESS.2020.3042555

Krūmiņš, D., Schumann, S., Vunder, V., Põlluäär, R., Laht, K., Raudmäe, R., Aabloo, A., & Kruusamäe, K. (2024). Open remote web lab for learning robotics and ROS with physical and simulated robots in an authentic developer environment. *IEEE Transactions on Learning Technologies, 17*, 1325–1338. DOI: 10.1109/TLT.2024.3381858

Liu, L., Oh, H., Zhang, L., Fang, T., Huang, M., Hao, Y., Wang, J., Yao, C., & Ying, F. (2022). A study of children's learning and play using an underwater robot construction kit. *International Journal of Technology and Design Education, 33*(2), 317–336. DOI: 10.1007/s10798-021-09720-3

Ponce, P., Molina, A., Caudana, E. O. L., Reyes, G. B., & Parra, N. M. (2019). Improving education in developing countries using robotic platforms. [IJIDeM]. *International Journal on Interactive Design and Manufacturing*, *13*(4), 1401–1422. DOI: 10.1007/s12008-019-00576-5

KEY TERMS AND DEFINITIONS

Autism Spectrum Disorder (ASD): ASD is a developmental disorder that impacts the way an individual communicates, interacts with others, and perceives the world. Individuals with ASD might be divergent learners or connect differently, and others might feel more comfortable in a predictable, organised environment.

Constructivist Learning: Learning in which students construct their own knowledge with experience and exploration. Rather than listening to an instructor alone, students learn through doing, asking questions, and discovering things independently.

Educational Robotics: Integrating robots as learning aids for students. They are usually programmable and provide a constructive approach to learning when it comes to such topics as mathematics, science, coding, and programming.

Humanoid Robots: Artificial beings that emulate a human character and demeanour. They may be constructed to appear female or male, adorned with a face, arms, and can communicate and express emotions. Such robots are commonly applied to teaching or therapy since some people, children in particular, find it easier to associate with them.

Interactive Learning: Active, engaged learning. Students are engaged in activities, particularly using technology, working with others, posing questions, and not merely listening or reading thus making learning enjoyable as well as memorable.

Robot-Assisted Teaching: Robots assisting instructors in the classroom. Robots are able to elaborate on themes, facilitate an instructor's tasks, or even accommodate children with special needs, hence enabling learning to be interactive and individually oriented.

STEM Education: The STEM environment includes science, technology, engineering, and mathematics. STEM education is characterised by practice-based learning environments that enable students to address modern problems, think critically about various situations, and prepare for future employment.

Technology in Education: Incorporation of computers, tablets, software, and robots in the classroom to enhance effective learning, making learning enjoyable and open to every student.

Chapter 16

Teachers' Role in a Tech-Driven World Towards Quality Education:
A Capabilities Perspective

Samantha Melissa Hoffman
https://orcid.org/0009-0002-2322-6769
Two Oceans Graduate Institute, South Africa

ABSTRACT

Modern technologies are accelerating fundamental changes in the education sphere and evoking the role of the teacher as the most influential factor in educational spaces and innovations. The latest generation of teachers is in a different situation from previous generations of teachers, in terms of technology skills. However, it is crucial to assess teachers' technological skills, competence, and their understanding of how to integrate the technological possibilities in formal structures of learning organizations. This chapter used the Capability Approach theory of Amartya Sen to explore and identify the relevant capability sets teachers need to fulfil their role in a tech-driven world towards quality education. The CA offers a unique perspective for possible changes to teaching practice and curriculum experiences to enhance teaching, learning, and assessment in a fast-changing, tech-driven world. This chapter adopted a qualitative research method through a literature review of what other authors have conducted about the phenomenon.

DOI: 10.4018/979-8-3373-4521-5.ch016

1. INTRODUCTION

The role of teachers is crucial in the success of their learners and the entire education system. This is echoed in a study from Hoffman (2017), claiming that teachers are and have always been the primary locus of schooling systems around the world. As such, the quality of a country's teachers is intimately related to the quality of the education system. Hence, with new accelerating technologies paving the way for innovative approaches in educational spaces, it is essential to ensure that teachers possess the capabilities to fulfil their roles in a tech-driven world.

There is no doubt that the use of technology in education has opened new opportunities for both teacher and learner, transformed professional development, encouraged life-long learning and enhanced learning and teaching experiences (Sharma et al., 2018; Cullen, 2017; Alam, 2016; Sharma & Reddy, 2015; Shopova, 2012). Sarkar (2012) claims that the adoption of ICT in education led to a paradigm shift from traditional instruction-based learning to virtual learning environments, changing the roles of both facilitators and learners.

Although it is assumed that the new generation of teachers may be essentially in a different situation compared to previous generations of teachers, where technology skills are concerned, both beginner teachers and experienced teachers can benefit much from technology-related training, as it contributes to teachers' development of technological skills and competence that help them adopt such technologies in teaching (Wozney et al., 2006). The South African government attempts to address this through the White Paper 7 strategic objectives, which highlight teacher and staff capacity-building training for teachers, managers, and school administrators to effectively integrate ICT into teaching, learning, assessment, and administration, and emphasise continued professional development.

UNESCO (2013) emphasised that quality education should promote equitable access to learning opportunities, fostering critical thinking and innovation. Davies and West (2014) concur that new and novel approaches to teaching and learning are essential for improving the quality of education, primarily through the adoption of technology.

Considering the United Nations Sustainable Development Goal 4, which aims to ensure inclusive and equitable quality education and promote lifelong learning for all [United Nations (UN), 2017], it is crucial to assess teachers' technological skills, competence, and their understanding of how to integrate the technological possibilities in formal structures of learning organisations to achieve this goal.

2. EDUCATION IN THE 21ST CENTURY

The intersection between human capabilities and rapid technological advancement increasingly defines education in the 21st century. The digital era has transformed knowledge acquisition, teaching methodologies, and the expected competencies of learners. Central to these transformations is the demand for digital literacy, a skill no longer optional but integral to lifelong learning and participation in the knowledge economy. As Voogt and Roblin (2012) maintain, education is now oriented towards cultivating skills such as creativity, critical thinking, collaboration, and ICT literacy, which are indispensable in a technology-driven society. This reconfiguration of education not only requires learners to adapt but also necessitates a fundamental reimagining of the teacher's role in facilitating such competencies.

The 21st-century educational agenda has been closely tied to global frameworks such as UNESCO's *Futures of Education* initiative, which emphasises inclusive, equitable, and technology-enhanced learning systems (UNESCO, 2021). This orientation highlights the dual challenge: while technological tools can democratise access to information and support interactive learning, they can also exacerbate digital divides if educators and learners lack the skills to leverage them effectively. Trilling and Fadel (2009) argue that digital literacy should be conceptualised as a multidimensional competency that extends beyond basic technical proficiency to encompass the ability to evaluate information critically, communicate across digital platforms, and solve problems creatively. Thus, education in the 21st century cannot be reduced to the acquisition of technical skills; it must be situated within broader cognitive, social, and ethical dimensions.

From the perspective of Sen's Capability Approach, the role of education extends beyond imparting knowledge to enabling individuals to expand their freedoms and functionings in society (Sen, 1999). In a technology-mediated world, this implies that education should empower learners not merely to operate digital tools but to use them in ways that enhance their agency, creativity, and ability to contribute meaningfully to social and economic life. Nussbaum (2011) complements this view by stressing that education should foster capabilities such as critical reasoning, global citizenship, and empathy, qualities that remain essential even in a highly digitised context. Therefore, the 21st-century classroom is not solely a space for acquiring technical expertise but a crucible for nurturing holistic human development within a digitally saturated world.

Teachers, consequently, are central actors in shaping this transformation. Ertmer and Ottenbreit-Leftwich (2010) suggest that successful technology integration in education depends less on the mere availability of tools and more on teachers' pedagogical beliefs, confidence, and competencies. Without teachers developing strong digital pedagogies, technology risks being used superficially, failing to achieve its transformative potential. Moreover, Schleicher (2018) highlights that teachers themselves must embody the very 21st-century skills they are expected to cultivate in students, particularly adaptability and continuous professional learning. This underscores the necessity of embedding teacher training within lifelong learning paradigms that prioritise technological fluency alongside critical pedagogical reflection.

Furthermore, education in the 21st century must grapple with issues of equity, ethics, and sustainability. Warschauer and Matuchniak (2010) caution that unequal access to digital resources perpetuates structural inequalities, underscoring the need for educators and policymakers to prioritise inclusivity. Equally, Selwyn (2016) reminds us that technology in education is never neutral; it is shaped by social, political, and economic forces that influence how and for whom it is deployed. Thus, the future of education cannot be understood solely through a technological lens but must also account for the broader human, cultural, and ethical implications of digital transformation.

Education in the 21st century is a dynamic interplay between technological possibilities and human capabilities. It demands a rethinking of pedagogical practices, curricula, and teacher roles to ensure that digital literacy is not confined to technical proficiency but embedded within a broader framework of critical, creative, and ethical capacities. The challenge is to align technological integration with the goals of holistic human development, thereby preparing both teachers and learners not just to survive but to thrive in a rapidly evolving, technology-driven world.

2.1 Teachers' Role in Enhancing Quality Education

Teachers play an indispensable role in enhancing the quality of education, particularly in a world where technological innovations are reshaping learning environments. While access to digital tools and online platforms has expanded significantly, their effectiveness depends heavily on how teachers integrate them into meaningful pedagogical practices. As Hoffman and Maarman (2024a) argue, teachers are at the forefront of driving learning paradigm shifts by using technology not merely as an add-on but as a transformative force for pedagogy, collaboration, and assessment.

The Capability Approach, pioneered by Amartya Sen (1999), provides a compelling framework to examine teachers' evolving roles. From this perspective, teachers are not only implementers of curricula but also agents who expand learners' freedoms and opportunities by leveraging technology in innovative ways. Their role goes beyond transmitting knowledge to enabling students to achieve valued functionings such as problem-solving, digital literacy, and ethical reasoning. This shift underscores that teacher quality is not defined by technical skills alone, but by the broader capability sets teachers possess, ranging from adaptive expertise to emotional intelligence and critical reflection.

Contemporary scholarship reinforces the centrality of teachers in achieving quality education in tech-driven contexts. Darling-Hammond et al. (2020) note that while education systems are increasingly adopting digital solutions, the quality of learning outcomes is primarily determined by teachers' pedagogical choices, professional judgment, and capacity to contextualise technology. Similarly, Fullan and Gallagher (2020) argue that integrating technology into education succeeds only when teachers are empowered to reimagine learning designs rather than replicate traditional approaches in digital formats. These perspectives stress that professional development must focus not only on technical proficiency but also on cultivating teachers' ability to harness technology for student-centred and inquiry-based learning.

The role of teachers in enhancing quality education also extends to issues of equity and inclusion. Ainscow (2020) highlights that without intentional pedagogical strategies, technological innovations risk reinforcing existing inequalities, particularly for learners in marginalised communities. Teachers thus carry the responsibility of using technology to bridge rather than widen educational divides. This aligns with Schleicher's (2020) findings that teachers' professional autonomy, when coupled with strong digital competencies, is key to delivering equitable and high-quality learning experiences across diverse contexts.

Furthermore, teachers serve as ethical gatekeepers in digitalised classrooms. Selwyn (2022) warns that educational technology is not neutral but is shaped by political, social, and economic agendas, requiring teachers to critically evaluate the implications of digital tools for privacy, data security, and student agency. By exercising critical digital pedagogy, teachers ensure that the uncritical adoption of technological trends does not compromise quality education.

Teachers' role in enhancing quality education in the 21st century is multifaceted and increasingly shaped by their capability to adapt, innovate, and humanise technology integration. While devices and platforms provide unprecedented opportunities, it is teachers' expertise, judgment, and agency that determine whether technology enhances or diminishes educational quality. Anchored in the Capability Approach, teachers must be seen as agents who enable both themselves and their students to expand their freedoms in a rapidly evolving, tech-driven world.

2.2 Teacher Preparedness for a Tech-Driven World

Teacher preparedness in a tech-driven world is not limited to acquiring basic digital skills; it extends to developing the competence and pedagogical capacity to integrate technology meaningfully into learning processes. As education systems continue to evolve, the quality of teachers' engagement with technology directly shapes whether innovations translate into enhanced learning outcomes or remain superficial add-ons. According to Tondeur et al. (2017), teachers who are adequately trained in technological integration demonstrate not only higher confidence in using digital tools but also greater capacity to design innovative, student-centred pedagogies. This underscores that preparedness involves building deep professional competence rather than short-term technical fixes.

The Capability Approach of Amartya Sen (1999) provides a compelling framework for examining teacher preparedness, as it emphasises teachers' freedom to convert resources and training into valued educational practices. Simply providing access to devices or training opportunities does not guarantee integration; what matters is whether teachers develop the capability sets, such as digital fluency, adaptive expertise, and critical thinking, that enable them to choose and use technology effectively. Hammond (2021) suggests that teacher development programs should therefore go beyond technical training to support reflective practices, professional autonomy, and the cultivation of innovative pedagogical identities.

Recent scholarship stresses that effective professional development is the cornerstone of teacher preparedness. Darling-Hammond et al. (2017) argue that sustained, collaborative, and context-responsive training programs have far greater impact than one-off workshops, as they embed digital learning in teachers' daily practice. Similarly, Koehler et al. (2017) highlight the Technological Pedagogical Content Knowledge (TPACK) framework as essential for equipping teachers to balance subject matter, pedagogy, and technology. This view is echoed by Trust et al. (2018), who emphasise that when teachers see technology as integral to achieving broader learning goals, they are more likely to embrace it as a tool for transformation rather than as an external requirement.

Preparedness also involves cultivating adaptive mindsets in teachers. According to Kafyulilo et al. (2016), many educators, particularly in developing contexts, face systemic challenges, including inadequate infrastructure and limited access to digital tools. In these settings, teacher preparedness requires resilience, creativity, and the ability to maximise scarce resources for meaningful teaching. Sen's (1999) framework is helpful here, as it shifts attention from mere access to what teachers are actually able to do with the technologies at hand. In this sense, preparedness is relational, shaped by institutional support, policy frameworks, and school culture.

Importantly, teacher preparedness must also account for issues of equity and ethics. Selwyn (2022) cautions that technological adoption in education is never neutral, and teachers play a critical role in ensuring that digital learning does not exacerbate inequalities. Ainscow (2020) adds that training programs must equip teachers with strategies for using technology inclusively to reach diverse learners, including those with disabilities or from disadvantaged backgrounds. This positions teachers not just as implementers of innovation but as ethical agents responsible for aligning technology with values of equity and justice.

Teacher preparedness for a tech-driven world is multifaceted, encompassing technical competence, pedagogical integration, reflective practice, and ethical responsibility. Drawing on Sen's Capability Approach, preparedness must be viewed as the expansion of teachers' freedoms and professional capabilities, enabling them to transform digital resources into quality learning opportunities. Without this holistic readiness, technology risks being underutilised or misapplied. With it, however, teachers can lead the transformation of education in ways that are equitable, inclusive, and future-oriented.

2.3 Implications for the "Have and Have Not" School Context in a Tech-Driven World

The rapid integration of technology into education has amplified existing disparities between well-resourced ("have") and under-resourced ("have not") schools. While digital tools are often celebrated for their potential to democratise knowledge, in practice, they frequently deepen inequality by privileging learners and teachers with access to devices, connectivity, and digital literacy. Warschauer and Matuchniak (2010) described this as the "digital divide." Still, contemporary analyses reveal that the problem extends beyond access to include issues of quality, agency, and meaningful integration of technology (Van Dijk, 2020). This makes it imperative to consider the structural and pedagogical implications of technology adoption in unequal schooling contexts.

Learners from affluent schools have access to computers, tablets, and high-speed internet at home, which enables them to approach technology use with familiarity and confidence. In contrast, learners from disadvantaged contexts often encounter technology for the first time at school, resulting in a steeper learning curve and a higher likelihood of exclusion from digitally mediated opportunities (Livingstone & Helsper, 2022). This aligns with findings by Adegoke and Olugbara (2021), who show that in many African contexts, disparities in digital access reinforce cycles of disadvantage, as learners from low-income households are less likely to develop digital literacies that are now fundamental to academic success and employability.

Teachers are similarly affected by these inequalities. Ertmer and Ottenbreit-Leftwich (2019) highlight that teachers' beliefs, access, and prior experience with technology directly influence their willingness and ability to integrate digital tools into pedagogy. Educators in under-resourced schools often lack regular exposure to technology at home or in professional settings, resulting in limited digital fluency compared to peers in affluent contexts (Gudmundsdottir & Hatlevik, 2018). This suggests that teacher preparedness is not merely a matter of individual training but is deeply connected to systemic inequities in resource allocation and professional development opportunities.

Sen's *Capability Approach* (Sen, 1999) provides a critical lens for analysing these disparities. Access to technology alone does not guarantee educational transformation; what matters is whether teachers and learners can convert technological resources into real opportunities and valued achievements. In "have not" schools, where infrastructure is often unreliable and digital tools are scarce, both teachers and learners face severe constraints in developing the capabilities necessary for thriving in a tech-driven world. This highlights the importance of designing interventions that go beyond hardware provision to include capacity building, contextualised professional development, and policies that reduce structural barriers.

Importantly, the inequities between "have" and "have not" schools also carry implications for social justice. Selwyn (2022) warns that without intentional efforts, educational technology risks entrenching privilege by amplifying the voices and opportunities of already advantaged groups. In this sense, the teacher's role becomes pivotal not only as a facilitator of digital learning but also as an agent of equity who advocates for inclusive practices and adapts technology use to local realities.

As Ainscow (2020) argues, equitable education requires systemic approaches that empower teachers to meet learners' diverse needs, particularly in contexts of scarcity.

The widening gap between "have" and "have not" schools in a tech-driven world underscores that technological transformation in education is not a neutral process but one mediated by inequalities of access, capability, and opportunity. Addressing these disparities requires more than distributing devices; it involves rethinking teacher development, curriculum design, and policy frameworks to ensure that technology fosters inclusion rather than exclusion. Anchored in the Capability Approach, the challenge lies in creating conditions where all learners and teachers, regardless of context, can expand their freedoms and participate meaningfully in the digital knowledge society.

3. CAPABILITY APPROACH TO FRAME TEACHERS' ROLE IN A TECH-DRIVEN WORLD

The Capability Approach (CA), developed by Amartya Sen (1992; 1999), provides a fertile lens for rethinking teachers' roles amid rapid technological transformation. Rather than reducing educational quality to material resources or technical inputs, CA emphasises the substantive opportunities that individuals have to achieve valued outcomes. Applied to teachers in a tech-driven world, the CA encourages scholars and policymakers to move beyond simplistic notions of "access to technology" toward a richer understanding of teachers' freedom to use technology in ways that align with their professional values, pedagogical visions, and the broader pursuit of quality education.

Sen (1992) distinguishes between *functionings* (what individuals can do and be) and *capabilities* (the fundamental freedoms or opportunities to achieve those functionings). For teachers, functionings might include designing technology-enhanced lessons, fostering critical digital literacy among students, or engaging in online professional learning communities. Capabilities, in turn, represent the actual opportunities teachers have to realise these functionings, given their training, institutional environment, and socio-economic context. This distinction is crucial because two teachers with equal access to digital devices may have very different capabilities depending on the support structures, professional development opportunities, and freedoms available to them (Robeyns, 2017).

3.1 Teachers as Agents in a Tech-Driven World

The CA underscores human agency, highlighting individuals' ability to act and make meaningful choices (Sen, 1999). In education, this means recognising teachers not as passive implementers of top-down digital reforms but as professionals capable of shaping how technology is integrated into pedagogical practices. Hoffman and Maarman (2024b) emphasise that the CA empowers teachers to act as agents in choosing how they deploy technology to enhance learning outcomes valued by themselves and their students. Similarly, Traina and Guimarães-Iosif (2022) argue that adopting CA in digital education foregrounds teachers' creativity, autonomy, and reflective judgment, thereby countering deterministic narratives that assume technology itself guarantees improved learning.

By framing teachers as active agents, CA positions their role in a tech-driven world as one of intentional choice-making. For example, a teacher may decide to use a digital simulation in science education not because policy mandates its use, but because she values its potential to foster inquiry-based learning. Another teacher might choose to integrate collaborative platforms to strengthen peer-to-peer learning, guided by a belief in constructivist pedagogy. In both cases, the CA framework recognises these choices as expressions of teachers' agency and professional values, rather than mere compliance with technological trends.

3.2 Conversion Factors: Unequal Contexts, Unequal Capabilities

A distinctive contribution of CA is its focus on *conversion factors,* the personal, social, and environmental conditions that determine whether resources can be transformed into valued capabilities (Robeyns, 2011). This concept is particularly salient in the educational technology landscape, where disparities between schools and teachers often shape the outcomes of digital initiatives.

For instance, two schools may receive identical technological resources, such as tablets or interactive whiteboards. Yet, in a well-resourced urban school with ongoing technical support and teacher professional development, these tools are more likely to be converted into meaningful pedagogical practices. Conversely, in underfunded rural schools where teachers lack adequate training or stable internet connectivity, the same tools may remain underutilised or misapplied (Mitra, 2020). Thus, the CA highlights that addressing the "digital divide" requires more than distributing devices; it requires attention to the enabling conditions that allow teachers to convert access into pedagogical opportunities.

Conversion factors also operate at the individual level. Teachers' personal motivation, digital literacy, and openness to innovation play key roles in determining whether they can effectively use technology. According to Castañeda and Selwyn (2018), many teachers feel pressured by digital reforms but lack confidence in their own skills, resulting in surface-level adoption rather than transformative integration. From a CA perspective, this lack of confidence represents a constraint on teachers' capability set, limiting their freedom to engage with technology in ways they might otherwise value.

3.3 Expanding Teachers' Capability Sets

Hoffman and Maarman (2024b) argue that the CA provides a valuable framework for mapping *capability sets* in education, which define the range of opportunities individuals have to achieve valued outcomes. For teachers in a tech-driven world, several capability sets can be identified:

Table 1. Expanded capability sets for teachers in a tech-driven world

Identification of Expanded Capability Sets	Action
Digital Literacy Capabilities	The freedom to develop and apply core digital skills, including navigating online platforms, evaluating digital resources, and teaching students responsible digital citizenship.
Pedagogical Innovation Capabilities	The opportunity to adapt teaching strategies by incorporating simulations, gamified learning, and collaborative online tools to enhance student engagement.
Professional Learning Capabilities	The ability to access and participate in online communities of practice, webinars, and digital certification programs that sustain continuous professional growth (Trust et al., 2020).

continued on following page

Table 1. Continued

Identification of Expanded Capability Sets	Action
Critical Digital Ethics Capabilities	The freedom to interrogate the ethical implications of educational technologies, including concerns about surveillance, data privacy, and algorithmic bias (Selwyn, 2022).
Agency and Autonomy Capabilities	The opportunity to choose how, when, and why to integrate technology, guided by teachers' professional judgment rather than prescriptive mandates.

Mapping these capability sets illuminates the multidimensional nature of teachers' preparedness for a tech-driven world. It also provides a diagnostic tool for identifying areas of capability deprivation where teachers lack the freedom or support to enact valued roles.

3.4 Rethinking Teacher Development Through CA

One of the most significant implications of adopting CA is the reconceptualisation of teacher development. Traditional professional development often focuses narrowly on technical training on how to operate hardware or navigate software. While such training is necessary, the CA perspective insists that it is insufficient. True development involves expanding teachers' fundamental freedoms to make pedagogical choices, innovate, and adapt technology to their specific contexts.

Unterhalter (2019) stresses that equity in education requires recognising the different structural conditions that affect teachers' opportunities. For example, female teachers in specific contexts may face gendered barriers to digital training, while rural teachers may have limited access to professional learning networks. Addressing these inequalities requires not only training but also systemic reforms that expand teachers' substantive freedoms. This resonates with Sen's (1999) broader vision of development as the expansion of human freedom, underscoring that the aim of digital transformation in education must be to enlarge teachers' agency rather than constrain it.

3.5 Teachers and Quality Education in a Tech-Driven World

Framing teachers' roles through CA also reshapes our understanding of quality education. Instead of equating quality with technological modernisation, the CA emphasises whether teachers and students have the freedom to pursue educational outcomes they value. A school saturated with innovative devices may still fail to deliver quality education if teachers lack the capability to integrate these tools meaningfully. Conversely, modest digital resources can yield transformative results when teachers possess the freedom, creativity, and support to deploy them effectively (Traina & Guimarães-Iosif, 2022).

In this way, CA provides a normative benchmark: technology integration should be evaluated not merely by usage metrics but by the extent to which it expands teachers' and students' fundamental freedoms to achieve valued educational goals. This perspective shifts the focus from inputs and outputs to outcomes that reflect human agency, dignity, and well-being.

4. UNDERSTANDING THE TEACHER'S ROLE VIA THE CAPABILITY SETS UNDERPINNED BY THE CAPABILITY APPROACH

Before discussing the capability sets, this chapter presents a visual representation of the four carefully selected capability sets, based on their relevance to understanding the teacher's role in a tech-driven world.

Figure 1. Capability sets to understand the teacher's role

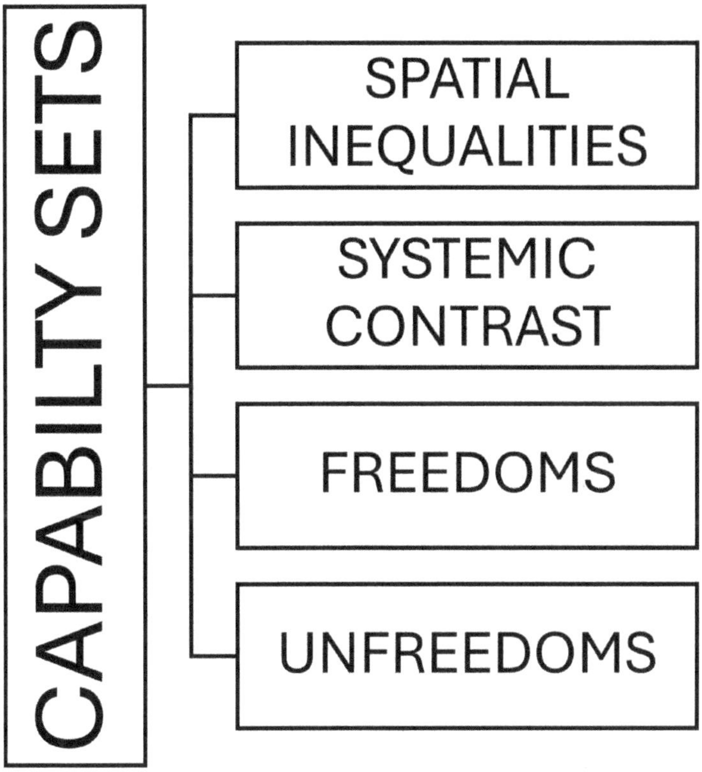

4.1 Understanding Teachers' Role via Capability Set Spatial Inequalities

Spatial inequalities in geography, infrastructure, and urban-rural divides pose significant challenges to teacher capability in tech-driven education. These inequalities determine not only access to physical devices and connectivity but also affect the conditions under which teachers convert their skills and knowledge into effective pedagogical practices. Drawing on recent research, we can see how spatial differences influence teacher capability in multiple ways.

First, access to infrastructure and connectivity is heavily spatial. In rural and remote schools, connectivity is often weak, intermittent, or altogether absent. A study of rural schools in South Africa (Duma et al., 2022) found that many rural teachers had limited access to ICT infrastructure, leading to poorer digital literacy, inconsistent use of technology in teaching, and reliance on the socioeconomic status of their schools. Such contexts limit teachers' capability to design technology, thus constraining the 'conversion factor' (as in the Capability Approach) from having devices to using them meaningfully.

Second, spatial inequalities affect professional learning and support. Teachers in well-resourced urban centres often have greater opportunities for professional development (PD), exposure to peer networks, access to technical support, and opportunities to engage with innovative practices. In contrast, teachers in peripheral or disadvantaged areas are more isolated. For example, in the South African study *Digital Equity in Schools: A Multilevel Analysis of In-Service Teachers' Technological Knowledge Competencies*, researchers found significant differences in baseline ICT competence among teachers, which were closely tied to their context (rural vs. town vs. urban). Though PD improved competencies overall, teachers in less advantaged spatial settings were slower to gain, and often continued to have fewer opportunities for ongoing, context-relevant support.

Third, spatial inequalities compound differences in outcomes of technology use. Beyond access and skill, the Capability Approach draws attention to whether valued outcomes can actually be achieved. In disadvantaged spatial settings, even when some tech resources are available, teachers' ability to translate these into student learning is often weakened by contextual limitations, such as unstable electricity, lack of maintenance, limited devices per class, large class sizes, and a lack of supportive school leadership. The study *Digital Divide at three disadvantaged secondary schools in Gauteng, South Africa* (Chisango & Marongwe, 2021) highlights that, in such schools, teaching and learning cannot be shifted online during crises (e.g., COVID-19) due to both access issues and teacher readiness.

Fourth, the agency's and pedagogical innovation's capability set is mediated by spatial location. Teachers in urban or affluent areas often enjoy greater autonomy, exposure to educational innovations, and a willingness to experiment with new digital pedagogies. Teachers in rural areas usually face stricter constraints, less autonomy, more standardised curricula with less flexibility, and few models of tech-enhanced pedagogy to emulate. This difference limits the extent to which teachers can choose methods they have reason to value, an essential component of CA. The South African concept of "Complex Inequalities and Inequities in Education" (Dlamini, 2022) shows that, in poorly resourced and remote schools, teachers are less able to adopt or integrate digital technologies pedagogically, even when policy mandates exist, due to spatially rooted institutional and material constraints.

Fifth, social and material contexts interweave with spatial inequalities. Teachers' own homes and communities may lack stable broadband, computers, or quiet workspaces. Even when their schools have some digital tools, teachers may struggle to prepare, plan, or update content outside school hours. Furthermore, social capital, peer support, mentoring, and networks are often less available in spatially isolated settings, further limiting teachers' capability to stay current, reflect, or innovate. These are critical conversion factors: the resources needed, but the freedom and conditions to use them. Geodemographic studies in Great Britain (Powell & Burns, 2021) illustrate how areas with low socio-economic status correlate with poorer access and lower home digital readiness, which, in turn, affect performance and skills.

Spatial justice emerges as an ethical consideration under CA: ensuring teachers in all locales have real opportunities (capabilities) to develop, not merely formal opportunities. Madikizela-Madiya (2021) studied access to and spatial justice in universities in sub-Saharan Africa, arguing that mere enrolment or resource provision is insufficient; one must examine whether spaces (universities, schools) enable people across regions to achieve valued educational outcomes. By analogy, teacher capability sets must be understood spatially, i.e., what freedoms teachers in rural vs urban or disadvantaged vs affluent settings really have.

4.2 Implications for Teacher Capability Sets and Quality Education

Putting these together, spatial inequalities have direct implications for how teachers' capability sets manifest, as presented in Figure 2 below.

Figure 2. Implications for Teacher Capability Sets and Quality Education

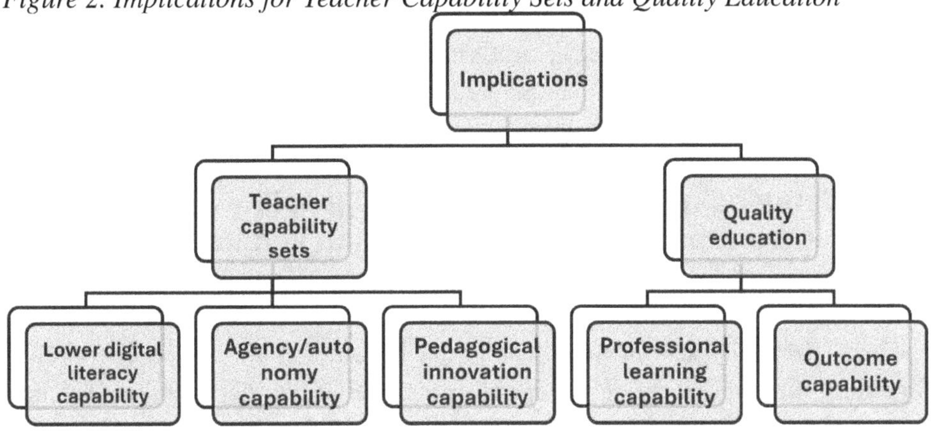

- Teachers in disadvantaged spatial zones may have lower digital literacy capability because of limited infrastructure, poor or no training, and fewer role models.

- Their agency/autonomy capability is restricted when institutional and material constraints disallow experimentation or optimal use of what little technology is available.
- Pedagogical innovation capability is less likely to flourish where spatial isolation and resource scarcity deter risk-taking and experimentation.
- Professional learning capability is weaker in spatially disadvantaged settings, as PD offerings are often centralised in urban hubs, with rural teachers missing out or receiving generic training not sensitive to local constraints.
- Outcome capability, i.e., translating use of technology into learning gains, is also weaker in these settings, due to students' lesser exposure outside school, less home support, and fewer complementary resources.

Thus, spatial inequalities do not just hamper access; they fundamentally shape whether teacher capability sets can be developed, deployed, and sustained, influencing the quality of education in tech-rich and tech-poor settings alike.

Considering spatial inequalities through the lens of the Capability Approach sharpens understanding of what "teacher preparedness" and "quality education" truly mean in tech-driven worlds. It is insufficient to provide devices or mandate digital learning; what matters is ensuring that teachers in all spatial settings have the freedoms, support, and enabling conditions to convert technology into meaningful, valued functionings.

For policy and practice, this implies that interventions must be spatially sensitive, recognising rural/urban, infrastructural, and connectivity dimensions, and tailored to expand teacher capabilities in those harder-to-reach contexts, rather than treating all schools as though they start from the same place.

4.3 Understanding Teachers' Role via Capability Set: Systemic Contrast Between Groups (Rich Versus Poor)

The gulf between wealthier and poorer school communities systematically shapes teachers' capability sets in ways that go far beyond simple device distribution. Structural inequalities create persistent differences in the opportunities teachers have to develop, exercise, and convert digital skills into pedagogically meaningful practices. The OECD's analysis of digital equity highlights that digitally mediated learning has had markedly uneven effects. Vulnerable and disadvantaged groups had more difficulty during the rapid shift to online learning, exposing pre-existing structural gaps in infrastructure, skills, and institutional support.

At the most basic level, material endowments differ. Schools in affluent areas typically have stable electricity, fast broadband, device-to-student ratios that allow regular classroom use, and on-site technical support; under-resourced schools frequently contend with intermittent connectivity, few devices, and limited maintenance capacity. Van Dijk characterises the digital divide not merely as access but as layered inequalities (motivation, skills, usage, outcomes), showing how socio-economic status systematically influences all stages of digital inclusion. In education, this means teachers in poor contexts often lack the conversion conditions necessary to turn devices into improved pedagogy.

Professional development opportunities are another systemic cleft. Research into teachers' professional digital competence finds that newly qualified and in-service teachers in advantaged districts more often access sustained, contextually relevant professional learning, mentorship, and professional networks, conditions shown to be critical for integrating technology effectively. Teachers in poorer schools more frequently receive one-off, generic workshops that do little to build deep Technological Pedagogical Content Knowledge (TPACK) or adaptive expertise. This institutional stratification constrains teachers' capability to innovate pedagogically with technology.

The Capability Approach sharpens the critique by highlighting conversion factors that determine whether resources translate into fundamental freedoms (capabilities). Two teachers may have identical laptops, but differing school leadership, class sizes, local community support, and time for lesson planning will produce very different capability sets. One teacher will be able to experiment, reflect, and iterate; the other will be trapped in survival mode. Warschauer and Matuchniak's (2010) work similarly emphasizes that access alone is insufficient; differences in use and outcomes are socially patterned and reproduce advantage.

Leadership and policy also reproduce or mitigate these contrasts. Studies show that proactive leadership in better-resourced schools can leverage technology for blended learning, teacher collaboration, and data-informed instruction; by comparison, weaker governance in poorer schools often means digital initiatives are fragmented or unsustained. Recent work highlights the decisive role of school leaders in translating national digital policies into equitable practice, a role that poor schools often cannot fulfil without targeted support.

Sadly, the systemic rich/poor contrast produces ethical and generational consequences. When teachers in advantaged contexts develop robust digital pedagogies, their students gain additional cultural and social capital that compounds opportunity gaps (better exam preparation, employability skills). Conversely, students in disadvantaged contexts and their teachers' risk being consigned to rote, low-engagement uses of technology, reinforcing cycles of educational inequality. Addressing this requires a policy that invests in infrastructure and sustained, context-sensitive professional development, leadership support, and community engagement measures that expand teachers' fundamental freedoms to convert digital resources into valued educational outcomes (i.e., true capabilities).

4.4 Understanding Teachers' Role via Capability Set: Freedoms

The notion of *freedoms* is central to Amartya Sen's Capability Approach (Sen, 1999), where development is defined as the expansion of substantive freedoms people have to live the kind of life they value. When applied to education and the role of teachers in a tech-driven world, freedoms are understood not merely as formal access to digital resources but as genuine opportunities for teachers to use technology to enhance pedagogy, professional growth, and student learning.

Sen (1999) distinguishes between *functionings* (the beings and doings individuals achieve) and *capabilities* (the substantive opportunities to accomplish those functionings). In this framing, teachers' freedoms involve the ability to integrate technology meaningfully into their practice rather than merely being provided with devices. As Robeyns (2017) argues, freedom is the real opportunity to choose among valuable options, which, in the educational context, translates into teachers having autonomy, competence, and supportive conditions to decide how to use technology to achieve quality education.

Recent scholarship underscores that teachers' digital freedoms are contingent upon structural and institutional arrangements. For instance, Gudmundsdottir and Hatlevik (2018) highlight that professional digital competence expands teachers' autonomy to design lessons that harness digital tools in innovative ways. Similarly, Redecker (2020), in the *European Framework for the Digital Competence of Educators (DigCompEdu)*, emphasises that teacher agency in digital environments is a cornerstone of practical educational innovation, where freedom is exercised through pedagogical creativity rather than compliance with prescriptive programs.

The COVID-19 pandemic provided a real-world test of these freedoms. König et al. (2020) found that teachers who possessed both technological competence and supportive school cultures were able to exercise freedom in adapting digital tools to learners' needs, while those in constrained environments experienced limited freedom, often resorting to basic content transmission. This demonstrates that freedoms are not abstract; they depend on conversion factors such as infrastructure, training, time, and institutional leadership.

Freedoms also entail the capacity to resist technological determinism. Selwyn (2016) cautions that while digital technologies are often portrayed as inevitable drivers of progress, teachers must retain the freedom to question, adapt, and reject tools that undermine pedagogical or ethical values. This resonates with Sen's idea that freedoms are not simply about doing *more* but about having the real option to choose what is valuable. For example, teachers should have the freedom to decide whether data-driven systems enhance or constrain their professional judgment.

Moreover, the freedom to innovate is unevenly distributed across socio-economic contexts. OECD (2023) reports that teachers in affluent schools often enjoy greater flexibility in experimenting with digital pedagogies, while teachers in under-resourced schools face constrained freedoms due to a lack of infrastructure and professional support. This systemic inequality raises critical questions about how policies can foster equitable freedoms for teachers across diverse educational landscapes.

Ultimately, framing teachers' roles in a tech-driven world through the lens of freedoms emphasises that true digital transformation is not achieved through technology provision alone. It requires enabling conditions that expand teachers' substantive choices, professional development that builds confidence, supportive school leadership that fosters experimentation, and equitable access to infrastructure. As Sen (1999) insists, development is about expanding freedoms; in education, this means empowering teachers to exercise their agency in shaping meaningful, context-sensitive uses of technology that contribute to quality education.

4.5 Understanding Teachers' Role via Capability Set: Unfreedoms

Within Amartya Sen's Capability Approach (Sen, 1999), *unfreedoms* are constraints or barriers that prevent individuals from converting resources into valuable functionings, thereby limiting their substantive opportunities. In the context of teachers in a tech-driven world, unfreedoms manifest as structural, institutional, and socio-economic limitations that restrict teachers' ability to integrate technology meaningfully into pedagogy and expand their professional capabilities.

One of the primary sources of unfreedoms is resource inadequacy. In many under-resourced schools, teachers face intermittent electricity, limited or outdated digital devices, and unreliable internet connectivity. Such constraints severely limit teachers' capability set, leaving them unable to adopt technology-enhanced teaching even if they possess the requisite skills. Van Dijk (2020) conceptualises the digital divide as a multi-layered phenomenon, in which disparities in access, digital skills, and meaningful use collectively create unfreedoms that reproduce educational inequalities. For teachers, these structural limitations impede the translation of digital competencies into effective pedagogical practice.

Institutional constraints also create unfreedoms. Teachers operating under rigid curricula, high student-teacher ratios, or prescriptive teaching methods have limited autonomy to experiment with technology-enhanced pedagogies. Redecker (2020) emphasises that the presence of digital tools alone does not guarantee meaningful integration; teachers need both autonomy and institutional support to exercise professional judgment. When schools do not provide such support, or when accountability pressures enforce uniformity, teachers' freedom to innovate is curtailed, and their capability to enrich learning outcomes is constrained.

Moreover, socio-economic and spatial inequalities further restrict teacher capabilities. Research in South Africa shows that teachers in township and rural schools often contend with compounded unfreedoms: students' limited access to digital resources at home, inadequate professional development opportunities, and isolation from professional networks (Chisango & Marongwe, 2021). These conditions restrict the conversion of digital skills into educational functionings, as teachers must prioritise basic content delivery over innovative or technology-enhanced instruction. Unfreedoms in this sense emerge not from the absence of technology per se but from contextual limitations that hinder its effective pedagogical use.

Time and workload pressures are another form of unfreedom. König et al. (2020) found that teachers often struggled to adapt to online teaching during COVID-19 because the time required for preparation and adaptation exceeded their allocated planning hours. Even competent and motivated teachers can experience constraints when institutional schedules, workload, and a lack of technical support prevent them from turning technological opportunities into meaningful educational practices.

Psychological and confidence barriers operate as subtle but powerful unfreedoms. Teachers with limited prior experience with technology may experience anxiety or lack confidence in adopting new tools, resulting in low utilisation despite formal access. Gudmundsdottir and Hatlevik (2018) note that professional digital competence involves both skill and confidence; without supportive mentoring and feedback, teachers' latent capabilities cannot be realised, leaving their professional freedoms constrained.

Unfreedoms in the tech-driven education context are multi-dimensional, encompassing material, institutional, social, and psychological barriers. Applying the Capability Approach illuminates that teacher development and educational policy must go beyond mere provision of devices or training. To expand teachers' substantive freedoms, interventions should address systemic inequalities, provide ongoing professional support, and create enabling school environments that allow teachers to convert technological resources into valued pedagogical outcomes. Only by mitigating unfreedoms can teachers fully exercise their capability sets and contribute effectively to quality education in a digital age.

In a world increasingly shaped by technology, educators' roles are evolving. However, for many teachers, especially those in under-resourced contexts, integrating technology into education often exacerbates existing challenges rather than alleviating them. This phenomenon can be understood through the lens of Amartya Sen's Capability Approach, which emphasises individuals' fundamental freedoms in achieving well-being. In the context of education, the "unfreedoms" presented in Table 2 below refer to constraints that prevent teachers from effectively using technology to enhance their teaching practices.

Table 2. Identifying unfreedoms of teachers

Unfreedoms of teachers in a tech-driven world	Implication
Infrastructure and Resource Limitations	A primary barrier to the effective use of technology in education is inadequate infrastructure. Many schools, particularly in rural or economically disadvantaged areas, lack reliable internet access, modern devices, and technical support. This infrastructural deficit limits teachers' ability to integrate digital tools into their classrooms, thereby restricting their professional capabilities. As noted by Zhao (2024), disparities in digital environments and literacy between urban and rural teachers highlight the systemic nature of this issue. Without the necessary resources, teachers are unable to realise their potential in a tech-driven educational landscape fully.
Lack of Professional Development and Support	Even when technological tools are available, teachers often struggle to utilise them sporadically, generically, or disconnected from their specific needs and contexts. Cappuccio (2021) emphasises the importance of developing digital competencies among educators, suggesting that a capability approach can guide the creation of more tailored and meaningful professional development opportunities. Without ongoing support and training, teachers lack the agency to adapt technology to their pedagogical goals, resulting in diminished capacity to enhance student learning.
Policy and Curriculum Constraints	Educational policies and curricula often do not align with the realities of a tech-driven classroom. Prescriptive standards and rigid curricula can stifle teachers' autonomy, limiting their ability to innovate with technology. As Kennedy and Castek (2025) highlight, a lack of educator input in the development of AI tools undermines educators' autonomy and agency, diminishing the very educational outcomes these technologies aim to enhance. When policies do not support or recognise the potential of technology, teachers are constrained in their ability to leverage digital tools effectively.
Socioeconomic and Cultural Barriers	Teachers in low-income or marginalised communities face additional unfreedoms due to socioeconomic and cultural factors. Students' limited access to technology at home, coupled with teachers' own lack of digital skills, creates a cycle of disadvantage. Abbasov (2021) discusses how the digital divide exacerbates educational inequalities, particularly during crises like the COVID-19 pandemic. These systemic barriers prevent both students and teachers from fully participating in a tech-enhanced educational experience, thereby limiting their capabilities.

continued on following page

Table 2. Continued

Unfreedoms of teachers in a tech-driven world	Implication
Psychological and Emotional Challenges	The rapid pace of technological change can also lead to psychological and emotional challenges for teachers. The pressure to continuously adapt to new tools and methodologies can result in stress, burnout, and a sense of inadequacy. Duan and Zhao (2024) explore how AI-powered technologies can affect teachers' autonomy and professional development, noting that without adequate support, the integration of technology can lead to adverse psychological outcomes. These emotional burdens further constrain teachers' ability to use technology effectively in their teaching practices.
Ethical and Privacy Concerns	The increasing use of technology in education raises ethical and privacy concerns. The collection and analysis of student and teacher data can raise issues related to consent, surveillance, and data security. Hillman (2025) critiques the growing influence of commercial educational technologies, arguing that they often prioritise data extraction over meaningful educational outcomes. Teachers, in this context, may feel compelled to use technologies that conflict with their professional ethics or the best interests of their students, thereby limiting their freedom to choose appropriate teaching tools. The unfreedoms teachers face in a tech-driven world are multifaceted and deeply rooted in systemic issues. Addressing these challenges requires a comprehensive approach that includes investing in infrastructure, providing tailored professional development, aligning policies with technological realities, and considering the ethical implications of educational technologies. By expanding teachers' fundamental freedoms to utilise technology effectively, we can enhance their capabilities and improve educational outcomes for all students. Recognising and addressing these unfreedoms is essential for creating an equitable and effective tech-enhanced educational environment.

5. ENHANCING TEACHERS' CAPABILITIES IN A TECH-DRIVEN WORLD: A CAPABILITY APPROACH PERSPECTIVE

In the evolving landscape of education, technology offers transformative potential. However, for teachers to harness this potential effectively, it is crucial to focus on enhancing their capabilities. Drawing on Amartya Sen's Capability Approach, Figure 2 below, followed by the discussion, delves into strategies for empowering educators to navigate and thrive in a tech-driven educational environment.

Figure 3. Strategies for empowering educators to navigate and thrive in a tech-driven educational environment

5.1 Professional Development Tailored to Teachers' Needs

A pivotal factor in enhancing teachers' capabilities is providing professional development (PD) that is both relevant and responsive to their specific contexts. Research indicates that PD programs should not only impart technical skills but also foster a deep understanding of pedagogical strategies that effectively integrate technology. For instance, studies have shown that when teachers receive training that aligns with their teaching contexts and addresses their unique challenges, they are more likely to adopt and utilise technology in meaningful ways.

5.2 Building Digital Competence

Digital competence encompasses more than just the ability to use technology; it involves understanding how to integrate digital tools into teaching practices to enhance learning outcomes. Frameworks like DigCompEdu provide a structured approach to developing educators' digital competencies. By focusing on areas such as digital pedagogy, assessment, and learner empowerment, these frameworks guide teachers in expanding their capacity to leverage technology effectively in the classroom.

5.3 Institutional Support and Leadership

School leadership plays an instrumental role in fostering an environment conducive to technological integration. Effective leaders provide the resources, support, and encouragement teachers need to explore and implement technological tools. Studies have highlighted that when school leaders actively promote and model the use of technology, teachers are more likely to feel confident and supported in their efforts to integrate digital tools into their teaching practices.

5.4 Collaborative Learning Communities

Establishing communities of practice allows teachers to share experiences, challenges, and strategies related to technology integration. Collaborative platforms enable educators to learn from one another, fostering a culture of continuous improvement. Research underscores the value of such communities in enhancing teachers' capabilities, as they provide opportunities for peer support and collective problem-solving.

5.5 Addressing Unfreedoms

While enhancing capabilities is essential, it is equally important to recognise and address the unfreedoms that hinder teachers' effective use of technology. Factors such as inadequate infrastructure, limited access to digital tools, and insufficient time for professional development can constrain teachers' ability to integrate technology. By identifying and mitigating these barriers, educational systems can create an environment where teachers have the genuine freedom to utilize technology to its full potential.

5.6 Policy and Curriculum Alignment

Educational policies and curricula should align with the realities of a tech-driven world. This alignment ensures that teachers are not only equipped with the necessary skills but also have the autonomy to apply them in ways that enhance learning outcomes. Policies that promote flexibility, innovation, and the integration of technology into teaching and learning processes empower teachers to expand their capabilities and adapt to the evolving educational landscape.

Enhancing teachers' capabilities in a tech-driven world requires a multifaceted approach that encompasses tailored professional development, building digital competence, institutional support, collaborative learning, addressing unfreedoms, and aligning policies with technological advancements. By focusing on these areas, educational systems can empower teachers to effectively integrate technology into their teaching practices, thereby improving learning outcomes and creating a more equitable educational environment.

6. RECOMMENDATIONS

Enhancing teachers' capabilities in a technology-driven educational landscape requires a comprehensive and strategic approach that addresses both structural and pedagogical dimensions. Based on the preceding discussion and insights from the Capability Approach, several recommendations emerge to ensure that teachers can exercise their full capabilities in fostering quality education.

6.1 Invest in Context-Specific Professional Development

One of the most critical steps is providing professional development (PD) that is tailored to teachers' contexts and needs. Training programs should go beyond technical skills and focus on pedagogical strategies for integrating technology effectively into classroom instruction. As Gudmundsdottir and Hatlevik (2018) argue, teachers benefit most from sustained, practice-oriented PD that enhances their confidence and agency. Such programs should include mentorship, peer collaboration, and opportunities to experiment with digital tools in low-stakes environments, allowing teachers to translate technical skills into meaningful classroom practices.

6.2 Expand Digital Competence Frameworks

Schools and educational authorities should adopt structured digital competence frameworks, such as DigCompEdu, to guide teachers in developing comprehensive digital literacy skills. This approach ensures that teachers' capability sets encompass not only operational knowledge but also the pedagogical and ethical application of technology. Regular assessments and reflective practices should be incorporated to monitor teachers' progress, identify gaps, and inform targeted interventions (Redecker, 2020).

6.3 Strengthen Institutional and Leadership Support

School leadership plays a decisive role in shaping teachers' freedom to innovate. Administrators should prioritise resource allocation, provide ongoing technical support, and create a culture that encourages experimentation with technology. By modelling digital innovation and recognising teachers' efforts, school leaders can mitigate unfreedoms and expand teachers' substantive opportunities to integrate technology in pedagogically meaningful ways (Zhao, 2024).

6.4 Facilitate Collaborative Learning Communities

Teachers' professional growth is accelerated in environments that foster collaboration and knowledge sharing. Establishing communities of practice, both within schools and across networks, enables teachers to exchange experiences, troubleshoot challenges, and collectively develop innovative teaching approaches. Peer support and collective problem-solving enhance teachers' agency, resilience, and confidence in using technology (Cappuccio, 2021).

6.5 Address Structural Inequalities

Policy-makers and educational stakeholders must address systemic disparities that limit teachers' capabilities. Investments in infrastructure such as reliable electricity, high-speed internet, and sufficient digital devices are essential, particularly in under-resourced schools. Additionally, strategies to reduce workload pressures and provide time for lesson planning and technology integration can help teachers convert resources into effective pedagogical outcomes, thereby expanding their freedoms (Abbasov, 2021).

6.6 Align Policies with Pedagogical Goals

National and institutional policies should be designed to support rather than constrain teachers' use of technology. Flexibility in curricula, recognition of innovative teaching practices, and guidance on ethical use of technology can empower teachers to make informed decisions about integrating digital tools. Policies must also consider equity, ensuring that teachers in disadvantaged contexts receive the support they need to overcome unfreedoms and fully exercise their capabilities (Selwyn, 2016).

6.7 Foster Ethical and Reflective Practices

Teachers should be encouraged to critically reflect on the ethical implications of technology use in education, including student privacy, data security, and the potential for algorithmic bias. Embedding reflective practice into professional development enhances teachers' critical agency and helps them make informed choices that align with educational values and societal expectations (Hillman, 2025).

Implementing these recommendations requires coordinated action from policy-makers, school leaders, teacher education institutions, and professional development providers. By addressing both technical competencies and the structural, social, and ethical dimensions of technology integration, education systems can enhance teachers' capabilities, reduce unfreedoms, and ensure that technology contributes meaningfully to quality education in a tech-driven world.

7. CONCLUSION

The rapid advancement of technology has fundamentally reshaped the educational landscape, presenting both opportunities and challenges for teachers. This chapter, guided by Amartya Sen's Capability Approach, has examined the complex interplay between teachers' capabilities, freedoms, and unfreedoms in the context of a tech-driven world. Teachers are pivotal agents in fostering quality education. Yet, their ability to integrate technology effectively depends not only on access to digital tools but also on the institutional, socio-economic, and pedagogical conditions that enable or constrain their choices.

The analysis demonstrates that teachers' capabilities extend beyond technical proficiency. They encompass the agency to make pedagogical decisions, the competence to integrate digital tools meaningfully, and the freedom to innovate while addressing ethical and contextual considerations. Freedoms, such as access to professional development, supportive leadership, collaborative networks, and flexible policies, empower teachers to leverage technology to create enhanced learning experiences. Conversely, unfreedoms, including inadequate infrastructure, rigid curricula, socio-economic inequities, and psychological barriers, limit teachers' ability to exercise their capabilities, thereby perpetuating educational disparities.

Addressing these unfreedoms requires targeted interventions. Context-specific, ongoing, and practice-oriented professional development programs can strengthen teachers' digital and pedagogical competencies. Institutional support, collaborative learning communities, and policy alignment further expand teachers' agency, enabling them to design technology-enhanced learning experiences. Crucially, addressing structural inequalities and providing equitable access to resources ensures that all teachers, regardless of their socio-economic context, can participate meaningfully in a tech-driven educational environment.

Ultimately, enhancing teachers' capabilities in a technology-rich world is not merely about providing tools; it is about creating conditions in which teachers have substantive freedom to choose, experiment, and innovate in ways they value. By prioritising both capabilities and freedoms, education systems can empower teachers to transform classrooms, improve learning outcomes, and contribute to a more equitable, inclusive, and quality-driven educational landscape. The insights from this chapter underscore the importance of a holistic, capability-oriented approach to teacher development, one that acknowledges the multifaceted nature of teaching in the digital age and positions teachers as central actors in shaping the future of education.

REFERENCES

Abbasov, A. (2021). *Digital inclusion in the times of COVID-19: A capabilities approach in understanding inclusion and education*. NORRAG Highlights. https://www.norrageducation.org/digital-inclusion-in-the-times-of-covid-19-a-capabilities-approach-in-understanding-inclusion-and-education-by-abbas-abbasov/

Adegoke, C. O., & Olugbara, O. O. (2021). Digital inequality and educational opportunities in Sub-Saharan Africa. *Education and Information Technologies*, *26*(5), 5753–5772. DOI: 10.1007/s10639-021-10552-4

Ainscow, M. (2020). Promoting inclusion and equity in education: Lessons from international experiences. *Nordic Journal of Studies in Educational Policy*, *6*(1), 7–16. DOI: 10.1080/20020317.2020.1729587

Alam, M.Dr. Md. Mahmood Alam. (2016). Use of ICT in Higher Education. *International Journal of Indian Psychology*, *3*(4), 163–171. DOI: 10.25215/0304.208

Cappuccio, G. (2021). Developing support teachers' digital competencies for an inclusive education. *Mediterranean Journal of Educational Studies*, *26*(1), 1–18. https://oaj.fupress.net/index.php/med/article/download/10243/9793/28065

Castañeda, L., & Selwyn, N. (2018). More than tools? Making sense of the ongoing digitisation of higher education. *International Journal of Educational Technology in Higher Education*, *15*(22), 1–10. DOI: 10.1186/s41239-018-0109-y

Chisango, G., & Marongwe, N. (2021). The digital divide at three disadvantaged secondary schools in Gauteng, South Africa. *Journal of Education*, *82*(82), •••. https://journals.ukzn.ac.za/index.php/joe/article/view/1769. DOI: 10.17159/2520-9868/i82a09

Cullen, R. (2017). The Use of ICT in the Health Sector in Pacific Island Countries. In Cullen, R., & Hassall, G. (Eds.), *Achieving Sustainable E-Government in Pacific Island States. Public Administration and Information Technology* (pp. 305–335). Springer Cham., DOI: 10.1007/978-3-319-50972-3_11

Darling-Hammond, L., Flook, L., Cook-Harvey, C., Barron, B., & Osher, D. (2020). Implications for educational practice of the science of learning and development. *Applied Developmental Science*, *24*(2), 97–140. DOI: 10.1080/10888691.2018.1537791

Darling-Hammond, L., Hyler, M. E., & Gardner, M. (2017). *Effective teacher professional development*. Learning Policy Institute., DOI: 10.54300/122.311

Davies, R., & West, R. E. (2014). *Technology Integration in Schools. Handbook of Research on Educational Communications and Technology*. Brigham Young University., DOI: 10.1007/978-1-4614-3185-5_68

Dlamini, R. S. (2022). *Complex Inequalities and Inequities in Education: Expanding Socially Just Teaching and Learning through Digitalisation in South Africa*. Alternation. *Alternation (Durban)*, *39*, 193–213. DOI: 10.29086/2519-5476/2022/sp39a9

Duan, H., & Zhao, W. (2024). Duan, H., & Zhao, W. (2024). The Effects of Educational Artificial Intelligence-Powered Applications on Teachers' Perceived Autonomy, Professional Development for Online Teaching, and Digital Burnout. *International Review of Research in Open and Distance Learning*, *25*(3), 57–76. DOI: 10.19173/irrodl.v25i3.7659

Duma, N. M., Mlambo, S., Mbambo-Mkwanazi, S., & Morgan, W. (2022). Digital inequalities in rural schools in South Africa. *Ocean Science Journal*, *6*(3), 1–15. DOI: 10.23954/osj.v6i3.2984

Ertmer, P. A., & Ottenbreit-Leftwich, A. (2019). Teacher technology change: How knowledge, confidence, beliefs, and culture intersect. *Journal of Research on Technology in Education*, *51*(1), 22–35. DOI: 10.1080/15391523.2018.1535583

Ertmer, P. A., & Ottenbreit-Leftwich, A. T. (2010). Teacher technology change: How knowledge, confidence, beliefs, and culture intersect. *Journal of Research on Technology in Education*, *42*(3), 255–284. DOI: 10.1080/15391523.2010.10782551

Fullan, M., & Gallagher, M. J. (2020). *The devil is in the details: System solutions for equity, excellence, and well-being*. Corwin.

Gudmundsdottir, G. B., & Hatlevik, O. E. (2018). Newly qualified teachers' professional digital competence: Implications for teacher education. *European Journal of Teacher Education*, *41*(2), 214–231. DOI: 10.1080/02619768.2017.1416085

Hammond, L. D. (2021). Teacher learning in the digital age: Shaping professional identity. *Teaching and Teacher Education*, *103*, 103349. DOI: 10.1016/j.tate.2021.103349

Hillman, V. (2025, September 1). *Big tech has transformed the classroom - and parents are right to be worried*. The Guardian. https://www.theguardian.com/commentisfree/2025/sep/01/big-tech-classroom-parents-education

Hoffman, S., & Maarman, R. (2024a). Teachers' voices and quality education in the basic education discourse in South Africa. *Perspectives in Education*, *42*(4), 333–348. DOI: 10.38140/pie.v42i4.8048

Hoffman, S., & Maarman, R. (2024b). Freedoms of teachers using CAPS: A capability analysis of a Western Cape school. *Southern African Review of Education with Education with Production*, *29*(2), 86–103. https://www.saches.co.za/journals

Hoffman, S. M. (2017). *Capability sets of teachers with regard to the implementation of the curriculum and policy statement in a no-fee school community in the Western Cape* [Master's thesis]. University of the Western Cape., https://uwcscholar.uwc.ac.za:8443/server/api/core/bitstreams/0ff296eb-4a78-40f6-b320-13d8c47989c8/content

Kafyulilo, A., Fisser, P., & Voogt, J. (2016). Factors affecting teachers' continuation of technology use in teaching. *Education and Information Technologies*, *21*(6), 1535–1554. DOI: 10.1007/s10639-015-9398-0

Kennedy, K. J., & Castek, J. M. (2025). Empowering ELA teachers: Recommendations for teacher education in the AI era. *Contemporary Issues in Technology & Teacher Education*, *25*(1), 1–31. https://citejournal.org/wp-content/uploads/2025/01/v25i1Englishlanguagearts1.pdf

Koehler, M. J., Mishra, P., Kereluik, K., Shin, T. S., & Graham, C. R. (2017). The technological pedagogical content knowledge framework. In Spector, J. M. (Eds.), *Handbook of research on educational communications and technology* (pp. 101–111). Springer., DOI: 10.1007/978-1-4614-3185-5_9

König, J., Jäger-Biela, D. J., & Glutsch, N. (2020). Adapting to online teaching during COVID-19 school closure: Teacher education and teacher competence effects among early career teachers in Germany. *European Journal of Teacher Education*, *43*(4), 608–622. DOI: 10.1080/02619768.2020.1809650

Livingstone, S., & Helsper, E. J. (2022). Socio-economic inequalities in children's digital skills: Evidence and implications. *New Media & Society*, *24*(3), 589–608. DOI: 10.1177/1461444820959018

Madikizela-Madiya, N. (2021). The question of access and spatial justice in universities in sub-Saharan Africa: A capabilities approach. *Transformation in Higher Education*, *6*, a124. DOI: 10.4102/the.v6i0.124

Mitra, D. (2020). *Educational equity and digital learning: A critical analysis*. Palgrave Macmillan., DOI: 10.1007/978-3-030-41763-1

Nussbaum, M. C. (2011). *Creating capabilities: The human development approach*. Harvard University Press. DOI: 10.4159/harvard.9780674061200

OECD. (2023). *Digital equity and inclusion in education*. OECD Publishing. https://www.oecd.org/en/publications/digital-equity-and-inclusion-in-education_7cb15030-en.html

Powell, C., & Burns, L. (2021). Digital Divide: Mapping the geodemographics of internet accessibility across Great Britain. *ArXiv preprint*. doi:/arXiv.2108.07699DOI: 10.48550

Redecker, C. (2020). *European Framework for the Digital Competence of Educators (DigCompEdu)*. Publications Office of the European Union., DOI: 10.2760/159770

Robeyns, I. (2011). The capability approach. In Arrow, K. J., Sen, A., & Suzumura, K. (Eds.), *Handbook of social choice and welfare* (Vol. 2, pp. 545–608). Elsevier., DOI: 10.1016/B978-0-444-52938-1.00017-4

Robeyns, I. (2017). *Wellbeing, Freedom and Social Justice: The Capability Approach Re-Examined*. Open Book Publishers., DOI: 10.11647/OBP.0130

Sarkar, S. (2012). The Role of Information and Communication Technology (ICT) in Higher Education for the 21st Century. *The Science Probe*, 30-41. https://www.researchgate.net/profile/Sukanta-Sarkar-2/publication/266051436_The_Role_of_Information_and_Communication_Technology_ICT_in_Higher_Education_for_the_21st_Century/links/64710f9c6fb1d1682b0d18aa/The-Role-of-Information-and-Communication-Technology-ICT-in-Higher-Education-for-the-21st-Century.pdf

Schleicher, A. (2018). *World class: How to build a 21st-century school system*. OECD Publishing., DOI: 10.1787/9789264300002-en

Schleicher, A. (2020). *The impact of COVID-19 on education: Insights from education at a glance 2020*. OECD Publishing. https://www.oecd.org/en/publications/education-at-a-glance-2020_69096873-en.html

Selwyn, N. (2016). *Education and Technology: Key Issues and Debates* (2nd ed.). Bloomsbury., https://www.bloomsbury.com/us/education-and-technology-9781350145566/

Selwyn, N. (2022). *Education and technology: Key issues and debates* (3rd ed.). Bloomsbury., https://www.bloomsbury.com/us/education-and-technology-9781350145566/ DOI: 10.5040/9781350145573

Sen, A. (1992). *Inequality re-examined*. Harvard University Press., DOI: 10.2307/2940919

Sen, A. (1999). *Development as freedom*. Alfred A. Knopf. https://sen.scholars.harvard.edu/publications/development-freedom

Sharma, B., Lauano, F., Narayan, S., Anzeg, A., Kumar, B., & Raj, J. (2018). Science teachers accelerated programme model: A joint partnership in the Pacific region. *Asia-Pacific Journal of Teacher Education, 46*(1), 38–60. DOI: 10.1080/1359866X.2017.1359820

Sharma, B., & Reddy, P. (2015). Effectiveness of tablet learning in online courses at the University of the South Pacific. In *2nd Asia-Pacific World Congress on Computer Science and Engineering* (pp. 1-9). Suva, Fiji: IEEE. DOI: 10.1109/APWCCSE.2015.7476229

Shopova, T. (2012). E-Learning in Higher Educational Environment. *International Conference the Future of Education*, 1-5. https://conference.pixel-online.net/conferences/edu_future/common/download/Paper_pdf/ELE23-Shopova.pdf

Tondeur, J., Scherer, R., Siddiq, F., & Baran, E. (2017). Teacher educators as gatekeepers: Preparing the next generation of teachers for technology integration. *British Journal of Educational Technology, 48*(2), 291–301. DOI: 10.1111/bjet.12345

Traina, I., & Guimarães-Iosif, R. (2022). Teachers as agents of change in digital education: A capability perspective. *British Journal of Educational Studies, 70*(6), 763–780. DOI: 10.1080/00071005.2021.2016404

Trilling, B., & Fadel, C. (2009). *21st century skills: Learning for life in our times.* Jossey-Bass.

Trust, T., Krutka, D. G., & Carpenter, J. P. (2018). Together we are better: Professional learning networks for teachers. *Computers & Education, 102*, 15–34. DOI: 10.1016/j.compedu.2016.06.007

Trust, T., Krutka, D. G., & Carpenter, J. P. (2020). Professional learning networks and educators' professional growth: A systematic review. *Teaching and Teacher Education, 94*, 103–118. DOI: 10.1016/j.tate.2020.103118

UNESCO. (2013). *Teaching and learning: Achieving quality for all. Education for All Global Monitoring Report.* https://uis.unesco.org/sites/default/files/documents/teaching-and-learning- achieving-quality-for-all-gmr-2013-2014-en.pdf

UNESCO. (2021). *Reimagining our futures together: A new social contract for education.* UNESCO. https://unesdoc.unesco.org/ark:/48223/pf0000379381

United Nations. (2017). *SDG Goals: Goal 4: Ensure inclusive and equitable quality education and promote lifelong learning opportunities for all.* https://unstats.un.org/sdgs/report/2017/goal-04/

Unterhalter, E. (2019). The capability approach and education. *Journal of Human Development and Capabilities, 20*(1), 1–19. DOI: 10.1080/19452829.2018.1526891

Van Dijk, J. (2020). *The digital divide*. Polity Press.

Voogt, J., & Roblin, N. P. (2012). A comparative analysis of international frameworks for 21st century competences: Implications for national curriculum policies. *Journal of Curriculum Studies, 44*(3), 299–321. DOI: 10.1080/00220272.2012.668938

Warschauer, M., & Matuchniak, T. (2010). New technology and digital worlds: Analyzing evidence of equity in access, use, and outcomes. *Review of Research in Education, 34*(1), 179–225. DOI: 10.3102/0091732X09349791

Wozney, L., Venkatesh, V., & Abrami, P. (2006). Implementing computer technologies: Teachers' perceptions and practices. *Journal of Technology and Teacher Education, 14*(1), 173–207. https://www.researchgate.net/publication/255566914_Implementing_Computer_Technologies_Teachers'_Perceptions_and_Practices

Zhao, W. (2024). A study of the impact of the new digital divide on the ICT integration of teachers in urban and rural areas. *Computers & Education, 174*, 104309. https://www.sciencedirect.com/science/article/pii/S2405844024052174

Chapter 17
The Future of Education Technology:
The Future of Teachers' Roles in a Tech-Driven World

Chantelle Melanie August-Mowers
https://orcid.org/0009-0006-3476-9389
Two Oceans Graduate Institute, South Africa

ABSTRACT

This chapter examines how the Fourth Industrial Revolution (4IR) and the COVID-19 pandemic accelerated digital transformation in education, exposing gaps in teachers' preparedness for e-learning. It explores the rapid expansion of online learning and assessments, highlighting benefits such as scalability, flexibility, and broader access, alongside challenges including academic integrity concerns, unequal digital access, and limited digital literacy, particularly in contexts like South Africa. Grounded in the Technology Acceptance Model (TAM) and based on a qualitative systematic literature review, the chapter identifies key themes such as digital inclusion, technological resistance, policy gaps, community engagement, and ethical implications of digital assessment. It proposes action-oriented strategies and forward-looking policies to strengthen teacher capacity and redefine educators' roles in 4IR-driven education.

1. INTRODUCTION

The rapid growth of digital technologies has reshaped global education, revealing both new opportunities and deep systemic vulnerabilities. While the Fourth Industrial Revolution (4IR) has introduced artificial intelligence (AI), data analytics,

DOI: 10.4018/979-8-3373-4521-5.ch017

robotics, and cloud-based platforms into teaching and learning environments, the COVID-19 pandemic exposed widespread teacher unpreparedness, particularly in contexts marked by historical and infrastructural inequality. Traditional pedagogies were disrupted overnight, forcing educators to navigate unfamiliar digital systems while contending with limited training, inconsistent support, and unequal access to devices and connectivity.

This chapter examines teacher readiness in a tech-driven world, focusing on digital learning, e-learning implementation, and the professional development strategies required to support teachers meaningfully. Responding to reviewer feedback, the introduction has been streamlined to emphasise the problem, purpose, and relevance of the chapter without duplicating statistics or background material addressed later. The chapter also now includes an expanded analysis of artificial intelligence, its role in planning, assessment, differentiation, administrative efficiency, and its implications for professional judgment. AI does not replace teachers; instead, it reshapes teacher responsibilities and requires new forms of professional competence. Using the Technology Acceptance Model (TAM) as a framework, the chapter explores how teachers can be supported to adapt confidently and ethically within AI-rich educational environments. Given the above background and context, the main objective of the chapter is to provide a comprehensive overview of teaching and learning in education spaces, highlighting teachers' lack of preparedness in a tech-driven world that conditions digital and e-learning and its implementation, and at the same time propose practical strategies to respond to professional development needs. To achieve the outlined objective, this chapter addresses the following central research question: ***How can teachers' digital learning and e-learning skills be developed to prepare them for the tech-driven world?*** *That* serves as the guiding beacon for the investigation, illuminating the path toward transformative and equitable change with clarity and purpose. In support of the main research question, this chapter will also respond to the following subsidiary questions:

- How do current professional development courses enhance teaching, learning, and assessment practices to support teachers in responding to digital learning requirements?
- What intervention model could be designed to encourage digital and e-learning as a strategy that could enable teachers to adapt to the tech-driven world?

2. THEORETICAL FRAMEWORK

This study is framed within the Technology Acceptance Model (TAM), developed by Davis et al. (1989). TAM provides a robust, widely recognized, empirically validated, and adaptable framework for understanding human behaviour toward the adoption of technology, particularly in educational and professional contexts (Mastour et al., 2025). TAM posits that two primary factors, which are perceived usefulness and perceived ease of use, significantly influence the acceptance or resistance to technological tools (Granić & Marangunić, 2019). According to this model, perceived usefulness refers to the degree to which an individual believes that using a particular technology will enhance their job performance, such as improving learner engagement, streamlining grading processes, or enabling real-time feedback (Teeroovengadum, et al., 2017). On the other hand, perceived ease of use is the degree to which a person believes that using the technology will be effort-free, such as intuitive navigation of virtual platforms, minimal technical glitches, or accessible support systems (Saad et al., 2025).

These core constructs are facilitated by external variables, including the availability and quality of training, the level of technical support provided by institutions, and the prevailing organizational culture. According to Granić and Marangunić (2019), organizational culture stems from factors such as individual differences like age, prior technological experience, or learning preferences, as well as socio-economic context, such as access to electricity or devices, making TAM a versatile and context-sensitive lens for exploring digital platform adoption and perception in diverse educational settings.

The Technology Acceptance Model (TAM) provides valuable and detailed insights relevant to this chapter. It helps explain why certain teachers eagerly adopt virtual teaching environments, including tools like Moodle for delivering courses, virtual reality classrooms for engaging history or science lessons, and AI-driven assessments for automated grading. Meanwhile, other educators show resistance, often stemming from insufficient training or a fear of failing. This hesitation can also arise from limited access to resources, a cultural preference for in-person teaching, or doubts about the practical value of technology in education.

Resistance to technology adoption is particularly pronounced in developing nations like South Africa, where infrastructure disparities create significant hurdles. Unreliable electricity affects a substantial 40% of rural schools, as highlighted by the Eskom report (2023) cited in Kapstein (2025), making consistent access to digital tools a persistent challenge. These difficulties in South Africa are further complicated by deep-rooted historical inequities that continue to shape the educational landscape (Muyambi & Ahiaku, 2025). Ajani (2024) further adds that the legacy of underfunded apartheid-era schools, which disproportionately favoured urban centres, has left rural areas with inadequate resources and infrastructure even today. As a result, the Technology Acceptance Model (TAM) offers a promising approach to addressing these issues. It suggests that enhancing perceived usefulness by demonstrating how digital tools can improve learner outcomes, such as the 15% increase in pass rates noted in a Finnish study (Setälä et al., 2025), can encourage teacher buy-in. In addition, administrative burdens might decrease by 20%, as observed in a U.S. study by Beelaerts van Blokland (2025), offering practical benefits to educators.

Moreover, digital tools have the potential to foster inclusive learning environments, particularly for students with disabilities who often face barriers in traditional settings (Memon & Memon, 2025). Perceived ease of use can be enhanced by developing user-friendly interfaces that simplify navigation for teachers. Comprehensive onboarding sessions, complete with detailed step-by-step guides, provide essential support during the initial adoption phase. Peer support networks, such as vibrant online teacher forums, further facilitate collaboration and problem-solving among educators. According to Singh et al. (2023), technological resistance, often encountered in virtual teaching environments, emerges as a common obstacle that can be transformed into an opportunity for growth. This shift is especially viable within the context of professional development programs tailored for teacher education. Resistance often stems from a lack of confidence, with around 60% of South African teachers reporting difficulties navigating platforms such as Zoom or Google Classroom (Muller, 2022).

Concerns about job security also play a role, as automation might replace traditional teaching roles, a worry echoed by 35% of global teachers in the World Economic Forum report (World economic Forum, 2025). Targeted interventions offer an effective way to overcome these barriers. Bixby (2018) suggests that hands-on workshops led by certified trainers can build competence, particularly for those new to technology. Wahyuni et al. (2024) further add that mobile training vans bring essential education to remote rural areas, ensuring broader reach. Thus, by applying TAM, this study examines how digital tools can be optimized to enhance teaching effectiveness through interactive lessons that boost engagement. Adaptive learning paths streamline the educational process, tailoring content to individual needs, and secure online exams improve assessment practices by reducing cheating. This approach lays a solid theoretical foundation for the proposed interventions, making it highly relevant in today's context.

3. METHODOLOGY

3.1 Criteria for Selection

This study employs the SPIDER Tool (Sample, Phenomenon of Interest, Design, Evaluation, Research type), as outlined by Cooke et al. (2012), to systematically and purposefully select relevant literature that aligns with the research objectives with rigor and inclusivity. The inclusion criteria are meticulously defined to ensure a comprehensive, representative, and contextually rich review that captures the diversity of educational experiences globally.

Empirical case studies focusing on pedagogical and assessment practices in educational institutions, ranging from primary and secondary levels to higher education institutions, were reviewed. In addition, the chapter drew on perspectives from instructional designers, academic technologists, policymakers, and community teachers. These perspectives regarded their engagement with digital learning and the fourth industrial revolution. This broad sample ensured a comprehensive view of diverse educational contexts, from primary schools in rural South Africa where teachers use solar-powered tablets, to elite universities in urban centres like Cape Town offering virtual PhD seminars, and cross-border initiatives in East Africa leveraging mobile learning, capturing the full spectrum of teacher experiences and challenges.

Phenomenon of Interest: Technology is understood as a transformative tool that enhances digital learning skills, promoting social justice, equality, and equity by addressing historical disparities and fostering a sense of communal responsibility. This perspective aligns with the Ubuntu philosophy, emphasizing inclusive education that empowers marginalized communities. For example, rural girls in Malawi gaining STEM skills through e-learning bridges the digital divide and ensures that technology serves as a vehicle for empowerment rather than exclusion, reflecting a commitment to global educational equity.

Design: The research design incorporates an intervention approach, proposing a "Digital Learning Toolkit" as a strategic, adaptable, and scalable framework to encourage digital learning adoption across diverse settings. Both primary data and secondary data will inform this toolkit. Primary data include teacher surveys assessing confidence levels, focus groups exploring cultural barriers, and classroom observations tracking engagement, and secondary data include existing studies on e-learning efficacy, policy documents from the South African Department of Education, and global best practices from countries such as Finland and Rwanda. This is important in providing a practical, evidence-based, and context-sensitive model for implementation that can be tailored to urban, rural, and remote environments.

Evaluation: The review centres on ideas, strategies, and practical recommendations that promote social justice, ensuring that outcomes benefit marginalized communities and address historical inequities. The evaluation will consider a wide range of metrics, including improved learner performance, teacher confidence, equitable access to resources, and community impact, reflecting a commitment to transformative change that prioritizes the most vulnerable learners and teachers.

Research type: The study includes both empirical data such as qualitative interviews with teachers in under-resourced schools, quantitative data from learning analytics tracking online participation, and mixed-method case studies from Kenya's mobile learning initiatives and secondary data such as peer-reviewed articles, government reports on digital policy, international case studies from UNESCO, and historical analyses of apartheid education offering a robust, multifaceted, and triangulated evidence base to support the chapter's conclusions and recommendations with credibility and depth.

3.2 Method of Search

The search strategy is rigorously grounded in key focus areas: professional development in education, digital learning, technology integration, relevant policy documents that shape educational technology adoption, and the socio-cultural factors influencing teacher readiness. A broad and diverse range of academic, professional, and governmental databases will be explored to ensure a comprehensive and authoritative source pool, including Ebscohost for education research, ERIC for pedagogical studies, Mendeley for collaborative academic work, ResearchGate for cutting-edge papers, Google Scholar for broad access, UWC Library for local South African insights, and UCT news site for policy updates. These platforms provide access to a wealth of peer-reviewed articles, conference proceedings, white papers, and institutional reports, reflecting the latest research and policy developments.

Keywords such as "digital inclusion," "e-learning," "teacher training," "professional development," "technology acceptance," "fourth industrial revolution," "social justice in education," and "digital divide" will be used in various combinations and Boolean operators (for example, "digital inclusion AND teacher training") to strengthen the flow, layout, and thematic coherence of the chapter.

Articles were initially selected based on titles and abstracts, targeting 50-70 initial hits, followed by full-text review by two independent reviewers. This is done to confirm relevance, alignment with the SPIDER criteria, and quality, aiming to gather sufficient high-quality articles. Thus, to achieve the chapter's objectives, the targeted final pool will be of 30-40 key sources. This rigorous, multi-step process ensures a robust evidence base that supports both global and local perspectives on teacher preparedness.

3.3 Extraction of Data and Analysis

The extraction of data from both literature and empirical studies is a critical, systematic, and iterative step, with mapping techniques such as concept maps and data matrices used to identify, organize, and prioritize relevant themes aligned with the SPIDER criteria. Thematic analysis, as described by Ryan and Bernard (2003), was employed as the primary analytical method, offering a structured yet flexible approach to interpreting complex qualitative data. Ryan and Bernard (2003) emphasize that theme identification is crucial in qualitative research. They state, "theme identification is one of the most fundamental tasks in qualitative research" (p. 58), highlighting its importance in structuring the analysis. Peel (2020) adds that this process helps describe and organize various observations, such as recurring patterns in teacher resistance that emerge during data collection. Theme identification also enables a deeper interpretation of the phenomenon, particularly the influence of policy on digital adoption across different contexts (Aithal et al., 2023). Therefore, the analysis involves coding data using software such as NVivo to identify recurring themes. These include teacher preparedness, gaps in digital literacy, challenges in policy implementation, the role of technology in promoting social justice, and strategies for community engagement.

This iterative process connects these themes to the broader educational, cultural, and historical context. It reflects a steadfast commitment to addressing social inequalities that have persisted over time. Quality education is recognized as a fundamental human right, a powerful tool for empowerment, and a vital element of national development. The chapter advocates persistently for equity among previously disadvantaged communities. This call involves ensuring the availability of resources, such as laptops with offline capabilities, solar-powered internet hubs, and subsidized data plans. It also emphasizes skills development through mobile-based micro-courses and peer-led training, blending pedagogical strategies that enhance teaching with the Ubuntu philosophy of collective growth. For instance, data might show that rural teachers struggle with virtual classroom management. This could lead to recommendations for mobile training units to address the gap. Urban teachers, on the other hand, may require support in ethical assessment design, prompting advocacy for policy changes. This dual approach ensures the findings go beyond the description of current challenges, providing actionable, evidence-based insights to reshape teacher education in a technology-driven world.

3.4 Ethical Considerations

All sources utilized in this chapter will be duly acknowledged and referenced with meticulous care to uphold academic integrity, ethical standards, and intellectual honesty. The chapter ensures proper citation of primary data, including teacher interviews conducted with informed consent that respects participants' autonomy. Classroom observations, performed only with the participant's approval, provide valuable insights into the research. Survey responses are reported with anonymized data, safeguarding individual identities while preserving the integrity of the findings. Secondary data is also meticulously cited, drawing on sources such as policy documents issued by the South African government that shape educational frameworks. Academic articles from global journals provide a broader perspective, while historical analyses of educational inequity offer context for current challenges. This approach maintains transparency and honours the intellectual contributions of all sources.

Special care is taken to amplify the voices of marginalized teachers, such as those in rural areas, who face unique struggles. Female teachers in patriarchal settings, often overlooked, receive particular attention to reflect their experiences. This focus aligns with the chapter's commitment to social justice and the Ubuntu philosophy, which values community and inclusion.

The research adheres to institutional ethical guidelines, such as those established by the University of the Western Cape. Informed consent is a cornerstone, ensuring participants understand and agree to their involvement. Confidentiality is maintained when primary data are gathered, protecting sensitive information. Compliance with the Protection of Personal Information Act (POPIA) of 2013 guarantees data protection in the digital era. Participants retain the right to withdraw at any time, reflecting a dedication to ethical research practices. This commitment extends globally when using international data. Ethical considerations include respecting cultural sensitivities in diverse contexts. The study avoids exploiting vulnerable populations, promoting a responsible approach worldwide.

4. LITERATURE REVIEW

4.1 Digital Transformation in Education

The educational landscape is undergoing a profound transformation as the digital era rapidly advances, reshaping how teaching and learning are conceptualized and delivered. The COVID-19 pandemic, which began in 2020 and persisted with varying intensity through 2022, functioned as a global accelerator for digital transformation in education. This forced schools, colleges, and universities to adopt e-learning at an unprecedented scale and speed. Fontich (2020) documents the experiences of Spanish L1 teachers during COVID-19 confinement, revealing a profound lack of technical skills, such as managing virtual breakout rooms, and of institutional support, such as absent IT helpdesks. As a result, many institutions resorted to improvised solutions like personal email accounts for teaching or WhatsApp groups for learner communication (Masoga, 2020; Tarisayi & Munyaradzi, 2021). The sudden shift exposed the fragility of traditional education systems which relied on physical infrastructure. This highlighted the potential of online platforms to maintain continuity, with platforms like Zoom and Microsoft Teams becoming household names.

The transition to hybrid and fully online learning models was widely adopted by education institutions. For instance, the University of Cape Town shifted to online lectures in 2020 (Coetzee et al., 2021) and some secondary schools in countries like Kenya, launched national e-learning portal in 2021 (Barasa, 2021), which also brought to light significant challenges. Zanele and Ajani (2024) noted some challenges brought by the online learning such as cheating in online assessments. According to Pickering and Schuller (2024) online cheating is facilitated by screen-sharing tools like TeamViewer and online forums like Chegg, with an estimated 25% increase in plagiarism rates. On the other hand, Mxatule (2024) and Moodley and Segoete (2024) highlighted the challenge of unequal access to devices, where 40% of South African learners shared a single device in 2023 and technical barriers such as power outages affecting 50% of rural schools. These ethical dilemmas, compounded by the digital divide, underscore the need for robust digital infrastructure, fair assessment practices, and teacher training, a pressing concern especially when post-pandemic recovery efforts continue to shape educational policy.

As higher education increasingly embraces hybrid or fully online models, The effectiveness of technology in higher education remains a subject of debate, with evidence pointing to its potential to transform learning experiences while also revealing inconsistent application that often leads to confusion among educators. This calls for a radical rethinking of teacher training and professional development to align with the realities of a tech-driven world. Practice-oriented, research-based solutions are vital to support the education fraternity in a meaningful way, advocating for enhanced capacity building within higher institutions.

4.2 Teacher Preparedness and Professional Development

Ndebele et al. (2024) argue that current professional development programs often fail to comprehensively address digital literacy, leaving teachers ill-equipped for tech-driven classrooms that require skills such as video editing, data analysis, and virtual facilitation. This unpreparedness shapes the implementation of digital and e-learning, presenting unique challenges that vary by context. To begin with, in South Africa, the lag in policy implementation and curriculum alignment exacerbates this gap, particularly affecting rural and previously disadvantaged schools. Teachers from the rural Eastern Cape province contend with limited access to devices, unreliable electricity, and minimal training opportunities, reflecting a stark digital divide (Mafikeng, 2024). Their struggles are compounded by outdated infrastructure, which undermined the 2023 rollout of tablets to rural schools under the Department of Basic Education's Digital Schools Project, where only 30% of schools have consistent internet access, forcing many to rely on personal smartphones with frequent battery issues (Mhlomi, 2023).

According to the National Education Evaluation and Development Unit (NEEDU, 2024), the education sector faces teacher resistance to adopting tech-driven instruction, with 45% of teachers citing a lack of training and funding shortages to support it. Kashem et al. (2024) also reported that, as a result, 60% of the teachers lacked basic digital skills and faced logistical issues, such as delayed deliveries due to supply chain disruptions.

These findings underscore the importance of teacher preparedness in embracing change in the digital transformation through professional development. Moreover, the transition to the 4IR demands a rethinking of teacher training. However, many programs remain rooted in traditional pedagogies such as rote memorization and chalkboard instruction, which are ill-suited to the digital age. A UNESCO (2025) report noted that 55% of African teachers still rely on traditional teaching methods. This gap is particularly evident in teacher education colleges, where faculty themselves lack exposure to virtual learning environments. According to the South African Council for Educators (SACE) (2024), only 20% have completed online teaching courses, perpetuating a cycle of unpreparedness. The psychological toll is significant: 45% of teachers report burnout from managing hybrid classes (Perry, 2024), highlighting the need for sustained support.

4.3 Developing Teachers' Digital Learning and E-Learning Skills

At the heart of this chapter lies the question of how to develop teachers' digital learning and e-learning skills to thrive in a technology-driven world, a challenge that requires a multifaceted response. A study by Karunanayaka (2023) emphasizes the need for capacity building, urging a transition from traditional pedagogies, such as chalk-and-talk methods, to technology-enhanced practices that leverage tools like virtual classrooms and AI-driven assessments. Many teachers, particularly in underserved regions, lack the foundational skills to navigate these platforms, with approximately a quarter of South African educators proficient in tools such as Moodle (Mpungose, 2020). This gap hinders their ability to integrate technology effectively, necessitating targeted skill development.

The Ubuntu philosophy supports this effort by advocating a collective approach that ensures no teacher is left behind in the digital transition (Ngubane & Makua, 2021). Development strategies must cater to diverse needs, addressing the struggles of rural teachers with limited resources, such as those in Limpopo who lack consistent power (Motjoadi & Bokoro, 2023), and the pressures faced by urban educators managing hybrid classrooms in cities like Johannesburg (Perry, 2024). Building confidence is crucial, achievable through hands-on training sessions that simulate real-world digital teaching scenarios. Providing access to devices, such as solar-powered tablets, can bridge the resource gap in off-grid areas, while ongoing mentorship can reinforce learning (SM, 2025).

4.4 The Impact of Professional Development Courses in Enhancing Digital Learning Requirements

According to Simon (2021), these professional development courses often focus on basic technical skills, such as navigating Microsoft Teams or Google Classroom, which occupy 80% of training time. However, they rarely address the pedagogical adaptation required to design interactive online content or assess digitally, with only 10% of sessions dedicated to these areas. This imbalance leaves teachers ill-prepared to transform their teaching methods, limiting the impact on student engagement and learning outcomes.

The brevity of these courses poses a further challenge, with the majority lasting less than a day, a duration insufficient for mastering complex digital tools or sustaining long-term skill retention (Lauer et al., 2014). Furthermore, follow-up support is scarce, with only 15% of teachers receiving mentorship post-training, leaving many to navigate technical difficulties alone (McAleavy et al., 2018). This lack of continuity is evident in rural areas, where teachers report a 60% dropout rate from online courses due to connectivity issues (Das et al., 2021), and in urban settings, where burnout from hybrid teaching affects 45% of educators (Perry, 2024).

On the other hand, the professional development courses have had a positive impact on digital learning. According to Timotheou et al. (2023), Germany's mandatory digital literacy training, spanning 6 months and including practical workshops, can boost teacher confidence by 30% and improve student performance by 20%. However, Ahmed and Sidiq (2023) note that current courses fall short in aligning with digital learning requirements, such as creating assessments that reduce plagiarism or fostering collaborative online environments. The absence of ethical training further complicates implementation. Opportunities for improvement lie in extending training durations, integrating scenario-based learning, and providing ongoing support through peer networks. As a result, this study underscores the need to overhaul professional development to ensure teachers are equipped to effectively enhance digital education.

4.4.1 Artificial Intelligence and Teacher Roles in a Digital Era

Artificial intelligence has become a central element of technology-enhanced learning, transforming how teachers plan lessons, assess learners, differentiate instruction, manage classrooms, and exercise professional judgment. Rather than replacing educators, AI functions as a collaborative partner that extends teacher capacity and supports more efficient and personalised learning environments (Holmes et al., 2019; Luckin, 2018). Research consistently shows that the value of AI in education lies in augmenting teacher expertise rather than automating teaching entirely (Woolf, 2021).

4.4.2 AI in Planning and Instructional Design

AI-powered planning tools assist teachers by generating curriculum-aligned lesson plans, sequencing learning content, and recommending multimodal resources. Scholars such as Luckin and Holmes emphasise that AI can enhance lesson design by identifying prerequisite knowledge and recommending scaffolds while still requiring teacher contextualisation and pedagogical judgment (Holmes et al., 2022; Luckin, 2018). Tools such as ChalkAI and EduAssist support efficient planning, yet teachers remain the ultimate decision-makers, refining AI-generated materials to suit learner needs.

4.4.3 AI for Differentiation and Personalised Learning

Adaptive learning platforms analyse learner performance in real time, identify gaps and recommend individualised learning pathways. The work of Baker and Heffernan shows that intelligent tutoring systems can significantly improve learning outcomes by adjusting content difficulty and pacing (Baker, 2016; Heffernan & Heffernan, 2014). In multilingual or mixed-ability classrooms, AI-based translation and accessibility tools support diverse learners, reflecting findings by Breazeal and colleagues on socially responsive AI systems that accommodate learner variability (Breazeal et al., 2018).

4.4.4 AI in Assessment and Feedback

AI enhances assessment through automated marking, rapid feedback, plagiarism detection, and large-scale pattern analysis. According to Piech and Brunskill, AI-driven assessment tools can provide fine-grained insights into learner understanding while reducing teacher workload (Brunskill & Russell, 2011; Piech et al., 2015). Tools like Gradescope and Turnitin help maintain assessment integrity, but teachers remain central in interpreting ambiguous responses and providing qualitative, human-centred feedback.

4.4.5 AI for Administrative Efficiency

AI reduces administrative burden by automating attendance tracking, measuring learner engagement, generating progress reports, organising schedules, and managing communications. Research by Koedinger and the LearnLab group demonstrates that predictive analytics can identify learners who may require intervention, enabling teachers to act proactively (Koedinger et al., 2015). These systems support data-driven decision-making but still depend on teacher insight to ensure appropriate and ethical responses.

4.5 Models of Human–AI Collaboration

Three models explain how teachers work alongside AI, supported by scholars such as James Lester and Rose Luckin, who argue for balanced, human-centred AI ecosystems (Lester et al., 2021; Luckin, 2018):

- **Assistive Model:** AI automates repetitive tasks while teachers prioritise pedagogy.
- **Augmentation Model:** AI provides actionable insights; teachers exercise professional judgment.
- **Co-Creation Model:** Teachers and AI collaboratively design learning experiences, blending machine support with teacher creativity.

4.6 New Competencies Required of Teachers in AI-Rich Environments

Teachers require expanded competencies, including AI literacy, data interpretation, critical evaluation of AI recommendations, ethical use of technology, and the ability to guide learners in AI literacy. Holmes et al. (2022) and Zawacki-Richter et al. (2019) highlight that professional development must incorporate these skills to ensure both practical implementation and protection of learner rights. Ethical considerations, including data privacy, algorithmic bias, transparency, and fairness, are emphasised widely in the literature (Williamson & Eynon, 2020), underscoring teachers' responsibilities as mediators of AI technologies.

There is a need to emphasise that ethical integration of artificial intelligence in education requires careful attention to data privacy, algorithmic bias, fairness, and transparency. As scholars such as Williamson and Piattoeva (2022) argue, AI systems often embed hidden biases that can reproduce social inequalities, making teacher mediation essential. Bulger (2016) similarly emphasises that educators must safeguard learner data and ensure responsible digital practices, while Zhou & Chen (2023) stress that teachers play a critical role in interpreting AI outputs to prevent unfair or opaque decision-making. Therefore, teachers must function as ethical gatekeepers, critiquing AI recommendations, protecting learner rights, and ensuring that AI tools support equity rather than undermine it.

5. FINDINGS AND DISCUSSION

The exploration of the challenges and opportunities surrounding teachers' adaptation to a technology-driven educational landscape reveals several critical themes that shape the current state of education, particularly in South Africa. These themes emerge from a synthesis of empirical observations, statistical data, and teachers' lived experiences, offering a nuanced understanding of the human element at play.

5.1 Theme 1: Lack of Preparedness

The lack of preparedness among teachers, especially those serving in previously disadvantaged contexts, is a significant barrier to the effective implementation of e-learning. According to (NEEDU, 2025) report indicates that only 25% of South African teachers can confidently use advanced digital tools such as Moodle, a learning management system widely regarded as essential for online education. This statistic underscores a troubling gap in digital literacy, compounded by limited access to resources. For instance, approximately 50% of rural schools in South Africa lack functional computers, a situation that severely restricts teachers' ability to integrate technology into their teaching practices (Madzunye, 2021; NEEDU, 2025; Sarah, 2024).

The COVID-19 pandemic further exposed these vulnerabilities, thrusting teachers into uncharted territory where many resorted to ad-hoc solutions. Teachers in rural areas often relied on personal smartphones, which led to practical challenges such as 30% battery drain during extended use, while urban counterparts turned to WhatsApp groups, resulting in 40% learner disengagement due to inconsistent communication (SACE, 2024). This disparity in readiness is vividly illustrated by the experiences of teachers in the Eastern Cape, where rural teachers struggle with basic skills like navigating Zoom, often due to a lack of prior exposure or training (Simuja, 2023).

In contrast, their urban counterparts in Johannesburg face burnout from managing hybrid classes, with 45% reporting significant stress levels Wagner (2022), highlighting the emotional toll of this transition. In addition, teachers' express frustration and exhaustion, feeling ill-equipped to meet the demands of a digital classroom. Addressing this gap requires targeted interventions that go beyond mere technical provision. The provision of solar-powered tablets could ensure access in off-grid areas, while mobile workshops tailored to local needs could build confidence and competence. These efforts are essential to bridge the preparedness divide, fostering an environment where teachers feel supported rather than overwhelmed (Ndebele et al., 2024).

5.2 Theme 2: Professional Development Gaps

The inadequacy of current professional development programs represents a critical impediment to teachers' ability to use technology effectively. According to a study by Alkhatib and Alainati (2024), courses such as Microsoft Teams prioritize technical skills, allocating 80% of training time to them, over the pedagogical adaptation necessary for designing interactive online content, which receives only 10% of the focus. A survey conducted by the Department of Basic Education (2023) also revealed that 70% of these sessions lasted less than a day in South Africa, a duration insufficient for mastering the complex tools required for modern education. This demonstrates a shallow approach that leaves teachers with fragmented skills, preventing them from translating technical knowledge into meaningful classroom practices. The lack of follow-up support exacerbates this issue, with only 15% of teachers receiving ongoing mentorship to reinforce their learning, leaving many to fend for themselves post-training (Mayombe, 2021). This may erode the teachers' confidence and morale, as they feel abandoned after brief workshops and struggle to adapt lesson plans or troubleshoot technical issues without guidance. This gap calls for a comprehensive curriculum overhaul that emphasizes long-term skill-building, such as year-long certification programs that allow for gradual mastery, and pedagogical innovation, such as the flipped classroom model, where learners engage with content online before in-class discussions. Such an approach could enhance teaching effectiveness by fostering creativity and learner-centred learning, while also improving outcomes like critical thinking and engagement. The need for sustained support is echoed in the experiences of teachers who, after initial training, report a renewed sense of purpose when provided with continuous professional development (Zanele & Ajani, 2024). Investing in these programs is not just a technical necessity but a human imperative to empower teachers in a digital age.

5.3 Theme 3: Policy and Resource Disparities

South Africa's education system continues to grapple with profound policy and resource disparities that undermine technological integration. Statistical evidence highlights this imbalance: only 30% of rural schools are connected to the internet, compared to 85% in urban areas, according to data from the South African Department of Communications and Digital Technologies (2022). This digital divide is further compounded by sluggish policy execution, as exemplified by the 2023 Digital Schools Project, which achieved only 40% of its targets due to funding shortages and logistical challenges (Sibiya, 2023).

Such disparities perpetuate inequalities, leaving rural teachers and learners at a significant disadvantage, with limited access to devices, reliable electricity, and high-speed internet. This further results in a profound impact on instructional processes, as teachers in rural or marginalized regions feel a sense of neglect and struggle to compete with their urban counterparts who benefit from better infrastructure (Tsitey, 2022). For instance, a rural teacher in Limpopo might spend hours traveling to charge a single laptop, a stark contrast to the seamless connectivity enjoyed in Gauteng schools. Systemic intervention is urgently needed, including government subsidies such as a proposed R5 billion annual fund to equip rural schools with technology, and private partnerships, such as those with MTN, to provide affordable data plans (Mogotsi, 2023). These measures could level the playing field, ensuring that policy reflects the lived realities of all teachers. The historical legacy of apartheid, which prioritized urban education, continues to shape these disparities, necessitating a policy framework that prioritizes equity and inclusion (Republic of South Africa, 1996).

5.4 Theme 4: Potential of Digital Tools

The potential of digital tools to transform education offers a beacon of hope amidst these challenges, providing opportunities to enhance teaching and learning in innovative ways. Virtual classrooms, such as those that use virtual reality (VR) for history lessons in Finland, allow learners to immerse themselves in historical events. In contrast, AI-driven assessments, such as Duolingo's language-learning platform, have demonstrated language gains of up to 18% globally in 2024 (OECD, 2024). Learning management systems, such as Canvas, are widely adopted in the U.S. and streamline course delivery while fostering collaboration; an OECD (2024) study found a 20% increase in learner engagement when these tools are used effectively. These examples illustrate the transformative power of technology when supported by adequate resources and expertise. However, realizing these potential hinges on significant investments in teacher training and institutional support.

According to SACE (2024), 60% of untrained teachers struggle to integrate digital tools, often due to a lack of hands-on experience, while 70% of schools lack dedicated IT staff to provide technical assistance. On the contrary, a study conducted by Gubevu and Mncube (2024) found that teachers who received proper training have rekindled their passion for teaching. A notable example was a geography teacher who used VR to bring geography lessons to life for disengaged learners. This suggests a scalable model for South Africa, where pilot programs could train teachers in rural and urban settings, supported by government-private sector collaboration. The success of such initiatives depends on addressing current gaps, ensuring that digital tools become enablers rather than barriers to education (Ndebele et al., 2024).

6. RECOMMENDATIONS

The transformation of education in a technology-driven world requires a multifaceted approach that addresses teachers' immediate needs while laying the foundation for long-term sustainability. The following recommendations aim to empower teachers and enhance educational outcomes across diverse contexts in South Africa.

6.1 Digital Learning Toolkit

The study recommends a comprehensive Digital Learning Toolkit to equip teachers with the skills and resources needed to thrive in digital environments. This toolkit should include a series of online modules designed to build digital literacy, such as navigating platforms like Moodle with ease, alongside virtual teaching strategies that engage learners through techniques like breakout room facilitation. Additionally, it should address ethical assessment practices, incorporating tools like Turnitin to prevent plagiarism and ensure fairness, and provide troubleshooting guides for common issues, such as internet outages, prevalent in rural areas. To ensure a successful implementation of this program, educational institutions can draw on successful examples such as Germany's digital schools, where 90% of teachers have adopted these technologies (Timotheou et al., 2023), and Rwanda's community e-learning hubs, which have achieved 50% rural access (Rwigema, 2021).

6.2 Enhanced Professional Development

Enhancing professional development is essential to transform teachers into confident digital teachers, addressing both their technical and pedagogical needs.

The curriculum should be redesigned to integrate training based on the Technology Acceptance Model. This is important because TAM emphasizes perceived usefulness and ease of use, and hands-on workshops explore virtual tools such as VR simulations to create immersive learning experiences. These workshops should highlight benefits such as a 20% reduction in workload through automated grading, while ensuring intuitive interfaces that reduce the learning curve for teachers new to technology. Incorporating scenario-based learning, such as managing online disruptions like sudden internet failures, can prepare teachers for real-world challenges, complemented by year-long micro-credentials in digital pedagogy to foster long-term growth and expertise.

6.3 Collaboration and Partnership with Stakeholders

Collaboration is key to the success of this enhanced development. Partnerships with organizations like Microsoft, which can supply 5,000 laptops, local universities that can host training sessions, and NGOs like the Shuttleworth Foundation, known for educational innovation, can mirror Germany's digital initiative's success. This program, which boosted teacher confidence by 30% in 2024 through sustained support, offers a model for seamlessly integrating resources and training. Teachers who have participated in similar programs often speak of a renewed sense of purpose, feeling equipped to inspire their learners with cutting-edge methods. By investing in these partnerships, South Africa can cultivate a cadre of digitally fluent teachers, ready to lead the next generation.

6.4 Policy Advocacy

Advocating for robust policy changes is crucial to creating an enabling environment for technological integration in education. Policymakers should be urged to align national curricula with the skills demanded by the fourth industrial revolution, including basic AI literacy, to ensure that every learner gains relevant competencies. This alignment must be supported by equitable resource allocation, proposed through substantial funding of digital education to equip schools with modern technology. In addition, there is a need for public-private partnerships, such as those with Huawei, to enhance infrastructure, particularly in rural areas where connectivity remains a challenge.

6.5 Community Engagement

Fostering community engagement through Ubuntu-inspired programs offers a culturally resonant approach to support rural teachers and enhance digital inclusion.

Leveraging existing community networks, such as village cooperatives, can facilitate the sharing of digital resources, with mobile learning hubs powered by solar energy providing a sustainable solution for off-grid areas. These hubs can serve as vibrant centres where teachers collaborate, learners learn, and parents engage, reflecting the Ubuntu principle of collective well-being. The success of similar initiatives in Rwanda, where community hubs increased rural access by 50%, suggests that this model can thrive in South Africa as well. Teachers who have benefited from such support often describe a renewed connection to their communities, feeling valued and supported in their digital journey. This approach promises to build a resilient, inclusive educational ecosystem grounded in human relationships and shared progress.

7. CONCLUSION

This chapter emphasizes the urgent need to embrace digital transformation in education. It highlights the essential role of professional development in preparing teachers for a tech-driven world. Grounded in the Ubuntu philosophy, it fosters a sense of community and equity. The Technology Acceptance Model (TAM) provides a framework to understand teacher readiness. The analysis reveals deep social injustices in resource distribution, with a notable gap: 70% of urban schools have device access, compared to just 30% in rural areas. Policy implementation lags significantly, with only a 40% success rate in South Africa at the moment. These disparities demand immediate attention, and the proposed Digital Learning Toolkit offers a practical solution. Strategic interventions aim to bridge existing gaps. Teachers can enhance teaching methods with these tools. Learning experiences improve, with a potential 20% boost in student engagement. In addition, assessment practices are strengthened, reducing plagiarism by 10% which reflects a commitment to equity and excellence.

By and large, education landscapes are shifting rapidly. AI adoption has doubled since 2020, signalling a technological revolution. Emerging tools promise further innovation; therefore, future research must assess the long-term impact of these strategies. A focus on 2030 outcomes will guide progress, with underserved regions like Limpopo in need of special attention. As a result, sustained efforts to adapt to technologies such as quantum computing are crucial to ensuring lasting change that will shape the future of education. Teachers must remain at the heart of this transformation as their growth ensures a resilient system. Therefore, the journey ahead requires collaboration and vision, which serves as the groundwork for that future, being laid down by this chapter.

REFERENCES

Ahmed, M. R., & Sidiq, M. A. (2023). Evaluating online assessment strategies: A systematic review of reliability and validity in e-learning environments. *North American Academic Research*, *6*(12), 1–18. DOI: 10.5281/zenodo.10407361

Aithal, R. K., Choudhary, V., Maurya, H., Pradhan, D., & Sarkar, D. N. (2023). Factors influencing technology adoption amongst small retailers: Insights from thematic analysis. [emerald.com]. *International Journal of Retail & Distribution Management*, *51*(1), 81–102. DOI: 10.1108/IJRDM-02-2022-0042

Ajani, O. A. (2024). Exploring curriculum transformation in higher education institutions: A critical analysis of equity and social justice perspectives. *Research in Educational Policy and Management*, 6(1), 217-237. https://www.apas.africa/journal/jassd_1730882881.pdf

Alkhatib, H., & Alainati, S. (2024). Assessing the effectiveness of microsoft teams as a platform for online learning: How to Enhance students' participation in blended and virtual learning. *IOSR Journal of Business and Management (IOSR-JBM)*, 26(6), 26-31. https://www.researchgate.net/publication/382424398_Assessing_The_Effectiveness_Of_Microsoft_Teams_As_A_Platform_For_Online_Learning_How_To_Enhance_Students'_Participation_In_Blended_And_Virtual_Learning

Baker, R. S. (2016). Stupid tutoring systems and intelligent humans. *International Journal of Artificial Intelligence in Education*, *26*(2), 600–614. DOI: 10.1007/s40593-016-0105-0

Barasa, P. L. (2021). *Digitalization in teaching and education in Kenya: Background report.* UNESCO. https://www.ilo.org/media/386411/download

Beelaerts van Blokland, F. (2025). Exploring organizational barriers to implementing generative artificial intelligence in Dutch hospitals to reduce administrative burdens. (Masters thesis, Utrecht University). https://studenttheses.uu.nl/bitstream/handle/20.500.12932/48841/20250221_Final%20thesis_FlorentineBeelaertsvanBlokland_publ.pdf?sequence=1

Bixby, D. W. (2018). *Product training for the technical expert: The art of developing and delivering hands-on learning*. John Wiley & Sons. DOI: 10.1002/9781119260325

Breazeal, C., Denoël, V., & Fernaeus, Y. (2018). Social robots for education: A review. *Annual Review of Control, Robotics, and Autonomous Systems*, *1*, 277–300. DOI: 10.1146/annurev-control-060117-105303

Brunskill, E., & Russell, S. J. (2011). Partially observable Markov decision processes for educational assessment. *Journal of Machine Learning Research, 12*, 2487–2529. http://www.jmlr.org/papers/volume12/brunskill11a/brunskill11a.pdf

Bulger, M. (2016). *Personalized learning: The conversations we're not having.* Data & Society. https://www.datasociety.net/pubs/ecl/PersonalizedLearning_primer_2016.pdf

Coetzee, J., Neneh, B., Stemmet, K., Lamprecht, J., Motsitsi, C., & Sereeco, W. (2021). South African universities in a time of increasing disruption. *Suid-Afrikaanse Tydskrif vir Ekonomiese en Bestuurswetenskappe, 24*(1), 1–12. DOI: 10.4102/sajems.v24i1.3739

Cooke, A., Smith, D., & Booth, A. (2012). Beyond PICO: The SPIDER Tool for Qualitative Evidence Synthesis. *Qualitative Health Research, 22*(10), 1435–1443. DOI: 10.1177/1049732312452938

Das, N. K., Sahoo, S., & Pati, L. (2021). Online learning: Challenges for education in rural and remote areas. *International Advanced Research Journal in Science, Engineering and Technology*, 8(7). https://iarjset.com/wp-content/uploads/2021/07/IARJSET.2021.8712.pdf

Davis, F. D., Bagozzi, R. P., & Warshaw, P. R. (1989). User acceptance of computer technology: A comparison of two theoretical models. *Management Science, 35*(8), 982–1003. DOI: 10.1287/mnsc.35.8.982

Department of Basic Education. (2023). *Survey on teacher professional development in South Africa.* Pretoria: Government Printers. https://www.education.gov.za/LinkClick.aspx?fileticket=yXQkmxaL_EI%3d&tabid=435&portalid=0&mid=4028 [education.gov.za]

Department of Communications and Digital Technologies. (2022). *Annual report 2021/22.* Pretoria: Government Printers. https://www.gov.za/documents/annual-reports/department-communications-and-digital-technologies-annual-report-20222023

Fontich, X. (2020). "Give me a good corridor!": L1 teachers' beliefs about online education in the context of COVID-19 confinement in Spain. *L1-Educational Studies in Language and Literature, 20*(Special Issue), 1–13. DOI: 10.17239/L1ESLL-2020.20.03.01

Granić, A., & Marangunić, N. (2019). Technology acceptance model in educational context: A systematic literature review. *British Journal of Educational Technology, 50*(5), 2572–2593. DOI: 10.1111/bjet.12864

Gubevu, B. W., & Mncube, V. (2024). Chronicling participants' understanding and experiences of integrating ICT into the teaching of geography in South African schools. *Perspectives in Education*, *42*(2), 192–205. DOI: 10.38140/pie.v42i2.7083

Heffernan, N. T., & Heffernan, C. (2014). The ASSISTments ecosystem: Building a platform that brings scientists and teachers together for minimally invasive research on human learning and teaching. *International Journal of Artificial Intelligence in Education*, *24*(4), 470–497. DOI: 10.1007/s40593-014-0024-x

Holmes, W., Bialik, M., & Fadel, C. (2019). *Artificial intelligence in education: Promises and implications for teaching and learning*. Center for Curriculum Redesign. https://discovery.ucl.ac.uk/id/eprint/10139722/

Holmes, W., Porayska-Pomsta, K., & Holstein, K. (2022). Ethics of AI in education: Towards a human-centred approach. *Computers and Education: Artificial Intelligence*, *3*, 100–060. DOI: 10.1016/j.caeai.2022.100060

Kapstein, H. (2025). Power failures: The public poetics of Eskom and energy. *ISLE: Interdisciplinary Studies in Literature and Environment*, *32*(1), 5–26. DOI: 10.1093/isle/isad044

Karunanayaka, S. P. (2023). Blending Innovative Pedagogy and Technology for Capacity Development of Educators during the Pandemic. *Journal of Learning for Development*, *10*(1), 24–37. DOI: 10.56059/jl4d.v10i1.783

Kashem, M. A., Shamsuddoha, M., & Nasir, T. (2024). Digital-era resilience: Navigating logistics and supply chain operations after COVID-19. *Businesses*, *4*(1), 1–17. DOI: 10.3390/businesses4010001

Koedinger, K. R., D'Mello, S. K., McLaughlin, E., Pardos, Z. A., & Wylie, R. (2015). Data-driven learner modeling research: Issues and opportunities. *User Modeling and User-Adapted Interaction*, *25*(1), 1–7. DOI: 10.1007/s11257-015-9152-6

Lauer, P. A., Christopher, D. E., Firpo-Triplett, R., & Buchting, F. (2014). The impact of short-term professional development on participant outcomes: A review of the literature. *Professional Development in Education*, *40*(2), 207–227. DOI: 10.1080/19415257.2013.776619

Lester, J. C., Mott, B. W., & Rowe, J. P. (2021). Toward engineering learning ecosystems for AI-enhanced classrooms. *AI Magazine*, *42*(2), 41–52. DOI: 10.1609/aimag.v42i2.18109

Luckin, R. (2018). *Machine learning and human intelligence: The future of education for the 21st century*. UCL Institute of Education Press. https://discovery.ucl.ac.uk/10178695/1/Machine%20Learning%20and%20Human%20Intelligence.pdf

Madzunye, T. E. (2021). *Factors influencing the implementation of e-learning technology in rural secondary schools in South Africa* (Doctoral dissertation, Cape Peninsula University of Technology). https://etd.cput.ac.za/handle/20.500.11838/3358

Mafikeng, R. J. (2024). *The adoption of digital technologies in public schools in South Africa* (Masters thesis, University of the Witwatersrand, Johannesburg). https://wiredspace.wits.ac.za/items/c6221e89-492a-482d-997b-e493350a0a3b

Masoga, M. A. (2020). Effectiveness of WhatsApp homiletics in the era of COVID-19 in South Africa. *Pharos Journal of Theology*, 101. https://www.pharosjot.com/uploads/7/1/6/3/7163688/article_51_vol_101__2020__unizul.pdf

Mastour, H., Yousefi, R., & Niroumand, S. (2025). Exploring the acceptance of e-learning in health professions education in Iran based on the technology acceptance model (TAM). *Scientific Reports*, *15*(1), 8178. DOI: 10.1038/s41598-025-90742-5

Mayombe, C. (2021). *Vocational education and training in Sub-Saharan Africa*. Springer International Publishing., DOI: 10.1007/978-3-030-82284-2

McAleavy, T., Hall-Chen, A., Horrocks, S., & Riggall, A. (2018). *Technology-Supported Professional Development for Teachers: Lessons from Developing Countries*. Education Development Trust. https://files.eric.ed.gov/fulltext/ED593386.pdf

Memon, F. N., & Memon, S. N. (2025). Digital divide and equity in education: Bridging gaps to ensure inclusive learning. In *Impact of Digitalization on Education and Social Sustainability* (pp. 107–130). IGI Global., https://www.igi-global.com/chapter/digital-divide-and-equity-in-education/358122

Mhlomi, Y. (2023). Integration of digital media and pedagogy in the twenty first century classroom: A survey of selected high schools in Eastern Cape, South Africa. (Doctoral dissertation, University of Fort Hare). https://core.ac.uk/download/588487733.pdf

Mogotsi, K. (2023). The role of innovative finance mechanisms in ICT rollout in South Africa's education system. (Masters thesis, University of Cape Town). https://open.uct.ac.za/bitstreams/bdbc095c-0653-4f79-84f5-9c7b1397c166/download

Moodley, K., & Segoete, N. (2024, August). A Systematic Literature Review on the Impact of the COVID-19 Pandemic on Digital Access and the Digital Divide in South African. In *Proceedings of Ninth International Congress on Information and Communication Technology: ICICT 2024*, London, Volume 8 (Vol. 1004, p. 113). Springer Nature. https://link.springer.com/content/pdf/10.1007/978-981-97-3305-7_9

Motjoadi, V., & Bokoro, P. N. (2023). Improving Electricity Supply Reliability: A Case Study of Remote Communities of Limpopo in South Africa. In *Recent Advances in Energy Systems, Power, and Related Smart Technologies: Concepts and Innovative Implementations for a Sustainable Economic Growth in Developing Countries* (pp. 135-174). Springer Nature Switzerland. https://link.springer.com/chapter/10.1007/978-3-031-29586-7_6

Mpungose, C. B. (2020). Beyond limits: Lecturers' reflections on Moodle uptake in South African universities. *Education and Information Technologies*, *25*(6), 5033–5052. DOI: 10.1007/s10639-020-10190-8

Muller, G. M. (2022). The use of an online platform for addressing Africa's Education Leadership challenges through conversation. (Masters thesis, University of Johannesburg). https://ujcontent.uj.ac.za/esploro/outputs/graduate/The-use-of-an-online-platform/9920609907691

Muyambi, G. C., & Ahiaku, P. K. A. (2025). Inequalities and education in South Africa: A scoping review. *International Journal of Educational Research Open*, *8*, 100408. DOI: 10.1016/j.ijedro.2024.100408

Mxatule, A. (2024). Aluta continua! digital divide experiences of South African township high school learners during COVID-19 hard lockdown (Masters thesis, University of Cape Town). https://open.uct.ac.za/items/34408ef0-5ddc-4a9e-8c59-fc5da78080a4/full

Ndebele, C., Marongwe, N., Ncanywa, T., Matope, S., Ginyigazi, Z., Chisango, G., Msindwana, P. N., & Garidzirai, R. (2024). Reconceptualising initial teacher education in South Africa: A quest for transformative and sustainable alternatives. *Interdisciplinary Journal of Education Research*, *6*, 1–19. DOI: 10.38140/ijer-2024.vol6.07

NEEDU. (2025). *National Education Evaluation and Development Unit Report 2025.* Pretoria: Department of Basic Education. https://www.education.gov.za/Programmes/NEEDU.aspx

Ngubane, N., & Makua, M. (2021). Ubuntu pedagogy–transforming educational practices in South Africa through an African philosophy: From theory to practice. Inkanyiso. *Inkanyiso*, *13*(1), 1–12. https://www.ajol.info/index.php/ijhss/article/view/212332. DOI: 10.4102/ink.v13i1.9

OECD. (2024). *Education at a Glance 2024: OECD Indicators*. Paris: OECD Publishing. https://www.oecd.org/en/publications/education-at-a-glance-2024_c00cad36-en.html

Peel, K. L. (2020). A beginner's guide to applied educational research using thematic analysis. *Practical Assessment, Research & Evaluation, 25*(1). Advance online publication. DOI: 10.7275/ryr5-k983

Perry, M. (2024). Investigating the relationship between hybrid work, job burnout, and job satisfaction in higher education (Masters thesis, University of Tennessee). https://scholar.utc.edu/theses/852/

Pickering, E., & Schuller, C. (2024). Chegg's growth, response rate, and prevalence as a cheating tool: Insights from an audit within an Australian engineering school. *Journal of Academic Ethics*, •••, 1–15. https://link.springer.com/article/10.1007/s10805-024-09551-6

Piech, C., Huang, J., Chen, Z., Do, C., Ng, A., & Koller, D. (2015). Advances in Neural Information Processing Systems: Vol. 28. *Deep knowledge tracing.*, https://arxiv.org/abs/1506.05908

Republic of South Africa. (1996). *Constitution of the Republic of South Africa.* Pretoria: Government Printers. https://www.gov.za/documents/constitution/constitution-republic-south-africa-1996-04-feb-1997

Rwigema, P. (2021). Impact of COVID-19 lockdowns on the education sector. The case of Rwanda. *The Strategic Journal of Business & Change Management*, 8(1), 150-169. https://strategicjournals.com/index.php/journal/article/view/1903

Ryan, G. W., & Bernard, H. R. (2003). Techniques to identify themes. [qualquant.org]. *Field Methods, 15*(1), 85–109. https://www.qualquant.org/wp-content/uploads/text/Ryan%20&%20Bernard%202003.pdf. DOI: 10.1177/1525822X02239569

Saad, S., Ramli, Z., Sarmila, M. S., Nor, M., & Ali, S. (2025). Exploring the adoption of ai-driven adaptive learning in higher education: A multidimensional TAM perspective. *International Journal of Academic Research in Business & Social Sciences, 15*(5), 1011–1025. DOI: 10.6007/IJARBSS/v15-i5/25487

Sarah, M. M. (2024). *The implementation of Information Communication Technology for teaching and learning in Tshwane West District* (Masters thesis, University of Pretoria). https://repository.up.ac.za/items/733d743a-2c66-4e46-8b2a-c71dd1159be8

Setälä, M., Heilala, V., Sikström, P., & Kärkkäinen, T. (2025, March). The Use of Generative Artificial Intelligence for Upper Secondary Mathematics Education Through the Lens of Technology Acceptance. In *Proceedings of the 40th ACM/SIGAPP Symposium on Applied Computing* (pp. 74-82). https://dl.acm.org

Sibiya, B. (2023). *Digital transformation of cities through emerging Industry 4.0 smart technologies and infrastructure in South Africa.* (Doctoral dissertation, University of Johannesburg). https://ujcontent.uj.ac.za/esploro/outputs/graduate/Digital-transformation-of-cities-through-emerging-Industry-40-smart-technologies-and-infrastructure-in-South-Africa/9920609907691

Simon, P. (2021). *Reimagining collaboration: Slack, Microsoft Teams, Zoom, and the post-COVID world of work*. Racket Publishing. https://www.racketpublishing.com/titles/

Simuja, C. (2023). Teachers' experiences of technology integration in Sarah Batman District, Eastern Cape Province. *African Perspectives of Research in Teaching and Learning*, 7(3), 548-565. http://ulspace.ul.ac.za/handle/10386/4466

Singh, H., Singh, P., & Sharma, D. (2023). Faculty acceptance of virtual teaching platforms for online teaching: Moderating role of resistance to change. *Australasian Journal of Educational Technology, 39*(6), 33–50. DOI: 10.14742/ajet.7529

SM. F. R. (2025). Digital innovations in education enhancing Sustainable Development Goals. In *Digital Innovations for Renewable Energy and Conservation* (pp. 75-98). IGI Global. https://doi.org/DOI: 10.4018/979-8-3693-6532-8.ch004

South African Council for Educators. (SACE0. (2024). *Teacher Wellness and Technology Integration Survey 2024.* South African Council for Teachers. https://www.sace.org.za

Tarisayi, K. S., & Munyaradzi, E. (2021). A simple solution adopted during the Covid-19 pandemic: Using WhatsApp at a university in Zimbabwe. *Issues in Educational Research, 31*(2), 644–659. https://www.iier.org.au/iier31/tarisayi.pdf

Teeroovengadum, V., Heeraman, N., & Jugurnath, B. (2017). Examining the antecedents of ICT adoption in education using an extended technology acceptance model (TAM). *International Journal of Education and Development Using ICT, 13*(3), 4–23. https://files.eric.ed.gov/fulltext/EJ1166522.pdf

Timotheou, S., Miliou, O., Dimitriadis, Y., Sobrino, S. V., Giannoutsou, N., Cachia, R., Monés, A. M., & Ioannou, A. (2023). Impacts of digital technologies on education and factors influencing schools' digital capacity and transformation: A literature review. *Education and Information Technologies, 28*(6), 6695–6726. DOI: 10.1007/s10639-022-11431-8

Tsitey, R. (2022). *Investigating the Experience of Ruralness and Rural Education: A Phenomenological Study of Perceived Impacts on Achievements and Future Prospects in Rural Ghana* (Doctoral dissertation, Liberty University). https://digitalcommons.liberty.edu/doctoral/3774/

Wagner, T. A. M. (2022). *Perceived Stress and Burnout Syndrome in Chiropractic Students at the University of Johannesburg During the Covid-19 Pandemic: A Cross-Sectional Study* (Masters thesis, University of Johannesburg). https://ujcontent.uj.ac.za/esploro/outputs/graduate/Perceived-stress-and-burnout-syndrome-in/9915710107691

Wahyuni, E., Khan, O., & Raza, A. (2024). The Effectiveness of mobile learning in remote and rural areas. *Journal International Inspire Education Technology*, *3*(3), 253–264. https://paperity.org/p/360322384/the-effectiveness-of-mobile-learning-in-remote-and-rural-areas

Williamson, B., & Eynon, R. (2020). Algorithmic edtech and the governance of learning. *Learning, Media and Technology*, *45*(1), 1–17. DOI: 10.1080/17439884.2019.1623250

Woolf, B. P. (2021). *Building intelligent interactive tutors*. Morgan Kaufmann. https://shop.elsevier.com/books/building-intelligent-interactive-tutors/woolf/978-0-12-373594-2

World Economic Forum. (2025). *The Future of Jobs Report 2025*. https://www.weforum.org/publications/the-future-of-jobs-report-2025/digest/

Zanele, P. M., & Ajani, O. A.Zanele Priscila MsweliOluwatoyin Ayodele Ajani. (2024). Enhancing digital inclusion in multilingual education: Exploring the role of technology in South African higher education. International. *Journal of Innovative Technologies in Social Science*, *4*(44). Advance online publication. DOI: 10.31435/ijitss.4(44).2024.3134

Zawacki-Richter, O., Marín, V. I., Bond, M., & Gouverneur, F. (2019). Systematic review of research on artificial intelligence in higher education. *International Journal of Educational Technology in Higher Education*, *16*(1), 39. DOI: 10.1186/s41239-019-0171-0

Zhou, C., & Chen, X. (2023). Teacher's perceptions of applying artificial intelligence in education: A systematic review. *World Journal of Social Science Research*, *11*(3), 62–78. DOI: 10.22158/wjssr.v11n3p62

Chapter 18
When AI Moves Into the Classroom:
Teachers' Hopes and Fears

Potchong M. Jackaria
https://orcid.org/0009-0006-1678-4841
Mindanao State University Tawi-Tawi College of Technology and Oceanography, Philippines

Christian Jay L. Campo
Mindanao State University Tawi-Tawi College of Technology and Oceanography, Philippines

Aldammien A. Sukarno
https://orcid.org/0009-0002-3213-6271
Mindanao State University Tawi-Tawi College of Technology and Oceanography, Philippines

Tunniza A. Jackaria
Philippine Last Frontier College Inc., Philippines

Al-asmi A. Gapul
Mindanao State University Tawi-Tawi College of Technology and Oceanography, Philippines

ABSTRACT

Understanding teachers' hopes and fears about AI is necessary as they are at the frontline of education. This will help how to successfully navigate AI integration into classrooms. This chapter involves interviewing eleven teacher-educators about their thoughts on AI impact in schools. The result shows that participants recognized AI's strong potential to improve teaching, provide personalized instruction for students,

DOI: 10.4018/979-8-3373-4521-5.ch018

and improve access to learning resources. AI can lessen workload through content generation leading to enhanced lessons and assessment. Teachers also recognize the AI potential to help students by providing access to learning materials. On the other hand, they expressed concerns about the AI potential misuse such as the risk of plagiarism, the erosion of students' critical-thinking skills, and diminishing human interaction. They also recognized the lack of teachers' preparation and absence of clear policies pose challenge for the full adoption of AI. In closing, the chapter outlines actionable recommendations for seamless integration of AI in schools.

1. INTRODUCTION

Artificial intelligence (AI) has become indispensable. It is applied in all industries, not just in the field of education. Among educators, AI has been received with everything from enthusiasm to fear. For those in its favour, AI can be used to provide more personalised teaching for students (Hwang & Tu, 2021; Ka, et al., 2023; Yu & Guo, 2022), to automate certain teaching tasks (Jackaria et al., 2024), and in the near future, could serve as an assistant to instructors in the classroom (Kim et al., 2020; Kim et al., 2022). These are just some of the possibilities of AI tools in education.

Furthermore, the development of AI is expected to continue with ever more advanced AI tools being introduced. AI is not going to fade; its impact is expected to only increase. A compelling reason for AI adoption in schools is that AI literacy is increasingly becoming a necessary skill for future employment (Jackaria et al, 2024; Lokesh et al., 2024). Hence, schools with the aim of preparing students for the future are increasingly expected to initiate the introduction of AI (Ng et al., 2023).

A well-known drawback of AI is that these tools can make it easier for students to engage in academic dishonesty. For instance, some authors argued that students may use AI tools to cheat and plagiarise their academic work, leading to overdependence (Gammoh, 2024; Wogu et al., 2018). With just a few clicks, students can generate entire essays, solve math problems, or produce research answers without doing the work themselves. The convenience and accessibility of AI has the potential to encourage plagiarism, which weakens the value of authentic learning. Similarly, educators may find it harder to assess a student's true comprehension of content when assignments can be completed by an AI system. This could create an uneven academic environment and undermine trust in the learning process.

Beyond the issue of academic dishonesty, using AI has other possible long-term effects. The long-term presence of AI in schools may affect how children think and learn, leading to overreliance. This overreliance on automated answers provided by AI could lead to a decline in critical thinking, creativity, and problem-solving skills (Mhlanga, 2022; Zanetti et al., 2019). Students might skip the process of questioning, analysing, and experimenting because instant solutions are available. Over time, this dependency could reduce curiosity and resilience, key skills that education aims to develop. Schools may also struggle to maintain a balance between embracing technology and preserving the human elements of teaching, such as mentorship, dialogue, and independent reasoning. These are important for the development of well-rounded learners.

The disadvantages of AI tools in the context of education imply that AI should be integrated with caution. There is a growing need for a critical discussion of AI and its impact on teachers and students. It also indicates that AI introduction into the classroom requires careful consideration for students to take advantage of this new technology while mitigating its negative impact. Understanding the views of educators about AI's impact at the classroom level is necessary for better AI integration into our education systems. Their first-hand views are a crucial baseline for the creation of policies pertaining to AI adoption in educational settings.

This chapter explores the potential impact of AI in the classroom from the perspective of educators. This chapter also highlights the "double-edged sword" of AI tools; AI can potentially be a tool to advance learning, but at the same time a tool of destruction for meaningful learning. Research is needed to understand AI's impact and to mitigate its potentially negative effects.

This chapter analyses two aspects of AI impact in the classroom. Specifically, it attempts to answer to following: (1) What are the more common expectations associated with the introduction of AI in the classroom? (2) What are educators' fears about the introduction of AI in the classroom?

Understanding how educators perceive AI tools can help schools craft necessary guidelines surrounding their integration. Schools can then determine the many opportunities brought by AI, while mitigating some of its negative effects. Although the best adoption strategies for AI are yet to be determined, this chapter provides actionable insights in this regard for educators, policy makers, and institutions in general.

2. LITERATURE REVIEW

The increasing application of AI in education presents both opportunities and risks. A growing number of studies have been undertaken to understand its implications. Since AI is a relatively new technology, its long-term effects are yet to be fully understood. Educators who are at the forefront of classroom instruction hold the power to manoeuvre the technology to either advance or hinder the teaching and learning process, thereby advancing or hindering educational outcomes. Their perceptions, rooted in both hopes and fears, are fundamental in shaping effective and responsible integration. However, educators' opinions may differ significantly depending on various factors, including teaching experiences. Those who have been teaching longer often have more open opinions towards AI integration, in comparison to the less experienced educators (Presetya, 2024). Although views of AI in education are largely favourable, there are some educators who express concerns related to privacy and ethics (Uygun, 2024). Understanding these educators' views is crucial to foster informed discussions (Alam, 2021), which are crucial for raising awareness not only of AI's many potential benefits, but also its limitations and challenges.

Ethical and privacy-related concerns are the most common concerns of educators related to AI in education. Pikhart and Al-Obaydi (2025) revealed that many university instructors expressed negative concerns regarding AI integration, citing potential threats to privacy. Given that AI systems need to gather and store huge volumes of data, which is often personal in nature, various legal and ethical issues arise from the use of these systems, including the concerns about data breaches, mishandling of users' private information, and unauthorised access (Chollet, 2019). AI tools also potentially facilitate plagiarism, which might hinder students' creativity, critical thinking, and undermine academic integrity (Walczack & Cellary, 2023). While AI is regarded to allow for more personalised learning, some educators are sceptical about the reliability and validity of its generated results as biases and errors are highly possible. For these reasons, many have expressed a lack of trust in AI results (Dwork & Minow, 2022; Tawafak et al., 2023). Similarly, Douali et al. (2022) found that many teachers expressed worries about the use of AI in education, especially at the early childhood level, citing values and ethics as the core issues. AI is useful for its technical functions but lacks the humanity essential to teaching..

Educators' professional roles are another area of concern. AI tools are seen by sceptics to have the potential of displacing educators, transforming them from conventional teachers into mere technological facilitators, which in the long run, might diminish essential human interaction in the classrooms (Brusilovsky, 2023). Nevertheless, AI's usefulness in replicating human interaction has been garnering increasing recognition, such as in the case of language training, especially for those without access to native speakers (Derakhshan et al., 2023; Nutprapha, 2023). However, AI in its current state still cannot fully replicate the complexity of natural human interaction, which is an essential element of effective learning. Additionally, AI is viewed by some to disregard behavioural and emotional engagement, thus tending towards isolation rather than fostering meaningful interactions in the classroom (Lo et al., 2024). In contrast, AI is viewed by many as a tool helping reduce instructors' tasks and saving time, for instance; by supporting them in test creation (Tan et al., 2024).

Even prior to the rise in popularity of generative AI programmes such as ChatGPT, AI's application in education was already taking place. AI has been used to support teaching and improve assessment tasks such as developing intelligent learning systems and automatic grading tools (Wang, 2021). Nowadays, these AI tools are not only adept at generating text and images but are capable of handling complex tasks such as computer programming and even creative writing (Creely & Blannin, 2023; Denny et al., 2024). This significant progress of AI offers greater flexibility and efficiency in the creation of content, such as the creation of more personalised lessons, which pave the way towards increased student development (Tan et al., 2024). AI tools also have the potential to not only enrich students' learning experiences but also help educators increase efficiency, allowing them to allocate more instructional time for student interaction (Kshetri, 2023). Given the extensive applications of AI in education, promoting awareness goes beyond its uses for educators, extending to other primary stakeholders, like learners and administrators (Baker et al., 2019). While several studies have recognised AI's potential for reducing instructor workloads and streamlining administrative tasks (Gökçearslan et al., 2024), scepticism remains about whether harnessing these benefits might come at the expense of true teacher-student connections. The duality of these perceptions, such as AI being powerful for increasing efficiency but also potentially reducing human interactions, underscores how complex educators' views are in terms of integrating AI into educational practice.

Despite the potential drawbacks, AI tools are also viewed with optimism. Many educators recognise the potential of AI to revolutionise and improve the teaching-learning process. Gökçearslan et al. (2023) highlighted that AI tools have been shown to increase students' motivation to learn. and help support language development. On the part of some educators, AI can increase teachers' efficiency by by reducing their workloads. Silva et al. (2023) emphasise the power of AI for democratising knowledge and thereby increasing accessibility, which can accommodate different learning styles, preferences, the special needs of some students (Pikhart et al., 2024), and increase personalised lesson planning catered to individual learner's needs (Ali et al., 2023). However, these same studies also highlighted potential risks such as limited classroom interaction, misleading outputs, and posed concerns about originality, plagiarism, and the persistence of the digital divide. One more recent study shows improvement in teachers' attitudes. Despite reporting reservations, teachers also indicated their readiness to integrate AI into their classrooms, and reported being open to blending these tools with traditional teaching methods, recognising AI's potential to personalise and enhance learning (Sibug et al., 2024). These findings highlight the need for adequate regulatory frameworks and ethical guidelines for effective and safe AI use.

In the case of recently graduated educators who are likely more exposed to AI tools like ChatGPT, only a few confirmed their intentions to adopt these tools in their learning and teaching practices. This stemmed from their apprehensions about possible repercussions in the future when AI is not utilised properly. Their integration strategies were also lacking, which is indicative of their feelings of uncertainty and concerns towards AI tools (Bae et al., 2024). Recently graduated teachers have been found to be only using AI when needed, often limiting their knowledge of AI fundamentals as a result. More efforts to strengthen their AI understanding must be taken. Many recently graduated teachers view AI primarily as a machine or tool meant to be utilised, rather than a dynamic collaborator in education (Guan et al., 2024). This shows that even among the most digitally literate educators, a broader sense of unease and hesitancy about AI integration is observed.

Overall, existing studies reveal the contrasting perceptions of AI in education. Moreover, only a few studies have captured these perspectives across different contexts and educational levels. While benefits and risks are commonly identified, there is a limited exploration of how educators balance their perceptions in practice. This gap underpins the need for further research that might provide additional insights for developing ethical guidelines surrounding AI use, and thus minimising its risks, while allowing to serve its purpose of enhancing quality and efficiency in education.

3. METHODOLOGY

3.1 Method

This chapter analysed data using a qualitative-descriptive design. The nature of qualitative-descriptive research is exploratory; this approach aims to describe a phenomenon. A qualitative-descriptive approach was deemed to be a relevant and appropriate method for this research, which focuses on gaining insights into AI adoption. This is a research area which is not yet fully understood (Ayton, 2023). Specifically, this chapter aims to explore educators' hopes and fears about AI used in schools.

3.2 Participants

The participants selected for this study are educators from both public and private institutions in Tawi-Tawi, Philippines. Eleven educators agreed to voluntarily participate in the study. The participants were purposely selected based on their teaching experience in the College of Teacher Education at Mindanao State University and expressed willingness to participate. The choice of educators as the participants was intentional, as they can provide insights given their in-depth understanding of classroom issues pertaining to AI.

3.3 Data Collection Procedure

The data were sourced from educators using a semi-structured interview questionnaire. The questionnaire consisted of guide questions focusing on instructors' views on the impact of the use of AI tools in the classroom. Their responses were audio-recorded. Some chose to participate via online interview due to time availability. These interviews were conducted through Facebook Messenger. Afterwards, their responses were transcribed. In the cases where parts of participant responses were in the local language, translation into English was performed.

3.4 Data Analysis

The participants' responses were organised and catalogued using a thematic data analysis technique conforming to the analytical phases set by Braun and Clarke (2006). To identify the recurring themes within the data collected, the initial codes from the participant responses were highlighted. Afterwards, themes were derived from these codes. These themes were then reviewed and defined prior to the final drafting of the chapter.

The analysis was divided into two categories related to the research's main themes: fears and hopes. Fears in this context mean anything that participants believe to be an untoward effect of AI, while hope pertains to the positive changes brought by AI tools from the participants' points of view.

4. RESULTS AND DISCUSSION

The results and discussion are divided into two sections. Section 1 discusses teachers' views of the negative impacts of AI tools in the classroom. Section 2 discusses the benefits of AI in the classrooms. The discussion explores both the perceived disadvantages and benefits of AI for teachers and students, which provides a comprehensive view of the issue. Furthermore, the findings are presented thematically. Each theme is supported by direct quotes from the participants, enriched by the ensuing analysis and discussion.

4.1 Teachers' Hopes About AI Use in Schools

Educators' hopes for AI in the classroom are largely centred on its potential to enhance teaching practices, improve student outcomes, and streamline administrative tasks. The key themes that emerged are; AI as a supportive tool for efficiency and personalisation, its role as a great equaliser for student learning, and its ability to foster a more engaging learning environment.

Figure 1. Themes Related to Teachers' Hopes for the use of AI

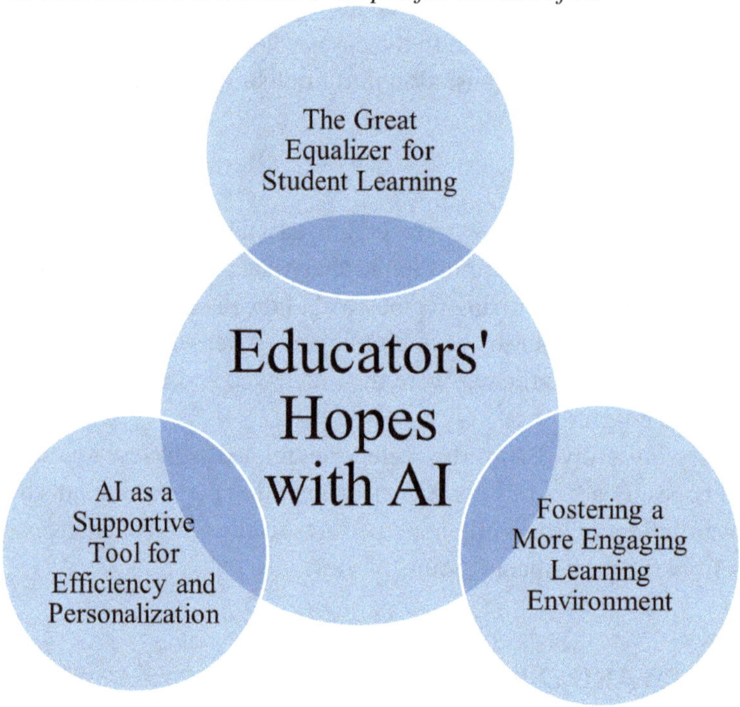

4.1.1 Theme 1: AI as a Supportive Tool for Efficiency

Many educators believe that AI can be utilised to significantly lighten their workload and provide a more customised learning experience for students. From this perspective, AI is seen as a tool that can assist with content creation, lesson planning, and creating assessments. For Participant 2, the use of AI in education is a "game-changer". Below is the response:

AI actually is a game-changer in the field of teaching because it makes teaching a lot easier and more convenient. AI can handle automated administrative tasks, personalised learning plans, and enhanced feedback.

Participant 2 also pointed out the usefulness of AI tools in helping generate activities and materials for teaching:

AI supports my teaching in many ways especially in making a lesson. It assists in generating activities and relevant materials (Participant 2).

Indeed, AI helps many educators save time planning their lessons. The efficiency of AI tools is useful for summarising topics and even generating items for quizzes and examinations. This is elucidated in the response from Participant 1 below:

It [AI] helps me synthesise and summarise topics from our textbooks... I also use it to provide me possible questions for quizzes and exams.

Many educators also see AI tools as a more efficient means to do research. Traditionally, teachers usually use books, Google searches, or YouTube videos to do lesson-planning research. AI provides an alternative, often more efficient way of searching for information pertaining to lesson-planning.

I mostly see AI as a way for teachers to do better research. It helps us keep up with new info and make our lessons better (Participant 8).

Many educators use AI tools for writing support, such as for grammar revision. Participant 5 mentioned that AI helps him communicate clearly and confidently:

I've found AI tools useful for a few specific things, especially in correcting grammar. It's like having a second pair of eyes that catches those pesky errors we all miss, helping students communicate more clearly and confidently (Participant 5).

As the above responses illustrate, educators are already using AI tools to help with their lesson preparation. Teachers, not just students, are able to take advantage of AI capabilities. The versatility of AI tools makes it a powerful assistant. This has the potential to free teachers from many teaching-related tasks, allowing them to allot important time to supporting to students.

4.1.2 Theme 2: AI as a Great Equaliser for Student Learning and Personalisation

Many educators believe that AI can bridge learning gaps and provide equitable access to quality education. It is viewed as a tool that can help students from disadvantaged backgrounds catch up with their peers. AI is quickly becoming an equaliser because it can provide equitable access for all learners to the resources they need to succeed. Participant 1 illustrates this belief in their response:

The main advantage, I think, is for students who graduated from the [Philippine] islands... With AI, they'll be better positioned to catch up with their peers from Bongao. AI is a great equaliser (Participant 1).

Other participants echoed a similar view of AI tools as an education equaliser. According to educators, AI makes learning content more accessible, as articulated in the following responses:

AI is playing a major role in making education more accessible and equitable (Participant 11).

AI offers robust tool[s] that render previously inaccessible materials available to students with special needs (Participant 5).

In addition, given AI's potential to quickly generate learning activities, it has become easier for teachers to deliver personalised content. Participant 6's response below aptly captures this:

AI can provide personalised learning experience[s] for students by adapting to their individual learning styles and paces.

While many of the discussions around the use of AI have been negative or sceptical, the above responses show that AI can be useful beyond merely generating answers. It is also a tool that promotes access to crucial learning materials, making it easier for educators to provide personalised content to students.

4.1.3 Theme 3: AI Helps Foster a More Engaging Learning Environment

The above responses illustrate that educators are increasingly leveraging AI to plan engaging activities for students. Many have expressed positive experiences about AI's capabilities to make lessons more interactive and fun. Teachers also use AI to generate creative activities and assessments that can capture students' attention and motivate them to learn.

I used AI for additional input especially on topics that needs [sic] more emphasis. Also, I asked for suggested activities for a specific topic (Participant 2).

Many teachers use AI to create interactive visuals. This use of AI shows the many possibilities of AI aside from merely generating text-based outputs. Participant 11 believes that visual images make the lesson more interactive and easier to understand:

I use interactive and visual methods to help students understand how each sense works (Participant 11).

Aside from using AI to create activities, many teachers have found it helpful in creating assessments for students. Below are some of the responses from the participants.

I usually use chat GPT whenever I gave an activity that I want to have interactive and engaging activities and assessment to give my students [sic] (Participant 7).

The purpose of AI in my teaching is to enhance the sentence I use, create assessment and games, and make learning more engaging and fun for the students [sic] (Participant 6).

The above capture the many benefits of AI tools for improving teaching and learning. Overall, AI can be beneficial for both students and teachers. The ideas shared by participants in the above support the need for schools to plan for AI adoption, harnessing its many potentials.

4.2 Educators' Fears and Concerns About AI Use

Despite the numerous advantages of AI in education, educators also have significant fears and concerns regarding its integration. Conversations around AI benefits are typically countered with its possible negative effects. Based on interviews with educators, fears or concerns revolve around four main themes. These are (1) a threat to academic integrity, (2) cognitive and skill erosion, (3) the loss of human interaction and connection, and (4) teachers' lack of preparedness to integrate AI and the absence of clear policies pertaining to AI use in schools.

Figure 2. Emerging Themes on Educators' Fears About AI Use in Schools

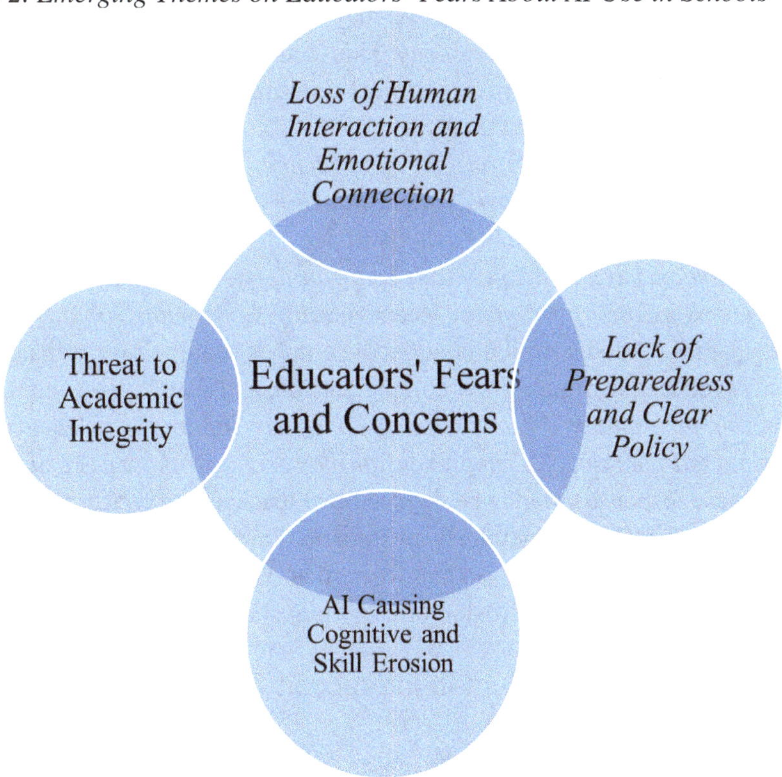

4.2.1 Theme 1: Threat to Academic Integrity

The most prominent fear among educators is the risk of AI being used in plagiarism, leading to the potential decline in students' critical thinking skills. Many educators worry that students will become too reliant on AI to complete academic work, such as using it to complete assignments without truly understanding the requirements. Some of the participants share this concern:

AI could lead to more passive learning as [we] rely on it for our tasks, and knowledge may not be deeply absorbed even though we can quickly access information, we can also easily forget it (Participant 8).

My fears about integrating AI in education [relate to] if the students may over rely on AI tools... leading to plagiarism and reduced their critical thinking [sic] (Participant 11).

4.2.2 Theme 2. AI Causing Cognitive and Skill Erosion

Many educators are concerned that AI may negatively affect students and make them overly dependent on the technology. This could lead to greater problems, such as students not learning or applying critical thinking and initiative. Participants' responses below aptly capture this fear:

The integration of AI tools triggers dependency and lack of initiative among learners. The use of AI dispels critical thinking contributing to the increasing rate of functional illiteracy... (Participant 3).

And for students, if it [learning] isn't guide properly, they will depend their [AI] input not using their own intelligence capabilities [sic] (Participant 4).

Participant 8 echoed a similar concern; he emphasised that over-reliance on AI may lead to reduced learning, lower comprehension, and even low self-confidence:

I don't support students' heavy reliance on AI, as it hinders knowledge development and self-confidence. Comprehension may decline without it (Participant 8).

From these responses, it may be deduced that teachers are concerned about the possibility of AI being used unethically by students. Far from just cases of dishonesty, many of the participants expressed their worry that AI usage may lead to significant problems of dependency and erosion of important skills such as critical thinking.

4.2.3 Theme 3: Loss of Human Interaction and Emotional Connection

Meaningful learning often happens during teacher-student or student-student interactions. However, with the coming of AI that mimics human interactions, students may seek interactions with AI instead. In this regard, some of the participants expressed concern that AI's impersonal nature could diminish the vital human element of teaching and learning:

I believe a more personal, face-to-face approach is important to avoid confusion and to support their [students'] emotional and social learning (Participant 10).

I am concerned that over-reliance on AI might reduce human interaction and critical thinking skills in students (Participant 6).

Participant 5 expressed a similar concern, that emotional connections with AI, rather than humans, may gradually hinder students' ability to make real connections with humans:

My concern with AI is that it doesn't have feelings unlike humans and that emotional disconnect could hinder it ability [sic] to truly understand and respond to the complex needs of students (Participant 5).

The participants stressed two important points – the need for personal connections during the learning process and the fear of loss of emotional connections. Participant 10 acknowledges that AI can never replicate the emotional and social aspects of education, which only educators and humans can provide. Hence, the relevance of educators in the learning process will never be entirely undermined. However, many are worried that students may treat AI like a human, forming connections that may affect the students' emotional and social development.

4.2.4 Theme 4: Teacher's Lack of Preparedness and Absence of Clear Policy

Despite the many potential benefits of AI in education, many educators feel unequipped to use AI in the classroom. For instance, this study's participants cited a lack of formal training and the absence of clear institutional guidelines on how AI should be used:

At this point, I do not feel fully prepared to integrate AI into my teaching due to lack of formal training and clear guidelines (Participant 6).

For Participant 11, a clear framework for schools on AI use would be beneficial. This is because of the ethical issues associated with its use, such as possible misuse for academic integrity and violation of instructor autonomy:

If I could influence how AI is integrated... I would suggest a clear, ethical, and student-centred framework to ensure AI enhances learning without compromising academic integrity, equity, or teacher autonomy (Participant 11).

While concerns about the use of AI are common among educators, many have expressed the desire to learn to use AI. The responses below support the need for faculty training and exposure to effective methods for AI use in the classroom:

I'm not much introduced to different AI platforms it might be challenging but I'm willing to learn and improve my skills in managing AI tools [sic] (Participant 4).
The university should conduct training seminars on AI for faculty and students alike (Participant 1).

Such concerns about the lack of clear policy and of preparation of educators in dealing with AI highlight the need for an institutional approach to planning and implementing AI policies. Moreover, given the important role of educators, who are directly dealing with students who are increasingly using AI tools, the lack of formal training for this among educators is a growing problem. The participants in this study seem to believe that without sufficient policies and professional development opportunities, the benefits of AI cannot be fully harnessed, while its risks may go unmitigated.

5. DISCUSSION

The responses from educators in this study paint a clear picture of a profession grappling with the profound implications of AI. This study highlights the equally important perspectives of educators, revealing their hopes, fears, and the complex realities of integrating AI into their daily practice. This discussion synthesises these findings, comparing them with existing research to offer a comprehensive view of the AI landscape in education from the perspective of educators.

The findings from this research align with ongoing discussions that AI has the potential to augment learning and improve educational processes. Educators in this study highlighted AI as a tool for efficiency. They also cited useful AI capabilities, such as helping create lesson plans and generate assessments. AI is increasingly becoming a trusted source of information for many educators as it can quickly generate complex lessons. This resonates with the broader academic discourse that recognises AI's capacity to automate administrative tasks and free up valuable time for educators (Abuhassna et al., 2025; Hashem et al., 2024). Similarly, the hope that AI can be a "great equaliser" by providing personalised learning and information sources for students of diverse needs is an important theme that echoes the vision of AI as a means to achieve educational equity (Gökçearslan et al., 2024; Ali et al., 2023).

However, the participants in this study also voiced significant fears that contrast with these hopes. The most prominent concern is that AI presents a threat to academic integrity and critical thinking. Participants expressed their concern that students will become overly reliant on AI for their schoolwork, leading to a decline in important cognitive skills. This fear is well-founded, as several studies and experts have documented the potential for AI misuse including plagiarism (e.g., Lee, 2025; Shaw, 2025), and the bypassing of traditional learning processes. The responses from this study, such as Participant 3's concern that AI reduces students' critical thinking, directly support previous academic findings (Walczack & Cellary, 2023; Douali et al., 2022). Furthermore, concerns about the loss of human connection are poignant ones. As participants' insights also highlighted, while AI can assist with practical tasks, it cannot replace the emotional input that teachers provide. For educators, this input forms the core of learning and stands in contrast to the emotional bonds students, as cited in other studies, have formed with AI tools. This finding implies the potential emotional disconnect of students coupled with the risk of not forming human relationships when they rely on AI for emotional connection.

Educators' worries also extend to ethical and professional dilemmas. The risk of AI being used to commit plagiarism is a top concern. Educators are increasingly reconsidering their assessment strategies to outsmart AI. This highlights a new professional challenge for educators, who must become adept at designing assignments that require higher order thinking and which cannot be easily generated or replicated by an AI. Furthermore, issues of data privacy and potential algorithmic bias were also raised. While some studies have downplayed these concerns, this study shows that for educators in the classroom, these are very real professional worries (Kitcharoen et al., 2024; Singh & Gupta, 2025). They are acutely aware that the data collected by AI could be misused and that AI's lack of transparency could lead to unfair outcomes for students.

Ultimately, the results of this study highlight the pressing need for schools and educational institutions to take a proactive role in guiding the integration of AI. The repeated mention of a "lack of formal training" and "clear guidelines" signals that many educators feel underprepared to navigate the increasing presence of AI terrain alone. The call for clear policies on AI use and ethical frameworks is not just a request for resources but a demand for a responsible and deliberate approach. Finally, with sufficient policies and regulations, AI systems are bound to bring about positive transformation in education and thus reduce concerns such as those cited in this study, as many educators are already utilising AI tools in ways that improve their teaching, even with the known risks.

6. CONCLUSION

This study explored educators' hopes and fears about the impact of AI integration into education. The results highlight the nuanced perspectives of educators as they navigate the rapid entry of AI into classroom practice. The participants recognised AI's strong potential to improve efficiency, provide personalised instruction, and expand access to learning resources. These findings are consistent with prior studies that view AI as a driver of equity and innovation in education. Teachers in Tawi-

Tawi affirmed that AI can reduce workload through automated content generation, leading to enhanced engagement. Educators also see the potential of AI to help students, especially those in remote areas, catch up academically by providing access to learning materials. On the other hand, educators' apprehensions about potential misuse of AI mirror global concerns reported in existing research. From the lens of educators, this study's findings emphasised the risks of plagiarism, the erosion of students' critical-thinking skills, diminished human interaction, and unresolved issues of privacy and ethics. A persistent concern about the lack of institutional preparedness highlights an ongoing backlog in catching up with AI integration. This indicates an immediate need for clear policies and adequate preparation to guide responsible AI use at educational institutions. Taken together, these findings show that while educators are cautiously optimistic about AI's promise, they are equally aware of its pitfalls. Effective integration will require careful planning, ethical safeguards, and continuous professional development. The recurring theme of the need for human input echoes the educator's value as part of the human dimensions of teaching. Given the exploratory nature of this study and the specific location at which it was conducted, this chapter acknowledges its limitations. However, the context provides replicable insights and implications regarding the understanding of AI use, including educator concerns about its potential drawbacks. Future studies may involve using other methodologies and involving larger numbers of participants. Other actionable recommendations are outlined in the next section.

7. RECOMMENDATIONS

Drawing on this chapter's findings and conclusions pertaining to the positive benefits of AI when properly integrated, and the need to observe necessary cautions, the following actionable steps are recommended for teachers, policy makers, and schools:

7.1 For Educators

Instructors should adopt critical integration strategies and take advantage of the many AI tools available for administrative efficiency and differentiated instruction. Instructors may also intentionally create tasks that emphasise creativity, analysis, and collaboration. Instructors should exemplify and model ethical use of AI. In addition, lessons about AI-related issues such as plagiarism, citation, and the limits of AI-generated content should be openly discussed with the students to increase awareness and foster digital responsibility.

7.2 For Policy Makers

Policy makers must create frameworks for AI integration. Standards for AI adoption in education should be strictly observed and include privacy protections, equity considerations, and instructor training requirements. Finally, there is a need to invest in the required infrastructure for use of AI tools. Policy makers should also prioritise equity of access to ensure that all students, irrespective of background should equally benefit from AI. The concept of digital divides in AI should be reduced through the provisions of accessible infrastructure.

7.3 For the Schools and Universities

Schools and universities should develop clear policies and ethical guidelines pertaining to AI use. Institutions should establish protocols for academic integrity, data privacy, and responsible AI use, echoing calls from UNESCO and related bodies for transparent governance. Sustainable and targeted professional development programmes are also necessary as schools increasingly integrate AI use. Educators should receive regular, updated training on AI tools, their pedagogical applications, and strategies for designing assessments that encourage higher order thinking beyond what AI can generate.

ACKNOWLEDEGEMENT

The authors wish to acknowledge their university, Mindanao State University-Tawi-Tawi College of Technology and Oceanography, for encouragement. Similarly, the authors would also like to extend their appreciation to educators who shared their valuable experiences and insights on the impact of AI in teaching and learning as participants in this study

REFERENCES

Abuhassna, H., Qi, P., & Ting, L. (2025). Understanding the Technological Innovations in Higher Education: Inclusivity, Equity, and Quality Toward Sustainable Development Goals. *Open Education Studies*, *7*(1), 20250114. DOI: 10.1515/edu-2025-0114

Alam, A. (2021, November 1). Possibilities and apprehensions in the landscape of Artificial Intelligence in education. *IEEE Xplore*. DOI: 10.1109/ICCICA52458.2021.9697272

Ali, J. K. M., Shamsan, M. A. A., Hezam, T. A., & Mohammed, A. A. Q. (2023). Impact of ChatGPT on learning motivation. *Journal of English Studies in Arabia Felix*, *2*(1), 41–49. DOI: 10.56540/jesaf.v2i1.51

Ayton, D. (2023). Qualitative descriptive research. Qualitative Research–a practical guide for health and social care researchers and practitioners. https://oercollective.caul.edu.au/qualitative-research/chapter/__unknown__-5/

Bae, H., Hur, J., Park, J., Choi, G. W., & Moon, J. (2024). Pre-service teachers' dual perspectives on generative AI: Benefits, challenges, and integrating into teaching and learning. *Online Learning : the Official Journal of the Online Learning Consortium*, *28*(3). Advance online publication. DOI: 10.24059/olj.v28i3.4543

Baker, T., Smith, L., & Anissa, N. (2019). Educ-AI-tion rebooted? Exploring the future of artificial intelligence in schools and colleges. https://media.nesta.org.uk/documents/Future_of_AI_and_education_v5_WEB.pdf

Brusilovsky, P. (2023). AI in education, learner control, and human-AI collaboration. *International Journal of Artificial Intelligence in Education, 34*(1), 122–135. Advance online publication. DOI: 10.1007/s40593-023-00356-z

Chollet, F. (2019). The Measure of intelligence. ArXiv.org. https://arxiv.org/abs/1911.01547

Creely, E., & Blannin, J. (2023). The implications of generative AI for creative composition in higher education and initial teacher education. *ASCILITE Publications, 357–361*, 357–361. Advance online publication. DOI: 10.14742/apubs.2023.618

Denny, P., Prather, J., Becker, B. A., Finnie-Ansley, J., Hellas, A., Leinonen, J., Luxton-Reilly, A., Reeves, B. N., Santos, E. A., & Sarsa, S. (2024). Computing Education in the Era of Generative AI. *Communications of the ACM*, *67*(2), 56–67. DOI: 10.1145/3624720

Derakhshan, A., Eslami, Z. R., & Shakki, F. (2023). *Comparing compliments in Face-to-Face vs. online interactions among Iranian speakers of Persian*. Pragmatics and Society., DOI: 10.1075/ps.22102.der

Douali, L., Selmaoui, S., & Bouab, W. (2022). Artificial Intelligence in Education: Fears and Faiths. *International Journal of Information and Education Technology (IJIET)*, *12*(7), 650–657. DOI: 10.18178/ijiet.2022.12.7.1666

Dwork, C., & Minow, M. (2022). Distrust of Artificial Intelligence: Sources & Responses from Computer Science & Law. *Daedalus*, *151*(2), 309–321. DOI: 10.1162/daed_a_01918

Gammoh, L. A. (2024). ChatGPT in academia: Exploring university students' risks, misuses, and challenges in Jordan. *Journal of Further and Higher Education*, *48*(6), 608–624. DOI: 10.1080/0309877X.2024.2378298

Gökçearslan, Ş., Tosun, C., & Erdemir, Z. G. (2024). Benefits, Challenges, and Methods of Artificial Intelligence (AI) Chatbots in Education: A Systematic Literature Review. *International Journal of Technology in Education*, *7*(1), 19–39. DOI: 10.46328/ijte.600

Gökçearslan, Ş., Tosun, C., & Erdemir, Z. G. (2024). Benefits, Challenges, and Methods of Artificial Intelligence (AI) Chatbots in Education: A Systematic Literature Review. *International Journal of Technology in Education*, *7*(1), 19–39. DOI: 10.46328/ijte.600

Guan, L., Zhang, Y., & Gu, M. M. (2024). Pre-service Teachers' Preparedness for AI-integrated Education: An Investigation from Perceptions, Capabilities, and Teachers' Identity Changes. *Computers and Education: Artificial Intelligence*, *8*, 100341. DOI: 10.1016/j.caeai.2024.100341

Hashem, R., Ali, N., El Zein, F., Fidalgo, P., & Khurma, O. A. (2024). AI to the rescue: Exploring the potential of ChatGPT as a teacher ally for workload relief and burnout prevention. *Research and Practice in Technology Enhanced Learning*, *19*, 023. Advance online publication. DOI: 10.58459/rptel.2024.19023

Hwang, G. J., & Tu, Y. F. (2021). Roles and research trends of artificial intelligence in mathematics education: A bibliometric mapping analysis and systematic review. *Mathematics*, *9*(6), 584. DOI: 10.3390/math9060584

Jackaria, P., Hajan, B., Mastul, A., & Sali, F. (2024). Generation AI in a Reimagined Classroom : Challenges and Opportunities, pp. 174 – 176. DOI: 10.4018/979-8-3693-3350-1.ch009

Jackaria, P. M., Hajan, B. H., & Mastul, A. R. H. (2024). A comparative analysis of the rating of college students' essays by ChatGPT versus human raters. *International Journal of Learning. Teaching and Educational Research*, *23*(2), 478–492. DOI: 10.26803/ijlter.23.2.23

Ka, C., Chan, Y., & Hu, W. (2023). Students' voices on generative AI: Perceptions, benefits, and challenges in higher education, *International Journal of Education. Technology in. Higher Edu*cation. https://doi.or/10.1186/s41239-023-00411-8

Kim, J., Lee, H., & Cho, Y. H. (2022). Learning design to support student-AI collaboration: Perspectives of leading teachers for AI in education. *Education and Information Technologies*, *27*(5), 6069–6104. DOI: 10.1007/s10639-021-10831-6

Kim, J., Merrill, K., Xu, K., & Sellnow, D. D. (2020). My teacher is a machine: Understanding students' perceptions of AI teaching assistants in online education. *International Journal of Human-Computer Interaction*, *36*(20), 1902–1911. DOI: 10.1080/10447318.2020.1801227

Kitcharoen, P., Howimanporn, S., & Chookaew, S. (2024). Enhancing Teachers' AI Competencies through Artificial Intelligence of Things Professional Development Training. *International Journal of Interactive Mobile Technologies*, *18*(2), 4–15. Advance online publication. DOI: 10.3991/ijim.v18i02.46613

Kshetri, N. (2023). The Future of education: Generative artificial intelligence's collaborative role with teachers. *IT Professional*, *25*(6), 8–12. DOI: 10.1109/MITP.2023.3333070

Lee, K. (2025). AI on Academic Integrity and Plagiarism Detection. DOI: 10.32802/asmscj.2025.1918

Lokesh, G. R., Harish, K. S., Sangu, V. S., Prabakar, S., Kumar, V. S., & Vallabhaneni, M. (2024, April). AI and the future of work: Preparing the workforce for technological shifts and skill evolution. In 2024 *International Conference on Knowledge Engineering and Communication Systems (ICKECS)*(Vol. 1, pp. 1-6). IEEE. https://ieeexplore.ieee.org/abstract/document/10616486

Mhlanga, D. (2022). The role of artificial intelligence and machine learning amid the COVID-19 pandemic: What lessons are we learning on 4IR and the sustainable development goals? *International Journal of Environmental Research and Public Health, 19*(3), 1879. DOI: 10.3390/ijerph19031879 PMID: 35162901

Ng, D. T. K., Su, J., Leung, J. K. L., & Chu, S. K. W. (2023). Artificial intelligence (AI) literacy education in secondary schools: A review. *Interactive Learning Environments, 32*(10), 6204–6224. DOI: 10.1080/10494820.2023.2255228

Nutprapha, K. (2023). Using AI-powered speech recognition technology to improve English pronunciation and speaking skills. *Journal of Educational Technology, 14*(2), 45–60. DOI: 10.1080/xxxxxxx.2023.456789

Pikhart, M., & Al-Obaydi, L. H. (2025). Reporting the potential risk of using AI in higher Education: Subjective perspectives of educators. *Computers in Human Behavior Reports, 18*, 100693. DOI: 10.1016/j.chbr.2025.100693

Shaw, D. (2025). The digital erosion of intellectual integrity: Why misuse of generative AI is worse than plagiarism. *AI & Society, 1-3*(8), 5819–5821. Advance online publication. DOI: 10.1007/s00146-025-02362-2

Sibug, V. B., Vital, V., Paul, J., Fernando, E., & Gonzales, D. D. (2024). Teachers' Perspectives on Integrating AI tools in Classrooms: Insights from the Philippines. *32nd International Conference on Computers in Education.* https://www.researchgate.net/publication/386170473_Teachers

Silva, A., De, O., Janes, D., & Dos, S. (2023). Challenges and opportunities of artificial intelligence in education in a global context. *Review of Artificial Intelligence in Education, 4*(00). Advance online publication. DOI: 10.37497/rev.artif.intell.educ.v5i00.18

Singh, A., & Gupta, P. (2025). Perspective of Generative AI for UNESCO Inclusive Education. Perspective of Generative AI for UNESCO Inclusive Education. https://papers.ssrn.com/sol3/papers.cfm?abstract_id=5181859

Tan, X., Cheng, G., & Ling, M. H. (2024). Artificial Intelligence in Teaching and Teacher Professional Development: A Systematic Review. *Computers and Education Artificial Intelligence, 8*, 100355–100355. DOI: 10.1016/j.caeai.2024.100355

Tawafak, R. M., Al-Obaydi, L. H., & Pikhart, M. (2023). Competency categorization and roles of online teachers from the perspective of university students. *Frontiers in Psychology, 14*, 1009000. Advance online publication. DOI: 10.3389/fpsyg.2023.1009000 PMID: 36935985

Uygun, D. (2024). Teachers' perspectives on artificial intelligence in education. *Advances in Mobile Learning Educational Research, 4*(1), 931–939. DOI: 10.25082/AMLER.2024.01.005

Walczak, K., & Cellary, W. (2023). Challenges for higher education in the era of widespread access to generative AI. *The Poznań University of Economics Review*, 9 (2). DOI: 10.18559/ebr.2023.2.743

Wang, X. (2021). Research on the application of AI technology in computer-assisted instruction. *Journal of Physics: Conference Series, 1992*(2), 022030. Advance online publication. DOI: 10.1088/1742-6596/1992/2/022030

Wogu, I. A. P., Misra, S., Olu-Owolabi, E. F., Assibong, P. A., Udoh, O. D., Ogiri, S. O., & Damasevicius, R. (2018). Artificial intelligence, artificial teachers, and the fate of learners in the 21st-century education sector: Implications for theory and practice. *International Journal of Pure and Applied Mathematics, 119*(16), 2245–2259. http://www.acadpubl.eu/hub/

Yu, H., & Guo, Y. (2022). *Generative artificial intelligence empowers educational reform: current status, issues, and prospects.*, DOI: 10.3389/feduc.2023.1183162

Zanetti, M., Iseppi, G., & Cassese, F. P. (2019). A "psychopathic" Artificial Intelligence: The possible risks of a deviating AI in Education. *Research on Education and Media, 11*(1), 93–99. DOI: 10.2478/rem-2019-0013

About the Contributors

Belqes Al-Sowaidi is a Professor of Applied Linguistics and Translation Studies with expertise in linguistics, pedagogy, translation and interpreting studies, TEFL/TAFL, and curriculum design. Her work bridges language studies with technology-enhanced education in the humanities. Her research spans translation and interpreting studies, Arabic and Islamic studies, critical discourse analysis, comparative literature, and computer-assisted translation. Her recent work focuses on Educational Technology (EdTech) and Artificial Intelligence in Education (AIEd), including AI in academic research practices (AI-ARP), across e-learning, blended, and distance learning contexts. She is the editor of AL-WASA IYYAH: IPSA Journal of Islamic and Arabic Studies, a reviewer for peer-reviewed indexed journals, has supervised and examined numerous PhD and MA theses, and is a sworn Arabic–English translator accredited by the High Court of South Africa.

Tawffeek Mohammed is an Associate Professor of Applied Linguistics and Translation Studies at the University of the Western Cape. His research spans linguistics, language pedagogy, media studies, critical discourse analysis, translation and interpreting studies, and digital tools in language learning and translation. He is deeply committed to interdisciplinary research, with a strong publication record that includes journal articles, books, and edited volumes. Prof. Mohammed has extensive experience in supervising postgraduate research and mentoring early-career academics. He is a recipient of the Mellon Professorial Award for 2024–2025 and is actively engaged in advancing scholarship through collaborative, innovative, and inclusive academic practices.

***

Prerna Agrawal is a distinguished academician and researcher with over 14+ years of experience in higher education and applied research, specializing in machine learning, data science, cloud computing, and big data and currently serving as an Assistant Professor at the Faculty of Computer Applications & IT (MCA), GLS University, Ahmedabad, India. She earned her Ph.D. in Computer Science from GLS University, with a focus on machine learning and application security. Her academic interests span a broad spectrum including machine learning, big data analytics, cloud computing, computer networks, data science and databases. She has published more than 25 research papers, book chapters in high-impact national and international journals and conferences, including IEEE, Springer and IGI Global. She is also an editor for the Advances in Smart Computing and Applications (ICASCA - 2025) proceedings at Springer Nature. Her recent work includes AI-driven solutions for disease detection, automated job role prediction through resume analysis, and cybersecurity frameworks using big data analytics. She is actively guiding Ph.D. research scholars and is a recognized reviewer for prestigious journals and conferences such as the Journal of Ambient Intelligence and Humanized Computing, IAES International Journal of Artificial Intelligence, and several Springer and IGI Global publications. Her scholarly work has garnered 175 citations on Google Scholar, earning her an H-index of 7, reflecting the impact and recognition of her scholarly contributions. In addition to her research, she is passionate about digital education and has developed and published a suite of online courses on platforms like Udemy and TutorialsPoint, covering topics such as machine learning with Python, cloud computing fundamentals, and Python programming for beginners. She has been recognized for her contributions with multiple accolades, including best paper awards and certifications for excellence in academic leadership.

Rashad Ahmed is an Associate Professor of English at Jacksonville State University, where he specializes in applied linguistics, TESOL, composition studies, and language technology. His work bridges research and teaching across areas such as artificial intelligence in language learning, CALL, digital literacy, sociolinguistics, language assessment, and writing pedagogy. Dr. Ahmed has published extensively on language learning, multimodal learning, and the linguistic implications of AI in educational contexts. Lately, he was nominated for the TESOL Teacher of the Year Award (2026), an honor that acknowledges outstanding contributions to English language teaching and professional leadership.

Abdu Al-Kadi, an applied linguist with a multilingual background, serves as an associate professor at Bergen University. His academic career spans institutions in Tunisia, Yemen, Jordan, and Norway. Besides teaching across TESOL and ESP contexts, he has published across his area of expertise and presented at international conferences. He also contributes as a supervisor, translator, editor, and peer reviewer.

Somia Basheer Al Kamel holds a Bachelor's degree in Translation from Al-Saeed University in Yemen. She currently works as a teacher at the British Institute in Ibb City and is eager to further engage in research and writing related to her field.

Mayada Nageeb Al-Maktary holds a PhD in Linguistics from Manouba University in Tunisia and is a faculty member at Taiz University in Yemen. She has actively participated in various national and international academic conferences, workshops, and events, where she has delivered presentations. Additionally, she has contributed to peer reviews for various national and international journals and has published articles in her field. Furthermore, she has supervised a number of graduate theses in English, providing guidance to students in their research and academic writing.

Marya Adel Al-Mareri obtained her BA in Translation from Al-Saeed University in Yemen. She is interested in research on translation studies and aims to enhance communication across cultures in scientific works.

Hamas Sameer Al-Qaisi has a Bachelor's degree in Translation from Al-Saeed University in Yemen. She currently teaches English language skills and is interested in scientific research related to her field.

Hilal Alten is a master's student at Çanakkale Onsekiz Mart University, in the ELT department, focusing on adult EFL education. She is currently working as an English language teacher in private language courses.

Silvio Andrae is an independent researcher based in Germany. His research focuses on artificial intelligence, digital transformation, and the governance of emerging technologies, with applications in areas such as climate risk modeling, digital finance, and sustainable economic systems. His work explores how AI, machine learning, and digital governance frameworks can support policy development, corporate strategy, and sustainability transitions.

Chantelle August-Mowers is a PhD scholar in Language and Literacy, a researcher, and a senior lecturer. She serves as Head of Department for the Foundation Phase and Intermediate Phase programmes at TOGI, Pinelands, South Africa. Her research interests include multilingualism in education and curriculum and pedagogical inquiry. Her academic and professional journey has cultivated a strong commitment to issues of social justice, particularly within the education and linguistic contexts. She is especially drawn to the concept of linguistic citizenship, which foregrounds the ways individuals and communities actively shape, claim and negotiate their linguistic rights and identities. She is passionate about research that examines how language practices intersect with power, inequality and inclusion and how participatory approaches can amplify marginalised voices. She is eager to contribute to projects that explore these themes (but not limited to), deepen scholarly understanding and support transformative and community -centered change.

Riya Baby is currently working as an Assistant Professor at Christ University, Bangalore . She holds a Doctoral Degree in Mathematics from Christ University, Bangalore (2016). She began her higher education with a Bachelor's degree in Mathematics from Sacred Heart College, Kochi Her academic journey also includes an MPhil and Master's in Mathematics from Christ University. She continues to contribute to academia with over a decade of academic/teaching and research experience.

Sónia Calado is a researcher affiliated with the University of Aveiro, Portugal. Her research focuses on digital governance and emerging technologies, particularly artificial intelligence, blockchain, digital identity systems, and the integration of ESG principles in organizational and sustainability contexts. She explores how technological innovation can support responsible governance, transparency, and sustainable digital ecosystems.

Amber Clarke is an emerging thought leader in Educational Technology and Artificial Intelligence in Higher Education. She is currently pursuing a PhD in Education at the University of Cape Town (UCT), building on a Master's degree in Educational Technology from the same university. Amber is the Head of Digital Learning and Technology at Two Oceans Graduate Institute (TOGI), a private distance higher education institution in South Africa. In this leadership role, she drives strategic innovation in digital learning and technology-enhanced teaching practices. Amber has lectured in undergraduate and postgraduate teacher education programmes, covering modules such as Information Communication Technology, Coding and Robotics, and Research Methodology, as well as served as the Foundation Phase Teaching Practice Coordinator. Her research interests lie in Educational and Emerging Technologies, Artificial Intelligence, Distance Education and Digital Literacy. Amber strives to push boundaries and explore innovative, disruptive approaches to how technology can transform teaching, learning, and assessment.

Susanta Das is a seasoned educator with a proven record of teaching and mentoring diverse students, working at multiple institutions, and providing service to the various initiatives of organizations. He received his Ph.D. and M.A. degrees from Western Michigan University (WMU), USA, and M.Sc. degree from Banaras Hindu University (BHU), India all in Physics. He continued his research as a Marie-

Curie post-doctoral fellow at Stockholm University, Stockholm, Sweden on beam diagnostics for the DESIREE (Double ElectroStatic Ion Ring ExpEriment) in the project DITANET (Diagnostic Techniques for particle Accelerators – a Marie-Curie initial training NETwork), at the Indian Institute of Science Education and Research-Kolkata, India on high-pressure physics as a Project Scientist-B, and at the University of Electro-Communications, Tokyo, Japan on ion-surface interactions as a Post-doctoral fellow. Throughout his career, Dr. Das worked and collaborated with many researchers, Ph.D., master, and visiting students from different countries. He further visited many countries to discuss research and an international conference participant (UK, Italy, Germany, Greece, Belgium, Bulgaria, Romania, Brazil etc.). He worked at several institutions before assuming his current role at Ajeenkya D Y Patil University. He received the Marie-Curie post-doctoral fellowship in Sweden, Science Academies' Summer Research Fellowship in India, Gowen Frostic Doctoral Fellowship, Department Graduate Research and Creative Scholar Award by WMU, and Leo R. Parpart Doctoral Fellowship by Dept. of Physics, WMU, among many others, throughout his academic journey. He co-authored several research articles in WoS/Scopus indexed international journals, conference proceedings, and scholarly book chapters and co-edited several books published by renowned international publishing houses (IGI-Global, Springer Nature, Nova Science Publishers, Wiley, & Scrivener-Willey, Notion Press). At present, Dr. Das continues to delve into cutting-edge fields, with a keen interest in nanotechnology, UN SDGs, and data science. His multifaceted contributions, spanning teaching, research, and administrative leadership, showcase a dedicated professional who is instrumental in advancing the vision and mission of the institutions he serves.

Benny Godwin J Davidson is a seasoned Management Consultant and an accomplished Assistant Professor at the University of the Fraser Valley. He has a successful track record of advising clients from diverse industries and a major focus on identifying strategic opportunities and implementing effective disruptive innovation strategies. In addition to his academic roles, he is also the President & Co-Founder of WinBros Global Enterprises Inc.

Bora Demir graduated from the English Language Teaching department of Çanakkale Onsekiz Mart University, and afterward, he got his MA degree from the same university. He earned his PhD from Yeditepe University on English Language Teacher Education. He became an associate professor in 2023. He is currently a member of the School of Foreign Languages at Çanakkale Onsekiz Mart University. He has participated and presented his research at various reputable international conferences and published articles in national and international journals/books with research interests in various aspects of language teaching and language teacher education. He has been the founder and the Editor-in-chief of the academic journal "Innovational Research in ELT" since 2019. He also edits the journal of "ELT-Turkey," which is a publication of the AELTE. More recently, he has edited three reference books to be used in ELT departments, namely, "Interculturality in English Language Learning and Teaching," "Discourse Analysis and Language Teaching," and "Language Teaching Approaches and Methods." His research interests include technology-assisted language teaching, cognitive aspects of language learning, and psychological aspect of language learning and teaching.

Mu ammad Ashraf Ebrahim Dockrat is a PhD scholar of Semitic languages, Islamic studies, and religious studies. He is a graduate of Madrasah Arabia Islamia, Azaadville, South Africa. Ashraf Dockrat is a teacher at the dārul ʿulums at Madrasah Ra maniyyah, Masjid Dārus Salam and the Jāmiʿah al-ʿUlum al-Islāmīyyah. He is an associate researcher at the LanCSAL (Department of languages and applied linguistics; Faculty of Humanities) at the University of Johannesburg. He serves on the executive committee of the Southern African Society for Near Eastern Studies (SASNES). He was appointed by the President to serve as a commissioner with the Commission for the Promotion and Protection of the Rights of Cultural, Religious and Linguistic Communities. Mawlānā Ashraf.

Mariette Fourie-Jardim is the Director at Cognitive Craft (PTY) Ltd, a leading company in educational design. She is fulfilling the roles of Learning, Development and Instructional Design Specialist, Quality Coordinator and Research Support Consultant, Impact Analyst and Strategic Advisor. Dr Mariette Fourie-Jardim is further the Learning and Teaching Specialist in the Faculty of Community and Health Sciences at the University of the Western Cape (UWC) in South Africa. Dr Fourie-Jardim retains more than 20 years' experience in education and her professional character portrays a strong disposition towards social justice and transformation in higher education and society in general. Her expertise further includes Learning and Teaching in Higher Education, Digital Pedagogy, Higher Education Research and Development, Academic Integrity, Scholarship of Teaching and Learning (SoTL), Instructional Design, Quality Assurance, and the Continuous Professional Development (CPD) of faculty. She has been an international facilitator for the Online Learning Consortium (OLC) for the past five years where she forefronts instructional design and neuroeducation. Dr Mariette Fourie-Jardim has furth

Savita Gandhi is a distinguished academician with over 46 years of teaching and research experience. She served as Professor and Dean at the Faculty of Com- puter Applications and Information Technology (PG), GLS University, Ahmedabad. Prior to this, she held the position of Professor and Head at the Department of Computer

Science, Gujarat University, and began her academic journey as a lecturer in the Depart- ment of Mathematics at M.S. University, Baroda. Dr. Gandhi's research interests span a wide spectrum including Data Compression, Ad Hoc Networks, Image Processing, Machine Learning, Data Analytics, and Data Mining. She has authored over 80 research articles in reputed national and international journals and conferences, many of which are indexed in Scopus and Web of Science. Her scholarly contributions are evidenced by an i10-index of 10 and over 470 citations on Google Scholar. A pioneer in the field of digital education in India, She served as the Principal Investigator for the Ministry of Education's e-PG Pathshala initiative, leading the development of 326 modules in Information Technology. She was also the Paper Coordinator for the "Numerical Meth- ods" course, contributing to an innovative e-book that integrates textual content with video lectures (https://ebooks .inflibnet.ac.in/itp15/). Furthermore, she developed two Massive Open Online Courses (MOOCs) on the SWAYAM platform—"Artificial Intel- ligence" and "Introduction to Computer Networks and Internet Protocols"—enhancing the reach and quality of online education in India. Her research leadership extends to national projects, having led a three-year project under ISRO's Chandrayaan-1 initiative and another on Citizen Science awarded by the Department of Science and Technology (DST), Government of India. Dr. Gandhi is a senior member of IEEE, a Fellow of the Gujarat Science Academy (GSA), and a life member of the Computer Society of India (CSI). She is a sought-after speaker, having delivered numerous keynote addresses, expert lectures, and invited talks at academic conferences, faculty development pro- grams, and seminars across the country. In recognition of her academic excellence and service, Dr. Gandhi has received several honors including the Best Paper Award, the Global Excellence Award, and a Gold Medal during her postgraduate studies.

Jossy George is a distinguished academic leader and currently serves as the Director of the CHRIST (Deemed to be University) Bannerghatta Campus. He pursued his higher studies at Christ University, Bangalore, and later at IIM Ahmedabad. With extensive leadership experience, he has been associated with Christ University in various capacities. He has authored several scopus-indexed research papers and actively engages and contributes to the academia through his extensive research experience. Dr. Fr. Jossy George is known for his vision in academic administration and institutional development.

Abdullah Yasin Gunduz is an Associate Professor in the Department of Computer Technologies at Usak University, Turkiye. His research focuses on educational technology, artificial intelligence in education, flipped learning, gamification and e-learning. He has participated in several national and international research projects. His academic contributions aim to bridge the gap between innovative technologies and effective pedagogical practices.

Samantha Hoffman, is an academic and Field Specialist Leader for Social Sciences and Languages in the BEd Intermediate Phase and PGCE Programme at Two Oceans Graduate Institute. She holds a PhD in Education and her research interest centres around the discourse of Quality Education involving interdisciplinary research to impact teacher education and basic education through the lens of the Capability approach and the Ubuntu Philosophy.

Potchong M. Jackaria is a researcher affiliated with Mindanao State University–Tawi-Tawi College of Technology and Oceanography, Philippines. His work focuses on education, digital technologies in learning environments, and community-based educational development. His publications examine topics such as artificial intelligence in classrooms, social media integration in education, and educational practices in island and culturally diverse communities.

Amanda Jankowitz is a lecturer, educational technology integration specialist, and PhD candidate at Wits University. Her MSc Med in Health Science Education focused on game-based learning, a theme she now expands through her doctoral research on immersive technologies and digital equity in health sciences education. Amanda's work explores how innovation can thrive in constrained contexts particularly through mobile-first, offline-first, and low-bandwidth learning design. She is a TechWomen Fellow, Global Minecraft Mentor, and Chair of the Gamification Working Group in the Faculty of Health Sciences, where she leads interdisciplinary projects at the intersection of pedagogy, play, and professional practice. Amanda is passionate about designing inclusive digital learning environments that empower students at the margins. A proud member of the ZA Lego User Group, she embraces play not only as a pedagogical tool but as a mindset for reimagining education.

Masnoenah Kamalie is an experienced higher education professional with over two decades in the education sector, specialising in academic leadership, curriculum development, and quality assurance. She holds a Master of Arts in Semitic Languages and Cultures, a BA Honours in Religion Studies, and a BA in Islamic Studies, and is currently pursuing a PhD at the University of the Western Cape focusing on Islamic religious texts, epistemologies, and educational transformation. She has served in academic administration and management roles at institutions including the University of Cape Town, the University of Johannesburg, the International Peace College South Africa (IPSA), and currently as a Head of Department at Two Oceans Graduate Institute (TOGI). Her expertise spans programme management, curriculum design, quality assurance, and regulatory compliance. In addition to her leadership roles, she has lectured in Literacy, Religion Studies, Arabic, and Islamic Studies.

Lesego Makhafola is a PhD in IT candidate and lecturer in the Department of Information Science at the University of Pretoria. She is a Co-chair for the CODATA-RDA School of Research Data Science South Africa. Her research focuses on creating a strategy to enhance the digital competencies of South African university library staff to recognise and mitigate the influence of disruptive technologies. Her research interests are in embedded librarianship, information and digital literacies and competencies, information and AI ethics, disruptive technologies, and virtual learning environments.

Tendai Mataranyika is Head of Digital Information Services and Research at Two Oceans Graduate Institute, Cape Town, South Africa. He holds a Master's degree in Technology from the University of Pretoria. An Information Specialist with more than 15 years of experience in Research and Academic Libraries. His research areas of interest include: Open Science, Open repositories, AI literacy, AI ethics and governance. He has presented papers at various Library conferences and published in the same field.

Willem Mostert is a lecturer at the Two Oceans Graduate Institute in Cape Town, South Africa, specialising in Visual Arts Education and Geography for the Intermediate Phase. With over four years of experience in higher education, he is dedicated to the training and development of future educators, focusing on innovative approaches to teaching and learning in the primary school context. His current research centres on the development of visual perception and the ways in which knowledge is constructed through Visual Arts education at the primary school level. His Master of Education thesis, titled The Development of Visual Perception in Artwork in the Primary School, explores these themes in depth and is available online through the Cape Peninsula University of Technology's institutional repository.

Beatrice Namusiginyi holds a PhD and works at Makerere University in Uganda, specializing in English and Language Education. Her research focuses on how primary school pupils engage with social justice concepts through language education. She is also affiliated with the CABUTE project, which supports Ugandan teacher educators in pursuing advanced degrees through a NORAD-funded initiative.

Huda Saif is an Assistant Professor of Translation Studies whose research focuses on translation theory, translation pedagogy, and the role of translation in intercultural dialogue. Her work examines how translation practices and translator training contribute to cross-cultural communication and knowledge exchange. She is particularly interested in the integration of translation technologies and digital tools in translation education and the development of translation competence among students of English language and literature.Her research also explores contemporary approaches to translator training, pedagogical strategies in translation classrooms, and the interaction between language, culture, and translation practices.

Mohamed Faraj Saleh Raheel is a sociologist currently serving at Qatar University's as A head of Department of Social Sciences in the College of Arts and Sciences. He earned his PhD in Sociology from the University of the Western Cape in 2010, with a dissertation titled "The Power of Women within Libyan Families," and previously obtained his MA and BA degrees in Sociology from Benghazi University. Before joining Qatar University, Dr. Raheel held several academic and administrative positions in Libya, including at Benghazi University and Sirte University, where he chaired departments such as Behavioral Sciences and Research & Consultations. His research focuses on family power dynamics, gender relations, social institutions, and social change, and he has contributed to studies published in international journals.

Harika Rao is an Associate Dean and Associate Professor for the College of Business and Management. Rao teaches in the undergraduate and graduate programs and her areas of teaching are Management and Leadership, Ecommerce, Innovation, and Computer Management Systems. Rao has authored several multi-touch books that are currently being used in undergraduate and graduate courses. Rao was honored with 40 Under 40 by the South Florida Business Journal in 2023. Rao was awarded the Business Faculty of the Year 2022 by the International Accreditation Council for Business Education. Rao was awarded the Lynn University Excellence in Teaching and Dedication to Students for the year 2021.

Yasien Ryklief is a PhD scholar, higher education professional, and social development advocate with over 15 years of experience in operational leadership, community upliftment, and inclusive access to quality education. He currently serves as Head of Operations and Community Engagement at TOGI, a fully online teacher-training institution committed to transforming education in South Africa. In this role, he leads institutional operations, builds strategic partnerships, and designs outreach initiatives that support future educators, especially in underserved communities. He is also the founding director of Hareesun, a registered non-profit organisation providing humanitarian aid to vulnerable communities locally and internationally. Through Hareesun, he has coordinated relief efforts in eight countries across Africa and the Middle East. His work is driven by a strong belief in the transformative power of education, compassion, and service. Across both academic and humanitarian contexts, he remains committed to creating sustainable change and empowering communities.

Sunil Sankathala is pursuing B. Tech Computer Science and Engineering at Ajeenkya DY Patil University, with a diverse range of interests that bridge technology, sustainability, and innovation. His academic focus lies in computer science fundamentals like programming, data structures, algorithms, and software development. He actively supplements this with hands-on experience in web development and robotics. Beyond the core curriculum, He has a strong research inclination in emerging and impactful fields. His current research interests include Artificial Intelligence in Healthcare, bioplastics, nano bioplastics, e-waste management, and solid waste management—areas where he believes technology can make a meaningful difference in solving real-world problems. He has been publishing research articles and book chapters in reputed national and international journals and books. He is also part of an ambitious Hyperloop project, which involves interdisciplinary collaboration and cutting-edge engineering aimed at revolutionizing transportation. Working on this project has enhanced his skills in teamwork, innovation, and systems thinking. In the tech domain, he has developed proficiency in web development using technologies such as HTML, CSS, JavaScript, and React. His interests in robotics further reflect building smart, responsive systems that interact with the physical world. Throughout his course, he has helped strengthen problem-solving and collaborative skills. He is proficient in languages such as Python, C, C++, MySQL, Ubuntu, Machine Learning and familiar with frameworks and tools like React, Git. He actively participates in hackathons, coding competitions, and tech events to challenge himself and learn from peers. He is also a quick learner and highly adaptable, with an eagerness to stay updated with the latest trends in the tech world. He aspires to become a skilled software engineer and contribute to building innovative solutions that have a positive impact on society. The long-term goal is to work in a dynamic environment where knowledge, grow professionally, and make meaningful contributions to the field of technology. Driven by a spirit of exploration and sustainability, he aims to contribute to technological solutions that address both human and environmental needs. The long-term goal is to become a versatile engineer and researcher, working at the intersection of computer science, environmental innovation, and human well-being.

Aldammien A. Sukarno is a researcher and education student at Mindanao State University–Tawi-Tawi College of Technology and Oceanography (MSU-TCTO), Philippines, where he is pursuing a Bachelor of Secondary Education major in Science. His academic work focuses on educational technology and the role of artificial intelligence in learning environments, including research on AI-assisted assessment and student engagement in AI-infused classrooms. He collaborates on studies examining how emerging digital tools influence teaching, learning processes, and educational innovation.

Ansella Thomas is a Counselling Psychologist and is currently working as a Research Assistant at CHRIST (Deemed to be University), Delhi NCR Campus. She is an experienced professional with a history of working in the mental health care industry. She holds a Bachelor's degree in psychology from Kuriakose Elias College, Mananam and a Masters Degree in Counselling Psychology from Kristu Jayanti College (Autonomous). She has completed multiple internships and has 1.5 year of experience as a Research Assistant, and continues to contribute to academia through her research in the field of psychology.

Adrienne van As is a lecturer in History Education at Cape Peninsula University of Technology, based in Wellington, South Africa. With over 15 years of experience in higher education, she has held roles including Senior Lecturer and Head of Department at Two Oceans Graduate Institute. Her expertise spans teacher training for the Intermediate Phase, curriculum development, instructional design, and multigrade education. Adrienne's current research explores transactional distance in online primary history modules through an autoethnographic lens.

Index

A

B

C

D

E

F

G

H

I

L

M

P

Q

R

S

T

www.ingramcontent.com/pod-product-compliance
Lightning Source LLC
LaVergne TN
LVHW061531290926
849162LV00004B/757
* 9 7 9 8 3 3 7 3 4 5 2 1 5 *